ORDNANCE MANUAL.

THE

ORDNANCE MANUAL

FOR

THE USE OF THE OFFICERS

OF THE

UNITED STATES ARMY.

SECOND EDITION.

Washington:
GIDEON & CO., PRINTERS.
1850.

ORDNANCE OFFICE,

WASHNGTON, *October* 14, 1847.

Captain A. MORDECAI,

Washington Arsenal.

SIR: The duty of arranging, preparing, and publishing drawings of a uniform system of Artillery, and of revising the Ordnance Manual and publishing a new edition, is assigned to you. * * * * * *

G. TALCOTT, *Lt. Col. of Ordnance.*

ORDNANCE BOARD.

WASHINGTON, *November* 15, 1849.

To Brig. Gen. TALCOTT,

Col. of Ordnance.

SIR: Under your instructions of the 27th ult., the Ordnance Board have carefully examined the Ordnance Manual, as revised by Major A. Mordecai for a new edition, in pursuance of your order dated October 14, 1847, and have made such alterations and additions as appeared to be required preparatory to the publication of the work.

R. L. BAKER, *Brevet Lieut. Col.*
J. W. RIPLEY, *Brevet Lieut. Col.*
J. SYMINGTON, *Major of Ordnance*
A. MORDECAI, *Brevet Major.*
B. HUGER, *Brevet Col.*
} ORD. BOARD.

ORDNANCE DEPARTMENT,

WASHINGTON, *November* 17*th*, 1849.

Hon. GEO. W. CRAWFORD,

Secretary of War.

It is respectfully recommended that the revised edition of the Ordnance Manual be printed for the use of the Army.

G. TALCOTT, *Bvt. Brig. Gen.*,

Colonel of Ordnance.

Approved, November 23, 1849:

G. W. CRAWFORD.

EXTRACTS *from the preface to the first edition of the Ordnanse Manual.*

"This work being designed chiefly for the use of those charged with the fabrication and care of the *materiel*, leaves untouched nearly all that relates to the personal service of Artillery, either in the field or in garrison." * * *

"It is earnestly requested that all officers of the Army, and especially those of the Ordnance Department, will avail themselves of every opportunity to verify the details and add to the information here given, and that they will communicate to the Colonel of Ordnance any corrections or amendments which it may appear advisable to make in a future edition of the work."

TABLE OF CONTENTS.

LIST OF PLATES.

INDEX.

A.

B.

Q.

R.

S.

W.

ERRATA.

Page 37—List of *Irons*, 5th line: For *links*, read *rings*.

" 133—12th line from the bottom; Add: 4 *notch plates*, fastened to the arcs, each by 4 *screws*.

" 217—First column of table: For 4, read 1.

" 218—1st line: For weight, read height.

" 428—*Equation of the Trajectory:* In the 2nd term of the second member, for x, read x^2.

" 437—19th line: The words "area of the" should be transposed to the beginning of the 18th line.

ORDNANCE MANUAL.

CHAPTER FIRST.

ORDNANCE.

The following are the kinds and calibres of ordnance used in the land service of the United States:

KIND OF ORDNANCE.		CALIBRE.	MATERIAL.	
GUNS	Field	6-pounder	Bronze	Plate 1.
GUNS	Field	12-pounder	Bronze	Plate 1.
GUNS	Siege and garrison	12-pounder	Iron	Plate 1.
GUNS	Siege and garrison	18-pounder	Iron	Plate 1.
GUNS	Siege and garrison	24-pounder	Iron	Plate 1.
GUNS	Seacoast	32-pounder	Iron	Plate 1.
GUNS	Seacoast	42-pounder	Iron	Plate 1.
HOWITZERS	Mountain	12-pounder	Bronze	Plate 1.
HOWITZERS	Field	12-pounder	Bronze	Plate 1.
HOWITZERS	Field	24-pounder	Bronze	Plate 1.
HOWITZERS	Field	32-pounder	Bronze	Plate 1.
HOWITZERS	Siege and garrison	8-inch	Iron	Plate 2.
HOWITZERS	Siege and garrison	24-pounder	Iron	Plate 10.
HOWITZERS	Seacoast	8-inch	Iron	Plate 2.
HOWITZERS	Seacoast	10-inch	Iron	Plate 2.
COLUMBIADS		8-inch	Iron	Plate 9.
COLUMBIADS		10-inch	Iron	Plate 9.
MORTARS	Light	8-inch	Iron	Plate 2.
MORTARS	Light	10-inch	Iron	Plate 2.
MORTARS	Heavy	10-inch	Iron	Plate 2.
MORTARS	Heavy	13-inch	Iron	Plate 2.
MORTARS	Stone mortar	16-inch	Bronze	Plate 2.
MORTARS	Coehorn	24-pounder	Bronze	Plate 2.
MORTARS	Eprouvette	24-pounder	Iron	Plate 2.

A 12-inch columbiad, of cast iron, has also been made for trial.

The plates and the tables of dimensions and weights refer to the latest patterns.

For the description of ordnance of former patterns, see the first edition of this Manual.

Nomenclature.

The forms of the several pieces of ordnance are shown in the Plates referred to in the last column of the preceding table.

Cannon made of bronze are commonly called *brass* cannon.

The *cascable* is the part of the gun in rear of the base ring; it is composed generally of the following parts: the *knob*, the *neck*, the *fillet*, and the *base of the breech*.

The *base of the breech* is a frustum of a cone, or a spherical segment, in rear of the breech.

The *base ring* is a projecting band of metal adjoining the base of the breech and connected with the body of the gun by a concave moulding.

The *breech* is the mass of solid metal behind the bottom of the bore, extending to the rear of the base ring.

The *reinforce* is the thickest part of the body of the gun, in front of the base ring; if there is more than one reinforce, that which is next to the base ring is called the *first reinforce;* the other, the *second reinforce*. In some howitzers, instead of a reinforce, there is a *recess* in the metal around the chamber, next to the base ring.

The *reinforce band* is at the junction of the first and second reinforces in the heavy howitzers and columbiads.

The *chase* is the conical part of the gun in front of the reinforce.

The *astragal* and *fillets*, in field guns, and the *chase ring* in other pieces, are the mouldings at the front end of the chase.

The *neck* is the smallest part of the piece, in front of the astragal or the chase ring.

The *swell of the muzzle* is the largest part of the gun in front of the neck. It is terminated by the muzzle mouldings, which, in field and siege guns, consist of the *lip* and the *fillet*. In the seacoast guns and heavy howitzers and columbiads, there is no fillet. In field and siege howitzers, and in mortars, a *muzzle band* takes the place of the swell of the muzzle.

The *face* of the piece is the terminating plane perpendicular to the axis of the bore.

The *trunnions* are cylinders, the axes of which are in a line perpendicular to the axis of the bore, and in the same plane with that axis.

The *rimbases* are short cylinders, uniting the trunnions with the body of the gun. The ends of the rimbases, or the *shoulders of the trunnions*, are planes perpendicular to the axis of the trunnions.

The *bore* of the piece includes all the part bored out, viz: the cylinder, the chamber, (if there is one,) and the conical or spherical surface connecting them.

The *chamber*, in howitzers, columbiads, and mortars, is the smaller part of the bore, which contains the charge of powder. In howitzers and columbiads the chamber is cylindrical; it is united with the large cylinder of the bore by a conical surface; the angles of intersection of this conical surface with the cylinders of the bore and chamber are rounded (in profile) by arcs of circles. In the 8-inch siege howitzer, the chamber is united with the cylinder of the bore by a spherical surface, in order that the shell may, when necessary, be inserted without a sabot.

A conical chamber which is joined to the cylinder of the bore by a portion of a spherical surface, (as in the 8-inch and 10-inch light mortars,) is called a *Gomer chamber*.

The *bottom of the bore* is a plane perpendicular to the axis, united with the sides (in profile) by an arc of a circle, the radius of which is one-fourth of the diameter of the bore at the bottom. In the columbiads, the heavy sea coast mortars, the stone mortar, and the eprouvette, the bottom of the bore is hemispherical.

The *muzzle*, or mouth of the bore, is chamfered to a depth of 0.15 inch to 0.5 inch, (varying with the size of the bore,) in order to prevent abrasion, and to facilitate loading.

The *true windage* is the difference between the true diameters of the bore and of the ball.

The axis of the *vent* is in a plane passing through the axis of the bore, perpendicular to the axis of the trunnions. In guns, and in howitzers having cylindrical chambers, the vent is placed at an angle of 80° with the axis of the bore, and it enters the bore at a distance from the bottom equal to one-fourth the diameter of the bore.

The diameter of the vent is *two-tenths* of an inch, in all pieces except the eprouvette in which it is *one-tenth*.

The vents of brass guns are bored in *vent pieces*, of wrought copper, which are screwed into the gun.

The *lock piece* is a block of metal at the outer opening of the vent, in some pieces of ordnance, to facilitate attaching a lock to the cannon.

The *natural line of sight* is a line drawn in a vertical plane through the axis of the piece, from the highest point of the base ring to the highest point in the swell of the muzzle, or to the top of the *sight*, if there is one.

The *natural angle of sight* is the angle which the natural line of sight makes with the axis of the piece.

The *dispart* is the difference of the semi-diameters of the base ring and the swell of the muzzle, or the muzzle band. It is therefore the tangent of the natural angle of sight, to a radius equal to the distance from the rear of the base ring to the highest point of the swell of the muzzle, the sight, or the front of the muzzle band, as the case may be.

The *preponderance* of the breech of the gun is the excess of weight of the part in rear of the trunnions over that in front: it is measured by the weight which it is necessary to apply in the plane of the muzzle to balance the gun when suspended freely on the axis of the trunnions.

The *handles* of the gun are placed with their centres over the centre of gravity of the piece.

The 6-pounder gun and the 12-pounder howitzer have no handles. The handle of a heavy mortar consists of a *clevis*, which is attached by a *bolt* to the *ear* of the mortar.

The *eprouvette mortar* is cast with a *sole*, which fits into a cast iron *bed plate*, bolted to the platform.

To designate a piece of ordnance.

State the kind, the calibre, (in inches if it be foreign ordnance,) the material, the weight, the inspector's initials, the number, the country in which it was made, the date, the place of fabrication, the founder's name, the name inscribed on it, its condition for service, the kind of chamber, if any; whether it has a vent piece, a lock piece, handles; the ornaments, and any particular marks which may serve to identify it.

PRINCIPAL DIMENSIONS AND WEIGHTS OF GUNS.

	IRON.					BRASS.	
	SEA COAST.		SIEGE AND GARRISON.			FIELD.	
	42	32	24	18	12	12	6
	Inches.	Inches.	Inches.	Inches.	Inches.	Inches.	Inches.
Diameter of the bore	7.	6.4	5.82	5.3	4.62	4.62	3.67
True windage	0.16	0.15	0.14	0.13	0.10	0.10	0.09
Length of bore	110.	107.6	108.	109.	103.4	74.	57.5
Ditto .....in diameters	**15.71**	**16.78**	**18.56**	**20.56**	**22.38**	**16.**	**15.67**
Length from rear of base ring to face of muzzle	117.	114.	114.	114.	108.	78.	60.
Whole length of the piece	129.	125.2	124.	123.25	116.	85.	65.6
Semi-diameter of the base ring	12.2	11.2	10.7	9.875	8.7	6.5	5.15
Semi-diameter of the swell of the muzzle	8.4	7.7	7.793	6.935	5.932	5.17	4.125
Distance between these two semi-diameters	115.	112.	111.	111.6	105.8	76.3	58.7
Natural angle of sight	....	....	1° 30′	1° 30′	1° 30′	1°	1°
Distance from rear of base ring to rear of trunnions	43.2	42.2	43.	43.50	42.	30.7	23.25
Diameter of the base ring	24.4	22.4	21.4	19.75	17.4	13.	10.3
Distance between the rimbases	22.	20.7	18.	16.8	14.8	12.	9.5
Length of the trunnions	6.5	6.	5.	4.75	4.5	3.5	2.8
Diameter of the trunnions	7.	6.4	5.82	5.3	4.62	4.62	3.67
Distance from axis of trunnions to face of muzzle	70.3	68.6	68.09	67.85	63.69	44.99	34.91
Weight .....pounds	8,465	7,200	5,790	4,913	3,590	1,757	884
Preponderance .....pounds	440	466	255	200	200	60	33

PRINCIPAL DIMENSIONS AND WEIGHTS OF COLUMBIADS AND HOWITZERS.

	COLUMB'DS.		HOWITZERS.							
	IRON.		IRON.				BRASS.			
			Sea Coast.		Siege and garrison.		Field.			Mountain.
	10-in.	8-in.	10-in.	8-in.	8-in.	24-pr.	32-pr.	24-pr.	12-pr.	12-pr.
	Inches	Inches	Inches	Inches	Inches	Inches	Inches	Inches	Inches	Inches
Diameter of the bore	10.	8.	10.	8.	8.	5.82	6.4	5.82	4.62	4.62
True windage	0.12	0.12	0.12	0.13	0.13	0.14	0.15	0.14	0.10	0.10
Length of bore, exclusive of chamber	99.00	100.	96.	85.5	38.5	53.25	64.	56.25	46.25	28.16
Ditto... in diameters	9.9	12.5	9.6	10.68	4.81	9.15	10.	9.66	10.	6.1
Diameter of the chamber	8.	6.4	7.	6.4	4.62	4.62	4.62	4.62	3.67	3.34
Length of the chamber	12.	11.	9.5	7.5	8.	4.75	7.	4.75	4.25	2.75
Length from rear of base ring to face of muzzle	120.	119.	112.	98.	52.	62.	75.	65.	53.	32.91
Whole length of the piece	126.	124.	124.25	109.	61.5	69.	82.	71.2	58.6	37.21
Semi-diameter of base ring	16.	13.	13.25	11.10	9.125	6.9	6.9	6.	5.	3.8
Semi-diameter of swell of muzzle	10.75	8.5	10.125	8.25	8.225	5.85	5.6	4.875	4.1	3.45
Distance between these semi-diameters	117.5	117.	109.5	96.	51.5	61.8	74.75	64.8	52.85	32.91
Natural angle of sight	1° 21′	1° 23′	......	......	1°	1°	1°	1°	1°	0° 37′
Distance from rear of base ring to rear of trunnions	41.5	41.5	41.	37.4	24.	24.69	30.7	27.5	23.25	15.
Diameter of base ring	32.	26.	26.5	22.2	18.25	13.8	13.8	13.8	12.	10.
Distance between the rimbases	31.	25.	25.	20.7	18.	12.8	12.	11.5	9.5	6.9
Length of the trunnions	9.	6.5	7.5	6.	5.	3.25	3.5	3.25	2.8	2.25
Diameter of the trunnions	10.	8.	8.	6.4	5.82	4.62	4.62	4.2	3.67	2.7
Distance from axis of trunnions to face of muzzle	73.5	73.5	67.	57.4	25.09	35.	41.99	35.4	27.91	16.56
Weight... pounds	15,400	9,240	9,500	5,740	2,614	1,476	1,920	1,318	788	220
Preponderance... pounds	470	350	450	380	460	70	125	112	51	30

PRINCIPAL DIMENSIONS AND WEIGHTS OF MORTARS.

	IRON.				BRASS.		IRON.
	HEAVY.		LIGHT.		Stone mortar.	Coehorn 24-pr.	Eprouvette.
	13-in.	10-in.	10-in.	8-in.			
	Inches.	Inches.	Inches.	Inches.	Inches.	Inches.	Inches.
Diameter of the bore	13.	10.	10.	8.	16.	5.82	5.655
True windage	0.13	0.13	0.13	0.12	......	0.14	0.025
Length of the bore, exclusive of the chamber	26.	25.	15.	12.	19.8	8.82	11.5
Ditto ... in diameters	**2.**	**2.5**	**1.5**	**1.5**	**1.24**	**1.51**	**2.**
Diameter of the chamber. Superior, (at the bottom of the shell in iron mortars,)	9.5	7.15	7.6	6.08	5.3	3.	1.5
Diameter of the chamber. Inferior	7.25	5.64	5.	4.	3.	2.	1.5
Length of the chamber	13.	10.	5.	4.	6.75	4.25	1.35
Whole length of the mortar	53.	46.	28.	22.5	31.55	16.32	
Distance from face of muzzle to front of trunnions	41.	37.	20.	16.5	20.	13.57	
Distance between the rimbases	36.	27.5	20.5	16.25	18.	7.5	
Length of the trunnions	8.5	6.5	5.	4.	6.	2.5	
Diameter of the trunnions	12.	9.	8.	6.	8.	2.75	
Weight ... pounds	11,500	5,775	1,852	930	1,500	164	220

OF THE MATERIALS FOR ORDNANCE.

Bronze.

Bronze for cannon, (commonly called *brass*,) consists of 90 parts of copper, and 10 of tin, allowing a variation of one part of tin, more or less. It is more fusible than copper, much less so than tin, more sonorous, harder, and less susceptible of oxidation, and much less ductile, than either of its components. Its fracture is of a yellowish color, with little lustre, a coarse grain, irregular, and often exhibiting spots of tin, which are of a whitish color. These spots indicate defects in the metal; but they seldom contain more than 25 per cent. of tin. The specific gravity of bronze is about 8,700, being greater than the mean of the specific gravities of copper and tin.

Pure copper is of a red color, inclining to yellow; it has a fine metallic lustre. Its fracture exhibits a short, even, close grain, of a silky appearance; it is very ductile and very malleable. The greater the purity of copper, the more malleable it is, and the finer the grain. Specific gravity from 8,600 to 9,000.

Pure tin is of a white color, a little darker than silver; it is malleable, and susceptible of being rolled into sheets, but it is not very ductile; it is very soft, and, when bent backwards and forwards, it gives a peculiar crackling sound, the distinctness of which is in proportion to the purity of the tin. Specific gravity, 7,290 to 7,320.

Analysis of bronze. Nitric acid dissolves the copper and converts the tin into an insoluble peroxide. Put into a small glass matrass 10 parts (say 100 grains) of bronze, in small particles, and 80 parts of very pure nitric acid, at 22° Beaumé's hydrometer, (specific gravity, 1,180;) heat it gradually to ebullition, and continue that heat until red vapors cease to come over. Let it settle; pour off the liquor, and add to the oxide of tin 20 parts of nitric acid; let it boil ten minutes; decant the liquor again, and repeat the same operation; dilute the first portion decanted with 2 or 3 times its volume of water, and pass it through a filter; do the same with the second and third portions. Then throw the oxide of tin on a double filter, the two parts of which are equal; wash the precipitate on the filter until the water that comes off no longer gives a blue color when heated with ammonia, and does not change the color of litmus paper. Spread the filter on paper, and dry it perfectly in a stove or a sand bath. Weigh it, adding the exterior filter to the weights, in order to ascertain the quantity of peroxide of tin which remains on the upper filter; 127 parts of peroxide give 100 parts of pure tin.

If lead is present, it will be dissolved by the acid. To detect it:—after the solution is cool, add sulphate of soda, in order to precipitate the lead in the state of an insoluble sulphate, 145 parts of which contain 100 of lead.

Cast Iron.

(*See also Chapter* 14.)

Iron for making cannon must be of the best quality of charcoal iron, made in a smelting furnace, with a cold blast, and should be selected particularly for its strength. It should be soft, yielding easily to the file or chisel; its fracture presenting an uniform appearance; color, dark grey; aspect, brilliant; chrystals of medium size.

When cast into cannon, it should approach that degree of hardness which resists the file and the chisel, but not too hard to be bored and turned without great difficulty. Its color a bright lively grey; chrystals small, with acute angles, and sharp to the touch; structure uniform, close, and compact. If the pig iron be too soft, coarse, and loose, its strength and density may be increased by remelting it once or twice, and by continuing it in fusion several hours, under a high heat.

But as the quality of cast iron cannot be accurately determined by an inspection of its fracture alone, samples taken from the pig iron, and from the sinking heads of cannon are submitted to practical tests. The mean specific gravity of pig iron is 7.00; and its tenacity is about 16,000 pounds to the square inch.

The following table shows some of the results obtained in the trials of samples from gun heads:

DATE.	DESIGNATION OF GUNS.				IRON.	
	Where made.	No.	Kind.	Weight.	Specific gravity.	Tenacity.
1846				lbs.		lbs.
April......	Richmond, Va.	28	32-pdr. S. C. guns.	7,200	7.204	26,396
July.......	do.	25	do. do.	7,200	7.226	28,462
June......	Pittsburgh, Pa.	33	8-inch columbiads.	9,237	7.227	27,133
September.	Pittsburgh, Pa.	7	8-inch navy guns.	6,280	7.299	32,445
November.	West Point, N.Y.	37	Siege mortars, howitzers & guns.	....	7.236	27,000
1847						
June......	Boston, Mass.	25	24-pdr. howitzers.	1,477	7.222	29,006
1848						
April......	Boston, Mass.	20	24-pdr. guns.	5,778	7.297	30,828
June......	West Point.	20	32-pdr. navy guns.	6,437	7.270	30,686
1849						
June......	West Point.	11	8-inch navy guns.	11,943	7.248	31,430
June......	Boston, Mass.	35	24-pdr. howitzers.	1,500	7.305	36,651
	Mean.......	241	....	....	7.248	29,693

In making guns from iron of which the quality is not known, a sample gun is made and proved to extremity, with gunpowder. The gun adopted for this proof is a long 9-pounder gun, of the same pattern as the 8-pounder used for the same purpose in France and Belgium. It is fired with the following series of charges, viz:

1st.	20 rounds,	3 pounds of powder,	1 ball.	Without wads.
2d.	20 "	4.5 " "	2 "	
3d.	10 "	4.5 " "	3 "	
4th.	5 "	9 " "	6 "	
5th.	-	18 " "	13 "	

In order that the iron shall be used for ordnance, the trial gun should sustain the first four series of rounds without breaking.

INSPECTION OF ORDNANCE.

Instruments.

1. *Star gauge.*—This is an instrument for measuring the diameter of the bore of a gun, at any part.

The head is of brass, with four steel sockets for the measuring points. Two of the sockets are soldered fast into the head; the other two are moveable. The moveable sockets and points are pushed out by means of two inclined cylinders, which are fastened to a stem, forming a conical slider. This slider tapers 0.35 in. in a length of 2.2 in.; so that by pushing the slider the 35th part of this length (about .06 in.) the distance between the moveable points is increased .01 in.

The slider is connected with a square steel rod, consisting of three parts, which are screwed together, according to the length of bore to be measured. This rod slides through a brass tube, which is also made in three pieces.

The tube is graduated, in inches and quarters, commencing at the measuring points, so as to indicate the distance of the latter from the muzzle of the gun.

The handle is of wood attached to a brass cylinder, or socket, through which the sliding rod passes. In the tube of the handle there is a slit, on the side of which a scale is marked, to indicate the movements of the measuring points. Each joint of the long tube has a mark, made on a small plate of silver, which shows the place of the zero on the scale, when the measuring points are adjusted to the true diameter of the bore. In this position the handle is fixed on the sliding rod by means of a screw clamp.

A *ring gauge*, for each calibre, is used for adjusting the instrument for use.

A *rest*, in the form of a T, is placed in the mouth of the gun, to keep the instrument in the axis of the bore. This rest has three slides, which can be adjusted to the different sizes of bore; the upright branch is moveable, for convenience of packing.

The star guage, its points and rest, are packed in one box, and the ring gauges in another.

2. *The cylinder staff.*—This is a round staff, made of mahogany, or other hard wood. It is in two parts, which are joined together by brass sockets and screws; each part has also a brass socket and screw at the outer end, to receive the *cylinder gauge*, *guide plate*, *measuring point*, and *searcher*. The staff is graduated, in inches and tenths, on a strip of brass let into it, on one side. These graduations are arranged to read the distances from the extemity of the measuring point, when it is screwed on the staff.

The cylinder staff is supported, at the muzzle of the piece, by a *half tompion* of wood, having in the centre a groove of the size of the staff. The *rest* for the star guage may be used also for this purpose.

3. The *cylinder gauge* is a hollow cylinder of wrought or cast iron, turned to the exact minimum (or true) diameter of the bore. The length of the cylinder is equal to its diameter. It has cross heads, at right angles to each other; one with a smooth hole of the same diameter as the cylinder staff; the other tapped for the screw of the staff socket.

4. The *searcher* is used to ascertain whether there are any cavities in the bore. It consists of four flat springs about 13 inches long, with sharp points, turned outwards at the end, attached to a socket on which the cylinder-staff is screwed.

5. The *guide-plate* is a circular iron plate 0.2 inch thick, and of the minimum diameter of the bore; it has a hole in the centre, with a thread by which it is screwed to the cylinder-staff; it serves to direct the measuring point to the centre of the bottom of the bore.

6. The *measuring point* is screwed on the end of the cylinder staff, over the guide-plate, to measure the depth of the bore; it is of iron, cylindrical in shape, so far as it screws on the end of the staff, and tapering down to the diameter of 0.75 inch.

7. The *trunnion-gauge* is an iron ring of the diameter of the trunnionsr which must pass over them and fit closely. The exterior diameter of this gauge serves to verify that of the rimbases.

8. The *trunnion-square* is a double square of wood, the distance between whose branches is the same as that between the rimbases of the gun; in the centre is a pointed sliding plate, with a thumb-screw to fasten it; the lowe, edges of the branches, which are shod with iron, are in the same plane, parallel to the upper edge of the connecting piece, so that when the square is placed with its branches resting on the trunnions, the upper edge of the connecting

piece is parallel to their axis. Each branch has also an iron plate projecting perpendicularly from one side to rest on the top of the trunnions. It is used to ascertain the position of the trunnions in relation to the axis of the bore and to each other.

9. The *trunnion rule*, for measuring the distance from the rear of the base ring to the rear of the trunnions.

10. *Callipers*, to measure diameters.

11. A *standard scale*, for verifying other instruments.

12. A wooden *rule*, to measure exterior lengths.

13. The *vent-gauges* are two pointed pieces of steel wire, 0.005 in. greater and less than the true diameter of the vent.

14. The *vent-searcher* is a hooked steel wire, about half the diameter of the vent.

15. A *rammer-head*, shaped to the form of the bottom of the bore, and furnished with a staff, is used to ascertain the interior position of the vent.

16. A *mirror; a wax taper; bees-wax.*

17. *Rammer*, *sponge*, and *priming wire*.

18. *Figure* and *letter stamps*, to affix the required marks.

Inspection of Iron Ordnance.

Cannon presented for inspection and proof, are placed on skids for the convenience of turning and moving them easily. They are first examined carefully on the exterior, to ascertain whether there are any flaws or cracks in the metal, whether they are finished as prescribed, and to judge, as well as practicable, of the quality of the metal. They must not be covered with paint, lacker, or any other composition. If it is ascertained that an attempt has been made to conceal any flaws or cavities by plugging, or filling them with cement, or any substance, the gun is rejected without further examination. After this preliminary examination, the inspector proceeds to verify the dimensions of the piece. The *interior of the bore* is first examined by reflecting the sun's rays into it from the mirror; or, if the sun is obscured, by a lighted wax taper or a lamp placed on the end of a rod, and inserted into the bore. The *searcher* is then introduced, and pushed slowly to the bottom of the bore and withdrawn, turning it at the same time; if one of the points hangs, the position of the hole is marked on the outside of the gun by noticing its distance from the muzzle, and its position in the bore; the size and figure of the cavity are found by taking an impression of it in *wax* placed on the end of a hook. The *cylinder-gauge*, screwed on the staff, is then pushed gently to the bottom of the cylindrical part of the bore and withdrawn; it must go to the bottom, or the bore is too small.

The *bore of the piece* is then measured with the star gauge. The measurements should be made at intervals of ¼ inch in the part of the bore occupied by the shot; at intervals of 1 inch in the rest of the bore in rear of the trunnions, and of about 1 calibre from the trunnions to the muzzle.

The *position of the trunnions*, with regard to the axis of the bore and to each other, is next ascertained.

To verify the position of the axis of the trunnions: set the trunnion-square on the trunnions, and see that the lower edges of its branches touch them throughout their whole length; push the slide down till it touches the surface of the piece, and secure it in that position by the thumb-screw; turn the gun over, and apply the trunnion square to the opposite side, and if, when the point of the slide touches the surface of the piece, the lower edges of the branches rest on the trunnions, the axis of the trunnions is in the same plane with the axis of the bore; if they do not touch the trunnions, their axis is above the axis of the bore by half the space between; and if the edges touch the trunnions, and the point of the slide does not touch the surface of the piece, their axis is below the axis of the bore. If the *alignment of the trunnions* be accurate, the edges of the trunnion-square will fit on them when applied to different parts of their surface; their diameter and cylindrical form, and the diameter of the rimbases, are verified with the trunnion-gauge.

To ascertain the length of the bore, screw the *guide-plate* and *measuring-point* on the cylinder staff, and push them to the bottom of the bore; place a *half-tompion* in the muzzle, and rest the staff in its groove; apply a *straight-edge* to the face of the muzzle, and read the length of the bore on the staff. The *exterior lengths* are measured by the *rule*, or by a *profile*, the accuracy of which is first verified. The *exterior diameters* are measured with the *callipers* and *graduated rule*. The *position of the interior orifice of the vent* is found from the mark made on the *rammer-head* by the *vent-gauge* inserted in the vent, while the rammer-head is held against the bottom of the bore—two impressions are taken. The position of the exterior orifice of the vent is also verified. The *vent* is examined with *gauges*, and with the *vent-searcher*, to ascertain if there are any cavities in it. In *mortars*, the dimensions of the *conical chambers*, and the *form of the breech*, may be verified with *patterns* made of plate iron. After the *powder proof*, the bore is washed and wiped clean, and the bore and vent are again examined, and the bore remeasured. The results of each of the measurements and examinations are noted on the inspection report against the number of the gun.

VARIATIONS ALLOWED IN THE DIMENSIONS OF IRON ORDNANCE.

		FIELD.	GARRISON, &c.
		Inches.	Inches.
IN THE BORE...	More than the prescribed diameter........	0.02	0.03
	Less than the prescribed diameter........	.00	.00
IN EXTERIOR DIAMETERS.	Where turned, more or less..............	.04	.05
	Where not turned, more................	.10	.20
	Where not turned, less.................	.05	.05
IN THE LENGTH.	Of the bore, more or less................	.10	.20
	From rear of base ring to face of muzzle, more or less	.10	.25
	Of the breech, including cascable, more or less..................................	.15	.20
	Of the base ring, more or less............	.05	.05
	Of the reinforce, more or less............	.10	.20
	Of the chase, including the muzzle, more or less..................................	.10	.15
	From rear of trunnions to rear of base ring, more or less, in different pieces.........	.10	.20
IN THE POSITION OF THE AXIS OF THE TRUNNIONS	above the axis of the bore......	.00	.00
	below the axis of the bore......	.20	.20
IN THE LENGTH OF THE TRUNNIONS,	more...............	.10	.10
	less................	.05	.05
Diameter of trunnions, less............................		.03	.04
In the distance between the rimbases, less.................		.05	.05
In the same gun, no variation is allowed in the position or in the alignment of the trunnions.			
IN THE VENT.......	Diameter, more.................	.005	.005
	Diameter, less..................	.00	.00
	Position of exterior orifice, more or less	.05	.05
	Position of interior orifice, more or less	.20	.20
DEPTH OF CAVITIES.	In the bore or vent..................	.00	.00
	On the exterior surface..............	.20	.25
	On the trunnions, within one inch of the rimbases....................	.10	.10
	On the trunnions elsewhere..........	.20	.25
In the eprouvette, no variation is allowed.			

The whole exterior surfaces of iron guns, columbiads, and howitzers are turned in the lathe, or dressed smooth in the parts which cannot be turned.

Inspection of Brass Ordnance.

Brass cannon are measured, and their dimensions recorded, as prescribed for iron cannon. *The exterior form and dimensions* are verified by the application of a *profile* cut out of sheet iron, of the exact shape of a longitudinal section of the piece. All brass ordnance, except stone mortars, should be bored under size from .04 to .05 inch, and after proof reamed out to the exact calibre. When the powder proof is finished, the bore should be cleaned and examined; the vent should then be stopped with a greased wooden plug, the muzzle raised, and the gun filled with water, to which pressure shall be applied to force it into any cavities that exist; or the water shall be allowed to remain in the bore about 24 hours. *The bore* must then be sponged dry and clean, and viewed with the *mirror* or *candle*, to discover if any water oozes from cracks or cavities, and also if any enlargement has taken place. The quantity of water that runs out of a crack or honey-comb will indicate the extent of the defect, and if it exceeds a few drops, the gun should be rejected, although the measured depth of the cavity may not exceed the allowance. If the water oozes out between the vent piece and the metal of the gun, a new vent piece must be inserted, and the gun again proved with one charge, and the water proof repeated. After the bore has been reamed out to the proper size, its dimensions are again verified, and an examination of the bore and vent is made, to detect any defects which may have been caused or developed by the proof. *Whitish spots* show a separation of the tin from the copper, and, if extensive, should condemn the piece. A *great variation from the true weight*, which the dimensions do not account for, shows a defect in the alloy. Any attempt to conceal cavities by filling them with screws, or by any other methods, should cause the rejection of the piece.

Brass cannon should be rejected for the following cavities or honey-combs:

Exterior.—Any hole or cavity 0.25 inch deep in front of the trunnions, and 0.2 inch deep at or behind the trunnions.

Interior.—From the muzzle to the reinforce, any cavity 0.15 inch deep. Any cavity from the reinforce to the bottom of the bore.

The specific gravity of the metal of brass ordnance should be occasionally ascertained, by taking that of some of the heaviest, and some of the lightest pieces, at each inspection.

The exterior surfaces of all brass ordnance are turned, or dressed smooth.

VARIATIONS ALLOWED IN THE DIMENSIONS OF BRASS ORDNANCE.

		Inch.
Length of bore, more or less		0.1
Diameter of bore	more	.02
	less	.00
Exterior position of vent, more or less		.05
Interior position of vent, more or less		.20
Diameter of vent	more	.005
	less	.00
Diameter of trunnions	more	.00
	less	.025
Length of trunnions	more	.10
	less	.05
Position of trunnions	*above* the axis of the gun	.00
	below the axis of the gun	.20
	out of alignment	.00
Distance from rear of base ring to rear of trunnions		.10
Distance between rimbases, less		.04
Length from the base ring to the muzzle, more or less		.10
Position of mouldings, more or less		.10
Any exterior diameter from the base ring to the muzzle inclusive, and diameter of rimbases, more or less		.04
Diameter of cascable, neck, and knob, more or less		.05

A proper discretion must be exercised in the inspection of ordnance; such slight imperfections as do not injure a piece for service may be disregarded, whilst the instructions should be strictly enforced with regard to defects which may impair its utility.

PROOF OF ORDNANCE.

Gunpowder for proving ordnance should be of the best quality, ranging not less than 250 yards by the eprouvette; it should be proved immediately before being used, unless it shall have been proved within one year previously, and there be no reason to suspect that it has become deteriorated.

The *cartridge bags* are made of woollen stuff, or of paper, the full diameter of the bore or chamber. They are filled by weight, and if not filled at the place where the guns are proved, each bag should be enveloped in a paper cylinder and cap, marked with the weight of powder and its proof range.

The *shot* must be smooth, free from seams and other inequalities that might injure the bore of the piece, and they must be of the true diameter given in the tables.

The *wads* are made of junk, as described in CHAPTER X.

PROOF OF IRON ORDNANCE.

Guns and *howitzers* are laid with the muzzle resting on a block of wood and the breech on the ground, or on a thick plank, giving the bore a small elevation.

Mortars are mounted on strong wooden frames or beds, at an elevation of 45°, supported by the trunnions.

In proving iron ordnance, after pricking the cartridge, prime with powder, or a tube, and place over the vent a piece of portfire, set in clay or putty, long enough to permit the man who fires it to reach a place of safety before the charge explodes.

Proof charges for Iron Guns.

FIRST AND SECOND ROUNDS.—A charge of *powder* equal to *one-half* of the weight of the shot; *two shot* and *one wad.*

THIRD ROUND.—A charge of *powder* equal to *one-third* of the weight of the shot; *one shot* and *one wad.*

In proving new guns, a compound shot, or a cylinder with hemispherical ends, of the true diameter of the shot, and equal in weight to the two shot, shall be used instead of them.

The wad is placed over the cylinder or the upper ball; the whole being well rammed.

Should any of the guns proved at one time fail to sustain the above proof, the remainder shall be again fired *twice* with a charge of powder equal to *one-half* of the weight of the shot, *one shot and one wad;* and if, in either or both of these trials, *one-fourth* of the whole number of guns should fail, the whole shall be rejected.

Other iron ordnance are fired with the following charges:

Columbiads.

10-inch.—1st round: 20 lbs. of powder, one 10-inch strapped shot, and one wad over the shot.
2nd round: 24 lbs. of powder, one 10-inch shell strapped.

8-inch.—1st round: 12 lbs. of powder, one 8-inch strapped shot and one wad.
2nd round: 15 lbs. of powder, one 8-inch shell strapped.

Howitzers.

SEA COAST.
- 10-*inch.*—2 rounds, with 15 lbs of powder, one 10-inch strapped shot, and one wad over the shot.
- 8-*inch.*—2 rounds, with 12 lbs. of powder, one 8-inch strapped shot, and one wad over the shot.

SIEGE AND GARRISON.
- 8-*inch.*—2 rounds, with 4 lbs. of powder, one 8-inch shot, and one wad over the shot.
- 24-*pdr.*—2 rounds, with 3 lbs. of powder, one 24-pdr. strapped shot, and one wad over the shot.

Mortars.

HEAVY....
- 13-*inch.*—2 rounds, with 20 lbs. of powder, and one 13-inch shot.
- 10-*inch.*—2 rounds, with 10 lbs. of powder, and one 10-inch shot.

LIGHT.....
- 10-*inch.*—2 rounds, with 5 lbs. of powder, and one 10-inch shot.
- 8-*inch.*—2 rounds, with $2\frac{1}{2}$ lbs. of powder, and one 8-inch shot.

Should any columbiad, howitzer, or mortar fail to sustain the above proof, the remainder of those offered at the same time shall be again fired *twice* with the same charges; and if, in either or both of these trials, *one-fourth* of the whole number should fail, the whole shall be rejected.

The *water proof*, as described for brass cannon, must also be applied occasionally to iron cannon, at the discretion of the inspector.

The bore and vent and the exterior surface of every piece which is approved, should be well covered with sperm oil immediately after the inspection.

PROOF OF BRASS ORDNANCE.

They are mounted on appropriate carriages or beds, and fired three times; *guns* and *howitzers* at an elevation of 5°, *mortars* at an elevation of 45°; with the following charges:

Field Guns.

A charge of *powder* equal to *one-third* of the weight of the shot, *one shot* and *one wad.*

Howitzers.

FIELD,
- 32-pdr.—$3\frac{1}{4}$ lbs. of powder, one strapped shot and one wad.
- 24-pdr.—$2\frac{1}{2}$ lbs. of powder, one strapped shot and one wad.
- 12-pdr.—$1\frac{1}{2}$ lbs. of powder, one strapped shot and one wad.

MOUNTAIN, 12-pdr.—$\frac{3}{4}$ lb. of powder, one strapped shot and one wad.

Mortars.

STONE MORTAR.—$2\frac{1}{2}$ lbs. of powder, covered by a wooden tompion 2 inches thick; a basket filled with alternate layers of stones and earth, weighing 100 lbs.

COEHORN, 24-pdr.—$\frac{3}{4}$ lb. of powder, and one 24-pdr. shot.

In proving brass cannon in service, or after they have been bored to the proper calibre, the shot should be wrapped in cloth or strong paper to save the bore as much as possible from injury.

MARKS.

All cannon are required to be weighed and to be marked, as follows, viz: the *number of the gun*, and *the initials of the inspector's name*, on the face of the muzzle; the numbers in a separate series for each kind and calibre at each foundry; the initial letters of the *name of the founder* and of the foundry, on the end of the right trunnion; the *year of fabrication* on the end of the left trunnion; the *foundry number* on the end of the right rimbase, above the trunnion; the *weight of the piece in pounds* on the base of the breech; the letters U. S. on the upper surface of the piece, near the end of the reinforce.

The natural line of sight, when the axis of the trunnions is horizontal, should be marked on the base ring and on the swell of the muzzle, whilst the piece is in the trunnion lathe.

Cannon rejected on inspection are marked X C, on the face of the muzzle; if condemned for erroneous dimensions which cannot be remedied, add X D; if by powder proof, X P; if by water proof, X W.

INJURIES CAUSED BY SERVICE.

Brass cannon are little subject to external injury, except from the bending of the trunnions sometimes after long service, or heavy charges.

Internal injuries are caused by the action of the elastic fluids developed in the combustion of the powder, or by the action of the shot in passing out of the bore. These effects generally increase with the calibre of the piece.

Of the first kind, which exhibit themselves in rear of the shot, are: *the enlargement of the bore* by the compression of the metal, which is seldom a serious defect; *corrosion of metal*, particularly at the angles, such as the inner orifice of the vent, or the mouth of a cylindrical chamber; *cracks*, from the yielding of the cohesion of the metal; *cavities*, cracks enlarged by the action of the gas, and by the melting of the metal; observable especially in the upper surface of the bore.

Injuries of the second kind, which appear in front of the charge, are : *The lodgment of the shot,* a compression of the metal on the lower side of the bore, at the seat of the shot, caused by the pressure of the fluid in escaping over the top of the shot. There is a corresponding *burr* in front of the lodgment and the motion thereby given to the shot causes it to strike alternately on the top and bottom of the bore, producing other *enlargements,* generally *three* in number; the first, on the upper side, a little in advance of the trunnions ; the second, on the lower side, about the astragal; the third, in the upper part of the muzzle; it is chiefly from this cause that brass guns become unserviceable; the extent of the injury varies according to the length of the bore. *Scratches* caused by the fragments of a broken shot, or the roughness of an imperfect one : *enlargement* of the muzzle by the striking of the shot in leaving the bore; *exterior cracks,* or longitudinal splits, caused by too great a compression of the metal on the interior.

The durability of brass cannon may be much increased by careful use, and by the precautions of *increasing the length of the cartridge,* or that of the *sabot,* or using *a wad over the cartridge,* in order to change the place of the shot ; by *wrapping the shot in woollen or other cloth,* or *in paper,* so as to diminish the windage and the bounding of the shot in the bore. In field *guns,* both brass and iron, the paper cap, which is taken off from the cartridge should always be put over the shot.

Iron cannon are subject to the above defects in a less degree than brass, except the corrosion of the metal, by which the vent especially is rendered unserviceable from enlargement. The principal cause of injury to iron cannon is the *rusting* of the metal, producing a roughness and enlargement of the bore, and an increase of any cavities or *honey combs* which may exist in the metal.

The service to which an iron cannon has been subjected may generally be determined by the appearance of the vent.

Spiking and unspiking cannon, and rendering them unserviceable.

To spike a piece, or to render it unserviceable: Drive into the vent a jagged and hardened steel spike with a soft point, or a nail without a head; break it off flush with the outer surface and clinch the point inside by means of the rammer. Wedge a shot in the bottom of the bore by wrapping it with felt, or by means of iron wedges, using the rammer or a bar of iron to drive them in ; a wooden wedge would be easily burnt by means of a charcoal fire lighted with the aid of a bellows. Cause shells to burst in the bore of brass guns, or fire broken shot from them with high charges. Fill a piece with sand over the charge to burst it. Fire a piece against another, muzzle to muzzle, or the muzzle of one to the chase of the other. Light a fire under the chase of a brass gun, and strike on it with a sledge to bend it. Break off the trunnions of iron guns; or burst them by firing them with heavy charges and full of shot, at a high elevation.

When guns are to be spiked temporarily, and are likely to be retaken, a *spring spike* is used, having a shoulder to prevent its being too easily extracted.

To *unspike a piece:* If the spike is not screwed in or clinched, and the bore is not impeded, put in a charge of powder of $\frac{1}{3}$ the weight of the shot and ram junk wads over it with a handspike, laying on the bottom of the bore a strip of wood with a groove on the under side containing a strand of quick match by which fire is communicated to the charge; in a brass gun, take out some of the metal at the upper orifice of the vent, and pour sulphuric acid into the groove for some hours before firing. If this method, several times repeated, is not successful, unscrew the vent piece, if it be a brass gun, and if an iron one, drill out the spike, or drill a new vent.

To drive out a shot wedged in the bore: Unscrew the vent piece, if there be one, and drive in wedges so as to start the shot forward, then ram it back again in order to seize the wedge with a hook; or pour in powder and fire it, after replacing the vent piece. In the last resort, bore a hole in the bottom of the breech, drive out the shot, and stop the hole with a screw.

Preservation of Ordnance.

Cannon should be placed together, according to kind and calibre, on skids of stone, iron, or wood, laid on hard ground, well rammed and covered with a layer of cinders, or of some other material, to prevent vegetation.

Guns and long howitzers.—The pieces should rest on the skids in front of the base ring and in rear of the astragal; the axis inclined at an angle of 4 or 5 degrees with the horizon, the muzzle lowest; the trunnions touching each other; or if space is wanting for that arrangement, the trunnion of one piece may rest on the adjoining piece, so that the axis of the trunnions is inclined about 45° with a horizontal line; the vent down, stopped with a greased wooden plug, or with putty or tallow. If circumstances require it, the pieces may be piled in two tiers, with skidding placed between them, exactly over those which rest on the ground; the muzzles of both tiers in the same direction and their axes preserving the same inclination.

Short howitzers and mortars.—On thick planks, standing on their muzzles, the trunnions touching, the vents stopped.

Iron ordnance should be covered on the exterior with a lacker impervious to water, (see Chap. VII ;) the bore and the vent should be greased with a mixture of *oil* and *tallow*, or of *tallow* and *beeswax* melted together and boiled to expel the water. The lacker should be renewed as often as requisite, and the grease at least once every year.

The lacker and grease should be applied in hot weather.

The cannon should be frequently inspected, to see that moisture does not collect in the bore.

ORDNANCE OF FOREIGN COUNTRIES.

The materials for the following table have been collected, with few exceptions, from the manuals of artillery in England, France, Belgium, Prussia, and Austria, and from memoranda obtained in Russia and Sweden.

The dimensions and weights are given in our own measures.

The column of *exterior length* shows the length from the rear of the base ring to the face of the piece, and the *length of bore* includes the chamber, when not otherwise mentioned.

In *England, France, Belgium*, and *Sweden*, howitzers and mortars take their denominations, as with us, from the diameter of the bore, or from the calibre of a gun of corresponding bore; in *Austria* and *Prussia*, from the weight of a stone ball of the calibre of the bore; in *Russia*, from the true weight of the shell.

ORDNANCE OF FOREIGN COUNTRIES.

DESIGNATION.		DIAMETER OF BORE.	DIAMETER OF BALL.		BRASS.			IRON.		
			High gauge.	Low gauge.	Length.		Weight.	Length.		Weight.
					Exterior.	Bore.		Exterior.	Bore.	
ENGLAND.		Inch.	Inch.	Inch.	Inch.	Inch.	Lbs.	Inch.	Inch.	Lbs.
BOMB CANNON.—	12-in. -	12.	11.88	11.80	–	–	–	100.	–	10,000
	10-in. -	10.	9.88	9.80	–	–	–	112.	110.	9,500
	8-in. -	8.12	7.95	7.9	–	–	–	130.	123.4	12,656
	8-in. -	8.05	7.95	7.90	–	–	–	108.	106.	7,280
	8-in. -	8.05	7.95	7.90	–	–	–	102.	100.	6,750
	8-in. -	8.05	7.95	7.90	–	–	–	96.	94.	5,824
GUNS.—	56-pdr. -	7.65	–	–	–	–	–	132.	124.87	10,864
	42-pdr. -	6.97	–	–	–	–	–	114.5	114.	9,520
	42-pdr. -	7.00	6.79	6.72	114.	–	7,280	114.	107.	7,300
New naval,	32 pdr. -	6.41	6.20	6.14	–	–	–	114.	109.	7,000
New naval,	32-pdr. -	6.37	6.20	6.14	–	–	–	108.	–	5,600
New naval,	32-pdr. -	6.35	6.20	6.14	–	–	–	102.	–	5,000
New naval,	32-pdr. -	6.35	6.20	6.14	–	–	–	96.	–	4,700
	24-pdr. -	5.82	5.63	5.58	114.	–	5,935	114.	107.41	5,600
	24-pdr. -	5.82	5.63	5.58	75.	–	2,700	108.	101.45	5.320
	18-pdr. -	5.29	5.12	5.07	69.	–	2,000	108.	101.75	4,700
	18-pdr. -	5.29	5.12	5.07	–	–	–	96.	89.74	4,200
	12-pdr. -	4.62	4.47	4.43	78.	74.55	2,000	102.	96.22	3,700
	12-pdr. -	4.62	4.47	4.43	60.	56.61	1,344	72.	–	2,350
	9-pdr. -	4.2	4.10	4.06	–	–	–	102.	96.48	3,200
	9-pdr. -	4.2	4.10	4.06	–	–	–	90.	84.44	2,912
	9-pdr. -	4.2	4.10	4.06	72.	67.74	1,512	84.	78.48	2,800
	6-pdr. -	3.66	3.56	3.53	84.	80.35	1,368	102.	96.96	2,600
	6-pdr. -	3.66	3.56	3.53	60.	57.47	672	72.	66.97	1,900
	3-pdr. -	2.91	2.83	2.80	72.	64.45	672			
	3-pdr. -	2.91	2.83	2.80	48.	46.00	336			
	3-pdr. -	2.91	2.83	2.80	36.	34.00	252			
	1-pdr. -	2.01	1.99	1.92	60.	60.00	280			
CARRONADES.—	68-pdr. -	8.05	7.95	7.9	–	–	–	64.	64.	4,032
	42-pdr. -	6.84	6.79	6.72	–	–	–	54.	54.	2,464
	32-pdr. -	6.25	6.2	6.14	–	–	–	48.	48.	1,900
	24-pdr. -	5.68	5.63	5.58	–	–	–	45.	45.	1,456
	18-pdr. -	5.16	5.12	5.07	–	–	–	40.	40.	1,120
	12-pdr. -	4.52	4.47	4.43	–	–	–	32.	32.	672
HOWITZERS.—	10-in. -	10.	9.88	9.8	48.	–	2,900	60.	58.75	4,480
	8-in. -	8.	7.90	7.82	37.	–	1,440	48.	46.80	2,350
	24-pdr. -	5.72	5.62	5.57	56.6	–	1,456			
	5½-in. -	5.62	5.62	5.57	33.	–	1,120	46.	..	1,680
	12-pdr. -	4.58	4.47	4.43	45.2	–	728			
	4 2-5-in.	4.52	4.47	4.43	22.	–	280			
MORTARS.—										
Sea,	13-in. -	13.	12.88	12.80	63.	–	9,192	52.	39.	11,200
Sea,	10-in. -	10.	9.88	9.80	56.	–	3,696	45.	35.	5,800
Land,	13-in. -	13.	12.88	12.80	43.50	–	2,800	36.	26.	4,100
Land,	10-in. -	10.	9.88	9.80	27.00	–	1,380	28.	20.	1,800
Land,	8-in. -	8.	7.90	7.82	21.	–	728	22.5	16.	900
Land,	5½-in. -	5.62	5.62	5.57	15.	12.	140			
Land,	4 2-5-in.	4.52	4.47	4.43	12.	10.	84			

FOREIGN ORDNANCE.

DESIGNATION.	DIAMETER OF BORE.	DIAMETER OF BALL.		BRASS.			IRON.		
		High gauge.	Low gauge.	Length.		Weight.	Length.		Weight.
				Exterior.	Bore.		Exterior.	Bore.	
FRANCE.	Inch.	Inch.	Inch.	Inch.	Inch.	Lbs.	Inch.	Inch.	Lbs.
GUNS.—									
48-pdr. -	7.404	7.329	7.248	152.17	-	11,775			
Siege and garrison. 24-pdr. -	6.011	5.878	5.804	127.33	121.53	6,067			
Siege and garrison. 16-pdr. -	5.264	5.130	5.056	122.34	117.26	4,432			
Siege and garrison. 12-pdr. -	4.775	4.686	4.620	115.48	110.87	3,432			
Siege and garrison. 8-pdr. -	4.175	4.088	4.021	104.24	100.21	2,345			
Field, 12-pdr. -	4.775	4.686	4.620	83.15	78.86	1,959			
Field, 8-pdr. -	4.175	4.088	4.021	72.49	68.74	1,279			
Field, 4-pdr. -	3.316	3.228	3.154	57.57	54.61	636			
Naval, 36-pdr. -	6.885	6.685	6.641	-	-	-	115.13	107.32	7,734
Naval, Long 30-pdr. -	6.485	6.307	6.263	-	-	-	110.91	104.01	6,684
Naval, Short 30-pdr. -	6.485	6.307	6.263	-	-	-	102.00	96.81	5,476
Naval, Long 24-pdr. -	6.004	5.826	5.782	-	-	-	108.74	101.90	5,519
Naval, Short 24-pdr. -	6.004	5.826	5.782	-	-	-	100.00	95.31	4,658
Naval, Long 18-pdr. -	5.463	5.308	5.264	-	-	-	102.34	95.94	4,543
Naval, Short 18-pdr. -	5.463	5.308	5.264	-	-	-	94.56	90.10	3,780
Naval, Long 12-pdr. -	4.775	4.641	4.597	-	-	-	95.94	90.35	3,230
Naval, Short 12-pdr. -	4.775	4.641	4.597	-	-	-	87.23	83.15	2,585
Naval, Long 8-pdr. -	4.175	4.064	4.020	-	-	-	102.34	97.45	2,573
Naval, Short 8-pdr. -	4.175	4.064	4.020	-	-	-	87.42	82.53	2,216
Naval, Long 6-pdr. -	3.790	3.679	3.635	-	-	-	89.55	85.11	1,868
Naval, Short 6-pdr. -	3.790	3.679	3.635	-	-	-	78.89	74.45	1,650
CARRONADES.—									
36-pdr. -	6.796	6.685	6.641	-	-	-	53.34	45.03	2,524
30-pdr. -	6.419	6.307	6.263	-	-	-	53.33	45.85	2,227
24-pdr. -	5.937	5.826	5.782	-	-	-	45.71	38.36	1,663
18-pdr. -	5.419	5.308	5.264	-	-	-	41.71	34.65	1,272
12-pdr. -	4.753	4.642	4.597	-	-	-	35.33	29.37	840
BOMB CANNON.—									
Naval, 10-in. -	10.630	-	-	-	-	-	124.00	110.84	11,000
Naval, 22-centm.	8,795	8.707	8.640	-	-	-	98.08	92.21	8 000
Naval, 17-centm.	-	6 730	6.683						
Naval, 16-centm.	-	6.352	6.305						
Naval, 15 centm.	-	5.871	5.824						
HOWITZERS.—									
Sea coast, 22 centm.	8.795	8.703	8.640	-	-	-	98.08	92.21	8,000
Siege, Old 8 in. -	8.795	8.703	8.624	37.05	33 85	1,182			
Siege, New 22 centm.	8.782	8.703	8.640	52.00	39.38	2,646			
Field, Old 6-in -	6.530	6.441	6.396	30.25	27.05	700			
Field, New 16-centm.	6.518	6.439	6.392	90.29	74.29	1,951			
Field, do. 15-centm.	5.958	5.879	5.832	67.54	63.60	1,281			
Mountain, 12-centm.	4.745	4.686	4.639	33.87	31.90	221			
MORTARS.—									
Gomer, 32-centm.	12.799	12.661	12.590	35 27	27.45	2,922			
Gomer, 27-centm.	10.790	10.712	10.641	30.29	22.83	2,296			
Gomer, 22-centm.	8.782	8.703	8.640	21.72	17.46	607			
Mountain, 15-centm.	5.958	5.879	5.832	16.70	14.10	154			
Stone mortar -	15.991	-	-	31.63	26.70	1,617			

DESIGNATION.	DIAMETER OF BORE.	DIAMETER OF BALL.		BRASS.			IRON.		
		High gauge.	Low gauge.	Length.		Weight.	Length.		Weight.
				Exterior.	Bore.		Exterior.	Bore.	
BELGIUM.	Inch.	Inch.	Inch.	Inch.	Inch.	Lbs.	Inch.	Inch.	Lbs.
GUNS.—									
Field, 6-pdr. -	3.760	3.678	3.591	-	60.16	1,045			
12-pdr. -	4.722	4.616	4.529	-	70.83	1,958			
Siege and garrison. 6-pdr. -	3.760	3.678	3.591	-	97.76	1,958	-	85.04	1,936
12-pdr. -	4.722	4.616	4.529	-	113.33	3,652	-	98.22	3,630
18-pdr. -	5.411	5.301	5.214	-	116.34	4,913	-	101.67	5,038
24-pdr.	5.974	5.860	5.773	-	119.48	6,270	-	106.16	6,204
HOWITZERS.— 15 centm.	5.974	5.860	5.773	-	60.34	1,111			
20 centm.	7.931	7.813	7.726	-	-	-	-	33.26	1,324
BOMB CANNON.—									
8-in. -	8.782	8.707	8.644	-	-	-	-	86.68	8,023
10-in. -	10.791	10.704	10.629	-	-	-	-	94.17	11,033
MORTARS.— 20 centm.	7.931	7.813	7.726	-	-	-	-	18.18	543
29 centm.	11.475	11.393	11.263	-	-	-	-	26.10	2,618
60 centm.	23.630	23.432	23.235	-	-	-	-	37.80	17,904
AUSTRIA.									
GUNS.—									
Mountain, 1-pdr. -	2.075	1.981	1.959	31.37	29.41	180			
3-pdr. -	2.957	2.849	2.827	31.64	29.16	296			
Field, 3-pdr. -	2.957	2.849	2.827	45.25	42.42	508			
6-pdr. -	3.724	3.594	3.562	57.00	53.43	842			
12-pdr. -	4.660	4.524	4.488	71.82	67.33	1,700			
18-pdr. -	5.311	5.173	5.137	82.22	77.71	2,514			
Siege and garrison. 6-pdr. -	3.724	3.594	3.562	-	-	-	92.47	88.90	1,566
12-pdr. -	4.660	4.524	4.488	112.22	108.01	3,276	111.85	106.61	3,445
18-pdr. -	5.311	5.173	5.137	123.32	118.50	4,735	117.86	111.76	4,789
24-pdr. -	5.827	5.691	5.655	130.08	124.78	6,130			
BOMB CANNON, 30-pdr. -	9.473	9.350	9.256	-	-	-	98.31	92.39	8,558
HOWITZERS, 7-pdr. -	5.870	5.755	5.698	34.55	31.70	598	34.55	31.70	498
10-pdr. -	6.634	6.512	6.418	35.71	31.68	913			
MORTARS.—									
Coehorn, 6-pdr. -	3.724	3.594	3.562	-	-	-	10.91	9.35	68
10-pdr. -	6.634	6.512	6.418	22.47	18.91	421			
30-pdr. -	9.494	9.350	9.256	27.77	22.63	1,141			
30-pdr. -	9.422	9.350	9.256	28.35	23.58	1,294			
60-pdr. -	11.922	11.763	11.663	32.44	25.97	2,167			
STONE MORTAR, 60 pdr. -	12.390	-	-	-	-	-	38.45	32.44	2,180
PRUSSIA.									
GUNS.—									
Field, 6-pdr. -	3.711	3.629	3.536	63.91	61.03	930			
12-pdr. -	4.680	4.573	4.460	80.40	76.64	1,874			
Siege and garrison. 3-pdr. -	2.948	2.886	2.804	57.72	55.00	607	-	-	800
6-pdr. -	3.711	3.629	3.536	-	-	-	59.79	55.66	1,019
12-pdr. -	4.680	4.573	4.460	106.68	102.57	3,066	107.20	101.84	3,054
24-pdr. -	5.855	5.752	5.639	119.17	113.39	5,890	119.17	112.46	5,897
24 pdr. -	5.855	5.752	5.639	71.94	67.21	2,828	72.87	67.21	2,842
HOWITZERS.—									
Field, 7-pdr. -	5.845	5.752	5.639	39.17	35.05	800			
10-pdr. -	6.741	6.633	6.520	42.26	38.40	1,200			
Siege and garrison, 25-pdr. -	8.927	8.834	8.710	54.80	53.66	3,416	54.80	53.66	3,426

FOREIGN ORDNANCE.

DESIGNATION.	DIAMETER OF BORE.	DIAMETER OF BALL.		BRASS.			IRON.		
		High gauge.	Low gauge.	Length.		Weight.	Length.		Weight.
				Exterior.	Bore.		Exterior.	Bore.	
PRUSSIA.—Continued	Inch.	Inch.	Inch.	Inch.	Inch	Lbs.	Inch.	Inch.	Lbs.
MORTARS.— Hand,	3.092	-	-	*	5.21	15½			
Hand,	4.618	4.573	4.460	†	7.63	39			
7-pdr. -	5.793	5.752	5.639	15.86	13.02	166			
10-pdr. -	6.690	6.633	6.520	20.61	15.97	393	21.64	15.97	627
25-pdr. -	8.906	8.834	8.710	26.29	21.65	909	27.83	21.65	1,129
50-pdr. -	11.184	11.102	10.978	36.69	29.89	1,775	37.87	29.89	2,165
Stone -	15.454	-	-	-		-	33.00	25.77	1,553
BOMB CANNON, 50-pdr. -	11.120	11.102	10.978	-	-	-	111.00	-	12,400
RUSSIA.									
GUNS.— Field, 6-pdr. -	3.762	3.646	3.609	-	51.13	802			
Field, 12-pdr. -	4.739	4.610	4.560	-	74.64	1,783			
Siege and garrison and sea coast, 3-pdr. -	2.996	2.920	2.880	-	-	-	51.00	48.00	681
6-pdr. -	3.762	3.646	3.609	-	-	-	82.70	79.00	1,665
12-pdr. -	4.739	4.610	4.560	-	100.00	3,492	104.00	99.00	3,300
18-pdr. -	5.426	5.300	5.210	-	108.75	4,814	114.00	106.50	5,680
24-pdr. -	5.972	5.860	5.784	-	119.70	6,485	126.00	118.00	7,600
30-pdr. -	6.443	6.320	6.240	-	-	-	129.00	121.15	9,080
36-pdr. -	6.837	6.750	6.650		-	-	136.00	127.70	10,500
HOWITZERS, (Likorna.)				-					
Field, 3-pdr. -	3.242	3.140	3.100	Exclusive of chamber.	28.37	240			
Field, 10-pdr. -	4.843	4.700	4.650		37.53	707			
Field, 10-pdr. -	4.843	4.700	4.650		42.38	780			
Field, 20-pdr. -	6.102	5.990	5.915		50.34	1,509	-	50.34	1,675
Siege and garrison, 40-pdr. -	7.688	7.575	7.476		63.90	3,170	-	63.43	3,476
MORTARS.—									
6-pdr. -	4.084	3.920	3.890		7.00	26			
80-pdr. -	9.650	9.570	9.490		14.50	1,311	-	16.00	1,927
200-pdr. -	13.150	13.050	12.950		18.81	3,243	-	21.83	4,900
BOMB CANNON.—									
20-pdr. -	6.000	5.990	5.915	-	-	-	92.00	87.00	3,300
40-pdr. -	7.700	7.575	7.476	-	-	-	116.00	110.00	5,600
96-pdr. -	9.000	8.900	8.820						
120 pdr. -	10.750	10.680	10.580						
SWEDEN.									
GUNS.— 3-pdr. -	3.015	2.922	2.887						
Field, 6-pdr. -	3.786	3.687	3.652	-	-	-	65.60	62.50	816
Field, 12-pdr. -	4.791	4.674	4.628	-	-	-	81.70	77.75	1,565
18-pdr. -	5.551	5.446	5.388						
24-pdr. -	6.112	5.994	5.924						
Ship, 30-pdr. -	6.560	6.455	6.385	-	-	-	74.00	70.00	3,636
Ship, 30-pdr. -	6.560	6.455	6.385	-	-	-	-	-	6,276
HOWITZERS.—									
Field, ‡ 12-pdr. -	4.791	4.674	4.628	-	-	-	53.77	50.62	830
Field, ‡ 24-pdr. -	6.112	5.994	5.924	-	-	-	68.39	64.53	1,550
MORTARS.— 7-in. -	8.905	8.765	8.695	-	-	-	33.78	29.23	1,050
Light 9-in. -	11.254	11.114	11.021	-	-	-	39.04	33.30	2,100
Heavy 9-in. -	11.254	11.114	11.021	-		-	52.84	44.66	4,800
11-in. -	12.855	12.715	12.598						

* Attached to a stock. † Cast with a bed plate. ‡ Not chambered.

CHAPTER SECOND.

SHOT AND SHELLS.

NOMENCLATURE, DIMENSIONS, WEIGHTS.

Diameters of gauges for Shot and Shells.

	13-in.	12 in	10-in.	8-in.	42	32	24	18	12	9	6	4	3	1
	In.	In.	In.	In.	In.	In.	In.	In.	In.	In.	In.	In.	In.	In.
Large - -	12.90	11.90	9.90	7.90	6.86	6.27	5.70	5.18	4.53	4.12	3.60	3.14	2.86	1.96
Small, new -	12.84	11.84	9.84	7.85	6.81	6.22	5.65	5.13	4.49	4.08	3.56	3 10	2.82	1.92
Small, old -	12.80	–	9.80	7.80	6.76	6.18	5.61	5.10	4.46	4.05	3.54	–	2.80	

For the manner of using these gauges, see *page* 31.

Shot.

	13-in.	12 in.	10-in.	8 in.	42	32	24	18	12	9	6	4	3	1
Diameter, in.	12.87	11.87	9.87	7.88	6.84	6.25	5.68	5.17	4.52	4.10	3.58	3.12	2 84	1.95
Weight, lbs.	294	231	128	65	42.7	32 6	24.4	18.5	12.3	9.25	6.1	4.07	3.05	1

Shells.

	For Columbiads & S. C. Howitzers.		For Mortars.			For Guns and Howitzers.				
	10-in.	8-in.	13-in.	10-in.	8-in.	42	32	24	18	12
	In.	In.	In.	In.	In.	In.	In.	In.	In	In.
Diameter - -	9.87	7.88	12.87	9.87	7.88	6.84	6.25	5.68	5.17	4.52
Thickness of sides and bottom. True -	2.	1.5	2.1	1.6	1.25	1.2	1.	0.9	0.9	0.7
Thickness of sides and bottom. Greatest	2.1	1.58	2.25	1.7	1.33	1.25	1.05	0.95	0.94	0.74
Thickness of sides and bottom. Least -	1.9	1.42	1.95	1.5	1.17	1.15	0.95	0.85	0.86	0.66
Thickness at fuze hole	3.	2.25	2.1	1.6	1.25	1.8	1.35	1.35	1.35	1.05
Diameter of fuze hole. Exterior	1.45	1.338	1.8	1.75	1.3	1.	0.9	0.9	0.9	0.9
Diameter of fuze hole. Interior	1.	1.	1.483	1.51	1.113	0.73	0.698	0.698	0.698	0.743
Distance between ears	6.	5.	7.	6.	5.	–	–	–	–	–
Weight, - - lbs.	101	50.5	197	87.5	44.5	31.	22.5	17	13.4	8.4

The 8-inch mortar shell is used for the siege howitzer.

The *ears* of a shell are holes for the points of the shell hooks, 0.5 inch in diameter, bored opposite to each other, and perpendicular to the axis of the fuze hole; the metal is cut out above them at the distance indicated in the table, in a direction perpendicular to the axis of the holes, which must remain 0.25 inch deep, with a thickness of 0.25 inch of metal above them, at the thinnest part.

Carcasses,

Are shells having three additional holes, of the same dimensions as the fuze hole, pierced at equal distances apart in the upper hemisphere of the shell, with their exterior openings tangent to the great circle which is perpendicular to the axis of the fuze hole.

	13-in.	10-in.	8-in.	42	32	24	18	12
Mean weight, lbs.	194	86	43	30	21.60	16	12.5	8

Spherical case shot.

	8-in.	42	32	24	18	12	6
	In.	In.	In.	In.	In.	In.	In.
Diameter..............	7.88	6.84	6.25	5.68	5.17	4.52	3.58
Thickness of metal at the sides. True.....	0.7	0.65	0.60	0.55	0.5	0.45	0.36
Thickness of metal at the sides. Greatest..	0.725	0.675	0.625	0.575	0.525	0.475	0.385
Thickness of metal at the sides. Least....	0.675	0.625	0.575	0.525	0.475	0.425	0.335
Thickness of metal at the fuze hole.............	1.6	1.5	1.5	1.1	1.1	0.75	0.75
Radius of reinforce at the fuze hole.............	3.0	2.75	2.5	2.3	2.1	1.8	1.4
Diameter of fuze hole. Exterior ...	1.2	1.2	1.2	0.9	0.9	0.9	0.9
Diameter of fuze hole. Interior	0.96	0.975	0.975	0.735	0.735	0.788	0.788
Mean weight.........lbs.	30.	20.32	16.	11.86	8.7	6.1	3.06

The thickness of metal at the fuze hole is supposed to be measured in the axis of the fuze hole between the spherical surfaces of the shell and of the reinforce.

The fuze holes of shells and spherical case shot taper 0.15 inch to 1 inch.

Grape shot.

	8-in.	42	32	24	18	12
	In.	In.	In.	In.	In.	In.
Diameter of large gauge.........	3.60	3.17	2.90	2.64	2.40	2.06
Diameter of small gauge........	3.54	3.13	2.86	2.60	2.36	2.02
Mean weight ....lbs.	6.1	4.2	3.15	2.4	1.8	1.14

Canister shot.

	NATURE OF ORDNANCE.								
	42-pdr. gun.	32-pdr. gun.	24-pdr. gun & 8 in. siege howitzer.	18-pdr. gun.	12-pdr. gun and 32 pdr. howitzer.	24-pdr. howitzer.	6-pdr. gun	12-pdr. howitzer. Field.	12-pdr. howitzer. Mountain.
	In.	In.	In.	In.	In.	In.	In.	In.	
Diameter of large gauge,	2.26	2.06	1.87	1.70	1.49	1.35	1.17	1.08	Musket ball.
Diameter of small gauge,	2.22	2.02	1.84	1.67	1.46	1.32	1.14	1.05	
Mean weight, lbs.	1.5	1.14	0.86	0.64	0.43	0.32	0.21	0.16	

Grenades.

Six-pounder spherical case shot may be used for *hand grenades*, and shells of any calibre for *rampart grenades*.

Lead balls.

DIAMETERS OF LEAD BALLS FROM 1 TO 32 TO THE POUND.

No. of balls to 1 lb.	Diameter.	No. of balls to 1 lb.	Diameter.	No. of balls to 1 lb.	Diameter.	No. of balls to 1 lb.	Diameter.
	In.		In.		In.		In.
1	1.670	9	0.803	17	0.650	25	0.571
2	1.326	10	.775	18	.638	26	.564
3	1.157	11	.751	19	.626	27	.557
4	1.051	12	.730	20	.615	28	.550
5	1.977	13	.710	21	.605	29	.544
6	.919	14	.693	22	.596	30	.537
7	.873	15	.676	23	.587	31	.531
8	.835	16	.663	24	.579	32	.526

For the mode of fabrication of lead balls, see CHAPTER X.

DIAMETERS OF CAST IRON BALLS FROM ¼ POUND TO 50 POUNDS WEIGHT.

Weight.	Diam.	Weight.	Diam.	Weight.	Diam.	Weight.	Diam.
Lbs. oz.	In.	Lbs.	In.	Lbs.	In.	Lbs.	In.
0 4	1.231	9	4.065	23	5.531	37	6.512
6	1.403	10	4.211	24	5.639	38	6.570
8	1.551	11	4.346	25	5.714	39	6.627
10	1.665	12	4.474	26	5.789	40	6.684
12	1.701	13	4.595	27	5.862	41	6.738
14	1.865	14	4.710	28	5.930	42	6.793
1	1.954	15	4.819	29	6.004	43	6.846
2	2.462	16	4.924	30	6.068	44	6.898
3	2.819	17	5.025	31	6.140	45	6.951
4	3.104	18	5.121	32	6.205	46	7.002
5	3.341	19	5.215	33	6.268	47	7.052
6	3.551	20	5.304	34	6.330	48	7.101
7	3.738	21	5.392	35	6.392	49	7.145
8	3.908	22	5.476	36	6.442	50	7.198

The specific gravity of shot and shells is about 7,000.

To find the weight of a cast iron shot or shell:

Multiply the cube of the diameter of the shot in inches, or the difference of the cubes of the exterior and interior diameters of the shell, by 0.134 for the weight in pounds.

For lead balls, the multiplier is 0.2142.

To find the diameter of a cast iron shot of a given weight:

Divide the weight in pounds by 0.134, and the cube root of the quotient will be the diameter in inches.

To find the quantity of powder which a shell will contain:

Multiply the cube of the interior diameter of the shell in inches by 0.01744, for the weight of powder in pounds.

INSPECTION OF SHOT AND SHELLS.

Shot and shells should be made of grey or mottled iron, of good quality, (see CHAP. XIV. *Cast iron.*) They must be cast in sand, and not in iron moulds; the shot from the latter are generally not spherical in form, nor uniform in size; they are also full of cavities, and are cracked by being heated.

Spherical case shot must be made with peculiar care, of the best quality of iron, in order that they may not be liable to break in the gun.

Shot.

INSPECTING INSTRUMENTS: One *large* and one *small gauge* and one *cylinder gauge* for each calibre: the cylinder gauge has the same diameter as the large gauge; it is made of cast iron, and is 5 calibres long. One *hammer*, weighing half a pound and having a flat face and a conical point. *Steel punches*.

One searcher, of steel wire No. 20, with a handle.

The shot should be inspected before they become rusty; after being well cleaned, each shot is placed on a table and examined by the eye to see that its surface is smooth, that the metal is sound and free from seams, flaws and blisters. If cavities or small holes appear on the surface, strike the point of the hammer or punch into them and ascertain their depth with the searcher; if the depth of the cavity exceed 0.2 inch, the shot is rejected; and also if it appear that an attempt has been made to conceal such defects by filling up the holes with nails, cement, &c.

The shot must pass in every direction through the large gauge and not at all through the small one; the founder should endeavor to bring the shot up as near as possible to the *large gauge* or to the *true diameter*.

N. B. The diameters of the small gauges have been recently increased, in order to produce greater uniformity in the dimensions of shot and shells, by reducing the limits of variation allowed in their fabrication. The new gauges are to be used only in the inspection of shot and shells to be hereafter made, and the projectiles now on hand are not to be rejected from service on account of passing through these gauges.

After having been thus examined, the shot are passed through the *cylinder gauge*, which is placed at an inclination of about 2 inches between the two ends and supported on blocks of wood in such a manner as to be easily turned from time to time, to prevent its being worn in furrows. Shot which *slide* or *stick* in the cylinder are rejected; the latter must be pushed out from the lower end with a wooden rammer.

Shot are proved by dropping them from a height of 20 feet on a block of iron, or rolling them down an inclined plane of that height, against another shot at the bottom of the plane.

The average weight of the shot is deduced from that of three parcels of 20 to 50 each, taken indiscriminately from the pile: some of those which appear to be the smallest should be also weighed, and they are rejected if they fall short of the weight expressed by their calibre more than one *thirty-second* part. They almost invariably exceed that weight.

Grape and Canister shot.

The dimensions are verified by means of a large and a small gauge attached to the same handle. The surface of the shot should be smooth and free from seams.

Shells and hollow shot.

INSPECTING INSTRUMENTS.—A *large* and *small guage* for each calibre, and a *cylinder gauge* for shells of 8 inches and under.

Callipers for measuring the thickness of the metal at the sides of the shell.

Callipers, to measure the thickness at the bottom of the shell.

Gauges for the dimensions of the fuze hole, and for the thickness of metal at the fuze hole.

A pair of hand bellows; a wooden plug to fit the fuze hole, and bored through to receive the nozzle of the bellows.

A hammer; a searcher; a cold chisel; steel punches.

The surface of the shell and its exterior dimensions are examined as in the case of shot. The shell is next struck with the hammer to judge by the sound whether it is free from cracks; the position and dimensions of the ears are verified; the thickness of metal is then measured at several points on the great circle perpendicular to the axis of the fuze hole, and at the bottom, and at the fuze hole. The diameter of the fuze hole, which should be accurately reamed, is then verified, and the soundness of the metal about the inside of the hole is ascertained by inserting the finger.

The shell is now placed on a trivet in a tub containing water deep enough to cover it nearly to the fuze hole; the bellows and plug are inserted into the fuze hole and the air forced into the shell; if there are any holes in the shell, the air will rise in bubbles through the water. This test also gives another indication of the soundness of the metal, as the parts containing cavities will dry more slowly than the other parts.

The mean weight of shells is ascertained in the same manner as that of shot.

Shot and shells rejected in the inspection are marked with a X, made with the cold chisel; on shot near the gate, and on shells, near the fuze hole.

PRESERVATION AND PILING OF BALLS.

Balls should be carefully lackered as soon as possible after they are received. For the composition of lacker and the manner of applying it, see CHAP. VII.

When it becomes necessary to renew the lacker, the old lacker should be removed by rolling or scraping the balls, which should never be heated for that purpose.

Balls are piled according to kind and calibre, under cover if practicable, in a place where there is a free circulation of air, to facilitate which the piles should be made narrow if the locality permits; the width of the bottom tier may be from 12 to 14 balls, according to the calibre.

Prepare the ground for the base of the pile by raising it above the surrounding ground so as to throw off the water; level it, ram it well, and cover it with a layer of screened sand. Make the bottom of the pile with a tier of unserviceable balls buried about two-thirds of their diameter in the sand; this base may be made permanent: clean the base well and form the pile, putting the fuze holes of shells downwards, in the *intervals*, and not resting on the shells below. Each pile is marked with the number of serviceable balls it contains.

The base may be made of bricks, concrete, stone, or with borders and braces of iron.

Grape and canister shot should be oiled or lackered, put in piles, or in strong boxes, on the ground floor, or in dry cellars; each parcel marked with its kind, calibre, and number.

To find the number of balls in a pile.

Multiply the sum of the three parallel edges by one-third of the number of balls in a triangular face.

In a square pile, one of the parallel edges contains but one ball; in a triangular pile, two of the edges have but one ball in each.

The number of balls in a triangular face is $\frac{n(n+1)}{2}$; n being the number in the bottom row.

The sum of the three parallel edges in a triangular pile is $n+2$; in a square pile, $2n+1$; in an oblong pile, $3\mathcal{N}+2n-2$; $\mathcal{N}$ being the length of the top row, and n the width of the bottom tier: or, $3m-n+1$; m being the length and n the width of the bottom tier.

If a pile consist of two piles joined at a right angle, calculate the contents of one as a common oblong pile, and of the other as a pile of which the three parallel edges are equal.

In the following Table of the number of balls in a pile, the second line shows the number in a triangular pile, the base of which is the corresponding number in the first line.

The other numbers show the contents of square and oblong piles; the length and width of the base being in the upper line and in the left hand column respectively.

TABLE OF THE NUMBER OF BALLS IN A PILE.

	2	3	4	5	6	7	8	9	10	11	12	13	14	15	16	17	18	19	20	21
Tri.	4	10	20	35	56	84	120	165	220	286	364	455	560	680	816	969	1140	1330	1540	1771
2	5																			
3	8	14																		
4	11	20	30																	
5	14	26	40	55																
6	17	32	50	70	91															
7	20	38	60	85	112	140														
8	23	44	70	100	133	168	204													
9	26	50	80	115	154	196	240	285												
10	29	56	90	130	175	224	276	330	385											
11	32	62	100	145	196	252	312	375	440	506										
12	35	68	110	160	217	280	348	420	495	572	650									
13	38	74	120	175	238	308	384	465	550	638	728	819								
14	41	80	130	190	259	336	420	510	605	704	806	910	1015							
15	44	86	140	205	280	364	456	555	660	770	884	1001	1120	1240						
16	47	92	150	220	301	392	492	600	715	836	962	1092	1225	1360	1496					
17	50	98	160	235	322	420	528	645	770	902	1040	1183	1330	1480	1632	1785				
18	53	104	170	250	343	448	564	690	825	968	1118	1274	1435	1600	1768	1938	2109			
19	56	110	180	265	364	476	600	735	880	1034	1196	1365	1540	1720	1904	2091	2280	2470		
20	59	116	190	280	385	504	636	780	935	1100	1274	1456	1645	1840	2040	2244	2451	2660	2870	
21	62	122	20	295	406	532	672	825	990	1166	1352	1547	1750	1960	2176	2397	2622	2850	3080	3311

TABLE OF OBLONG PILES—Continued.

	2	3	4	5	6	7	8	9	10	11	12	13	14	15	16	17	18	19	20	21
22	65	128	210	310	427	560	708	870	1045	1232	1430	1638	1855	2080	2312	2550	2793	3040	3290	3542
23	68	134	220	325	448	588	744	915	1100	1298	1508	1729	1960	2200	2448	2703	2964	3230	3500	3773
24	71	140	230	340	469	616	780	960	1155	1364	1586	1820	2065	2320	2584	2856	3135	3420	3710	4004
25	74	146	240	355	490	644	816	1005	1210	1430	1664	1911	2170	2440	2720	3009	3306	3610	3920	4235
26	77	152	250	370	511	672	852	1050	1265	1496	1742	2002	2275	2560	2856	3162	3477	3800	4130	4466
27	80	158	260	385	532	700	888	1095	1320	1562	1820	2093	2380	2680	2992	3315	3648	3990	4340	4697
28	83	164	270	400	553	728	924	1140	1375	1628	1898	2184	2485	2800	3128	3468	3819	4180	4550	4928
29	86	170	280	415	574	756	960	1185	1430	1694	1976	2275	2590	2920	3264	3621	3990	4370	4760	5159
30	89	176	290	430	595	784	996	1230	1485	1760	2054	2366	2695	3040	3400	3774	4161	4560	4970	5390
31	92	182	300	445	616	812	1032	1275	1540	1826	2132	2457	2800	3160	3536	3927	4332	4750	5180	5621
32	95	188	310	460	637	840	1068	1320	1595	1892	2210	2548	2905	3280	3672	4080	4503	4940	5390	5852
33	98	194	320	475	658	868	1104	1365	1650	1958	2288	2639	3010	3400	3808	4233	4674	5130	5600	6083
34	101	200	330	490	679	896	1140	1410	1705	2024	2366	2730	3115	3520	3944	4386	4845	5320	5810	6314
35	104	206	340	505	700	924	1176	1455	1760	2090	2444	2821	3220	3640	4080	4539	5016	5510	6020	6545
36	107	212	350	520	721	952	1212	1500	1815	2156	2522	2912	3325	3760	4216	4692	5187	5700	6230	6776
37	110	218	360	535	742	980	1248	1545	1870	2222	2600	3003	3430	3880	4352	4845	5358	5890	6440	7007
38	113	224	370	550	763	1008	1284	1590	1925	2288	2678	3094	3535	4000	4488	4998	5529	6080	6650	7238
39	116	230	380	565	784	1036	1320	1635	1980	2354	2756	3185	3640	4120	4624	5151	5700	6270	6860	7469
40	119	236	390	580	805	1064	1356	1680	2035	2420	2834	3276	3745	4240	4760	5304	5871	6460	7070	7700

CHAPTER THIRD.

ARTILLERY CARRIAGES.

NOMENCLATURE.

The nomenclature and the tables of dimensions and weights given in this chapter, apply to the latest patterns adopted. The parts are enumerated generally in the order in which they are put together.

The classification adopted for bolts, nuts, chains, nails, screws, &c., is shown in the tables following the nomenclature.

FIELD GUN CARRIAGES.—*Plate* 3.

There are three gun carriages for field artillery, viz:

One for the 6-pounder gun and the 12-pounder howitzer.

One for the 24-pounder howitzer.

One for the 12-pounder gun and the 32-pounder howitzer.

The parts of these carriages are all similar, differing only in their dimensions.

Wood.

1 *stock*, in two pieces; 2 *dowels;* 2 *cheeks;* 1 *axle body.*

Irons.

2 *trail handles.*
2 *bolts* and 2 *nuts* for do.
1 *lock-chain bolt*, 1 *washer*, and 1 *nut.*
1 *eye-plate for lock-chain.*
1 *lock-chain*, No. 5, 3 *links*, 1 *toggle.*
1 *lunette*, for the trail.
1 *trail-plate;* 2 *rivets.*
12 *nails*, for lunette and trail plate.
1 *large pointing ring and plate.*
2 *bolts* and 2 *nuts*, for do.
1 *small pointing ring.*
2 *bolts* and 2 *nuts*, for do.
2 *wheel guard plates.*
10 *nails*, for do.
2 *prolonge hooks.*
8 *nails*, for do.
1 *stop*, for rammer head.
4 *nails*, for do.
1 *ear-plate*, for worm.
2 *nails*, for do.
1 *key*, for worm.
1 *key chain;* 1 *eye pin.*
1 *eye plate*, for sponge and rammer chains.
2 *screws*, for eye-plate.
2 *chains and hasps*, for sponges and rammers.
2 *turnbuckles*, (BRASS.)
2 *stud plates*, for turnbuckles.
2 *trunnion plates.*
20 *nails*, for do., in 6-pdr. and 24-pdr. howitzer carriage.
28 *nails*, in 12-pdr. carriage.
2 *chin bolts;* 2 *bevel washers* and 2 *nuts.*
2 *key bolts;* 2 *nuts.*
6 *cheek bolts;* 4 *washers;* 6 *nuts.*
2 *cap squares;* 2 *eye pins.*
2 *cap-square chains;* 2 *eye pins.*
2 *cap-square keys.*
2 *key chains;* 2 *eye pins.*
2 *D rings*, for handspikes.
4 *staples*, for D rings.
1 *linstock-socket.*
6 *nails*, for do.

FIELD-GUN CARRIAGES—*Irons*—(Continued.)

6 *rondelles*, (CAST IRON.)
3 *assembling bolts*.
3 *washers* and 3 *nuts*, for do.
1 *washer hook*, for lock chain.
2 *washer hooks*, for handspikes.
1 *axletree;* the *arms*, the *stop*.
2 *under straps*.
1 *axle strap*.
1 *bevel washer*, for 6-pdr. axle strap.
3 *axle strap bolts ;* 3 *nuts*.

2 *axle bands*.
6 *nails*, for do.
1 *box for elevating screw*, (BRASS.)
2 *bolts*, for do.; 2 *washers ;* 2 *nuts*.
1 *elevating screw*.
2 *shoulder washers*, } for axletree.
2 *linch washers*, }
2 *linch pins*.

2 WHEELS.

LIMBER.—*Plate* 4.

The same limber is used for all field carriages.

Wood.

1 *axle body*.
2 *hounds*.
1 *fork*.
1 *splinter bar*.

4 *foot board brackets*.
2 *foot boards*.
1 *pole*.
1 *pole prop*.

Iron.

8 *screws*, for foot board brackets.
20 *nails*, for foot boards.
4 *rivets* and 4 *burrs*, for hounds.
4 *plates*, for stay pins; 8 *nails*.
1 *axletree*.
1 *pintle hook*.
3 *bolts*, for do.; 2 *washers ;* 3 *nuts*.
1 *stay plate*, for limber chest.
2 *nails*, for do.
1 *pintle key*.
1 *key chain ;* 1 *eye pin*.
1 *tar bucket hook ;* 2 *nails*.
2 *bolts*, for hounds; 2 *washers ;* 2 *nuts*.
2 *under straps*.
4 *bolts*, for under straps ; 4 *nuts*.
2 *axle bands ;* 6 *nails*.
2 *end bands*, for splinter bar.
4 *rivets*, for do.
2 *bolts*, for hounds and splinter bar.
4 *washers* and 2 *nuts*, for do.
1 *eye plate*, for pole prop socket.
2 *middle bands*, for splinter bar.
4 *trace hooks*.
1 *fork strap*.

2 *bolts*, for splinter bar and fork.
2 *nuts*, for do.
1 *pole prop socket ;* 1 *rivet*.
1 *pole prop ferrule ;* 1 *rivet*.
1 *pole prop chain ;* 1 *toggle*.
1 *eye pin*, for pole prop chain.
1 *burr*, for eye pin.
2 *stay pins*, for ammunition chest.
2 *keys*, for stay pins.
2 *key chains ;* 2 *eye pins*.
1 *rivet* and 1 *burr*, for end of pole.
1 *pole bolt ;* 2 *washers ;* 1 *nut*.
1 *pole strap* and 3 *rivets*.
2 *pole chains ;* the *links ;* the *ring*.
1 *muff*, for pole yoke.
1 *collar*, for muff; in two parts.
2 *branches*, for pole yoke; 2 *rings*.
2 *bolts*, for collar and branches.
1 *washer*, for muff; 1 *key*.
2 *shoulder washers*.
2 *linch washers*.
2 *linch pins*.

2 WHEELS, No. 1.
1 AMMUNITION CHEST.

WHEELS.

There are two Nos. of wheels for field carriages. No. 1, for the *6-pounder gun carriage*, the *caisson*, the *forge*, the *battery wagon*, and for the *limbers* of all field carriages. No. 2, for the *24-pdr. howitzer* and the *12-pdr. gun carriages.* These wheels are of the same form and height, and they fit on the same axle-tree arm; they differ only in the dimensions of their parts, and consequently in strength and weight.

Wood.	*Iron.*
1 *nave.*	2 *brow bonds*; 2 *end bands.*
14 *spokes.*	12 *nails*, for bands.
7 *fellies.*	1 *tire.*
7 *dowels.*	7 *tire bolts*; 7 *washers*; 7 *nuts.*
	1 *nave box*, (CAST IRON.)

AMMUNITION CHEST.—*Plate* 4.

The same ammunition chest is adapted to the limber and to the caisson.

For the interior arrangement of the chests, for different kinds of ammunition, see CHAPTER XI.

Wood.

2 *sides.*	1 *frame for cover*; 2 *sides*; 2 *ends.*
2 *ends.*	1 *panel for cover.*
1 *principal partition.*	1 *cover lining.*
1 *bottom.*	

Iron.

34 *cut nails*, for sides, ends and bottom.	2 *front stays*; 4 *rivets*; 8 *screws.*
4 *screws*, for the bottom.	2 *hinges*; 4 *rivets*; 20 *screws.*
60 *copper nails*, for cover lining.	2 *hinge plates*; 4 *screws.*
4 *corner plates*, for ends and sides.	1 *hasp*; 1 *rivet*; 5 *screws.*
2 do. for ends and bottom.	1 *hasp plate*; 2 *screws.*
1 do. for side and bottom.	2 *handles*; 8 *rivets*
96 *screws*, for corner plates.	14 *copper washers*, for rivets.
1 *assembling bolt*; 1 *nut.*	56 *copper tacks*, for washers.
1 *turnbuckle*, (BRASS.)	1 *cover*, (SHEET COPPER.)
1 *washer plate*, for do.; 2 *screws.*	216 *copper tacks*, for cover.
1 *back stay*; 6 *screws.*	

CAISSON.—*Plate* 4.

Wood.

1 *middle rail.*	1 *front foot board.*
2 *side rails.*	1 *rear foot board.*
1 *cross bar.*	1 *axle body.*
1 *bolster*, for front foot board.	1 *stock.*

CAISSON—*Iron.*

2 *nails*, for front foot board.
1 *bolt*, for do.; 2 *washers*; 1 *nut*.
6 *nails*, for rear foot board.
1 *middle assembling bar*.
2 *bolts*, 2 *washers*, and 2 *nuts*, for do.
1 *carriage hook*.
1 *rear assembling bar*.
2 *bolts*, 2 *washers*, and 2 *nuts*, for do.
1 *bridle*, for rear of middle rail.
4 *nails*, for the bridle.
1 *spare wheel axle*; the *body*, 2 *ribs*, 1 *washer*, 3 *rivets*.
1 *chain and toggle*, for spare wheel axle.
2 *stays*, for the same; 2 *nuts*.
1 *stay bolt*; 1 *nut*.
1 *foot bolt*; 1 *nut*.
1 *lock chain bridle*.
1 *lock chain and toggle*.
2 *bolts*, for lock chain bridle.
2 *washers* and 2 *nuts*, for do.
1 *lock chain hook*; 2 *nails*.
1 *axletree*.
2 *under straps*.
4 *bolts*, for under straps; 4 *nuts*.
2 *axle bands*; 6 *nails*.
2 *rivets* for the stock; 2 *burrs*.
1 *lunette*; 12 *nails*.
2 *lunette bolts*; 2 *nuts*.
1 *key plate*, for spare pole.
1 *spare pole key*.
1 *key chain*; 1 *eye pin*.
2 *wheel guard plates*; 10 *nails*.
1 *stock stirrup*.
2 *bolts*, for do.; 2 *washers*; 2 *nuts*.
1 *axle strap*.
1 *spare pole ring*.
3 *bolts*, for axle strap; 3 *nuts*.
8 *plates*, for stay pins; 16 *nails*.
4 *stay pins*.
4 *stay pin keys*.
4 *key chains*; 4 *eye pins*.
1 *ring bolt*, for spare handspike.
2 *washers* and 1 *nut*, for ring bolt.
1 *key plate*, for handspike; 2 *nails*.
1 *key plate*, for shovel; 2 *nails*.
2 *keys*, for handspike and shovel.
2 *key chains*; 2 *eye pins*.
2 *staples*, for tool handles.
2 *shoulder washers*.
2 *linch washers*.
2 *linch pins*.

2 WHEELS, No. 1.
2 AMMUNITION CHESTS.

TRAVELLING FORGE.—*Plate* 5.

Body and Bellows House.

Wood.

2 *side rails*.
1 *front cross bar*; 2 *pins*.
2 *middle cross bars*; 6 *pins*.
1 *rear cross bar*; 2 *pins*.
1 *middle rail*; 4 *screws*.
1 *axle body*.
1 *stock*.
4 *floor boards*; 16 *screws*.
4 *corner studs*; 8 *pins*.
1 *front board*, for iron room; 2 *pins*.
2 *side studs*; 4 *pins*.
2 *plates*.
1 *front end stud*.
2 *end boards*, for roof; 10 *screws*.
2 *roof bows*; 4 *screws*.
2 *side linings*, for iron room; 12 *nails*
1 *rear end*, for iron room.
2 *groove cleats*, for cover of iron room 6 *screws*.
1 *sliding cover*, for iron room; 6 *boards* and 2 *battens*; 36 *nails*.
2 *braces* for the bellows arms; 6 *screws*
1 *cap for coal box*; 5 *screws*.
10 *boards*, for sides of bellows house.
7 *boards*, for the roof.
272 *nails*, for sides and roof.
1 *prop*, for the stock.
1 *bellows pole*.

Forge Body.—*Iron.*

1 *axletree.*
2 *axle bands; 6 nails.*
2 *under straps.*
4 *bolts*, for do.; 4 *washers; 4 nuts.*
2 *rivets*, for stock; 2 *burrs.*
1 *lunette; 12 nails.*
1 *vice bolt; 1 nut.*
1 *middle lunette bolt; 1 nut.*
1 *prop bolt; 1 nut.*
1 *prop socket; 1 rivet.*
1 *prop ferrule; 1 rivet.*
1 *chain and toggle*, for forge prop; 1 *eye pin.*
1 *stock stirrup.*
2 *bolts*, for stock stirrup; 2 *nuts.*
1 *bolt*, for cross bar and stock.
1 *washer* and 1 *nut*, for do.
1 *axle strap.*
2 *bolts*, for do.; 2 *nuts.*
2 *wheel guard plates; 10 nails.*
2 *stud plates*, for coal box.
2 *rivets* and 2 *screws*, for do.
2 *keys*, for coal box.
2 *key chains; 2 eye pins.*
1 *lock chain hook; 2 nails.*
1 *bellows pole hook; 2 nails.*
1 *staple*, for bellows pole.
2 *front stay plates*, for bellows arms.
6 *screws*, for do.
2 *rear stay plates; 2 bolts; 2 thumb nuts.*
1 *front for bellows house*, } 169 *tacks.*
1 *cover*, for cross bar; }
1 *guard for stock*; 18 *tacks.*
1 *stud*, for bellows pole; 4 *screws.*
1 *cover for roof*, (SHEET COPPER;) 315 *copper tacks.*
1 *fire place*; 6 *plates* of iron joined by 59 *rivets.*
1 *air back*, (CAST IRON;) 4 *bolts*, for the box and back of air chamber.
5 *bolts*, for fastening the air back; 5 *nuts.*
1 *bucket hook; 2 rivets.*
3 *plates*, for side rails and cross bar.
10 *bolts*, for do.; 8 *washers* and 10 *nuts.*
1 *lock chain.*
1 *lock chain bridle.*
1 *brace*, for fire place; 4 *rivets.*
1 *bellows pole strap; 2 rivets; 3 screws.*
1 *bellows pole chain.*
2 *shoulder washers.*
2 *linch washers.*
2 *linch pins.*

2 WHEELS, No. 1.

Bellows.

Wood.

3 *bellows planks.*
2 *cross heads; 12 screws.*
2 *ribs;* each of 2 *sides*, 1 *end*, 1 *cross bar;* fastened with 8 *clout nails.*
2 *valves; 2 battens; 16 nails.*
4 *cleats*, for the bellows arms.
16 *screws*, for cleats.

Iron.

6 *butt hinges; 36 screws.*
2 *arms; 4 rivets; 8 screws.*
1 *hook; 3 rivets; 4 screws.*
1 *wind pipe*, consisting of an *elbow*, a *collar*, and a *joint pipe* of *brass;* and a *bent pipe*, of *sheet copper.*

Leather.

4 *hinges*, for the ribs.
2 *hinges*, for the valves; 2 *straps.*
393 *copper tacks*, for hinges.
1 *bellows leather*, for the sides.
617 *bellows nails.*
Safes, for the heads of the nails.

To put the bellows in its place: Remove the coal box from the back of the bellows house; take out the two stay plates at the lower ends of the rabbets in the braces; put the projecting ends of the upper bellows arm in the rabbets, and slide them up until the ends of the lower arm come into their places; put on the stay plates, and fasten them down with the thumb nuts. Screw the brass elbow pipe into its place, through the hole in the sheet iron front of the bellows house; put in the copper pipe and screw up the collar which connects it with the elbow pipe.

Coal Box.

Wood.

2 *sides*, 2 *ends*, 1 *bottom* } rabbeted together and fastened with 50 *cut nails*.	1 *top piece*; 7 *screws*. 1 *lid*; 2 *clamps* for lid.

Iron.

4 *corner plates*; 60 *screws*.	1 *turnbuckle*.
2 *end straps*; 2 *rivets*; 4 *screws*.	1 *hasp*; 1 *rivet*; 3 *screws*.
2 *handles*; 4 *washers* and 4 *nuts*.	1 *cover*, (SHEET COPPER;) 185 *copper tacks*.
1 *stud plate*, for turnbuckle; 2 *rivets*.	2 *hinges*; 4 *rivets*; 16 *screws*.

Limber Chest.

This chest differs from the ammunition chest in the following points, viz:

It has no principal partition, and instead of the assembling bolt, with the washer plate and turnbuckle, it has a *hasp staple and plate*, fastened by 2 *rivets*. The *back stay* is fastened by 1 *rivet* and 6 *screws*. The heads of the rivets are not covered with copper washers.

For the interior arrangement of the chest, see CHAPTER XI.

BATTERY WAGON.—*Plate* 6.

The battery wagon carries tools, spare parts of carriages, spare harness, and other stores required for the service of a battery in the field, and for repairs.

Wagon Body.

Wood.

2 *lower side rails*.	1 *stock*.
5 *cross bars*; 10 *pins*.	2 *cleats*, for the till; 6 *screws*.
3 *floor boards*; 36 *nails*.	1 *bottom*, for the till.
1 *axle body*.	1 *side*, for the till; 11 *nails*.
2 *upper side rails*.	2 *sides*, for forage rack.
2 *sides*; 2 *ends*.	3 *bars*, for forage rack; 6 *pins*.

Wagon Body.—*Iron.*

2 *rivets*, for lower rails; 2 *burrs*.
8 *side studs;* 14 *rivets*.
1 *spare stock hook;* 1 *button*.
1 *spare stock stirrup*.
4 *grooves*, for ends.
2 *assembling bolts;* 2 *nuts*.
12 *groove bolts;* 12 *nuts*.
3 *bolts*, for side studs; 3 *washers;* 3 *nuts*.
1 *turnbuckle bolt;* 1 *washer;* 1 *nut*.
1 *turnbuckle*, (BRASS.)
1 *hook*, for cover prop; 1 *burr*.
1 *eye pin*, for cover hasp; 1 *burr*.
2 *stays*, for upper rails; 4 *screws*.
2 *end studs;* 6 *rivets*.
1 *bolt*, for front end stud; 1 *nut*.
1 *washer* and 1 *nut*, for rear end stud.
1 *mortise plate;* 8 *screws*.
1 *axletree*.
2 *under straps*.
4 *bolts*, for do.; 4 *nuts*.
1 *bolt*, for front of right side rail.
2 *washers* and 1 *nut* for do.
2 *bolts*, for lock chain bridle.
1 *washer* and 2 *nuts* for do.
1 *lock chain*.
1 *lock chain bridle*.
1 *lock chain hook;* 2 *nails*.
2 *rivets*, for stock; 2 *burrs*.
1 *lunette;* 12 *nails*.
2 *lunette bolts;* 2 *nuts*.
2 *wheel guard plates;* 10 *nails*.
1 *stock stirrup*.
2 *bolts*, for do.; 2 *nuts*.
2 *bolts*, for stock and cross bars.
2 *washers* and 2 *nuts*, for do.
2 *washer plates*, for rails; 4 *screws*.
2 *forage rack chains;* each of 1 *ring*, 32 *links*, and 1 *hook*.
2 *forage rack bands;* 2 *rivets;* 22 *screws*.
4 *washer plates*, for forage rack sides.
4 *rivets*, for do.
2 *forage rack bolts;* 2 *washers;* 2 *nuts*.
2 *shoulder washers*.
2 *linch washers*.
2 *linch pins*.

2 WHEELS, No. 1.

Wagon Cover.

Wood.

2 *side rails*.
2 *end rails*.
2 *end studs;* 2 *pins;* 4 *rivets*.
2 *end boards;* 14 *screws*.
1 *ridge pole*.
9 *cover boards;* 36 *cut nails*.

Iron.

4 *corner squares;* 16 *screws*.
2 *end bows;* 36 *rivets*.
2 *middle bows;* 2 *rivets;* 36 *screws*.
4 *joint bolts;* 4 *nuts*.
2 *plates and staples;* 2 *rivets;* 2 *screws*.
1 *cover prop*, to support the cover.
1 *hasp*.
3 *hinges*.
6 *bolts*, 6 *nuts, and* 6 *rivets*, for hinges.

The roof is covered with strong linen canvass, which is fastened with 264 *copper nails*, with strips of *leather* under their heads.

Limber Chest.

This chest is like that of the travelling forge. For the interior arrangement of the wagon body and the limber chest, see CHAPTER XI.

SIEGE CARRIAGES.

GUN CARRIAGE.—*Plate* 7.

There are three gun carriages for siege artillery, viz:

One for the 12-pounder gun;

One for the 18-pounder gun;

One for the 24-pounder gun and the 8-inch howitzer.

These carriages are constructed in the same manner, differing only in their dimensions.

When the 8-inch howitzer is mounted on the 24-pounder carriage, a *quoin* is used, instead of the elevating screw; the howitzer being too short to rest on the screw.

Wood.

1 *stock*, in two pieces; 2 *dowels*.
2 *cheeks*.
1 *axle body*.
1 *breech bolster*.

Iron.

1 *assembling bolt*; 2 *washers*; 1 *nut*.
1 *manœuvring bolt*; 2 *collars*.
4 *washers* and 2 *nuts*, for do.
6 *rondelles*, (CAST IRON.)
2 *assembling bolts*; 4 *washers*; 2 *nuts*.
1 *lock chain bolt*; 2 *washers*; 1 *nut*.
1 *lock chain* and *toggle*.
1 *shoe*; 1 *key*, for shoe.
2 *trunnion plates*.
2 *chin bolts*; 2 *bevel washers*; 2 *nuts*.
2 *key bolts*; 2 *nuts*.
4 *cheek bolts*; 4 *washers*; 4 *nuts*.
2 *travelling trunnion bolts*.
2 *washers*; 2 *nuts*, for do.
2 *trunnion plate bolts*; 2 *nuts*.
2 *cap squares*; 2 *eye pins*.
2 *cap square chains*; 2 *eye pins*.
2 *cap square keys*.
2 *key chains*; 2 *eye pins*.
1 *axletree*.
2 *understraps*.
1 *axle strap*.
2 *bolts*, for axle strap; 2 *nuts*.
2 *axle bands*; 6 *nails*.
1 *lock chain hook*; 2 *washers*; 1 *nut*.
1 *hook*, for the shoe.
1 *cheek plate*, for do.; 3 *screws*.
1 *box*, for elevating screw, (BRASS.)
2 *bolts*, for do.; 2 *washers*; 2 *nuts*.
1 *elevating screw*.
1 *strap staple*; 1 leather strap and buckle.
2 *wheel guard plates*; 12 *nails*.
1 *lunette*; the *rondelle*; 3 *rivets*.
2 *lunette bolts*; 2 *washers*; 2 *nuts*.
1 *trail plate*; the *guard plate*; 6 rivets.
29 *nails*, for trail plate.
2 *bolster bolts*; 2 *washers*; 2 *nuts*.
2 *shoulder washers*, for axletree.
2 *linch washers*.
2 *linch pins*.

2 WHEELS.

WHEEL.

The same wheel is used for all the siege gun carriages and their limbers.

Wood.

1 *nave;* 14 *spokes;* 7 *fellies;* 7 *dowels.*

Iron.

2 *brow bands;* 2 *end bands;* 12 *nails;* 1 *tire;* 7 *tire bolts;* 7 *washers;* 7 *nuts;* 1 *nave box*, (BRASS.)

LIMBER.—*Plate* 7.

Wood.

1 *fork;* 2 *hounds;* 1 *splinter bar;* 1 *pole;* 1 *leading bar.*

Iron.

1 *rivet bolt*, for fork; 2 *washers;* 1 *nut.*
1 *axletree.*
1 *pintle plate;* 7 *nails.*
1 *sweep bar.*
2 *bolts*, for ears of sweep bar.
2 *washers;* 2 *nuts*, for do.
1 *axle strap.*
1 *lashing chain;* 4 *rings;* 1 *hook.*
6 *axle-strap bolts;* 2 *washers;* 6 *nuts.*
2 *understraps.*
4 *bolts*, for do.; 2 *washers;* 4 *nuts.*
1 *pintle;* 1 *nut.*
2 *end bands*, for splinter bar; 4 *rivets.*
2 *middle bands*, for do.
4 *trace hooks*, for splinter bar.
1 *bridle*, for front of fork.
2 *bolts*, for splinter bar and fork.
2 *nuts*, for do.
2 *bolts*, for splinter bar and hounds.
4 *washers* and 2 *nuts*, for do.
1 *bridle*, for middle of fork; 4 *nails.*
1 *rivet*, for the pole; 1 *burr.*
1 *eye plate*, for pole.
2 *pole chains.*
1 *ferrule*, for end of pole.
1 *pole clasp;* 1 *clasp bolt.*
2 *bolts*, for eye plate; 3 *washers;* 2 *nuts.*
2 *bolts*, for pole and fork.
4 *washers* and 2 *nuts*, for do.
1 *middle band*, for leading bar; 2 *rivets.*
1 *hook*, for do.
1 *double trace hook*, for middle band.
2 *end bands*, for leading bar; 4 *rivets.*
2 *trace hooks*, for end bands.
2 *axle shoulder washers.*
2 *linch washers.*
2 *linch pins.*

2 WHEELS.

MORTAR WAGON.

This wagon is designed for the transportation of siege mortars and their beds, or of guns, or large shot and shells.

The limber and the wheels are the same as those of the gun carriage.

Wood.

2 *middle rails.*
1 *front transom;* 2 *dowels.*
1 *middle transom.*
1 *rear transom.*
2 *side rails.*
1 *rear cross bar.*
6 *middle cross bars.*
2 *front cross bars.*
2 *bottom planks;* 12 *nails.*
1 *axle body.*
1 *windlass.*
2 *handspikes.*
1 *muzzle bolster.*
6 *stakes.*
A *frame*, for balls, when required.

Iron.

1 *assembling bar.*
2 *handspike hooks;* 4 *nails.*
1 *assembling bolt;* 2 *washers;* 1 *nut.*
1 *eye plate*, for lashing chain.
1 *bolt*, for do.; 2 *washers;* 1 *nut.*
1 *bolt*, for front transom.
2 *washers;* 1 *nut*, for do.
2 *manœuvring staples.*
2 *cross-bar plates.*
12 *bolts*, for do.; 9 *washers;* 12 *nuts.*
1 *lock-chain bridle.*
1 *bolt*, for do.; 1 *nut.*
1 *lock chain;* 1 *shoe;* 1 *key.*
1 *trail plate;* 11 *nails.*
1 *lunette;* 1 *reinforce plate;* 4 *rivets.*
1 *bridle*, for the pintle.
3 *bolts*, for lunette and bridle; 3 *nuts.*
2 *wheel guard plates;* 12 *nails.*
1 *axletree.*
2 *understraps.*
4 *bolts*, for do.; 4 *nuts.*
4 *bolts*, for middle rails and axle body.
4 *nuts*, for do.; 2 *axle straps.*
1 *breech hurter;* 4 *nails.*
6 *stake sockets;* 6 *pins.*
5 *pins*, for muzzle bolster.
10 *bolts*, for do.; 10 *washers;* 10 *nuts.*
2 *lock-chain hooks;* 2 *washers;* 2 *nuts.*
1 *tar-bucket hook;* 2 *nails.*
4 *handspike socket plates;* 32 *nails.*
2 *bands*, for windlass; 6 *nails.*
2 *journal boxes*, (BRASS.)
2 *journals.*
4 *journal plates;* 4 *nails.*
4 *bolts*, for do.; 4 *nuts.*
2 *roller hooks.*
2 *handspike straps;* 4 *rivets.*
2 *axle shoulder washers.*
2 *linch washers.*
2 *linch pins.*

2 WHEELS.

BARBETTE CARRIAGES.—*Plate* 8.

The barbette carriage consists of a *gun carriage* and a *chassis*, or traversing carriage.

The carriages for pieces of the following calibres are similar to each other, with some slight exceptions, mentioned in the nomenclature, viz: for the 12-pounder, 18-pounder, 24-pounder, 32-pounder, and 42-pounder guns, and for the 8-inch and 10-inch sea coast howitzers. The carriages for the columbiads are not yet definitively arranged.

Some chassis have been arranged, for use in peculiar situations, with the pintle under the middle transom, and others with the pintle under the rear transom.

GUN CARRIAGE.

Wood.

2 *uprights.*
2 *braces.*
1 *front transom.*
1 *middle transom.*
1 *rear transom.*
1 *transom and axle tie* ; 2 *dowels.*
1 *elevating bed* ; 2 *dowels.*
1 *axle body.*

Iron.

2 *trail rivet bolts;* 2 *washers;* 2 *nuts.*
2 *rivet bolts*, for uprights.
4 *washers* and 2 *nuts*, for do.
2 *cheek bolts;* 2 *washers;* 2 *nuts.*
2 *bevel washers*, for do. (CAST IRON.)
1 *lunette.*
4 *assembling bolts*, 8 *washers* and 4 *nuts*, for 12-pdr., 18-pdr., and 24-pdr. carriages.
6 *assembling bolts*, 12 *washers* and 6 *nuts*, for other carriages.
2 *transom and tie bolts*, 1 *washer;* 2 *nuts.*
For 8-inch howitzer: 2 *washers.*
1 *bed-plate bolt;* 1 *washer;* 1 *nut.*
For 8-inch howitzer: 2 *bolts;* 2 *washers;* 2 *nuts.*
1 *bed plate*, for elevating screw.
1 *nut*, for elevating screw; 4 *handles.*
1 *elevating screw.*
1 *axletree.*
2 *axle stirrups;* 2 *bridles;* 4 *nuts.*
1 *clamp washer*, for 12 and 18-pdr. carriages.
1 *axle and tie brace*, for larger calibres.
2 *axle and tie bolts.*
1 *double washer*, for do.; 2 *nuts.*
1 *bolt*, for middle transom and tie; 1 *nut.*
2 *washers*, for do., in 12 and 18-pdr. carriages.
1 *washer*, in other carriages, except 8-inch howitzer.
2 *manœuvring bolts;* 2 *washers;* 2 *nuts.*
2 *collars*, 2 *cheek plates*, and 2 *screws*, for 12, 18, and 24-pdr. carriages.
4 *collars*, 4 *cheek plates*, and 4 *screws*, for other carriages.
2 *manœuvring staples.*
2 *trunnion plates.*
4 *trunnion plate bolts;* 4 *nuts.*
2 *rollers* (CAST IRON.)
2 *axle shoulder washers.*
2 *linch washers.*
2 *linch pins.*

2 WHEELS.

WHEEL.

WOOD: 10 *spokes.*

IRON: 1 *nave* (CAST IRON); 1 *tire;* 10 *tire nails.*

BARBETTE—CHASSIS.

Wood.

2 *rails.*
2 *hurters;* 4 *nails.*
2 *counter hurters;* 4 *nails.*
1 *front transom.*
1 *middle transom.*
1 *rear transom.*
1 *tongue.*
1 *prop.*

Iron.

2 *rail plates;* 30 *screws.*
4 *bolts*, for do.; 4 *washers;* 4 *nuts.*
4 *rivets*, for hurters; 4 *burrs.*
6 *rivet bolts*, for front and middle transoms.
6 *washers* and 6 *nuts*, for do.
1 *friction plate;* 10 *nails.*
1 *transom and tongue brace*, for 32-pdr. and higher calibres.
2 *hurter and rail bolts;* 4 *washers;* 2 *nuts.*
2 *front transom and rail bolts;* 2 *nuts.*
2 *middle transom and rail bolts.*
2 *washers* and 2 *nuts*, for do.
For 32-pdr. and higher calibres: 4 *bolts;* 4 *washers;* 4 *nuts*, for do.
4 *counter hurter and rail bolts;* 4 *nuts.*
2 *fork sockets.*
2 *fork plates;* 12 *nails.*
2 *bolts*, for rear transom and fork plates.
2 *nuts*, for do.
1 *manœuvring loop;* 2 *nails.*
1 *loop bolt;* 1 *nut.*
3 *transom and tongue bolts.*
3 *washers*, and 3 *nuts*, for do.
2 *prop plates;* 4 *nails.*
1 *prop bolt;* 1 *key.*
2 *forks.*
2 *fork bolts;* 2 *nuts.*
2 *traverse wheels* (CAST IRON.)
For 32-pdr. and higher calibres, add:
4 *pipes* (CAST IRON.)
2 *pipe bolts;* 4 *washers;* 2 *nuts.*

1 PINTLE.

PINTLE CROSS.

WOOD: 2 *cross pieces*—1 *pintle bolster*, fastened to the cross by 4 *octagonal wooden pins* 1 inch thick.

IRON: 1 *bolster plate*, (cast iron;) fastened to the bolster by 4 *bolts*—4 *washers* and 4 *nuts*, for do.

1 *pintle*—1 *washer* and 1 *key* for do.

In temporary batteries, a circular platform of plank is required for the wheels of the chassis to traverse on.

In permanent batteries, the bolster plate, the pintle and the traversing circle are fixed in masonry.

CASEMATE CARRIAGES.

Each carriage consists of a *gun carriage* and a *chassis*.

The carriages for 24, 32, and 42-pounder guns, and the 8-inch Columbiad, are similar to each other, differing only in their dimensions.

A special carriage is arranged for mounting the 24-pounder iron howitzer in the flanks of casemate batteries.

GUN CARRIAGE.—*Plate* 9.

Wood.

2 *cheeks*, each in two pieces.
2 *dowels*, for do.
1 *front transom.*
1 *rear transom.*
1 *slide; 2 dowels.*
1 *axletree.*
2 *guides.*

Iron.

8 *cheek bolts; 10 washers; 8 nuts.*
2 *trunnion plates.*
4 *bolts*, for do.; 4 *nuts.*
1 *elevating screw.*
1 *bed plate*, for screw, (CAST IRON.)
1 *nut*, for do., (BRASS.)
1 *pinion*, for do., (BRASS.)
1 *shaft*, for pinion; 1 *set screw.*
1 *cheek washer; 3 screws.*
1 *handle*, for shaft, (CAST IRON.)
1 *washer* and 1 *nut*, for do.
2 *bed plate bolts; 2 washers; 2 nuts.*
2 *bolts*, for rear transom and slide.
2 *washers* and 2 *nuts*, for do.
1 *trail roller*, (CAST IRON.)
1 *roller shaft.*
2 *eccentrics*, for roller shaft.
2 *roller bolts; 2 washers; 2 nuts.*
2 *trail handles.*
4 *assembling bolts; 4 washers; 4 nuts.*
8 *axle skeans; 16 nails.*
2 *axle shoulder plates; 10 nails.*
2 *axle bands; 8 nails.*
2 *understraps.*
4 *guide bolts; 8 washers; 4 nuts.*
2 *linch pins.*

2 *truck wheels*, (CAST IRON.)

CHASSIS.—*Plate* 9.

Wood.

2 *rails.*
2 *counter hurters; 2 dowels.*
1 *front transom.*
1 *rear transom.*
1 *tongue.*
1 *prop; 2 pins.*

Iron.

2 *bolts*, for rear transom and rails.
2 *washers* and 2 *nuts* for do.
2 *bolts*, for front transom and rails.
2 *washers* and 2 *nuts*, for do.
2 *bolts*, for counter hurters and rails.
2 *washers* and 2 *nuts*, for do.
2 *rivet bolts*, for the tongue.
1 *double washer* and 2 *nuts*, for do.
2 *bolts*, for front transom and tongue.
2 *washers* and 2 *nuts*, for do.
1 *tongue fork.*
1 *front transom strap.*
1 *rear transom and tongue brace.*
2 *brace bolts; 2 nuts.*
8 *journal boxes*, (BRASS.)
8 *caps*, for do.; 16 *screws.*
4 *traverse wheels*, (CAST IRON.)
2 *rail plates; 8 screws; 54 nails.*
2 *rail plate bolts; 2 washers; 2 nuts.*
1 *tongue.*
2 *tongue bolts; 2 nuts.*

1 *pintle*, (CAST IRON.)

24-POUNDER HOWITZER CARRIAGE, FOR FLANK CASEMATES.

Gun Carriage.—*Plate* 10.

WOOD: 2 *cheeks*.

Iron.

2 *trail handles*; 4 *washers*; 4 *nuts*.
2 *manœuvring rings*.
2 *eye bolts*, for do.; 2 *nuts*.
2 *trail plates*; 8 *nails*.
2 *cheek bolts*; 2 *washers*; 2 *nuts*.
2 *trunnion plates*.
2 *bolts*, for do.; 2 *washers*; 2 *nuts*.
4 *key bolts*; 4 *nuts*.
1 *front transom* } (CAST IRON.)
1 *rear transom* }
3 *assembling bolts*; 6 *washers*; 3 *nuts*.
2 *understraps*.
2 *roller forks*; 2 *keys*.
2 *rollers*, (BRASS.)
2 *fork bolts*; 2 *nuts*.
2 *cap squares*; 4 *eye pins*.
4 *cap square keys*; 4 *key chains*.
1 *trail roller*, (CAST IRON.)
1 *roller journal*.
2 *eccentrics*, for do.
2 *journal plates*, (BRASS;) 4 *screws*.
1 *roller handspike*.
1 *elevating screw*.
1 *box* and 1 *pinion* for do., (BRASS.)
1 *shaft*, for pinion; 1 *set screw*.
1 *handle*, for shaft; 1 *screw*.
1 *cheek washer*; 3 *screws*.

Chassis.—*Plate* 10.

Wood.

2 *rails*.
1 *front transom*; 4 *dowels*.
2 *middle transoms*; 4 *pins*.
1 *rear transom*; 4 *dowels*.

Iron

3 *assembling bolts*; 6 *washers*; 3 *nuts*.
1 *collar*, for middle assembling bolt.
1 *upper pintle plate*.
1 *lower pintle plate*.
5 *bolts*, for pintle plates; 5 *nuts*.
1 *hurter plate*; 4 *screws*.
2 *counter hurter plates*; 8 *screws*.
2 *counter hurters*; 2 *washers*; 2 *nuts*.
1 *prop*.
2 *prop bolts*; 2 *nuts*.
1 *brace*, for the prop.
1 *brace bolt*; 1 *nut*.
1 *fork*, for traverse wheels.
2 *fork and prop bolts*; 2 *nuts*.
2 *traverse wheels*, (CAST IRON.)
2 *traverse wheel bolts*; 2 *nuts*.

1 *pintle*.

MORTAR BEDS.

Beds for 8-inch and 10-inch Siege Mortars.

WOOD.—1 *bolster*, for the quoin.

IRON.—2 *cheeks*, 1 *middle transom*, and 1 *front transom*, in one piece, (CAST IRON.)
4 *manœuvring bolts*, cast in place.
2 *cap squares*; 4 *cap square straps*; 4 *bolts*; 4 *keys*.
2 *bolster bolts*; 2 *nuts*.

Platform for Siege Mortars.

WOOD: 6 *sleepers;* 18 *deck planks;* 72 *dowels.*
IRON: 12 *eye bolts.*

Coehorn Mortar Bed.

WOOD: The *bed* is a block of oak wood, in 1 or 2 pieces.
IRON: 2 *assembling bolts;* 4 *washers;* 2 *nuts.*
2 *cap squares;* 2 *bolts;* 2 *nuts.*
4 *handles;* 4 *bolts;* 4 *nuts.*

Eprouvette Mortar Bed and Platform.

The *bed plate* for the eprouvette mortar is of cast iron.

The plate is let into a *platform* of oak wood, formed of one or two pieces, strengthened by 2 *bolts*, with 4 *washers* and 4 *nuts.*

This wooden platform is fastened with 4 *bolts*, No. 7, to a block of stone, of the same dimensions as the wood, which is firmly imbedded in the ground.

MACHINES.

FIELD AND SIEGE GIN.

Wood.

2 *legs.*
1 *pry pole.*
3 *braces.*
6 *assembling pins.*
1 *windlass.*
5 *handspikes.*

Iron.

6 *rivets*, for braces; 6 *burrs.*
1 *tongue;* 3 *rivets.*
2 *head straps;* 4 *rivets;* 16 *screws.*
1 *assembling bolt;* 2 *washers;* 1 *nut.*
2 *screws*, for washers.
2 *sheaves*, (BRASS.)
1 *sheave bolt;* 1 *key.*
2 *oval washers*, for do.; 2 *screws.*
1 *key bolt*, for pry pole.
1 *chain*, for do.; 1 *eye pin.*
2 *journal boxes.*
8 *bolts* for do.; 8 *washers;* 8 *nuts.*
2 *gudgeons*, for windlass; 2 *keys.*
4 *bands*, for windlass; 16 *nails.*
2 *bands*, for legs; 4 *nails.*
3 *bands*, for pry pole; 6 *nails.*
3 *points*, for legs and pry pole.
1 *handle*, for pry pole.
2 *washers*, for do.; 6 *screws.*
1 *pry pole tongue;* 2 *rivets;* 2 *burrs.*

Single Pulley Block.

1 *sheave*, (BRASS;) 2 *straps;* 1 *cross head;* 1 *hook;* 3 *bolts;* 3 *nuts.*

GARRISON GIN.—*Plate* 11.

Wood.

2 *legs;* 2 *bevel blocks.*
1 *pry pole.*
11 *cleats*, for pry pole; 22 *nails.*
1 *windlass.*

Iron.

6 *bands*, for legs and pry pole.
18 *nails*, for bands.
2 *rivet bolts;* 2 *nuts.*
2 *braces.*
4 *brace bolts;* 8 *washers;* 32 *nails.*
4 *keys*, for brace bolts.
4 *key chains;* 4 *eye pins.*
3 *points*, for legs and pry pole.
1 *pry pole handle.*
2 *washers*, for do.; 8 *nails.*
1 *clevis.*
1 *clevis bolt;* 1 *pin.*
2 *keys*, for clevis bolt.
2 *key chains;* 2 *eye pins.*
2 *journal boxes*, (BRASS;) 8 *screws.*
2 *pawls.*
2 *bolts*, for do.; 2 *washers;* 2 *nuts.*
2 *journals*, for windlass.
6 *bands*, for windlass; 24 *nails.*
2 *ratchets*, (CAST IRON;) 4 *nails.*

Pulley Blocks.

They are made with one, two, three, or four sheaves.

IRON: 2 *straps;* 2 *cross heads*, with 2 *eyes* riveted in them; 4 *nuts*, for cross heads; 1 *hook*, welded into one of the eyes; 1 *sheave bolt;* 1 *nut.*

The *partitions;* the *sheaves*, (BRASS.)

CASEMATE GIN.

It is made like the garrison gin, differing from it only in the dimensions of some parts. The pry pole has but 6 *cleats*, for steps.

SLING CART.—*Plate* 12.

Wood.

1 *axletree;* 1 *bolster;* 1 *pole;* 2 *hounds;* 1 *pole prop.*

Iron.

1 *lower axle skean.*
2 *upper axle skeans.*
6 *rivets*, for skeans.
2 *bands*, for axle arms.
4 *washer plates*, for hooks; 16 *nails.*
4 *hooks;* 4 *washers;* 4 *nuts.*
2 *stirrups*, for axle and bolster.
2 *bridles*, for do.; 4 *nuts.*
1 *bed plate*, for screw, (CAST IRON.)
2 *bolts*, for do; 2 *nuts.*
1 *hoisting screw.*
1 *nut*, for screw, (BRASS.)
1 *handle*, for screw.
2 *rivets*, for pole; 2 *burrs.*
1 *pole strap;* 12 *nails.*
3 *bolts*, for do.; 3 *nuts.*
2 *bolts*, for axle and hounds; 2 *nuts.*
3 *bands*, for hounds; 6 *nails.*
2 *bolts*, for hounds and pole.
4 *washers* and 2 *nuts*, for do.
1 *cascable chain* and *hook.*
1 *pole staple;* 2 *washers;* 2 *nuts.*
1 *eye pin*, for pole prop.
2 *washers* and 1 *nut*, for do.
1 *socket*, for pole prop; 1 *rivet.*
1 *ferrule*, for do.; 1 *rivet.*
1 *chain and toggle*, for do.
1 *eye pin*, for pole prop chain.
2 *axle shoulder washers.*
2 *linch washers.*
2 *linch pins.*

1 *sling chain and hook.*
2 *trunnion chains.*

2 WHEELS.

Sling Cart.—Wheel.

WOOD: 1 *nave;* 16 *spokes;* 8 *fellies;* 8 *dowels.*

IRON: 4 *nave bands;* 12 *nails.*
1 *tire;* 8 *tire bolts;* 8 *washers;* 8 *nuts.*
2 *nave boxes,* (CAST IRON.)

CASEMATE TRUCK.

This truck is designed for transporting guns in casemate galleries, or through posterns.

WOOD: 2 *rails;* 3 *transoms;* 1 *handle.*

IRON: 1 *rear transom plate;* 2 *rings,* for drag ropes; 4 *nails.*
1 *front transom plate;* 2 *rings,* for drag ropes; 6 *nails.*
6 *bolts,* for rails and transom plates; 6 *nuts.*
2 *fork plates,* for rear wheels; 8 *nails.*
1 *fork socket,* for front wheel; it is round, to allow the fork to turn.
3 *forks* and 3 *bolts,* for wheels.
1 *fork plate,* for front wheel.
1 *tongue,* fastened to the front fork plate by 1 *bolt* and 1 *nut.*
3 *truck wheels,* (CAST IRON,) like the traverse wheels of the barbette chassis.

HAND CART.

WOOD: 1 *bolster,* for axletree; 2 *lower side rails.*
3 *cross bars;* 2 *upper side rails;* 2 *end rails;* 6 *side studs;* 6 *end studs.*
5 *bottom boards.*

IRON: 70 *wood screws,* for fastening the sides, ends, and bottom.
1 *axletree;* 2 *bolts,* for do.; 2 *nuts.*
2 *props;* 4 *bolts,* for do.; 4 *nuts.*
2 *shoulder washers;* 2 *linch washers;* 2 *linch pins.*
2 WHEELS.

Wheel.

WOOD: 1 *nave;* 12 *spokes;* 6 *fellies.*

IRON: 2 *nave bands;* 6 *nails.*
1 *tire;* 6 *tire bolts;* 6 *washers;* 6 *nuts.*
1 *nave box.*

STORE TRUCK.

This is a common hand truck, used in store-houses, for moving boxes, &c.

LIFTING JACK.

A geared screw jack, for lifting heavy weights.

WOOD: 1 *bed plate.*

IRON: 2 *rivet bolts*, for bed plate; 4 *washers;* 2 *nuts.*
2 *eye plates*, for braces; 6 *screws.*
1 *stand*, (CAST IRON;) 4 *steadying points*, for the stand.
2 *braces;* 2 *brace bolts.*
1 *hoisting screw;* 1 *plate*, fastened to the foot by 3 *screws.*
1 *nut* and 1 *pinion*, for hoisting screw, (BRASS;) 1 *shaft*, for the pinion; 1 *set screw;* 1 *crank;* 1 *nut.*
1 *handle* (wood;) 1 *washer* and 1 *nut*, for do.
1 *cap plate;* 4 *bolts*, for do.

LEVER JACK.

The lever jack is an adjustable fulcrum, with a long lever.

WOOD: The *stand* (OAK) consists of 1 *bed*, 2 *uprights*, 1 *transom*, and 2 *pins.*
1 *lever.*

IRON: 1 *transom bolt;* 2 *washers* and 1 *nut*, for do.
1 *fulcrum bolt;* 1 *chain*, for do; 1 *eye pin.*
2 *lever plates;* 12 *screws.*

Weights.

Store truck	80 pounds.
Lifting jack	160 "
Casemate gallery truck	600 "

Principal dimensions and weights of Field Gun Carriages and Limbers.

DIMENSIONS		6-pdr. Gun and 12-pdr. Howtzr.	24-pdr. Howtzr.	12-pdr. Gun and 32-pdr. Howtzr.
		In.	In.	In.
Distance between the inside of the trunnion plates......		9.6	11.65	12.15
Diameter of the trunnion holes....................		3.7	4.25	4.65
Depth of the centre of trunnion hole below the upper face of the trunnion plate........................		1.	0.95	0.95
Distance of axis of trunnions in rear of axis of axletree, the piece being in battery on horizontal ground......		0.5	1.	0.8
Distance from axis of trunnions to axis of axletree....		14.65	16.2	16.6
Height of axis of trunnions above the ground.........		43.1	44.8	45.2
Vertical field of fire, above the horizontal line.	Gun	12°	......	13°
	Howitzer...	13°	13°	12°
Vertical field of fire, below the horizontal line.	Gun.......	8°	......	7°
	Howitzer...	5°	8°	5°
Distance between the points of contact of trail and wheels with the ground line....................		74.4	79.8	79.8
Distance from front of wheels to end of trail, the piece being in battery..............................		116.6	122.75	122.75
Distance of the muzzle of the piece in battery from the front of the wheels.	Gun, in front of wheels....	5.91	......	15.70
	Howitzer, front of wheels	......	5.9	12.7
	Howitzer, rear of wheels	1.09		
Length of gun carriage without wheels...............		104.4	111.4	113.5
Length of limber without wheels....................		161.2	161.2	161.2
Length of limber without wheels or pole............		52.85	52.85	52.85
Length of limber with wheels and pole..............		173.08	173.08	173.08
Distance between the centres of the axletrees of gun carriage and limber............................		96.	101.7	101.7
Length of the carriage limbered up..................		269.08	274.78	274.78
Distance from the muzzle of the piece, when limbered, to the front of pole.	Gun	279.1	......	294.
	Howitzer.....	272.1	283.78	291.
Whole length of the axletree.......................		78.84	78.84	78.84
Track of the wheels...............................		60.	60.	60.
Height of wheel...................................		57.	57.	57.
Dish of finished wheel.............................		1.5	1.5	1.5
		Lbs.	Lbs.	Lbs.
WEIGHTS.	Gun carriage, without wheels............	540	736	783
	Limber without wheels or ammunition chest	335	335	335
	Ammunition chest, without divisions.	165	165	165
	One wheel. Gun carriage.............	180	196	196
	One wheel. Limber.................	180	180	180
	Gun carriage complete, without implements	900	1128	1175
	Limber complete, without implements.....	860	860	860
	Gun carriage and limber, without implements	1760	1988	2035

Principal dimensions and weights of Siege Gun Carriages & Limbers.

DIMENSIONS.	12-pdr. Gun.	18-pdr. Gun.	24-pdr. Gun & 8-in. Howztr.
	In.	In.	In.
Distance between the inside of the trunnion plates.....	14.95	16.95	18.15
Diameter of the trunnion holes.....................	4.65	5.35	5.85
Depth of centre of trunnion hole below the upper face of trunnion plate..............................	1.1	1.2	1.4
Distance of axis of trunnions in rear of axis of axletree, the piece being in battery on horizontal ground......	3.	2.5	2.75
Distance from axis of trunnions to axis of axle tree....	22.45	22.85	23.25
Height of axis of trunnions above the ground.........	52.2	52.6	53.
Vertical field of fire..... above the horizontal line. Gun.......	13°	12°	12°
Vertical field of fire..... above the horizontal line. Howitzer...	......	......	15°
Vertical field of fire..... below the horizontal line. Gun.......	4°	4°	4°
Vertical field of fire..... below the horizontal line. Howitzer...	......	......	10°
Distance between the points of contact of the wheels and trail with the ground line.......................	100.	101.	101.
Distance from the front of the wheels to the end of the trail, the piece being in battery..................	141.	142.	142.
Distance of the muzzle of the piece in battery from the front of the wheels.. Gun, in front of the wheels	30.74	35.35	35.34
Distance of the muzzle of the piece in battery from the front of the wheels.. Howitzer, in rear of wheels	......	......	7.66
Length of gun carriage, without wheels..............	130.	133.	133.6
Length of limber, without wheels...................	176.65	176.65	176.65
Length of limber, without wheels or pole............	59.8	59.8	59.8
Length of limber, with wheels and pole..............	184.9	184.9	184.9
Distance between the centres of the axletrees of gun carriage and limber...............................	94.	96.	96.
Length of the carriage, limbered up..................	278.9	280.9	280.9
Distance from the muzzle of the gun, in its travelling position, to front end of pole.......................	285.15	291.42	290.
Whole length of the axletree.........................	81.8	81.8	81.8
Track of the wheels..................................	60.	60.	60.
Height of wheel......................................	60.	60.	60.
Dish of finished wheel...............................	2.	2.	2.
	Lbs.	Lbs.	Lbs.
WEIGHTS. Gun carriage, without wheels	1440	1542	1714
WEIGHTS. Limber, without wheels..................	585	585	585
WEIGHTS. One wheel............................	404	404	404
WEIGHTS. Gun carriage, complete, without implements	2248	2350	2522
WEIGHTS. Limber, complete.......................	1393	1393	1393
WEIGHTS. Gun carriage and limber, without implements	3641	3743	3915

Field and Siege Wagons.

DIMENSIONS AND WEIGHTS.	Caisson.	Forge.	Battery Wagon.	Mortar Wagon.
	In.	In.	In.	In.
Length	125.5	130.	154.	143.6
Distance between the axletrees of carriage and limber	92.	97.8	112.93	102.95
Whole length, when limbered up	274.7	279.	303.13	287.85
Height, above the ground	58.75	70.5	73.55	60.
	Lbs.	Lbs.	Lbs.	Lbs.
Weight: Carriage body, without wheels	432	997	910	984
Weight: Limber, without wheels or chest	335	335	335	585
Weight: One wheel	180	180	180	404
Weight: Carriage and limber, complete, without implements or spare parts	1,982	2,217	2,130	3,185

INTERIOR DIMENSIONS.	Length.	Width.	Depth.	Weight.
	In.	In.	In.	Lbs.
Ammunition, or limber chest, without divisions	40.	18.	14.75	165
Travelling forge. Iron room	40.	32.	7.5	
Travelling forge. Coal box	31.	13.	17.	100
Battery wagon, body	98.8	36.	22.	
Mortar wagon, floor	63.85	40.		

Mortar Beds.	Siege.		Coehorn.	Eprouvette.
	8-inch.	10-inch.		
	In.	In.	In.	In.
Length	42.	51.8	31.	22.
Exterior width, including manœuvring bolts	34.	40.	15.	22.
Weight.....pounds	920	1830	132	280

Weight of platform for siege mortars, made of yellow pine—837 lbs.

Principal dimensions and weights of Barbette Carriages.

DIMENSIONS.	12-pdr. Gun.	18-pdr. Gun.	24-pdr. Gun.	32-pdr. Gun and 8-in. Howitzer.	42-pdr. Gun.
	In.	In.	In.	In.	In.
Distance between the inside of the trunnion plates	14.9	16.9	18.1	20.8	22.1
Diameter of the trunnion holes	4.65	5.35	5.85	6.45	7.05
Depth of the centre of trunnion hole below upper face of trunnion plate	1.	1.	1.	1.	1.
Horizontal distance of axis of trunnions in rear of axis of axletree	3.9	3.9	4.	4.1	4.2
Distance of axis of trunnions from axis of axletree	41.3	41.3	42.	43.4	44.1
Height of the axis of trunnions, in battery, above the traverse circle	71.76	71.76	73.45	75.77	77.47
Horizontal distance from axis of trunnions to axis of elevating screw { Gun	43.1	44.5	44.25	43.9	44.8
Horizontal distance from axis of trunnions to axis of elevating screw { Howitzer	....	....	....	39.	
Vertical field of fire { above the horizontal line	11°	11°	11°	11°	11°
Vertical field of fire { below the horizontal line	5°	5°	5°	5°	5°
Length of gun carriage, from front of wheels to rear of lunette	89.5	89.5	90.75	90.75	92.05
Whole length of the axletree	57.76	57.76	59.76	66.06	68.31
Distance between the exterior faces of the gun carriage wheels	55.70	55.70	57.70	64.	66.25
Inclination of the chassis in 100 inches	5.	5.	5.	5.	5.
Whole length of the chassis	184.06	184.06	183.38	182.86	182.71
Width of the chassis between the outside of the rails	43.	43.	45.	51.30	53.5
Horizontal distance from centre of pintle to front end of rails	9.5	9.5	9.5	9.5	9.5
Horizontal distance from centre of pintle to rear end of chassis	174.3	174.3	174.22	173.76	173.66
Horizontal distance from centre of pintle to centre of traverse wheels	120.33	120.33	120.33	120.33	120.33
Horizontal distance from centre of pintle to the face of the piece, in battery { Gun	59.	63.15	63.29	63.70	65.30
Horizontal distance from centre of pintle to the face of the piece, in battery { Howitzer	....	....	....	52.5	

Principal dimensions and weights of Barbette Carriages—Continued.

DIMENSIONS.	12-pdr. Gun.	18-pdr. Gun.	24-pdr. Gun.	32-pdr. Gun and 8-in Howitzer.	42-pdr. Gun.
	In.	In.	In.	In.	In.
Horizontal distance from centre of pintle to axis of axletree, the piece being in battery	0.8	0.8	0.8	0.8	0.8
Horizontal distance from centre of pintle to axis of axletree, the piece recoiled to counter hurters	113.07	113.07	113.	112.53	112.43
Diameter of gun carriage roller	13.	13.	13.	13.	13.
Diameter of gun carriage wheel	43.5	43.5	43.5	43.5	43.5
Diameter of traverse wheel of chassis	15.	15.	15.	15.	15.
	Lbs.	Lbs.	Lbs.	Lbs.	Lbs.
WEIGHTS. Gun carriage, without wheels or rollers	780	800	1073	1327	1400
One gun carriage roller	135	135	135	146	146
One gun carriage wheel	308	308	308	308	308
Chassis, without traverse wheels or forks	1100	1100	1420	1836	2000
One traverse wheel and fork	97	97	97	97	97
Pintle—new pattern	17	17	17	17	17
Gun carriage, complete, without implements	1666	1686	1959	2213	2308
Chassis, complete, without pintle	1294	1294	1614	2030	2194

Principal dimensions and weights of Casemate Carriages.

DIMENSIONS.	24-pdr. Gun.	32-pdr. Gun.	42-pdr. Gun.	8-in. Columbiad.	24-pdr. Howitzer.
	In.	In.	In.	In.	In.
Distance between the inside of the trunnion plates, measured in the axis of trunnion holes	18.52	21.26	22.56	25.10	12.95
Diameter of the trunnion holes	5.85	6.45	7.05	8.05	4.65
Depth of axis of trunnion hole below the upper face of trunnion plate	0.75	0.75	0.75	0.75	0.
Horizontal distance of axis of trunnions in rear of axis of axletree	1.90	1.90	1.90	3.00	
Distance of axis of trunnions from axis of axletree	26.32	27.51	28.21	28.31	
Height of axis of trunnions, in battery, above the traverse circle	48.75	49.95	50.65	50.65	48.25
Vertical field of fire { above the horizontal line	9°	8°	8°	8°	
Vertical field of fire { below the horizontal line	4°	4°	4°	4°	
Length of gun carriage, from front of cheeks to rear of trail roller	67.35	67.35	67.35	67.20	48.25
Whole length of the axletree	48.50	53.	55.05	57.60	
Distance between the exterior faces of gun carriage trucks	40.	44.50	46.55	49.10	
Inclination of the chassis in 100 inches	7.35	7.35	7.35	7.35	5.83
Whole length of chassis, (including 3 inches for the tongue fork)	189.15	189.15	189.15	189.15	151.
Width of chassis between the outsides of the rails	40.	44.50	46.76	49.16	22.
Length of rear transom of chassis	59.50	64.	66.26	68.66	
Horizontal distance from centre of pintle to front end of rails, upper side	49.94	49.94	49.94	49.94	7.
Horizontal distance from centre of pintle to middle of rear transom of chassis	193.40	193.40	193.40	193.40	
Horizontal distance from centre of pintle to rear end of chassis	235.	235.	235.	235.	144.

Principal dimensions and weights of Casemate Carriages—Continued.

DIMENSIONS.	24-pdr. Gun.	32-pdr. Gun.	42 pdr. Gun.	8-in. Columbiad.	24-pdr. Howitzer.
	In.	In.	In.	In.	In.
Horizontal distance from centre of pintle to centre of rear traverse wheels	194.5	194.5	194.5	194.5	120.
Horizontal distance from centre of pintle to centre of front traverse wheels	62.5	62.5	62.5	62.5	
Horizontal distance from centre of pintle in rear of face of the piece, in battery	0.52	1.03	2.73	4.83	25.6
Horizontal distance from centre of pintle to axis of axletree — piece in battery	65.67	65.67	65.67	65.67	
Horizontal distance from centre of pintle to axis of axletree — piece recoiled to counter hurters	177.13	177.13	177.13	177.13	
Diameter of gun carriage truck wheel	20.	20.	20.	20.	3.8
Diameter of rear traverse wheels, (mean)	15.90	15.90	15.90	15.90	6.
Diameter of front traverse wheels, (mean)	7.84	7.84	7.84	7.84	
	Lbs.	Lbs.	Lbs.	Lbs.	Lbs.
WEIGHTS. Gun carriage, without truck wheels	908	1064	1120	1128	
WEIGHTS. One gun carriage truck wheel	223	223	223	223	
WEIGHTS. Chassis, without traverse wheels	2120	2430	2575	2600	
WEIGHTS. One rear traverse wheel	99	99	99	99	
WEIGHTS. One front traverse wheel	30	30	30	30	
WEIGHTS. One pintle	92	92	92	92	50
WEIGHTS. Gun carriage, complete, without implements	1354	1510	1566	1574	620
WEIGHTS. Chassis, complete, without pintle	2378	2688	2833	2858	660

Sling Carts.		Large.	Hand.
		In.	In.
Length from rear of wheels to front end of pole		242.4	160.75
Length of axletree		92.	75.50
Height of wheels		96.	72.
Distance between the wheels, on the ground		58.75	60.4
		Lbs.	Lbs.
Weight.	One wheel	701	
	Whole weight, without sling chains	2282	1115
	Trunnion chain and rings	23	
	Sling chain	84	

Gins.		Field and siege.	Garrison.	Casemate.
		In.	In.	In.
Length of legs		175.5	256.5	172.5
		Lbs.	Lbs.	Lbs.
Weight of pry pole		55	224	175
Weight of gin, without blocks		455	823	642
Weight of pulley blocks.	Single	37		
	Double	....	65	65
	Triple	....	84	84

BOLTS, NUTS, AND WASHERS.

In the following Table the letters indicate the form of the head of the bolt, as follows:

A. Bolt with round (cylindrical) head, chamfered; square under the head.

B. Round head, not chamfered; to be let into wood; square under the head.

C. Countersunk head; bolt square under the head.

D. Convex, or rose head; square under the head.

E. Square head, chamfered; round under the head; nut let into wood.

F. Round head, chamfered; applied to wood; round under the head.

G. Round head, not chamfered; to be let into wood; round under the head.

H. Countersunk head; bolt round under the head.

Table of Bolts, Nuts, and Washers.

Nos.		1	2	3	4	5	6	7	8	9
BOLTS.		In.	In.	In.	In.	In.	In.	In.	In.	In.
Diameter of bolt		0.375	0.5	0.625	0.75	1.	1.125	1.25	1.375	1.5
Diameter of head	A	.85	1.1	1.4	1.7	2.3	2.5	2.75	3.	3.25
	B	1.	1.25	1.5	1.875	2.5	2.75	3.	3.5	3.75
	C. D. H.	0.7	0.875	1.06	1.25	1.625				
	E.	.75	1.	1.25	1.5	2.	2.25	2.5	2.75	3.
	F. G.	1.125	1.5							
Thickness of head	A. B. E. F. G.	0.3	0.375	.5	.6	.75	.8	.9	1.	1.1
	C. D. H.	.25	.3	.35	.4	.5				
Chamfer of head, A. E. F.		.1	.125	.16	.19	.25	.28	.31	.344	.375
Length of square, under the heads A. B. C. D.		.375	.5	.625	.75	1.	1.125	1.25	1.375	1.5
Usual length of thread cut		.75	1.	1.25	1.5	2.	2.25	2.5	2.75	3.
Number of threads to the inch		13	13	13	10	8	8	8	7	7
NUTS	Square.	.75	1.	1.25	1.5	2.	2.25	2.5	2.75	3.
	Thickness.	.375	.5	.625	.75	1.	1.125	1.25	1.375	1.5
	Chamfer.	.1	.125	.16	.19	.25	.28	.31	.344	.375
	Diagonal.	1.06	1.41	1.77	2.12	2.83	3.16	3.54	3.87	4.24
WASHERS	Diameter.	1.25	1.6	2.	2.45	3.15	3.5	4.	4.375	4.75
	Thickness.	0.125	.125	.125	.19	.19	.19	.25	.25	.25
	Width of chamfer.	.1	.1	.12	.16	.16	.17	.23	.25	.25
	Depth of chamfer.	.06	.06	.06	.1	.1	.1	.125	.125	.125

Rivets.

		Nos......	1	2	3	4
			In.	In.	In.	In.
Diameter of body			0.2	0.25	0.375	0.5
Diameter of head	B.		....	.75	1.125	1.5
	C. D.		....	.5	.7	.875
	H.		.75			
Thickness of head	B.		....	.2	.25	.375
	C. D.		....	.2	.25	.3
	H.		.125			
BURRS.	Diameter		.75	.75	1.125	1.5
	Thickness		.125	.2	.25	.375
	Exterior diameter of countersink		.3	.45	.6	.7
	Depth of countersink		.1	.15	.17	.25

B. Head not chamfered; to let into wood. D. Rose head; resting on iron.
C. Countersunk head; to let into iron. H. Rose head; resting on wood.

Wrought Nails.

	Nos....	1	2	3	4	REMARKS.
		In.	In.	In.	In.	
Body; diameter or thickness		.25	.3	.375	.5	C. Square nail, with countersunk head.
Heads C. D.	Diameter....	.5	.6	.7	.875	D. Round nail, with rose head.
	Thickness...	.2	.25	.25	.3	

Cut Nails.

Nos....	2*d.*	2*d.*	4*d.*	6*d.*	8*d.*	10*d.*	12*d.*	20*d.*
Length....Inches	1.	1.25	1.5	2	2.5	3	3.5	4
Number in 1 lb....	550	450	340	150	100	60	40	25

Spikes are large nails, *wrought* or *cut:* the size is designated by the length in inches.

Bellows nails and *clout nails* are short wrought nails, with large heads, slightly convex; they are used chiefly for nailing leather, canvass, &c., on wood.

Bellows nails 1.13 inch long, 0.1 inch thick, with heads .75 inch to 1 inch in diameter, should weigh about 120 to 1 lb.

Tacks are classed by the length in inches, or by the weight of 1,000, in ounces.

Sprigs, brads, finishing nails, are classed by the length in inches.

Wood Screws.

Wood screws are classed by the length in inches, and by the No. which indicates the size of the wire, or body of the screw.

The following table of dimensions, derived from measurements of the screws made by the New England Screw Company, at Providence, Rhode Island, will be found convenient for reference.

No.	Diameter of body.	Head.		No. of threads to 1 in.	Remarks.
		Diameter.	Thickness.		
	In.	In.	In.		
3	0.10	0.20	0.06	24	The length of thread cut is two-thirds the length of the screw.
4	.11	.22	.065	24	
5	.13	.26	.075	20	
6	.15	.30	.08	20	
7	.16	.32	.085	18	
8	.17	.34	.09	14	
9	.19	.38	.095	13½	
10	.20	.40	.10	13	
11	.21	.42	.11	12	
12	.22	.44	.12	11	
13	.23	.46	.13	11	
14	.24	.48	.14	10	
15	.25	.50	.15	10	
16	.26	.52	.16	9½	
17	.27	.54	.17	9	
18	.28	.56	.18	8½	
20	.30	.60	.20	8	
21	.32	.64	.21	8	
22	.35	.70	.22	7½	
24	.38	.76	.24	7	
26	.40	.80	.26	7	

Rings.

Designation.		Thickness of wire.	Exterior diameter of ring.	Remarks.	
		In.	In.		
No. 1	A.	0.2	1.4	Welded.	These are the rings most commonly used in field and siege carriages, with the chains Nos. 1, 2 & 3.
	B.	.2	1.	Coldshut.	
No. 2	A.	.25	1.5	Welded.	
	B.	.25	1.25	Coldshut.	

Chains.

No.	Thickness of iron.	LINKS.			Proof weight.	REMARKS.
		Kind.	Length.	Width.		
	In.		In.	In.	Lbs.	
1	0.15	Twisted.	1.1	0.6	400	All chains are welded.
2	.2	Twisted.	1.25	.75	800	
3	.25	Twisted.	1.6	1.1	1,200	
4	.25	Straight.	2.	1.	1,500	
5	.375	Straight.	3.	1.5	2,500	
6	.5	Straight.	3.	1.75	5,000	
7	.625	Straight.	3.4	2.25	6,500	

Eye Pins.

There are three sizes of eye pins used in field and siege carriages, as follows:

Nos......	1	2	3
	In.	In.	In.
Diameter of stem......	0.3	0.375	0.5
Diameter of eye.......	.25	.3	.375

Sheet metals and Wire.

Sheet metals and metallic wires are designated by *Nos.* corresponding with the thickness, as indicated by the ordinary iron wire gauge. These gauges do not exactly agree with each other, but the following table shows very nearly the thickness corresponding with the several Nos.

No.	Thickness.	No.	Thickness.	No.	Thickness.	No.	Thickness.
	In.		In.		In.		In.
1	0.313	9	0.161	17	0.057	25	0.023
2	.292	10	.143	18	.052	26	.02
3	.271	11	.125	19	.047	27	.018
4	.25	12	.113	20	.042	28	.016
5	.233	13	.1	21	.037	29	.014
6	.216	14	.088	22	.031	30	.012
7	.2	15	.075	23	.028		
8	.18	16	.063	24	.025		

Bills of timber for Field Carriages.

NAMES OF PARTS.		No. of pieces.	ROUGH DIMENSIONS OF EACH PIECE.			CONTENTS.		Kind of wood.
			Long.	Wide.	Thick.	Each piece.	Total	
GUN CARRIAGES.			In.	In.	In.	Sup. ft.	Sup. ft.	
For 6-pr. gun and 12-pr. howitzer.	Stock	2	100	9.25	4.5	28.90	57.80	Oak.
	Cheeks ..	2	40	13.5	3.5	13.12	26.24	Do.
	Axle body	1	50	7.	6.	14.58	14.58	Do.
							98.62	
For 12-pr. gun, 24-pr. and 32-pr. howitzers	Stock	2	108	11.	5.75	47.44	94.88	Do.
	Cheeks ..	2	50	16.	4.	22.22	44.44	Do.
	Axle body	1	50	7.	7.	17.01	17.01	Do.
							156.33	
WHEELS, Nos. 1 & 2.								
Nave		1	16	14.	Round	17.09	17.09	Do.
Spokes..................		14	32	3.5	2.	1.55	21.70	Do.
Fellies..................		7	27	7.	3.5	4.59	32.13	Do.
							70.92	
LIMBER.								
Axle body		1	50	9.	6.	18.75	18.75	Do.
Hounds..................		2	56	4.5	3.25	5.68	11.36	Do.
Fork		1	40	9.25	4.	10.27	10.27	Do.
Splinter bar		1	72	4.25	3.5	7.43	7.43	Do.
Brackets		4	9	2.3	1.6	......	......	Cuttings.
Front foot board		1	46	8.75	1.13	3.14	3.14	Oak.
Rear foot board		1	46	5.	1.13	1.86	1.86	Do.
Pole...	Large end..... / Small end	1	132	4.5 / 3.25	4.5 / 3.25	14.11	14.11	Oak or ash.
Pole prop		1	30	2.25	2.25	1.05	1.05	Hickory.
							67.97	
AMMUNITION CHEST.								
Ends..................		2	22	17.	1.31	3.40	6.80	Walnut.
Sides..................		2	44	17.	1.31	6.80	13.60	Do.
Principal partition........		1	22	17.	1.31	3.40	3.40	Do.
Cover frame.	Sides ..... / Ends	2 / 2	69	3.75	2.	3.59	7.18	Do.
Bottom		1	44	20.	1.31	8.00	8.00	Oak.
Panel for cover..........		1	42	17.5	2.	10.21	10.21	Poplar.
Cover lining............		1	42	20.	0.5	2.91	2.91	Poplar.
							52.10	

Bills of timber for Field Carriages.

NAMES OF PARTS.	No. of pieces.	ROUGH DIMENSIONS. OF EACH PIECE.			CONTENTS.		Kind of wood.
		Long.	Wide.	Thick.	Each piece.	Total.	
CAISSON.		In.	In.	In.	Sup.ft.	Sup.ft.	
Middle rail	1	76	5.75	4.75	14.41	14.41	Oak.
Side rails	2	78	5.	3.25	8.79	17.58	Do.
Stock	1	84	6.	4.75	16.62	16.62	Do.
Axle body	1	50	6.	6.	12.50	12.50	Do.
Cross bar	1	40	4.	3.	3.33	3.33	Do.
Foot board bolster	1	14	4.	1.25	.48	.48	Do.
Front foot board	1	42	7.5	2.13	4.65	4.65	Do.
Rear foot board	1	42	5.	1.25	1.82	1.82	Do.
						71.39	
FORGE—*Body.*							
Side rails	2	96	4.75	3.75	11.87	23.74	Oak.
Middle rail	1	50	4.75	4.25	7.01	7.01	Do.
Stock	1	90	6.	4.75	17.81	17.81	Do.
Axle body	1	50	7.25	6.	15.10	15.10	Do.
Front cross bar	1	40	3.5	3.5	3.40	3.40	Do.
Rear middle cross bar	1	40	3.5	3.5	3.40	3.40	Do.
Front middle cross bar	1	40	10.	3.5	9.72	9.72	Do.
Rear cross bar	1	40	3.	3.	2.50	2.50	Do.
Floor boards	4	48	8.	1.25	3.33	13.32	Do.
Roof bows	2	42	9.	1.25	3.28	6.56	Do.
Corner studs	4	36	3.5	2.5	2.19	8.75	Do.
Side studs	2	36	3.	2.5	1.88	3.75	Do.
Plates	2	46	3.	2.5	2.39	4.78	Do.
Front end stud	1	22	6.	1.25	1.14	1.14	Do.
Front of iron room	1	40	9.5	1.25	3.30	3.30	Do.
Rear of iron room	1	36	3.	1.25	0.94	.94	Do.
Lining of iron room	2	44	8.5	1.	2.59	5.18	Do.
Cleats for grooves	2	44	2.	1.	0.61	1.22	Do.
Braces	2	48	4.	2.	2.67	5.34	Do.
Front end of roof	1	42	10.	1.75	5.10	5.10	Walnut.
Rear end of roof	1	42	12.	1.75	6.13	6.13	Do.
Cap for coal box	1	36	2.5	1.25	0.78	.78	Do.
Boards for sides	10	42	7.	0.75	1.53	15.30	White pine.
Boards for roof	7	46	7.	.75	1.68	11.75	Do.
Boards for sliding cover	6	36	8.	.75	1.50	9.	Do.
Prop for stock	1	30	2.25	2.25	1.05	1.05	Hickory.
Bellows pole	1	57	2.	2.	1.58	1.58	Do.
						187.65	

Bills of timber for Field Carriages.

NAMES OF PARTS.	No. of pieces.	ROUGH DIMENSIONS OF EACH PIECE.			CONTENTS.		Kind of wood.
		Long.	Wide.	Thick.	Each piece.	Total.	
FORGE—*Bellows.*		In.	In.	In.	Sup. ft.	Sup. ft.	
Upper and lower planks...	4	34	15.	2.	7.08	28.32	Poplar.
Middle plank............	2	44	15.	2.	9.17	18.34	Do.
Cross heads..............	2	32	3.5	3.	2.33	4.66	Do.
Ribs. Sides............	4	36	3.	1.	0.75	3.00	Do.
Ribs. Ends............	2	32	3.	1.	0.67	1.34	Do.
Ribs. Cross bars.......	2	32	2.25	1.	0.50	1.00	Do.
Cleats..................	4	7	2.75	.75	......	......	Cuttings.
Valves..................	2	9	9.	.75	0.42	.84	Walnut.
Battens for valves........	2	9	4.5	.75	0.21	.42	Do.
Coal box.						57.92	
Sides and top piece.......	2	36	24.	1.38	8.28	16.56	Walnut.
Ends....................	2	16	24.	1.38	3.68	7.36	Do.
Lid.....................	1	36	14.	1.25	4.37	4.37	Do.
Clamps for lid............	2	14	2.5	1.25	.30	.60	Do.
Bottom..................	1	36	15.	1.31	4.91	4.91	Oak.
BATTERY WAGON—*Body.*						33.80	
Lower side rails..........	2	116	6.5	4.	20.94	41.88	Oak.
Upper side rails..........	2	108	3.	3.	6.75	13.50	Do.
Stock...................	1	108	6.	6.	27.00	27.00	Do.
Axle body...............	1	50	6.25	6.25	13.56	13.56	Do.
Front cross bar...........	1	40	5.5	5.	7.64	7.64	Do.
Front middle cross bars...	2	40	4.25	4.	4.72	9.4d	Do.
Rear middle cross bar.....	1	38	4.	2.5	2.64	2.64	Do.
Rear cross bar	1	40	4.	3.5	3.88	3.88	Do.
Floor boards.............	3	106	11.5	1.25	10.58	31.74	Wh. pine.
Sides of body............	2	108	21.5	1.38	22.25	44.50	Do.
Side of till..............	1	104	11.5	1.25	10.38	10.38	Do.
Bottom of till............	1	104	10.	1.25	9.02	9.02	Do.
Cleats for till.............	2	10	1.25	1.	......	......	Cuttings.
Ends of body............	2	40	24.	1.38	9.20	18.40	Walnut.
Forage rack sides.........	2	36	5.5	2.	2.75	5.50	Oak.
Forage rack bars.........	3	46	3.25	1.	1.03	1.03	Do.
Cover.						240.11	
Side rails................	2	108	3.	3.	6.75	13.5	Oak.
Ridge pole...............	1	108	3.	3.	6.75	6.75	Do.
End rails................	2	42	3.	3.	2.63	5.25	Do.
End studs	2	18	2.5	1.5	0.47	.94	Do.
End boards..............	2	42	13.5	1.25	4.91	9.82	Walnut.
Roof boards	9	108	7.	0.75	3.94	35.44	Wh. pine.
						71.70	

Bills of timber for Siege Carriages.

NAMES OF PARTS.	No. of pieces.	ROUGH DIMENSIONS OF EACH PIECE.			CONTENTS.		Kind of wood.
		Long.	Wide.	Thick.	Each piece.	Total.	
GUN CARRIAGES.		In.	In.	In.	Sup. ft.	Sup. ft.	
12-PDR. Stock	2	130.	11.5	7.	72.67	145.34	Oak.
12-PDR. Cheeks	2	55.	19.5	5.5	40.96	81.92	
12-PDR. Axle body	1	48.	9.5	8.5	26.92	26.92	
12-PDR. Bolster	1	14.	6.5	6.5	4.11	4.11	
						258.29	
18-PDR. Stock	2	132.	11.5	8.	84.33	168.66	
18-PDR. Cheeks	2	60.	20.	5.75	47.92	95.84	
18-PDR. Axle body	1	48.	9.5	8.5	26.92	26.92	
18-PDR. Bolster	1	14.	6.5	6.5	4.11	4.11	
						295.53	
24-PDR. Stock	2	132.	11.5	8.75	92.24	184.48	
24-PDR. Cheeks	2	60.	20.5	6.25	53.39	106.78	
24-PDR. Axle body	1	48.	9.5	8.5	26.92	26.92	
24-PDR. Bolster	1	16.	6.5	6.5	4.70	4.70	
ONE WHEEL.						322.88	
Nave	1	19.	16.	Round	26.53	26.53	
Spokes	14	32.	4.25	2.5	2.36	33.04	
Fellies	7	28.	8.	4.5	7.	49.00	
LIMBER.						108.57	
Fork	1	60.	11.	7.25	33.23	33.23	
Hounds	2	50.	5.	3.75	6.51	13.02	
Splinter bar	1	70.	4.	3.75	7.29	7.29	
Pole. Large end / Small end	1	142.	5.5 / 4.	5.5 / 4.	22.25	22.25	
Leading bar	1	70.	4.	3.75	7.29	7.29	
MORTAR WAGON.						83.08	
Middle rails	2	142.	8.	5.75	45.36	90.72	
Front transom	1	28.	7.	3.75	5.10	5.10	
Middle transom	1	4.	4.	3.12	......	....	Cuttings.
Rear transom	1	4.	6.7	5.9	......	....	
Side rails	2	92.	7.5	5.	23.96	47.92	Oak.
Rear cross bar	1	42.	4.5	3.	3.94	3.94	
Middle cross bars	6	16.	4.5	3.	1.5	9.00	
Front cross bars	2	14.	4.5	2.5	1.09	2.18	
Bottom planks	2	78.	8.	2.	8.67	17.34	
Axle body	1	48.	9.5	8.5	26.92	26.92	
Windlass	1	36.	6.5	6.5	10.56	10.56	
Muzzle bolster	1	12.	6.5	6.5	3.52	3.52	
Stakes	6	20.	3.5	3.25	1.58	9.48	
Handspikes	2	56.	4.	4.	6.22	12.44	Hickory.
						239.12	

Bills of timber for Barbette Carriages.

	NAMES OF PARTS.	No. of pieces.	ROUGH DIMENSIONS OF EACH PIECE.			CONTENTS.		Kind of wood.
			Long.	Wide.	Thick.	Each piece.	Total.	
	GUN CARRIAGE.		In.	In.	In.	Sup.ft.	Sup.ft.	
12 AND 18-POUNDERS.	Uprights	2	52.	17.	5.5	33.76	67.52	Oak.
	Braces	2	83.	12.5	5.5	39.62	79.24	
	Front transom	1	23.	12.	9.	17.25	17.25	
	Mid. transom	1	23.	9.	8.	11.5	11.5	
	Rear transom	1	23.	13.	10.25	21.28	21.28	
	Transom and axle tie	1	82.	11.	8.	50.11	50.11	
	Elevating bed	1	28.	8.	6.	9.33	9.33	
	Axle body	1	35.	9.	8.5	18.59	18.59	
	Spokes for two wheels	20	22.	4.25	4.25	2.76	55.20	
							330.02	
	CHASSIS.							
	Rails	2	148.	12.5	7.5	96.35	192.70	
	Hurters Counter hurters	2 2	28.	7.	5.25	7.14	14.28	
	Front transom	1	48.	9.	9.	27.	27.	
	Middle transom	1	48.	9.	7.	21.	21.	
	Rear transom	1	42.	9.	8.	21.	21.	
	Tongue	1	192.	10.5	8.5	119.	119.	
	Prop	1	36.	8.	4.	8.	8.	
							402.98	
	GUN CARRIAGE.							
24-POUNDER.	Uprights	2	52.	17.75	5.75	36.85	73.70	Oak.
	Braces	2	83.	13.	5.75	43.09	86.18	
	Front transom	1	24.	12.	9.	18.	18.	
	Middle transom	1	24.	9.	9.	13.5	13.5	
	Rear transom	1	24.	14.	11.	25.66	25.66	
	Transom and axle tie	1	84.	11.	9.	57.75	57.75	
	Elevating bed	1	28.	9.	6.	10.5	10.5	
	Axle body	1	36.	9.	8.5	19.12	19.12	
	Spokes for two wheels	20	22.	4.25	4.25	2.76	55.20	
							359.61	
	CHASSIS.							
	Rails	2	148.	13.5	8.5	117.93	235.86	
	Hurters Counter hurters	2 2	28.	8.	5.25	8.16	16.32	
	Front transom	1	51.	9.	9.	28.68	28.68	
	Middle transom	1	51.	9.	8.	25.5	25.5	
	Rear transom	1	42.	9.	8.	21.	21.	
	Tongue	1	192.	11.5	9.5	145.66	145.66	
	Prop	1	36.	9.	4.	9.	9.	
							482.02	

Bills of timber for Barbette Carriages.

	NAMES OF PARTS.	No. of pieces.	ROUGH DIMENSIONS OF EACH PIECE. Long.	Wide.	Thick.	CONTENTS. Each piece.	Total.	Kind of wood.
			In.	In.	In.	Sup.ft.	Sup.ft.	
32-POUNDER AND 8-INCH HOWITZER.	GUN CARRIAGE.							
	Uprights	2	54.	18.25	6.75	46.19	92.38	Oak.
	Braces	2	84.	14.5	6.75	57.09	114.18	
	Front transom	1	27.	12.	9.	20.25	20.25	
	Middle transom	1	27.	11.	9.	18.56	18.56	
	Rear transom	1	27.	14.	12.	31.5	31.50	
	Transom and axle tie	1	84.	11.	10.	64.16	64.16	
	Elevating bed { 32-pdr.	1	28.	10.	6.	11.66	11.66	
	Elevating bed { 8-inch.	1	28.	10.	8.	15.55	15.55	
	Axle body	1	42.	9.	8.5	22.31	22.31	
	Spokes for two wheels.	20	22.	4.25	4.25	2.76	55.20	
	Total. { 32-pdr.						430.20	
	Total. { 8-inch.						434.09	
	CHASSIS.							
	Rails	2	148.	14.5	9.5	141.57	283.14	
	Hurters	2	28.	9.	5.25	9.19	18.38	
	Counter hurters	2						
	Front transom	1	57.	11.	9.	39.19	39.19	
	Middle transom	1	57.	11.	10.	43.54	43.54	
	Rear transom	1	48.	9.	9.	27.	27.	
	Tongue	1	192.	12.5	10.5	167.70	167.70	
	Prop	1	36.	10.	4.	10.	10.	
							588.95	
42-POUNDER.	GUN CARRIAGE.							
	Uprights	2	55.	19.	7.25	52.61	105.22	Oak.
	Braces	2	87.	15.	7.25	65.70	131.40	
	Front transom	1	28.	13.	9.	22.75	22.75	
	Middle transom	1	28.	11.5	9.	20.12	20.12	
	Rear transom	1	28.	15.	12.	35.	35.00	
	Transom and axle tie.	1	85.	11.	11.	71.42	71.42	
	Elevating bed	1	29.	11.	6.	13.29	13.29	
	Axle body	1	45.	9.	8.5	23.90	23.90	
	Spokes for two wheels.	20	22.	4.25	4.25	2.76	55.20	
							478.30	
	CHASSIS.							
	Rails	2	148.	15.5	10.5	167.27	334.54	
	Hurters	2	28.	10.	5.25	10.20	20.40	
	Counter hurters	2						
	Front transom	1	60.	11.	9.	41.25	41.25	
	Middle transom	1	60.	11.	11.	50.41	50.41	
	Rear transom	1	48.	9.	9.	27.	27.	
	Tongue	1	192.	13.5	11.5	207.	207.	
	Prop	1	36.	11.	4.	11.	11.	
							691.60	

Bills of timber for Casemate Carriages.

	NAMES OF PARTS.	No. of pieces.	ROUGH DIMENSIONS OF EACH PIECE.			CONTENTS.		Kind of wood.
			Long.	Wide.	Thick.	Each piece.	Total.	
	GUN CARRIAGE.		In.	In.	In.	Sup.ft.	Sup.ft.	
24-POUNDER.	Cheeks	2	132.	15.5	5.75	81.69	163.38	Oak.
	Front transom	1	24.	16.5	6.	16.50	16.50	
	Rear transom	1	28.	18.5	6.5	23.38	23.38	
	Slide	1	28.	18.5	8.5	30.57	30.57	
	Axletree	1	58.	9.	7.	25.37	25.37	
	Guides	2	40.	7.	6.	11.66	23.32	
							282.52	
	CHASSIS.							
	Rails	2	162.	12.5	11.5	161.71	323.42	
	Counter hurters	2	17.	6.	5.25	3.72	7.44	
	Front transom	1	50.	16.5	14.5	83.07	83.07	
	Rear transom	1	68.	16.5	14.5	112.97	112.97	
	Tongue	1	200.	12.5	11.5	199.65	199.65	
	Prop	1	27.	12.	12.	27.00	27.00	
							753.55	
	GUN CARRIAGE.							
32-POUNDER.	Cheeks	2	132.	16.	6.5	95.33	190.66	Oak.
	Front transom	1	26.	16.5	6.5	19.36	19.36	
	Rear transom	1	30.	18.5	6.5	25.05	25.05	
	Slide	1	30.	18.5	8.5	32.76	32.76	
	Axletree	1	58.	9.	7.	25.37	25.37	
	Guides	2	40.	7.	6.	11.66	23.32	
							316.52	
	CHASSIS.							
	Rails	2	162.	14.	12.	189.00	378.00	
	Counter hurters	2	17.	6.	5.25	3.72	7.44	
	Front transom	1	54.	16.5	14.5	89.71	89.71	
	Rear transom	1	72.	16.5	14.5	119.62	119.62	
	Tongue	1	200.	14.	12.5	243.05	243.05	
	Prop	1	27.	12.	12.	27.00	27.00	
							864.82	

Bills of timber for Casemate Carriages.

	NAMES OF PARTS.	No. of pieces.	ROUGH DIMENSIONS OF EACH PIECE.			CONTENTS.		Kind of wood.
			Long.	Wide.	Thick.	Each piece.	Total.	
	GUN CARRIAGE.		In.	In.	In.	Sup.ft.	Sup.ft.	
42-POUNDER.	Cheeks	2	132.	16.5	7.	105.87	211.74	Oak.
	Front transom	1	28.	16.5	7.	22.46	22.46	
	Rear transom	1	32.	18.5	7.	28.77	28.77	
	Slide	1	32.	18.5	8.	32.89	32.89	
	Axletree	1	62.	9.	7.	27.12	27.12	
	Guides	2	40.	7.	6.	11.66	23.32	
							346.30	
	CHASSIS.							
	Rails	2	162.	14.5	12.5	203.90	407.80	
	Counter hurters	2	17.	6.	5.25	3.72	7.44	
	Front transom	1	56.	16.5	14.5	93.04	93.04	
	Rear transom	1	74.	16.5	14.5	122.94	122.94	
	Tongue	1	200.	14.5	12.5	251.73	251.73	
	Prop	1	27.	12.	12.	27.00	27.00	
							909.95	
	GUN CARRIAGE.							
8-INCH COLUMBIAD.	Cheeks	2	132.	16.5	7.	105.87	211.74	Oak.
	Front transom	1	30.	16.5	7.	24.06	24.06	
	Rear transom	1	30.	18.5	7.	26.97	26.97	
	Slide	1	30.	18.5	8.	30.83	30.83	
	Axletree	1	62.	9.	7.	27.12	27.12	
	Guides	2	40.	8.	6.	13.33	26.66	
							347.38	
	CHASSIS.							
	Rails	2	162.	14.5	12.5	203.90	407.80	
	Counter hurters	2	17.	6.	5.25	3.72	7.44	
	Front transom	1	58.	16.5	14.5	96.36	96.36	
	Rear transom	1	76.	16.5	14.5	126.27	126.27	
	Tongue	1	200.	14.5	12.5	251.73	251.73	
	Prop	1	27.	12.	12.	27.00	27.00	
							916.60	
24-PDR. HOWITZER.	*Gun car'ge*—Cheeks	2	50.	15.5	4.25	22.87	45.74	
	Chassis. Rails	2	161.	11.	8.5	104.53	209.06	
	Chassis. Transoms	4	......	......	......	......	......	Cuttings.

Bills of timber for Gins and Sling Cart.

NAMES OF PARTS.	No. of pieces.	ROUGH DIMENSIONS OF EACH PIECE.			CONTENTS.		Kind of wood.
		Long.	Wide.	Thick.	Each piece.	Total.	
FIELD AND SIEGE GIN.		In.	In.	In.	Sup. ft.	Sup. ft.	
Legs	2	180	6.5	5.5	44.69	89.38	Spruce or ash.
Pry pole	1	180	5.5	5.5	37.81	37.81	
Windlass	1	68	9.	9.	38.25	38.25	Oak.
Braces. Upper	1	48	4.75	2.75	4.35	4.35	Oak plank.
Braces. Middle	1	72	4.75	2.75	6.53	6.53	
Braces. Lower	1	102	4.75	2.75	9.25	9.25	
						185.57	
GARRISON GIN.							
Legs and pry pole. Large end	3	264	9.	9.	113.21	339.63	Spruce.
Legs and pry pole. Small end			6.5	6.5			
Two bevel blocks	1	40	10.	9.	25.	25.00	
Windlass	1	104	11.	11.	87.39	87.39	Oak.
Cleats	11	12	4.25	3.	1.06	11.66	Oak plank.
						463.68	
CASEMATE GIN.							
Legs. Large end	2	180	12.5	9.5	100.33	200.66	Spruce.
Legs. Small end			6.5	6.5			
Pry pole. Large end	1	180	9.	9.	77.03	77.03	
Pry pole. Small end			6.5	6.5			
Windlass	1	101	11.	11.	84.88	84.88	Oak.
Cleats	6	12	4.25	3.	1.06	6.36	Oak plank.
						368.93	
SLING CART.							
Axletree	1	102	11.	9.	70.13	70.13	Oak.
Bolster	1	66	9.	9.	37.13	37.13	Do.
Hounds	2	80	9.	5.	25.	50.	Do.
Tongue. Large end	1	198	7.5	6.	48.13	48.13	Do.
Tongue. Small end			5.	5.			
TWO WHEELS. Naves	2	21	19.	Round	41.34	82.68	Do.
TWO WHEELS. Spokes	32	48	5.25	2.75	4.81	153.92	Do.
TWO WHEELS. Fellies	16	39	9.	5.5	13.4	214.4	Oak plank.
						656.39	

Bills of iron for Field Carriages.

Kind of carriage.	Width.	Thick-ness.	Length.	Weight.	REMARKS.
	In.	In.	Feet.	Lbs.	
6-PDR. GUN CARRIAGE.	0.15	Round	2.81	0.18	For chains No. 1.
	0.2	Round	8.50	.90	2.3 feet for chains No. 2.
	0.25	Round	1.1	.18	
	0.375	Round	18.	6.62	
	0.5	Round	7.2	4.70	
	0.625	Round	4.10	4.18	
	0.75	Round	10.86	15.96	
	0.875	Round	0.65	1.30	
	1.	Round	2.58	6.73	
	1.5	Round	2.17	12.78	
	2.	Round	1.46	15.28	Hammered.
	0.25	0.25	2.21	.46	
	0.3	0.3	7.87	2.36	
	0.75	0.375	1.33	1.25	Hammered.
	1.0	0.375	0.23	.29	
	1.0	0.5	1.5	2.52	
	1.0	1.0	0.58	1.94	
	1.25	0.5	2.16	4.53	
	1.25	0.625	0.84	2.20	Hammered.
	1.25	0.75	0.7	2.20	
	1.375	0.05	3.0	.70	
	1.375	0.25	0.33	.38	
	1.5	0.25	3.75	4.72	
	1.5	0.375	.46	.86	
	1.5	0.5	1.16	2.92	Hammered.
	1.5	0.625	1.66	5.22	Hammered.
	1.5	0.75	3.3	12.47	Hammered.
	1.5	1.5	.59	4.46	Hammered.
	1.75	0.25	.93	1.36	
	2.0	0.125	.33	.27	
	2.0	0.75	.93	4.68	
	2.0	1.	.5	3.36	Hammered.
	2.0	1.25	.38	3.19	Hammered.
	2.5	0.188	1.66	2.60	
	2.5	0.875	.33	2.42	
	2.5	1.25	1.5	15.75	Hammered; or 2 drafts for cap squares.
	2.5	1.5	1.66	20.91	Hammered; or 2 drafts for trunnion plates.
	2.5	1.75	.5	7.35	Hammered.
	2.75	0.5	10.23	47.26	
	3.25	0.375	0.39	1.23	
	3.75	0.15	.5	.95	
	3.75	0.2	.44	1.11	

Bills of iron for Field Carriages.

Kind of carriage.	Width.	Thickness.	Length.	Weight.	REMARKS.
	In.	In.	feet.	Lbs.	
6-PDR. GUN CARRIAGE—Continued.	3.75	0.25	0.38	1.19	
	5.	0.25	.83	3.48	
	5.5	0.2	1.5	5.53	
				136.00	2 drafts for axletree.
				28.00	1 draft for lunette.
				404.93	
	1.0	0.375	0.21	.26	Steel for lunette.
				17.00	4 small rondelles } Cast iron.
				13.00	2 large rondelles } Cast iron.
				30.00	
				8.00	Brass box of elevat'g screw.
				.42	Brass for turnbuckles.
				8.42	
24-POUND'R HOWITZER CARRIAGE.	0.15	Round	2.81	0.18	For chain No. 1.
	0.2	Round	9.80	1.03	2.3 feet for chain No. 2.
	0.25	Round	1.08	.18	
	0.375	Round	19.6	7.21	
	0.5	Round	7.54	4.93	
	0.625	Round	4.50	4.59	
	0.75	Round	1.42	2.08	
	0.875	Round	0.65	1.30	
	1.0	Round	15.83	41.32	
	1.5	Round	0.5	2.94	
	2.0	Round	3.58	37.48	Hammered.
	0.25	0.25	2.21	.46	
	0.3	0.3	7.88	2.36	
	0.75	0.375	1.33	1.25	Hammered.
	1.0	0.375	0.23	.29	
	1.0	0.5	1.5	2.52	
	1.0	1.0	0.58	1.94	
	1.25	0.5	2.16	4.53	
	1.25	0.625	0.84	2.20	Hammered.
	1.25	0.75	0.71	2.23	
	1.375	0.05	4.0	.92	
	1.375	0.25	0.33	.37	

Bills of iron for Field Carriages.

Kind of carriage.	Width.	Thick-ness.	Length.	Weight.	REMARKS.
	In.	In.	feet.	Lbs.	
24-POUND'R HOWITZER CARRIAGE—Continued.	1.5	0.25	4.0	5.04	
	1.5	0.5	1.08	2.72	Hammered.
	1.5	0.625	1.66	5.22	Hammered.
	1.5	0.75	0.37	1.39	Hammered.
	1.5	1.5	0.59	4.46	Hammered.
	1.75	0.25	0.93	1.36	
	1.75	0.375	3.5	7.70	
	2.0	0.125	0.33	.28	Hammered.
	2.0	0.75	0.92	4.63	
	2.0	1.0	4.0	26.88	Hammered.
	2.0	1.25	0.38	3.19	Hammered.
	2.5	1.75	0.5	7.35	Hammered.
	2.75	1.	0.33	3.04	
	3.0	0.5	11.23	56.59	
	3.0	1.25	1.84	23.18	Hammered; or 2 drafts for cap squares.
	3.0	1.5	2.33	35.22	Hammered; or 2 drafts for trunnion plates.
	3.25	0.188	2.57	5.24	
	3.25	0.375	0.30	1.22	
	3.75	0.15	0.5	.94	
	3.75	0.2	0.57	1.43	
	3.75	0.25	0.38	1.19	
	5.0	0.25	0.83	3.48	
	6.0	0.2	1.5	6.04	
				200.	Draft for axletree.
				37.	Draft for lunette.
				567.10	
	1.0	0.375	0.21	0.26	Steel for lunette.
				17.	4 small rondelles } Cast iron.
				13.	2 large rondelles } Cast iron.
				30.	
				8.	Brass for box of elevating screw.
				.42	Brass for 2 turnbuckles.
				8.42	

Bills of iron for Field Carriages.

Kind of carriage.	Width.	Thickness.	Length.	Weight.	REMARKS.
	In.	In.	Feet.	Lbs.	
12-PDR. GUN CARRIAGE.	0.15	Round	2.81	0.18	For chains No. 1.
	0.2	Round	9.80	1.03	2.3 feet for chains No. 2.
	0.25	Round	1.08	.18	
	0.375	Round	19.60	7.21	
	0.5	Round	7.54	4.93	
	0.625	Round	4.73	4.82	
	0.75	Round	1.42	2.08	
	0.875	Round	0.65	1.30	
	1.0	Round	15.83	41.32	
	1.5	Round	0.5	2.94	
	2.0	Round	3.58	37.48	Hammered.
	0.25	0.25	2.21	.46	
	0.3	0.3	7.88	2.36	
	0.75	0.375	1.33	1.25	Hammered.
	1.0	0.375	.23	.29	
	1.0	0.5	1.5	2.52	
	1.0	1.0	.58	1.04	
	1.25	0.5	2.16	4.53	
	1.25	0.625	0.84	2.20	Hammered.
	1.25	0.75	0.71	2.23	
	1.375	0.05	4.00	.92	
	1.375	0.25	0.33	.37	
	1.5	0.25	4.00	5.04	
	1.5	0.5	1.08	2.72	Hammered.
	1.5	0.625	1.66	5.22	Hammered.
	1.5	0.75	.37	1.39	Hammered.
	1.5	1.5	.59	4.46	Hammered.
	1.75	0.25	.93	1.36	
	1.75	0.375	.5	1.10	
	2.0	0.125	.33	.28	Hammered.
	2.0	0.75	0.92	4.63	
	2.0	1.0	4.00	26.88	Hammered.
	2.0	1.25	0.38	3.19	Hammered.
	2.5	1.75	0.5	7.35	Hammered.
	2.75	1.0	0.33	3.04	
	3.0	1.25	1.84	23.18	Hammered; or 2 drafts for cap squares.
	3.0	1.5	2.33	35.22	Hammered; or 2 drafts for trunnion plates.
	3.2	0.5	7.23	38.86	
	3.25	0.188	2.17	4.42	
	3.25	0.375	0.30	1.22	
	3.25	0.5	5.00	27.30	
	3.75	0.15	0.5	.94	

Bills of iron for Field Carriages.

Kind of carriage.	Width.	Thick-ness.	Length.	Weight.	REMARKS.
	In.	In.	Feet.	Lbs.	
12-PDR. GUN CARRIAGE—Continued.	3.75	0.2	0.57	1.43	
	3.75	0.25	0.38	1.19	
	5.0	0.25	0.83	3.48	
	6.5	0.2	1.5	6.54	
				200.	Draft for axletree.
				42.	Draft for lunette.
				574.08	
	1.0	0.375	.21	0.26	Steel for lunette.
				17.	4 small rondelles, } Cast iron.
				13.	2 large rondelles, } Cast iron.
				30.	
				8.	Brass for box of elevating screw.
				.42	Brass for 2 turnbuckles.
				8.42	
WHEEL No. 1.	0.5	Round	2.93	1.91	
	0.25	0.25	1.63	0.34	
	1.0	0.5	0.58	0.97	
	1.25	0.25	5.83	6.12	
	1.5	0.25	4.67	5.88	
	1.625	0.125	1.00	0.68	
	2.75	0.5	15.00	69.30	In one piece; for tire.
				85.20	
				15.5	Cast iron for nave box.
WHEEL No. 2.	0.5	Round	3.15	2.06	
	0.25	0.25	1.63	0.34	
	1.0	0.5	0.58	0.97	
	1.25	0.25	6.29	6.60	
	1.5	0.25	5.33	6.72	
	1.625	0.125	1.00	0.68	
	2.75	0.625	15.00	86.55	In one piece; for tire.
				103.92	
				15.5	Cast iron for nave box.

Bills of iron for Field Carriages.

Kind of carriage.	Width.	Thickness.	Length.	Weight.	REMARKS.
	In.	In.	Feet.	Lbs.	
LIMBER.	0.15	Round	2.08	0.13	For chains No. 1.
	0.2	Round	3.67	.38	2.3 feet for chains No. 2.
	0.25	Round	4.95	.80	2.33 feet for chains No. 3.
	0.375	Round	11.8	4.34	
	0.5	Round	1.30	.85	
	0.625	Round	1.80	1.83	
	0.75	Round	4.75	6.98	
	0.875	Round	0.30	.60	
	1.0	Round	2.69	7.02	
	1.25	Round	1.08	4.41	
	1.625	Round	0.75	5.18	
	0.25	0.25	2.3	.48	
	0.3	0.3	1.19	.35	
	0.5	0.25	0.17	.07	
	0.5	0.5	0.95	.80	
	1.0	0.25	0.93	.78	
	1.0	0.5	3.33	5.59	Hammered.
	1.0	0.1	0.5	1.68	Hammered.
	1.25	0.25	4.19	4.40	Hammered.
	1.25	0.5	2.67	5.60	
	1.25	0.625	1.15	3.01	
	1.25	0.75	0.71	2.23	Hammered.
	1.25	1.25	1.0	5.25	
	1.5	0.125	1.0	.63	
	1.5	0.5	2.17	5.46	Hammered.
	1.5	0.625	2.12	6.67	Hammered.
	1.5	0.75	.38	1.43	
	1.75	0.375	1.0	2.20	
	1.75	0.5	0.5	1.47	
	2.0	0.125	1.33	1.11	
	2.5	0.188	0.54	.85	
	2.5	0.5	3.84	16.12	
	2.5	1.5	0.5	6.30	
	2.75	0.5	0.54	2.49	
	3.0	0.625	0.5	3.15	
	3.5	2.5	0.84	24.69	Hammered; middle piece for axletree.
	4.25	0.25	0.75	2.67	
				120.	2 drafts for axletree.
				25.	Draft for pintle hook.
				283.	
	1.0	0.375	0.21	0.26	Steel for pintle hook.

Bills of iron for Field Carriages.

Kind of carriage.	Width.	Thick-ness.	Length.	Weight.	REMARKS.
	In.	In.	Feet.	Lbs.	
AMMUNITION CHEST.	0.375	Round	1.5	0.55	
	0.5	Round	3.16	2.06	
	0.75	Round	4.13	6.07	
	1.0	Round	0.25	.65	
	1.0	0.5	0.08	.13	
	1.C	1.0	2.00	6.72	
	1.5	0.375	1.73	3.26	
	1.5	0.75	4.58	17.31	
	1.5	1.0	0.2	1.00	
	1.5	1.5	1.0	7.56	
	1.75	0.75	0.33	1.45	
	15.5	0.1	4.0	20.50	
				67.26	
	25.0	No. 24	4.	9.50	Sheet copper for cover.
				0.21	Brass for turnbuckle.
CAISSON.	0.15	Round	8.53	0.50	For chains No. 1.
	0.2	Round	4.08	0.43	
	0.25	Round	0.71	.11	
	0.375	Round	15.04	5.53	
	0.5	Round	0.63	.41	
	0.875	Round	1.02	2.04	
	1.0	Round	4.49	11.71	
	1.25	Round	2.61	10.67	
	0.25	0.25	2.92	.61	
	0.3	0.3	6.23	1.87	
	1.0	0.25	1.75	1.47	
	1.0	0.5	1.5	2.52	
	1.0	1.0	2.79	9.37	Hammered.
	1.125	0.25	0.19	.18	
	1.25	0.5	3.18	6.68	
	1.25	0.625	3.1	8.12	Hammered.
	1.25	0.75	0.70	2.20	Hammered.
	1.5	0.125	2.0	1.26	
	1.5	0.25	3.0	3.78	
	1.5	0.5	0.33	.83	
	1.5	0.625	.83	2.61	Hammered.
	1.5	0.75	1.33	5.02	Hammered.
	1.5	1.5	1.33	10.05	

Bills of iron for Field Carriages.

Kind of carriage.	Width.	Thickness.	Length.	Weight.	REMARKS.
	In.	In.	Feet.	Lbs.	
CAISSON—Continued.	2.0	0.125	1.67	1.40	
	2.0	0.5	0.75	2.52	
	2.31	0.25	0.69	1.33	
	2.5	0.5	7.0	29.40	
	3.0	0.5	6.46	32.55	
	3.5	0.25	0.5	1.47	
	3.5	1.0	3.17	37.27	Hammered; or 2 drafts for lunette.
	4.0	0.25	0.84	2.82	
	4.25	1.25	1.5	26.77	
	5.75	0.5	0.48	4.63	
	6.0	0.5	0.5	5.04	
				136.	2 drafts for axletree.
				369.17	
FORGE.	0.15	Round	1.5	0.09	For chain No. 1.
	0.2	Round	3.75	.38	2.3 feet for chain No. 2.
	0.25	Round	0.57	.93	
	0.375	Round	19.48	7.17	
	0.625	Round	0.24	.24	
	0.5	Round	3.51	2.29	
	0.75	Round	4.58	6.73	
	0.875	Round	0.58	1.16	
	1.0	Round	1.88	4.90	
	1.25	Round	3.48	14.23	
	1.5	Round	0.3	1.76	
	2.5	Round	0.67	10.96	
	0.25	0.25	1.32	.28	
	0.3	0.3	6.23	1.88	
	0.5	0.25	.17	.07	
	0.625	0.375	.79	1.89	
	0.75	0.75	1.0	.63	
	1.0	0.25	1.25	1.05	
	1.0	0.375	0.84	1.06	
	1.0	0.5	2.75	4.62	
	1.25	0.25	0.5	.52	
	1.25	0.375	0.88	1.38	
	1.25	0.5	4.31	9.05	
	1.25	0.625	1.56	4.08	Hammered.
	1.25	0.75	0.7	2.20	
	1.25	1.0	1.0	4.20	Hammered.

Bills of iron for Field Carriages.

Kind of carriage.	Width.	Thick-ness.	Length.	Weight.	REMARKS.
	In.	In.	Feet.	Lbs.	
FORGE—Continued.	1.25	1.25	0.5	2.62	
	1.5	0.25	3.17	4.00	Hammered.
	1.5	0.375	1.88	3.55	
	1.5	0.5	5.66	14.26	
	1.5	0.75	2.42	9.14	Hammered.
	1.5	1.0	0.66	3.32	Hammered.
	1.625	0.125	1.25	.85	
	1.75	0.75	0.33	1.45	Hammered.
	2.0	0.125	1.17	.98	
	2.0	0.15	0.84	.84	
	2.0	0.25	0.67	1.12	
	2.0	0.5	1.5	5.04	
	2.0	1.0	0.83	5.58	Hammered.
	2.0	1.375	2.17	20.03	Hammered.
	2.25	0.15	0.33	.37	
	2.5	0.5	7.5	31.50	
	2.625	0.25	1.0	2.20	
	3.0	0.625	0.5	3.15	Hammered.
	3.5	1.0	3.17	37.27	Hammered; or 2 drafts for lunette.
	4.0	0.25	0.84	2.82	
	10.	No. 12	3.4	12.5	Sheet iron.
	13.25	No. 11	2.58	14.25	Sheet iron.
	27.	No. 8	7.5	122.00	Sheet iron.
	28.	No. 24	5.	11.85	Russia sheet iron.
				136.	2 drafts for axletree.
				530.44	
	0.75	0.5	0.67	0.84	Cast steel.
	1.0	0.25	0.33	.27	Spring steel.
				36.5	Cast iron air back.
				6.	Brass for windpipe.
	22.5	No. 24	7.33	15.75	Sheet copper; in 2 sheets 44 in. long.
	18.5	No. 24	3.04	5.25	Sheet copper.
	20.	No. 18	0.05	1.90	Sheet copper.
				22.90	

Bills of iron for Field Carriages.

Kind of carriage.	Width.	Thickness.	Length.	Weight.	REMARKS.
	In.	In.	Feet.	Lbs.	
BATTERY WAGON.	0.25	Round	26.08	4.25	24.7 feet for chains No. 4.
	0.375	Round	20.3	7.47	
	0.5	Round	6.92	4.52	
	0.625	Round	1.92	1.95	
	0.75	Round	6.22	9.14	
	1.0	Round	1.38	3.60	
	1.25	Round	2.60	10.63	
	1.5	Round	3.11	18.31	
	0.25	0.25	0.44	.09	
	0.3	0.3	6.23	1.88	
	0.75	0.375	1.38	1.29	
	1.0	0.125	6.25	2.62	
	1.0	0.25	8.41	7.06	
	1.0	0.375	5.92	7.46	
	1.0	0.5	1.5	2.52	
	1.0	1.0	2.84	9.54	Hammered.
	1.125	0.25	1.12	2.11	
	1.25	0.25	0.38	.40	
	1.25	0.375	1.71	2.68	
	1.25	0.5	2.18	4.58	
	1.25	0.625	0.73	1.91	Hammered.
	1.25	0.75	0.71	2.23	Hammered.
	1.5	0.25	11.25	14.17	
	1.5	0.375	1.5	2.83	
	1.5	0.5	0.33	.83	
	1.5	0.75	2.47	9.32	Hammered.
	1.5	1.0	0.83	4.18	
	1.625	0.5	16.67	45.50	
	2.0	0.125	0.83	.70	
	2.0	0.75	0.5	2.52	
	2.5	0.188	1.67	2.62	
	2.5	0.5	5.33	22.38	
	3.5	1.0	3.17	37.27	Hammered; or 2 drafts for lunette.
	3.75	0.15	8.48	16.02	
	4.0	0.25	0.83	2.79	
	5.25	0.25	0.65	2.87	
	5.5	0.375	1.66	11.50	
				136.00	2 drafts for axletree.
				417.74	
				0.21	Cast brass for turnbuckle.

Bills of iron for Siege Gun Carriages.

Width	Thickness.	12-POUNDER.		18-POUNDER.		24-POUNDER.		REMARKS.
In.	In.	Feet.	Lbs.	Feet.	Lbs.	Feet.	Lbs.	
0.2	Round	2.29	0.24	2.29	0.24	2.29	0.24	For chains No. 2.
0.25	Round	5.17	.84	5.17	.84	5.17	.84	3 feet 6 inches for
0.375	Round	9.03	3.32	9.03	3.32	9.03	3.32	chains No. 3.
0.5	Round	.62	.40	.62	.40	.62	.40	
0.625	Round	13.05	13.31	13.05	13.31	13.05	13.31	
0.75	Round	7.40	10.88	7.46	10.96	7.52	11.05	
1.0	Round	3.	7.83	3.	7.83	3.	7.83	
1.125	Round	2.17	7.18	2.17	7.18	2.17	7.18	
1.25	Round	18.57	75.95	17.12	70.01	18.11	74.07	
1.5	Round	2.18	12.84	4.64	27.33	4.91	28.92	
2.0	Round	.5	5.23	.5	5.23	.5	5.23	
2.375	Round	1.58	23.32	1.58	23.32	1.58	23.32	Hammered.
2.5	Round	2.04	33.37	2.04	33.37	2.04	33.37	
3.0	Round	.33	7.77	.33	7.77	.33	7.77	
0.25	0.25	1.33	.28	1.33	.28	1.33	.28	
0.3	0.3	3.17	.95	3.17	.95	3.17	.95	
0.375	0.375	8.75	4.11	8.75	4.11	8.75	4.11	
1.	0.5	.38	.64	.38	.64	.38	.64	
1.25	0.625	.21	.55	.21	.55	.21	.55	
1.25	1.25	1.67	8.77	1.71	8.97	1.73	9.08	
1.5	0.125	.5	.31	.5	.31	.5	.31	
1.5	0.375	5.0	9.45	5.0	9.45	5.0	9.45	
1.5	0.625	2.42	7.62	2.42	7.62	2.42	7.62	
1.5	0.75	1.71	6.46	1.71	6.46	1.71	6.46	
1.75	0.5	.58	1.70	.58	1.70	.58	1.70	
2.0	0.75	.58	2.92	.58	2.92	.58	2.92	
2.0	1.0	.67	4.50	.67	4.50	.67	4.50	
2.5	0.188	1.67	2.62	1.67	2.62	1.67	2.62	
2.5	1.25	5.33	55.95	4.42	46.41	4.42	46.41	Hammered.
2.75	1.5	......	......	.93	12.89	.93	12.89	Hammered.
3.0	0.625	.93	5.86	.93	5.86	.93	5.86	
3.5	0.25	.58	1.70	.58	1.70	.58	1.70	
3.5	0.375	.58	2.56	.58	2.56	.58	2.56	
3.5	0.625	.96	7.04	.96	7.04	.96	7.04	
3.5	2.	.29	6.82	.29	6.82	.29	6.82	
3.75	2.	.38	9.57	.38	9.57	.38	9.57	
4.0	0.25	4.33	14.54	4.33	14.54	4.33	14.54	
4.0	0.5	1.23	8.26	1.23	8.26	1.23	8.26	
4.0	0.625	3.17	26.63	......	......	......	......	In one piece.
4.0	0.75	3.06	30.84	......	......	......	......	In one piece.
Forward....		......	423.13	......	377.84	......	383.69	

Bills of iron for Siege Gun Carriages.

Width	Thick-ness.	12-POUNDER.		18-POUNDER.		24-POUNDER.		REMARKS.
In.	In.	Feet.	Lbs.	Feet.	Lbs.	Feet.	Lbs.	
Forw'd.	......	......	423.13	......	377.84	......	383.69	
4.25	0.625	......	......	3.46	30.86	......	......	In one piece.
4.25	0.75	......	......	3.13	33.52	......	......	Do.
4.75	0.25	.40	1.60	.40	1.60	.40	1.60	Do.
4.75	0.625	......	......	......	......	3.38	33.70	Do.
4.75	0.75	......	......	......	......	3.13	37.46	Do.
5.	0.625	.42	4.41	.42	4.41	.42	4.41	
5.75	0.5	.75	7.24	.75	7.24	.75	7.24	
6.5	0.25	1.08	5.89	1.08	5.89	1.08	5.89	
9.0	0.5	3.25	49.14	3.25	49.14	3.25	49.14	In one piece.
5.75	0.375	0.79	......	0.79	......	0.79	......	Steel for shoe.
Drafts....		......	26.3	......	29.2	......	36.14	2 trunnion plates.
		......	16.	......	17.7	......	20.45	2 cap squares.
		......	222.	......	222.	......	222.	1 axletree.
		......	16.5	......	16.5	......	16.5	1 lunette.
		......	21.5	......	21.5	......	21.5	1 shoe.
			793.71	......	817.4	......	839.72	
Cast iron.		......	43.5	......	43.5	......	43.5	2 rondelles.
		......	52.5	......	52.5	......	52.5	4 rondelles.
		......	96.	......	96.	......	96.	
Cast brass ..		......	15.37	......	15.37	......	15.37	Box for screw.

Bill of iron for one Siege Carriage Wheel.

Width.	Thickness.	Length.	Weight.	REMARKS.
In.	In.	Feet.	Lbs.	
0.75	Round	4.33	6.36	
0.25	0.25	2.12	.44	
1.5	0.375	7.66	14.48	
1.5	0.75	.87	3.29	
1.75	0.375	6.08	13.37	
2.5	0.188	1.46	2.29	
4.	0.75	15.5	156.24	Tire; in one piece.
			196.47	
Cast brass....................			24.	Nave box.

Bill of iron for one Siege Carriage Limber.

Width.	Thickness.	Length.	Weight.	REMARKS.
In.	In.	Feet.	Lbs.	
0.25	Round	2.92	0.47	
0.5	Round	14.83	9.70	
0.75	Round	15.58	22.90	
1.0	Round	1.5	3.91	
1.25	Round	2.71	11.08	
0.3	0.3	1.04	.31	
0.375	0.375	1.83	.86	
1.0	0.5	.17	.28	
1.125	0.25	.09	.08	
1.5	0.5	0.5	1.26	
1.5	0.625	2.42	7.62	
1.5	0.75	3.21	12.13	
1.75	0.5	1.33	3.91	
2.	0.2	.83	1.11	
2.	0.5	1.33	4.46	
2.5	0.188	3.33	5.23	
2.5	0.5	.83	3.48	Hammered.
2.5	0.625	6.08	31.92	Hammered.
2.5	1.25	.21	2.20	
2.5	2.5	.96	20.16	Hammered.
2.75	0.625	5.33	30.75	
3.0	0.625	3.	18.90	
3.5	0.625	.96	7.05	Hammered.
4.0	0.75	4.	40.32	
5.5	1.	.83	15.34	
			222.00	Draft for axletree.
			36.50	Draft for pintle plate.
			513.93	

Bill of iron for one Mortar Wagon.

Width.	Thickness.	Length.	Weight.	REMARKS.
In.	In.	Feet.	Lbs.	
0.25	Round	0.42	0.06	
0.375	Round	8.79	3.23	
0.5	Round	.62	.40	
0.625	Round	17.46	17.81	
0.75	Round	17.87	26.27	
1.	Round	2.92	7.62	
1.25	Round	.83	3.39	
1.5	Round	2.75	16.20	
1.625	Round	1.08	7.46	
0.25	0.25	8.03	1.68	
0.3	0.3	8.40	2.53	
0.375	0.375	3.32	1.56	
1.	0.25	.42	.35	
1.	0.5	.37	.62	
1.25	0.2	2.89	2.43	
1.25	0.625	1.67	4.37	
1.5	0.375	1.08	2.04	
1.5	0.5	.58	1.46	
1.5	0.625	2.42	7.62	
1.5	0.75	4.21	15.91	
2.	0.125	2.	1.68	
2.	0.75	.58	2.92	
2.	2.	.50	6.72	
2.5	0.188	3.12	4.90	
2.5	0.375	6.	18.90	
2.5	0.5	1.67	7.01	
2.5	0.625	.50	2.62	Hammered.
2.75	0.5	5.17	23.88	
3.	1.5	.29	4.38	
3.375	0.5	7.33	41.56	
3.5	0.625	.92	6.56	
3.75	0.75	3.21	30.33	
4.	0.75	.42	4.23	
5.	0.3	.92	4.63	
5.5	0.3	3.58	19.83	
6.	0.3	1.	6.04	
6.	0.75	.75	11.34	
6.5	0.25	1.08	5.89	
6.5	0.3	.60	3.93	
8.	0.5	.80	10.75	
			222.00	Draft for axletree.
			21.50	Draft for shoe.
			584.61	
5.75	0.375	0.79	5.72	Steel for shoe.
			3.5	Brass, for two journal boxes.

Bill of iron for one 12-pdr. or one 18-pdr. Barbette Carriage.

SIZE OF IRON.		GUN CARRIAGE.		CHASSIS.		TOTAL.		REMARKS.
Wide.	Thick.							
In.	In.	Feet.	Lbs.	Feet.	Lbs.	Feet	Lbs.	
0.5	Round	2.25	1.47	11.96	7.82	14.21	9.29	
0.75	Round	4.82	7.08	......	......	4.82	7.08	
1.	Round	18.28	47.72	12.85	33.53	31.13	81.25	Add 8 in. for 18-pdr
1.5	Round	.33	1.94	......	......	.33	1.94	
2.	Round	3.5	36.64	3.75	39.26	7.25	75.90	
2.375	Round	1.75	25.83	1.33	19.63	3.08	45.46	Hammered.
0.25	0.25	......	......	7.75	1.63	7.75	1.63	
0.5	0.5	7.92	6.65	......	......	7.92	6.65	
0.75	0.125	......	......	.12	.03	.12	.03	
1.0	0.5	.17	.28	.92	1.54	1.09	1.82	
1.0	1.0	2.83	9.50	......	......	2.83	9.50	
1.5	0.3	......	......	1.64	2.49	1.64	2.49	
1.5	0.375	......	......	.50	.94	.50	.94	
1.5	0.5	5.17	13.02	......	......	5.17	13.02	
1.5	0.75	2.08	7.86	......	......	2.08	7.86	
1.5	1.5	1.00	7.56	......	......	1.00	7.56	
1.625	0.125	.27	.18	1.33	.90	1.60	1.08	
2.0	0.25	......	......	18.80	31.61	18.80	31.61	
2.0	0.4	......	......	1.21	3.24	1.21	3.24	
2.0	0.75	5.17	26.05	......	......	5.17	26.05	
2.0	1.	3.20	21.50	2.83	19.02	6.03	40.52	
2.5	0.188	.83	1.30	......	......	.83	1.30	
3.0	0.5	1.30	6.55	......	......	1.30	6.55	
3.0	1.0	.37	3.73	......	......	.37	3.73	
3.0	1.25	......	......	5.5	69.30	5.5	69.30	
3.25	0.188	4.80	9.79	2.40	4.89	7.20	14.68	
3.25	0.25	1.62	4.42	......	......	1.62	4.42	
3.5	0.5	......	......	2.80	16.46	2.80	16.46	
4.0	0.5	1.19	7.99	......	......	1.19	7.99	
4.	1.0	.79	10.61	......	......	.79	10.61	
4.	1.5	1.16	23.41	......	......	1.16	23.41	
4.5	0.5	3.94	29.78	......	......	3.94	29.78	
4.5	0.875	22.67	299.69	......	......	22.67	299.69	2 pieces, 11 ft. 4 in.
5.	0.5	......	......	1.6	13.44	1.6	13.44	
6.625	0.25	......	......	1.62	9.0	1.62	9.0	
8.	1.	......	......	1.58	42.47	1.58	42.47	
•			141.	......	......	......	141.	Draft for axletree.
			751.55	......	316.89	......	1068.75	+1.75 lb. for 18 pdr
Cast iron..		......	4.	......	......	......	4.	2 bevel washers.
		......	270.	......	......	......	270.	2 rollers.
		......	206.	......	......	......	206.	2 naves.
		......	......	......	130.	......	130.	2 traverse wheels.
		......	480.	......	130.	......	610.	
Cast brass...		......	11.	......	......	......	11.	Nut for screw.

Bill of iron for one 24-pdr. Barbette Carriage.

SIZE OF IRON.		GUN CARRIAGE.		CHASSIS.		TOTAL.		REMARKS.
Wide.	Thick.	Feet.	Lbs.	Feet.	Lbs.	Feet.	Lbs.	
In.	In.							
0.5	Round	2.35	1.54	12.96	8.47	15.31	10.01	
0.75	Round	4.94	7.26	......	......	4.94	7.26	
1.0	Round	15.52	40.50	13.69	35.73	29.21	76.23	
1.125	Round	4.21	13.93	......	......	4.21	13.93	
1.5	Round	.33	1.94	......	......	.33	1.94	
2.	Round	2.5	26.17	3.75	39.26	6.25	65.43	
2.25	Round	1.08	14.31	......	......	1.08	14.31	
2.375	Round	1.75	25.83	1.33	19.63	3.08	45.46	Hammered.
0.25	0.25	......	......	7.75	1.62	7.75	1.62	
0.5	0.5	7.92	6.65	......	......	7.92	6.65	
0.75	0.125	......	......	.12	0.03	.12	.03	
1.0	0.5	.16	.27	.91	1.52	1.07	1.79	
1.125	1.125	3.14	13.34	......	......	3.14	13.34	
1.5	0.3	......	......	1.64	2.49	1.64	2.49	
1.5	0.375	......	......	0.5	.94	.5	.94	
1.5	0.5	5.16	13.	......	......	5.16	13.00	
1.5	0.75	2.92	11.03	......	......	2.92	11.03	
1.5	1.5	1.0	7.56	......	......	1.0	7.56	
1.625	0.125	.27	.18	1.33	.90	1.60	1.08	
2.0	0.25	......	......	18.71	31.43	18.71	31.43	
2.0	0.4	......	......	1.21	3.24	1.21	3.24	
2.0	0.75	5.17	26.05	......	......	5.17	26.05	
2.0	1.0	2.54	17.07	2.83	19.01	5.37	36.08	
2.25	1.125	.83	7.05	......	......	.83	7.05	
2.5	0.188	.83	1.30	......	......	.83	1.30	
3.0	0.5	3.10	15.62	......	......	3.10	15.62	
3.0	1.0	.37	3.73	......	......	.37	3.73	
3.0	1.25	......	......	5.5	69.30	5.5	69.30	
3.25	0.188	2.94	5.99	2.39	4.88	5.33	10.87	
3.5	0.25	1.62	4.76	......	......	1.62	4.76	
3.5	0.5	......	......	2.87	16.87	2.87	16.87	
3.625	0.188	1.8	4.10	......	......	1.8	4.10	
4.	0.5	1.27	8.53	......	......	1.27	8.53	
4.	1.0	.8	10.75	......	......	.8	10.75	
4.	1.5	1.17	23.61	......	......	1.17	23.61	
4.5	0.875	22.67	299.69	......	......	22.67	299.69	2 pieces, 11 ft. 4 in.
4.75	0.5	4.15	33.11	......	......	4.15	33.11	
5.	0.5	......	......	1.6	13.44	1.6	13.44	
6.625	0.25	......	......	1.66	9.23	1.66	9.23	
8.0	1.0	......	......	1.58	42.48	1.58	42.48	
			147.	......	......	......	147.	Draft for axletree.
			791.87	......	320.16	......	1112.34	
Cast iron..		......	6.	......	......	......	6.	2 bevel washers.
		......	270.*	......	130†	......	400.	*2 rollers, †2 wh'ls.
		......	206.	......	......	......	206.	2 naves.
		......	482.	......	130.	......	612.	
Cast brass..		......	11.	......	......	......	11.	Nut for screw.

Bill of iron for one 32-pounder Barbette Carriage.

SIZE OF IRON.		GUN CARRIAGE.		CHASSIS.		TOTAL.		REMARKS.
Wide.	Thick.							
In.	In.	Feet.	Lbs.	Feet.	Lbs.	Feet.	Lbs.	
0.5	Round	2.60	1.70	14.96	9.78	17.56	11.48	
0.75	Round	2.50	3.67	......	......	2.50	3.67	
1.00	Round	23.51	61.36	27.52	71.82	51.03	133.18	
1.25	Round	4.56	18.65	......	......	4.56	18.65	
2.	Round	3.50	36.64	5.0	52.35	8.50	88.99	
2.375	Round	1.75	25.83	1.33	19.63	3.08	45.46	Hammered.
2.5	Round	1.17	19.14	......	......	1.17	19.14	
0.25	0.25	......	......	7.75	1.62	7.75	1.62	
0.5	0.5	7.92	6.65	......	......	7.92	6.65	
0.75	0.125	......	......	.14	.04	.14	.04	
1.0	0.5	.16	.27	.91	1.52	1.07	1.79	
1.25	1.25	3.81	20.00	......	......	3.81	20.00	
1.5	0.3	......	......	1.64	2.49	1.64	2.49	
1.5	0.375	......	......	.50	.94	.50	.94	
1.5	0.5	5.17	13.	......	......	5.17	13.	
1.5	0.75	1.33	5.02	......	......	1.33	5.02	
1.625	0.125	.27	.18	1.33	.90	1.60	1.08	
2.0	0.25	......	......	18.62	31.28	18.62	31.28	
2.0	0.4	......	......	1.21	3.24	1.21	3.24	
2.0	0.75	5.17	26.05	......	......	5.17	26.05	
2.0	1.0	3.87	26.00	3.67	24.66	7.54	50.66	
2.0	2.0	1.17	15.72	......	......	1.17	15.72	
2.5	1.25	.83	8.71	......	......	.83	8.71	
3.0	0.5	3.10	15.62	2.98	15.01	6.08	30.63	
3.0	1.	.44	4.44	......	......	.44	4.44	
3.0	1.25	......	......	5.5	69.30	5.5	69.30	
3.25	0.188	5.06	10.32	4.	8.16	9.06	18.48	
3.5	0.5	......	......	3.32	19.52	3.32	19.52	
4.0	0.5	2.42	16.26	......	......	2.42	16.26	
4.0	1.0	.79	10.62	......	......	.79	10.62	
4.0	1.5	1.17	23.61	......	......	1.17	23.61	
4.125	0.25	2.04	7.06	......	......	2.04	7.06	
4.25	0.25	3.25	11.60	......	......	3.25	11.60	
4.5	0.875	22.67	299.69	......	......	22.67	299.69	2 pieces, 11 ft. 4 in.
5.5	0.5	4.56	42.13	......	......	4.56	42.13	
6.625	0.25	......	......	1.66	9.23	1.66	9.23	
7.0	0.5	......	......	.67	7.88	.67	7.88	
8.0.	1.0	......	......	1.58	42.48	1.58	42.48	
			205.	......	......	......	205.	Draft for axletree.
			934.94	......	391.85	......	1326.79	
Cast iron .		......	7.5*	......	50.†	......	57.5	*2 wash's †4 pipes.
		......	292.‡	......	130.‖	......	422.	‡2 rollers, ‖2 wh'ls.
		......	206.	......	......	......	206.	2 naves.
		......	505.5	......	180.	......	685.5	
Cast brass ..		......	11.	......	......	......	11.	Nut for screw.

Bill of iron for one 8-inch Howitzer Barbette Carriage.

SIZE OF IRON.		GUN CARRIAGE		CHASSIS.		TOTAL.		REMARKS.
Wide.	Thick.							
In.	In.	Feet.	Lbs.	Feet.	Lbs.	Feet.	Lbs.	
0.5	Round	2.60	1.70	14.96	9.78	17.56	11.48	
0.75	Round	5.12	7.53	......	......	5.12	7.53	
1.0	Round	22.55	58.85	27.52	71.83	50.07	130.68	
1.25	Round	4.56	18.65	......	......	4.56	18.65	
1.5	Round	.33	1.94	......	......	.33	1.94	
2.0	Round	3.25	34.03	5.0	52.35	8.25	86.38	
2.375	Round	1.75	25.83	1.33	19.63	3.08	45.46	Hammered.
2.5	Round	1.17	19.14	......	......	1.17	19.14	
0.25	0.25	......	......	7.75	1.62	7.75	1.62	
0.5	0.5	7.92	6.65	......	......	7.92	6.65	
0.75	0.125	......	......	.14	.04	.14	.04	
1.0	0.5	.16	.27	.91	1.52	1.07	1.79	
1.25	1.25	3.81	20.00	......	......	3.81	20.00	
1.5	0.3	......	......	1.64	2.49	1.64	2.49	
1.5	0.375	......	......	.50	.94	.50	.94	
1.5	0.5	5.17	13.00	......	......	5.17	13.00	
1.5	0.75	.16	.60	......	......	.16	.60	
1.625	0.125	.27	.18	1.33	.90	1.60	1.08	
2.0	0.25	......	......	18.62	31.28	18.62	31.28	
2.0	0.4	......	......	1.21	3.24	1.21	3.24	
2.0	0.75	5.17	26.05	......	......	5.17	26.05	
2.0	1.0	3.71	24.93	3.67	24.66	7.38	49.59	
2.0	2.0	1.17	15.72	......	......	1.17	15.72	
2.5	0.188	.42	.66	......	......	.42	.66	
2.5	1.25	.83	8.71	......	......	.83	8.71	
3.0	0.5	3.10	15.62	2.98	15.01	6.08	30.63	
3.0	1.0	.37	3.73	......	......	.37	3.73	
3.0	1.25	......	......	5.5	69.30	5.5	69.30	
3.25	0.188	4.79	9.77	4.0	8.16	8.79	17.93	
3.5	0.5	......	......	3.32	19.52	3.32	19.52	
4.0	0.5	2.42	16.26	......	......	2.42	16.26	
4.0	1.0	.62	8.33	......	......	.62	8.33	
4.0	1.5	1.17	23.61	......	......	1.17	23.61	
4.125	0.25	2.04	7.06	......	......	2.04	7.06	
4.25	0.25	3.25	11.60	......	......	3.25	11.60	
4.5	0.875	22.67	299.69	......	......	22.67	299.69	2 pieces, 11 ft. 4 in.
5.5	0.5	4.56	42.13	......	......	4.56	42.13	
6.625	0.25	......	......	1.66	9.23	1.66	9.23	
7.0	0.5	......	......	.67	7.88	.67	7.88	
8.0	1.0	......	......	1.58	42.48	1.58	42.48	
			205.	......	......	......	205.	Draft for axletree.
			927.24	......	391.86	......	1319.10	
Cast iron ..		......	7.5*	......	50.†	......	57.5	*2 wash's †4 pipes.
		......	292.‡	......	130.‖	......	422.	‡2 rollers, ‖2 wh'ls.
		......	206.	......	......	......	206.	2 naves.
		......	505.5	......	180.	......	685.5	
Cast brass ...		......	11.	......	......	......	11.	

Bill of iron for one 42-pounder Barbette Carriage.

SIZE OF IRON.		GUN CARRIAGE.		CHASSIS.		TOTAL.		REMARKS.
Wide.	Thick.							
In.	In.	Feet.	Lbs.	Feet.	Lbs.	Feet.	Lbs.	
0.5	Round	2.69	1.76	15.80	10.33	18.49	12.09	
0.75	Round	2.5	3.67	......	......	2.5	3.67	
1.0	Round	25.65	66.95	30.31	79.11	55.96	146.06	
1.25	Round	4.74	19.38	......	......	4.74	19.38	
2.0	Round	3.5	36.64	5.	52.35	8.5	88.99	
2.375	Round	1.75	25.83	1.33	19.63	3.08	45.46	Hammered.
2.5	Round	1.17	19.14	......	......	1.17	19.14	
0.25	0.25	......	......	7.75	1.63	7.75	1.63	
0.5	0.5	7.92	6.65	......	......	7.92	6.65	
0.75	0.125	......	......	.14	.04	.14	.04	
1.0	0.5	.17	.28	......	......	.17	.28	
1.25	1.25	3.94	20.68	......	......	3.94	20.68	
1.5	0.3	......	......	1.64	2.49	1.64	2.49	
1.5	0.375	......	......	.5	.94	.5	.94	
1.5	0.5	5.17	13.02	.92	2.32	6.09	15.34	
1.5	0.75	1.33	5.02	......	......	1.33	5.02	
1.625	1.25	.27	.18	1.33	.90	1.60	1.08	
2.0	0.25	......	......	18.59	31.22	18.59	31.22	
2.0	0.4	......	......	1.21	3.24	1.21	3.24	
2.0	0.75	5.17	26.05	......	......	5.17	26.05	
2.0	1.0	3.87	26.00	3.67	24.66	7.54	50.66	
2.0	2.0	1.17	15.72	......	......	1.17	15.72	
2.5	1.25	.83	7.05	......	......	.83	7.05	
3.0	0.5	3.10	15.62	2.99	15.01	6.09	30.63	
3.0	1.0	.37	3.73	......	......	.37	3.73	
3.0	1.25	......	......	5.5	69.30	5.5	69.30	
3.25	0.188	5.06	10.32	4.0	8.16	9.06	18.48	
3.5	0.5	......	......	3.42	20.11	3.42	20.11	
4.0	0.5	2.42	16.26	......	......	2.42	16.26	
4.0	1.0	.79	10.62	......	......	.79	10.62	
4.0	1.5	1.17	23.61	......	......	1.17	23.61	
4.125	0.25	2.04	7.06	......	......	2.04	7.06	
4.5	0.875	22.67	299.69	......	......	22.67	299.69	2 pieces, 11 ft. 4 in.
4.75	0.25	3.25	12.97	......	......	3.25	12.97	
6.	0.5	4.58	46.16	......	......	4.58	46.16	
6.625	0.25	......	......	1.66	9.23	1.66	9.23	
7.	0.5	......	......	.67	7.88	.67	7.88	
8.	1.0	......	......	1.58	42.48	1.58	42.48	
			213.	......	......	......	213.	Draft for axletree.
			953.06	......	401.03	......	1354.09	
Cast iron.		......	7.5*	......	49.†	......	56.5	*2 wash's, †4 pipes
		......	292.‡	......	130.‖	......	422.	‡2 rollers, ‖2 wh'ls
		......	206.	......	......	......	206.	2 naves.
		......	505.5	......	179.	......	684.5	
Cast brass...		......	11.	......	......	......	11.	Nut for screw.

Bill of iron for one 24-pounder Casemate Carriage.

SIZE OF IRON. Wide	Thick.	GUN CARRIAGE. Feet.	Lbs.	CHASSIS. Feet.	Lbs.	TOTAL. Feet.	Lbs.	REMARKS.
In.	In.	Feet.	Lbs.	Feet.	Lbs.	Feet.	Lbs.	
0.375	Round	4.25	1.56	......	......	4.25	1.56	
0.5	Round	.16	.10	1.37	0.89	1.53	.99	
0.75	Round	6.16	9.05	1.12	1.64	7.28	10.69	13.5 in. for pintle.
1.	Round	33.23	86.73	10.39	27.11	43.62	113.84	
1.5	Round	10.44	61.49	......	......	10.44	61.49	
2.	Round	5.00	52.35	5.66	59.33	10.66	111.68	26.5 in. for traverse wheels.
2.375	Round	1.12	16.53	......	......	1.12	16.53	
3.25	Round	.42	11.61	......	......	.42	11.61	
0.3	0.3	......	......	12.5	3.78	12.50	3.78	
0.75	0.375	3.5	3.29	......	......	3.5	3.29	
1.0	0.5	......	......	.16	.26	.16	.26	
1.25	0.2	3.08	2.59	......	......	3.08	2.59	
1.25	0.375	2.83	4.44	......	......	2.83	4.44	
1.5	0.75	1.87	7.06	......	......	1.87	7.06	
1.625	0.125	......	......	.19	.12	.19	.12	
2.	0.25	......	......	5.42	9.10	5.42	9.10	
2.	0.75	2.33	11.74	......	......	2.33	11.74	
2.	1.0	3.33	22.38	2.33	15.65	5.66	38.03	
2.	1.25	.66	5.54	......	......	.66	5.54	
2.5	0.188	1.5	2.35	......	......	1.5	2.35	
3.0	0.2	1.	2.01	......	......	1.	2.01	
3.0	0.5	......	......	7.35	37.04	7.35	37.04	
3.25	0.188	5.83	11.89	2.89	5.90	8.72	17.79	
3.5	0.188	.29	.64	......	......	.29	.64	
4.75	0.5	8.66	69.10	......	......	8.66	69.10	
5.	0.375	......	......	22.66	142.75	22.66	142.75	2 pieces, 11 ft. 4 in.
1 draft......		......	......	......	28.	......	28.	Tongue fork.
1 do.		......	......	......	83.	......	83.	Tongue.
			382.45	......	414.57	......	797.02	
Cast iron...........			54.5	......	......	......	54.5	Bed plate.
Do............			11.	......	......	......	11.5	Handle for screw.
Do............			13.	......	......	......	13.	Roller.
Do............			446.	......	......	......	446.	2 truck wheels.
Do............			......	......	60.	......	60.	2 wheels.
Do............			......	......	198.	......	198.	2 do.
Do............			......	......	92.	......	92.	Pintle.
			525.	......	350.	......	875.	
Cast brass..........			12.	......	......	......	12.	Nut for screw.
Do............			2.	......	......	......	2.	Pinion for screw.
Do............			......	......	44.	......	44.	8 journal boxes.
			14.	......	44.	......	58.	

Bill of iron for one 32-pounder Casemate Carrriage.

SIZE OF IRON.		GUN CARRIAGE.		CHASSIS.		TOTAL.		REMARKS.
Wide.	Thick.							
In.	In.	Feet.	Lbs.	Feet.	Lbs.	Feet.	Lbs.	
0.375	Round	4.25	1.56			4.25	1.56	
0.5	Round	.16	.10	1.62	1.05	1.78	1.15	
0.75	Round	6.16	9.05	1.12	1.64	7.28	10.69	13.5 in. for pintle.
1.	Round	35.88	93.64	10.77	28.10	46.65	121.74	
1.5	Round	10.68	62.90			10.68	62.90	
2.	Round	5.	52.35	5.66	59.33	10.66	111.68	26.5 in. for tra-
2.375	Round	1.12	16.53			1.12	16.53	verse wheels.
3.25	Round	.42	11.61			.42	11.61	
0.3	0.3			12.50	3.78	12.50	3.78	
0.75	0.375	3.5	3.29			3.5	3.29	
1.	0.5			.16	.26	.16	.26	
1.25	0.2	3.08	2.59			3.08	2.59	
1.25	0.375	2.83	4.44			2.83	4.44	
1.5	0.75	1.87	7.06			1.87	7.06	
1.625	0.125			0.19	.12	.19	.12	
2.	0.25			5.42	9.10	5.42	9.10	
2.	0.75	2.33	11.74			2.33	11.74	
2.	1.	3.33	22.38	2.33	15.65	5.66	38.03	
2.	1.25	.66	5.54			.66	5.54	
2.5	0.188	1.50	2.35			1.50	2.35	
3.	0.2	1.	2.01			1.0	2.01	
3.	0.5			7.70	38.81	7.70	38.81	
3.25	0.188	5.83	11.89	2.89	5.90	8.72	17.79	
3.5	0.188	.29	.64			.29	.64	
5.	0.375			22.66	142.75	22.66	142.75	2 pieces, 11 ft. 4 in.
5.5	0.5	8.75	80.85			8.75	80.85	
1 draft......					28.		28.	Tongue fork.
1 do.......					83.		83.	Tongue.
			402.52		417.49		820.01	
Cast iron..........			54.5				54.5	Bed plate.
Do.............			11.5				11.5	Handle for screw.
Do.............			14.				14.	Roller.
Do.............			446.				446.	2 truck wheels.
Do.............					60.		60.	2 wheels.
Do.............					198.		198.	2 do.
Do.............					92.		92.	Pintle.
			526.		350.		876.	
Cast brass.........			12.				12.	Nut for screw.
Do.............			2.				2.	Pinion for screw.
Do.............					44.		44.	8 journal boxes.
			14.		44.		58.	

Bill of iron for one 42-pdr. or one 8-in. Columbiad Carriage.

SIZE OF IRON.		GUN CARRIAGE.		CHASSIS.		TOTAL.		Remarks.
Wide.	Thick.							
In.	In.	Feet.	Lbs.	Feet.	Lbs.	Feet.	Lbs.	
0.375	Round	4.25	1.56	......	......	4.25	1.56	
0.5	Round	.16	.10	1.64	1.08	1.80	1.18	
0.75	Round	6.16	9.05	1.12	1.64	7.28	10.69	13.5 in. for pintle.
1.0	Round	37.54	97.98	10.98	28.65	48.52	126.63	
1.5	Round	10.77	63.43	......	......	10.77	63 43	
2.	Round	5.	52.35	5.66	59.33	10.66	111.68	26.5.in for traverse wheels.
2.375	Round	1.12	16.53	......	......	1.12	16.53	
3.25	Round	.42	11.61	......	......	.42	11.61	
0.3	0.3	......	......	12.50	3.78	12.50	3.78	
0.75	0.375	3.5	3.29	......	......	3.50	3.29	
1.0	0.5	......	......	.16	.26	.16	.26	
1.25	0.2	3.08	2.59	......	......	3.08	2.59	
1.25	0.375	2.83	4.44	......	......	2.83	4.44	
1.5	0.75	1.87	7.06	......	......	1.87	7.06	
1.625	0.125	......	......	.19	.12	.19	.12	
2.0	0.25	......	......	5.42	9.10	5.42	9.10	
2.0	0.75	2.33	11.74	......	......	2.33	11.74	
2.0	1.0	3.33	22.38	2.33	15.65	5.66	38.03	
2.	1.25	.66	5.54	......	......	.66	5.54	
2.5	0.188	1.50	2.35	......	......	1.50	2.35	
3.0	0.2	1.	2.01	......	......	1.00	2.01	
3.0	0.5	......	......	8.08	40.72	8.08	40.72	
3.25	0.188	5.83	11.89	2.89	5.90	8.72	17.79	
3.5	0.188	.29	.64	......	......	.29	.64	
5.	0.375	......	......	22.66	142.75	22.66	142.75	2 pieces, 11 ft. 4 in.
6.	0.5	9.08	91.52	......	......	9.08	91.52	
1 draft......		......	......	......	28.	......	28.	Tongue fork.
1 do......		......	......	......	83.	......	83.	Tongue.
			418.06	......	419.98	......	838.04	
Cast iron............			54.5	......	......	......	54.5	Bed plate.
Do			11.5	......	......	......	11.5	Handle for screw.
Do			14.	......	......	......	14.	Roller.
Do			446.	......	......	......	446.	2 truck wheels.
Do			......	......	60.	......	60.	2 wheels.
Do			......	......	198.	......	198.	2 do.
Do			......	......	92.	......	92.	Pintle.
			526.	......	350.	......	876.	
Cast brass..........			12.	......	......	......	12.	Nut for screw.
Do			2.	......	......	......	2.	Pinion for screw.
Do			......	......	44.	......	44.	8 journal boxes.
			14.	......	44.	......	58.	

Bill of iron for one 24-pdr. Howitzer Casemate Carriage.

SIZE OF IRON.		GUN CARRIAGE.		CHASSIS.		TOTAL.		REMARKS.
Wide.	Thick.							
In.	In.	Feet.	Lbs.	Feet.	Lbs.	Feet.	Lbs.	
0.15	Round	3.75	0.37	......	......	3.75	0.37	
0.2	Round	2.33	.32	......	......	2.33	.32	
0.5	Round	3.08	2.01	......	......	3.08	2.01	
0.625	Round	1.83	1.86	......	......	1.83	1.86	
0.75	Round	4.16	6.11	2.54	3.73	6.70	9.84	
0.875	Round	.87	1.74	......	......	.87	1.74	
1.0	Round	15.92	41.55	5.67	14.79	21.59	56.34	
1.375	Round	1.06	5.23	......	......	1.06	5.23	
1.5	Round	.50	2.94	1.87	11.01	2.37	13.95	
2.	Round	2.04	21.35	.75	7.85	2.79	29.20	
3.	Round	......	......	2.12	49.95	2.12	49.95	
3.25	Round	.42	11.61	......	......	.42	11.61	
0.3	0.3	1.66	.50	......	......	1.66	.50	
1.0	0.5	.17	.28	......	......	.17	.28	
1.25	0.75	......	......	1.	3.15	1.	3.15	
1.5	0.375	.25	.47	......	......	.25	.47	
1.5	0.75	1.	3.78	1.87	7.07	2.87	10.85	
1.625	0.125	.27	.18	......	......	.27	.18	
1.75	1.75	1.	10.29	......	......	1.	10.29	
2.0	0.75	.58	2.92	......	......	.58	2.92	
2.0	1.0	3.33	22.38	3.33	22.38	6.66	44.76	
2.5	0.188	1.02	1.60	.67	1.05	1.69	2.65	
2.5	0.5	......	......	2.75	11.55	2.75	11.55	
2.5	0.75	......	......	4.42	27.84	4.42	27.84	
2.5	2.	......	......	1.	16.80	1.	16.80	
3.0	0.5	......	......	5.25	26.46	5.25	26.46	
3.25	0.188	2.12	4.32	1.58	3.22	3.70	7.54	
3.25	0.25	.54	1.47	.83	2.26	1.37	3.73	
3.25	0.5	2.72	14.85	......	......	2.72	14.85	
3.25	1.0	5.33	58.20	......	......	5.33	58.20	
6.0	0.75	......	......	.58	8.77	.58	8.77	
12.0	0.5	......	......	1.	20.16	1.	20.16	
			216.33	......	238.04	......	454.37	
Cast iron		......	160.	......	......	......	160.	Front transom.
Do		......	200.	......	......	......	200.	Rear transom.
Do		......	12.	......	......	......	12.	Roller for trail.
Do		......	......	......	28.	......	28.	2 traverse wheels.
			372.	......	28.	......	400.	
Cast brass		......	15.	......	......	......	15.	2 rollers.
Do		......	.5	......	......	......	.5	2 journal plates.
Do		......	12.	......	......	......	12.	Nut for screw.
Do		......	2.	......	......	......	2.	Pinion for screw.
			29.5	......	......	......	29.5	

Bill of iron for Field and Siege Gin.

PARTS.	Width.	Thickness.	Length.	Weight.	REMARKS.
	In.	In.	In.	Lbs.	
Chain, No. 2	0.2	Round	42.	0.36	
Rivets and nails	.375	Round	129.	3.95	
Bolts, No. 3, and keys for gudgeons	.625	Round	71.	6.03	
Key bolt	.75	Round	10.	1.22	
Bolts, No. 5, eye pin and handle	1.	Round	27.	5.87	
Sheave bolt	1.25	Round	16.	5.45	
Bolts for pulley block	1.5	Round	8.	3.92	
Cross head for pulley block	2.5	Round	3.5	4.77	
Collars for gudgeons	0.5	0.5	16.	1.12	
Nuts, No. 3	1.25	.625	10.	2.18	
Bands	1.5	.25	212.	22.26	
Nuts, No. 4	1.5	.75	5.	1.57	
Hook for pulley block	1.75	1.75	12.	10.29	Hammered.
Washers, No. 3	2.	0.125	18.	1.26	
Bevel washer	2.	.625	3.	1.05	
Gudgeons and points	2.	2.	29.	32.48	
Oval washers	2.5	0.125	13.	1.14	
Head straps	2.5	.31	32.	7.	
Straps for pulley block	2.5	.5	30.	10.50	
Pry pole tongue	3.5	1.	12.	11.76	Hammered.
Journal boxes	3.5	1.75	24.	41.16	
Tongue plate	5.5	0.5	16.	12.32	Hammered.
				187.66	
Three sheaves for pulleys				24.	Brass.

Bill of iron for one Garrison or Casemate Gin.

PARTS.	Wide.	Thick.	Long.	Weight.	REMARKS.
	In.	In.	Feet.	Lbs.	
Key chains, No. 1	0.15	Round	7.5	0.52	This bill includes the materials for one double and one triple pulley block.
Rings	0.2	Round	2.5	0.27	
Rivet bolts, No. 1	0.5	Round	1.66	1.08	
Pin for clevis bolt	0.75	Round	0.41	0.60	
Eye pins	0.875	Round	0.83	1.66	
Bolts, No. 5, and pry pole handle	1.	Round	3.33	8.69	
Bolts, No. 3, for pawls	1.25	Round	0.70	2.86	
Braces and clevis	1.5	Round	22.5	132.52	
Clevis bolt	1.75	Round	2.25	18.02	
Bolt heads, No. 5, and points for legs	2.	Round	4.	41.88	
Nails, No. 3	0.375	0.375	9.41	4.42	
Nuts, No. 1	1.	0.5	0.16	0.26	
Keys for braces	1.25	0.125	1.16	0.60	
Nuts, No. 3, and pawls	1.25	0.625	2.54	6.65	
Eyes for pulley blocks	1.25	1.25	2.	10.50	
Keys for clevis bolt	1.5	0.125	1.16	0.73	
Nuts, No. 4	1.5	0.75	0.75	2.83	
Hooks for blocks	1.75	1.75	1.83	18.83	Hammered.
Washers, No. 3	2.	0.125	0.33	0.27	
Middle bands for windlass	2.	0.25	14.58	24.49	
Collars for points	2.	1.	2.	13.44	
Journals	2.	2.	1.66	22.31	
Washers for handle	3.	0.188	0.5	0.94	
Washers, No. 5	3.25	0.188	2.16	4.40	
End bands for windlass	3.5	0.25	5.33	15.67	
Lower bands for legs	4.	0.25	5.08	17.06	
Cross heads for blocks	4.	1.25	2.33	39.14	Hammered.
Upper bands for legs	6.	0.25	4.12	20.76	
Partitions for blocks	8.	0.25	2.75	18.48	
Straps for blocks	8.	0.37	5.	50.40	
				480.28	
Two ratchets	.....	.....	.....	39.	Cast iron.
Two journal boxes	.....	.....	.....	13.	Cast brass.
Five sheaves	.....	.....	.....	60.	
				73.	

Bill of iron for one Sling Cart.

PARTS.	Wide.	Thick.	Long.	Weight.	REMARKS.
	In.	In.	Feet.	Lbs.	
Pole prop chain, No. 1........	0.15	Round	3.75	0.26	
Rings, No. 1................	0.2	Round	0.31	0.03	
Rivets, No. 2................	0.25	Round	0.50	0.08	
Chain, No. 5, and rivets, No. 3.	0.375	Round	9.06	3.33	
Pole rivets...................	0.5	Round	0.50	0.32	
Bolts, No. 4, chains & pole staple	0.75	Round	89.58	131.68	
Eye pin, No. 1..............	0.875	Round	0.14	0.28	
Bolts, Nos. 2 and 5, and rings..	1.	Round	9.91	25.86	
Bolt heads, No. 4, and eye pin*.	1.5	Round	1.	5.86	* Pole prop.
Screw handle................	1.75	Round	5.33	42.69	
Bolt heads, No. 5............	2.	Round	0.50	5.23	
Nails, No. 3.................	0.375	0.375	12.04	5.66	
Toggle for pole prop chain.....	0.5	0.25	0.16	0.06	
Axle washers, upper skeans, nuts No. 2, and chain hook.	1.	0.5	11.25	18.90	
Burrs for pole rivets..........	1.125	0.25	0.18	0.17	
Nuts, No. 3.................	1.25	0.625	0.10	0.26	
Bolster hooks................	1.25	1.25	2.33	12.23	
Axle bands..................	1.3	0.2	2.50	2.17	
Nuts, No. 4.................	1.5	0.75	3.25	12.28	
Hook for sling chain..........	1.5	1.	1.33	6.70	Hammered.
Axle hooks..................	1.5	1.5	2.50	18.90	
Pole prop ferrule.............	1.75	0.375	0.66	1.45	
Linch pins...................	1.75	0.625	0.83	3.04	
Washers, No. 3..............	2.	0.125	0.33	0.27	
Bands for hounds and pole.....	2.	0.25	10.	16.80	
Brow bands for naves........	2.	0.375	16.33	41.00	
Lower skean & stirrups, (in part)	2.	0.5	10.	33.60	
Bridles......................	2.	0.625	1.58	6.63	
Stirrups and pole straps.......	2.	0.75	4.83	24.34	
Nuts, No. 5.................	2.	1.	0.66	4.43	
Upper skeans................	2.25	0.5	0.66	2.49	
Nuts, No. 7.................	2.25	1.25	0.37	3.49	
Washers, No. 4.............	2.5	0.188	4.58	7.19	
End bands, for naves.........	2.5	0.375	13.82	43.52	
Lower axle skean—body......	3.	0.5	3.41	17.18	
Hoisting screw, (in one piece)..	3.	3.	3.83	115.81	Hammered.
Washers, No. 5.............	3.25	0.188	0.54	1.10	
Pole prop socket.............	3.5	0.625	1.25	9.18	
Socket of screw handle.......	3.5	2.25	1.	25.88	Hammered.
Washers, No. 7..............	4.	0.25	0.66	2.21	
Washers for axle & bolster hooks	4.5	0.375	2.33	13.18	
Two wheel tires..............	4.5	0.875	50.	661.00	In 4 pieces.
Lower axle skean—middle part.	6.	0.5	1.	10.08	
				1336.82	
Bed plate for screw...........	......	......	......	42.	Cast iron.
Nave boxes for two wheels....	......	......	......	60.	Cast iron.
				102.	
Nut for hoisting screw........	......	......	......	14.	Cast brass.

CHAPTER FOURTH.

ARTILLERY IMPLEMENTS AND EQUIPMENTS.

NOMENCLATURE, DIMENSIONS, WEIGHTS.

Rammer Heads.

Rammer heads are made of ash, maple, birch, beech, elm, gum, or other tough woods; the head is bored $\frac{2}{3}$ of its length with a hole 0.25 inch less than the diameter of the staff, which enters with a tenon. The staff is driven into the head and fastened with a *pin* of hard wood 0.3 inch diameter: the neck has a *copper band* 0.5 inch wide and 0.05 inch thick, fastened with 3 *copper nails.*

Rammer heads for howitzers are countersunk, to receive the fuzes, in ramming shells.

Dimensions.

KIND.	Length.	DIAMETER.	
		Body.	Neck.
	In.	In.	In.
42-pounder gun, 10-inch sea coast howitzer, and 10-inch columbiad	7	6.13	3.
32-pounder gun, 8-inch sea coast howitzer, and 8-inch columbiad	6.4	5.6	3.
24-pounder gun	5.8	5.1	3.
18-pounder gun	5.3	4.64	3.
12-pounder gun, 8-inch siege howitzer, 24-pounder and 32-pounder howitzers, 13-inch and 10-inch mortars, (heavy,)	5.5	4.	2.5
6-pounder gun, 12-pounder field howitzer, 10-inch mortar, (light,) 8-inch mortar and stone mortar	4	3.24	2.5

Sponge Heads.

Diameter, 1 inch less than the calibre of the piece ; this is the size required for the wove woollen sponge.

KIND.	Length.	Diameter.
	In.	In.
10-inch columbiad.. Bore	8.	9.
10-inch columbiad.. Chamber	8.	7.
8-inch columbiad.. Bore	8.	7.
8-inch columbiad.. Chamber	8.	5.4
42-pounder gun and 10-inch sea coast howitzer	8.	6.0
32-pounder gun and 8-inch sea coast howitzer	8.	5.4
24-pounder gun	8.	4.8
18-pounder gun	8.	4.3
12-pounder gun, 8-inch siege howitzer, 24-pounder and 32-pdr. howitzers, 13-inch and 10-inch mortars, (heavy)	7.5	3.6
6-pounder gun, 12-pounder howitzer, 10-inch mortar, (light,) 8-inch mortar and stone mortar	7.5	2.7

Sponge heads are made of elm or poplar, &c. The head is bored $\frac{2}{3}$ of its length, with a hole 0.25 inch less than the body of the staff which is inserted with a tenon and fastened by 2 hard wood *pins* 0.3 inch diameter.

Sponges.

Sponges are made of coarse, well twisted woollen yarn, woven into a warp of strong hemp or flax thread, after the manner of Brussels carpet ; the loops are 0.75 inch long.

They are woven in webs with selvages between them, which being cut, the sponges are sewed to fit formers of the same dimensions as the sponge heads. One end of the sponge is drawn together with strong twine and a tuft of woollen yarn is inserted at the centre of the gather or folds; a circular piece of strong canvass is stitched inside of the bottom; the other end, after receiving the sponge head, is nailed to it around the staff with 6 *copper nails*, 1 inch long; 3 *copper nails* should also be driven into the bottom of the sponge, to secure it to the head.

Similar sponges are made by working the yarn with needles into canvass bags, but the wove sponges are equally good and less expensive.

Sponges are likewise made of sheep skin alum-dressed, with the wool on; but they are inferior to those made of yarn.

For dimensions of sponges, see Table of sponge heads.

Sponge Covers.

They are made of Russia duck or canvass, painted the same color as the gun carriage.

The lengths are:

For the 6-pounder sponge.............................. 9 inches.
" 12-pounder and 18-pounder sponge............... 11 "
" 24-pounder, 32-pounder, and 42-pounder sponge... 12 "

The interior diameter is equal to the calibre of the piece. A *hem* 0.5 inch wide around the top, receives a *cord* 0.2 inch diameter, by which the mouth is drawn together and tied around the sponge staff: a *loop* of canvass 0.75 inch wide is sewed on the end of the cover, to draw it off by.

The covers are marked in white, with the calibre of the gun.

Ladle Heads.

DIMENSIONS.		42-pdr.	32-pdr.	24-pdr.	18-pdr.	12-pdr.
		In.	In.	In.	In.	In.
Whole length..................		7.	6.4	5.8	5.3	4.6
Diameters.	Above the shoulder..	6.7	6.1	5.5	5.	4.3
	Below the shoulder..	6.6	6.	5.4	4.9	4.2
	Neck..............	3.	3.	3.	3.	2.5

Ladle heads are made of the same kinds of wood, and are fastened to the staves in the same manner, as rammer heads.

Rammer, ladle, and sponge heads should be saturated, when new, with linseed oil, to prevent splitting from alternate wetting and drying in service.

Ladles.

Ladles are used for siege, garrison, and sea-coast guns only. They are made of sheet copper, No. 18.

DIMENSIONS.	42-pdr.	32-pdr.	24-pdr.	18-pdr.	12-pdr.
	In.	In.	In.	In.	In.
Whole length..................	16.5	15.35	14.1	13.1	11.2
Length of band, developed	20.75	18.85	16.95	15.4	13.2
Width of scoop, developed	14.	12.8	11.6	10.6	9.2
Width of band, (included in whole length).....................	2.5	2.5	2.5	2.5	2.0

Towards the mouth of the ladle the copper is spread a little, so as to increase the diameter of the ladle 0.3 inch: the corners are rounded with a radius of from 2 inches to 3.5 inches. To stiffen the ladle, the copper is *planished*, after being bent and brazed. The ladle is attached to the head by 6 to 10 *copper nails*, 1 inch long, driven in two rows around the body, about 1 inch apart.

Worms.

DIMENSIONS.		Siege and garrison.	Field.
		In.	In.
Length of socket and neck		5.5	5.5
Length of one branch from neck to point, (developed)		16.	13.
Depth of socket		4.5	4.5
Exterior diameter of socket at top		1.75	1.5
Diameter of neck		0.8	0.7
Thickness of the iron of the socket		0.125	0.125
Diameter of branches at the neck, (tapering to a point)		0.6	0.5
Length of socket and worm, complete		9.5	9.
Diameter of worm complete, (exterior circle)		4.	3.
Size of iron for worms	Length	7.	6.
	Width	3.	3.
	Thickness	0.5	0.5
Weight of worm ......lbs.		1.75	1.5

The staff is pointed to fit the conical form of the socket, driven in hard and fastened by 2 *iron rivets* 0.25 inch diameter.

Staves.

Staves for implements are made of tough ash.

The diameter of the tenon is 0.25 inch less than that of the staff; its length, $\frac{2}{3}$ of that of the head into which it is inserted.

For field guns, field and siege howitzers and mortars, the rammer and sponge heads are on the same staff; for other pieces, on separate staves.

For the coehorn mortar, the body of the staff forms the rammer and sponge head.

Dimensions of Staves for Implements.

KIND.	Diameter.	LENGTH, INCLUDING TENONS.			
		For Sponge.	For Rammer.	For Ladle.	For Worm.
	In.	In.	In.	In.	In.
42-pounder sea coast gun..........	1.75	125.33	125.66	111.66	123.
32-pounder sea coast gun..........	1.75	125.33	125.86	113.01	123.
24-pounder siege and garrison gun..	1.75	125.33	126.07	113.47	123.
18-pounder siege and garrison gun..	1.75	125.33	126.23	115.43	123.
12-pounder siege and garrison gun..	1.75	125.5	126.17	117.36	123.
10-inch columbiad.. Bore........	1.75	115.33	125.66		
10-inch columbiad.. Chamber....	1.75	125.33	125.66		
8-inch columbiad.. Bore........	1.75	115.33	125.86		
8-inch columbiad.. Chamber....	1.75	125.33	125.86		
10-inch sea coast howitzer.........	1.75	125.33	125.66		
8-inch sea coast howitzer.........	1.75	105.33	105.86		
8-inch siege howitzer	1.5	51.67	51.67		
24-pounder casemate howitzer......	1.5	75.67	75.67		
12-pounder field gun ; 32-pounder & 24-pounder field howitzers......	1.5	91.67	91.67	......	82.5
6-pounder field gun, and 12-pounder field howitzer.................	1.5	73.17	73.17	......	67.5
13-inch and 10-inch heavy mortars..	1.5	39.67	39.67		
10-inch light mortar; 8-inch mortar, and stone mortar..............	1.5	30.17	30.17		
24-pounder coehorn mortar........	1.5	18.	18.		

For other cannon than those of the patterns described in CHAP. 1 staves may be made of such a length that the finished implement shall be 18 inches longer than the bore of the piece.

Lengths and weights of Finished Implements.

KIND.	Length.	WEIGHT.			
		Sponge.	Rammer.	Ladle.	Worm.
	In.	Lbs.	Lbs.	Lbs.	Lbs.
42-pounder sea coast gun.............	128.	10.25	9.75	13.75	7.5 (42- to 12-pounder)
32-pounder sea coast gun.............	128.	10.	8.4	13.15	
24-pounder siege and garrison gun......	128.	9.65	8.15	12.4	
18-pounder siege and garrison gun......	128.	8.7	8.	10.	
12-pounder siege and garrison gun......	128.	7.8	7.35	7.8	
10-in. columbiad. Sponge for bore.....	118.	12.			
10-in. columbiad. Sponge for chamber..	128.	11.			
10-in. columbiad. Rammer	128.	......	9.75		
8-in. columbiad. Sponge for bore.....	118.	10.25			
8-in. columbiad. Sponge for chamber..	128.	10.			
8-in. columbiad. Rammer............	128.	......	8.4		
10-inch sea coast howitzer............	128.	10.25	9.75		
8-inch sea coast howitzer.............	128.	8.5	7.		
8-inch siege howitzer.................	56.	3.7 (sponge and rammer)			
24-pounder casemate howitzer..........	80.	5.			
12-pr. field gun; 32-pr. and 24-pr. field howitzer... Sponge and rammer.	95.	5.8			
12-pr. field gun; 32-pr. and 24-pr. field howitzer... Worm....	87.	....		......	4.25
6-pr. field gun, and 12-pr. field howitzer .... Sponge and rammer..	77.	4.5			
6-pr. field gun, and 12-pr. field howitzer .... Worm....	72.	....		......	3.6
13-inch and 10-inch heavy mortars......	44.	3.2			
10-inch light, 8-inch and stone mortars..	34.	2.			
24-pounder coehorn mortar............	18.	0.8			

Plank for 100 *Implement Staves.*

KIND.	Number of planks.	DIMENSIONS.			CONTENTS.	
		Width.	Thickness.	Length.	Each plank.	Total.
		In.	In.	In.	Sup. ft.	Sup. ft.
Siege and garrison.....	17	14.	2.	132	25.66	436.22
Field.... 12-pounder..	17	12.5	1.75	102	15.49	263.33
Field.... 6-pounder..	17	12.5	1.75	84	12.76	216.92

Bills of timber for 100 Implement Heads.

KIND.	RAMMER HEADS.			SPONGE HEADS.			LADLE HEADS.		
	Square.	Length.	Contents.	Square.	Length.	Contents.	Square.	Length.	Contents.
	In.	Feet.	Sup. ft.	In.	Feet.	Sup. ft.	In.	Feet.	Sup. ft.
42-pounder.	6.625	66	241.40	6.5	72	253.5	7.25	66	289.09
32-pounder.	6.125	60	187.58	6.	72	216.0	6.5	60	211.25
24-pounder.	5.75	53	146.02	5.25	72	165.37	6.	53	159.0
18-pounder.	5.125	50	109.44	4.75	72	135.37	5.5	50	126.04
12-pounder.	4.5	50	84.37	4.125	68	96.42	4.75	50	94.01
6-pounder.	3.75	40	46.87	3.25	68	59.85			

Handspikes.

Trail handspike, for field carriages; (hickory, young oak;) whole length 53 inches—the *large end* rounded, diameter 2.2 inches; largest diameter 3 inches—the *small end*, diameter 1.5 inch—the *stop*, iron, projecting 0.3 inch; distance from the large end to the farthest side of the stop 9 inches; the stem clinched in the wood and filed down smooth—the *strap*, iron, fastened by 1 *rivet;* the middle of it 9 inches from the small end—the *ring*, round iron, 1.5 inch diameter.

Manœuvring handspike, for garrison and sea coast carriages and for gins, (hickory, young oak.) Whole length 66 inches; length of the *square* 19 inches; *chamfered part* (8 square) 12 inches; the remainder round. Diameter at the upper end 1.8 inch—upper end of the square, 3 inches—lower end, 2.36 inches. For siege service and other heavy work, the handspike is made 84 inches long—weight 12 lbs.

Shod handspike. Upper end 1.75 inch diameter; the lower end of the round part, 2.5 inches—square 2.5 inches by 3 inches. The end rounded on one side, and shod with an iron *shoe* fastened with 3 *rivets*. Length of round part 4 feet—square 14 inches. It is particularly useful in the service of mortars and of casemate and barbette carriages.

Truck handspike, for casemate carriages, (wrought iron;) whole length 42 inches—*point*, conical, 4 inches; *body*, cylindrical, 12 inches; the handle round. Diameter at the ends 1.1 inch—body 1.4 inch.

Roller handspike, for casemate carriages. It is made of 1 inch round iron; the point conical, 1.5 inch long, tapered to 0.85 inch diameter—whole length 34 inches.

LINSTOCK; (ash or oak;) length of wood 31.5 inches—diameter of head 1.5 inch—a hole 0.75 inch diameter 1.5 inch below the top; the lower end pointed and shod with iron.

PORT-FIRE STOCK. The *port-fire socket* made of cast brass 2.75 inches long; socket 0.75 inch diameter, with a circular plate in the bottom; a *stud* at the top for a thumb screw; 1.25 inch of the lower part forms the *stock socket*, in which the stock is secured with 1 *rivet*—the *thumb-screw*, to hold the port-fire, the end riveted inside; the *hook*, 8 inches from the top, to hang in the loop of the port-fire case—the *stock* (ash or oak) 22.5 inches long; diameter 1 inch. Whole length 24 inches.

PASS BOX, (white pine, 0.75 inch thick)—interior dimensions 7 inches square by 14 inches long; one side turns on 2 *hinges*, and is fastened with a brass *hook* and a *staple*—a wooden *handle* is set diagonally on one end.

BUDGE BARREL, for use in forts and batteries; *staves* (oak) 0.4 inch thick—*bottom* (oak) in 1 or 2 pieces, 0.4 inch thick—4 *hoops* (sheet copper, No. 18) 48 inches long, 1.1 inch wide, and confined to the barrel each by 5 *rivets* 0.2 inch thick; they are joined by 2 *rivets*, or brazed together—height of barrel, 20 inches; exterior diameter at ends, 13 inches; at bilge, 15 inches—*cover* (bag leather) 18 inches high and 40 inches wide, secured to the barrel under the upper hoop by 5 *nails*, and by the 5 *rivets* through the hoop—2 *cords* 0.6 inch thick, 6 feet long, passing through holes in the cover at 1.5 inch from the top, to draw the mouth together; the ends of the cords pass through a *cap* or *hood* 9 inches deep, sliding on the cords.

GUNNER'S HAVRESACK: (bag leather,) 2 *sides* 13 inches high, 13 inches wide at bottom, 14 inches at top of flap—end and bottom *gussets* 5 inches wide—*flap* 8 inches deep, with a *strap* 7 inches long passing through a *buckle* sewed to the front side—*shoulder belt* 1.5 inch wide, one part 12 inches long, with a *buckle and loop;* the other, 36 inches long.

PORT-FIRE CASE: (sole leather,) to contain 12 port-fires; length of *case* 15.6 inches; interior diameter 2.75 inches—*cover* 5.8 inches high, with two *loops* for the belt—1 *loop* on the cover and 1 on the case, for port-fire stock—*belt*, 1 inch wide with a *buckle* and *strap* like that of the haversack, and a *pocket* for the port-fire cutters; length of long strap 55 inches, short strap 28 inches; the straps are sewed on the case so as to be below the top when the case is empty.

TUBE POUCH: the sides 4.25 inches high, 7.25 inches long—2 *ends* 0.9 inch wide at bottom, 2 inches at top—the inner *cover*—the *flap*, 8 inches deep, with its *strap*, and brass *button* attached to the bottom of the pouch—2 *loops* for the belt to pass through—the *belt*, 1.37 inch wide and 42 inches long, with a *buckle and loop* at one end. The priming wire and gunner's gimlet are carried with the tube pouch in the loops, attached by a twine, or in small loops on the inside of the flap.

PRIMING HORN: the *horn* about 13 inches long, 3 inches diameter at the bottom, and 1 inch at the neck—the *bottom* (poplar or ash) 1 inch thick, hollowed out on the exterior for the convenience of filling, having a hole 0.75 inch diameter, with a *screw plug* in the centre—the *stopper*, a conical piece of wood, mean diameter, 0.4 inch. Instead of the stopper the horn may have a *brass mouth piece*, closed by a *valve*, which is held fast by a *spring*. The *strap* (leather) 1 inch wide and 48 inches long, sewed to the neck of the screw plug in the bottom, and to the neck of the horn, or to a ring on the brass mouth piece. The horn should contain at least 1 lb. of powder.

PRIMING WIRE: iron wire 0.175 inch diameter, formed with a ring 2 inches diameter at the head, and pointed; length of stem, for siege and garrison guns, 14 inches; length for field guns, 8 inches.

GUNNER'S GIMLET, like the priming wire, terminating in a gimlet point.

VENT PUNCH: the *body* (steel wire) 0.175 inch diameter, 4.3 inches long—*head* 0.175 inch thick, 1 inch octagonal, with a hole 0.2 inch diameter in the middle.

THUMBSTALL: (buckskin,) *cushion*, stuffed with hair, 2.5 inches long, 1 inch thick—the *strap* 3 inches long—the *string* 12 inches.

PORT-FIRE CUTTER: *blades* (steel) 2.37 inches long, with a notch 1 inch long and 0.4 inch deep in one of them, 1 inch from the joint—*handles* with bows 2 inches by 1 inch—whole length 7 inches.

TANGENT SCALE: (sheet brass, No. 13,) *flanch* 0.5 inch wide, cut to fit the base ring of the piece; upper edge cut into notches for each ¼ degree elevation.

Table of Tangent Scales for Field Guns and Howitzers.

ELEVATION.	GUNS.		HOWITZERS.		
	6-pdr.	12-pdr.	12-pdr.	24-pdr.	32-pdr.
	In.	In.	In.	In.	In.
1° 15′	0.256	0.333	0.252	0.289	0.331
2°	1.025	1.334	0.945	1.138	1.310
3°	2.051	2.670	1.870	2.271	2.618
4°	3.077	4.006	2.791	3.400	3.920

PENDULUM HAUSSE; or tangent scale.

The *scale* is made of sheet brass No. 13. At the lower end is a brass bulb, filled with lead. The *slider* is of thin brass, and is retained in any desired position on the scale by means of a brass set screw with a milled head. The scale is passed through a slit in a piece of steel, with which it is connected by a brass screw, forming a pivot on which the scale can vibrate laterally; this slit is made long enough to allow the scale to take a vertical position in any ordinary cases of inequality of the ground on which the wheels of the carriage may stand. The ends of this piece of steel form two journals, by means of which the scale is supported on the seat attached to the gun, and is at liberty to vibrate in the direction of the axis of the piece.

The *seat* is of iron, and is fastened to the base of the breech by 3 *screws*, in such a manner that the centres of the two journal notches shall be at a distance from the axis equal to the radius of the base ring.

A *muzzle sight*, of iron, is screwed into the swell of the muzzle of guns, or into the middle of the muzzle ring of howitzers. The height of this sight is equal to the dispart of the piece, so that a line from the top of the muzzle sight to the pivot of the tangent scale is parallel to the axis of the piece; consequently, the vertical plane of sight passing through the centre line of the scale and the top of the muzzle sight, will be also parallel to the axis, in any position of the piece; the tangent scale will, therefore, always indicate correctly the angle which the plane of sight makes with the axis.

The seat for suspending the hausse on the gun is adapted to each piece, according to the varying inclination of the base of the breech to the axis. The hausse, the seat and the muzzle sight, are marked for the kind of gun to which they belong. The hausse, when not in use, is carried in a leather pouch suspended to a shoulder strap.

The graduations on the scale are the tangents of each quarter of a degree, to a radius equal to the distance between the muzzle sight and the centre of the journal notches, which are, in all cases, one inch in rear of the base ring.

Tangent scales for Pendulum Hausses for field guns and howitzers.

	FOR GUNS.		FOR HOWITZERS.			
	6-pdr.	12-pdr.	12-pdr.	24-pdr.	32-pdr.	
	In.	In.	In.	In.	In.	
Radius of base ring	5.15	6.5	5.0	6.0	6.9	
Dispart ...	1.025	1.33	0.9	1.125	1.3	Height of muzzle sight.
Tang. 1°	1.042	1.349	0.931	1.138	1.310	
2°	2.084	2.698	1.862	2.275	2.621	
3°	3.124	4.046	2.792	3.412	3.933	
4°	4.164	5.392	3.722	4.548	5.248	
5°	5.203	6.737	4.650	5.683	6.566	

GUNNER'S PERPENDICULAR. This is made of sheet brass; the lower part is cut in the form of a crescent, the points of which are made of steel; a small spirit level is fastened to one side of the plate, parallel to the line joining the points of the crescent, and a slider is fastened to the same side of the plate, perpendicular to the axis of the level. The instrument is useful in marking the points of sight on siege guns and mortars, when the platform is not perfectly level.

CANNON LOCK. Hidden's patent.

The *seat* is of cast brass; it is attached to the gun, on the left side of the vent, by means of two steel *steady pins* and *one screw pin*, if the gun has no lock piece; a small brass *roller* is set into the rear end of the seat for the lanyard to pass round.

The *hammer* is of brass, with a cone of hardened steel screwed into the head, and fastened by a rivet; the hole for the pin on which the hammer turns is oblong, so that the head of the hammer is drawn back by the same pull of the lanyard which causes it first to strike the primer on the vent.

The *lanyard* is a piece of sash cord .25 in. thick and 6 feet long; one end is secured to the shank of the hammer by a knot; the other end carries an iron *toggle*, which serves for a handle, and also for a wrench to turn the screw pin that fastens the lock to the gun.

For guns that have lock pieces, the seat of the lock is made with a flanch to fit the side of the lock piece, to which it is fastened by *two bolts*, with thumb nuts.

LOCK COVER. It is made of black bridle or harness leather. The cap which covers the lock is 7 in. long, 3. in. wide, and 3 in. high. *Two billets* and *two buckle straps,* with black buckles, fasten it on the gun; the length of the straps being proportioned to the diameter of the piece.

VENT COVER, for field pieces without locks; (leather) 6 inches long, 4 inches wide, with a *copper pin* riveted to it, 0.175 inch diameter, and 2 inches long—2 *straps,* 1 inch wide, with *buckles.* The length of the strap varies with the size of the piece. In permanent batteries sheet lead may be used for vent covers.

FUZE SETTER; (brass) *the handle,* upper end slightly rounded—the *cup* 2.1 inches diameter; depth 0.3 inch. Whole length 5 to 6 inches.

FUZE MALLET; (dog wood or oak) in one piece; *head* 5.5 inches long, 4 inches diameter—*handle* 7.5 inches long, 1.25 inch diameter.

FUZE SAW; (tenon saw,) 10 inch blade.

FUZE RASP; 12 inch wood rasp.

FUZE AUGER, for boring out the composition to any required depth: *bit* 0.2 inch diameter sliding in a brass *socket* graduated to 10ths of an inch, and held by a thumb screw in the side—*handle,* of hard wood.

FUZE GIMLET; common gimlet 0.2: used for boring across the composition instead of sawing off the fuze.

SHELL-PLUG SCREW; (iron) *stem* 3 inches long, cut with a deep, sharp thread —*eye* 2 inches diameter.

FUZE-PLUG REAMER. A conical steel reamer, for reaming the holes for paper uzes, in the wooden fuze plugs.

FUZE EXTRACTOR. The inner *screw* and its *stem* are made of steel, and riveted into the *handle,* which is of iron. The stem is contained in a *hollow screw* of steel, which is worked up and down by means of an iron *nut* with *two handles;* the screw being prevented from turning by a slot and a *feather* in the frame; the nut is kept in place by 4 *iron set screws,* the points of which enter into a groove in the nut. The *frame* is of cast brass.

In using this fuze extractor, the inner stem is screwed into the fuze or plug to be extracted, by means of the upper handle, and it is lifted out by turning the nut of the hollow screw.

GUNNER'S PINCERS. Made of iron, with steel jaws 1 inch wide; whole length 10.5 inches.

GUNNER'S CALLIPERS. Made of sheet brass, with steel points. The graduations show the diameters of guns and of shot, linear inches, degrees of the circle, &c.

GUNNER'S QUADRANT; (wood) a graduated *quadrant* of 6 inches radius attached to a rule 23.5 inches long. It has a *plumb line* and *bob,* which are carried, when not in use, in a hole in the end of the rule, covered by a brass plate.

MAUL, for driving pickets; *head* (elm or hickory) 6 inches diameter, 8 inches long—*handle* (ash) 1½ inch diameter, 24 inches long, with an iron band on each end, 1 inch wide, ¼ inch thick.

POINTING WIRE, for mortars; (iron wire No. 7) 20 inches long.

QUOIN for siege mortars; (oak) length 19.5 inches; height 7.85 inches; *handle*, 6 inches long.

CHOCK for casemate carriage; small wedge with a handle on one side.

PLUMMET, for mortars—*line* and *bob*.

SCRAPER, for do.; (iron) *handle* 0.5 inch by 0.3 inch square, 27 inches long—one end formed like a *spoon;* the other, a *scraper.*

SPATULA, for mortars; (ash or hickory,) *handle* 16.5 inches long—*blade* 6 inches—*square end* 3 inches long.

SPLINTS; (white pine) 6 inches long, 0.25 inch thick at the large end, 1 inch wide.

WIPER, for the chambers of mortars; tow cloth, 1 yard square.

GUNNER'S SLEEVE, for mortars; (serge or flannel.)

BASKET, for mortar implements— of strong wicker work, 18 inches in diameter, 12 inches deep.

TARPAULINS are made of two sizes: large, 15 feet by 12 feet; small, 5 feet square. For the manner of painting them, see CHAPTER VII.

TOMPIONS, for 8-inch siege howitzers and mortars, and 10-inch mortar.

BROOM, for mortar batteries, (hickory or birch.)

SHELL HOOKS; (iron) 2 *branches* 0.5 inch diameter, in shape of an *S*, joined by a *rivet;* upper end of the branches connected by 2 *small rings*, 1.25 inch diameter, and 1 *large ring* 3.4 inches diameter: straight *points*, to insert into the ears of the shell 0.5 inch diameter, 0.75 inch long—whole length of branches 12.48 inches.

TOW HOOK; (iron,) *handle* 0.4 inch diameter, 13 inches long; *hook* 1 inch—the other end forms a *hammer* 0.6 inch diameter, 2 inches long.

Used for unpacking ammunition chests.

FUNNEL, for filling shells; (copper or tin,) diameter of *funnel* 3.3 inches—diameter of *pipe* 0.7 inch—length of pipe 2 inches.

POWDER MEASURES. They are made of sheet copper, from No. 16 to No. 20. The bottom is made with a flanch .1 inch deep, turned downwards, and it is brazed or soldered to the sides.

Interior dimensions of cylindrical Powder Measures.

Contents.	Diameter and height.	Contents.	Diameter and height.
Lbs. oz.	In.	Lbs. oz.	In.
0 1	1.337	2 0	4.240
0 2	1.685	2 8	4.571
0 4	2.122	3 0	4.857
0 8	2.673	4 0	5.346
1 0	3.368	4 8	5.560
1 4	3.628	6 0	6.120
1 8	3.855	8 0	6.736

PROLONGE; 3.5 inch hemp rope of 4 strands; on one end, a *toggle* and 3 *round links* in a *thimble*—on the other end, a *hook* and *thimble*—from the end of the hook to the centre of 1st *ring*, 31 inches; from centre of 1st to centre of 2d *ring*, 8 feet; from centre of 2d ring to end of toggle, 16 feet. Whole length of prolonge 26 feet 7 inches—the *toggle* of round iron 0.75 inch diameter, 7.5 inches long, with an eye in the centre—*toggle rings* of 0.5 inch round iron; the ring that enters the thimble is 3 inches, the other two 2.75 inches exterior diameter—*hook* 5.5 inches long; *eye* of 0.5 inch round iron, exterior diameter 2.5 inches; body of hook 0.75 inch diameter, tapering to a point—*thimbles* 1.1 inch interior diameter—*prolonge rings* of 0.6 inch round iron, 4.5 by 3.5 inches; the concave flattened part that is lashed to the rope is 2 inches long, lashed with marline.

SPONGE BUCKET, for field gun carriages. It is made of sheet iron, No. 13; the top and bottom are turned over the sides, and fastened each by *four rivets.* Diameter 7.8 inches; height 9 inches.

The *float* is of wood, fastened by *two rivets* to a cross bar; it is put in before the top is fastened on. The *handle* of the float is fastened to it with *two rivets,* and it is connected with the bail of the bucket by a *chain.* The *bail* is fastened to the bucket by *two ears,* each held by *three rivets.* A *toggle,* which is fastened to the bail by *two links* and a *swivel,* serves to attach the bucket to the eye of the axle strap on the gun carriage.

TAR BUCKET. The bucket is made of sheet iron, No. 13, like the sponge bucket. The *cover* is fastened to the top by a rivet on which it turns, and it is kept closed by shutting over a stud riveted into the top. The *ears* are fastened to the bucket each by *three rivets;* a *ring,* for suspending the bucket on its hook, is connected with the ears by *two chains.* Diameter of bucket 7.2 inches; height 8 inches.

WATER BUCKET, for the travelling forge. The *staves* and the *bottom* are of oak; there are sixteen staves, and the bottom is made of not more than two pieces. *Three hoops*, made of hoop iron, No. 16; each hoop is joined together with *two rivets*, No. 1, and fastened to the bucket with *two rivets*. *Two ears* let into the sides, and fastened each by *one rivet*. The *bail* has a *link* connected with it by a *swivel*. Diameter at top 11 inches; bottom 10.25 inches; height 11 inches.

WATER BUCKET, for garrison service. It is made in a similar manner with the preceding, except that the bail has no link and swivel attached to it. Diameter at top 10.25 inches; bottom, 13.5 inches; height 11 inches.

WATERING BUCKET, for field service, made of sole leather. The bottom is of two thicknesses, fastened to each other with 25 *copper rivets*, and to the sides with 61 *rivets;* the side seams fastened with 28 *rivets*, all 0.5 inch long. A rim of sheet copper, No. 24, is fastened on the upper edge with 14 *copper rivets;* 2 *ears* for the bail, fastened each with 4 *rivets*, 0.62 inch long. The *bail* is of round iron 0.5 inch thick. Interior diameter of the bucket at top 12 inches; at bottom, 10 inches; height 9 inches.

SHOVEL—*blade* sheet iron, pointed with steel—length 12 inches; width 10.5 inches—*handle* (ash) 1.5 inch thick at bottom, and 1.25 inch at top; length 45 inches—*ring*, 1.5 inch diameter, secured by a *strap* to the handle at 9 inches from the upper end.

PICKAXE; iron, pointed at both ends with steel—length of each blade 6.5 inches; width of edge of axe 3 inches—*handle* (hickory) about 1.5 inch by 1.25 inch, and 30 inches long.

FELLING AXE—*blade* with steel edge, length 7.25 inches; width of top 3.5 inches, of edge 4.75 inches; thickness at top 0.75 inch, at the eye 1.25 inch; size of the eye 2.25 inches by 0.75 inch—*handle* (hickory) 27 inches long.

HAND BILL, OR BILL HOOK; (iron with steel edges)—*blade*, whole length 8.25 inches; width in the middle 3 inches, near the shank 2.7 inches; thickness 0.25 inch—*hook* 1 inch long—*shank* 8 inches long—*handle* (hickory) 7.5 inches long.

DRAG ROPE; 4 inch rope 28 feet long, with a *thimble* worked in a loop at one end, and a *thimble and hook* at the other end—6 *handles*, wood, 12 inches long, 1.5 inch in diameter, fastened in the rope at the distance of 4 feet apart, and at the same distance from the ends of the rope.

MEN'S HARNESS; 4 inch rope 18 feet long, with *thimbles* and a *hook* like the drag rope—instead of handles, 10 *loops* made of strips of bag leather 5 feet long, 2.75 inches wide, are fastened to the rope in pairs, each pair being secured in place by two knots worked on the rope; the first pair of loops at 3 feet from he hook; the others, at a distance of 3½ feet apart.

SCREW JACK; for field service. The *stand*, (cast iron;) the *hoisting screw;* the *nut;* 2 *handles;* the *cap plate*, fastened on the top of the stand by 4 *screws*. Height of the stand 19 inches; length of screw 15 inches; handles 7.25 inches each.

Weights af Implements and Equipments.

KIND.		Weight.
		Lbs.
Woollen sponges.	42-pdr..	0.7
	32-pdr..	0.65
	24-pdr..	0.5
	18-pdr..	0.4
	12-pdr..	0.35
	6-pdr..	0.25
Sponge covers....	42-pdr..	0.28
	6-pdr..	0.14
Trail handspike............		7.25
Manœuvring handspike.....		8.25
Shod handspike and long manœuvring handspike .		12.
Truck handspike...........		18.5
Roller handspike...........		7.
Linstock...................		0.9
Port-fire stock		0.65
Pass box...................		7.
Budge barrel		15.5
Gunner's havresack		1.86
Port-fire case..............		1.55
Tube pouch		0.95
Priming horn..............		0.86
Priming wire..............		0.08
Gunner's gimlet...........		0.08
Vent punch................		0.08
Thumbstall		0.003
Port-fire cutter............		0.77
Tangent scale..............		0.21
Pendulum hausse and case ..		0.65
Cannon lock...............		2.75
Lock cover................		0.9
Vent cover................		0.45
Lanyard for friction primers.		0.10
Fuze setter................		2.66
Fuze mallet................		2.75
Fuze saw		0.75
Fuze rasp..................		0.75
Fuze auger.................		0.3
Fuze gimlet................		0.1
Shell plug screw		0.31

KIND.		Weight.
		Lbs.
Fuze plug reamer		0.3
Fuze extractor..............		3.53
Gunner's pincers...........		0.85
Gunner's callipers..........		0.5
Gunner's quadrant, wood ...		0.84
Gunner's perpendicular.....		0.6
Maul......................		10.
Pointing wire..............		0.08
Quoin, for siege mortars		7.
Chock.....................		1.4
Plummet..................		1.
Scraper....................		2.3
Spatula		0.75
Splint		0.03
Gunner's sleeve............		0.25
Basket....................		4.
Tarpaulins	Small...	9.
	Large ..	54.
Mortar tompions.	8-inch .	5.
	10-inch .	7.
Broom (hickory)...........		3.75
Shell hooks................		2.
Tow hooks		0.6
Funnel....................		0.32
Powder measures.	4 oz.....	0.3
	8 oz.....	0.5
	1 lb.....	0.75
	3 lbs....	1.6
Prolonge..................		18.
Sponge bucket.............		10.
Tar bucket................		7.
Water bucket, wood........		10.
Watering bucket, leather....		8.
Shovel....................		4.75
Pickaxe		6.5
Felling axe................		6.
Hand bill		2.
Drag rope.................		16.5
Men's harness.............		23.
Screw Jack................		25.

Preservation and arrangement in Store.

Implements collected together according to kind and calibre, in a dry place, arranged on shelves or racks, in bundles or bunches, or in boxes, according to their nature, with marks and labels showing the kind and number of the articles.

Sponges, rammers, ladles and worms complete, placed on pins in a vertical frame, or suspended vertically or horizontally by racks or hooks, from the joists, supported so as not to bend.—When in separate parts, the *heads* piled on shelves or on the floor, and the *staves* tied up in bundles, according to kind and calibre.

The *woollen sponges* should be preserved from moths by means of camphor, pepper, &c., or by being sealed up in strong paper bags.

Handspikes, in square piles, heads and points alternating.

Leather Equipments—hung on pins or hooks, in dry and cool rooms.

All wood painted, except tool handles—Iron either painted or oiled—See CHAPTER VII.

Sappers and miner's tools, arranged in piles, the iron coated with varnish—See CHAPTER VII.

CHAPTER FIFTH.

ARTILLERY HARNESS.—Plate 13.

The construction of the field carriages requires a harness different, in some respects, from that of common wagons. The limber having no sweep bar, the pole is supported directly by the wheel horses, by means of a chain which connects the hames with the pole yoke of the limber; and, in order to diminish the weight at the end of the pole, the leading bars are dispensed with, the traces of the leaders being attached to those of the wheel horses.

The same harness is perfectly adapted also to the siege carriages; but, as these are arranged for draught in the ordinary manner, common wagon harness may be used with them, if necessary.

Black leather is used for the harness, when not otherwise specified ; it should be of the best quality, and the strongest leather is selected for the parts which are exposed to the greatest strain, such as traces and breeching. The leather is sewed with strong waxed thread, in double stitch, with about eight stitches to the inch. The seam along an edge is 0.15 inch or 0.2 inch from the edge. The awls should be small for the thread. The ends of the thread should be well fastened before they are cut off.

Straps, or other pieces which have buckles or iron loops attached to them, are generally doubled on a length equal to twice their width, to receive the buckle or loop, which is fastened by two seams. The double end is shaved down.

Standing loops are placed close to the buckles. Their ends are shaved down, brought together, and fastened between the two parts of the strap, if it is doubled.

The tongue holes for buckles are made with a punch corresponding to the size of the tongue. Their distance apart is generally equal to the width of the strap, and the first hole is at double that distance from the end of the strap. This end is shaved down and reduced in width, to facilitate its entrance into the buckle.

The buckles, loops, rings, and hooks are of wrought iron japanned, (black.) The buckles are all made with rollers.

NOTE.—A *layer* is a piece of leather sewed upon another piece, to strengthen it.

A *chape* is a piece used to fasten a buckle or a loop to a strap, or other piece of leather.

A *billet* is a strap which enters a buckle.

A *safe* is a piece of leather placed under a buckle, &c., to prevent it from chafing.

Head Gear.

The head gear is made of strong, black bridle leather, not less than 0.1 inch thick.

HALTER. *One crown piece*, having a billet at each end, for the buckles of the cheek straps.

Two cheek straps. Each of them is sewed to a square *iron loop*, and has at the upper end a *buckle*, with *one standing* and *one sliding loop*.

One brow band, having a loop at each end, through which the crown piece passes.

One nose band, sewed to the same loop as the cheek straps.

Two chin straps. They are doubled, and are sewed to the loops of the cheek straps, and also to another *square iron loop* in rear.

One throat strap. It is made double and sewed to the last mentioned iron loop; its upper end is formed into a loop to receive the throat lash.

One throat lash, with *one buckle*, *one standing* and *one sliding loop* on the left side. It passes through the loops in the brow band and the throat strap.

One chain, (common halter chain.) It consists of about 65 links, No. 1, connected by *two rings* and a *swivel*. It is fastened by a ring to the loop which connects the chin straps of the halter. The other end of the chain has a *toggle* and a *loose ring*, to hitch with. Whole length of chain, 4½ feet.

BRIDLE. *One crown piece.* It is split at each end, so as to form, at one end, *two billets* for the buckles of the cheek straps, and at the other, one billet and one buckle strap, with a *buckle* and a *standing loop* for the *throat lash*.

One brow band, formed into a loop at each end for the crown piece to pass through.

Two cheek straps. Each of them is sewed at the lower end into an *iron loop*, and has at the upper end a *buckle*, with *one standing* and *one sliding loop*, to fasten it to the crown piece. *Two billets* for attaching the bit to the loops of the cheek straps. Each billet has a *buckle* with *one standing* and *one sliding loop*.

Two reins. Each rein is sewed to a *billet*, which has a *buckle*, a *standing* and a *sliding loop*, for attaching it to the bit. The short rein is on the near side, and has a *buckle*, a *standing* and a *sliding loop*, for the billet of the long rein.

THE BIT. It is made of iron, tinned. The *bars* are riveted into the *cheek pieces*. There should be different degrees of severity in the curve of the *port mouth*. The width of the bit, between the cheeks, also varies for three sizes, viz: 4⅞ inch, 5 inch, and 5¼ inch; about three-fifths being of the medium size.

The *curb chain* consists of 19 links, diminishing in size from the middle towards each end. It is attached by an *S* to the right cheek piece, and by a *hook* to the left.

Driver's Saddle.

WOOD. The frame of the tree is made of beech, and consists of the *pommel*, the *cantle*, and *two side bars*, which are notched into the pommel and cantle. The frame is covered with *canvas*, which is glued on and painted.

IRON. *Two pommel plates.* The upper one is fastened by *six rivets* passing through both plates; the lower one by two additional *rivets* in each end, one of which holds one end of the stirrup bar. *One cantle plate*, fastened on the under side of the cantle and the side bars by *ten rivets*.

Two stirrup bars. The front end fastened to the pommel by one of the rivets of the lower pommel plate; the rear end fastened to the side bar by *one rivet*. The *stay* is formed of a piece of iron bent round the stirrup bar, and fastened to the side bar by *one rivet*. There is a roller on each side of the stay, for the stirrup and girth billets to pass over.

Two loops, with rollers; one fastened to the pommel, the other to the cantle, by two of the rivets which hold the plates. The saddle tree is covered with hemp webbing and strong tow linen, stretched on and nailed to the tree.

LEATHER. The *seat* is covered with black upper leather, and stuffed with deer's hair. *Two skirts* are sewed, with welts, to the cover of the seat. *Two iron loops*, for holster straps, are fastened to the front of the saddle by leather loops which pass through slits in the skirts, and are nailed to the tree.

Two inner skirts, or flaps, nailed to the side bars, protect the pad from being chafed by the stirrup and girth leathers. The *pad* is made of russet sheep skin, lined with strong linen, and faced with black sheep skin; it is stuffed with deer's hair, and quilted.

Two iron loops, for cloak straps, are fastened by leather loops, which are nailed to the under side of the cantle.

One billet, for the collar strap, is sewed to the upper loop on the pommel.

Two girth billets, and *two billets* for the trace loops, are sewed on the stirrup bars, behind the middle stay.

Two stirrup leathers pass over the stirrup bars in front of the stay; the *buckle*, with *one standing* and *one sliding loop*, is sewed to the thin end of the strap, which is doubled and stitched, on a length of 8 inches, where it passes through the eye of the stirrup.

The *girth* is of thick black leather. It has a *buckle* and a *standing loop* fastened to each end by a layer.

The pommel and the cantle are plated with *sheet brass*, No. 20, fastened with brass tacks.

Valise Saddle.

WOOD: The frame of the tree is made like that of the driver's saddle, except in its dimensions.

IRON: The *lower pommel plate* is fastened by *ten rivets*, six of which also hold the *upper plate*. These plates have holes in them for the shank of the bridle hook. The hole in the upper plate is square; that in the lower, round.

The *cantle plate* is fastened under the cantle with *eight rivets*.

The *hook* for the reins is fastened to the top of the pommel by a *nut*. The end of the shank should be riveted over the nut.

Two loops, for the collar strap and the crupper, are fastened to the pommel and cantle, as in the driver's saddle. *Four oval rings*, for the valise straps, are fastened by staples which are driven into the tree; two of them in the side bars and two in the cantle.

LEATHER: The *seat* and the *pad* are formed as in the driver's saddle, but the seat is not stuffed. The *skirts* are joined in a similar manner to the cover of the seat.

The *girth* is of leather, and is sewed to the off skirt of the saddle; it has a *buckle* and *two loops*, fastened to it by a layer. A *billet* for the girth is sewed to the near skirt.

Two billets, for the trace loops, pass through the skirts, and are nailed to the side bars.

Two valise straps, each with a *buckle*, a *standing* and a *sliding loop*.

A *billet* for the collar strap is sewed to the iron loop on the pommel.

The *crupper strap* is double. It is sewed to the iron loop on the cantle, and has another *loop*, with a roller, attached to the rear end, for the back strap of the crupper to pass through, so that the same crupper may fit both saddles.

Valise.

The valise is made of black bridle leather, and lined with cotton ticken. The lining is pasted to the inside of the valise; it is sewed round the borders of the outer cover, forming a pocket which has an opening in the middle. The *inner flap* is held down by a *strap* passing through *six staples* of iron wire, No. 12, and fastened by a *buckle* and *loop;* a strip of leather is stitched over the inner ends of the staples.

The ends of the valise are double.

The *cover* is fastened down by *three billets* and *three buckle straps* and *loops*. The *handles* are of leather, rounded and sewed into the ends. *Two loops*, 1 inch wide, for the valise straps to pass through, are sewed to the bottom of the valise.

Whip.

The *stock* is of hickory or of raw hide, about 30 inches long. It is covered with braided leather. A *loop* for the hand is fastened to the butt of the whip.

The leather should be well fastened together at the small end. A *lash* of thread is tied on, and not plaited in with the leather.

Leg Guard.

The *body* is made of stout kip leather; *two layers* are stitched to the upper and lower parts. The *under strap*, to pass under the foot, is sewed to the bottom. *Four leg straps*, each with a *buckle* and a *loop*, are fastened to the body of the leg guard, under the plate. The billet ends of these straps pass through slits in the body.

The *plate* is of iron 0.1 inch thick, and is fastened to the body with *five rivets.*

Nose Bag.

The *bottom* is made of stiff leather, 6 inches diameter and 4 inches deep, to which a bag of strong linen is sewed. Width of bag at the top, 15 inches; whole height, 15 inches. The head strap, 1 inch wide, has a buckle strap 6 inches long, and a billet 34 inches long, sewed to the bag.

Draught Harness.

THE COLLAR. The *rim* is made of bridle leather, and stuffed with uncut rye straw. The *belly*, made of upper leather, in two pieces, is stuffed with straw cut into pieces not longer than $\frac{1}{4}$ inch. The collars are of 2 sizes, 17 and 20 inches; they are made open at the top, and the size is further varied by *two buckle straps* and *two billets* sewed to the open ends. A *pad*, made of black sheep skin, stuffed with deer's hair, protects the neck of the horse from being chafed by these straps.

THE HAMES are made of iron, and painted black. The *branches* have studs forged on them to receive the bolts of the *joint loops* for the trace tugs; these loops turn freely on the bolts. *Two links*, for supporting the breast strap, are welded into the eyes of the bolts.

Two rings, for the trussing straps, are welded into the rectangular eyes at the upper ends of the branches. The branches are joined together, at the lower ends, by a *clasp* which is made fast to the off branch. The *chain* and *toggle*, for connecting the pole yoke with the hames, are fastened to the hames clasp.

Two leather safes are sewed round the branches, under the joint loops, to protect the collar from being chafed by the trace tugs.

Two trace tugs, made of four layers of leather, 0.63 inch thick, are stitched into the joint loops and into *two loop rings* through which the traces pass.

Two trussing straps, each with *one buckle*, *one standing*, and *one sliding loop*, pass through the rings in the upper ends of the hames. They are used for trussing up the harness.

One hames strap, with a *buckle* and *two loops*, connects the two branches together at the top.

One collar strap, having *one buckle* and *one loop*, passes round the hames strap, and is buckled to the billet on the pommel of the saddle, to keep the collar in place.

THE TRACES, for the wheel and the leading harness, are alike, except in the length of the leather part.

The leather trace is made of three layers of leather, making a thickness of 0.63 inch. An *iron loop* is fastened to each end with *three rivets*, 0.25 inch thick.

The trace chains are made of iron 0.3 inch diameter. The front chain has *five links* and a *toggle*. The rear chain has *fourteen links*, *four rings*, (oval,) and a *toggle*.

Two trace loops. The loop is formed by doubling the leather. It has at the upper end a *buckle* and a *standing loop*, by means of which it is connected with the billet on the saddle. At the lower end of each trace loop is an *iron loop*, to which the belly band is sewed. The *belly band* is made in two parts, one being a billet, and the other having a *buckle* and a *standing loop*.

One loin strap, for supporting the traces. It is the same for the wheel and the leading harness, except in length. A *layer* is sewed under the middle of the wheel loin strap, forming a loop through which the back strap of the crupper passes. Each end of the loin strap is buckled into a *loop*, like those just described, through which the trace passes.

THE CRUPPER. The *dock* is made of a piece of leather, 3.5 inches wide and 14 inches long, which is doubled and rounded, without being stuffed. A *buckle* and a *standing loop* are sewed to each end. The *body* of the crupper is split, at the rear end, into two billets which connect it with the buckles of the dock. At the other end are a *buckle* and *four loops* for the billet of the back strap. A *layer*, 10 inches long, is sewed on the body, leaving an opening for the hip strap to pass through; a short *layer* is inserted under the first, in rear of this opening. The *back strap* is sewed in under the first layer in front of the opening for the hip strap. The back strap, passing through the loop in the middle of the loin strap, and through the iron crupper loop on the saddle, returns to the buckle on the body of the crupper. A *sliding loop* holds the two parts together, near the saddle.

Breeching.

The breech strap is made of thick harness leather. A *layer*, also of stout leather, is stitched on the outside of the strap. A *buckle* and *three standing loops* are fastened, at each end, by both these pieces of leather, which are turned back three or four inches and stitched down. *Two iron loops* are fastened by chapes sewed to the breech strap.

Four tugs, for the hip straps, are fastened to the breech strap; two of them in the buckles, and two in the iron loops. These tugs are made double, and have each a *buckle* and *three standing loops* attached to them. A *safe* is sewed to the inside of each tug, to prevent it from chafing the horse.

The hip strap is made in one piece, split at each end into two billets which buckle into the tugs of the breech strap.

The breast strap is made of three layers put together in such a manner as to make the strap 0.63 inch thick in the middle, and 0.5 inch at the ends, where it is buckled to the breech strap. The breast strap is supported by the iron loops on the hames, and by the trace loops attached to the saddle. An *iron loop*, with an eye for the pole chain hook, slides on the middle part of the breast strap; it is covered with leather, to prevent it from chafing the strap.

The *pole chain hook* is like the trace hook of the limber; it is welded into the eye of the sliding loop, and forms a direct connection between the pole and the breeching, independently of the collar and hames.

Harness required for each horse.

PARTS.		WHEELERS.		LEADERS.		Weight.
		Near side.	Off side.	Near side.	Off side.	Lbs.
Halter		1	1	1	1	3.5
Bridle		1	1	1	1	3.
Driver's saddle		1	......	1	......	18.
Valise saddle and valise		......	1	......	1	11.5
Collar and hames		1	1	1	1	16.
Pair of traces	Wheel	1	1	......	......	9.5
	Leading	......	......	1	1	11.5
Trace loops and belly band		1	1	1	1	1.
Loin straps and trace loops.	Wheel	1	1	......	......	1.
	Leading	......	......	1	1	1.
Crupper		1	1	1	1	0.75
Breeching, hip strap and breast strap		1	1	......	......	8.5
Leg guard		1	......	......	......	2.25
Whip		1	......	1	......	0.5
Nose bag		1	1	1	1	1.15
		Lbs.	Lbs.	Lbs.	Lbs.	
WEIGHT.	For each horse	65.15	55.9	56.4	49.4	
	Set for 2 horses	121.05		105.8		

PLATE 13 represents the harness of each horse complete. It shows the manner in which the parts are put together, and also the manner of hitching the horses to the carriage.

Dimensions of the principal leather parts of artillery harness, with the number and size of buckles.

Parts.		Number.	Width.	Length. Cut.	Length. Finished.	Buckles. No.	Buckles. Width
			In.	In.	In.		In.
Halter.	Crown piece	1	1.25	30	30		
	Cheek straps	2	1.25	12.5	8	2	1.25
	Brow band	1	1.25	21	15		
	Nose band	1	1.25	18.5	14		
	Chin straps	2	1.25	12	5.25		
	Throat strap	1	1.25	13.5	6.25		
	Throat lash	1	1.	44	42	1	1
Bridle.	Crown piece	....	1.75	....	31		
	(Crown piece and throat lash)	1	......	44			
	Throat lash	....	.75	....	42	1	.75
	Brow band	1	1.	23	16		
	Cheek straps	2	1.	12.5	8	2	1
	Bit billets	2	1.	12	9	2	1
	Reins, long	1	1.	60	60		
	Reins, short	1	1.	42	40	1	1
	Billets for reins	2	1.	9	9	2	1
Driver's Saddle.	Flaps	2	7.	14			
	Skirts	2	15.5	24.5			
	Billet for collar strap	1	1.25	10	8		
	Girth billets	2	1.25	17	15		
	Trace loop billets	2	1.25	17	15		
	Stirrup leathers	2	1.5	64	56	2	1.5
	Girth	1	2.5	45	45	2	1.25
Valise Saddle.	Skirts	2	11.	15	15		
	Girth billet	1	2.5	26	26		
	Girth	1	2.5	41	41	1	1.5
	Trace loop billets	2	1.25	18	18		
	Billet for collar strap	1	1.25	10	8		
	Crupper strap	1	1.25	11	5		
	Valise straps	2	1.	37	35	2	1
Valise.	Body	1	18.	25			
	Ends	2	6.25	7.25			
	Inner flap	1	4.	16			
	Strap for flap	1	.88	18	18	1	.88
	Cover	1	.10	20.3			
	Buckle straps	3	.88	4	2	3	.88
	Billets for buckle straps	3	.88	7.5	7.5		

Table of Dimensions—Continued.

PARTS		Number.	Width.	LENGTH.		BUCKLES.	
				Cut.	Finished.	No.	Width
			In.	In.	In.		In.
LEG GUARD.	Body	1	.17	20.5			
	Foot strap	1	.88	14	14		
	Leg straps	4	.75	26	24	4	0.75
COLLAR AND HAMES.	Collar billets	2	1.	11	11	2	1.
	Trace tugs	2	1.75	17	7		
	Trussing straps	2	1.	34	32	2	1.
	Hames strap	1	1.25	21	18	1	1.25
	Collar strap	1	1.25	15	9	1	1.25
TRACES AND STRAPS.	Wheel traces	2	1.75	50	50		
	Leading traces	2	1.75	96	96		
	Trace loops	2	1.25	21	9	2	1.25
	Belly band	1	1.25	31	25	1	1.25
		1	1.25	16	13		
	Loin straps, wheel	1	1.25	48	48		
	leading	1	1.25	60	60		
	layer	1	1.25	6	6		
	loops	2	1.25	23	10	2	1.25
CRUPPER.	Dock	1	3.5	14	14	2	0.88
	Body	1	1.75	20	20	1	1.25
	Layer for body	1	1.25	10	10		
	Back strap	1	1.25	31	31		
BREECHNIG.	Breech strap	1	2.5	48	42	2	1.75
	Layer for breech strap	1	1.75	50	42		
	Tugs	4	1.25	13	6	4	1.25
	Safes	4	2.25	6	6		
	Hip strap	1	2.5	48	48		
	Breast strap	1	1.75	......	150		

Leather, &c., required for 1 set of wheel and 1 set of leading harness, for 2 horses each.

Harness leather	8 sides.
Bridle leather	5½ sides.
Collar	6 sides.
Horse skin	2 sides.
Russet sheep skins	6½
Black sheep skins	2
Deer's hair	12 lbs
Hemp webbing	5 yds.

1 side of collar leather makes 14 whips.

Preservation of Harness in Store.

The store houses should be well ventilated, not too dry, but free from dampness. The different articles should be arranged according to kind and class, separated or in bundles according to their nature, so placed as to touch each other and the walls as little as possible, having a free circulation of air about them—*saddles* on trestles or bars—*collars* hung on pins—*hames*, with their straps, and *traces* with chains and hooks, hung up ; the traces hanging vertically—*side pipes* and *belly bands* piled on the floor or on shelves—*surcingles* and *breast straps* stretched on racks—*halters, bridles, reins*, &c., hung up in bundles of five or ten—*hames straps, collar straps*, &c., hung up in bundles of ten or twenty—*bits, curb chains, trace hooks*, in boxes.

All these articles should be examined and cleaned at least four times a year.

The leather articles are brushed and greased with *neat's foot oil*, as often as their condition requires: if they have a reddish hue, mix a little lamp black with the oil. First brush the leather carefully, then pass over it a sponge wet with luke warm water ; grease it slightly on the hair side, applying the oil with a soft brush before the leather is quite dry. In general, new leather is not greased until it has been in store three years, unless it should be found to require it. Iron parts which are not japanned or tinned, or from which the coating is rubbed off, are greased with tallow.

CHAPTER SIXTH.

MOUNTAIN ARTILLERY.

The carriage and most of the equipments for mountain service being of a peculiar kind, all the details relative to them are collected, for more convenient reference, in this chapter.

The ordnance for mountain service is the light 12-pdr. howitzer, described in Chapter I.

The gun carriage is adapted to transportation on a pack horse; but for occasional draught when the roads permit, it is furnished with a thill, which is used with the same saddle that carries the pack.

GUN CARRIAGE.—*Plate* 14.

Wood: 1 *stock*, in two pieces; 2 *dowels;* 1 *axletree.*

Iron.

3 *assembling bolts;* 4 *washers;* 3 *nuts.*
2 *washer hooks*, (drag hooks.)
2 *trunnion plates;* 6 *nails.*
2 *bolts*, for do.; 2 *nuts.*
2 *chin bolts;* 2 *nuts.*
2 *key bolts;* 2 *nuts.*
2 *cap squares;* 2 *eye pins.*
2 *cap square chains;* 2 *eye pins.*
2 *cap square keys.*
2 *key chains;* 2 *eye pins.*
2 *implement hooks.*
2 *staples*, for straps.
1 *lunette;* 2 *rivets;* 6 *nails.*
1 *trail plate;* 6 *nails.*
1 *knee*, for trail plate; 2 *rivets.*
1 *handspike staple.*
2 *friction plates*, for shaft; 4 *nails.*
1 *box*, for elevating screw.
2 *bolts*, for do.; 2 *washers;* 2 *nuts.*
1 *elevating screw.*
1 *axle skean.*
1 *axle bolt;* 2 *washers;* 1 *nut.*
2 *rivets*, for axle arms; 4 *burrs.*
2 *ferrules*, for axle arms; 2 *rivets.*
2 *axle bands;* 4 *nails.*
2 *understraps.*
2 *linch pins.*

2 wheels.

Wheel.

Wood: 1 *nave;* 12 *spokes;* 6 *fellies;* 6 *dowels.*
Iron. 4 *nave bands;* 12 *nails.*
1 *tire;* 6 *tire bolts;* 6 *washers;* 6 *nuts.*
1 *nave box*, (brass.)

Thill.

WOOD: 2 *shafts;* 1 *cross bar.*

IRON: 1 *cross bar plate;* 2 *bolts* and 2 *nails*, for do.; 4 *rivets;* 11 *screws.*
1 *supporting bar.*
1 *key;* 1 *key chain;* 1 *eye pin.*
2 *staples;* 4 *burrs*, for do.

In attaching the thill to the gun carriage the supporting bar is laid on the trail plate, near the handspike staple, and the knee in rear of the lunette rests on the cross bar plate, the holes for the key in these two pieces corresponding with each other.

IMPLEMENTS AND EQUIPMENTS.

One handspike, (HICKORY OR OAK.) At the small end it has a *strap* fastened by *two rivets*, forming a loop by which to hang the handspike on its hook. At eight inches from the other end there is a *stop* like that on the handspike of a field carriage. A *loop of rope* fastened in two holes at the middle of the handspike serves to assist in placing the gun on the pack saddle. Length 45.58 inches.

One sponge and rammer. The *staff* (ASH) has a tenon at one end for the rammer head, which is fastened by one wooden pin, and at the other for the sponge head, fastened by two pins. The rammer head is countersunk at the end, to avoid striking the fuze in ramming a shell. The neck has a *copper band*, fastened by *three nails*. Diameter of rammer head 3.24 inches; of sponge head 2.5 inches. Whole length 49 inches.

Near the rammer head an *eye pin* is riveted into the staff, for the purpose of attaching the implement to the carriage, and in the middle of the staff is a *loop of rope*, like that in the handspike, and for a similar use.

One linstock. Diameter 1 inch; length 24 inches.

One havresack. *One tube pouch*, for primers. *One ditto*, for fuzes. *One sponge cover.* *One priming wire.* *One gunner's gimlet.* *One vent cover.* *One fuze plug reamer.* *One gunner's pincers.* *Two lanyards*, for friction tubes. *One small tarpaulin.*	} Like those for field service, CHAP. IV.

PACK SADDLE.—*Plate* 14.

Wood: *Two arcs*, for the frame. They are made each of three pieces, glued together and fastened by *six screws* in the front arc, and *eight screws* in the rear arc.

Two transoms. They have circular notches for the trunnions of the gun to lie in. They are fastened to the arcs by bolts which traverse their whole length, and by *one screw* in each end.

One cross bar. It is let into the transoms, and fastened to them by *two screws* in each end.

Two inner side bars. They are fastened to the arcs by *three screws* in each end.

Two outer side bars. They are mortised into the arcs. Each of these bars has a piece of leather nailed on the outside, where the lashing rope passes round it, for securing the pack on the saddle.

Two round bars. They connect the lower ends of the arcs, to which they are joined by round tenons and mortises, and fastened by *one screw* in each end. This screw serves also to strengthen the bearing notch for the ammunition chest.

Iron. *Two arc plates*. They are fastened on the outside of the arcs, each by *two rivets* and by the assembling bolts. They have hooks at each end, for attaching the lashing chains of the ammunition and tool chests. Each plate has a *staple* riveted to it in the middle. To the staple on the front plate a wooden button is strapped, to hook the bridle on. The crupper strap is attached to the staple on the rear plate.

Two assembling bolts. They pass through the transoms, connecting the front and rear arcs together. *Two nuts* for these bolts.

Four staples, for confining the lashing straps. They are fastened to the arcs by *two rivets* in each.

Leather. *Four billets*, for lashing straps. They are fastened near the head of the arcs, each by *one screw* and a staple.

Four buckle straps, for the same. They are fastened to the inside of the arcs, at the lower end, each by *one screw*.

Two buckle straps, for the billets of the shoulder straps. They are fastened to the front arc, each by *one screw* and *two nails*.

One cover, (bridle leather.) It is stretched over the inner side bars and nailed to the inside of the arcs. A strip of thin leather is put under the heads of the nails. Two flaps, of harness leather, are sewed to the lower ends of the cover.

Two thill straps. They pass over the round bars and form loops for the shafts of the gun carriage.

One lining, (thick black leather.) It is nailed to the inside of the arcs and sewed to the flaps of the cover, below the round bars.

Six girth billets. They are sewed to the lining, three on each side of the saddle.

Four iron loops, for the breeching and breast straps. They are held by leather loops which are sewed to the lining.

One girth, (strong hemp webbing.) It has three buckles sewed to each end, with leather loops.

One pad. The upper side is made of sheep skin; the lining, of strong canvas. It is stuffed with straw and deer's hair and stitched in the usual manner. The pad is fastened to the lining of the saddle with ten leather thongs.

HARNESS.—*Plate* 14.

The same harness is used for the packs and for draught, except that the lashing girth and lashing rope are not required for the latter purpose.

The harness is made of black leather, like that for field artillery.

Bridle.

One crown piece. One end is split into two billets, and the other into a billet and buckle strap, for the throat lash and cheek pieces.

One buckle and *one standing loop*, for the throat lash.

One buckle and *loop*, attached to the top of the crown piece; for the billets of the winker straps.

One brow band. It is formed into a loop at each end, through which the crown piece passes.

Two cheek straps. Each strap has *two buckles* and *five standing loops.* The upper end of the strap is buckled to the billet of the crown piece; the lower end passes through the ring of the bit.

Two winkers. They are sewed to the cheek straps and supported at the front part by *two straps*, which are fastened in the buckle at the top of the crown piece.

One leading rein. It is sewed into the ring on the right end of the bit, and passes through the other ring. A *wooden button* is sewed into a loop at the loose end of the rein, with a leather washer inside of it.

THE BIT. It consists of a *bar* and *two rings*, made of iron and tinned.

Halter.

The halter and its chain are like those used for the field artillery.—CHAP. V

Crupper.

The dock, with a *buckle* and *loop* at each end, by which it is connected with *the body* of the crupper, the rear end of the latter being split into two billets for that purpose.

The back strap. It is sewed to the crupper and passes through the staple on the rear arc plate of the saddle. *One buckle*, with *three standing loops* and a *sliding loop*, for the billet of the back strap.

The loin strap passes between the back strap and the body of the crupper. The ends are two billets to which the breeching is buckled.

Breeching.

The breech strap. To each end of it is sewed a *side strap*, with a *buckle* and *four standing loops.* These side straps pass through two iron loops on the pack saddle, or through the staples in the shafts, when the harness is used for draught.

Two buckle straps. Each strap has a *buckle* and *three standing loops.* It is fastened to the breech strap by an *iron loop* and a *chape.* A *safe* is sewed under each strap, its whole length. These buckle straps receive the billets of the loin strap which support the breeching.

Breast Strap.

The breast plate. A *billet strap*, with a *buckle* and *three loops*, is sewed to each end of the breast plate. These billets are buckled into the front iron loops on the pack saddle, or into the staples on the shafts, when the harness is used for draught.

Two shoulder straps. They are sewed to the breast plate, which they support by means of the buckle straps on the front of the pack saddle.

Lashing Girth and Rope.

The girth is a broad piece of thick leather, to each end of which an *iron hook* is fastened. *The lashing rope;* $2\frac{1}{2}$ inch rope, 10 feet long; it is used, with the girth, to secure the pack on the saddle.

AMMUNITION.

The ammunition for the mountain howitzer consists of *shells*, *spherical case shot* and *canisters*, to all of which the cartridge is fixed, by means of a sabot.

For instructions relative to the manner of fixing the ammunition, see CHAP. X.

The charge of powder is uniformly 8 oz.

The cartridge bag is made of woollen stuff:

Diameter of circular bottom, cut	4	inches.
Length of rectangle	10.42	"
Height	5	"
Diameter of cartridge finished	2.8	"

Sabots.

DIMENSIONS.		For shell or Sph. case.	For Canister.
		In.	In.
Whole height		2.7	3.75
Height of conical part		2.	2.55
Diameter of conical part.	Top	4.2	4.52
	Bottom	3.24	3.24
Diameter at the bottom of the sabot		2.8	2.8
Cavity for the shell.	Depth	1.3	
	Radius of curvature	2.26	
Cylinder for tin canister.	Diameter	....	4.47
	Height	....	0.5
Distance from middle of groove to bottom of sabot		0.55	0.55
Width of groove		0.3	0.3
Depth of groove		0.15	0.15

Straps and Rings for Shells.

The shell or spherical case is fixed to the sabot by means of 4 *straps* of tin which are hooked into slits in a *ring* of tin round the fuze hole, and are fastened to the sabot, each by 2 *iron tacks.*

Diameter of ring..	Exterior	2.25	inches.
	Interior	1.15	"
Width of straps		0.45	"
Length of strap		7.5	"

Caps for Cartridges.

The cartridge is covered with a paper cap.

Height of paper for cap		4.55	inches.
Width (cylinder developed)		10.	"
Flat former for cap.	Length, exclusive of handle	6.	"
	Width at large end	4.50	"
	Width at small end	4.45	"
	Thickness	0.15	"
Height of cap		2.9	"
Cylindrical former for choking caps	Diameter.	2.9	"
	Height	9.	"

Shells and Spherical Case Shot.

The shells and spherical case shot are the same as for other pieces of the same calibre.

The fuzes are like those for field service, viz: The composition is contained in a paper case, which is inserted, at the moment of firing, into a wooden plug previously driven into the fuze hole.

These fuzes being all of the same length, the time of burning is regulated by the proportions used in making the fuze composition; see CHAPTER X.

The 2 second fuzes are colored *black;* the 3 second, *red;* 4 second, *green.*

After the shell or spherical case has been strapped to the sabot, it is charged with powder; the fuze plug is then driven in, and the hole for the paper fuze reamed out. This hole is then stopped with a plug of tow, pressed in hard. The wooden plug should project about .1 inch from the fuze hole.

Charge of shell	7	oz. rifle powder.
Charge of spherical case	4½	oz. rifle powder.
	78	musket balls.

Canisters.

The canister for the mountain howitzer is filled with musket balls; its dimensions and weight are as follows:

Length of tin for the cylinder, (lap included)	14.4	inches.
Height of do	4.	"
Interior diameter of cylinder	4.47	"
Diameter of plates	4.42	"
Thickness of bottom iron plate	0.25	"
Thickness of sheet iron cover	0.07	"
Number of balls in each tier	37	
Number of tiers of balls	4	
Whole number of balls	148	
Height of finished canister, including sabot	6.85	inches.
Weight of finished canister, including sabot	11.2	lbs.

Fixed Ammunition.

DIMENSIONS AND WEIGHTS.	Shell.	Spherical case.	Canister.
	In.	In.	In.
Height of shell straped, or canister with sabot....	5.92	5.92	6.85
Height of round of fixed ammunition	8.17	8.17	9.1
	Lbs.	Lbs.	Lbs.
Weight of projectile, strapped and loaded........	9.2	11.	11.2
Weight of round of fixed ammunition...........	9.8	11.6	11.8

Primers.

Friction tubes are generally used for the mountain howitzer, for which they are particularly convenient, in dispensing with the lock. But the lock with percussion primers may be used, or the common tube and match.

Packing Ammunition.

DIMENSIONS AND WEIGHTS OF BOXES.	Shells.	Spherical case.	Canisters.
	In.	In.	In.
Interior dimensions. Length..................	27.5	27.5	27.5
Interior dimensions. Width..................	9.25	9.25	9.25
Interior dimensions. Depth..................	8.5	8.5	9.5
Number of rounds in a box..................	12.	12.	12.
	Lbs.	Lbs.	Lbs.
Weight of ammunition......................	117.6	139.2	141.6
Weight of box packed......................	150.	172.	175.

The ammunition is placed upright in the box; the projectiles below, with thin strips of wood under the shells and spherical case, to prevent the fuzes from bearing on the bottom.

For further instructions, relative to the manner in which the boxes are made and packed, see CHAP. X.

In each box there are placed, with the ammunition:

6, 2-second fuzes..(*black*) ..
12, 3-second fuzes..(*red*).... } for the shells and spherical case.
6, 4-second fuzes..(*green*)..

10 priming tubes; 1 port-fire; 2 yards slow match.

AMMUNITION CHEST.

WOOD: 2 *ends;* 2 *sides;* 1 *bottom.*—1 *panel* and 2 *clamps,* for the lid.
2 *beckets,* for the handles; 8 *screws.* 2 HANDLES, of 1 inch rope.

IRON: 1 *brace;* 1 *screw* —1 *stud plate;* 1 *rivet;* 1 *screw;* 1 *turnbuckle.*
4 *corner plates;* 40 *screws;*—2 *hinges;* 26 *screws.*
2 *lashing chains;* 2 *bridles;* 4 *rivets.*—1 *hasp;* 4 *screws.*
1 LINEN COVER, painted, and fastened with 160 copper tacks.
2 *leather loops,* for linstock; 8 *screws.*

INTERIOR DIVISIONS: 8 *long cleats,* for supporting the upper tier of ammunition; they are glued to the sides and fastened by 32 *nails.* 8 *short cleats,* fastened with 8 *screws* and 16 *nails.*

MANNER OF PACKING. The chest contains 8 rounds of fixed ammunition, viz: 2 *shells,* 5 *spherical case,* and 1 *canister.* Four of the spherical case are placed in the bottom tier, with the balls down; the remaining spherical case, the shells, and the canister in the upper tier, with the cartridges down; the canister in the right hand end of the chest. In each chest are placed:

2-second fuzes, (*black*)	4
3-second fuzes, (*red*)	7
4-second fuzes, (*green*)	3
Priming tubes	5
Friction primers	10
Port-fire	1
Slow match	2 yards.

The fuzes and primers wrapped in water proof paper, and the whole load well packed in tow.

A supply of friction primers, equal to half the number of rounds of ammunition belonging to the battery, should be carried in reserve.

Implements and Equipments for each Carriage.

1 handspike } on the carriage.
1 sponge and rammer }
1 sponge cover, on the sponge.
1 vent cover, on the gun.
1 linstock, in the loops on the ammunition chest.
1 havresack, } on the pack, with the ammunition chests.
1 tube pouch, }
1 fuze pouch, }
1 small tarpaulin, }
1 priming wire, in the tube pouch.
1 gunner's gimlet, } in the fuze pouch.
2 lanyards for friction tubes, }
1 gunner's pincers, } in tool chest A.
1 fuze plug reamer, }

PORTABLE FORGE.

The *hearth* is of sheet iron, No. 13, bent into a hollow form, and riveted to an iron *frame*. The *back* of the hearth is bent under the bottom and riveted to it. The *border* of the hearth is bent round the back, and is riveted to it and to the frame. The *back* of the fire place is of sheet iron, No. 13, connected with the back of the hearth by *two brass hinges*, which are riveted to each. The *edges* of both the back pieces are stiffened by strips of sheet iron riveted to them. An *air back* is formed by a piece of sheet iron, No. 7, bent hot into a convex shape, and riveted to the inside of the back plate of the fire-place. A *button*, turning on an axis which is riveted to the outside of the back plate, serves to fasten this plate to a stud in the front border of the hearth, when the back is turned down on its hinges.

The frame is supported by *three legs*, which are connected with it by bolts, so that they can be folded up close to the frame. The front leg is divided into two branches, which are bolted to *two eye pieces* that are riveted to the sides of the frame. The two other legs are connected together by a cross bar, with a nut at each end. This bar supports also the fork in which the bellows handle works. The legs of the frame have round tenons at the lower ends, with shoulders which rest on three socket plates attached to the side of the forge chest, for the forge to stand on when set up for use.

The bellows handle is of iron, with a wooden head. It is attached to a *fork* which fits in a square hole in the cross bar joining the rear legs of the frame. The lower end of the handle is hooked into a *connecting rod* attached to the rear end of the bellows; it is fastened to this rod by a sliding *catch* which is secured by a thumb screw. When the bellows is dismounted, this rod is hooked into an eye on the upper side of the bellows, to keep it closed.

THE BELLOWS. The frame consists of an *upper*, a *lower*, and a *middle plank*, (walnut) and *two ribs*, (poplar,) connected by a *cross head*, as in a common smith's bellows. There are valves in the middle and the lower plank.

A *bar* of iron, attached to the middle plank, terminates in two journals, which support the bellows, fitting in the joints of the rear legs of the frame of the forge.

The *nozzle*, of sheet iron, is inserted into the cross head, above the middle plank. It enters into a *cast iron pipe* which is attached to the rear of the forge back by means of a *bridle* bolted to the back plate of the hearth.

A *handle* is attached to a *plate* which is fastened on the upper bellows plank. A *leaden weight* of one pound is attached to the inside of the lower plank by the rivets which hold the eye plate on the connecting rod.

The *bellows leather* (calfskin) is fastened to the planks by small bellows nails.

THE FORGE BUCKET is of sheet iron, stiffened with a band at top, and furnished with a handle.

THE ANVIL is fitted into a *block* of tough oak, or other hard wood, and fastened by an *iron pin*. The block has a *band* round the top. *Two rings* fastened by *staples* serve for handles.

THE COAL SACK is made of strong leather. It is 14 inches in diameter and 18 inches high; it is closed at the top by a leather strap passing through slits in the sack.

TOOL CHESTS.

Chests for the Forge and Smith's Tools.

The forge and the smith's tools are packed in two chests, which are alike, except in the interior divisions. The forge chest has socket plates, for the legs of the forge to stand on.

WOOD, (walnut.) *Two ends* and *two sides*, dovetailed together. *One bottom* let into the ends and sides and fastened by *thirty-two nails*. *One lid*, made with two *end clamps*, like that of the ammunition chest.

IRONS. *Four corner plates*, of sheet iron, No. 18, fastened each by *eighteen screws*.

Two handles. The straps are turned under the bottom of the chest. They are fastened each by *one rivet* and *four screws*.

Two hinges. The short strap is fastened to the inside of the lid by *one rivet* and *three screws*. The long straps are bent under the bottom of the chest and fastened, each by *three rivets* and *eleven screws*. Two of these rivets hold the *bridle for the lashing chain*, which is placed at the same distance from the bottom as in the ammunition chest.

One hasp. The strap is let into the inside of the cover and fastened with four screws.

One hasp staple and *plate*. The staple is riveted into the plate, which is fastened to the box with *two rivets*.

One linen covering, like that of the ammunition chest.

Three socket plates, fastened on the back of the forge chest, each by *four screws*. They have holes in them for the legs of the frame of the forge to stand in, when it is mounted for use.

Contents of the Forge Chest and manner of packing.

The legs are folded up close to the frame, and the back of the fire-place is turned down on the hearth and fastened by its catch.

The bellows is closed and fastened by the connecting rod, the handle being detached.

The fire-place and *frame* are placed against the back of the chest, the hearth outwards. They are kept in place by a clamp which fits, over the top of the frame, into an iron staple fastened by two screws to the back of the chest.

The *bellows* is placed on its side, with its top against the front of the chest. One journal goes into a hole in a cleat screwed to the bottom. The nozzle is supported by a notched board which is framed into a cleat screwed on the bottom of the chest, and it is held fast by a buckle strap passing through a staple in the board. A clamp, with a hole for the upper journal, goes across the top of the bellows, and is held by staple plates screwed to the front and back of the chest.

The bellows handle hangs on a cleat in the front of the box, towards the right hand, the hook downwards.

One wrench, (for nuts Nos. 1 and 4,) in two iron brackets on the right end of the chest, near the front.

One hand hammer, *One riveting hammer.*	With handles.	Placed upright near the wrench.
One fore punch, *One creaser.*	On same handle.	

Ten pounds of horse shoe nails, in two strong linen bags, packed in tow, in the vacant space to the right of the bellows.

Contents of Smith's Tool Chest and manner of packing.

The anvil and its block are placed in the bottom of the chest ; the head of the anvil in a mortise made in a cleat screwed on the bottom. The block is fastened by a leather strap and buckle to an iron staple in the bottom of the chest.

One water bucket, (iron,) on the anvil block, resting on a moveable cleat which is hollowed out to fit the block and the bucket.

One pair shoeing pincers,
One vice. } In a wooden cleat, on the front of the chest.

One nailing hammer,
One shoeing hammer,
One splitting chisel. } In iron brackets, against the front of the chest.

One pair tongs,
One pritchel, } In a triangular cleat, in the left front corner.

One hardie,
One clinching iron,
One shoeing knife. } In a wooden rack, on the left end.

One poker,
One shovel,
One rake,
One nail punch. } In two wooden racks, on the back of the chest.

One buttress, hung on two hooks in the front of the upper shovel rack, and held fast by a wooden button.

One toe knife, in two cleats, on the back of the chest, near the top.

One rasp,
One square file. } In two racks, on the back of the chest, near the left end.

Two flat files fastened by two cleats and a button to the inside of the lid.

Ten pounds of horse shoe nails, in two bags; one on the bottom at the left end, the other in the water bucket.

The bags of horse shoe nails should be distributed in the two chests so as to equalize and adjust the weight on each side. They should be packed in tow, to prevent injury to the tools.

Carriage maker's Tools and Stores.

The tools and stores for the use of carriage makers, in repairing the carriages and equipments, are packed in two chests, which are like those for the ammunition, but without the interior divisions.

The hasp and *hasp staples* are like those of the forge chest.

The two chests are designated by the letters A and B.

Contents of Carriage maker's Tool Chests.

Chest A.	Chest B.
1 claw hatchet,	1 hand axe,
1 nailing hatchet,	1 claw hatchet,
2 firmer chisels, ½ and ¾ inch,	1 nailing hatchet,
1 trying square,	2 firmer chisels,
1 bevel,	1 firmer gouge,
2 augers, ½ and ⅝ in., and one handle,	1 pair compasses,
1 riveting hammer,	1 trying square, six inches,
1 hand saw,	1 scriber,
1 jack plane,	1 riveting hammer,
1 screw driver,	1 mallet,
1 rule, (two feet,)	3 gimlets,
3 gimlets,	1 screw driver,
2 hand saw files,	1 wood rasp,
2 wood files, twelve inch,	1 oil stone,
2 sickles,	6 brad awls,
1 gunner's gimlet,	2 sickles,
1 priming wire,	1 gunner's gimlet,
1 gunner's pincers,	1 priming wire,
1 fuze plug reamer,	2 papers tacks, 8 oz. and 12 oz.
2 papers of sprigs, 1 in. and 1½ inch,	½ lb. twine,
2 papers of tacks, 8 oz. and 12 oz.,	25 leather thongs,
60 wood screws, ¾ inch, No. 9,	36 wood screws, 1½ in. & 1 in., No. 14,
2 lbs. sash cord,	12 do 2 in., No. 16,
½ lb. twine.	12 nuts, No. 1; 2, No. 2; 6, No. 4.
	12 washers, No. 1.

The sickles are fastened to the front and back of the chests, (inside,) with small cleats at the necks and points. The other articles are securely packed in tow, the edges of the cutting tools being carefully wrapped up, to prevent injury.

Dimensions and Weights of gun carriage and equipment.

DIMENSIONS.	
Gun Carriage.	Inches.
Distance between the inside of trunnion plates	7.
Diameter of trunnion holes	2.75
Depth of axis of trunnions below upper face of trunnion plate	0.62
Distance of axis of trunnions in rear of axis of axletree, the piece being in battery, on horizontal ground	2.5
Distance from axis of trunnions to axis of axletree	8.5
Height of axis of trunnions above the ground	27.
Vertical field of fire { above the horizontal line	9°
Vertical field of fire { below the horizontal line	7°
Distance between the points of contact of wheels and trail with the ground line	43.7
Distance from front of wheels to end of trail, the piece being in battery	71.8
Distance of the muzzle of the piece, in battery, in rear of wheels	2.44
Length of gun carriage, without wheels	61.
Length of thill	73.
Whole length of the axletree	38.25
Track of the wheels	30.2
Height of wheel	38.
Dish of finished wheel	2.
Ammunition Chest, or *Carriage maker's Tool Chest.* { Interior length	32.8
" width	4.75
" depth	9.35
Forge Chest, or *Smith's Tool Chest.* { Interior length	32.8
" width	8.
" depth	16.25
WEIGHTS.	Pounds.
Howitzer	220
Gun carriage, without wheels	157
One wheel	65
Handspike	5
Sponge and rammer	3
Gun carriage complete, with implements	295
Thill	30
Bridle	3
Halter	3.5
Pack saddle and harness	44
Lashing girth and rope	3
Ammunition chest, or carriage maker's tool chest, empty	20
Forge chest, or smith's tool chest, empty	42
Ammunition chest, packed	112
Forge chest, packed	115
Smith's tool chest, packed	117
Coal sack, filled with charcoal	25
Carriage maker's tool chests { A	45
Carriage maker's tool chests { B	45

Packs.

1. The howitzer and the thill of the carriage. Weight 250 pounds.

2. The gun carriage, with wheels and implements. Weight 295 pounds.

3. Two ammunition chests, with the havresack, tube pouch, and fuze pouch, covered with the tarpaulin. Weight 238 pounds.

4. The two forge chests. Weight 232 pounds.

5. The two chests for carriage makers tools, (90 pounds,) with the coal sack, (25 pounds.) Weight 115 pounds.

The same kind of pack saddle serves for each of these packs. Weight of saddle and harness, complete, 53 pounds.

Bill of Timber for Mountain Howitzer Carriage, &c.

NAMES OF PARTS.	Number of pieces.	DIMENSIONS OF EACH PIECE, (ROUGH.)			REMARKS.
		Length.	Width	Thickness.	
Gun carriage body.		In.	In.	In.	
Stock	2	66	9.	7.	Oak.
Axletree	2	44	5.	3.	Young, tough hickory.
Two wheels.					
Nave	2	11	9.	Round	Oak.
Spokes	24	20	2.5	1.5	Do.
Fellies	12	21	5.5	2.5	Do.
One thill.					
Shafts	2	72	3.	2.25	Ash.
Cross-bar	1	33	3.5	2.25	Do.
One ammunition chest.					
Sides and ends	2	44	11.	1.	Poplar.
Bottom	1	36	7.	1.	Do.
Cover and partitions	1	66	8.	1.	Do.
One pack saddle.					
Arcs	1	50	12.	1.25	Ash or beach.
Transoms	1	20	12.	1.75	Do.
Cross bar	1	14	6.	1.25	Do.
Side bars	1	42	12.	0.75	Do.
Round bars	2	20	1.5	1.5	Hickory.
One handspike	1	50	2.5	2.5	Hickory.

Bill of Iron for Mountain Howitzer Carriage.

NAMES OF PARTS.	Width.	Thickness.	Length.	Weight.	REMARKS.
Gun carriage body.	In.	In.	In.	Lbs.	
Cap square and key chains No. 1..	0.15	Round	25.	0.13	
Rivets No. 2, nails No. 1, and staples	.25	Do.	54.	0.73	
Nails No. 2....................	.3	Do.	18.	0.36	
Handspike staple, bolts No. 1, and rivets No. 3................	.375	Do.	44.	1.35	
Implement hooks, and bolt No. 3..	.625	Do.	11.	0.94	
Bolts No. 4.....................	.75	Do.	84.	10.30	
Eye pins No. 1.................	.875	Do.	7.	1.16	
Elevating screw.................	1.75	Do.	11.	7.34	Hammered.
Nuts No. 1.....................	0.75	0.375	1.5	0.12	Do.
Handspike strap and linch pins....	1.	0.5	16.	2.24	
Washers No. 1................	1.25	0.125	2.5	0.11	
Axle bands....................	1.25	0.2	34.	2.38	
Cap square keys................	1.25	0.25	3.	0.26	
Nut No. 3.....................	1.25	0.625	1.25	0.27	
Heads of key and chin bolts......	1.25	0.75	16.	4.20	Hammered.
Nuts No. 4.....................	1.5	0.75	11.	3.47	
Ferrules for axletree............	2.	0.25	15.	2.10	
Washer hooks.................	2.	0.375	8.	1.68	
Understraps....................	2.	0.5	36.	10.08	
Handles for elevating screw.......	2.	1.25	5.	3.50	
Trunnion plates and cap squares...	2.25	1.	42.	26.46	Hammered.
Washers No. 4..................	2.5	0.188	10.	1.31	
Knee of lunette.................	2.5	1.	4.	2.80	Hammered.
Trail plate......................	4.	0.2	12.5	2.80	
Axle skean	4.	0.375	38.	15.96	
Lunette.........................	4.	0.5	18.	10.08	
				112.13	
Box for elevating screw	.....	.....	.....	3.0	Brass.
Two wheels.					
Band nails No. 1................	0.25	Round	48.	0.65	
Tire bolts No. 1................	0.375	Do.	42.	1.29	
Brow bands....................	0.75	0.125	96.	2.50	
Nuts No. 1.....................	0.75	0.375	10.	0.78	
End bands.....................	1.	0.2	82.	4.59	
Washers No. 1..................	1.25	0.125	15.	0.65	
Tires..........................	2.00	0.375	240.	50.40	
				60.86	
Nave boxes....................	.....	.....	.....	10.0	Brass.

Bill of Iron for Mountain Howitzer Carriage.—Continued.

NAMES OF PARTS.	Width.	Thickness.	Length.	Weight.	REMARKS.
Thill.	In.	In.	In.	Lbs.	
Key chain No. 1	0.15	Round	12.	0.06	
Rivets No. 2	0.25	Do.	12.	0.16	
Staples	0.375	Do.	26.	0.80	
Bolts No. 2	0.5	Do.	7.	0.38	
Key	0.75	Do.	4.	0.49	
Supporting bar	1.	0.5	48.	6.72	
Cross bar plate	2.75	0.25	30.	5.78	
				14.39	
Ammunition Chest.					
Chains, and rivets No. 2	0.25	Round	43.	0.60	
Hinges and hasp strap	1.	0.375	38.	4.00	
Bridles and brace	1.	0.5	4.	0.56	
Hasp	1.	0.625	3.5	0.61	
Turnbuckle plate	1.5	0.1	3.5	0.15	
Corner plates	2.4	No.18.	40.	1.35	
				7.27	
Turnbuckle	......	......	......	0.10	Brass.
Pack Saddle.					
Staples and rivets	0.25	Round	12.	0.16	
Bolts	0.375	Do.	37.	1.13	
Nuts	0.75	0.375	1.25	0.10	
Arc plates	1.25	0.2	36.	2.52	
				3.91	

Ranges of Mountain Howitzer.

Charge.	Ball.	Elevation.	Range.	REMARKS.
0.5 lb.	Shell	0°	170 yds.	
		1	300	
		2	392	
		2° 30′	500	Time 2 seconds.
		3	637	
		4	785	Time 3 seconds.
		5	1005	
0.5	Sph. case	0°	150	
		2° 30′	450	Time 2 seconds.
		3	500	
		4	700	Time 2.7 seconds.
		4° 30′	800	Time 3 seconds.
0.5	Canister	4° to 5°	250	

CHAPTER SEVENTH.

PAINTS, LACKERS, ETC.

COMPOSITION AND PREPARATION.

The proportions are given for 100 parts by weight of prepared colors, &c., when not otherwise designated.

A gallon of Linseed oil weighs	7.5	lbs.
Spirits of turpentine	7.25	"
Japan varnish	7.	"
Sperm oil	7.12	"
Neatsfoot oil	7.63	"

Boiled Oil.

Raw linseed oil	103.
Copperas	3.15
Litharge	6.3

Put the copperas and litharge in a cloth bag and suspend it in the middle of the kettle. Boil the oil $4\frac{1}{2}$ hours, with a slow, even fire, so that it may not be burnt: then let it stand and deposit the sediment.

Dryings.

Mixture of copperas and litharge taken from the boiled oil	60
Spirits turpentine	56
Boiled oil	2

The mixture taken from the boiled oil to be ground, and mixed with the turpentine and oil.

Putty.

For filling cracks in wood:

Spanish whiting, pulverized	81.6
Boiled oil	20.4

Made into a stiff paste. If not intended for immediate use, raw oil should be used, as the putty made with boiled oil hardens quickly.

Another kind of putty for the same purpose is made by mixing fine sifted oak saw dust with linseed oil which has been boiled until it assumes a glutinous consistency.

White paint.

	For inside work.	For outside work.
White lead, grouud in oil	80	80
Boiled oil	14.5	9
Raw oil		9
Spirits turpentine	8	4

Grind the white lead in the oil, and add the spirits of turpentine.

New wood work requires about 1 lb. to the square yard, for 3 coats.

Lead color.

White lead, ground in oil	75.
Lampblack	1.
Boiled linseed oil	23.
Litharge	0.5
Japan varnish	0.5
Spirits turpentine	2.5

The lampblack and the litharge are ground separately upon the stone, in oil, then stirred into the white lead and oil; the turpentine and varnish are added as the paint is required for use, or when it is packed in kegs for transportation.

Black paint.

Lampblack	28
Litharge	1
Japan varnish	1
Linseed oil, boiled	73
Spirits turpentine	1

Grind the lampblack in oil; mix it with the oil, then grind the litharge in oil and add it, stirring it well into the mixture. The varnish and turpentine are added last. The paint is used for the iron work of carriages.

Olive Paste.

Yellow ochre, pulverized	68.
Lampblack	1.1
Boiled oil	37.
Spirits turpentine	0.4

Make a thick paste with the ochre and oil, in a paint pot, and with the lampblack and oil in another; grind them together in small portions, and keep the mixture in a tin vessel.

Liquid Olive Color.

Olive paste	61.5
Boiled oil	29.5
Spirits turpentine	5.5
Dryings	3.5
Japan varnish	2.

Stirred together in a paint pot.

Brainard's Paint.

Dissolve 10 lbs. of shellac in 10 gals. of boiling water, adding 30 oz. of sal æratus. Mix this solution with an equal quantity of paint prepared in the usual manner. This paint is economical and durable.

Quantity of paint required for a carriage.

KIND OF CARRIAGE.	Lead color.	Olive.	Black.
	Lbs.	Lbs.	Lbs.
Field gun carriage and limber, with implements	6	10	0.75
Caisson, with limber and implements, &c.	8	15	0.8
Forge, with limber	6	10	1.
Battery wagon, do.	7	13	0.9
Casemate carriage and chassis, with implements	7	14	0.75
Barbette carriage and chassis, with mplements	6	11	1.

A priming of lead color and two coats of olive color are applied to new wood work, and 1 coat of lead color and 1 of black, to the iron work.

Paint for Tarpaulins.

A square yard takes 2 lbs. for 3 coats.

1.—*Olive.*—Liquid olive color 100
Beeswax 6
Spirits turpentine 6

Dissolve the beeswax in the spirits of turpentine, with a gentle heat, and mix the paint warm.

2.—Add 12 oz. of beeswax to 1 gallon of linseed oil, and boil it two hours; prime the cloth with this mixture, and use the same, in place of *boiled oil*, for mixing the paint. Give two coats of paint.

Grey, or *Stone Color*, (for Buildings.)

	1st.	2nd.
White lead, in oil	78.	100.
Boiled oil	9.5	20.
Raw oil	9.5	20.
Spirits of turpentine	3.	
Turkey umber	0.5	
Lampblack	0.25	0.25
Yellow ochre		3.

Mixed like the lead color.

A square yard of new brick work requires, for 2 coats, 1.1 lb.; for 3 coats, 1.5 lb.

Cream Color, (for Buildings.)

	1st coat.	2nd coat.
White lead, in oil	66.66	70.
French yellow	3.33	3.33
Japan varnish	1.33	1.33
Raw oil	28.	24.5
Spirits turpentine	2.25	2.25

square yard of new brick work requires, for 1st coat, 0.75; for 2nd coat, 0.3 lb.

Wash for Buildings.

Boil half a bushel of flaxseed in 5 gallons of water, and use this for slaking 1.5 gals. of lime. Add 1 gal. of salt, 1 gal. of fine sand, and as much water as may be necessary to thin it. Stir it frequently to prevent the sand from settling.

To give this wash a *cream color*, add yellow ochre; for a *grey or stone color*, add lampblack, previously deadened with whiskey, and a small quantity of ochre.

Linseed oil, with a small quantity of glue mixed in it, is sometimes used, instead of flaxseed.

To make the wash incombustible, add 1 lb. of alum and ¾ lb. of potash.

Lacker for Iron Ordnance.

1.—Black lead, pulverized	12
Red lead	12
Litharge	5
Lamplack	5
Linseed oil	66

Boil it gently about twenty minutes, during which time it must be constantly stirred.

Lacker for Iron Ordnance.

2.—Umber, ground	3.75
Gum shellac, pulverized	3.75
Ivory black	3.75
Litharge	3.75
Linseed oil	78.
Spirits of turpentine	7.25

The oil must be first boiled half an hour. The mixture is then boiled 24 hours, poured off from the sediment and put in jugs corked.

3.—Coal Tar, (of good quality,)	2 gals.
Spirits turpentine	1 pint.

The turpentine to be added in small quantities during the application of the lacker.

In applying lacker, the surface of the iron must be first cleaned with a scraper and a wire brush, if necessary, and the lacker applied hot, in two thin coats, with a paint brush. It is best done in summer.

Old lacker should be removed with a scraper, or by scouring, and not by heating the guns or balls, by which the metal is injured.

About 5 gallons of lacker are required for 100 field guns and 1,000 shot; about 1 quart for a sea-coast gun.

Lacker for Iron Ordnance, (used in the British service.)

Anti-corrosion	40 lbs.
Grant's black, ground in oil	4 "
Red lead, as a dryer	3 "
Linseed oil	4 gals.
Spirits turpentine	1 pint.

This mixture when well stirred and incorporated, will be fit for use; but as by long keeping in this state it becomes hard, no more should be mixed than may be required for immediate use.

Anti-corrison:—Slag from iron foundries, pounded	12
Chalk	12
Soot, common	1

Lacker for Small Arms, or for Water Proof Paper.

Beeswax	13 lbs.
Spirits turpentine	13 gals.
Boiled linseed oil	1 "

All the ingredients should be pure and of the best quality. Heat them together in a copper or earthen vessel, over a gentle fire, in a water bath, until they are well mixed.

Lacker for bright Iron Work.

Linseed oil, boiled	80.5
Litharge	5.5
White lead, ground in oil	11.25
Rosin, pulverized	2.75

Add the litharge to the oil; let it simmer over a slow fire 3 hours; strain it, and add the rosin and white lead; keep it gently warmed, and stir it until the rosin is dissolved. Apply it with a paint brush.

Varnish for Holsters, Scabbards, &c., (or Patent Leather.)

For 1st and 2nd coats:

Prussian blue, in lumps	4.
Sugar of lead	0.7
Aqua fortis	0.7
Linseed oil boiled	70.
Spirits turpentine	24.6

The ingredients, except the turpentine, are boiled together in an *iron* kettle 8 hours, when the mixture will assume a brilliant black color. When the varnish is nearly cool, stir in the turpentine. The kettle in which the varnish is made should be of a capacity to hold double the quantity of varnish to be boiled.

For the 3d or finishing coat.—COPAL VARNISH.

Gum copal, (in clean lumps)	26.5
Boiled linseed oil	42.5
Spirits turpentine	31.

This varnish is made in a *copper* vessel, smallest at top, in the form of a still.

Put the copal in the vessel, set it on a charcoal fire for one hour, in which time it will melt, and all the watery particles will evaporate. Add the oil whilst the copal is warm, but not boiling hot. When nearly cool, add the turpentine, which will give it a proper consistency for use.

For 5 lbs. copal and the proper proportions of oil and turpentine, the vessel should hold six gallons.

Japan Varnish.

Litharge	4
Boiled oil	87
Spirits turpentine	2
Red lead	6
Umber	1
Gum shellac	8
Sugar of lead	2
White vitriol	1

Japan varnish is generally purchased from the paint sellers. It is made by boiling over a slow charcoal fire, for five hours, all the ingredients, except the turpentine, and a small portion of the oil; the latter is added as required to check the ebullition and allay the froth which rises to the surface. It must be continually stirred with a wooden spatula, and great care is necessary to prevent it from taking fire.

The turpentine is added after the varnish is nearly cool, and it is stirred well in. The varnish must be put in demijohns or close cans, and kept tightly corked.

Grease for Carriage Wheels.

Hog's lard, softened, (if fresh,) by working it.

If this cannot be procured, *tallow* or other grease may be used; if hard, it should be melted with fish oil.

About 1 lb. of grease is required for four wheels.

Booth's Patent Grease for Railway Axles.

Water	1 gal.
Clean tallow	3 lbs.
Palm oil	6 lbs.
Common soda	½ lb.

Or, Tallow	8 lbs.
Palm oil	10 lbs.

To be heated to about 210°, and to be well stirred until it cools down to 70°.

CHAPTER EIGHTH.

SMALL ARMS AND ACCOUTREMENTS.

NOMENCLATURE.

Percussion Musket.—Plate 15.

BARREL. 1st reinforce (from the breech to the corner of the flats and ovals 1.89 in.;) 2d reinforce (to the lower band, 8.8 in.;) chase (to the top of the upper band, 28.66 in.;) muzzle, *bayonet stud*, breech, flats and ovals, cone seat, fence, vent, bore, thread for breech screw, thread for the cone.

BREECH SCREW. Plug, with its thread; tenon, shoulders, tang, tang screw hole, notch for side screw, chamfer.

TANG SCREW: shoulder.

CONE: screw thread, shoulder, square, cone, vent.

BAYONET. *Blade:* point, face flute, back flutes, edges of back and blade, corners, elbow, neck.—*Socket:* muzzle end, bridge end, bridge, mortice, shoulder for the clasp, stop pin.—*Clasp:* body, studs, bridge, groove, *stop*, *clasp-screw*.

LOCK. *Lock plate:* front and rear ends, middle, sides, bolsters, chamfer, convex; 3 holes, for the pivots of the main spring, and bridle, and for the arbor of the tumbler; 6 screw holes; 1 mortise for the sear spring stud.—*Hammer:* body, head, comb, countersink, slit, tumbler hole—*Tumbler:* body, friction shoulder, arbor, square, pivot, hook, half-cock notch, cock notch, screw hole—*Tumbler screw.*—*Bridle:* body, eye, pivot, three holes for the tumbler pivot, sear screw and bridle screw—*Bridle screw.*—*Sear:* body, eye, nose, tang, screw hole, friction shoulder—*Sear screw.*—*Sear spring:* blade (upper and lower branch and elbow,) eye, stud, notch, chamfer, screw hole—*Sear spring screw.*—*Main spring:* blade (upper and lower branch and elbow,) hook, pivot, eye, (rest and point,) chamfer, screw hole.—*Main spring screw.*

TWO SIDE SCREWS.

In all the screws the parts are: the stem, the head, the slit, the thread.

MOUNTINGS. *Upper band:* body, pipe for the rod, back, upper and lower straps, creases, *sight*, groove, tang, hole for the band spring pivot.—*Upper band spring:* stem, wire, shoulder, pivot.—*Middle band:* body, stud, creases, hole for the swivel rivet.—*Middle band swivel:* wire, eye, holes in the eye, rivet.—*Middle band spring:* stem, wire, shoulder.—*Lower band:* body, tang, creases.—*Lower band spring:* same as middle band spring.—*Side plate:* body, eyes and holes for the side screws.—GUARD.—*Guard plate:* body, bolsters, trigger stud, 2 holes for the guard bow, 2 for wood screws, 1 for tang screw, 1 for trigger-screw.—*Guard bow:* body, pillars, stems with their screw threads, swivel stud and hole; 2 *nuts* for stems—*Swivel and rivet.*—*Trigger:* blade, tang or finger piece, hole for the screw.—*Trigger screw*—*Two wood screws* for guard plate.—*Butt plate:* body, toe, heel, corners, tang, screw holes.—*Two wood screws* for butt plate.

RAMROD.—Stem, head, screw.—*Ramrod spring:* stem, eye, spoon.—*Pin* for rod spring.—*Stop* for rod.

STOCK.—Butt, comb, handle, head, facings, 1st and 2nd reinforce, chase, shoulders for the lower and middle bands; *grooves* for the barrel and ramrod; *beds* for the tang and tenon, lock, side plate, guard plate, nuts of the guard bow and trigger stud, butt plate, rod spring and band springs; *mortices* for the trigger and rod stop; *holes* for the rod, the side screws, tang screw, guard screws, butt plate screws, band springs, and pin for the rod spring.

IMPLEMENTS.—*Screw-driver,* with cone wrench.—*Wiper*—*Ball-screw*—*Spring-vice.*

Materials of which the parts are made.

Steel: Tumbler, sear, lock springs, band springs, ramrod spring, ramrod, blade of the bayonet, screw-driver, wiper, and ball screw.

Brass: Sight.

Wood: Stock (black walnut.)

Iron: Socket of the bayonet, and all the other parts not enumerated under the three preceding heads.

NOTE.—The brass for parts of small arms is composed of 80 copper, 17 zinc, and 3 tin.

Flint Musket.—Pattern of 1840.

(See first edition of Ordnance Manual.)

This arm is like the new percussion musket, except in the parts relating to the mode of priming, viz:

BARREL. Omit *cone seat,* and *cone.*

LOCK. Omit *hammer.*

Add: *Pan* (brass)—*pan screw*—*battery* and *battery screw*—*battery spring* (steel)—*battery spring screw*—*cock*—*upper jaw*—*flint screw.*

Flint Musket.—Pattern of 1822.

Of this kind are most of the muskets in store at the Arsenals, which are now being altered to percussion. The bayonet has no *clasp*.

BARREL: *bayonet stud.*
BREECH SCREW.
TANG SCREW.
BAYONET: blade, socket.

LOCK.
- *Lock plate; 2 side screws.*
- *Pan; pan screw.*
- *Battery; battery screw.*
- *Battery spring.*
- *Battery spring screw.*
- *Cock; upper jaw; flint screw.*
- *Tumbler; tumbler screw.*
- *Bridle; bridle screw.*
- *Sear; sear screw.*
- *Sear spring; sear spring screw.*
- *Main spring; main spring screws.*

TWO SIDE SCREWS.

MOUNTINGS.
- *Upper band; sight.*
- *Upper band spring.*
- *Middle band.*
- *Middle band swivel* and *rivet.*
- *Middle band spring.*
- *Lower band.*
- *Lower band spring.*
- *Side plate.*
- GUARD: *guard plate; guard bow.*
- *Swivel* and *rivet.*
- *Trigger; trigger pin.*
- *Guard plate screws*, (2.)
- *Butt plate; 2 butt plate screws.*

RAMROD.
STOCK.

IMPLEMENTS.—*Screw-driver—Wiper—Ball-screw—Spring-vice.*

Materials.

Steel: Face of the battery, lock springs, ramrod, blade of the bayonet, screw-driver, wiper, and ball screw.

Brass: Pan and sight.

Wood: Stock.

Iron: Bayonet socket, back of the battery, and all the other parts not enumerated under the three preceding heads.

Alteration of Flint Muskets to Percussion.

THE BARREL is altered: 1st, by closing the vent in the side, and boring a new vent on the upper part of the barrel; 2nd, by upsetting a *cone seat* in the metal of the barrel, and putting in a *percussion cone.* The screw thread of the cone for altered muskets is a little shorter than that for the new muskets, so that it may not project into the bore.

THE LOCK is altered: 1st, by removing the *cock*, the *battery, battery screw, battery spring, and battery spring screw;* 2nd, by cutting off the *pan*, near the face of the lock plate, filling up the hollow of the remaining part with brass, soldered in, and dressing off the upper surface even with the top of the lock plate; 3d, replacing the cock by a *percussion hammer*; 4th, filling up the holes of the battery screw and the battery spring screw with pieces of those screws, rounded on the outer end, and filling the pivot hole of the battery spring with wire.

Percussion Rifle.

BARREL: *sight, guide, grooves, bands. Cone. Breech screw; tang screw.*
LOCK: *lock plate; hammer; tumbler; tumbler screw; bridle; bridle screw; sear; sear screw; sear spring; sear spring screw; main spring; main spring screw.*
TWO SIDE SCREWS.
MOUNTINGS: *upper band,* with *swivel stud.*
Upper band swivel, and *rivet.*
Upper band spring.
Lower band; lower band spring.
Side plate.
Guard plate; guard bow and nuts.
Guard bow swivel and rivet.
Trigger; trigger screw.
Guard plate screw.
Butt plate; 2 butt plate screws.
Box plate; the lid and the strap joined by a *hinge* and *rivet.*
Three box plate screws.
Box plate spring; screw, for do.
Box plate catch; 2 rivets.
RAMROD: *rod spring and pin; stop.*
STOCK: *patch box.*
IMPLEMENTS: *screw driver,* with cone wrench; *wiper; ball screw; spring vice; bullet mould.*

Materials.

Steel: Cone, guide, tumbler, sear, lock springs, band springs, rod spring, box spring, ramrod, (except the head,) screw driver, wiper, ball screw. Some of the barrels are also now made of cast steel.

Brass: Sight, bands, guard plate, guard bow, side plate, butt plate, box plate and strap, head of ramrod.

Wood: Stock.

Iron: Parts not enumerated under the preceding heads.

Cavalry Musketoon—Percussion.

BARREL: *swivel stud; cone; breech screw; tang screw; swivel.*
LOCK: same as for rifle.
TWO SIDE SCREWS.
MOUNTINGS: *upper band* and *sight.*
Upper band spring.
Lower band; swivel bar stud.
Swivel bar; ring; screw; nut.
Side plate.
Guard plate; guard bow, and *nuts.*
Trigger; trigger screw.
2 guard plate screws.
Butt plate; 2 butt plate screws.
RAMROD: *head; button.*
RAMROD SWIVEL: *2 side bars; screw; axis.*
STOCK.
IMPLEMENTS, same as for the musket.

Materials.

Steel: Cone, tumbler, sear, lock springs, band spring, ramrod, (except the head,) screw driver, wiper, and ball screw.

Brass: Bands, side plate, guard plate, guard bow, butt plate.

Wood: Stock.

Iron: Head of ramrod and all the other parts not enumerated under the three preceding heads.

Artillery Musketoon—Percussion—Plate 15.

BARREL—*Bayonet stud; cone.*
Breech screw; tang screw.
LOCK—Same as for rifle.
TWO SIDE SCREWS.
MOUNTINGS: *Upper band and sight.*
Upper band spring.
Lower band, and swivel stud.
Lower band spring.
Lower band swivel and rivet.
Side plate.
Guard plate; guard bow and nuts.
Trigger; trigger screw.
2 guard plate screws.
Swivel plate and stud; 2 screws.
Swivel and rivet.
Butt plate; 2 butt plate screws.
Ramrod spring, and pin.
Ramrod stop.
STOCK.
IMPLEMENTS, the same as for the musket.

N. B.—The musket bayonet may be used with this arm.

Materials.

Steel: Cone, tumbler, sear, lock springs, band springs, ramrod, screw driver, wiper, and ball screw.

Brass: Sight. *Wood:* Stock. *Iron:* The remaining parts.

Sapper's Musketoon—Percussion.

This arm is the same as the artillery musketoon, with the addition of an *upper band stud* on the barrel, and a *catch stud* on the upper band, for the sword bayonet.

SWORD BAYONET: *Blade*, (steel;) *gripe and guard*, (brass) in one piece; slot for the catch stud; socket for the barrel; *clasp* and *clasp screw*, similar to those on the musket bayonet—*Scabbard*, (leather) with brass *band and tip.*

Pistol—Percussion—Plate 15.

BARREL: *Sight; swivel stud. Cone.* BREECH SCREW: *Tang screw.*

LOCK: Same parts as for the musket and rifle. TWO SIDE SCREWS.

MOUNTINGS: *Band and side plate*, in one piece—*guard plate—guard plate screw—trigger—trigger screw—guard bow—guard bow nuts—butt plate—butt plate screw.*

RAMROD: Button—*head*, riveted on.

RAMROD SWIVEL: *Two side bars—1 screw—1 cross bar*, riveted into the side bars.

STOCK.

IMPLEMENTS: *Screw driver and cone wrench—wiper—ball screw—spring vice—bullet mould.*

Materials.

Steel: Cone, tumbler, sear, lock springs, ramrod, (except the head,) screw driver, wiper, and ball screw.

Brass: Sight, band and side plate, guard plate, guard bow, butt plate.

Wood: Stock.

Iron: Head of ramrod and the remaining parts.

The tumbler of the pistol is now made with a *safety notch*, in place of the half cock notch.

Hall's Carbine—Percussion—Plate 15.

This is a cavalry carbine, which loads at the breech by means of a moveable chamber called the *receiver*.

BARREL: *Ramrod stud, sight, guide.*

TWO SUPPORTERS: Each with 2 holes for supporter screws, 2 holes for side screws, 1 for swivel bar and 1 for chock screws—4 *supporter screws;* the heads are countersunk in the supporters, and they are dressed smooth and flush with the outer face of the supporters, which are permanently connected with the barrel by these screws, and by being soldered in place.

TWO CHOCKS: 2 *chock screws.*

RECEIVER AND LOCK: Bore, shoulder for the chocks, cone seat, vent, slot for the side screw, mortise for the lock, studs for the catch—*Cone—Hammer and tumbler*, in one piece; slit for the link—*tumbler screw—sear and trigger*, in one piece; slot for side screw—*sear screw—sear spring—sear spring screw—link—link screw—main spring—main spring screw—catch—catch screw—catch spring—catch spring screw.*

TWO SIDE SCREWS: One of them is the axis of the receiver; the other passes through the supporters and the butt piece.

BUTT PIECE—*Butt piece screw*, passing through the supporters and the butt piece.

APRON: Lining of the stock, at the junction of the barrel and receiver—*Stop*, riveted to the apron, for the receiver to rest on. The apron and stop have a screw hole tapped to receive the front guard plate screw.

MOUNTINGS: *Upper band—ramrod spring*, riveted to the upper band—*upper band spring—lower band*, with stud for swivel bar—*swivel bar;* the rear end is a side screw for the supporters—*swivel screw—swivel ring—guard plate;* 2 studs for the catch lever—*guard bow—guard bow nuts—catch lever and pin—three guard plate screws—butt plate—2 butt plate screws.*

RAMROD.

STOCK.

IMPLEMENTS: *Screw driver and cone wrench—wiper—spring vice—bullet mould.*

Materials.

Steel: Chocks; hammer and tumbler; link; sear part of trigger; all the springs; ramrod.

Brass: Sight; bands; guard plate; guard bow; butt plate.

Wood: Stock.

Iron: The remaining parts.

For description of *Hall's Rifle*, (flint lock,) see first edition of Ordnance Manual.

Principal Dimensions and Weights of Small Arms.

DIMENSIONS.	FLINT MUSKET.		PERCUSSION.						
	1822.	1840.	Musket.	Rifle.	Cavalry Musketoon.	Artillery Musketoon.	Sapper's Musketoon.	Pistol.	Hall's Carbine.
	In.	In.	In.	In.	In.	In.	In.	In.	In.
BARREL. — Diameter of the bore	0.69	0.69	0.69	0.54	0.69	0.69	0.69	0.54	0.52
BARREL. — Variation allowed, *more*	0.015	0.015	0.01	0.01	0.01	0.01	0.01	0.01	0.01
BARREL. — Diameter at the muzzle	0.82	0.85	0.85	0.90	0.85	0.85	0.85	0.70	0.75
BARREL. — Diameter at breech, between the flats	1.25	1.25	1.25	1.15	1.25	1.25	1.25	1.	1.
BARREL. — Length, without the breech screw	42.0	42.	42.	33.	26.	26.	26.	8.5	21.
RECEIVER. — Diameter of chamber	.....	.....	.....	.....	.....	.....	.....	.....	0.56
RECEIVER. — Depth of chamber	.....	.....	.....	.....	.....	.....	.....	.....	2.10
BAYONET, length of the blade	16.	18.	18.	.....	.....	18.	22.		
RAMROD, length	41.96	41.70	41.70	33.	25.70	25.70	25.70	8.7	19.50
ARM COMPLETE. — Length, without bayonet	57.64	57.80	57.80	48.8	41.	41.	41.	14.3	40.
ARM COMPLETE. — Length, with bayonet fixed	73.64	75.80	75.80	.....	.....	59.	62.1		
WEIGHTS.	Lbs.	Lbs.	Lbs.	Lbs.	Lbs.	Lbs.	Lbs.	Lbs.	Lbs.
BARREL, without breech screw	4.	4.19	4.25	5.17	2.94	2.94	2.95	1.03	3.55
LOCK, with side screws	1.23	1.22	0.85	0.55	0.58	0.58	0.58	0.43	
BAYONET	0.73	0.64	0.68	.....	.....	0.68	2.33		
ARM COMPLETE. — Without bayonet	9.34	9.78	9.14	9.68	7.22	7.02	7.02	2.73	8.14
ARM COMPLETE. — With bayonet	10.10	10.42	9.82	.....	.....	7.70	9.35		
Flint lock altered to percussion—deduct	0.24	0.24							

INSPECTION OF SMALL ARMS.

All the materials used in the manufacture of arms must be of the best quality, and they should be tested by the inspectors, according to the methods indicated in CHAPTER XIV.

The wood for gun stocks should be seasoned at least 3 years and kept in a dry place 2 years before being worked; it must be free from knots and sap, and no wood which is *brash* or light, (cut from old trees,) or worm eaten, or in any degree decayed, or which is cut across the grain at the handle of the stock, or which is kiln dried, should be used or received.

The following rules for inspection apply more particularly to the percussion musket, when not otherwise stated, but the principles and most of the details of the inspection are the same for all fire arms, whether made at the national armories, or by contract at private establishments.

The attention of the inspecting officers should be directed, as much as possible, to the operations of the workmen in the course of the fabrication of arms.

Each component part is first inspected by itself and afterwards the arm in a finished state.

The materials and the forms and dimensions of all the parts must conform strictly to those of the established patterns; the workmanship and finish must be equal to those of the model arms, and the several parts must be browned, blued, case hardened, or polished as in the standard model.

The forms and dimensions of the parts are verified by means of the following gauges:

List of Verifying Gauges for the Percussion Musket.

Each set of gauges is distinguished by the letter with which it is marked. The pieces of the same set are numbered as in the following list.—In some cases *each groove* of a gauge is numbered; for instance, those of the barrel, rod, and bayonet gauges: these numbers will not be found on the list.

No.	FOR BARRELS.
1	1 Stock gauge for the length of the barrel and rod.
2	1 Groove gauge for the diameters of the barrel.
3	1 Standard plug, } for the calibre of the barrel.
4	1 Limit plug, } for the calibre of the barrel.
5	1 Taper plug, } for the calibre of the barrel.
6	1 Tap and die for the barrel and breech screw.
7	1 Standard tap and die for the cone seat and cone.
8	1 Tap gauge for the depth of thread in the cone seat.
9	1 Groove gauge for the finished barrel and breech screw.
10, 11	2 Gauges for the exterior of the cone seat.
12	1 Receiving gauge for the barrel and breech screw.

No.	MUSKET—BARREL—*Continued.*
13	1 Gauge for the vent.
14	1 Receiving gauge for the muzzle.
15	1 Groove and tap gauge for the cone.
	FOR LOCKS.
16	1 Pattern for lock plates.
17	1 Groove gauge for lock plates.
18	1 Receiving and groove gauge for tumblers.
19	1 Receiving and groove gauge for bridles.
20	1 Receiving and groove gauge for sears.
21	1 Size gauge for the hole in the sear.
22	1 Groove gauge for hammers.
23	1 Gauge for the set and length of the hammers.
24	1 Receiving gauge for hammers.
25	1 Gauge drift for tumbler holes.
26	1 Groove gauge for main spings.
27	1 Groove gauge for sear springs.
28	1 Groove and tap gauge for the lock screws, and for all the screws except the wood screws.
29	1 Gauge for depth of tumbler screw hole.
30	1 Receiving gauge for finished locks.
	FOR MOUNTINGS AND OTHER PARTS.
31	1 Pattern and receiving gauge for butt plates.
32	1 Groove gauge for butt plates.
33	1 Groove gauge for bands.
34	1 Gauge mandril for lower bands.
35	1 Gauge mandril for middle bands.
36	1 Gauge mandril for upper bands.
37	1 Groove and receiving gauge for guard plate bow and nuts.
38	1 Tap gauge for tang screw hole, trigger stud, and guard bow nuts.
39	1 Receiving gauge for guards.
40	1 Receiving and groove gauge for triggers.
41	1 Receiving and groove gauge for lower and middle band springs.
42	1 Receiving and groove gauge for upper band springs.
43	1 Receiving and groove gauge for side plates.
44	1 Receiving and groove gauge for rod springs and wire pins.
45	1 Groove and plug gauge for swivels.
46	1 Groove gauge for breech plate and guard screws, (wood screws.)
47	1 Receiving gauge for bayonets.
48	1 Scabbard gauge for bayonets.
49	1 Groove gauge for bayonets.
50	1 Plug for bayonet sockets.
51	1 Groove and plug for bayonets and socket clasps.
52	1 Groove and pattern gauge for bayonet necks.
53	1 Grooved and tapped gauge for rods.
54	1 Groove gauge and pattern for rod stop.
55	1 Apparatus for testing lock springs; consisting of a stock, scale beam, and brass pods weighing 10 pounds.
56	1 Gauge for the angle of the stock, and positions of the bands on the finished musket.

No.	MUSKET—APPENDAGES.
57	2 Hand screw drivers for locks.
58	2 Hand screw drivers for guard bow nuts and trigger screws.
59	1 Hand screw driver for side screws.
60	1 Iron brace with screw drivers.
61	1 Cone wrench.
62	1 Charger for first proof charge—1-18th of a pound.
63	1 Charger for second do. 1-22nd do.
64	1 Bench hammer.
65	1 Punch for wire pins.
66	1 Punching wire.
67	1 Pair of small steel callipers.
68	1 Steel square divided into inches and decimals of an inch.

Gauges for Percussion Rifle.

	BARREL.
1	Stock gauge for length of barrel and rod.
2	Groove gauge for barrel.
3	Standard plug for calibre of barrel.
4	Limit plug for calibre of barrel.
5	Tap for barrel.
6	Die for breech screw.
7	Receiving gauge for breech screw and barrel.
8	Groove gauge for adjusting breech screw.
9	Receiving gauge for barrel, and plug with screws for verifying the thread for the cone.
10	Groove gauge for cone seat.
11	Plug gauge for vent.
12	Groove gauge for guide and sight of barrel.
13	Charger for 1-28th lb. powder.
14	Charger for 1-32nd lb. powder.
	CONE.
15	Groove gauge, with holes, for size of cone.
16	Plug gauge, with 3 points for the 3 sections of the cone orifice.
17	Plug gauge for cone orifice, middle and upper end.
18	Tap grinder for making chasers for cone screw thread.
19	Tap grinder for making chasers for the breech screw thread.
	LOCK.
20	Receiving gauge, with holes, for lock plate.
21	Pair of patterns for lock plate.
22	Pattern for interior of lock plate.
23	Pattern for bevel of lock plate.
24	Groove gauge lock plate.
25	Pattern for the hole for scar spring stud.
26	Pattern with axis pivot for hammer.
27	Plug gauge and sweep for the cup and position of hammer.
28	Plug for the axis hole and cup of hammer.
29	Groove gauge for hammer.
30	Receiving gauge with grooves and holes for tumblers.

No.	RIFLE—LOCK—*Continued.*
31	Pattern for tumbler.
32	Plug gauge for depth of screw hole in tumbler.
33	Receiving gauge with grooves for bridle and pin for pivot hole in bridle.
34	Receiving gauge with grooves, &c., for sears.
35	Groove gauge with patterns, &c., for lock springs.
36	Groove and tap gauge for lock, tumbler, side, and box spring screws.
37	Gauge, with holes, for tumbler, axis pivot and main spring, and bridle pivot.
38	Apparatus for testing lock springs.
	MOUNTINGS.
39	Receiving gauge for breech plates.
40	Groove gauge with square for breech plate.
41	Gauge plug for lower bands.
42	Gauge plug for upper bands.
43	Groove gauge for bands.
44	Plug gauge for orifice of rod hole and band spring pivot hole in upper bands.
45	Receiving gauge for guard plates.
46	Groove gauge with pattern for guard bow.
47	Groove gauge tapped, and with holes for guard plate, guard bow, and guard bow nuts.
48	Receiving and groove gauge for trigger.
49	Receiving and groove gauge for lower band spring.
50	Receiving and groove gauge for upper band spring.
51	Receiving gauge with pattern for side plate.
52	Groove gauge with plug for swivels.
53	Groove and tap gauge for tang, breech plate, guard and trigger screws.
54	Groove and tap gauge for ramrods.
55	Receiving and groove gauge for rod spring and pin.
56	Groove gauge and pattern for box.
57	Groove gauge for box spring and catch.
58	Gauge for angle of stock.
59	Gauge for handle and comb of stock.
60	Screwplate for cone thread, side, lock, tang, box spring, trigger, and rod screws.
	APPENDAGES.
61	Hand screw driver for lock screws.
62	Hand screw driver for guard bow nuts.
63	Hand screw driver for trigger screw.
64	Hand screw driver for side and breech plate screws.
65	Bench hammer.
66	Punch for wire pins and band springs.

Gauges for the Percussion Pistol.

	FOR THE BARREL.
1	Groove gauge for rough barrel.
2	Tap and die for breech screw.
3	Tap for cone seat.
4	Gauge and die for cone thread
5	Gauge pin for vent.

No.	PISTOL—BARREL—*Continued.*
6	Plug for calibre of barrel.
7	Groove gauge for finished barrel.
8	Receiving gauge for barrel, with pin for cone seat.
9, 10	Gauges for exterior of cone seat.
11	Gauge for length of barrel and rod, and for the rod and swivel.
12	Groove and size gauge for cone.
	LOCK.
13	Groove gauge for lock plate.
14	Pattern for lock plate.
15	Gauge pin for pivots of bridle and main spring.
16	Groove gauge for hammer.
17	Pattern gauge for hammer.
18	Gauge for tumbler hole and length of hammer.
19	Groove and receiving gauge for tumbler.
20	Gauge for depth of tumbler screw hole.
21	Groove and receiving gauge for bridle.
22	Groove and receiving gauge for sear.
23	Gauge pin for screw hole in sear.
24	Groove and pattern gauge for main spring.
25	Groove and pattern gauge for sear spring.
26	Receiving gauge for lock.
27	Apparatus for testing lock springs.
28	Groove and tap gauge for screws.
	FOR MOUNTINGS, ETC.
29	Receiving gauge for breech plate.
30	Groove gauge for breech plate and band.
31	Receiving gauge for guard.
32	Groove gauge for guard plate and bow.
33	Gauge for trigger mortise and stud.
34	Groove and receiving gauge for trigger.
35	Groove and receiving gauge for side plate.
36	Receiving gauge for band.
37	Groove gauge for stock.
38	Gauge for length and shape of finished arm.
	APPENDAGES.
39	Brace with screw drivers and cone wrench.
40, 41, 42	Hand screw drivers, for slit screws.
43	Screw driver for guard bow nut.
44	Hand hammer.
45	Sheel square.
46	Charger for 1st proof charge, 1-32nd lb.
47	Charger for 2nd proof charge, 1-40th lb.

Inspection of barrels.

The first inspection of the barrel is made after it is reduced to the dimensions required for proof, which are verified by the proper gauges for that purpose: these dimensions are nearly the same as those of the finished barrel (not more than 0.003 in. greater in the exterior diameter, and 0.003 in. less in the diameter of the bore,) leaving only sufficient surplus metal (about 1½ oz. in a musket barrel) to enable the workman to dress the barrel in fine boring and to remove the marks made in straightening the barrel after proof. The thread for the breech screw in the barrel must be cut and the bayonet stud brazed on. The inspector will see that the exterior and interior dimensions of the barrel are correct; that there are no interior hammer marks, ring bores, cinder holes, flaws, cracks or other defects, which will not disappear in the finishing, and that the thread of the breech screw is accurately cut.

The barrels rejected for defects that cannot be remedied will be stamped on the upper side, in a line with the vent, with the mark of condemnation, which will be in all cases the letter *C*. If the defect is of such a nature as not to prevent the use of the barrel for a shorter arm, when cut off, the mark will be made on the defective part.

Proof. The barrels which pass this inspection will then be proved by being fired twice, with the following charges:

KIND OF BARREL.	1st charge.			2nd charge.			Size of ball.		Size of wad.
	Powder.	Balls.	Wads.	Powder.	Balls.	Wads.	Weight.	Diam.	Square.
	Lbs.	No.	No.	Lbs.	No.	No.	Lbs.	In.	In.
Musket	1-18th	1	2	1-22nd	1	2	1-15th	0.676	4.
Musketoon	1-22nd	1	2	1-28th	1	2	1-15th	0.676	4.
Hall's carbine..	1-28th	2	2	1-32nd	1	2	1-32nd	0.525	3.25
Rifle.........	1-28th	2	2	1-32nd	1	2	1-32nd	0.525	3.25
Ristol	1-32nd	1	2	1-40th	1	2	1-32nd	0.525	3.25

One wad is placed on the powder and the other on the ball, (the upper ball when there are two,) and the charge is well rammed with copper rods. The wad occupies, when rammed, about ¾ in. in the length of the barrel.

The barrels are closed for proof either with their breech screws, (in which case the vent must be drilled before proof,) or with *proving plugs* having vents in them.

The barrels of Hall's arms, being without threads for breech screws, are closed with smooth proving plugs 0.7 in. long, fitting tight to the barrel: the plug is held in its place by a wedge bearing against a stirrup attached to a collar which rests against the shoulder of the barrel; these barrels are proved before the supporters are attached to them; they are loaded at the muzzle like other barrels.

Rifle barrels are proved before being rifled.

Musket powder will be used for proving the barrels of muskets and musketoons; rifle powder for all the others; the powder must be of the best quality, giving a range of not less than 250 yards by the mortar eprouvette; it must be proved immediately before being used, unless it shall have been proved within one year, and the inspector has no reason to suppose that it has become deteriorated.

The measures for the proof charges should be of a conical form, with the mouth as small as may be convenient, in order that there may be less variation in the quantity of powder; their dimensions will be determined by the rule in CHAPTER X.

Before commencing the proof of barrels, the inspector will satisfy himself as to the quality and proof of the powder, the size of the balls and of the wads.

The inspector will observe the greatest caution in having the barrels properly loaded; for which purpose, after they are placed on the proving bed, he will pass a ramrod into each barrel, to verify the accuracy of the charge.

After the discharge he will again pass the ramrod into each barrel, and those which have missed fire will be pricked and primed and discharged, before proceeding to the second proof charge.

After the second proof charge, the inspector will examine the barrels which have burst and note the cause of defect, whether in the materials or workmanship.

He will then examine those which have not burst, and he will mark, as condemned, any which are evidently defective; the others will receive the proof stamp, viz: the initials of the inspector's name with the letter *P* under them, placed on the left side of the barrel, just above the left flat, and about 1 in. from the breech. The barrels will be immediately washed clean, in hot water, and dried, after which they will be again carefully examined.

They will now be inspected in the interior and on the exterior; the inspector will reject such as are too large in the bore, and such as have holes, cross cracks, scales, seams or ring bores; he will examine the brazing of the bayonet stud and see that the barrel is not notched too deep, or indented inside.

The barrels having been reduced to their ultimate dimensions, straightened and completely finished, are again strictly inspected to verify the straightness of the bore, the exterior and interior diameters, their weight, (which should not vary more than 1 oz. from the standard weight,) the taps for the breech screw and cone, the size, position and direction of the vent.

The straightness of the barrel may be ascertained by holding it up to the light and reflecting a straight edge on the different parts of the bore, by which means an experienced eye readily detects any inaccuracy in the bore. The small or *standard* plug should pass freely through the whole length of the barrel including the threads for the breech screw, and the bore should not admit the large or *limit* plug.

The *grooves of rifle barrels* should be carefully examined to see that they are formed according to the pattern, and that they are even and uniform throughout.

The *breech screws* will be examined to see that they are of the proper dimensions, are sound in every part, and have good threads; those of the new model are not case hardened. The screw must be tried in the barrel, to see that it occupies all the threads in the tap of the barrel, and that it is not loose after entering three threads.

The *vent* should enter the bore of the barrel clear of the end of the breech screw.

Marks. Barrels condemned for defects detected after proof, or at any time in the course of inspection, are marked with the letter *C*, struck in deeply; those finally received are stamped in addition to the proof mark, with the letters *U. S.*, on the top of the barrel 1 in. from the breech, and the *Year* of fabrication underneath those lettters, in the direction of the axis of the barrel, ending at the breech.

Report of Inspection of Barrels.

After the inspection of each lot of barrels the inspector will make a statement, showing:

1. The number of barrels offered for proof.
2. The number rejected before proof.
3. The number burst in proof.
4. The number rejected after proof, for flaws, cross cracks, or other defects.
5. The number received after the proof and inspections.
6. The number rejected on inspection of the finished arm.

These statements furnish the materials for the reports of inspection required by the Ordnance Regulations.

Cones.

Verify the dimensions exterior and interior, and the thread of the screw.—See that the upper part of the cone is properly hardened and free from cracks or flaws.

Locks.

Examine all the limbs to see that they are sound, well filed, and of the proper form; try the temper of the hardened parts with a fine cut file.

Hammers. Verify the dimensions and form carefully with the proper gauges, see that they are properly case hardened, especially in the head and cup for the cone.

Tumblers must be verified separately with great care, and their hardness tested.

Springs. The strength of the lock springs, as indicated by the weights they require to bend them up to the cock notch, is nearly as follows:

Main spring of musket ....85 lbs.
Do. pistol........... .74 "
Sear spring....................20 "

Screws. Examine the forms of the stems and heads of all screws and the cutting of the threads, and gauge them; see that they are properly hardened.

Lock plates. Verify with the proper gauges the form and dimensions, the accuracy of the position of the holes and the threads of those which are tapped; see that the plate is sound and free from cracks and flaws, especially about the tumbler hole, and that it is well hardened.

Finished locks. The locks having been put together, see:

1st. That they are clean in the inside.

2d. That the sear works freely when the sear screw is driven as far as it will go, and that the nose is sufficiently strong and falls properly into the notches of the tumbler.

3d. That the bridle has no cracks or flaws about the holes for the tumbler-pivot and screws.

4th. That the springs are well bent and of good proportions; that the fixed branches fit close to the lock plate, and that the moveable branches swing clear of it without having too much play.

5th. That the slits of the screw heads are not defective.

6th. That the arbor and pivot of the tumbler fit accurately in their holes.

7th. That the hook of the tumbler does not fall below the edge of the lock plate when the cock is down.

8th. That the notches of the tumbler are sound and smooth, and that the tumbler fits and turns well.

9th. That the hammer fits well on the square of the tumbler, and that it does not rest on the lock plate when screwed up tight, and that it has the proper set in relation to the cone.

10th. That all the parts work well together.

Marks. The place and year of fabrication are marked on the face of the lock plate, in rear of the hammer; at the national armories an *eagle* and the letters *U. S.* are stamped on the lock plate; at private armories, the letters *U. S.*, with the name of the contractor.

Mountings.

The forms and dimensions are verified with the appropriate gauges and patterns. The rod springs should not be so stiff as to endanger splitting the stock. The trigger should be well fitted to the guard plate, with as little lateral play as is consistent with its free movement. The form, size, and threads of the screws should be carefully examined. The letters *U. S.* are marked on the tang of the butt plate.

Ramrods.

The temper of the rod is tested by springing it in four directions with the point resting on the floor. The musket ramrod should bend 6 inches from a right line joining the ends; the rod should spring back perfectly straight without setting. Its soundness and freedom from flaws and cross cracks are ascertained by the sound it gives when suspended by one end and gently struck with a piece of metal, and by passing it over the edge of a block of wood, or the closed jaws of a vice, pressing down the ends at the same time and turning the rod so as to present every side successively to inspection. Rifle and pistol rods are subjected to the last tests only. The diameter of the rod and the tap of the screw for the wiper are verified with the proper gauges. The length is also verified.

Marks. The rods approved are marked with a small stamp near the head.

Bayonets.

The form and dimensions of the bayonet are verified with the proper gauges; the temper is tried by springing the bayonet attached to the barrel, the point resting on the floor. In case of doubt, the temper of the bayonet is definitely proved in the following manner:

Two iron staples are fixed in a piece of oak plank on a work bench, $16\frac{5}{8}$ inches apart; one of them serves as a bridge and has notches to receive the blade, the other serves as a staple for holding the point of the bayonet close to the plank: the bayonet is fixed on a barrel to the butt of which is fastened a brass ball weighing 6 lbs., so that by inserting the point of the blade in the staples, the face and back resting alternately on the bridge, the blade sustains a weight of 9 lbs., which springs it about $\frac{5}{6}$ of an inch. In this situation the blade is also examined to detect flaws and cross cracks. It should not remain bent after this trial.

The inspector then seizes the blade near the point and strikes the elbow smartly on the work bench, to ascertain that the welding is sound.

If the proof shows no defects, he verifies the dimensions and bore of the socket and the accuracy of the channels. He examines the dimensions of the clasp, to see that it fits well to the shoulder; that it turns evenly, without binding in any part; that the stop is well placed and firmly set; that the clasp screw and its thread in the stud of the clasp are well cut; that the elbow has the proper form and dimensions.

Marks. Bayonets are marked on the face of the blade, near the neck, with the letters *U. S.;* those approved are marked on the neck with the inspector's stamp; those rejected for defects that cannot be remedied are marked with the stamp of condemnation.

Stocks.

The examination of the stock will be directed:

1st. To the quality of the wood; that it has good straight grain, is well seasoned and free from sap and worm holes.

The degree of seasoning is indicated by the smell of the wood at a fresh cut place—by the appearance of the lock and barrel, &c., when removed from the stock; they will be rusted by unseasoned wood—by rolling a thin shaving between the fingers, it will crumble if the wood be well seasoned, otherwise it will be tough and will bend.

The medium weight of a well seasoned musket stock is 2 lbs.: a stock made of good walnut will not weigh *less* than 1 lb. 13 oz.

2nd. To the workmanship; that it is free from splits, especially about the barrel groove and heading; that it has not been split and glued up; that the grooves and beds are of the proper forms and dimensions; that the roundings for the bands are smooth and accurate; that the handle and comb are of the proper size and form; that the stock has the proper *fall* or crook, and is of the right length; that the holes are well drilled, and that those for the wood screws have good threads.

In examining the bed of the lock, see:

1st. That all the edges are sharp and smooth.

2nd. That the beds of the sear screw and sear spring screw are not bored down to the trigger or to the breech screw.

3d. That the beds of the main spring and main spring screw do not penetrate to the barrel.

4th. That the hole for the tang of the sear is as small as possible, so that the sear shall not be wood bound.

5th. That the wires fit well in their holes.

Marks. The stocks inspected are marked on the left side with the stamp of approval, (the initials of the inspector's name,) or of condemnation, as the case may be.

Appendages.

Ball screws and wipers are examined by screwing them on a piece of ramrod furnished with a handle, to verify the accuracy of the screw thread ; the temper of the branches is tested by pressing the points on a piece of hard wood, in which proof they should spring back to their proper form.

Screw drivers, by inserting the blades in a vice, or in a slit made for the purpose, and twisting them with the hand. Test the strength and size of the cone wrench, by putting it on a square socket and wrenching it by hand.

Other implements are examined by applying the appropriate patterns &c., and their soundness may be further tested by striking them a smart blow with a hammer.

Finished arms.

Finished arms offered for inspection must be taken entirely to pieces, and each part must be examined as above directed; if the parts have been previously inspected, see that they have suffered no subsequent injury. This being done, the arms will be put together and examined in their complete state. Some of the arms in every lot should be put together by the inspector himself.

The inspector will examine the finished arms on every side, to see that the parts are well fitted together—he will verify the principal dimensions and forms by means of the appropriate gauges and patterns.

Barrel. The diameter of the bore must be verified with the standard and limit gauges. The barrel should enter the groove of the stock to the depth of half its diameter, and should bear well in the whole length of the groove, particularly at the breech. The vent should be accurate in its dimensions, position and direction, and a wire should be passed into the vent through the cone, to see that it is free. The cone should be examined, to see that it is sound. The shoulders of the breech screw should fit close to the end of the barrel, and it must be free from cracks or flaws about the tang screw hole; the tang screw should be perpendicular to the tang. The bore of the barrel should be clean and bright.

Ramrod. The temper and the screw of the ramrod are tried as before directed, also by dropping it into the barrel, which will test soundness and length ; the fitting of the groove is ascertained by drawing and returning the rod smartly several times, to see that it holds well and does not stick too tight; the musketoon, pistol and carbine ramrods should hold more firmly than that of the musket—the ramrod must bear on the rod stop, and in that position its head should not project beyond the end of the barrel; it should fill the groove well; the open part of the groove should be in the centre of the stock, the covered part in the middle of the thickness of the stock between the outside and the bottom of the barrel groove, and the rod should not interfere with the front side screw.

Bayonet. The socket of the bayonet should be a little below the muzzle of the barrel at the upper end, and should clear the upper band about 0.05 in. Work the clasp to see that the ramrod does not interfere with it, that it bears well on the shoulders, that the clasp screw holds well, that the stop is firmly fixed, and that the clasp moves evenly without binding; the blade of the bayonet should set outwards a little towards the point. To try the strength and temper of the bayonet when fixed: spring it smartly in four directions, towards the back and face and each edge, resting the point on the floor, and grasping the butt of the stock with the right hand and the middle of the barrel with the left. Examine the fitting of the bayonet to the barrel and see that the inside of the socket is clean and free from rust, and that the bayonet stud is well brazed and of the right dimensions.

Lock. Examine carefully the action of the lock; snap the hammer on the cone, to see that it fits well. Let the hammer down several times, to judge of the working of the lock.

See also: 1st, that the interior parts are not wood bound.

2nd. That the hammer stands off (0.02 in.) from the lock plate.

3d. That it does not go off at half cock, when the trigger is pulled hard.

4th. That it goes neither too hard nor too easily when cocked.

5th. That it does not stop at half cock.

6th. That the trigger is steady at cock and half cock, and free when the hammer is down.

7th. That the fall of the hammer is not stopped by the heel of the tumbler, before it touches the cone.

8th. That the hammer has sufficient sweep; and that it falls evenly, without a jerk.

Examine the soundness of the hammer at the tumbler hole.

In examining a finished lock by itself, observe the rules laid down above; see that the lock plate fits accurately in its bed and that the wood around it is full and sound.

Mountings. The front part of the trigger at half cock should be nearly perpendicular to the surface of the guard plate; the slit for the trigger should be of the exact width, so that the trigger shall have no lateral motion.

It is important that the guard plate should bear firmly on the wood in every part; as otherwise, by driving the tang screw too hard, the trigger might be brought too close to the sear and the action of the lock be thus interfered with.

The butt plate should be well fitted, in the centre of the stock.

The bands should fit smoothly at the shoulders and closely to the stock and barrel, but not so tight as to require a great effort to remove them. The band springs should not be too deeply set; they should spring back freely when pressed down; the holes for the wires should not interfere with the barrel or ramrod grooves.

All the mountings should fit smoothly to the stock. The stock should have the proper fall or crook, which is ascertained by applying the pattern and by trying the piece in the position of aiming.

By sighting along the barrel it will be seen whether it is well stocked, whether the upper band is well placed and the sight central, and the bayonet well set.

See also below: *Inspection of arms in service.*

SPECIAL INSTRUCTIONS FOR THE INSPECTION OF HALL'S CARBINES.

The foregoing rules for inspection of arms are to be observed here as far as they are applicable; such as those relating to the quality of materials and workmanship; the proving of barrels and ramrods; gauging the parts and ascertaining that they are sound; that their forms and dimensions agree in all respects with those of the standard models, and that they are not inferior in finish to those models.

The following instructions apply exclusively to arms of Hall's patent.

These arms should be fabricated in such a manner that the component parts of all the arms of the same kind shall interchange, or fit equally well together. In order to test the accuracy of the work in this respect, examine and gauge the various component parts belonging to any number of arms offered for inspection, and cause the arms to be put together by taking the parts promiscuously from the whole number examined. Take then a certain proportion of the finished arms (say 10 in every hundred of the first 400 arms, after that about 10 in 400,) and interchange the component parts of each of these lots of 10, as follows:

2nd. Apply each receiver to one and the same arm—ascertain that the joint between its muzzle and the breech of the barrel is a little open, (from 0.004 in.

to 0.008 in.) so as to admit of one thickness of common writing paper without jamming it, and two thicknesses of the same, jamming and holding them tight. Also, ascertain that its catch fits well to the catch plate below, and that when the receiver is pressed hard down, the space between the catch notch and the catch plate is not less than 0.008 in. nor more than 0.016 in.—that the receiver admits of a little motion, or has between it and the chock on each side of it a play of not less than 0.004 in. nor more than 0.008 in.

Ascertain that the opening on each side between the receivers and the supporters, in rear of the chocks, is not less than 0.008 in., nor more than 0.016 in.

That the opening between the rear end of the receiver and the butt piece, and between the front part of the shoulders (before the chocks) and the supporters, is not less than 0.016 in. nor more than 0.03 in. That the receiver opens and shuts with ease, and that the trigger which is attached to it passes through the guard freely and clear of the end of the mortise in the guard, both in front and rear, and that when the piece is cocked and the receiver shut, the trigger stands $\frac{1}{8}$ of an inch from the guard behind.

3d. Apply one catch plate to all the stocks; put in a receiver and ascertain that it fits the catch: also, apply all the catch plates to one and the same stock and receiver, ascertaining that each one fits.

4th. Apply all the catches to each receiver and ascertain that the catch fits on the plate below; that the opening between the hook of the catch and the catch plate is correct as before stated.

5th. Apply all the chocks to one and the same arm and ascertain that the opening or joint formed between the receiver and the barrel is within the limits before prescribed. Apply one and the same pair of chocks to each arm, and ascertain that the opening in the joint between the receiver and the barrel is the same as before.

6th. Apply all the butt pieces to one and the same arm ascertaining that each one fits alike and corresponds well with the ends of the supporters, with the wood of the stock and with the screw holes through the stock and the supporters—then apply one and the same butt piece to all the arms and ascertain the same points as before.

7th. Apply all the butt plates to one and the same stock, but without turning in the screws, except in a few of the plates, otherwise the hold of the screw in the wood will be injured; but ascertain that the holes in the plate correspond with those in the stocks at the same time that its outer edges correspond with the outside of the stock—then apply one and the same butt plate to all the stocks and ascertain that it fits alike to each, turning in the screws in this latter case.

8th. Apply all the guards to one and the same stock, ascertaining that each fits the wood well around its edges and at the holes—then apply one and the same guard to each of the stocks, ascertaining that it fits as before.

9th. Apply each set of bands to one and the same stock and barrel, ascertaining that they go moderately tight only, and so nearly alike as to make good and close work—then apply one and the same set of bands to all the arms and ascertain the same points with each, and that the bands fit well to the stocks and barrels and to the band springs.

10th. Apply all the barrels, with one and the same set of bands, to one and the same stock, putting the bands fully to their places to ascertain that they go neither too tight nor too loose, which will be the case when they admit of being shoved by the hand to within a quarter of an inch of their respective places; ascertain that the supporters fit the stocks and the butt pieces—then apply one and the same barrel with the same set of bands to each of the stocks, observing the same particulars.

11th. Ascertain that the supporters are securely fastened to the barrels with two screws in each, and with good solder over the whole extent of the supporter where it comes in contact with the barrel—to determine this point, put a little oil above the junction of the supporter and the barrel, then grasp both supporters with one hand, holding the barrel with the other, and spring them inwards several times; if the soldering is not sound, the oil will be seen to issue from between the supporters and the barrel.

12th. Test the guides, ascertaining that they slide equally easy in their respective dove-tails in all the barrels, first applying all the guides to one barrel and then one of them to all the barrels.

13th. Examine the receiver and the various parts attached to it by applying in the first place all the hammers to one and the same receiver, ascertaining that each one falls fairly down on the cone; then apply one and the same hammer to all the receivers; and thus proceed to test the accuracy of all the different parts of the lock attached to the receiver, applying all of the different component parts to one and the same receiver, and one of each of the component parts to all the receivers.

GENERAL DIRECTIONS.

The inspector is not restricted to the particular examinations above mentioned; he will make any other examinations which he may deem necessary to ascertain the quality of any part of the arms and their conformity to the standard models; if he discovers or suspects any attempts on the part of the workmen to cover or conceal serious defects, he will subject the arms to the most severe scrutiny, in order to detect such defects.

In the inspection of contract arms, the inspector will judge of the quality of materials and workmanship by the rules which govern in like cases at the national armories; that is, he will reject such arms or parts of arms as would be condemned at the national armories, and he will receive such as would be approved at the national armories; without exacting, in any case, more rigid conditions than are enforced at those establishments.

The ordnance officer charged with the inspection of arms, or the master armorer at a national armory, will cause at least *one in twenty* of each lot of arms passed by a sub-inspector to be taken to pieces in his presence, and he will examine them strictly, agreeably to the foregoing directions, before affixing his stamp of approval on the finished arms, all of which must be examined by him.

Marks: As a general rule, every part condemned on inspection will be indelibly marked with the letter *C*, and every principal part approved will be marked with the initials of the inspector's name. Care must be taken that the marks of approval are not stamped so deep as to be injurious.

Finished arms approved on inspection will be marked on the left face of the stock with the initials of the name of the principal inspector, and the year of inspection.

BROWNED ARMS.

The barrels of rifles and carbines are browned at the armories before being received for the service; the *locks, ramrods, band springs, triggers, receivers* and *screws* are not browned. The parts of these arms should be thoroughly inspected before browning, and the finished arm after being browned.

Instructions for Browning Arms.

Materials for Browning Mixture.

1½ oz. spirits of wine.
1½ oz. tincture of steel.
¼ oz. corrosive sublimate.
1½ oz. sweet spirits of nitre.
1 oz. blue vitriol.
¾ oz. nitric acid.

To be mixed and dissolved in 1 quart of soft water—the mixture to be kept in *glass bottles* and not in earthen jugs.

Previous to commencing the operation of browning, it is necessary that the barrel or other part should be made quite bright with emery or a fine smooth file, (but not burnished,) after which it must be carefully cleaned from all greasiness; a small quantity of pounded lime rubbed well over every part of the barrel is the best for this purpose. Plugs of wood are then to be put into the muzzle of the barrel and into the vent, and the mixture applied to every part with a clean sponge or rag. The barrel is then to be exposed to the air for twenty-four hours; after which time it is to be well rubbed over with a *steel scratch card* or *scratch brush*, until the rust is entirely removed; the mixture may then be applied again, as before, and in a few hours the barrel will be sufficiently corroded for the operation of scratch brushing to be repeated. The same process of scratching off the rust and applying the mixture is to be repeated twice or three times a day for four or five days, by which time the barrel will be of a very dark brown color.

When the barrel is sufficiently brown and the rust has been carefully removed from every part, about a quart of boiling water should be poured over every part of the barrel, in order that the action of the acid mixture upon the barrel may be destroyed and the rust thereby prevented from rising again.

The barrel, when cold, should afterwards be rubbed over with linseed oil or sperm oil. It is particularly directed that the steel scratch card or scratch brush be used in the place of a hard hair brush, otherwise the browning will not be durable, nor have a good appearance.

The browning mixture is applied to other parts of arms in the same manner as to the barrels.

About 6 quarts of browning mixture are required for 1,000 barrels.

To remove old browning: Plug the vent and the muzzle of the barrels; immerse the browned parts for one hour in boiling lime water or lye, to remove the varnish or grease; wipe them and put them in vinegar, in a wooden trough, for half an hour or an hour, when the browning may be rubbed off with a rag.

PACKING SMALL ARMS.

Box for 20 *Percussion Muskets.* Plate 16.

The box is made of well seasoned pine boards 1 in. thick; the sides and bottoms lap over the ends. 4 *corner pieces* (oak) 2.25 in. wide, 1.125 in. thick; the width of the corner piece is placed against the end of the box; a rabet is cut in each piece to receive the ends of a board 4.5 in. wide and .125 in. thick, which forms the inner lining of the implement pocket. 2 *end linings*, between the corner pieces, 8.75 in. deep, leaving vacant spaces above them, between the corner pieces, 4.5 in. deep, for the implements. They are fastened to the ends, each with two nails.

Interior dimensions of the box: Length, between the end linings, 59.25 in.; width, 15.75 in.; depth, 13.25 in.

The *ends* are fastened with nine 8d nails in two rows, in each corner piece. Each *side* is fastened with five 12d nails in each end, three 10d nails, and one 2 in. screw No. 14, (above the nails) in each corner piece. The *bottom* is fastened to each end and lining, with twelve 10d nails, and to each side with ten 10d nails and two 2 in. screws. The top is fastened with two 2 in. screws to each end, and four to each side. Two holes are bored in each end, 6 in. apart and 8 in. from the bottom, to receive *rope beckets*, .5 in. thick and 18 in. long, which are inserted and fastened by a knot countersunk in the end, before the linings are nailed on.

Two grooves, 1 in. wide and .25 in. deep, are cut in each side of the box, close to the corner pieces, to receive the packing stuff.

4 *bayonet clamps* 1 in. thick; two of them are 1 in. deep; the others, 1.5 in. They have each ten notches on the under side to receive the blades of the bayonets, and they are fastened to the bottom of the box, each with 2 screws. The small clamps are placed 3.4 in. apart, in the clear; the large ones, 5.5 in. apart.

4 *muzzle clamps*, 1 in. thick and 2.25 in. wide; each clamp has 5 holes for the muzzles of the barrels and 5 for the heads of the ramrods. They are placed in the grooves; the lower clamps fastened to the ends of the box at the bottom, each with two nails; the others sliding in the grooves.

4 *butt clamps*, 2 in. thick, 2.25 in. wide. They have rabets 1 in. thick at the ends, to slide in the grooves, and each clamp has 5 sloping notches 1 in. deep, 1.5 in. wide at top, and 2 in. at bottom, to receive the butts of the muskets.

2 *middle clamps*, 1.125 in. thick, 2 in. wide, with rabets to fit the grooves—they are laid in flat.

2 *top clamps*, 2 in. thick, 3.125 wide, with rabets 1 in. thick at each end, to slide in the grooves. The cover presses on them and keeps the muskets tight.

To pack a box of Muskets.

Unfix the bayonets and let down the hammers.

The small bayonet clamps being fastened down, place the points of the bayonets in their notches, the bayonets lying on the edge of the blade; then put in the large clamps and screw them down.

Place the lower tier of ten muskets; the muzzles and ramrods in the holes in the lower end clamps, the butts resting on the opposite clamp; put two lower butt clamps in the grooves over the butts of the lower tier of muskets, and over them the two middle clamps. Place the upper muzzle clamps in the grooves; insert the upper tier of muskets like the lower; put in the upper butt clamps and the top clamps.

Put the implements in the pockets provided for them, and screw on the cover.

Packing box for 20 Rifles.

Rifles are packed in the same manner as muskets, the box being made like the musket box except in its dimensions, and omitting the *bayonet clamps.*

Interior dimensions of rifle box: Length between the end linings 50 in.; width 16.75 in.; depth 12.5 in.

Packing box for 50 Pistols. Plate 16.

The form and dimensions of the box are represented in the plate.

The muzzles and the heads of the rods are inserted in holes countersunk in the side of the box, the handle of the stock being confined by 4 *clamps*, which slide in grooves made in the ends of the box.

The implements are placed in a small compartment provided for them, at the top of the box.

Interior dimensions of pistol box: Length 42.25 in.; width 14.5 in.; depth 12 in.

Weights of boxes of Arms packed.

20 muskets, percussion	290	lbs.
20 do. flint	300	"
20 rifles, percussion	275	"
50 pistols, do.	190	"

Packing Arms with Straw.

In the field, or under other circumstances, when the proper arm chests are not on hand, it may sometimes be necessary to pack arms in this manner.

The interior dimensions of a box for 20 muskets may be the same as for the regular packing box.

The straw should be long, perfectly dry, and free from dust; *rye straw* is the best; *hay* should not be used: about 25 lbs. of straw are required to a box.

To prepare the musket for packing: oil it; let down the hammer, pass the bayonet up to the socket into the guard bow, on the right side, in front of the trigger. Make a rope of about 40 straws, slightly twisted, and 40 in. long; wrap it about the musket, commencing on top of the hammer, going round the bayonet below, again over the hammer and round the piece in front of the guard, then over the socket of the bayonet near the neck, and wrapping the rest around the handle of the stock.

Lay a bed of straw 2 in. thick in the bottom of the box; in the middle and at 6 in. from the ends, place three cushions of straw 6 in. thick and 12 in. wide.—Put in a tier of 10 muskets crossing each other, the butts resting alternately against the ends of the box, the guards uppermost, and the hammers bearing on the cushions. Put small trusses of straw under the upper and middle bands, by raising the muskets at one end and then pressing them down between the others. Pack, between the butts, wads of straw 8 in. long, made of a handful of straws folded in three; cover the guards and guard bows with the ends of the straw that forms these wads, which will be still about 12 in. long. Put in another tier of 10 muskets in the same manner, making the cushions 4 in. thick. Pack the implements in straw in the vacant spaces. Fill the box with straw, so that the cover shall require strong pressure to keep it down. Put two hoops round the box, at 18 in. from the ends.

Other arms, swords, &c., are packed in a similar manner.

Arms should not be wrapped in paper, unless it be oiled, as it attracts moisture more readily than straw does.

PRESERVATION OF ARMS IN STORE.

Arrangement and Manner of Storing Arms.

Arms are kept at the Arsenals either in the boxes in which they are received from the armories, or in racks.

Those of each kind are kept separate and they are arranged according to the model, the place and year of fabrication, and the time when they were last cleaned.

New arms are kept distinct from those which have been repaired.

Each parcel should have a label indicating the kind, number, model, date of their receipt in store, and of their being last cleaned.

The manner of keeping arms at the arsenals is determined by the chief of the Ordnance Department, according to the peculiar circumstances of each case, and racks are constructed for them only in pursuance of special authority from the Ordnance office; without such authority they are kept in boxes. The form and arrangement of the racks vary with those of the room in which they are placed, so as to use the space to the best advantage, and give light and air to every part of the room. The usual arrangement of racks for muskets is to establish two rows of double racks, two tiers high, perpendicular to the length of the room, leaving alleys around the room next to the walls, and in the centre, if necessary. The bayonets are passed through the middle band swivel, the socket covering the top of the ramrod. Other racks of a similar kind may be made for *rifles*, *carbines*, &c. ***Pistols*** are suspended by the guard bows, on hooks driven into the faces of the musket racks, or into the joists, or into strips attached to the walls of the building.

When there are neither racks nor boxes prepared, the arms are stored in dry rooms, arranged in rows apart from the walls, standing on their muzzles and supported by frames to prevent them from pressing too much on each other. The bayonets should be unfixed and passed through the swivel. They should be covered with tarpaulins or cloths, if necessary, to protect them from dust.

Arms of peculiar kinds and arms to be repaired, are kept separate from others; as also arms unserviceable or condemned to be broken up.

Limbs and spare parts intended for repairs of arms should be kept in store by themselves, in a dry place, classed according to the kind of arms and to the model and year of fabrication, and labeled accordingly.

Musket and *rifle barrels* and other long barrels, standing on their muzzles; the piles covered from the dust with tarpaulins supported so as not to touch the barrels. *Pistol barrels, bayonets*, and other small parts, in drawers or boxes, properly labeled. *Stocks*, in square piles, in the attic or upper story of the building.

Care of Arms in Store.

Arms when received at an arsenal should be unpacked and carefully examined, to detect any damage suffered in transportation; they should be cleaned and oiled, if they require it. Those arms which are not to be placed in racks should be returned to the boxes, laid in loosely but safely, and the cover slightly fastened down, so that they can be readily examined.

All arms in store should be frequently examined, to see that they do not become rusty. Those which are found to be rusted should be immediately cleaned and again oiled. Browned arms, if affected with specks of rust, should be rubbed hard with linseed oil, and if the appearance of the browning indicate that the acid is not neutralized, care should be taken to examine the arms again within a short time, as it may be found necessary to remove and renew the browning; but this operation should not be performed without special authority from the chief of the Ordnance Department, on the report of a duly authorized inspector.

Arms which are to be repaired should be oiled and taken care of in the same manner as serviceable arms. Irreparable arms, the parts of which can be used for repairs, should be oiled. Similar remarks apply to spare parts for repair of arms.

Sperm oil should be used for greasing arms.

Empty boxes from which the arms in racks are taken should be kept with all the parts belonging to them in the attics or other dry situations.

The store houses for arms should be aired in clear dry weather.

Issuing Arms.

The Ordnance Regulations prescribe the manner of issuing arms to the troops, under the various circumstances of service, and to the States, for arming the militia.

All arms issued from an arsenal should be carefully examined before delivery, cleaned and put in good order; if intended for transportation, they should be oiled, if necessary, after cleaning, and carefully packed.

PRESERVATION OF ARMS IN SERVICE.

The officers, non-commissioned officers, and soldiers should be instructed and practised in the nomenclature of the arms, the manner of dismounting and mounting them, and the precautions and care required for their preservation.

Each soldier should have a screw driver and a wiper, and each squad of 10, a wire and a tumbler punch, and a spring vice. No other implements should be used in taking arms apart or in setting them up.

In the inspection of arms, officers should attend to the qualities essential to service, rather than to a bright polish on the exterior of the arms. The arms should be inspected in the quarters at least once a month, with the barrel and lock separated from the stock.

Taking Arms to pieces.

To take apart the altered percussion musket, pattern of 1822.—1. The bayonet—2. The ramrod—3. The side screws—4. The side plate—5. The lock—6. The upper band—7. The upper band spring—8. The middle band—9. The middle band spring—10. The trigger wire—11. The trigger—12. The tang screw—13. The lower band—14. The lower band spring—15. The barrel—16. The guard screws—17. The guard—18. The butt plate screws—19. The butt plate.

In the musket of the model of 1840, and in the new percussion musket, the trigger screw and trigger are taken off after the guard, then the pin for the ramrod spring, and the ramrod springs.

Order in which the lock is taken apart.—Cock the piece and put the spring vice, or clamp, on the main spring. 1. The main spring screw—2. The main spring—3. The sear spring screw (before turning this screw entirely out, strike the elbow of the spring with the screw driver, so as to disengage the pivot from its mortise)—4. The sear spring—5. The sear screw—6. The sear—7. The bridle screw—8. The bridle—9. The tumbler screw—10. The tumbler (it is driven out with the punch inserted in the screw hole)—11. The hammer.

The lock and the musket are put together in the inverse order of taking them apart.

The tumbler screw has a larger head than any other lock screw. The other four lock screws are distinguished by their lengths, which are in the following order, beginning with the shortest, viz: 1. Main spring screw—2. Sear spring screw—3. Bridle screw—4. Sear screw. The two side screws are of nearly equal length; the point of the rear one is flat, that of the front one rounded. There are two sizes for the threads of these screws; the first for the side screws, the second for all the others.

Before replacing the screw, put a small drop of *sperm oil* in the screw hole or on the point of the screw; put a drop of oil also on the arbor and pivot of the tumbler; between the moveable branches of the springs and the lock plate; on the hook and notches of the tumbler, after the lock is put together. Take care that the screws are not turned in too hard, so as to make the limbs bind; to insure this, try the motion of each limb before and after its spring is mounted, and see that it moves freely without friction.

The soldier should never take the lock apart, take off the guard, or take out the cone, except when a non-commissioned officer considers it necessary. The band and rod springs, and the butt plate should not be taken off unless it is impossible to clean them in place· The breech screw should be taken out only by an armorer, and *never* in ordinary cleaning; the same remark applies to the bayonet clasp of the new musket, which should be frequently oiled.

Cleaning and care of Arms.

For the iron and steel parts, when much rusted, use fine emery, sifted and moistened with oil ; when slightly rusted, use rotten stone or brick dust, sifted very fine, moistened likewise with oil. *For the brass parts*, use rotten stone or fine brick dust, moistened with vinegar or water; these parts should not be greased. Make use of a hard brush, or a piece of soft wood, such as white pine or cedar. Remove the dirt from the screw holes by screwing a piece of soft wood into them. Wipe the parts clean with a linen rag, (leaving a *little oil* on the inner parts of the lock,) but never *burnish* them.

To clean the exterior of the barrel, lay it flat on a bench or table or piece of board, in order to avoid bending it. The practice of cleaning a bright barrel by supporting it at the two ends and rubbing it with a strap or buff stick, or with the ramrod to burnish it, is highly pernicious, and should be strictly prohibited. After firing, the barrel should be always washed; when the water comes off clear, wipe the barrel dry, and then pass into it a rag moistened with oil.

To take off the barrel: after removing the bands and the tang screw, hold the stock and barrel lightly with the left hand, about 6 inches from the breech, the barrel down, with the muzzle about an inch from the ground ; strike with the right hand on the handle of the stock until the barrel is disengaged from its groove, supporting the barrel with the left hand until it can be seized by the right hand and separated from the stock.

To change the cone, when it is broken or worn out : after removing the old cone, enter the new one carefully with the fingers, before using the wrench, in order to avoid bruising the thread in the barrel.

It is very important to use no other implements than those before mentioned. By using nails to drive out the wires, their holes are enlarged. The main spring should never be heated for the purpose of either raising or lowering its temper; this destroys the elasticity of the spring and the lock no longer gives fire.

The notches of the tumbler, the hook of the mainspring, and, in general, all the joints of the lock, should be frequently oiled, after first wiping off the hard grease and the dust.

Browned arms are cleaned by rubbing them hard with an oiled rag until the oil is well incorporated with the browning ; or by rubbing them with bees wax on a rag or cork.

Care of Hall's Carbines.

The peculiar construction of these arms renders it necessary to observe certain precautions in the use of them, besides those which are required generally for the preservation of small arms.

To take the arm apart. Turn out the front side screw and remove the receiver, then turn out the other side screw, loosen the bands and take off the barrel. The order in which the other mountings are detached from the stock is not important.

To take the lock apart. Detach the limbs in the following order: 1, the sear spring screw; 2, the sear screw; 3, the sear; 4, the sear spring; 5, the main spring screw, (after compressing the main spring with the spring vice, and detaching it from the link;) 6, the main spring; 7, the hammer screw; 8, the hammer; 9, the link screw; 10, the link.

To put the arm together. The mountings are attached to the stock before the barrel is put in, observing that the butt piece screw should not be turned in hard until the barrel is in place.

To put the lock together. Place the sear spring and turn its screw loosely in; put in the main spring and its screw, and then the hammer; hook the link to the main spring with the aid of the spring vice; put in the sear and its screw, and then turn in the sear screw and sear spring screw tight. The tumbler screw and the sear screw should be turned in very tight; the other screws are left rather loose.

The greatest attention must be paid to the chocks, by which the recoil of the receiver is checked, and the opening between it and the barrel regulated. This opening should be such as to admit one thickness of common writing paper, and to bind two thicknesses; if the opening becomes, from any cause, too great, it may be diminished by inserting a thin slip of metal in the notch of the supporter, behind one chock or both, as may be required.

The shoulders of the receiver must always bear firmly against both chocks; *the piece should never be fired without the chocks being in place,* as in that case the opening between the receiver and the barrel becomes much too great, a part of the charge is perhaps lost, the effect of the remainder much lessened, and the stock almost inevitably destroyed by the blast, and by the undue strain which it suffers from the recoil of the receiver.

If by frequent firing the receiver becomes foul so as to close with difficulty, or not to admit the ball readily, its easy action may be restored by slightly wetting it and wiping the bore with the finger, and the muzzle with the palm of the hand.

INSPECTION OF ARMS IN SERVICE, OR WHICH HAVE BEEN IN SERVICE.

Implements. Standard and limit gauges for the bore, limit gauges for the exterior of the barrel, and a screw plate with taps for the holes of the lock plate.

The following are the principal points to be attended to in the inspection of arms :

1st. *The arms being taken to pieces and cleaned.*

Barrel. *Defects for which the barrel must be condemned as unfit for service.* The large gauge entering the whole length of the barrel. The small or standard gauge not entering, unless the diminution of the bore is caused by the barrel being indented or bent, defects which may be remedied. A diminution of the exterior diameter at the breech or at the muzzle, so as to enter the small receiving gauges : this diminution is 0.1 inch at the breech ; 0.03 inch at the muzzle for arms with bayonets, and 0.045 inch for arms without bayonets. A diminution of more than 0.25 in the length of a pistol barrel, or 0.5 inch in the lengths of other barrels. Splits, cross cracks, and other serious defects, caused either by bad workmanship or by use.

Examine the barrel carefully to see if it has any of the above defects, and if so, mark them with a file, when not very apparent—see if the bayonet stud is broken or too much worn—if the cone seat is perfect, and its thread in good order, and the vent unobstructed. If the breech screw is not tight after entering 5 or 6 threads, or if it can be screwed down by hand without the use of a wrench—if the threads are not sharp and sound—if the plug does not fill up the whole box of the female screw—if the tang is broken or cracked at the screw hole—or if, when the breech screw is in, the tang is not even with the upper surface of the barrel, a new breech screw is required.

Cone. Examine the chamfered end of the cone to see that it is not broken or bruised ; examine also the thread and the vent.

Bayonet. A bayonet is considered unserviceable if the blade is 1 inch too short —see if it is sound and perfect in all its parts, and if it fits the barrel—also, if the clasp is in good order and turns freely.

Lock. See if the fixed branches of the *springs* fit close to the lock plate, if the moveable branches are clear of it, and if any of the parts are wood bound.

Have the springs and the bridle of the tumbler renewed when their pivots are broken. There should be an equal space between the lock plate and the sear, the tumbler and the hammer.

If the *sear* rubs on the plate, have it adjusted. The friction of the *tumbler* may be caused by the bridle being badly pierced, in which case renew the bridle.

If the hammer rubs on one side only, have it adjusted; if it rubs every where, the arbor of the tumbler does not project sufficiently, and the tumbler should be renewed. If the *notches of the tumbler* are broken, or the edges too blunt, have them dressed; if the hook of the tumbler projects beyond the edge of the lock plate when the hammer is let down, the tumbler should be renewed. The arbor and the pivot of the tumbler should fit well in their holes. Examine the *sear* closely, and have it renewed when the nose is too thin or is worn on the side next the lock plate, although it may be perfect on the exterior. If the hammer is not steady, the tumbler should be renewed. Try the action of the hammer, to see that it explodes the cap with certainty.

Renew the *lock plate* when the holes are too much worn to be dressed over. Renew every limb that is broken or cracked, the screws which are too much worn, or of which the stems are bent, or the slits too much enlarged.

Mountings. See if the parts are complete and sound.

If the *tang screw* does not fit tight in the screw hole of the guard plate, renew whichever part is defective.

Ramrod. See if it is sound and has a good thread, and is of the proper length, otherwise replace it.

Stock. Examine carefully the *bed of the lock*, and the holes for the band springs. Press the thumb against the *facings*, to see if they are split at the holes for the side screws, and renew the stock if it is split there or at any other part, to an injurious extent.

2nd. The arms complete,

Are inspected according to the rules before laid down for the inspection of finished arms; due allowance being made for the necessary wear in service.

REPAIRS OF ARMS AT ARSENALS.

When arms which have been in the hands of the troops are turned into store at an arsenal, they should be inspected by a master armorer, under the supervision of an officer, and classed as follows:

1st. *Serviceable arms.*
2nd. *Arms requiring repairs.*
3rd. *Irreparable arms.*

Arms requiring repairs are classified according to their kinds and models, and to the extent of the repairs required. Each arm should be marked with a number, and the requisite repairs should be noted on the register of inspection, to guide the workmen and to govern the issue of spare parts required for repairs.

Repairs prohibited. The following repairs being always imperfect, the parts requiring them should be replaced: cutting off a barrel—brazing a patch on a barrel—brazing a tang on the breech screw—brazing a bolster on a lock plate—reaming out the hole for the arbor of the tumbler—brazing a piece for a tumbler hole or a shoulder on the hammer—hammering in the edge of the hole to make it fit tight on the square of the tumbler—putting a pivot to a tumbler—twisting the square of the tumbler to increase the sweep of the hammer—straightening the arbor—brazing a ramrod—splicing a stock.

The spare parts furnished from the armories are in general *filed and finished*, except hardening and tempering. The screws are finished and hardened.

The parts of Hall's arms are supplied in a finished state.

Fitting new parts. To adjust a new lock, the flat of the barrel should not be filed, but the bolsters of the lock plate should be ground.

The *barrel* should not be touched with a file, except in dressing the flat on the side of the lock, when it has been injured by rust. *In replacing the bayonet stud,* avoid cutting too deep into the barrel and producing a projection inside; try the small gauge in the barrel after the operation. *In fitting a new bayonet,* dress out the groove of the socket and ream out the socket if necessary.

To replace a lock plate: Use the old plate as a gauge for filing and piercing the new one, in order that it may fit well in the stock, &c. *In fitting a hammer,* dress out the tumbler hole to make it fit the tumbler; set the hammer parallel to the plate. Let it down on the cone and correct the set of the hammer if necessary. *In adjusting a tumbler,* dress the square or the notches only, and never diminish the thickness. *In fitting a sear,* adjust the dimensions and curve of the nose according to the set of the tumbler and hammer. *To dress a tumbler or a sear,* the limb should be first softened if necessary, and after being fitted, it should be hardened and tempered blue. *In cutting the tumbler and sear screws,* cut them so that they cannot be driven in too far. *In fitting a guard plate, side plate, or butt plate,* do not file away the edges so that they shall not fit the beds.

Braze sights and bayonet studs only, and no other pieces; the solder is composed of two parts of brass and one of zinc, without any tin.

Irreparable Arms.

Arms are considered *irreparable* when both the barrel and stock are unfit for service; or when the arms require very extensive repairs and the parts can be made useful for repairs of other arms. They can be broken up only by special authority, and they should therefore be oiled and preserved, in order to be submitted to an inspector, as prescribed in the Ordnance regulations.

When arms are broken up, the parts are classed either as *serviceable, reparable,* or *unserviceable;* those of the last class should be turned into store as *scrap iron or steel, &c.*

Number and kind of Armorer's Tools required for any number of workmen, from 1 to 12, at an Arsenal for repairs.

Number of workmen -	1	2	3	4	5	6	7	8	9	10	11	12
TOOLS.												
Awls—wire	3	3	3	3	3	3	6	6	6	6	6	6
Band-sets, for muskets, rifles and pistols	1	1	1	1	1	1	2	2	2	2	2	2
Brace, drill, } Iron	1	1	1	1	1	1	1	1	1	1	1	1
Brace, band, } Iron	1	2	3	4	5	6	7	8	9	10	11	12
Bitts—ramrod } for do.	3	3	3	3	3	3	6	6	6	6	6	6
" centre } for do.	6	6	6	6	6	6	12	12	12	12	12	12
" chambering } for do.	3	3	3	3	3	3	3	3	3	3	3	3
" bayonet boring	1	1	1	1	1	1	1	1	1	1	1	1
" side screw do.	3	3	3	3	3	3	6	6	6	6	6	6
" guard screw do.	3	3	3	3	3	3	6	6	6	6	6	6
" butt screw do.	3	3	3	3	3	3	6	6	6	6	6	6
Brushes, hard	2	2	2	2	2	2	4	4	4	4	4	4
Brushes, hand (bench)	1	1	1	1	1	1	2	2	2	2	2	2
Callipers, pairs	1	1	1	1	1	1	2	2	2	2	2	2
Centre punch	1	2	3	4	5	6	7	8	9	10	11	12
Chisels, cold	3	6	9	12	15	18	21	24	27	30	33	36
Chisels, stocker's	12	12	12	12	12	12	24	24	24	24	24	24
Chisels, bottoming or foot	2	2	2	2	2	2	4	4	4	4	4	4
Compasses, pairs	1	1	1	1	1	1	2	2	2	2	2	2
Countersinks, pairs	3	6	9	12	15	18	21	24	27	30	33	36
Clamps, spring for do.	3	3	3	3	3	3	3	3	3	3	3	3
Clamps, for bands do.	2	2	2	2	2	2	2	2	2	2	2	2
Clamps, for swivels do.	3	3	3	3	3	3	3	3	3	3	3	3
Drill-bow	1	1	1	1	1	1	2	2	2	2	2	2
Drills, assorted	12	12	12	12	12	12	24	24	24	24	24	24
Dies, sets	9	9	9	9	9	9	9	9	9	9	9	9
Drifts, cock	3	3	3	3	3	3	6	6	6	6	6	6
Dividers, spring	1	1	1	1	1	1	1	1	1	1	1	1
Floats, barrel and rod for do.	3	3	3	3	3	3	6	6	6	6	6	6
Fleams, (or sliders)	2	2	2	2	2	2	4	4	4	4	4	4
Files, assorted	12	24	36	48	60	72	84	96	108	120	132	144
Glue pot	1	1	1	1	1	1	1	1	1	1	1	1
Gouges, stocker's	12	12	12	12	12	12	24	24	24	24	24	24
Grinders, assorted	30	30	30	30	30	30	30	30	30	30	30	30
Gauges, lock for do.	8	8	8	8	8	8	8	8	8	8	8	8
Gauge, wire	1	1	1	1	1	1	1	1	1	1	1	1
Hooks, spring	1	2	3	4	5	6	7	8	9	10	11	12
Hammers, bench	2	4	6	8	10	12	14	16	18	20	22	24
Knives, drawing, (stocker's)	2	2	2	2	2	2	4	4	4	4	4	4
Levelers	2	2	2	2	2	2	4	4	4	4	4	4
Mandrils, swivel for do.	1	1	1	1	1	1	1	1	1	1	1	1
Mandrils, band, sets of	3	3	3	3	3	3	3	3	3	3	3	3
Nippers, pairs	1	2	3	4	5	6	7	8	9	10	11	12
Pliers, pairs	1	1	1	1	1	1	2	2	2	2	2	2
Planes, assorted, stocker's	7	7	7	7	7	7	14	14	14	14	14	14
Reamers, for do.	12	24	36	48	60	72	84	96	108	120	132	144
Rods, wiping	1	1	1	1	1	1	2	2	2	2	2	2
Rods, rifling	1	1	1	1	1	1	2	2	2	2	2	2
Rifflers	2	2	2	2	2	2	4	4	4	4	4	4
Stakes	1	2	3	4	5	6	7	8	9	10	11	12
Saws, hack	1	2	3	4	5	6	7	8	9	10	11	12
Stocks, die	2	2	2	2	2	2	2	2	2	2	2	2
Stocks, drill	1	1	1	1	1	1	2	2	2	2	2	2
Set-punch	1	2	3	4	5	6	7	8	9	10	11	12
Scraper, barrel—musket, rifle and pistol	2	2	2	2	2	2	4	4	4	4	4	4
Screw-drivers	3	6	9	12	15	18	21	24	27	30	33	36
Screw plates	3	3	3	3	3	3	3	3	3	3	3	3
Squares, iron	2	2	2	2	2	2	2	2	2	2	2	2

Number and kind of Armorer's Tools—Continued.

NUMBER OF WORKMEN - -	1	2	3	4	5	6	7	8	9	10	11	12
TOOLS.												
Tongs, pairs - - - - -	7	7	7	7	7	7	7	7	7	7	7	7
Taps, cone—sets - - - -	1	1	1	1	1	1	2	2	2	2	2	2
Taps, lock screws—musket, rifle and pistol	6	6	6	6	12	12	12	12	18	18	18	18
Taps, side screws— do. -	6	6	6	6	12	12	12	12	18	18	18	18
Taps, breeching - do. - -	9	9	9	9	9	9	9	9	9	9	9	9
Vices, barrel - - - - -	1	1	1	1	1	1	1	1	1	1	1	1
Vices, bench - - - - -	1	2	3	4	5	6	7	8	9	10	11	12
Vices, hand - - - - -	1	2	3	4	5	6	7	8	9	10	11	12
Wrenches, breech and tap—musket, rifle and pistol - - - - -	4	4	4	4	4	4	4	4	4	4	4	4
Wrenches—hammer - - -	1	1	1	1	1	1	1	1	1	1	1	1
Wrenches—cone - - - -	1	1	1	1	1	1	2	2	2	3	3	3

Spare parts required for the repair of 1000 *Percussion Muskets, for one year, in the field.*

PARTS.	New pattern.	Pattern of 1822 altered.	PARTS.	New pattern.	Pattern of 1822 altered.
Barrels..............	2	2	Middle band swivels...	75	75
Breech screws.........	20	20	Middle band springs....	30	30
Tang screws..........	50	50	Lower bands..........	30	30
Cones................	75	75	Lower band springs ...	30	30
Bayonets	75	75	Side plates...........	30	30
Bayonet clasps........	100		Guard plates..........	10	10
Clasp screws..........	100		Guard bows	10	10
Locks................	2	2	Guard bow nuts.......	50	
Lock plates...........	6	6	Guard bow swivels	75	50
Hammers	75	75	Triggers	25	25
Tumblers.............	75	75	Trigger screws........	25	
Tumbler screws	125	125	Trigger pins	......	25
Bridles	25	25	Guard plate screws.....	75	75
Bridle screws	125	125	Butt plates...........	5	5
Sears................	40	40	Butt plate screws......	25	25
Sear screws...........	125	125	Ramrods..............	100	100
Sear springs..........	125	125	Ramrod springs.......	50	
Sear spring screws.....	125	125	Rod spring pins.......	50	
Main springs	125	125	Ramrod stops.........	10	
Main spring screws....	125	125	Stocks	50	50
Side screws...........	200	200	Screw drivers.........	75	75
Upper bands..........	50	50	Wiperrs	75	75
Upper band springs....	75	75	Ball screws...........	25	25
Middle bands.........	30	30	Spring vices..........	25	25

Spare parts required for the repair of 1000 *Percussion Rifles, Musketoons, and Pistols, during one year, in the field.*

PARTS.	Rifle.	Cavalry Musketoon.	Pistol.
Barrels	2	2	
Guides	25		
Sights	10		
Breech screws	10	10	5
Tang screws	30	25	10
Cones	50	50	50
Locks	2	2	
Lock plates	2	2	
Hammers	25	25	20
Tumblers	20	20	20
Tumbler screws	100	100	50
Bridles	20	20	15
Bridle screws	50	50	25
Sears	20	20	15
Sear screws	50	50	25
Sear springs	50	50	25
Sear spring screws	50	50	25
Main springs	50	50	25
Main spring screws	50	50	25
Side screws	100	100	50
Upper bands with swivels	10	10	
Upper band swivels and rivets	50		
Upper band springs	30	30	
Lower bands	10	10	10
Lower band springs	20		
Swivel bars	....	20	
Swivel bar rings	....	40	
Swivel bar nuts	....	20	
Side plates	10	10	10
Guard plates	10	10	5
Guard bows	20	20	10
Guard bow nuts	40	40	20
Guard bow swivels and rivets	50		
Triggers	10	10	5
Trigger screws	10	10	5
Guard plate screws	50	50	25
Butt plates	2	2	10
Butt plate screws	20	20	25
Box plates, with catches	5		
Box plate screws	10		
Box plate springs	10		
Box plate spring screws	10		
Ramrods	50	25	25
Ramrod heads	25	10	10
Ramrod springs and pins	10	10	

Spare parts of Arms.—Continued.

Parts.	Rifle.	Cavalry Musketoon.	Pistol.
Ramrod stops	5	5	
Ramrod swivel: side bars	....	100	50
Ramrod swivel: screws	....	50	25
Ramrod swivel: cross heads	....	50	25
Ramrod swivel: rivet burrs	....	100	
Stocks	30	30	20
Screw drivers	50	50	25
Wipers	50	50	25
Ball screws	10	10	5
Spring vices	10	10	5
Bullet moulds	10	....	10

Spare parts required for the repair of 1000 *Hall's Carbines (percussion) for one year, in the field.*

Parts.	No.	Parts.	No.
Barrels and supporters complete	2	Aprons and stops	10
Chocks	50	Upper bands	10
Chock screws	100	Ramrod springs	10
Receivers	2	Upper band springs	10
Cones	50	Lower bands	10
Hammers	50	Swivel bars	20
Tumbler screws	50	Swivel screws	20
Sears	20	Swivel rings	20
Sear screws	25	Guard plates	10
Sear springs	50	Guard bows	10
Sear spring screws	50	Guard bow nuts	20
Links	50	Catch levers and pins	20
Link screws	50	Guard plate screws	50
Main springs	50	Butt plates	5
Main spring screws	50	Butt plate screws	10
Catches	25	Ramrods	50
Catch screws	25	Stocks	100
Catch springs	25	Screw drivers	25
Catch spring screws	25	Wipers	25
Side screws	100	Spring vices	5
Butt pieces	10	Bullet moulds	10
Butt piece screws	25		

For the repair of the Artillery Musketoon :

The same parts as for the Cavalry Musketoon, with the following exceptions :

Omit : *Swivel bars, rings,* and *nuts.*

Add : Swivel plate and studs............................25
Swivel plate screws..............................50
Swivels and rivets...............................50
Lower band springs...............................20

For the repair of arms in the hands of troops in garrison, take about one-half of the number of parts required for arms in the field.

Spare parts required for repairs, if not obtained from arms that are broken up, are supplied from the armories, on requisitions made in the manner pointed out by the regulations of the Ordnance Department.

Durability and strength of Musket Barrels.

The United States musket barrel being much like the French musket barrel, the following remarks relative to the latter, (extracted from the *Aide Memoire,*) will apply to the former. It is to be observed that the charge of the French musket was formerly 162 grains Troy, priming included, (or 146 grains, exclusive of priming,) and is therefore considerably greater than our present service charge.

The regulation fixing the duration of small arms in the French service at 50 years, is founded on the durability of the barrel, which is the most important part of those arms. Experience has shown that a musket barrel will bear 25,000 discharges without becoming unserviceable, and even in time of war a musket is not fired more than 500 times a year. The wear caused by firing is therefore small, and the principal cause of the rejection of barrels is the diminution of 0.09 inch in the diameter at the breech. With good management and care, that diminution will take place very slowly, and it ought not generally to occur in the space of 50 years.

It has also been ascertained, by direct trials, that the strength of the barrel furnishes every requisite security against the accidents of service and the want of care on the part of the soldier; and that, even after being reduced in diameter 0.09 inch at the breech, it is still perfectly safe against the effect of the charge. In experiments made in 1806, barrels reduced 0.13 inch at the breech, bore a double and triple charge with one ball, or 2 cartridges placed one over the other.

Other trials were made in 1829, at the manufactory of Mutzig, on arms sent there for repairs, which had been a greater or less time in the hands of the troops. They furnished the following results :

1st. When a musket barrel is charged with a single cartridge, placed in any part of it, or with 2 or even with 3 cartridges, inserted regularly, without any interval between them, there is no danger of bursting; with 4 cartridges inserted regularly over each other, or with 2 or even 3 cartridges placed over each other with slugged balls, (or balls *driven* in, as in a rifle,) there is danger only in case of some defect of fabrication, or some deterioration in the barrel—with more than 4 cartridges inserted regularly one over another, or with 2, 3, and 4 cartridges with intervals between them, it is not safe to fire.

2nd. No danger of bursting is occasioned by leaving a ball screw in the barrel. There may be danger from a plug of wood driven tight into the muzzle, when the barrel has been loaded with 2 cartridges; or from a cork rammed into the barrel to a certain distance from the charge, with another cartridge over it.

Snow, clay, and sand, which may be accidentally introduced into the barrel are not dangerous, if they lie close to the charge; but they are so, when there is a space between them and the charge; in this case sand is the most dangerous, then clay and snow.

Balls or pieces of iron inserted over the charge, were not attended with danger when placed close to the charge, even when their weight amounted to 1¼ lb.; but there is danger from a piece of iron 0.5 inch square, weighing ¼ lb., if placed 20 inches or more from the breech.

3d. A barrel with a defect which might have escaped the inspector at the armory, bore the explosion of 3 cartridges, regularly inserted. After mutilation, which may have caused a reduction of metal in some parts, it may still be used without danger.

Finally, the diminutions of exterior diameter which may be produced in ordinary service are never sufficient to be dangerous. In these trials, barrels originally 0.272 inch thick at the breech, did not burst when loaded with 2 cartridges, until the thickness was reduced to 0.169 inch, and with one cartridge to 0.091 inch.

SWORDS AND SABRES.

NOMENCLATURE.

Cavalry Sabre.—Plate 15.

BLADE. Shoulder, back, edge, bevel, point, curvature, large groove, small groove ; *tang*, riveting.

HILT. *Surmounting* (brass,) notch for the guard, back, rivet cap, hole for the tang of the blade—*gripe*, wooden body, (birch or maple,) leather covering, (calf skin blackened,) wires, (brass,) notch for the guard, ridges, shoulder, hole for the tang of the blade—GUARD ; *front branch*, hook ; *back branch; middle branch; plate*, mortise for the tang, flange, bead, lip.

SCABBARD. (sheet steel)—*Body*, back, front, sides, holes for the rivets—*Mouth piece*, rim, springs, rivet holes ; 2 *rivets*—2 *Bands*, knob, eye for the ring—2 *Rings*—*Tip*, front branch, back branch.

The same sabre, with gilt mountings, for cavalry officers.

Sabre for Mounted Artillery.—Plate 15.

BLADE. With but one groove.

HILT. *Guard*, one branch terminating in a scroll ; the plate has 2 countersinks, one for the gripe, the other for the scabbard.

SCABBARD. *Spring*, fastened to the back by 1 *rivet*—no mouth piece.

In other respects the nomenclature is the same as that of the cavalry sabre.

The same sabre, with ornamented gilt mountings, for mounted officers of artillery and infantry.

Foot Artillery Sword.—Plate 15.

BLADE. Straight, two edged, narrower nearer the hilt than in the middle—*Body* (or blade proper,) shoulder, shoulder rounding, ridges, point, bevels, edges—*Tang*, its rounding and riveting, three holes for the gripe rivets.

HILT. (brass, in one piece)—Cross, knob and panel of the cross, mortise for the tang, gripe, fillet, necks, swell, knob with an *eagle* on each side, bolster and hole for the tang rivet, grooves and ridges, three holes and bolsters for the gripe rivets—3 *Rivets* (iron.)

SCABBARD. (harness leather, jacked, blackened, and varnished,)—*Body*, edges, inner and outer sides—*Mountings* (brass.)—*Ferrule*, stud, bead, cap—*Safes* (buff leather)—4 *Nails* for the ferrule and safes—*Tip*, bead, knob—4 *Nails* for the tip.

Infantry Sword.—Plate 15.

BLADE. (Straight, cut and thrust)—Back, edge, groove, bevel, point.

HILT. *Surmounting* (brass,) notch for the hook of the guard, rivet cap, shoulder for the ferrule, hole for the tang ; 2 *ferrules*—*Gripe*, wooden body, hole for the tang—*Covering* (sheet brass,) grooves and ridges.

GUARD, in one piece ; *branch*, hook and its shoulder ; *plate*, flange, bead ; *knob*.

SCABBARD. (Leather)—*Ferrule and hook*, (brass,)—*Tip* (brass,) body, front branch, back branch.

This sword is for the non-commissioned officers of foot troops; a similar one, without the guard *plate* and with a blade 26 *inches long*, for musicians.

The sword for *officers not mounted* is also of the same pattern, with ornamented gilt mountings and a silver gripe; the inner half of the guard plate is made with a *hinge*.

Principal dimensions and weights of Swords and Sabres.

DIMENSIONS.	Cavalry sabre.	Artillery sabre.	Artillery sword.	Infantry sword.
	In.	In.	In.	In.
Whole length of the sword or sabre in its scabbard	43.25	38.6	26.	38.75
Length of the blade proper	36.	32.	19.	32.
Length of the scabbard	37.25	33.	20.	32.5
Width of the blade in the middle	1.1	1.06	1.8	0.72
Versed sine of the curvature of the blade in the middle	1.5	2.32		
Versed sine of the curvature of the blade in proof	7.5	6.5	....	6.5
WEIGHTS.	Lbs. oz.	Lbs. oz.	Lbs. oz.	Lbs. oz.
Weight of the sword or sabre, complete	4 8	4 1½	3 3	2 5
Weight of the finished blade	1 5	....	1 9	
Weight of the scabbard	2 2	....	10	

PROOF AND INSPECTION OF SWORDS AND SABRES.

1st. The dimensions and form of the *blade* are verified by comparing it with the model, and by applying the appropriate gauges and patterns, for the length, width and thickness at several points, and the curvature, if any.

2nd. The *blade* is then proved as follows :—1st. The point is confined by a staple, and the blade is bent on each of the flat sides over a cylindrical block, the curvature of which is that of a circle 35 inches diameter, the curvature of the part next the tang being reduced by inserting a wedge 0.7 inch thick at the head and 14 inches long. 2nd. It is struck twice, on each of the flat sides, on a block of oak wood the curvature of which is the same as the above. 3d. It is struck twice on the edge and twice on the back across an oak block 1 foot in diameter. 4th. The point is placed on the floor and the blade bent until it describes an arc having the versed sine indicated in the above table. After these trials the blade is examined to see that it is free from flaws, cracks, or other imperfections, and that it is not *set*, that is to say, does not remain bent.

The blade of the *Artillery sword* is proved by striking each of the sides and edges twice on a flat block of hard oak wood.

The stamp of approval or condemnation is placed on the side of the blade, below the tang.

3d. The form, dimensions and workmanship of the *mountings* are examined and compared with the model. After the blade is mounted, the sword is again examined, and it is struck 4 times on a hard block of wood to test the strength of the mountings. The quality of the brass mountings may be tested by breaking a certain number, not more than 4 in each hundred, which should be taken from the pieces rejected for erroneous dimensions.

4th. The form, workmanship, and finish of the *scabbards* are examined and compared with the model, and their fitting to the blades tested. The sewing of leather scabbards and the fastening of the ferrules and tips will be particularly examined.

Steel scabbards are proved by letting fall on them, from a height of 18 inches, an iron weight of two pounds, 1 inch square at the base: 1st, on one side just above the upper band; 2nd, on the same side, 6 inches from the tip; 3d, on the opposite side, just above the lower band. In this proof the scabbard should not remain indented. The nature of the material (whether iron or steel) may be tested, if there is any doubt, by using nitric acid which will leave a black spot on the steel but not on the iron.

PACKING SWORDS AND SABRES.

Packing boxes for swords and sabres are made on the same principles as those for muskets and other small arms, being furnished with packing boards or partitions made with grooves to receive the scabbards near the hilt and near the point; the swords are placed in their scabbards, with the hilts and points alternately towards each end of the box; except the Artillery swords, two of which are placed in the length of the box, their points resting on a packing board in the middle. Number packed in a box:

30 Cavalry sabres. 50 Artillery swords.
50 Artillery sabres. 50 Infantry swords.

CLEANING SWORDS AND SABRES.

The iron and brass parts of swords and sabres are cleaned in the same manner as those of muskets. When the oil on the blade of a sword is dried up, it will leave a spot which may be removed by covering it with oil and rubbing it smartly, after a short time, with a linen rag. When a leather scabbard has become wet, draw the blade and dry the scabbard slowly without heating it; wipe the blade dry and pass an oiled rag over it and the scabbard, before returning the blade. Oil the blades of arms in store, and also the scabbards, especially on the seams.

ACCOUTREMENTS.

Infantry Accoutrements.

CARTRIDGE BOX, (black bridle leather.) Length 7.2 inch; width 1.6 inch; depth in front, 5.8 inch—*inner cover*, (light upper leather,) 4 inches wide, with end pieces sewed to it, so as to cover the ends of the box—*flap*, 8.5 inches wide at bottom, 8 inches at top, with a button hole *strap* sewed near the bottom—*brass button*, riveted to the bottom of the box—*implement pocket* (light upper leather) sewed to the front of the box; 6 inches long, 3.5 inches deep, with a *flap*, *strap*, and *loop*—2 *loops*, on the back of the box, near the top, for the shoulder belt to pass through. 2 *roller buckles* (japanned, black,) for the belt; sewed to the bottom of the box. Two TINS, each with *one lower division*, 3 inches by 3.3 inches, open in front, to contain a bundle of 10 cartridges, and 2 *upper divisions*, 2.7 inches deep, one of 2 inches by 1.35 inch for 6 cartridges; the other 1.35 inch square, for 4 cartridges. The edges of the tin are turned over and soldered down, to prevent them from cutting the cartridges. All the tin linings should be made to slide freely in the boxes.

CARTRIDGE BOX PLATE: (brass,) oval, 3.5 inches by 2.2 inches, with the letters U. S. stamped on it—2 *eyes*, of iron wire, for fastening the plate to the flap of the box.

CARTRIDGE BOX BELT: (buff leather,) width, 2.25 inches; length, 55.5 inches, clear of the 2 *billets* for buckles, which are each 4.25 inches long and 0.875 inch wide.

CARTRIGE BOX BELT PLATE: (brass,) circular, 2.5 inches diameter, stamped with an *Eagle;* 2 *eyes*, of iron wire.

CAP POUCH: (black bridle leather,) length and depth 3 inches; width 1.25 inch—*inner cover*, with end pieces—*flap*, made of the same piece as the back, with a button hole strap at the bottom—*brass button*, riveted under the bottom of the pouch—2 *loops*, sewed to the back, 2.25 inches long, to admit a waist belt, of 2 inches—*lining*: a strip of sheepskin, with the wool on, 1.5 inch wide, glued with fish glue, and sewed to the back, at the mouth of the pouch.

CONE PICK: (steel wire, No. 18,) 1.5 inch long, with a ring handle 0.5 inch diameter; it is carried in a loop in the inner left hand corner of the cap pouch.

BAYONET SCABBARD: (black bridle leather.) Length, including the ferrule and tip, for the bayonets of the model of 1822, 18 inches; for bayonets of model of 1840, 19.5 inches. *Ferrule and tip*, brass. *Frog:* (buff leather,) sewed to a socket of black leather which is fastened to the top of the scabbard—the frog slides on the waist belt.

WAIST BELT: (buff leather) width 1.5 in.; length 38.5 in.; a *loop* at one end.

WAIST BELT PLATE, (brass) oval, 2.8 in. long by 1.6 in. wide, stamped with the letters U. S. 1 *stud* and 1 *hook* (brass.)

GUN SLING, (russet, bag leather) width 1.25 in.; length 46. in.; 1 *standing and* 1 *sliding loop—hook*, (brass) fastened to the sling with 2 *brass rivets*.

SWORD SHOULDER BELT, for non-commissioned officers—(buff leather)—width 2.3 in.; length of short branch 17 in.; long branch 40 in.—1 *standing loop*, on long branch—*Frog* for sword.

SHOULDER BELT PLATE—like the cartridge box belt plate, except in having 3 *hooks*, instead of eyes.

Rifle Accoutrements.

CARTRIDGE BOX. The leather parts are like those of the infantry cartridge box; length 7.2 in., depth in front 5 inches, width 1.6 in. *Two loops* are placed upright on the back of the box, to receive a 2 in. waist belt. The *tin lining* has 2 lower divisions, each 3.3 in. long by 2.8 in. deep, and 5 upper divisions, 1.35 in. square by 2.1 in. deep.

CARTRIDGE BOX PLATE. Like the infantry waist belt plate, except in having instead of a stud and a hook, 2 *eyes*, to fasten it to the flap of the box.

CAP POUCH. CONE PICK. WAIST BELT. 2 in. wide. WAIST BELT PLATE: like infantry cartridge box plate, with 2 *studs* and a *hook*. GUN SLING. SWORD SHOULDER BELT, for non-commissioned officers.	In other respects the same as for the infantry.

POUCH, (light upper shoe leather,) 7 in. wide at bottom, 6.6 in. at top, 5.5 in. deep, made with *gussets* at the sides and bottom—*partition*—*flap*, 2.7 in. deep, with a *strap* and leather *button* on the front side—2 *loops*, (japanned iron,) 0.9 in. wide and 0.7 in. long, for the belt rings.

FLASK. *Body* (copper bronzed,) length 7 in., greatest width 4 in., thickness 2 in.; diameter at top 1.7 in.—*inner charging tube*, (brass) 0.57 in. diameter, 1 in. long—*outer charging tube* 0.65 in. diameter, 1.75 in. long—*valve and spring*—2 *rings* for belt, (copper.)—Flask holds 8 oz. of powder: maximum charger 100 grains, minimum 75 grains—Weight of flask complete, 13 oz.

FLASK-AND-POUCH BELT, (buff leather,) 1.5 in. wide—*belt*, 26 in. long—2 *straps* at each end, 13.5 in. long, 0.6 in. and 0.9 in. wide, to which the pouch and flask are attached by *brass hooks*, riveted to the straps.

Cavalry Accoutrements.

CARTRIDGE BOX, for carbine or musketoon; like the rifle cartridge box.

PISTOL CARTRIDGE BOX. It is like the carbine cartridge box, except in its dimensions; length 6.2 in., width 1.3 in., height in front 3.5 in.—*inner cover*, 3.5 in. wide—*flap*, 6.6 in. wide at top, 6.8 in. at bottom, 6 in. deep—*Tins:* 2 lower divisions, 2 in. deep, 2.9 in. long, 1.2 wide; 5 upper divisions, 1.2 wide by 1.15 in. long and 1.5 in. deep.

CARTRIDGE BOX PLATE, for carbine or pistol cartridge box; the same as for the rifle.

CAP POUCH, } the same as for the infantry.
CONE PICK, }

SABRE BELT (buff leather)—*Waist belt*, 2 inches wide, 36 in. to 40 in. long—1 *square loop* and 2 *D rings* (brass,) for attaching the slings and shoulder strap—1 *shoulder strap*, 1.125 in. wide, 41 in. long, with 2 *hooks*, brass—2 *sabre* slings 1.125 in. wide; front sling 17 in. long, rear sling 34 in.—4 *studs* for do., brass—1 *sabre hook*, brass wire.

SABRE BELT PLATE—Like the rifle waist belt plate.

SWORD KNOT (buff leather)—*Strap* 1 in. wide, 36 in. long; one end of the strap is fastened to a *tassel* 3 in. long; the other end is passed through the tassel after going round the guard of the sabre, and is fastened by one of the tags of the tassel—1 *sliding loop*.

CARBINE SLING, (buff leather.) Length 56 in., width 2.5 in.—1 *buckle* and 1 *tip*, brass—*swivel* and *D* with *roller*, bright iron, 2.62 in. wide—*link* and *hook*, iron—*guard-spring*, steel.

HOLSTERS. *Pipe* (sole leather, black); diameter of cylindrical part 2 in.; length of do. 7.5 in.; width of the mouth, 4.8 in.; depth, 2.2 in.; whole length, 14.5 in.—*pocket*, (light upper leather,) 3.2 in. long, 2.5 in. deep, lined with *tin* and covered with a *flap*—5 *cylindrical divisions*, diameter 0.6 in., each for one cartridge—1 *centre piece* forming the backs and connecting the two holsters, (bridle leather, black,) length 22 in., width 5.75 in.—2 *straps* 14 in. long, 0.75

wide, with 2 buckles, to attach the holsters to the saddle—2 *surcingle loops*, (light bridle leather, black,) 1.5 in. wide, 3.5 in. long, doubled.

Two holster covers, (black leather;) 10 in. long, 9.5 in. wide over the cartridge-pocket—*straps*, 4 in. long, 1 in. wide, to button on 2 *brass studs* on the holster pipes.

Artillery Accoutrements.

For Mounted Artillery.

Sabre belt (buff leather) 1.7 in. wide, 36 to 40 in. long—2 *leather loops*, sewed on the outside of the belt for attaching 2 *brass loops* for the slings—2 *sabre slings*, like those on the cavalry sabre belt—4 *studs* for do.—1 *sabre hook.*

Sabre belt plate, (brass,) circular, 1.4 in. diameter, lettered *U. S.;* it slides on the belt and is fastened by a *brass hook* and a *sliding loop*—the plate hooks in a *ring* 1.95 in. exterior diameter, attached to the left side of the belt.

Sword knot. Like that for cavalry.

For Foot Artillery.

Sword belt (buff leather) 1.7 in. wide, made in three pieces; *long branch*, 24 in.; *frog piece* 4.5 in.; *short branch*, 4 in.; they are united together by 2 *loops*, brass—*frog*, 3.5 in. deep, 2.5 in. wide at top and 2.3 in. at bottom, suspended to the loops by 2 *slings* 1.3 in. wide and 3.5 in. long.

Belt plate, the same as for the sabre belt of mounted artillery.

This belt is also used by the non-commissioned officers of infantry, when armed with the foot artillery sword.

Sapper's Accoutrements.

Sword belt, (buff leather,) 2 inches wide, 36 to 40 inches long. *Frog*, sliding on the waist belt; width of the loop for the belt 3 inches; width at the bottom 4 inches.

Belt plate, like that for the artillery.

Cartridge box and plate,
Cartridge box belt and plate,
Cap pouch,
Cone pick,
} the same as for the infantry.

Spare parts required for repair of Side Arms and Accoutrements, for one year, in the field.

For 1000 *non-commissioned officers or musicians' swords.*

100 tips for scabbards.
20 ferrules and hooks.
40 guard bows.
50 belt plates.

For 1000 *Infantry accoutrements.*

50 tips for bayonet scabbards.
25 cartridge box plates.
50 cartridge box belt plates.
100 waist belt plates
100 cone picks.

For 1000 *Cavalry carbine slings.*

150 swivels.
150 swivel springs.

MATERIALS REQUIRED FOR MAKING ACCOUTREMENTS.

Leather.

19 Infantry cartridge box belts 200 Infantry bayonet frogs 45 Infantry waist belts 34 Rifle waist belts 33 Rifle pouch-and-flask belts 15 Cavalry sabre belts 20 Foot artillery sword belts 20 Horse artillery sabre belts 20 Carbine slings 70 Sword knots	Either of these can be cut out of one hide of *buff leather.*

40 Gun slings—out of one butt of *bag leather.*
8 Pairs of holsters—out of one side of *heavy sole leather.*
11 Infantry cartridge boxes—except pockets and inner covers—out of one side of *heavy bridle leather.*

27 Bayonet scabbards 40 Cap pouch fronts 10 Carbine cartridge boxes 12 Pistol cartridge boxes (except ends) 10 Holster centre pieces 60 Pairs of holster straps 70 Surcingle loops	Out of one side of *light bridle leather.*
12 Rifle pouches. 50 Pockets for infantry cartridge boxes 50 Inner covers for do do. 40 do. for cap pouches 40 Tops for do.	Out of one side of *light upper shoe leather.*

MATERIALS FOR ACCOUTREMENTS—*Continued.*

Thread.

100 Infantry cartridge boxes	1.25 lbs.	*Shoe thread,* green, No. 10, waxed with rosin wax.
100 Carbine ..... do.	1.0 "	
100 Pistol ..... do.	0.9 "	
100 Holsters	1.25 "	
100 Rifle pouches	0.75 "	
100 Gun slings	0.13 "	
100 Infantry waist belts	0.06 "	*Shoe thread,* No. 3, half bleached, waxed with beeswax.
100 Artillery sword belts	0.8 "	
100 Sabre belts	0.33 "	
100 Rifle pouch belts	0.13 "	

Metals.

For 100 *sets of Cavalry sabre belt mountings.*

100 Sabre hooks	2.5 lbs. brass wire, No. .
100 Loops	4 lbs. brass wire, No. 10.
100 Large hooks	4 lbs. sheet brass, No. 11.
100 Small hooks	1.5 lb. sheet brass, No. 14.
200 Rings	4 lbs. brass wire, No. 10.
400 Rivets	0.375 lb. brass wire, No. 15.
400 Studs	cast brass.
100 Belt plates	*See* below.

Tins for 100 *carbine cartridge boxes.*

75 sheets of sing'e tin. 1 lb. tinner's solder, (2 tin to 1 lead.)

Tins for 100 *pistol cartridge boxes.*

48 sheets of single tin. 1 lb. solder.

Tins for 100 *pairs of holsters.*

4½ sheets of single tin.	These tins may be cut from the remnants of the sheets required for 100 infantry cartridge boxes.
1 lb. solder.	

Tins for 100 *Infantry cartridge boxes.*

125 sheets of single tin. 1 lb. tinner's solder.

For 100 *plates for Infantry cartridge boxes, cavalry sabre belts, and rifle waist belts.*

4 lbs. sheet brass, No. 26.
7 lbs. do. No. 14, for sabre belt plate hooks.
1 lb. do. No. 5, for do. studs.
0.625 lb. iron wire, No. 14.
4 lbs. soft solder, (1 tin to 2 lead.)

For 100 *ferrules for bayonet scabbards.*

3 lbs. sheet brass, No. 25.
4.7 lbs. brass wire, 0.45 in. thick.
0.14 lb. copper wire, No. 15.
0.2 lb. spelter.

For 100 *Infantry cartridge box belt plates.*

3.75 lbs. sheet brass, No. 26.
0.844 lb. iron wire, No. 14.
4 lbs. soft solder.

For 100 *plates for Infantry waist belts and for carbine and pistol cartridge boxes.*

3 lbs. sheet brass, No. 26.
3 lbs. do. No. 14, for waist belt plate hooks.
0.75 lb. iron wire, No. 14, for cartridge box plates.
3 lbs. soft solder.

For 100 *gun sling hooks and rivets.*

1.5 lb. sheet brass, No. 14.
0.16 lb. brass wire, No. 15.

For 100 *Artillery sword belts.*

200 loops..8.5 lbs. brass wire, No. 10
100 small hooks..............................1.5 lb. sheet brass, No. 14.
200 rivets......................................0.14 lb. brass wire, No. 15.

For 100 *Artillery sabre and sword belt plates.*

25 lbs. pig brass.

For 100 *Rifle pouch and flask belts.*

4 lbs. sheet brass, No. 15.
0.66 lb. brass wire, No. 15.

WEIGHT OF ACCOUTREMENTS.

100 Infantry cartridge boxes and plates....................176 lbs.
100 Cartridge box belts and plates.............................63 "
100 Cap pouches and cone picks...............................13 "
100 Bayonet scabbards and frogs...............................27 "
100 Waist belts and plates for infantry.........................32 "
100 Gun slings..15 "
100 Non-commissioned officers' shoulder belts and plates....60 "
100 Rifle or carbine cartridge boxes and plates...............118 "
100 Rifle waist belts and plates..................................56 "
100 Rifle pouches...43 "
100 Rifle flasks..81 "
100 Rifle flask and pouch belts...................................27 "
100 Pistol cartridge boxes and plates...........................81 "
100 Cavalry sabre belts and plates...............................115 "
100 Carbine slings and swivels.................................110 "
100 Pairs of holsters and covers.................................250 "
100 Mounted artillery sabre belts and plates....................97 "
100 Foot artillery sword belts and plates.........................73 "
100 Sappers' sword belts and plates..............................63 "

CHAPTER NINTH.

GUNPOWDER.

MATERIALS.

Saltpetre.

Saltpetre, nitre, nitrate of potassa, is composed of 53.45 nitric acid and 46.55 potassa—its specific gravity is 2,090—it melts at 660°, and is decomposed at a red heat—100 parts of water, at the temperature of 32°, dissolve 13.32 parts of nitre; at 59°, 25.49 ; at 86°, 45.90 ; at 104°, 63.80 ; at 140°, 110.70 ; at 176°, 170.80 ; at 212°, 246.15. Saltpetre crystallizes generally in six-sided prisms, terminated by six-sided pyramids, or in needles deeply striated—its taste is cool, saline, and slightly bitter—when thrown on burning charcoal it melts and deflagrates violently.

Saltpetre occurs naturally in great quantities, on the surface of the earth in India and other warm countries, and in the limestone caves of Virginia, Georgia, Tennessee and Kentucky ; in the last named State, it is also found in the form of what is termed *rock ore*, being sand stone containing a very large proportion of nitre. This salt is formed spontaneously by the decomposition of animal and vegetable substances in moist situations, and on this principle artificial nitre beds are made for its production. Saltpetre obtained from any of these sources may be separated from the greater part of the foreign salts and earthy matter by lixiviation with wood ashes and evaporation. The nitrous earth of India yields about one-fifth of its weight of nitre; that of the nitre caves, from one to ten pounds of nitre to the bushel, and the rock ore as much as 20 or 30 pounds to the bushel. The best artificial nitre beds afford annually about a quarter of a pound of nitre to a bushel of earth. Nearly all the saltpetre used in the United States, for the manufacture of gunpowder, is obtained from India, whence it is imported in a crystalized state, called *grough saltpetre*, containing generally from 6 to 12 per cent. of foreign salts, earths, and water.

Test of grough saltpetre : To a pound of grough saltpetre add a pint of water, saturated with pure saltpetre ; stir the mixture for ten minutes with a glass rod, and decant the liquor on a filter ; wash the saltpetre a second time in the same manner, with half a pint of the saturated solution, and pour the whole on the filter ; let it drain, and then dry it perfectly by placing it first on a bed of some absorbent matter, such as ashes or lime, and then by evaporation in a glass vessel over a gentle fire. The saturated solution having taken up only the foreign salts, what remains on the filter, (allowing 2 per cent. for earthy matter and the saltpetre left by the saturated water,) is the quantity of pure saltpetre contained in the pound of grough. As the changes of temperature during the operation may affect the quantity of pure saltpetre remaining on the filter, it is proper to perform a corresponding operation, at the same time and under the same circumstances, on a like quantity of pure saltpetre ; the gain or loss thus ascertained will show the correction to be made in the former result.

Refining Saltpetre.

Saltpetre to be used in the manufacture of gunpowder requires to be freed from the impurities present in its crude state. This may be done by boiling it in pure water and filtering the liquor through canvass bags. The method of refining on a large scale, at the refinery of Paris, is as follows :

First washing.—This first operation is performed on 11,660 lbs. of grough saltpetre, containing about 6 per cent. of foreign salts and 6 per cent. of water and earthy matters. This is washed with 4,400 lbs. of water saturated with pure saltpetre, obtained in previous operations ; if that is not at hand, pure water may be used : stir it well, and at the end of 12 hours rake up the saltpetre towards one side of the vessel, and let the water run off at the opposite side, carrying with it the foreign salts ; this is afterwards treated as mother water. After this washing the saltpetre contains only 1 per cent. of foreign matter, and the quantity is reduced to 11,000 lbs.

Melting. In a boiler of the capacity of about 900 gallons, dissolve 10,000 lbs. of the saltpetre from the first washing in 300 gallons of water, at a moderate heat, putting in first three-fourths of the saltpetre with a proportional quantity of water, and adding the rest in three successive parts. Prepare a solution of 36 oz. of glue in 4½ gallons of water, and when ebullition is about to commence in the boiler, pour in three-fourths of the solution of glue diluted with twice its bulk of water, and skim carefully ; then add 22 gallons of water, in order to diminish the density of the liquid, and to allow the foreign salts and earthy matters to pass through it, and settle at the bottom, or to rise in scum ; this is called *a washing*. Throw into the boiler one-third of the remainder of the saltpetre and the rest of the glue diluted with four gallons of water ; skim for about one hour—make a second washing, and about two hours after, a third—continue the skimming and evaporation, increasing the heat, until there remains in the boiler but one part of water to four of saltpetre—let the liquor stand for some hours, keeping up a sufficient heat to prevent crystallization, and then draw it off into the crystallizing vat.

CRYSTALLIZATION. The liquor is kept in constant agitation by means of rakes, to prevent the formation of large crystals. Draw off the mother water when its temperature is reduced to 104°, and let the saltpetre drain for some hours.

WATERING. When taken from the crystallizer the saltpetre contains not more than 1-500th of foreign salts; it is put into boxes capable of containing about 4,800 lbs.; on each of these boxes pour, with watering pots, 220 gallons of water, one-third at a time—the two first waterings are allowed to remain on the saltpetre two hours before being drawn off through openings in the bottom of the box; the third merely passes through the saltpetre.

DRYING. After these waterings the saltpetre contains but 1-18000th of hydrochlorates. It is left to drain several days, and then dried in drying vats at a low heat, being constantly stirred.

PACKING. If designed for transportation, the saltpetre when thoroughly dried, being then perfectly white and in small grains, is passed through a sieve of fine wire gauze and packed in barrels. A 100 lbs. powder cask will hold about 132 lbs. of saltpetre.

Saltpetre is also well preserved in cakes, which are made by fuzing the refined saltpetre in iron pots, and casting it into moulds of convenient size; the cakes are 12 in. square and 6 in. thick, weighing about 70 lbs.; six are packed in a box 12.75 in. × 12.75 in. × 38 in.; gross weight 465 lbs. This method of treating saltpetre has the advantage of expelling from it the water of crystallization; but it requires a little more work to pulverize the saltpetre afterwards, in making powder.

The mother water, as it issues from the crystallizer, is received in basins where it cools and deposites saltpetre, which is added to that which has undergone the first washing in another operation; the rest is evaporated to obtain grough saltpetre.

The water used for watering the refined saltpetre is kept to make the first washing of the grough saltpetre, or else it is added to the mother water.

The scum which is obtained in melting is called *foul scum*. Put about 4,400 lbs. of it into a boiler with 265 gallons of water; heat it gradually until it begins to boil; skim and allow it to settle; then draw off the liquor which, in cooling, will deposite grough saltpetre. On the residuum, whilst still hot, pour about 250 gallons of water and add the *second scum*, so as to fill the boiler; after this has been boiled, skimmed, and allowed to settle, draw off the clear liquor and add it to the mother water. Add the last scum and the dregs to the materials for lixiviation.

Thus, 11,660 lbs. of grough saltpetre furnish 8,000 lbs. of pure, dry saltpetre, besides, 200 lbs. remaining in the scum, 1,200 lbs. in the mother water, and 1,000 lbs. in the washings, which are obtained in the subsequent operations; in all, 10,400 lbs. of pure saltpetre.

TEST OF REFINED SALTPETRE. In order to be used in the manufacture of gunpowder, saltpetre should not contain more than 1-3000th of chlorides.—To test this, dissolve 200 grains of saltpetre in the least possible quantity (say 1000 grains) of tepid distilled water; pour on it 20 grains of a solution of nitrate of silver containing 10 grains of the nitrate to 1033 grains of water, that being the quantity required to decompose 200-3000ths of a grain of muriate of soda; filter the liquid and divide it into two portions—to one portion, add a few drops of the solution of nitrate of silver; if it remains clear, the saltpetre does not contain more than 1-3000th of muriate of soda—to the other portion, add a small quantity of solution of muriate of soda; if it becomes clouded, the saltpetre contains less than 1-3000th. By using the test liquor in very small quantities, the exact proportion of muriate of soda may be ascertained; at the refinery of Paris it does not exceed 1-18000th of the saltpetre, and this degree of purity is attained also at the refinery of Messrs. Dupont. Saltpetre for the best sporting powder is refined a second time, and contains not more than 1-60000th part of chlorides.

Charcoal.

Charcoal obtained from light woods is the best for the manufacture of gunpowder, being more easy to pulverize. *Willow* and *poplar* are used for this purpose in the United States.

The wood must be sound, and should not be of more than 3 or 4 years growth, and about 1 inch in diameter; branches larger than that should be split up. It is cut in the spring, when the sap runs freely, and is immediately stripped of its bark. The smaller branches are used for fine sporting powder.

The operation of charring may be performed in pits, but the method now almost universally pursued in making charcoal for gunpowder is that of *distillation*. For this purpose the wood is placed in an iron vessel, generally of a cylindrical form, to which a cover is luted; an opening, with a pipe, is made to convey off the gaseous and liquid products, and the wood is thus exposed to the heat of a furnace.

The charcoal thus obtained should retain a certain degree of elasticity, and should have a *brown* color, the wood not being entirely decomposed; it retains the fibrous appearance of the wood, and the fracture is irridescent. As it readily absorbs 1-20th of its weight of moisture, it should be made only in proportion as it is required for use. Wood contains generally about 52 per cent. of carbon, but distillation furnishes not more than 30 to 40 per cent. of charcoal.

The specific gravity of charcoal triturated under heavy rollers is about 1,380; but in sticks, as it comes from the charring cylinders, it rarely exceeds 300.

Sulphur.

Pure sulphur is of a citron yellow color and shining fracture ; it crackles when pressed in the hand. The specific gravity of native sulphur is 2,033; that of sulphur refined by sublimation 1,900; its specific gravity is diminished by trituration. Sulphur melts at 220°, but at 320° it takes the consistency of paste; it sublimes at 680°. It is insoluble in water, but soluble in oils and in alcohol.

Sulphur is generally found in great quantities in the neighborhood of volcanoes; it may also be obtained from metallic ores (pyrites) and other sources. Most of that used in the United States is obtained from the French refineries.

Crude sulphur, as extracted by the first sublimation from the ore, contains about 8 per cent. of earthy matter. It is purified by a second sublimation, from which it is collected in the form of powder, called *flowers of sulphur*, or it is melted and run into moulds, making *roll brimstone*. It may also be refined, but not so thoroughly, by being simply melted and skimmed.

Pure sulphur is entirely consumed in combustion, and its purity is thus easily tested by burning about 100 grains in a glass vessel; the residuum should not exceed a small fraction of a grain.

MANUFACTURE OF GUNPOWDER.

Proportions of Ingredients.

		Saltpetre.	Charcoal.	Sulphur.
	By the Atomic theory....	74.64	13.51	11.85
IN THE UNITED STATES:				
	For the military service.	76 75	14 15	10 10
	For sporting...........	78 77	12 13	10 10
IN ENGLAND:	For the military service...	75	15	10
	For sporting...........	78 75	14 17	8 8
IN FRANCE:	For the military service...	75	12.5	12.5
	For sporting.............	78	12	10
	For blasting.............	62	18	20
IN PRUSSIA:	For the military service...	75	13.5	11.5

Fabrication.

This consists essentially in the following operations: *pulverizing the ingredients, incorporation, compression, granulation, drying, glazing, dusting.*

POUNDING MILL. In this method of fabrication the first three operations are performed at the same time by the pestles. A mill contains generally 20 or 24 mortars and pestles in two rows; the pestle weighs 90 lbs., and falls 16 inches fifty-five times in a minute; the lower part of the pestle is made of bronze or of very hard wood. The mortars are nearly spherical and are dug out of a piece of oak, having a piece of harder wood in the bottom.

Each mortar receives about 20 lbs. of composition. The stamping is continued about 11 hours. The proper charge of charcoal in small pieces is first put in, with a quantity of water equal to one-tenth of the weight of composition, say 1 quart; after this has been pounded half an hour, at the rate of 40 strokes a minute, add the saltpetre and then the sulphur, previously pulverized in a mill or rolling barrel and sifted. Mix the materials with the hand, and for the first quarter of an hour let the stamping continue at 40 strokes a minute; at the end of each hour the composition is passed from each mortar into the next—at the 6th or 8th *change,* add half a pint of water. During the last two hours no change is made, in order that the composition may form into cake. When taken from the mortar it is dried, so as to reduce the contained moisture to about 4 per cent.; it is then grained.

ROLLING BARRELS. In order to lessen the duration and danger of pounding in the mortars, the materials may be pulverized and mixed in rolling barrels, before being put under the pestles.

These rolling barrels are about 44 in. diameter and 22 in. long on the interior; they are made of strong leather or hides stretched over a frame the slats of which project inwardly about 0.5 in. and are 9 in. apart; the elasticity of the leather prevents the composition from adhering to the sides, which it would do in wooden barrels. Each barrel contains 100 lbs. of balls about 0.25 in. diameter, made of zinc, or of an alloy of 75 copper and 25 tin; the barrel revolves 25 or 30 times in a minute. The charge of composition is half the weight of the balls.

For the purpose of pulverizing, the charcoal and sulphur are rolled together for two hours. For incorporation, the saltpetre is added in the state in which it comes from the refinery, and the mixture is rolled two hours more; it is then placed under the pestles, adding 10 per cent. of water, and it is beaten for 3 hours only.

Press. Instead of being put in the pounding mill, the composition from the rolling barrels may be spread in thin layers, moistened with 10 per cent. of water distributed very equally with a fine watering pot or a brush, and subjected to pressure by a hydraulic or screw press, by which means it is brought to the state of a cake. The composition is sometimes subjected to the press after being incorporated in the pounding mill, or in the cylinder mill.

Cylinder mills. These mills, first used in England, and now generally adopted in the manufacture of gunpowder, supply the place of pounding mills in performing at the same time the operations of pulverizing, incorporating, and pressing the composition. They consist of two cylinders, of marble or cast iron, weighing about 5 tons each, rolling in a circular trough of the same material, the inner diameter of which is about three feet; a wooden plough follows the cylinders, to bring the powder towards the centre of the trough. The cylinders revolve 10 times in a minute, and run from 1 to 3 hours on each charge of 50 lbs. of composition.

Granulation. The composition being formed into *cake*, by any of the above methods, the next process is to break it up into grains; to facilitate this, it is aired or partially dried; it is then put into a graining sieve formed of parchment pierced with holes, where it is broken up by the action of a lenticular disc of hard wood, weighing about 5 lbs., being 8.5 in. in diameter, 2.75 in. thick in the middle, 2 in. at the edge. The sieve is shaken by hand, or by machinery, in such a manner that the disc may move round it against the border, and the grains pass through the holes as fast as they are sufficiently reduced. Another method of graining is to pass the cake between wooden rollers. The grains thus formed are sifted, to separate those which are too coarse or too fine, and also to separate from each other the different kinds of grains for *cannon*, *musket*, and *rifle* powder.

Diameter of the holes in the sieve for			
	Cannon powder..	Maximum	0.100 in.
		Minimum	0.070 in.
	Musket.........	Maximum	0.070 in.
		Minimum	0.050 in.
	Rifle............	Maximum	0.035 in.
		Minimum	0.025 in.

Glazing is necessary, in order to enable gunpowder to resist the effects of shaking in transportation, and of exposure to the moisture of the air. All the powder made for the Ordnance Department is glazed. This operation is performed by enclosing the powder, containing about 3 per cent. of moisture, in a large glazing barrel which makes 15 or 20 revolutions in a minute; a charge of 500 lbs. is thus treated for about 24 hours or less, according to the effect required.

Drying. Gunpowder is dried in two ways—1st, in the open air; the powder is spread upon sheets laid on tables placed in a suitable situation where it remains 10 or 12 hours, being frequently stirred to expose it thoroughly to the sun: in summer, it requires to be sometimes covered in the heat of the day, to prevent the loss of the sulphur—2ndly, in a drying house, where the powder is exposed, in layers from 1 in to 4 in. thick, to a current of air heated to about 140°, by means of a furnace or by hot water pipes.

DUSTING. After powder has been glazed and dried, it is sifted in fine sieves, or through bolting cloths, in order to clean it thoroughly, and to cool it before being barreled. The dust and small grains obtained in this and previous operations are again pressed or worked over to make inferior powder, or mixed with a portion of fresh composition in the mills.

ROUND POWDER may be made in an expeditious manner as follows: Fix a powder barrel on a shaft passing through its two heads, the barrel having ledges on the inside; to prevent leakage, cover it with close canvas glued on, and put the hoops over the canvas. Put into the barrel 10 lbs. of sulphur in lumps and 10 lbs. of charcoal, with 60 lbs. of zinc balls, or of small shot, (down to No. 4, 0.014 in. in diameter nearly;) turn it by hand or otherwise, 30 revolutions in a minute. To 10 lbs. of this mixture thus pulverized add 30 lbs. of saltpetre, and work it two hours with the balls; water the 40 lbs. of composition with 2 quarts of water, mixing it equally with the hands; granulate with the graining sieve. The grains thus made, not being pressed, are too soft. To make them harder, put them into a barrel having 5 or 6 ledges projecting about 0.4 in. inside; give it at first 8 revolutions in a minute, increasing gradually to 20. The compression will be proportionate to the charge in the barrel which should not, however, be more than half full; continue this operation until the density is such that a cubic foot of the powder shall weigh 855 oz., the mean density of round powder; strike on the staves of the barrel from time to time to prevent the adhesion of the powder.

Sift the grains and dry the powder as usual; that which is too fine or too coarse is returned to the pulverizing barrel.

This powder is round and the grain is sufficiently hard on the surface, but the interior is soft, which makes it unfit for keeping, and may cause it to burn slowly. This defect may be remedied by making the grains at first very small, and by rolling them on a sheet or in a barrel, watering them from time to time, and adding the pulverized composition in small portions; in this way, the grains will be formed by successive layers; they are then separated according to size, glazed and dried.

It appears from experiments that the simple incorporation of the materials makes a powder which gives nearly as high ranges with the cannon as grained powder; the incorporated dust from the rolling barrel may therefore be used in case of necessity. Gunpowder burns at the temperature of 575° to 600° Fahr.

DENSITY OF GUNPOWDER.

The density of gunpowder may be approximately determined by taking the weight of a given quantity; this is called the *gravimetric density*, and the measure used for the purpose a *gravimeter*. The gravimetric density may be expressed by the weight of a cubic foot in ounces, and a convenient form for the gravimeter is a brass cylindrical measure, 4 inches in diameter and 5.093 inches in height, containing 64 cubic inches, or 1-27th of a cubic foot. The weight of the contents should be ascertained with the powder loose and shaken; the difference gives an indication of the relative irregularity and size of grain.

The gravimetric density of unglazed powder (French) made in pounding mills, is about 840. The following results were obtained from some of the best powder made in cylinder mills:

SIZE OF GRAIN.		Specific gravity.	No. of grains of powder in 10 grs. Troy.	Weight of 1 cubic foot.		Cubic inches in 1 lb. loose
				Loose.	Shaken.	
				oz.	oz.	
U. S.	Cannon........	1,912	150	929	1,039	30.
	Musket........	4,983	1,100	896	1,012	30.8
	Rifle..........	....	6,000	900	1,060	30.7
	Sporting.........	2,012	73,000	1,047	1,197	26.5
English—	Cannon........	1,970	174	874	993	31.6

The specific gravities stated in the above table were obtained by means of alcohol; the results are not perfectly accurate, as the method is liable to some objections. The following method of ascertaining the specific gravity of gunpowder is pursued in the French manufactories, but it is also not free from objections. The specific gravity of the sporting powder of the above table obtained by this method is 1,890, and that obtained approximately, by direct measurement and weight of pieces of dried mill cake, is about 1,920.

Determination of the Specific Gravity of Gunpowder.

The instrument used for this purpose is a cylindrical glass vessel of uniform diameter, the edges of which are well ground, and to which is adapted a cover of polished glass accurately ground on the surface, so as to close the vessel her-metrically. The diameter of the vessel is 3 in., and its weight 4.5 in. With a good balance take the exact weight of the vessel and cover.—Fill the vessel with distilled water and cover it so as entirely to exclude the air; this may be effected by pouring in the water until it runs over the sides of the vessel, and then sliding the cover on—wipe the vessel and the cover perfectly dry, without disturbing the cover so as to admit air in the vessel.—Ascertain the weight of the vessel thus filled, and deducting its weight when empty, set down the weight of distilled water which it contains, which weight we will designate by W. Now wipe the vessel and cover perfectly dry, and ascertain in the same manner the weight W', which the vessel will contain of water saturated with nitre, such as is used in testing the purity of saltpetre—pour out three-fourths of the saturated solution, and having weighed 1500 grains of powder free from dust, pour it *slowly* into the saturated solution, so that the air between the grains of powder may escape—then fill the vessel with the solution, and cover it as before; wipe it dry and ascertain the weight. From the weight thus found, subtract that of the vessel and cover, and that of the powder; the remainder will be the weight of the saturated solution in the vessel; deduct this weight from that W', of the saturated solution, before obtained, and the difference will be the weight w', of the quantity of the solution which occupies the same space as the given quantity of powder. Then $W' : W :: w' : w$, the weight of distilled water which would have been displaced by the powder; and this weight is to that of the powder as the specific gravity of distilled water is to the specific gravity of the powder. Repeat the operation three times, and take the mean result.

Alcohol may be used in the same manner, instead of saltpetre water.

PACKING POWDER.

Government powder is packed in barrels of 100 lbs. each. Powder barrels are made of well seasoned white oak, and hooped with hickory or cedar hoops which should be deprived of their bark; the cedar is not so liable as hickory or white oak to be attacked by worms, and it should therefore be used in preference, or the hoops may be prepared by immersion in a solution of corrosive sublimate. The hoops should cover two-thirds of the barrel. The diameter of the bung-hole is 1.25 in.—Instead of a bung on the side, a screw hole 1.5 inch in diameter is sometimes made in the head of the barrel; it is closed by a wood screw with an octagonal head which must not project beyond the ends of the staves; under the head of the screw is a washer of thin leather steeped in a solution of beeswax in spirits of turpentine. This screw plug renders it unnecessary to take out the head of the barrel, and the hoops may therefore be secured with copper nails; for transportation, a piece of cloth should be glued over the head of the plug.—Some barrels have been made with six copper hoops, and others with 4 copper and 8 or 10 cedar hoops; the copper hoops are 1 in. wide, and $\frac{1}{8}$ of an inch thick, fastened with two rivets, and nailed each with 3 copper nails, 0.625 in. long —Average weight of a hoop $2\frac{1}{4}$ lbs.

In 1836, some barrels were made water proof by a lining of India rubber cloth, to ascertain its efficiency in preserving the powder in damp situations, or in the exposure of service in the field. This lining appears to have had an injurious effect on the powder, when exposed to heat and moisture, in consequence of the affinity of the caoutchouc for sulphur.

Dimensions of Powder Barrels.

Whole length ....20.5 inches
Length, interior, in the clear.......................18 "
Interior diameter at the head......................14 "
Interior diameter at the bilge......................16 "
Thickness of the staves and heads ....0.5 "
Weight of the barrel with cedar hoops.............25 lbs.

The barrels have generally 12 hoops, 14 to 16 staves, and 2 or 3 pieces in each head. The above dimensions are calculated so that, with 100 lbs. of powder, there shall be a vacant space in the barrel, allowing the powder to shake, in order to prevent its caking—the barrel would contain about 120 lbs. of powder, settled by shaking.

INSPECTION AND PROOF OF POWDER.

Gunpowder should be of an even grain, angular and irregular in form; it should be so hard as not to be easily crushed by pressure with the finger; it should, when new, leave no trace of dust when poured on the back of the hand, and should leave no beads or foulness when flashed, in quantities of 10 grains, on a copper plate. The size of the grain for each kind of powder is tested in the following manner:

There are three sieves or gauges for each size of grain, made by piercing round holes in thin sheets of brass. The sizes of these holes are as follows:

	CANNON.			MUSKET.			RIFLE.		
	No. 1.	No. 2.	No. 3.	No. 4.	No. 5.	No. 6.	No. 6.	No. 7.	No. 8.
	In.	In.	In.	In.	In.	In.	In.	In.	In.
Maximum.	0.100	......	......	0.06	......	......	0.035		
Medium...	......	0.085	......	......	0.05	......	......	0.03	
Minimum .	......	......	0.070	......	......	0.035	......	......	0.025

Cannon powder, sifted through the gauges Nos. 1, 2, and 3, should leave not more than 6 per cent. on No. 1; not more than 20 per cent. should pass through No. 3; and of the remainder, not more than one-half should pass through No. 2. This would give about 150 grains of powder in a weight of 10 grs. troy.

Musket powder should all pass through No. 4; about one-half should pass through No. 5; and nearly one-fourth through No. 6. This would give about 2,000 or 2,500 grains of powder in 10 grs. troy.

Rifle powder should all pass through No. 6; not more than one-fifth through No. 8; and not more than two-fifths through No. 7. This would give about 12,000 or 15,000 grains of powder in 10 grs. troy.

Ordinarily, the uniformity and size of grain will be judged of by mere inspection.

The powder in each barrel is proved. For this purpose a sample of about 3½ oz. is taken from each; this is conveniently done by means of an *extractor*, which is a copper tube about 1 inch interior diameter, and 18 inches long, pointed at the bottom, and having a valve at the lower end, or an opening about 9 inches from that end, by covering which with the hand the powder may be poured out of the mouth of the tube; the sample is put into a tin canister marked with a number, a corresponding one to which is inscribed with chalk on the barrel; from these samples, the charges for the eprouvette are weighed on the proving ground, as they are required.

The platform for the mortar eprouvette should be a block of oak timber firmly established on a foundation of masonry, with which it is connected by strong bolts; to this block the iron bed plate is fixed by the three bolts provided for that purpose, the plate being also let into the wood about 1.5 inch, to avoid bending the bolts. The ground where the balls are to fall should be free from stones and not too hard.

The eprouvettes are provided with 3 service balls and a standard ball, (marked No. 1,) by means of which, and of the standard powder accompanying each eprouvette, the mortar and the service balls should be verified from time to time.

The eprouvette, being washed clean and dried by firing a scaling charge, is placed on its bed, in a vertical position, in which it is supported by a wedge or prop; the vent is stopped with a copper wire having a shoulder to prevent it from projecting into the chamber, and the charge of powder is introduced through a long funnel which is supported on the bottom of the bore, at the mouth of the chamber; the ball is then carefully lowered down by means of a hook, and the mortar placed on its bed, care being taken not to jar it roughly; it is primed with a small strand of quick match, and fired without delay. Two charges are fired in this way from each sample of powder, and if the ranges differ more than 20 yards, a third charge is fired, and the two nearest ranges are used in obtaining the mean range. The mortar is scraped and wiped after each discharge, and it is washed and dried, as at first, after about 8 shots.

The general mean range of new powder proved at any one time must be not less than 250 yards; but no powder ranging below 225 yards is received. The powder in magazines is considered unserviceable if it does not range over 180 yards.

With the eprouvettes, as adjusted in 1837, good cannon powder ranges from 280 to 300 yards, and small grain powder, from 300 to 320 yards.

INSPECTION REPORT. The report of inspection should show the place and date of fabrication and of proof—the kind of powder and its general qualities; as, hard or soft, round or angular, whether free from dust or not, of uniform or irregular grain—its gravimetric density—the separate ranges and the mean range—the condition of the mortar and the ball—the state of the weather.

MARKS. Each barrel is marked on one head with the place and year of manufacture, and with the kind of grain, *cannon*, *musket*, or *rifle;* on the other head, with the year in which it was proved and the proof range, leaving room for subsequent proofs, which are marked in the same manner.

Remarks.

Although the above is the established mode of proof and inspection for Government powder, it cannot be disguised that a very imperfect test of the relative projectile force of gunpowder is thereby afforded. Slight variations in the density of powder, which would but little affect its strength, when fired in large quantities, produce great difference in the proof range; and variations in the size of the grain cause still greater irregularities in the range, the powder being in other respects the same. In general, gunpowder of *small grain* and *low specific gravity* gives the highest range in the eprouvette, whilst recent experiments with the ballistic pendulum have shown that the greatest initial velocity, in a shot from a heavy gun, is produced by powder of *great specific gravity* and of *coarse grain.*

PENDULUM EPROUVETTE. The best mode of testing the projectile force of gunpowder is undoubtedly that of ascertaining its effects when used in the same quantities in which it is to be employed in service. This method has been partially adopted by establishing, at Washington Arsenal, a cannon pendulum and a musket pendulum, which are used for proving samples of powder sent from the manufactories. The apparatus shows the initial velocity of a ball fired from a cannon or a musket.

In proving cannon powder, the initial velocity of a ball of medium weight and windage, with a charge of *one-fourth* its weight of powder, should be:

From a 24-pounder garrison gun, not less than 1,600 feet.

From a 12-pounder field gun, not less than 1,550 feet.

From a 6-pounder field gun, not less than 1,500 feet.

In proving small arm powder, the initial velocity of a musket ball, with a charge of 120 grains, should be:

With musket powder, not less than 1,500 feet.

With rifle powder, not less than 1,600 feet.

With fine sporting powder, not less than 1,800 feet.

HYGROMETRIC QUALITIES. The susceptibility of powder to absorb moisture may be judged of by exposing 1 lb. to the air, in a moist place, (such as a cellar which is not too damp,) on a glazed earthen dish, for 15 or 20 days, stirring it sometimes so as to expose the surface better; the powder should be previously well dried, at a heat of about 140°. Well glazed powder, made of pure materials, treated in this way, will not increase in weight more than 5 parts in 1000, or a half of one per cent. Such powder kept in casks in a dry magazine will absorb about 8-10ths of 1 per cent. of moisture. A sample thus kept for 15 years, in a common barrel, was found to lose but 9-10ths of 1 per cent. in drying.

A more accurate and expeditious method of comparing the hygrometric qualities of different samples of powder is to expose them to air saturated with moisture. For this purpose, samples of about 1,500 grains weight may be placed in a shallow tin pan, 9 in. × 6 in., set in a tub, the bottom of which is covered with water; the pan of powder should be placed about 1 inch above the surface of the water, and the tub covered over. In this manner any sample of powder may be compared with another of known good quality. Good powder, made of pure materials, will not absorb more than 2½ per cent. of moisture in 24 hours.

QUICKNESS OF BURNING. The relative quickness of two different powders may be judged of by burning a train laid in a circular, or other groove which returns into itself, made in a piece of hard wood; one-half of the groove, being filled with each kind of powder, and fire communicated at one of the points of meeting of the two trains, the relative quickness is readily deduced from observation of the point at which the flames meet. For this purpose it is necessary that the two powders compared should be of equal grain, and the method is best applied to the comparison of fine grained powders which can be laid evenly in the groove; for such powder, a groove whose cross section is a semicircle of $\frac{1}{8}$ of an inch diameter, and its length 20 feet, divided into tenths of a foot, will be found convenient.

Analysis of Gunpowder.

Whatever may be the mode of proof adopted, it is essential, in judging of the qualities of gunpowder, to know the mode of fabrication, and the proportions and degree of purity of the materials; the latter point may be ascertained by analysis.

To determine the quantity of saltpetre. In a vessel of tinned copper, like a common coffee pot, dissolve 1,000 grains of powder, well dried before weighing, in 2,000 grains of distilled water, and heat it until it boils—let it stand a moment, and then decant it on a piece of filtering paper, doubled exactly in the middle; repeat this operation four times—at the 4th, instead of decanting, pour the whole contents of the vessel on the filter—drain the filter, and wash it several times with 2,000 grains of water heated in the vessel, using in all these operations 10,000 grains of water. After passing through the filters, this water contains in solution all the saltpetre, the quantity of which is ascertained by evaporating to dryness. Dry the double filter with the mixture of coal and sulphur, and take the weight of this composition by using the exterior filter to ascertain the weight of that on which the composition remains; this weight serves to verify that of the saltpetre, and to estimate the loss in the process. By expelling the sulphur from this composition by heat, the quantity of coal, and consequently of sulphur, may be found; but this operation is tedious and delicate.

To determine the quantity of sulphur directly. Mix and beat in a mortar 10 grains of dry powder, 10 of subcarbonate of potash, 10 of saltpetre, and 40 of chloride of sodium—put this mixture in a vessel (capsule) of platinum or glass, on live coals, and when the combination of the materials is completed, and the mass is white, dissolve it in distilled water, and saturate the solution with nitric acid—decompose the sulphate which has been formed, by adding a solution of chloride of barium, in which the exact proportions of the water and the chloride are known. According to the atomic proportions, the quantity of sulphur will be to that of the chloride of barium used, as 20.12 to 152.44.

To determine the quantity of charcoal directly. Mix 1,000 grains of powder with an equal quantity of caustic potash, (or of subcarbonate of soda or potash,) and a little water; boil the mixture for some time, and pour it on a double filtering paper—when the liquor, which is of a deep yellow color, is filtered, wash the filter several times with distilled water, until the water comes off tasteless, or until it gives no precipitate with acetate of lead—then dry the charcoal and weigh it. Repeat the operation two or three times. The results thus obtained may be verified by composing a powder in the proportion indicated, and analyzing it in the same way; the new results will show the corrections necessary in the first.

Restoring unserviceable powder.

When the quantity of water absorbed by gunpowder does not exceed 7 per cent., the powder may be restored by drying; this may even be effected in the magazine, if it is dry, by means of ventilation, or by the use of the chloride of lime for 20 or 30 days. Quick lime may be used, but the use of it is attended with danger, on account of the heat evolved in slaking.

When powder has absorbed from 7 to 12 per cent. of water, it may still be restored by drying in the sun or in a drying house; but it remains porous and friable, and unfit for transportation: in this case it is better to work it over. In service, it may be worked by means of the rolling barrels, as described for making round powder.

When powder has become mixed with dirt or gravel, or other foreign substances which cannot be separated by sifting, or when it has been under water, or otherwise too much injured to be re-worked, it must be melted down, to obtain the saltpetre by solution, filtration, and evaporation.

PRESERVATION, STORAGE AND TRANSPORTATION.

In the powder magazines the barrels are generally placed on the sides, three tiers high, or four tiers, if necessary; small skids should be placed on the floor, and between the several tiers of barrels, in order to steady them, and chocks should be placed at intervals on the lower skid to prevent the rolling of the barrels. The powder should be separated according to its kind, the place and date of fabrication, and the proof range. Fixed ammunition, especially for cannon, should not be put in the same magazine with powder in barrels, if it can be avoided.

In a room 13 or 14 feet wide, the barrels may be arranged in a double row in the centre, two alleys 2½ feet wide, and 2 single rows 6 to 12 inches from the walls; in this way the marks of each barrel may be seen, and any barrel can be easily reached. In a room 12 feet wide, an equal number of barrels may be placed in two double rows, with a central alley of 3 feet, and 2 side alleys, next the walls, of about 10 in. each: there should be an unincumbered space of 6 or 8 feet at the door or doors of the magazine.

Should it be necessary to pile the barrels more than 4 tiers high, the upper tiers should be supported by a frame resting on the floor; or the barrels may be placed on their heads, with boards between the tiers.

Besides being recorded in the magazine book, each parcel of powder should be inscribed on a ticket attached to the pile, showing the entries and the issues.

For the preservation of the powder, and of the floors and lining of the magazine, it is of the greatest importance to preserve unobstructed the circulation of air, under the flooring as well as above. The magazine should be opened and aired in clear, dry weather; the ventilators must be kept free; no shrubbery or trees should be allowed to grow so near as to protect the building from the sun. The moisture of a magazine may be absorbed by chloride of lime suspended in an open box under the arch, and renewed from time to time; quick lime, as before observed, is dangerous.

The sentinel or guard at a magazine, when it is open, should have no fire arms, and every one who enters the magazine should take off his shoes, or put socks over them; no sword, or cane, or any thing which might occasion sparks should be carried in.

Barrels of powder should not be rolled for transportation; they should be carried in hand barrows, or slings made of rope or leather. In moving powder in the magazine a cloth or carpet should be spread; all implements used there should be of wood or copper, and the barrels should never be repaired in the magazine. When it is necessary to roll the powder for its better preservation and to prevent its caking, this should be done, with a small quantity at a time, on boards, in the magazine yard.

In wagons, barrels of powder must be packed in straw, secured in such a manner as not to rub against each other, and the load covered with thick canvas.

LIGHTNING RODS.

Extracted from a Report of the French Academy of Sciences.

In a lightning rod there may be distinguished two principal parts; the pointed *stem*, and the *conductor* with its roots.

The stem or upper part of the rod is a bar of square or round iron, or copper, drawn out into a pyramidal or conical form, 13 to 20 feet high, (according to the height of the building and of the surrounding objects,) and from 1.25 in. to 2 in. thick at the base, in order to give it sufficient stiffness in proportion to its height. The upper end is made of a conical brass rod 20 in. long, gilt at the top, or pointed with platinum which is united to the brass with silver solder, the joint strengthened by a small brass collar. The iron and brass rods are joined together by an iron dowel, screwed into both, and secured by iron pins. The brass point may be used without being gilt or armed with platinum.

The *stem* should be made, if possible, in one piece; if it becomes necessary to divide it, the joint should be at about one-third of the height from the bottom; the two parts connected together by a tapering tenon in the upper piece, and a corresponding mortise below, secured by an iron pin; or, the two parts may be screwed together. At the bottom of the stem, above the roof, is a shoulder or flanch to throw off the rain water which might otherwise follow down the rod into the roof; just above this flanch the stem is rounded about 2 in. in height, to receive a hinged collar with two *ears*, between which the end of the conductor is secured by a bolt; or the stem and the conductor may be connected by a *square collar* or *strap*, and a bridle, which is fastened over the conductor by two nuts screwed on the ends of two branches of the strap which pass through holes in the bridle; the back of this strap has a *branch* projecting upwards, which is secured by a bolt to a *fork* formed in the end of the conductor.

The stem is fixed to the building in various ways, according to circumstances. The best method is to attach it to a chimney or gable, where it may be secured by straps passing round the chimney, or through the wall, keyed inside against an iron bar. On an arch, the stem terminates in three or four branches or *feet* which are leaded into the masonry.

The *conductor* is made of bars of square or round iron or copper, from 0.5 in. to 1 in. thick, connected together by a bevel joint in the form of a Z, fastened by 2 pins; or the bars may be screwed together. The conductor runs parallel to the roof, from 4 in. to 6 in. above it, and is supported, at intervals of about 10 feet, by *forks*, the lower ends of which are not pointed, but flattened and bent at a right angle and nailed to a rafter, to prevent the filtration of water into the wood; the rod is held in each fork by a rivet through the branches above the rod.

The conductor follows the cornice of the building without touching it, and descends in like manner along the wall, to which it is fastened by *cramps* or *staples*. About 18 in. below the surface of the ground, it is bent perpendicularly to the wall and extended in that direction about 15 feet, when it passes into a well, or if water is not met with, into a pit 15 feet deep, which may be filled with loose paving stones, if it is not convenient to let it remain as a well.

To facilitate the transmission of the electric fluid, and to prevent the rod from becoming rusty, it is enclosed in a trough filled with well burnt charcoal, which should be packed about 1.5 in. thick all round the rod; this trough may be made of bricks, or of stone, tiles, wood, &c. The conductor passes out of this trough through the sides of the well; if the latter is within the building, the conductor should pass through the wall under ground. The communication should not be made with a well or cistern which is resorted to for use.

The conductor terminates generally in two or three *prongs*, which should be so placed, if possible, as to be always immersed in water not less than 2 feet; in a dry well, the prongs should be covered with charcoal well rammed, and the rod within the well should be enclosed in a pipe or trough filled with charcoal. In rock or dry ground, if the conductor cannot be led into moist earth, increase the number of branches. Lead the rain water, if practicable, over or through the trough which contains the rod, and into the well.

Chains or *ropes of metallic wire* may be used for conductors, and are convenient in some situations, but rods are preferable. Copper wire is better than iron for this purpose.

The greatest care must be taken, both in fixing the rod and in its subsequent preservation, to keep the communication perfect through every part of it; otherwise it will be *dangerous* instead of useful.

It is considered that a lightning rod can protect a circular space the radius of which is double the height of the rod above the roof of the building; but when it is attached to an elevated part of the building, such as a tower or steeple, it is safer to rely on its protection to the extent only of its height above the body of the building, and to erect others for protecting the more distant parts.

A building is better protected by two rods of 15 to 20 feet high placed at a distance equal to the sum of their radii of action, than by one rod of double the height.

All the large pieces of metal about a building, such as metallic coverings of the roof, ridges, fastenings, gutters, and long bars, should communicate with the conductor through bars or wires about 0.25 in. thick; it is better, in this respect, not to use such materials in building when they are not indispensable; nothing is to be apprehended from the common iron work of buildings, as hinges, locks, &c.

The conductor should be carried to the ground in the shortest line; one conductor may sometimes be made to communicate with two stems, without increasing its diameter: there should be not less than two conductors for *three* stems or points; the feet of several conductors may be made to communicate with each other.

Conductors should be generally placed on the side towards the prevalent storms; the walls of that side being oftenest wet by the rain might otherwise cause accidents, by acting as imperfect conductors.

Lightning rods for powder magazines are attached to *masts* or poles planted from six to ten feet from the walls of the building: the *stem* of the rod need not be thicker than the conductor nor more than six feet high, but the mast should be of such a height that the point of the stem may be about fifteen feet above the building.

CHAPTER TENTH.

AMMUNITION AND MILITARY FIREWORKS.

LABORATORY.

Buildings.

The rooms required for a laboratory are :

1. *Furnace room,* for casting bullets and making compositions requiring the use of fire.
2. *Cartridge rooms,* for making paper and flannel cartridges of all kinds.
3. *Filling room,* for filling cartridges for cannon and small arms.
4. *Composition room,* for mixing compositions.
5. *Driving room,* for driving rockets, portfires, fuzes, &c.
6. *Packing room,* for putting up ammunition for transportation or storage.
7. *Carpenter's shop.*
8. *Magazine,* or storehouse for powder and fixed ammunition, &c.

These rooms are sometimes arranged, for greater security, in separate buildings, protected by trees or traverses of earth ; but it is more convenient to have them under one roof, (except the furnace room, the carpenter's shop, and the magazine,) or connected by covered passages. The laboratory should be apart from inhabited buildings. The size of the rooms must be regulated by the number of artificers to be accommodated, and in small establishments, the number of rooms may be reduced, as the same room may be used, at different times, for different purposes.

In a large establishment, such as an arsenal of construction, the arrangements of the laboratory will be necessarily modified by the facilities for work, afforded by other parts of the establishment.

Fixtures and Furniture.

1. *Furnace room.* Furnaces; work benches; platform balance, or large scales; a tinner's bench and tools, with a vice, an anvil and a chest for tools; a smith's shovel and poker; stools, &c.

2. *Cartridge rooms.* A table for making cartridges for small arms, 12 feet long and 2½ feet wide, for 12 men or boys to work at, and the length in that pro-

portion for any greater number; tables for cutting paper and flannel, and for rolling cases on; choker for rocket cases; press for rocket and portfire cases; benches for cartridge tables; stools. Closets should be partitioned off from these rooms and furnished with cases, drawers, racks, and shelves, for materials and tools.

3. *Filling room.* A shelf 2 feet wide for weighing on; other shelves with closets under them; tables with raised borders for filling, folding, &c.; budge barrels, or powder barrels with copper hoops and covers; stools for seats; foot stools; a step ladder; stands and gutters for emptying powder barrels.

4. *Composition room.* Shelf for weighing on; shelves, drawers and closets; tables; mealing tables, with raised borders; stools for seats; foot stools; step ladder.

5. *Driving room.* Blocks set in the ground or pavement, through the floor; benches and stools.

In favorable weather, a porch attached to the building, or a tent, may be used for a driving room.

6 *Packing room.* Tables, benches and stools; platform balance.

7. *Carpenter's shop.* Turning lathe and tools; carpenter's benches and tools.

8. *Magazine.* Shelves and frames, for boxes and barrels.

Furnaces.

Two kinds of furnaces are used in a laboratory : in the first, the flame circulates around both the bottom and sides of the kettle; in the second, it comes in contact only with the bottom; the latter are used for compositions of which gunpowder forms a part.

Furnaces are built of bricks. The kettle is of cast iron, about 2 feet in diameter at the top, having a rounded bottom and a flange about 4 inches wide around the top, or else strong handles, to set it by. The bottom is 0.75 in. thick, and the sides 0.5 in. By setting it in an iron plate pierced with holes, encircling the bottom, a furnace of the first kind may be converted into one of the second kind by stopping the holes.

In the field, furnaces may be built with sods, or sunk in the earth, if bricks cannot be readily procured.

Furnace built with sods. Let the kettle rest on a trivet, the feet of which may stand on any piece of flat iron, such as the bottom of a shot canister, or stand for grape; the bottom of the kettle about 1 foot from the ground; build round it with sods; the door of the furnace is 10 in. square; the flue of the chimney, opposite to the door, 6 inches square, and commencing about 6 in. from the ground; the first part of the flue inclined at an angle of about 15°, the rest vertical and placed, if circumstances permit, against a wall; the top of the door and of the flue may be supported by small bars of iron.

Furnace sunk in the earth. The edge of the kettle should be 1 foot above the ground, and the bottom 1 foot above the hearth of the furnace; the earth is dug out so as to give access to the door; the flue is bored out on the opposite side, with a crowbar; it commences 6 in. above the hearth and comes out of the ground 18 in. from the furnace, whence it is carried horizontally about 13 feet.

In furnaces of the second kind mentioned above, the trivet may be omitted, and the kettle may rest on the sod or earth, for about 1 inch all round.

Tools and Implements.

The following list of laboratory tools and implements shows the kinds and proportions which may be required for a large laboratory and for a park of artillery :

KIND.	QUANTITY.	
	Laboratory.	Park.
Adze, copper, weighing 5 lbs.	1	1
Bench, for drawing the loads of shells.	1	
Bench stake	1	
Bick iron	1	
Blocks, for driving fuzes of different calibres	72	
Blocks, for driving signal rockets and portfires	6	
Blocks, for punches	2	
Blocks, for cutting on	1	
Bottles, with ground glass stoppers	4	
Boxes, for 12 workmen making cartridges, 3 to each	36	
Bowls, wooden, various sizes	12	4
Bowls, earthen, glazed, large	6	
Braces and bits	2	1
Brushes, of various kinds	18	4
Buckets	6	
Callipers, various sizes	3	1
Chargers, copper, for fuzes	36	18
Chargers, copper, for portfires	4	2
Chargers, copper, for signal rockets	6	2
Chargers, copper, for cartridges for small arms, (revolving)	4	1
Chisels, brass, for unloading shells	6	3
Compasses, common	3	1
Compasses, spring	2	1
Coopers' drivers, copper and wood	2	2
Crowbar	1	1
Cutting boards	6	
Dippers	6	

KIND.	QUANTITY.	
	Laboratory.	Park.
Dredging boxes	6	2
Drifts, of iron, pointed with copper or brass, for driving portfires	12	
Drifts, for driving fuzes for 13 in. and 10 in. shells; long and short	24	8
Drifts, for driving fuzes for 8 in. shells and howitzers; long and short	24	8
Drifts, for driving signal rockets, sets for 2 pdr	1	
Drifts, do. do. for 1 pdr	2	1
Drifts, for driving serpents, iron	6	2
Formers, of iron or wood, for portfire cases	6	
Formers, for rocket cases, sets for each calibre	2	1
Formers, for serpents	6	2
Formers, for leaders	2	
Formers, for small arm cartridges, of each calibre, 1 to each workman	20	20
Formers, for cylinders and caps, for each calibre	2	1
Formers, for mortar cartridges, do.	1	
Formers, for pots for rockets, do.	1	1
Formers, for cutting pots on, do.	1	1
Formers, for cones for rockets do.	1	1
Formers, for wads, do.	1	
Fork, iron, for dipping pitched facines	1	
Funnels, of copper and tin, various kinds	28	10
Fuze setters	2	10
Fuze extractors	2	1
Gauges, steel, for shot and shells; for each calibre	2	2
Gauges, double, for grape and canister, do.	1	1
Gauges, do. for cartridge formers, do.	1	1
Gauges, do. for priming tubes	4	1
Gauges, of sheet iron, for shot blocks; for each calibre	1	1
Gauges, do. for canister bottoms, do.	1	
Gauges, do. for canisters, do.	1	
Gauges, of copper or wood, for cannon cartridges	1	1
Gimlets	2	2
Gimlets for priming rockets	6	3
Glue pot and brush	1	
Gunner's callipers	.....	1
Gunner's pincers	3	3
Hammers, iron, hand, for strapping shot, &c.	13	4
Hammers, copper	2	1
Handbarrows, with rope or leather bottoms, for powder barrels	2	
Hatchet	1	1
Hooks for unpacking ammunition boxes	6	3
Implements for making paper fuzes—sets	4	1

KIND.	QUANTITY.	
	Laboratory.	Park.
Kettles, iron, for melting lead	2	1
Kettles, iron, for firestone, &c.	2	
Kettles, iron, for pitch	1	1
Kettles, copper, for paste	2	1
Knives, for cutting paper, large and small	12	6
Knives, block	1	
Ladles, iron, for lead, pitch, &c.	5	1
Ladles, copper, for saltpetre, &c.	1	
Lanterns	5	5
Letter punches, (stencils,) set	1	1
Mallets, for driving fuses and portfires	48	20
Mallets, for driving rockets	6	4
Mallets, carpenter's	2	
Measures, for powder, from 8 lbs. to 4 oz.	22	12
Measures, gallon, quart, pint, half pint, and gill	5	5
Mortar and pestle, bronze	1	1
Mortar, marble, with pestle of hard wood	1	
Moulds, for balls and buckshot, sets	6	6
Moulds, for incendiary balls, different calibres	4	
Moulds, brass, (or cylinders of copper or tin,) for portfires	4	
Moulds, for rockets, of each calibre	2	1
Mullers, wooden	4	2
Needles, of various kinds	150	50
Nippers, for cutting wire	2	1
Nippers, for trimming balls	6	3
Palms, for sewing canvass	4	2
Paste brushes	12	12
Patterns, for cartridge papers for small arms	4	2
Patterns, tin, of each kind and calibre for paper cartridges	1	1
Patterns, do. do. for flannel cartridges	1	1
Patterns, do. do. for canisters	1	
Pans, copper, various sizes	18	6
Pitchers, stone	6	
Pliers, flat, for twisting wire	4	2
Press, for paper and pasteboard	1	
Profiles, of sheet iron, for shot blocks, for each calibre	1	
Punches	6	
Punches, for piercing shot straps	12	6
Punches, centre	4	
Punches, for fuze caps; for 13 in., 10 in., 8 in., and 24-pdr., 2 ea.	8	
Rasps, for wood	6	6
Reels, or frames, for quick match	2	
Rocket stand	1	
Rolling boards, for portfire cases, &c.	4	
Rules, carpenter's	2	1
Rules, iron, for cutting by	8	2
Sand stones, for sharpening knives	6	2

KIND.	QUANTITY.	
	Laboratory.	Park.
Scale of 1 foot, (diagonal,) divided into inches and 100ths	1	1
Scales, copper, large, small, and medium ; or spring balances	5	2
Scissors and shears of different sizes; one pair for each cartridge maker	12	12
Scoops, copper, for taking up materials	6	4
Screw drivers	4	2
Scribers	4	2
Shell plug screws	4	2
Sieves, hair, Nos. 1, 2, 3, and 4, with frames	4	4
Sieves, bolting cloth	2	2
Screens, for demolition of cartridges for small arms	2	
Shovels	2	
Skimmer, copper, for saltpetre	1	
Soldering furnaces and irons	2	1
Socks, pairs	60	
Spatulas, steel, for saltpetre, &c	3	1
Spatulas, for fire stone	6	
Spatulas, for packing ammunition boxes	24	2
Spoke shave	1	
Spools, for twine	40	
Squares, wooden	6	2
Squares, iron	2	1
Stamps for flannel cartridges, for each calibre	1	
Tarpaulins	4	2
Thimbles	6	6
Tinner's crease	1	
Tinner's shears	2	1
Trestles, pairs	2	
Trivets, iron	2	
Tubs, for the demolition of cartridges for small arms	1	
Tubs, common	6	
Tubs, for making slow match, &c., (casks sawed in two)	6	
Twisting machine, for match rope, &c	1	
Watering pots	2	1
Weights, sets for each balance or pair of scales	1	1
Wires, brass, for piercing priming tubes	1000	100
Yard stick	1	1

Powder Measures.

Made of sheet copper; those for use in the park should be made without handles, for the convenience of putting them up in a nest; their form is cylindrical, the interior diameter and height being equal.

To find the diameter and height of a cylinder to contain a given quantity of gunpowder: Multiply the weight in pounds by

38.2 for cannon powder....... } of medium density,
39.4 for musket or rifle powder }

and take the cube root of the product.

DIMENSIONS OF POWDER MEASURES.

Weight of powder.		Diameter and height.	Weight of powder.		Diameter and height.
lbs.	oz.	In.	lbs.	oz.	In.
0	1	1.337	2	0	4.240
0	2	1.685	2	8	4.571
0	4	2.122	3	0	4.857
0	8	2.673	4	0	5.346
1	0	3.368	4	8	5.560
1	4	3.628	6	0	6.120
1	8	3.855	8	0	6.736

Precautions against accidents.

Avoid, as much as possible, the use of iron in the construction of the buildings, fixtures, tables, &c., of the laboratory; sink the heads of iron nails if used, and paste paper or putty over them; cover the floor with oil cloth or carpets; have it frequently swept.—Let the workmen in the powder room wear socks, and take them off when they go out.—Keep no more than the requisite quantity of gunpowder in the laboratory, and have the ammunition and finished work taken to the magazine.—Let powder barrels be carried in hand barrows made with leather, or with slings of rope or canvass, and the ammunition in boxes.—Let every thing that is to be moved be lifted, and not dragged or rolled on the floor.—Never drive rockets, portfires, &c., in a room where there is any powder or composition, except that used at the time.—Never enter the laboratory at night, unless it is indispensable, and then use a close lantern, with a wax or oil light carefully trimmed.—Allow no smoking of tobacco near the laboratory.

MATERIALS.

NOTE. The proportions are by *weight*, and the temperatures in degrees of Fahrenheit's thermometer.

SALTPETRE. For use in the laboratory, saltpetre must be reduced to fine powder, or else to very minute crystals. It is best pulverized in the rolling barrels at the powder mills, but it may be pulverized by hand in the laboratory, as follows: Put into a *rolling barrel* 50 lbs. of dry refined saltpetre, and 100 lbs. of composition balls; turn the barrel for two hours and a half at 30 revolutions a minute, striking it, at the same time, with a mallet to prevent the saltpetre from adhering to the sides. Separate the balls by means of a brass wire screen, and the foreign substances, with a hair sieve.

Saltpetre may also be pulverized by pounding it in a brass mortar, or by solution, as follows: Put 14 lbs. of refined nitre, with 5 pints of clear water, in a broad and shallow copper pan over a slow fire, and, as the nitre dissolves, skim off the impurities; stir the solution with a wooden spatula until the water is all evaporated, when the nitre will be very white and fine. Should it boil too much, the pan must be lifted from the fire and set upon wet sand or earth, and the saltpetre should be stirred until it dries, to prevent it from adhering to the pan.

CHARCOAL. To make charcoal fit for laboratory use: Bury an iron kettle in the earth, to within 4 inches of the edge; put small pieces of wood against the sides; set fire to them, and add wood as it burns, covering that which is already charred; stir it with a poker, from time to time, until the kettle is full of charcoal; then put on a cover, and when vapor ceases to come over, cover it with earth; at the end of 48 hours take out the charcoal, and separate the wood which is imperfectly charred.

Charcoal should be kept in close barrels, in a dry place. For use, when not previously pulverized, it is put into a rolling barrel with 4 times its weight of bronze balls, and run for half an hour; it is then screened and bolted. It may be pulverized also in a leather bag, in which it is beaten about five minutes with a maul; the bag should be well filled; it is held on a block and turned occasionally by one man whilst another pounds it. Charcoal for signal rockets, being used coarse, is beaten about 15 blows, and passed through a coarse and a fine sieve, using that which remains on the latter; charcoal from hard wood answers best for this purpose.

SULPHUR. When melted sulphur is to be used, care must be taken that it does not become thick, which occurs at about 320°. It is pulverized by being rolled 4 hours in a rolling barrel, with twice its weight of balls, or by being pounded in a mortar and sifted. Roll brimstone is used for melting, and flowers of sulphur may be used instead of roll sulphur pulverized, but is not so good.

Gunpowder. For compositions, gunpowder is *mealed*, either by rolling it for 2 hours with once and a half its weight of balls, or by beating it an equal length of time in a leather bag, or by grinding it with a muller, on a mealing table.

Mealed powder, and pulverized saltpetre, charcoal and sulphur, are generally obtained from the powder mills.

Lead. Specific gravity 11,352—melts at 600°.

Pigs of lead frequently contain foreign matters; the fraud is easily detected by immersing the pig in a vessel of water with straight sides, so that the quantity of water displaced by the lead may be easily measured; the weight of the lead should be equal to that of the water displaced, multiplied by 11.352.

Lead melted in contact with air is soon covered by a coat of grey oxide, which rapidly increases in thickness. The formation of this oxide, or of dross, is prevented by covering the lead with powdered charcoal or rosin.

To reduce the oxide of lead. Put in a kettle about 50 lbs. of lead, with 1-10th of its weight of powdered charcoal or grease; cover the kettle, and raise to a red heat; stir the mass, and add gradually more coal, as it assumes a yellow color, using in all 1-6th of the weight of oxide; dip out the lead with an iron ladle, and pour it into iron moulds or pans. After having obtained in this way two-thirds of the weight of oxide, in lead, throw the dross into a tub of water and wash it, to separate the ashes and coal; dry the remaining oxide and grains of lead, and put them in the ladle with 1-20th of their weight of rosin; raise it to a red heat, set fire to the rosin, shake the ladle, and pour off the lead; a further addition of rosin will produce more lead; 1-14th of the weight of dross is generally used. Tallow may be used in place of rosin.

When the quantity of dross is considerable, it may be reduced in a similar manner, in a small cupola furnace.

Acetate of lead, (*sugar of lead*,) is used for making slow match; it is a white efflorescent salt, of a sweet taste, very soluble in water.

Plumber's solder, (*soft solder*,) is an alloy of lead with $\frac{1}{2}$ or $\frac{1}{3}$ of tin; used for soldering tin.

Antimony. Specific gravity 6,700—melting point 809°; it is easily reduced to powder, and by its combustion with sulphur produces strong light and heat, with a blue or white flame. Antimony is never found pure in the shops; that which is sold under the name of *regulus of antimony* always contains a little sulphuret of antimony, arsenic, and sometimes sulphuret of iron.

Copper, (see *page* 8,) being but slightly acted on by saltpetre, is employed for powder measures, utensils for refining saltpetre, &c. Copper vessels should not be exposed to a great heat, or used for heating compositions containing sulphur; the copper would be rapidly oxydized, or would combine with the sulphur, and there would be danger of explosion.

Bronze is used for utensils and implements liable to blows, or acting by percussion.

Brass wire, for screens and sieves.

Acetate of copper, (*verdigris*,) is used to make slow match which gives a strong coal and a slight green flame.

Copper filings give reddish sparks and a greenish blue flame.

Zinc. Specific gravity 6,860—melts at 680°—is volatilized at a red heat. Heated to 400°, it may be pulverized under the hammer. It gives a bluish flame; an alloy of zinc and antimony pulverized gives beautiful blue drops. The oxide of zinc, (*flowers of zinc*,) produces the appearance called gold rain.

Iron. Filings and thin chips give very brilliant sparks and stars, the effects of which depend on the size of the particles used; the filings must be made when wanted, or be very carefully preserved from rust.

Steel. Filings and small pieces of steel give the most brilliant sparks.

Cast iron, pulverized, gives very large red sparks, (*Chinese fire.*) White metal, or fragments of thin pots are to be preferred; to facilitate pulverization, heat the iron red and throw it into cold water.

Sheet iron. Choose the softest and most pliant; to make it bend easily it must be annealed by heating to a dull red, in a fire of shavings, and letting it cool on a bed of hot ashes sheltered from the wind.

Tin should be very pliant, of a smooth surface, free from rust, having a white and homogeneous fracture.

For the five preceding articles, see Chap. XIV.

LABORATORY PAPER.

No.	Kind.	Dimensions of sheets.	No. of sheets in a bundle.	Weight of a bundle.	Articles made with one bundle.	Quantity required for a stated number of articles.		
						No. of articles.	No. of sheets.	Weight.
		Inches.		Lbs.				Lbs.
1	For ball cartridges -	13 by 16½	1,000	20				
	musket - -	-	-	-	12,000 Cartridges -	1,000	83⅓	1.66
	rifle - - -	-	-	-	16,000 Do. -	1,000	62½	1.25
	pistol - - -	-	-	-	24,000 Do. -	1,000	41⅔	0.83
2	For wrappers - -	18 by 20	1,000	36				
	musket or rifle cartridges - -	-	-	-	6,000 Wrappers -	100	16⅔	0.6
	pistol - - -	-	-	-	9,000 Do. -	100	11	0.4
3	For blank cartridges	15 by 20	1,000	30				
	musket - -	-	-	-	20,000 Cartridges -	1,000	50	1.5
	wrappers for do. -	-	-	-	4,000 Wrappers -	100	25	0.75
4	For port fires - -	19 by 28	500	65	1,000 Cases - -	1,000	500	65.
	1.8-in. rockets -	-	-	-	200 Do. - -	100	250	32.5
	2-in. rockets -	-	-	-	125 Do. - -	100	400	52.
5	For fixed ammunition for field guns -	23⅛ by 24	500	60				
	6-pdrs - .	-	-	-	2,000 Cylinders 2,000 Caps	100 each	25	3.
	12-pdrs -	-	-	-	1,000 Cylinders 1,000 Caps	100 each	50	6.
	18-pdrs - -	-	-	-	600 Cylinders 600 Caps	100 each	83⅓	10.
6	For cannon cartridges	19 by 23	500	70				
	24-pdrs - -	-	-	-	500 Bags - -	100	100	14.
	32-pdrs - -	-	-	-	333⅓ Do. - -	100	150	21.
	42-pdrs - -	-	-	-	333⅓ Do. - -	100	150	21.

No. 1 should be well sized, smooth, strong, and of even thickness ; thickness of bundle pressed, 4 inches.

No. 2, of strong materials, with very little sizing.

No. 3, of ordinary materials, smooth, well sized, and colored *blue*.

Nos. 4, 5, and 6, of best materials, even and well sized.

The several kinds to be packed in bundles ; Nos. 1, 2, 3, in bundles of 1,000 sheets each ; the others, in bundles of 500 sheets ; all without folding. The dimensions given above are such as the sheets are required to have when trimmed for use.

A *ream* of paper is 20 *quires* of 24 *sheets* each.

Proof of laboratory paper. Cut a strip 4 in. wide and one foot long, in the weakest direction of the fibre of the sheet; make a loop by lapping the ends of the strip and pressing them between two rollers fixed in a frame; suspend a scale-pan by means of a hook attached to the ends of another roller resting in the bottom of the loop; these strips should sustain, before breaking, the following weights:

No.	Lbs.	No.	Lbs.
No. 1	85½	No. 4	180
2	101	5	225
3	67½	6	315

PARCHMENT, used principally for fuze caps. *Parchment paper* may be substituted for it.

PASTEBOARD, is made of 2 or 3 sheets of paper pasted together; about 50 of the sheets of pasteboard are put under press for one hour, then dried separately in the shade, and put again in the press for one hour, before they become thoroughly dry.

PASTE. *Flour paste* is made best of rye flour. Sift the flour and mix it with 8½ times its weight of water; heat it gently, stir it, and let it boil for three-quarters of an hour; when it becomes ropy, pour it into bowls, and pass it through a sieve before it is quite cold. The flour yields 7 times its weight of paste. Time required to make it, one hour and a half.

Starch paste. Mix wheat starch with twice its weight of water; pour it gradually into 6½ times its weight of boiling water, and let it boil for 10 minutes, stirring it all the time; then proceed as before. Starch yields 8 times its weight of paste. Time required, 1 hour.

Paste for pasteboard. Mix the flour or starch with 12 times its weight of water; this yields 9 times the weight of flour, and 11 times the weight of starch.

The addition of 1-16th of glue makes the paste fit for pasting sheets of parchment together, or for pasting paper on wood. Dissolve the glue separately, and pour it into the cold water with which the flour or starch is mixed.

These different kinds of paste should be used cold. A supply for not more than 2 or 3 days should be made at one time, but it may be preserved longer by adding alum in the proportion of 1-10th of the weight of flour. The depredations of rats may be prevented by dissolving a like proportion of colocinth in the water with which the paste is made.

GLUE, should be hard, dry, transparent, of a brownish red color, and free from smell. It is dissolved in its own weight of boiling water. A glue pot with a water bath should be used, to avoid burning the glue.

Isinglass solution. Dissolve 4 oz. of isinglass in 3 pints of boiling water; it is used sometimes in making quick match.

Flannel, wildbore, or serge, for cartridge bags, should be made entirely of wool—it should be soft, closely woven, and not frayed—the width should be even in the same piece; that ¾ yd. wide is convenient and the most common—the colors are to be preferred in the following order; green, grey, yellow, blue, red, white; reject black, which is almost always burnt and weak. Wildbore and serge are to be preferred to flannel. Fabrics of cotton and flax are not used, because the powder sifts through them, and they are more apt than woollen stuffs to leave fire in the gun.

Canvas. Take the strongest and closest woven; used for sacks for fire balls, bags for rolling leaden balls, and in case of need, for shot straps.

Twine, should be strong, smooth, and well twisted—0.03 in. thick for bundling cartridges, &c., and for sewing fire balls—from 0.06 in. to 0.08 in., for fixing ammunition, &c.

Thread, for infantry cartridges; of unbleached flax, two strands, strong and even. If home-made, it should be gently boiled for one hour in a weak lye and washed in pure water. Excellent hemp thread is obtained from the manufactories, more even, stronger and cheaper than the home-made; it is conveniently wound in balls, and may be used without spooling it.

Rope, should be even and well twisted; that most commonly used in the laboratory is *white hemp rope* from 1 in. to 1.5 in. in girth. (See Chap. XIV.)

Miscellaneous materials. *Spirits of turpentine, rosin, turpentine, tar, pitch,* (See Chap. XIV,) *petroleum, bees-wax, tallow,* are used in compositions for lighting and incendiary purposes; *linseed oil,* in mixing some compositions, and *gum arabic* in others, to give them body and tenacity. The latter retards combustion; the solution should be prepared as it is wanted, being liable to spontaneous decomposition.

Alcohol (Spirits of Wine,) *brandy* or *whisky,* and *vinegar,* are used for mixing compositions in which saltpetre enters, because that salt is but slightly soluble in those liquids.

Lamp black is employed to give a train of rose colored fire in the air; *common salt,* for yellow flames; *flint glass,* in powder, for white fires; *mica,* for rose colored sparks; *oxide of zinc,* for blue flames.

Solutions of phosphate of ammonia and alum, are used for rendering *paper* and *cloth* incombustible.

Other materials, used for particular purposes, will be mentioned under their proper heads.

FLINTS.

The best flints are translucent, with a smooth surface, of a uniform tint of light yellow or brown color, and slightly conchoidal fracture. They are generally obtained from England or France.

The parts of a flint are: the *edge* or *bevel*, the *back*, the *sides*, the *face*, slightly convex, and the *bed* or lower face, slightly concave; in using the flint, the bevel is placed uppermost. There are three sizes for military service; *musket*, *rifle*, and *pistol*, flints. A good musket flint will last for more than 50 fires. Flints are issued to the troops in the proportion of 1 flint to 20 rounds.

DIMENSIONS.	MUSKET.		RIFLE.		PISTOL.	
	Min.	Max.	Min.	Max.	Min.	Max.
	In.	In.	In.	In.	In.	In.
Whole length	1.20	1.50	0.97	1.20	0.93	1.10
Width	1.08	1.13	0.79	0.88	0.83	0.92
Thickness at the back	0.26	0.33	0.20	0.29	0.21	0.27
Length of the bevel	0.39	0.55	0.41	0.71	0.30	0.42

The rifle and the musketoon take the same flint. In the inspection of flints, first verify their dimensions with a gauge, giving the maximum and minimum dimensions; see that the bevel is free from spots and irregularities of surface, that the face and bed are nearly parallel, and have not too great a curvature.

Packing Flints.

Flints are usually packed, for sale, in large casks, or in barrels about the size of powder barrels; the latter will hold about 7,500 musket, 13,700 rifle, and 14,700 pistol flints.

In service, they are packed in boxes of the following dimensions:

KIND OF FLINTS.	Interior dimensions of the box.				Flints in each box.		Total weight of box packed.
	Length.	Width.	Depth.	Cubic contents.	Number.	Weight.	
	In.	In.	In.	In.		Lbs.	Lbs.
Musket	24	11.5	8.75	2,415	5,000	111	129
Rifle	24	11.5	4.75	1,311	5,000	66	82
Pistol	24	11.5	3.25	897	5,000	42	55

The weights vary according to the kind of flint, the black and inferior kind being the heaviest.

The boxes should be made of pine boards 1 inch thick, planed on both sides, and dovetailed at the corners. The length and width of all flint boxes are the same; the depth only is varied to give the required capacity to boxes for different descriptions of flints. If any parcel of one denomination shall be found larger or smaller than usual, the depth of the boxes should be increased or diminished so as to contain them conveniently. A rope handle (or becket) is to be inserted in each end of the box. In boxing a large parcel, it will not be necessary that the contents of each box should be actually counted, if the flints are nearly uniform in size; after counting out accurately four or five parcels, of 5,000 each, from any cask, let each be separately weighed, and take the mean weight of the counted parcels as the basis for determining the quantity for each box, when taken from the same cask. After the flints are placed in the boxes, all the interstices are to be filled with dry sand, in order to exclude the air from them as much as possible; and for the same purpose, the boxes should be well made, of seasoned wood, and with close joints. Each box should be plainly marked on the end with the number and description of flints contained in it, and with the year in which they were manufactured, if this be known; if not known, then with the year in which they were procured.

Flints should not be placed in the upper stories of a building, but in the basement or cellar where the air is damp and cool.

CARTRIDGES FOR SMALL ARMS.

KIND.		BALLS.		CHARGES OF POWDER.				REMARKS.
		Diameter.	Number in 1 pound.	Weight.	Number in 1 pound.	Ratio to wgt. of ball.	Blank cartridges.	
		In.		Grains			Grains	
PERCUSSION.	Musket	0.65	17	110	64	1-4th	75	Musket powder.
	Musketoon...	0.65	17	75	93	1-5th	75	
	Hall's carbine	0.525	32	75	93	1-3d	60	Rifle powder.
	Rifle........	0.525	32	75	93	1-3d	60	
	Pistol........	0.525	32	30	233	1-7th	30	

Buckshot are 0.31 in. in diameter; weight, about 150 or 155 to 1 lb.

Cartridges are made either with *single ball*, 1 *ball and* 3 *buckshot*, or sometimes with 12 *buckshot*, and they are designated accordingly.

Making Balls.

To cast balls. 6 men required to each kettle; 2 to cast the balls, 1 to extract and roll, and 3 to trim them.

Tools and utensils. 1 *iron kettle*, fixed in a furnace as before described—2 *iron ladles*, 0.10 in. thick, 3.5 in. diameter, with a lip on the left side and a handle 18 in. long a little bent—1 *bench*, of 4 in. plank—6 *moulds*, (brass,) with double rows for 6 or 8 balls on each side, or for 8 balls and 15 buckshot; placed on the bench—1 *mallet*—1 *double ball-gauge;* the diameter of one ring is 0.002 in. greater than, that of the other 0.0015 less than, the true calibre of the ball—3 *nippers;* one arm is bent and fixed in the bench, the other is about 5 in. longer and has a wooden handle; the jaws are of steel, two inches wide, tempered and ground sharp; they may be so formed as to cut the gate according to the spherical surface of the ball. Under the jaws of the nippers is a hole in the bench, through which the balls fall into *boxes* placed to receive them—1 *rolling barrel*, 2 feet long and 1 foot diameter, made of hard thick staves, with but little bilge, and hooped with iron; it has a small scuttle in the bilge, with hinges and a hasp and staple; the barrel has a gudgeon in each head, and is turned by a crank in a frame to which a hopper may be attached. Instead of the rolling barrel, 2 strong *canvas bags* may be used; they should be 5 feet long and 16 in. in diameter, suspended horizontally by 4 cords attached to the joists of the building—1 *screen*, (sheet iron,) the holes of which are of the diameter of the largest calibre gauge; it is supported by gudgeons which turn in a frame, or in the tops of two stakes driven in the ground.

Casting. Weigh the lead; fill the kettle and cover it; as the lead melts add more, until it comes within 3 inches of the edges of the kettle; then cover it with a layer of powdered charcoal 1 in. thick; push the heat until paper in contact with the lead is inflamed by it; this requires from 1 to 2 hours.

Immerse the ladle and fill it about ¾ full of lead covered with charcoal, which is kept back by a piece of wood, in running the lead; fill all the moulds on one side, then turn them and fill the other side; the first castings are thrown back into the kettle, being imperfect from the moulds being cold; the diameter of some of the balls is verified from time to time, with the gauges; the moulds must be carefully cleaned when it is perceived that the lead sticks to them, and if any moulds give imperfect balls, they must be filled with copper.

Extract the balls and trim them; in cutting, the ball should be gently pressed with the left fore-finger against the nippers, the gate being placed between the jaws.

TO SMOOTH THE BALLS. Put 100 lbs. of them into the rolling barrel, and roll them for 3 minutes; or 50 lbs. into a bag and shake it five minutes; then run them through the screen, putting in 50 lbs. at a time; those which remain on the screen are re-cast.

With the above force 30,000 to 35,000 musket balls are made in 11 or 12 hours.

With proper care in observing the instructions, 100 lbs. of lead will give from 96 to 98 lbs. of balls.

PRESSED BALLS. Lead balls are now generally made by compression, by means of machinery; either at the arsenals or at private establishments. These balls are more uniform in size, smoother and more solid than the cast balls. *Compressed buckshot* are also readily obtained from private shot works.

PACKING. Balls are packed in boxes made of 1 in. boards, 9 in. square inside and 5 in. deep, containing 100 lbs. of balls or buckshot; they should be marked on one end with the weight and kind of balls, the place and date of fabrication; the top is fastened with six 2-inch screws, and the boxes must be hooped with iron for transportation.

Making Cartridges.

DIMENSIONS OF PAPER FOR CARTRIDGES.		SHEETS.		TRAPEZOIDS.			
		Length.	Breadth.	Height.	Long side.	Short side.	Number in one sheet.
		In	In.	In.	In.	In.	
MUSKET.	Single ball, or ball and buck-shot	16.5	13	4.33	5.25	3	12
	Blank	20	15	4	4.75	2.75	20
	12 buckshot	16.5	13	5.5	5	3	9
RIFLE	Ball	16.5	13	4	4.25	2.25	16
	Blank	20	15	3	4.25	2.25	30
PISTOL	Ball	16.5	13	2.75	4.25	2.25	24
	Blank	20	15	2.5	4.25	2.25	36

TO CUT THE PAPER. 1 Cutter, 1 assistant.

Implements. 1 *Cutting board,* 30 in. square—1 *pattern,* of hard wood or iron, of the dimensions of each of the papers—1 *rule,* of hard wood, 33 in. long,

1.5 in. wide, and 0.5 in. thick, to cut by—2 *laboratory* (shoe) *knives*—2 *sand stones*, for sharpening knives on.

The paper is first cut into strips of a width equal to the length of a trapezoid, and then into trapezoids, by means of the patterns; cut about 12 sheets at a time. A cutting machine, like that used by bookbinders, facilitates the operation, when many hands are employed.

TO MAKE THE CYLINDERS. 1 Master; 10 men to roll the cylinders; 1 to fill them, 4 to fold, 4 to bundle. Boys or girls from 12 to 18 years of age may be advantageously employed.

Implements and utensils, for each workman for making cylinders: 2 *boxes* for the empty cylinders, made of ½ in. boards; interior dimensions, 20 in. long, 8 in. wide, and 5 in. high, without a cover; they are placed upon the sides, facing the front of the cartridge table which is furnished with brackets to receive them, and also with a small enclosure or *locker* for balls, at the right hand of each workman—1 *spool of thread*, turning on a vertical iron spindle fixed in the table near the shot locker ; 1 lb. of thread is required for 10,000 single ball musket cartridges, being 8½ inches to a cartridge— 1 *choking string*, made by twisting together 4 or 5 cartridge threads ; fastened to the edge of the table, at the right hand of the workman—1 *pair of scissors*, to cut the thread—1 *former*, cylindrical, of hard wood, of the same diameter as the ball ; one end convex, the other concave, to receive one-third of the ball ; length 6 or 7 inches.

Take the paper in the left hand, the former in the right; lay the paper on the table, with the side perpendicular to the bases towards the workman, the broad end to the left; place the former with its convex end at the broad end of the paper; turn it so as to envelop it with the paper, then with the right hand laid flat upon the paper, roll all the paper upon the former ; seize it with the left hand, and with the choking string in the right hand, take one turn around the cylinder at about half an inch from the end, to which distance the end of the former is withdrawn ; hold the former firmly in the left hand, and draw gently upon the choking string, pressing at the same time, with the left fore-finger, upon the projecting end of the cylinder, thus folding it neatly down upon the end of the former. Having choked the cylinder, carry it to the right side, and with the twine in the right hand, take two turns and a half hitch firmly around the part that has been choked ; withdraw the former and introduce the ball, following it to the end of the cylinder with the former reversed ; raise the whole again, and with the same thread, (which is never cut until the cartridge is finished,) take two half hitches just upon the upper side of the ball, between it and the concave end of the former. The operation is expedited by rolling the ball placed in the concave end of the former and choking the paper over it. Cut the thread and place the cartridge in the box which stands fronting the workman.

For ball and buckshot cartridges. Roll and choke the paper, put in 3 buckshot, follow them with the former, and take a half hitch of thread over them; then insert the ball as before.

Buckshot cartridges have 4 tiers of 3 buckshot each, inserted like the first, with a half hitch between them, and finishing with a double hitch.

For rifles, the ball is prepared by being enveloped in a square piece of fine *muslin*, or of soft thin *leather*, or of *bladder*, tied over it and leaving a projecting end about ½ in. long, which, after being trimmed with scissors, is introduced into the paper cylinder which is choked over it and fastened by two turns and a double hitch.

1,000 patches require about 4 yards of muslin.

Cylinders for blank cartridges are made by folding down the paper over the concave end of the charger, touching the fold with a little paste, and pressing it on a ball imbedded in the table for that purpose.

To FILL THE CYLINDERS. 1 Man to fill, 4 to fold, 4 to bundle.

Implements and utensils. 1 Large *copper pan* for powder.

1 *Charger* for each kind of cartridge, made of thin copper, with a handle at the top. The chargers are conical:

Dimensions of chargers.	110 grs.	75 grs.	30 grs.
	In.	In.	In.
Diameter { top	0.8	0.7	0.5
Diameter { bottom	0.6	0.5	0.4
Height	1.35	1.25	0.85

1 *Funnel*, copper, of the following interior dimensions:

	In.
Diameter of funnel, { superior	1.75
Diameter of funnel, { inferior	0.5
Diameter of pipe	0.5
Height of funnel	1.
Length of pipe	1.25

The funnel has a ring handle 0.6 in. diameter.

A charger, for filling cartridges much more expeditiously, is made by attaching to a large brass funnel two charging cylinders which communicate with one discharging pipe at the lower end. These cylinders are alternately filled and emptied by a reciprocating motion of the funnel pipe.

1 *Folding box* for each calibre, made with only two sides; width equal to 5 times the diameter of the ball, height equal to twice that diameter. Two strips of wood nailed on the table will answer the same purpose more conveniently.

Take the boxes full of cartridge cylinders to the table in the filling room; as they are filled, incline the cylinders over from the empty ones; when all in one box are full, fold the paper down over the powder by two rectangular folds, and place the cartridges before the men who are to bundle them.

BUNDLING. Put a wrapper in the folding box and place in it 2 tiers of 5 cartridges each, parallel to each other and to the short sides of the wrapper, the balls alternating; wrap the cartridges, whilst in the folding box, by folding the paper over them; tie them, first in the direction of the length, then of the breadth, with a bit of twine fastened in a single flat knot.

A package of 12 *percussion caps* is placed in each bundle of 10 cartridges, at the end of the bundle.

The case for the caps is made like a cylinder for a rifle cartridge; it is choked at one end and tied; when the caps are inserted it is folded like a cartridge.

Dimensions of bundles of Percussion Cartridges.

KIND OF CARTRIDGE.		Length, (height of cartridge.)	Breadth.	Thickness.
		In.	In.	In.
Musket	Ball	2.6	3.1	1.35
	Buck and ball	2.90	3.1	1.35
	Buck shot	3.1	3.1	1.35
	Blank	1.83	3.1	1.35
Musketoon	Ball	2.5	3.1	1.35
	Buck and ball	2.18	3.1	1.35
	Buck shot	2.43	3.1	1.35
	Blank	1.39	3.1	1.35
Rifle	Ball	3.	2.6	1.15
	Blank	1.9	2.6	1.15
Hall's Carbine	Ball	2.1	2.6	1.15
	Blank	1.58	2.6	1.15
Pistol	Ball	2.	2.6	1.15
	Blank	1.12	2.6	1.15

Wrapping paper is but slightly sized, with a view to its being immersed, before using it, in a varnish made of bees-wax, linseed oil and spirits turpentine, for the purpose of making the paper water proof.—See CHAPTER VII.

1000 lbs. of paper require :

Bees-wax..............................133 lbs.,
Spirits of turpentine.....................135 gallons,
Linseed oil..............................10 gallons.

With the above mentioned force, 10,000 musket cartridges are made and bundled in 10 hours, being 1000 for each maker of cylinders.

Packing Cartridges.

Ball cartridges are packed in boxes to contain 1000 each. Blank cartridges may be packed in powder barrels.

Interior dimensions of packing boxes for 1000 *Percussion Cartridges.*

KIND.	Depth.	Length.	Width.	WEIGHT.	
				Empty.	Packed.
	In.	In.	In.	Lbs.	
Musket, buck and ball.......	6.75	15.5	11.75	12.	107
Musketoon, ball.............	6.75	15.5	9.	11.5	100
Rifle, ball..................	5.75	13.	11.75	11.	60
Hall's Carbine..............	5.75	13.	11.	9.	55
Pistol, ball.................	5.75	13.	8.	7.	45

The boxes are made of 1 in. white pine boards, and are furnished with wooden brackets or handles nailed to the ends ; the lids fastened with four $1\frac{3}{4}$ in. screws. They are painted olive color. The kegs or boxes should be lined with strong water proof paper, and the bundles of cartridges must be closely packed, so as not to shake in transportation. Each keg or box should be marked, on both ends, with the number and kind of cartridges ; on the inside of the cover, with the place and date of fabrication.

AMMUNITION FOR FIELD SERVICE.—*Plate* 17.

The charges of powder are contained in *cartridge bags*.

The projectile is attached to a block of wood called a *sabot*.

For the guns and the 12-pounder howitzer, the cartridge and the projectile are attached to the same sabot, making together *a round of fixed ammunition*.

For 32 *and* 24-*pounder howitzers*, the projectile is separate from the charge, and the cartridge is attached to a block of wood, called a *cartridge block*.

Charges of Powder.

KIND.	FOR GUNS.		FOR HOWITZERS.		
	12-pdr.	6-pdr.	32-pdr.	24-pdr.	12-pdr.
	Lbs.	Lbs.	Lbs.	Lbs.	Lbs.
For shot.................	2.5	1.25	–	–	–
For spherical case or canister.	2.	1.	2.5	2.	1.
For shells. { Small charge...	–	–	2.5	2.	} 1.
For shells. { Large charge...	–	–	3.25	2.5	

Cartridge Bags.

The best materials for cartridge bags are wildbore, merino, and bombazette. The stuff should be composed entirely of wool, free from any mixture of thread or cotton, and of sufficiently close texture to prevent the powder from sifting through; that which is not twilled is to be preferred. Flannel is used when the other materials cannot be conveniently obtained.

MAKING CARTRIDGE BAGS. A cartridge bag for field service is made of a rectangle which forms the cylinder, and a circular piece which forms the bottom.

DIMENSIONS.	12-pdr. gun; 32 & 24-pdr. howitzers.	6-pdr. gun, and 12-pdr. howitzer.	REMARKS.
	In.	In.	
Length of rectangle (cylinder developed)..............	14.2	11.4	1 in. allowed for seam.
Height..................	10.	7.25	0.5 in. do.
Diameter of bottom.........	5.25	4.37	1 in. do.

The length of the rectangle (development of the cylinder) should be taken in the direction of the length of the stuff, as it does not stretch in that direction.

One hundred 12-pounder cartridge bags require about 27 yards of stuff of single width, (22 inches.)

One hundred 6-pounder bags take about 15 yards.

IMPLEMENTS. *Tables—patterns*, of hard, well seasoned wood, or of sheet iron or tin for the rectangles and bottoms—*scissors—chalk*, or *colored crayons*.

A marker and his assistant spread a piece of stuff on a table, and with the patterns trace out the rectangles and bottoms; a cutter follows and cuts them out with scissors.

Sewing. The bags are sewed with woollen yarn, with 12 stitches to an inch; they are stitched within half an inch of each edge, and the two edges of the seam are turned down on the same side and basted, to prevent the powder from sifting through; the edges of the bottom are basted down upon the sides. Bags for fixed ammunition are sewed to within 3 in. of the mouth, for 12-pdrs.; to within 2.75 in., for 6-pdrs.; all others, up to the mouth.

Cartridge bags when filled should pass through the small shot gauge of their calibre; those used for patterns should be thus verified. The empty bags should be measured by laying the bag, flattened out, between two marks on a table, showing the width of the pattern bag; a variation of 0.1 in. greater or less is allowed. Reject those sewed with too large stitches.

Bags for immediate use, or for blank cartridges, may be formed by sewing together two rectangular pieces with semicircular ends; the stuff is marked, for cutting and sewing, with stamps of the following dimensions:

		CALIBRES....	12-pdr.	6-pdr.
			In.	In.
Stamps,	for cutting,	Width	7.6	6.
		Length, including semicircular ends.	10.5	8.5
	for sewing,	Width	6.6	5.2
		Length, including semicircular ends.	10.	8.

These stamps are made of 1 in. boards of the dimensions of the cutting stamp, with a handle in the middle of one side; to the edges of the board is fastened a strip of tin or copper projecting about $\frac{3}{4}$ in. on the side opposite to the handle; another strip is inserted in like manner in a groove parallel to the edges of the board, at the distance indicated for the sewing stamp; the edges of these strips are made rough, to retain the chalk or paste used for marking.

Packing. Cartridge bags are preserved from moths by being packed with pounded camphor and black pepper, or dipped in water with arsenic dissolved in it. Or, they may be sealed up, in bundles of 50, in cases made of cartridge paper, carefully closed with strips of thin paper pasted over the seams. Each bundle is marked with the number and kind of bags.

They may be preserved from moisture by being enveloped in water proof paper, as above recommended for cartridges for small arms.

Cartridge Blocks.—Plate 17.

Cartridge blocks are cylinders of wood to which the cartridges of howitzers are attached, to give them a better finish, and to increase the length of the smaller charges, so that they may fill the chamber of the piece, and may be less apt to turn in the bore.

They are made of *poplar*, *linden*, or other soft wood.

DIMENSIONS.	32-PDR. HOWITZER.		24-PDR. HOWITZER.	
	Small charge.	Large charge.	Small charge.	Large charge.
	In.	In.	In.	In.
Diameter....................	4.15	4.15	4.15	4.15
Height......................	2.	0.75	1.	0.5
Distance from middle of groove to bottom of block.........	0.4	0.375	0.4	0.25
Width of groove.............	0.3	0.3	0.3	0.3
Depth of groove.............	0.15	0.15	0.15	0.15

Sabots—Plate 17.

Sabots are made of *poplar*, *linden*, or other light, close grained wood; the stuff should be clear of knots and splits, and it must be well seasoned.

Sabots for shot and spherical case, for guns, have *one groove* for attaching the cartridge—those for gun canisters, and for the 12-pdr. howitzer shells, spherical case and canisters, have *two grooves*. These grooves are .3 in. wide and .15 in. deep. The corners of the grooves and bottom are slightly rounded.

Sabots for the 32 and 24-pdr. howitzers have no grooves; they are furnished with *handles*, made of cord about .15 in. thick, passing through two holes in the sabots, .25 in. diameter, and fastened by knots countersunk on the inside.

The dimensions of finished sabots are verified with appropriate gauges.

DIMENSIONS OF SABOTS.	12-PDR. GUN.		6-PDR. GUN.		32-PDR. HOWTZR.		24-PDR. HOWTZR.		12-PDR. HOWTZR.	
	Shot and sph. case.	Canister.	Shot and sph. case.	Canister.	Shells and sph. case.	Canister.	Shells and sph. case	Canister	Shells and sph. case.	Canister.
	In.	In.	In.	In	In.	In.	In.	In.	In.	In.
Whole height - - - - - -	2.	2.25	1.55	2.25	2.4	4.75	2.4	4.45	3.2	4.45
Greatest diameter - - - - - -	4.35	4.52	3.35	3.58	5.6	6.24	5.3	5.68	4.27	4.52
Diameter of bottom of conical part -	-	-	-	-	4.5	4.5	4.6	4.6	3.6	3.6
Height of conical part - - - -	-	-		-	2.4	4.	2.4	3.75	2.	2.75
Diameter at bottom of sabot - - -	4.15	4.15	3.2	3.2	4.5	4.5	4.6	4.6	3.2	3.2
Cavity for ball. { Depth - - - -	1.5	-	1.	-	1.5	-	1.5	-	1.3	
Cavity for ball. { Radius of curvature -	2.26	-	1.8	-	3.12	-	2.84	-	2.26	
Height of cylinder for tin - - -	-	0.5	-	0.5	-	0.75	-	0.7	-	0.5
Diameter of do. - - - - - -		4.47	-	3.53	-	6.19	-	5.63	-	4.47
Distance from middle of lower groove to bottom of sabot - - - -	0.4	0.4	0.4	0.4	-	-	-	-	0.4	0.4
Distance between centres of grooves -	-	0.8	-	0.8	-	-	-	-	0.5	0.5
Distance between holes for handles -	-	-	-	-	1.5	2.3	1.5	2.3		
Length of cord for handle - - -	-	-	-	-	12.	20.	12.	19.		

Straps.

Straps are made of sheet tin ; they are cut with shears and straightened with a wooden mallet, upon a block of lead.

For shot, there are two straps crossing at right angles, one passing through a slit in the middle of the other. *For shells,* there are four straps soldered to a *ring* of tin, or fastened to it by cutting 4 slits in the ring, into which the upper ends of the strap are hooked and turned down on the inside of the ring.

DIMENSIONS.		FOR SHOT.		FOR SHELLS AND SPH. CASE.			
		12-pdr.	6-pdr.	32-pdr.	24-pdr.	12-pdr.	6-pdr.
		In.	In.	In.	In.	In.	In.
STRAPS..	Width.........	0.45	0.35	0.6	0.55	0.45	0.35
	Length.........	12.75	10.	10.5	9.00	7.50	5.5
RINGS...	Exterior diam..	.....	.....	2.3	2.3	2.3	2.3
	Interior do..	.....	.....	1.2	1.15	1.15	1.15

Strapping Shot and Shells.

UTENSILS AND IMPLEMENTS. 1 *bench*—2 *pans*, containing *nails* 0.55 in. long, with strong flat heads 0.2 in. diameter—*boxes* and *barrels*, for straps and sabots—4 *hammers*, for strapping—1 *common hammer*—4 *punches*—*shot gauges*, of each calibre—1 *gauge* for each calibre, 0.04 in. greater than the largest shot gauge, through which the shot should pass after it is strapped—*tow* or *rags*, for wiping balls—1 *wheelbarrow*—1 *tarpaulin*, if the shop has not a plank floor.

A helper knocks off the scales from the balls with a hammer, cleans and dries the interior of the shells, if requisite, wipes the balls, and gauges them both before and after they are strapped. The workman inserts the roughest part of the shot in the cavity of the sabot, and strikes a few blows on the bottom of the sabot to make the shot enter; he can tell by the sound if the shot touches the bottom of the cavity; if it does not touch, he tries another sabot. With the edge of the hammer he bends one end of the strap which is not slit into the groove of the sabot, punches and nails it; he fastens the other end in the same manner, cutting off the superfluous length; he then nails the other strap, and with his hammer sets them both in, close to the ball, at the top of the sabot.

The sabots for 32 and 24-pounder field howitzers having no groove, each strap is fastened by one nail on the side and 2 under the bottom of the sabot. Two men can strap, in 10 hours, 130 shot, or 75 shells, cutting the tin from the sheet.

If tin or sheet iron cannot be procured, straps may be made of *strong canvas*, 1 inch wide, sewed at the point of crossing. The part of the ball which is to be inserted in the sabot is dipped in glue; the straps are also glued to the ball; the ends are doubled into the groove and secured by two nails in each end. Another method is to wrap round the ball a band of canvass 1 inch wide, one half of which is glued to the ball, the other to the sabot; or, the shot may be kept in place by merely tying the cartridge bag over the top of it.

Fuze Plugs.—Plate 17.

The fuzes for field shells and spherical case are inserted, at the moment of loading the gun, into wooden *fuze plugs*, previously driven into the shells.

These plugs are made of *beech*, perfectly seasoned and dried, so that they may not shrink after they are driven.

DIMENSIONS.		For 32-pdr. spherical case.	For other shells and spherical case.	REMARKS.
		In.	In.	
Exterior diameter,	at top.....	1.25	0.95	Exterior taper .15 in. to 1 in.
	at bottom..	1.025	0.75	
Interior diameter.	at top.....	0.50	0.50	Interior taper .05 in. to 1 in.
	at bottom..	0.425	0.4325	
Height.....................		1.5	1.35	

Charging Shells.

CHARGES.		32-pdr.		24-pdr.		12-pdr.		REMARKS.
		Lbs.	oz.	Lbs.	oz.	Lbs.	oz.	
Powder required	to fill the shell.........	1	5	1		0	8	Rifle or musket powder is used in preference to cannon powder
	to burst the shell........	0	11	0	8	0	5	
	to blow out the fuze plug	0	2	0	2	0	1	
	for service charge.......	1		0	12	0	7	

MATERIALS. *Rifle or musket powder—Fuze plugs.*

IMPLEMENTS. 1 *Funnel—Powder measures,* to hold the required charges—1 *small mallet*—1 *Fuze plug reamer.*

The shells having been properly cleaned and dried, and attached to the sabots, pour in the charge of powder; drive in the fuze plug with the mallet, until the top of it is within .1 in. of the surface of the shell; be careful that the plug is not split in driving. Ream out the fuze hole in the plug, with a careful steady hand; if the hole is properly reamed, the fuze will project about .15, when pressed in with the thumb. Stop up the hole in the fuze plug, by inserting a wad of dry tow, which should be pressed in firmly with a round stick.

Spherical Case Shot.

CHARGE.	8-in.	42	32	24	18	12	6
Number of musket balls......	486	306	225	175	120	78	38
Bursting charge of powder, oz.	15	9	8	6	5	4.5	2.5
Weight of shot loaded.....lbs.	59.5	39	30.13	22.75	16.3	11.	5.5

The shot having been cleaned and strapped to the sabot, put in the balls. In order to get in the whole number of balls, it is sometimes necessary, when the shell is nearly full, to push the upper balls aside, with the finger, or with a stick. Pour in the charge of powder, shaking it down among the balls. Insert the fuze plug, ream out the hole and stop it with tow, in the same manner as for common shells.

Canisters.—Plate 17.

A canister for field service consists of a tin cylinder attached to a sabot and filled with cast iron shot. For the dimensions of *Canister Shot,* see CHAP. II.

To form the cylinder, the tin is lapped, from .3 to .5 in. and soldered. The cylinder is fastened to the sabot with 6 or 8 nails .5 in. to .75 in. long. A plate of rolled iron is placed on the sabot, and the canister is closed with a sheet iron cover; the top of the cylinder is cut into strips .4 in. to .5 in. long, and turned down over the cover.

The tin is .02 in. to .025 in. thick. (Double tin.)

DIMENSIONS OF CANISTERS.	FOR GUNS.		FOR HOWITZERS.		
	12	6	32	24	12
	In.	In.	In.	In.	In.
Length of tin for cylinder, (developed)..	14.40	11.5	20.	18.3	14.4
Height of ditto..................	6.65	5.4	7.1	6.3	5.2
Interior diameter of cylinder	4.45	3.53	6.19	5.63	4.45
Diameter of plates for bottom and cover	4.40	3.48	6.14	5.58	4.40
Thickness of bottom plate.............	0.25	0.25	0.25	0.25	0.25
Thickness of sheet iron cover..........	0.07	0.07	0.10	0.10	0.07
Height of finished canister, includ'g sabot	8.	6.75	10.5	9.55	8.75
Number of tiers of shot...............	4	4	4	4	4
Number of shot in each of 3 lower tiers.	7	7	12	12	12
Number of shot in 4th tier............	6	6	12	12	12
Whole number of shot................	27	27	48	48	48
	Lbs.	Lbs.	Lbs.	Lbs.	Lbs.
Weight of finished canister............	14.8	7.32	28.5	21.25	10.8

A variation of 0.05 in. more or less, is allowed in the diameter of the iron bottom.

The exterior diameter of each canister must be verified with the maximum shot gauge of the calibre, and the interior, with a cylinder of a diameter 0.02 in. less than that given in the table, which should enter the canister, otherwise it is rejected.

Before filling the canister, dip the tin cylinder into a lacker of bees-wax dissolved in spirits of turpentine, to prevent it from rusting. Coat the balls and the plates with paint or coal tar.

Filling canisters. Place the canister upright on a bench; insert the iron bottom and place it flat on the sabot; put in a tier of balls, fill the interstices with dry sifted saw dust, pack it with a pointed stick so that the balls will hold by themselves, and throw out the loose saw dust; place another tier of balls and proceed in the same manner until the canister is filled; cover the upper tier with saw dust; put on the cover and on it place one of the iron bottoms furnished with a handle, and strike it with a small mallet in order to compress the saw dust; then remove this bottom and turn down the slit pieces of the canister over the cover, with a hammer. When the canister is finished, verify its diameter with the maximum shot gauge of the same calibre.

Cylinders and Caps.

For the greater security of field ammunition, the cartridges are covered with paper cylinders and caps. The cap is drawn off at the moment of loading the piece, and in using solid shot it may be placed over the shot, to diminish the windage. A cylinder and a cap are formed together by folding the paper over a *former*, which allows a lap of about 0.75 inch for pasting. The requisite length for the cylinder is cut off from the smaller end; the rest forms the cap, which is *choked* at the end from which the cylinder is cut.

DIMENSIONS.		FOR GUNS.		FOR HOWITZERS.		
		12	6	32	24	12
		In.	In.	In.	In.	In.
Paper for a cylinder and a cap.	Length, developed...	14.4	11.6	14.4	14.4	11.6
	Height............	12.5	11.5	12.	10.	8.
Height of cylinder	For large charge....	5.	4.	5.25	3.5	
	For small charge....	4.	3.5	5.	3.	3.
Formers for cylinders and caps.	Length (exclusive of handle)..........	15.	13.	Same as 12-pdr. gun		Same as 6-pdr. gun
	Width at upper end.	6.71	5.25			
	Width at lower end..	6.6	5.17			
	Thickness..........	0.15	0.15			
Cylindrical formers for choking caps.	Length............	10.	10.			
	Diameter..........	4.3	3.3			

The choking former should be bored through the axis with a ½ inch hole, to facilitate drawing off the cap; one end is rounded.

Fixing Ammunition.

IMPLEMENTS AND UTENSILS: *Barrels* for powder—1 *funnel*—1 *set of powder measures*—1 *straight edge*, to strike the measures with—*barrels*—*tubs*, formed of barrels sawed in two, or *boxes* for the cartridge bags—2 *tarpaulins*—2 *benches*—12 *choking sticks*, 6 with holes in them and 6 slit—6 *knives*—6 *handbarrows*, with four legs and a box, and *tarpaulins* to cover them—*calibre gauges*, for the cartridge bags and for fixed ammunition; they may be made of wood—6 *stools*—1 *wheelbarrow*—1 *mallet*—1 *copper chisel*—1 *copper drift*, or a *wrench*, to open powder barrels.

For dimensions of powder measures, see *page* 235.

Fixing shot, or spherical case, for field guns. The bags should be filled in the small magazine or filling room, and carried, after being shaken and gauged, to the finishing room. One of the gaugers takes a filled bag with one hand, squeezing the bag upon the powder; he strikes with the other hand on the top and bottom of the bag, twisting the mouth of the bag down upon the powder at the same time; he then tries it with the small gauge, through which it should pass with not more than 0.25 inch play; should it not do this, the bag is emptied and rejected. These bags, filled and gauged, are placed upright in a tub or box, and carried by the gaugers into the finishing room, where the men are placed in pairs, sitting astride on a bench, facing each other. One of them opens a bag and levels the powder, the other inserts the sabot of a strapped shot square upon the powder and draws up the end of the bag over the shot; the first man passes about 4 feet of twine through the pierced stick, and makes two turns and a double hitch with the end at the top of the sabot; he makes a knot in the end of the twine, inserts it into the slit in the other choking stick, and tightens the double hitch by rolling the twine on the sticks and bearing upon the sabot; he then takes out the end of the twine from the slit, ties it in a hard knot, which he tightens with the assistance of the choking stick, and cuts the twine off near the knot. The second man turns down the mouth of the bag over the sabot and the first makes a similar tie in the groove; he makes another tie below the sabot, the twine being lodged between it and the powder, to prevent the latter from sifting in between the bag and the sabot; he then runs the paper cylinder over the cartridge and sabot, leaving about 2 inches of the end of the cartridge uncovered, and he makes a tie, similar to the others, in the groove of the sabot. He now holds the shot in the left hand and examines it, striking the sabot with the right hand, if necessary, to bring it straight; if the shot is properly fixed, the sabot and the bag will be on the same axis; the seams should be between two straps, and the knots should be neither on the seams nor on the straps.

The assistants pass the cartridges through the large gauge, which is 0.04 inch larger than the large gauge for the shot. If the size is correct, they put on the paper cap, lay the cartridges on their sides in the box of the handbarrow, and carry them to the magazine. Those which will not pass through the gauge are handed back to the fixers, who cut the strings and put them up anew.

Canisters for field guns are fixed in the same manner as shot, except that the first tie is made in the upper groove of the sabot; the cylinder is tied in the lower groove. The caps must be cut somewhat shorter than those for shot cartridges.

For the 12-pdr. field howitzer: The shells, spherical case, and canisters, are fixed in the same manner as the gun canisters.

For the mountain howitzer: The sabots having but one groove, the first tie is omitted, and the cartridge is covered with a cap only.

For the 32-pounder and 24-pounder howitzers: The cartridge is not attached to the projectile. The cartridge block is inserted with the grooved end next to the powder, and a tie made in the groove; the mouth of the bag is then turned down, and another tie is made between the cartridge block and the powder; the superfluous part of the bag is cut off, and the cartridge is covered with its cylinder and cap, as in other cases.

When the shot is attached to the sabot by a single band of canvas, or when it is placed in the sabot without any strap, the cartridge bag is drawn over it and tied on top; for this purpose, the bag should have an additional length of from 2½ to 3 inches.

When sabots cannot be obtained, place upon the powder a layer of tow about 0.2 in. thick, forming a bed for the shot; tie the bag over the shot and around the tow; the bag requires to be 1 inch longer than for strapped shot.

Dimensions and weights of Fixed Ammunition.

DIMENSIONS.		FOR GUNS.		FOR HOWITZERS.		
		12	6	32	24	12
		In.	In.	In.	In.	In.
Height of charge of powder; including cartridge blocks for 32 and 24 pdr howitzers	Large charge	5.	4.	7.4	5.9	3.25
	Small charge	4.	3.25	7.4	5.4	
Height of strapped shot or shell		5.02	4.13	7.14	6.58	6.42
Height of canister with sabot		8.	6.75	10.5	9.55	8.75
Height of a round of fixed ammunition, with cap.	Shot	10.4	8.43			
	Shell	.....	.....	.....	.....	10.
	Spherical case	9.5	7.8	.....	.....	10.
	Canister	12.4	10.3	.....	.....	12.3
WEIGHTS.		Lbs.	Lbs.	Lbs.	Lbs.	Lbs.
Cartridge, including cartridge block	Large charge	2.56	1.3	3.88	2.7	
	Small charge	2.06	1.05	3.1	2.34	1.05
Shot, strapped		12.75	6.28			
Shell, strapped and charged		.....	.....	24.6	18.8	9.35
Spherical case, strapped and charged		11.43	5.75	31.	23.	11.3
Canister with sabot		14.8	7.32	28.5	21.25	10.8
Round of ammunition, complete	Shot	15.4	7.6			
	Shell, with small ch'ge	.....	.....	27.7	21.15	10.5
	Spherical case	13.5	6.82	34.1	25.34	12.5
	Canister	16.91	8.4	31.6	23.6	11.85

Packing Field Ammunition.

Packing boxes for field ammunition are made of well seasoned stuff, (generally white pine,) 1.25 in. thick, dovetailed at the corners. The top of the box is fastened with six 2 in. screws; the box has two handles of $1\frac{3}{4}$ in. rope, attached to brackets at the ends.

The boxes are painted olive color on the outside, and the kind of ammunition is marked on both ends, in large white letters. The place and date of fabrication are marked on the inside of the cover.

Dimensions and Weights of Packing Boxes.

KIND OF AMMUNITION.		No. of rounds.	INTERIOR DIMENSIONS.			WEIGHT.	
			Length.	Width.	Depth.	Empty.	Packed.
For Guns.			In.	In.	In.	Lbs.	Lbs.
12-PDR.	Shot	8	17.5	10.5	9.5	23	148
	Spherical case.	8	17.5	9.5	9.5	22	132
	Canister	8	18.4	12.5	9.5	24	161
6-PDR.	Shot	14	24.	8.75	7.75	25	133
	Spherical case.	14	24.	8.25	7.75	24	118
	Canister	14	25.5	10.5	7.75	26	146
For Howitzers.							
32-PDR.	Shells	4	12.75	12.75	12.	23	136
	Spherical case.	4	12.75	12.75	12.	23	162
	Canister	4	12.75	12.75	15.5	25	158
24-PDR.	Shells	6	17.25	11.5	11.5	25	155
	Spherical case.	6	17.25	11.5	11.5	25	180
	Canister	6	17.25	11.5	14.75	26	170
12-PDR.	Shells	12	27.5	9.25	10.5	30	160
	Spherical case.	12	27.5	9.25	10.5	30	183
	Canister	12	27.5	9.25	12.5	31	177

* The above weights are those of white pine boxes.

Contents of each packing box for Field Ammunition.

KIND OF AMMUNITION.	FOR GUNS.	
	12-pdr.	6-pdr.
SHOT.		
Shot fixed	8	14
Priming tubes	5	5
Portfires	1	1
Slow match . . . yds	1.5	1.5
SPHERICAL CASE.		
Shot fixed	8	14
Priming tubes	5	5
Portfires	1	1
Slow match . . . yds	1.5	1.5
Fuzes { black, 2 sec.	3	7
Fuzes { red, 3 sec.	8	14
Fuzes { green, 4 sec.	3	7
Fuzes { yellow, 5 sec.	3	
CANISTER.		
Canisters fixed	8	14
Priming tubes	5	5
Portfires	1	1
Slow match . . . yds	1.5	1.5

KIND OF AMMUNITION.	HOWITZERS.		
	32-pdr.	24-pdr.	12-pdr.
SHELLS.			
Shells fixed	....	....	12
Shells strapped	4	6	
Cartridges, { small charge	4	6	
Cartridges, { large charge	1	1	
Priming tubes	3	3	5
Portfires	1	1	1
Slow match . . . yds	1.5	1.5	1.5
Fuzes { black, 2 sec.	2	2	6
Fuzes { red, 3 sec.	4	6	12
Fuzes { green, 4 sec.	2	2	6
Fuzes { yellow, 5 sec.	2	2	
SPHERICAL CASE.			
Shot fixed	....	....	12
Shot strapped	4	6	
Cartridges, small charge.	4	6	
Priming tubes	3	3	5
Portfires	1	1	1
Slow match . . . yds	1.5	1.5	1.5
Fuzes { black, 2 sec.	2	2	6
Fuzes { red, 3 sec.	4	6	12
Fuzes { green, 4 sec.	2	2	6
Fuzes { yellow, 5 sec.	2	2	
CANISTER.			
Canisters fixed	....	....	12
Canisters with sabots	4	6	
Cartridges, small charge	4	6	
Priming tubes	3	3	5
Portfires	1	1	1
Slow match . . . yds	1.5	1.5	1.5

Manner of packing Ammunition Boxes.

FOR GUNS. *Shot, spherical case and canisters, fixed:* Laid in two tiers across the box, the shot or canisters alternating with the cartridges at each side. The shot or canisters of the upper tier rest on those of the lower, and not on the cartridges.

FOR 32-PDR. AND 24-PDR. HOWITZERS. *Shells and spherical case shot:* Placed upright, the balls down, resting on strips of wood about .25 in. thick, placed lengthwise of the box and nailed to the bottom, so as to prevent the fuze plugs from bearing on the bottom of the box. The balls are held down by small strips of wood tacked with sprigs to the sides of the box, over the sabots. The cartridges are laid on top of the sabots.

Canisters are packed in the same manner, omitting the strips of wood in the bottom of the box.

FOR 12-PDR. FIELD AND MOUNTAIN HOWITZERS. *Shells and spherical case shot, fixed:* Placed upright, the balls down, resting on strips of wood, as for the other howitzers.

Canisters are packed in the same manner, resting on the bottom of the box.

In all the boxes, the small stores are placed in the vacant spaces on top of the ammunition.

The fuzes of each color are put up in a bundle, wrapped in water-proof paper of corresponding color, and marked with the time of burning. All the fuzes for a box are put in one parcel, wrapped with water-proof paper, and marked: FUZES.

A layer of tow is placed in the bottom of each box, and the whole contents are well packed in tow, filling the box so as to be pressed down by the cover. About 3 lbs. of tow are required for a box.

AMMUNITION FOR SIEGE AND GARRISON SERVICE.

Cartridges.

The ordinary service charge of powder for heavy guns is *one-fourth* the weight of the shot; but the charge varies according to circumstances, from *one-third* the weight of the shot, (for a breaching battery,) to *one-sixth* of that weight, for firing double shot or hot shot, and still less, for ricochet firing. The charges for mortars and howitzers vary according to the required range.

Cartridge bags for siege and garrison service are usually made of woollen stuff. These are cut in two pieces, in the form of a rectangle with semicircular ends, which are sewed together to form the bag, as described in making bags for field service. See *page* 250, for the manner of making and preserving them.

Dimensions of Cartridge Bags.

	GUNS.					COLUMBIADS		HOWITZERS.		
									Sea coast.	
	42-pdr.	32-pdr.	24-pdr.	18-pdr.	12-pdr.	10-in.	8-in.	Siege 8-in.	10-in	8-in.
Charge of powder - pounds	10.5	8.	8.	6.	4.	20.	12.	4.	12.	8.
	In.	In.	In.	In.	In.	In.	In.	In.	In.	In.
Diameter of chamber - - -	7.	6.4	5.82	5.3	4.62	8.	6.4	4.62	7.	6.4
Length of chamber - - -	-	-	-	-	-	12.	11.	8	9.5	7.5
Diameter of cartridge - - -	6.	5.5	5.	4.6	4.2	7.5	6.	4.2	6.5	6.
Length of 1 lb. of powder in a cartridge - - - - -	0.98	1.16	1.45	1.75	2.	0.63	0.98	2.	0.83	0.98
Width of cutting stamp - -	10.35	9.55	8.75	8.15	7.6	12.7	10.35	7.6	11.15	10.35
Width of sewing stamp, and of the finished bag - - -	9.35	8.55	7.75	7.15	6.6	11.7	9.35	6.6	10.15	9.35
Whole length of bag, cut - -	18.	18.	18.	17.	14.	24.	20.	14.	18.	15.
Length of cartridge filled - -	11.	10.5	12.	11.	9.	14.	12.5	9.	11.	9.
Quantity 5-4 stuff for 100 bags, yds.	30	27	25	23	14	36	30	14	31	20

PAPER BAGS. Cartridge bags for heavy ordnance may be made entirely of paper. The bottom is circular; one end of the paper forming the cylinder is cut into slips about 1 in. long which are pasted over the paper bottom, on a cylindrical former.

The dimensions of the formers and of the paper are easily obtained from the foregoing table. The formers must be bored through the axis, to facilitate drawing off the bag.

When a paper bag is filled, the open end is folded down about ¾ in. wide, and this fold is rolled on itself down to the powder, and the part which projects beyond the cylinder is turned in on the top of it.

These bags are apt to leave paper burning in the gun, for which reason those made of woollen stuff are preferable.

For columbiads and sea-coast howitzers, the cartridge should always occupy the whole length of the chamber; for this purpose, in firing with reduced charges, *a cartridge block* is placed in the bag, over the powder. The length of this block for any charge is easily deduced from the length occupied by 1 lb. of powder, as given in the above table.

For mortars, cartridge bags may be made in the same manner as for guns, their dimensions corresponding to those of the chamber of the mortar. But as the charge is generally poured loose into the chamber, the bag being used only for carrying it to the mortar, a gun cartridge bag of any convenient size may be used for mortar service.

For firing hot shot, cartridge bags are made double, by putting one bag within another; care must be taken that the bags are free from holes.

For ricochet firing or other occasions when very small charges are required, a cartridge bag for a piece of an inferior calibre may be used. Or else, after the charge is poured into the bag, place on it another bag filled with hay, pressing it with the hands to reduce the diameter; after having shaken this bag down and rolled and flattened the empty part of the two bags, tie them with woollen yarn, like a bundle of musket cartridges, placing the knot on top.

For proving ordnance, cartridge bags are made of woollen stuff for small calibres, and of paper for heavy ordnance. They should be of the full diameter of the bore or chamber.

Strapping Shells.

Sabots for shells for heavy guns, howitzers and columbiads, are made of plank.

DIMENSIONS OF SABOTS.	SIEGE AND GARRISON GUNS.					SEA COAST HOWITZERS.		COLUMBIADS.	
	42	32	24	18	12	10-in.	8-in.	10-in.	8-in.
	In.	In.	In.	In.	In.	In.	In.	In.	In.
Whole height	2.	1.5	1.5	1.5	1.5	2.	2.	2.	2.
Greatest diameter / Diameter at bottom	6.58	6.	5.43	4.92	4.35	7.75	6.79	8.41	6.79
						6.75	6.15	7.75	6.15
Cavity for the ball. Depth	1.	0.75	0.75	0.75	1.	1.	1.	1.	1.
Cavity for the ball. Radius of curv.	3.42	3.12	2.84	2.58	2.26	4.93	3.93	4.93	3.93
STRAPS. Width	0.65	0.6	0.55	0.5	0.45	1.	0.75	1.	0.75
STRAPS. Length	21.	19.	17.5	16.	14.	29.	23.5	29.	23.5

One of the straps has a slit in the middle for the other strap to pass through. Two rings, or loops of tin, 0.38 inch diameter, are soldered securely to the slit strap of the howitzer and columbiad shells, for the purpose of attaching a handle made of cord 0.15 inch to 0.25 inch thick.

The shells are placed in the sabot, and the straps put on in such a manner that the fuze hole may fall in one of the angles, between two straps, and that the axis of the fuze hole may stand at an angle of about 45° with that of the sabot. The eyes of the shell should not be covered by the straps. The straps are fastened at each end with 2 *nails* in the side, and 2 in the bottom of the sabot.

In loading the piece, care must be taken to place the fuze hole in the upper part of the bore.

Canisters.

A canister for a siege and garrison gun, is made by turning one end of the tin cylinder over the iron bottom, from 0.25 in. to 0.38 in. wide, according to the calibre; the other end is cut into strips 0.5 in. long, to turn down on the cover when the canister is filled. The cover for these canisters is of sheet iron .1 in. thick; it has a handle 3.75 in. long by 1.75 in. wide, made of iron wire No. 9, fastened to the cover by a strap of sheet iron, 2 in. long 1.75 in. wide, secured by two rivets 0.15 in. thick. The bottom plate is of cast iron, 0.5 in. thick.

For dimensions of *Canister Shot,* see CHAP. II.

Canisters for 8-inch siege and sea-coast howitzers, are attached to sabots, of the following dimensions:

8-INCH CANISTER SABOTS.	SIEGE.	SEA-COAST.	
	In.	In.	
Whole height	4.68	5.	
Greatest diameter	7.85	7.85	
Diameter at the bottom	*	6.4	* Bottom hemispherical.
Diameter of cylinder for the tin	7.8	7.8	
Height of do.	0.75	0.75	

Dimensions and weights of Canisters.

DIMENSIONS.	FOR SIEGE AND GARRISON GUNS.					FOR 8-IN. HOWITZERS.	
	42	32	24	18	12	Siege.	S.coast
	In.	In.	In.	In.	In.	In.	In.
Length of tin for cylinder, developed	21.5	20.	18.3	16.7	14.4	25.1	25.1
Height of ditto	9.6	9.	8.25	7.7	6.75	8.6	8.6
Interior diameter of cylinder	6.78	6.19	5.63	5.12	4.47	7.8	7.8
Diameter of plates	6.73	6.14	5.58	5.07	4.42	7.75	7.75
Height of finished canister	8.7	8.1	7.35	6.8	6.	12.03	12.35
Number of tiers of shot	4	4	4	4	4	4	4
Number of shot in each of the 3 lower tiers	7	7	7	7	7	12	12
Number of shot in 4th tier	6	6	6	6	6	12	12
Whole number of shot	27	27	27	27	27	48	48
WEIGHT, finished canister, Lbs.	48.	37.	29.	23.	15.	53.5	54.5

Grape.

For the dimensions of *Grape Shot*, see CHAPTER II.

A STAND OF GRAPE consists of 9 shot, put together by means of 2 *cast iron plates*, 2 *rings* and 1 *pin* and *nut*.—See *Plate* 17.

DIMENSIONS.	8-in.	42	32	24	18	12
	In.	In.	In.	In.	In.	In.
Diameter of plates	7.85	6.83	6.24	5.68	5.17	4.52
Thickness of plates	0.6	0.6	0.5	0.5	0.4	0.4
Interior diameter of rings	6.55	5.73	5.16	4.75	4.26	3.8
Diameter of round iron for rings and pin	0.6	0.5	0.5	0.38	0.38	0.32
Length of pin, including tapped part	14.7	9.25	8.7	7.88	7.18	6.12
Height of stand, between the outsides of the plates	9.85	8.75	8.2	7.5	6.8	5.8
WEIGHTS.	Lbs.	Lbs.	Lbs.	Lbs.	Lbs.	Lbs.
Plates	13.6	10.2	8.	6.75	4.56	3.44
Pin, nut, and rings	4.75	2.8	2.5	1.81	1.12	0.69
Stand, complete	74.5	51.25	39.75	30.61	22.15	14.84

The square of the nut is 2 diameters of the pin; its thickness, 1 diameter. The head of the pin is countersunk flush with the bottom of the lower plate, which has a *slot* to prevent the pin from turning when the nut is screwed on. Each plate has on the inside 3 beds for the shot, of a depth equal to half the thickness of the plate; they are made in the form of a spherical segment, the curvature of which is the same as that of the shot; their centres are on equidistant radii, midway between the edge of the pin hole and that of the plate. In the upper plate are 2 holes 0.25 in. diameter, placed opposite to each other at 0.5 in. from the edge of the plate, to receive a rope handle.

For the 8-inch sea-coast howitzer, the stand of grape must be attached to a conical sabot. The sabot is 4.25 in. long, 7.85 in. diameter at the large end, and 6.4 in. at the small end. The sabot may be fastened to the lower plate with screws, or the pin may be made long enough to pass through it; or else the sabot may be inserted into the piece separately from the stand of grape.

Filling Shells for Mortars.

CHARGES FOR MORTAR SHELLS.		13-in.		10-in.		8-in.	
		Lbs.	oz.	Lbs.	oz.	Lbs.	oz.
Charge..	of the shell filled with powder........	11		5		2	9
	to burst the shell..................	6		2		1	
	to blow out the fuze................	0	6	0	5	0	4
Ordinary service charge.	Cannon powder......	7		3		1	12
	Incendiary match, or other composition ..	0	8	0	6	0	6

1 Man to fill, 1 helper.

MATERIALS. *Cannon powder—incendiary match*—pieces of *fire stone* 3 in. long, or other incendiary composition—*loaded fuzes—tow*.

IMPLEMENTS AND UTENSILS. 1 *pair of shell hooks*—1 *handspike*—2 *hand hammers*—2 *scrapers*, (pieces of sword blade)—2 *tow hooks*—2 *pairs of pincers*—*rags* —1 *chisel* and 1 *mallet*, to clean the shells and break up any hard substance that may be found in the interior—2 *searchers*, for sounding cavities—*shell gauges*— 1 *grate*, to dry the shells on—1 *fuze saw*—1 *gimlet*—a *ring of rope*, or a hollow block—1 *funnel*—*powder measures*—1 *tub*, or vessel for powder—2 *baskets*, for the composition and fuzes—1 *rasp*—1 *fuze setter*, and 1 *mallet*.

TO CHARGE A SHELL. Clean the shell inside and out; gauge it; see that it has no holes or fissures deep enough to cause its rejection; that the fuze hole is well reamed, and that there are no flaws around it on the inside; if the shell is wet, heat it slightly and let it cool slowly.

Cut the fuze to the proper length, according to the range, by resting it in a groove made in the block, the saw running in a cut made for it; or bore the fuze through with a gimlet, perpendicularly to the axis, at the proper length.

Place the shell on the block or ring of rope; pour in the powder and introduce the incendiary composition; try the fuze, which should enter $\frac{3}{4}$ of its length; cover the head of the fuze with tow, and drive it with the fuze setter and mallet, so that the head of the fuze shall project not more than 0.2 in. to 0.4 in.

Shells are generally filled and the fuzes driven in the battery magazines, as they are required.

Charges for Shells for Columbiads and heavy Guns.

CHARGE OF POWDER.	COLUMBIADS.				GUNS.									
	10-in.		8-in.		42		32		24		18		12	
	Lbs.	oz.	Lbs.	oz.	Lbs.	oz.	Lbs.	oz.	Lbs.	oz.	Lbs.	oz.	Lbs.	oz.
To fill the shell - -	3	4	1	12	1	8	1	5	1	0	0	11	0	8
To burst the shell - -	1	6	1	0	0	12	0	11	0	8	0	7	0	5
To blow out the fuze plug -	0	10	0	8	0	6	0	2	0	2	0	1⅛	0	1
For ordinary service - -	3	0	1	8	1	4	1	0	0	12	0	10	0	7

The *fuzes* for these shells are made with paper cases, and are inserted at the time of loading the piece.

The *fuze plugs* are made of wood, or of brass, driven or screwed into the fuze hole; they are covered with a cap of peculiar construction which contains the priming of the fuze. The size of the plug is indicated by that of the fuze hole in the shell.

The bursting charge is poured into the shell through the hole in the fuze plug.

Wads.

Wads for proving cannon are made of *junk.*

IMPLEMENTS. 1 *wad mould* with two holes for each calibre; made of cast iron cylinders set in oak, or of two strong pieces of oak strapped with iron and joined by a hinge—1 *drift* for ditto—1 *maul.*

DIMENSIONS OF MOULDS.	10 in.	8 in.	42	32	24	18	12	6
	In.	In.	In.	In.	In.	In.	In.	In.
Diameter of moulds, large hole -	9.75	7.8	6.8	6.2	5.65	5.12	4.48	3.55
Diameter of moulds, small hole -	9.4	7.5	6.5	5.9	5.3	4.8	4.1	3.2
Thickness of upper block - - -	10.	8.	7.	6.4	5.8	5.3	4.6	3.7
Thickness of lower block - - -	5.	4.	4.	4.	4.	4.	4.	4.
Width of blocks - - - -	17.	15.	13.	12.	11.5	11.	10.	9.
Diameter of cylindrical drift - -	8.5	7.3	6.2	5.6	5.	4.5	3.8	2.9
Height of do. do. - -	24.	24.	24.	24.	24.	24.	24.	24.

MAKING WADS. The junk, after having been picked, is compressed by being beaten in the smaller mould until it assumes the requisite dimensions; it is then taken out, by raising the upper part of the mould, and closely wrapped with rope yarn passed over it in the direction of the axis of the cylinder and fastened by a few turns round the middle of the wad; after which it is placed in the large mould and again beaten with the maul and drift; the diameter of the wad when finished is verified with a wooden gauge corresponding to the large gauge of the shot.

DIMENSIONS AND WEIGHTS OF WADS.	10-in.	8-in.	42	32	24	18	12	6
	In.	In.	In.	In.	In.	In.	In.	In
Diameter and height of wad	9.75	7.8	6.8	6.2	5.65	5.1	4.4	3.5
	Lbs. oz.	Lbs. oz.	Lbs. oz.	Lbs. oz.	Lbs. oz.	Lbs. oz.	Lbs. oz.	Lbs. oz.
Weight of wad - -	16 8	8 8	5 10	4 6	3	2 6	1 8	0 13
Quantity of junk required for 100 wads . -	1650	850	562	437	300	237	150	87

An addition of 3 per cent. to the quantity required may be allowed for waste, tar, &c.

Wads for firing hot shot, and for other like purposes, may be made of *hay* wrapped with rope yarn ; they are fabricated in the same manner as junk wads.

Ring wads (or *grommets*, as they are called in the naval service,) have been found very serviceable in increasing the accuracy of fire, and they are to be preferred where the object of a wad is merely to retain the ball in its place. They consist of a ring of rope yarn, about 0.7 in. thick, with two pieces of strong twine tied across it, at right angles with each other. The size of the ring is the full diameter of the bore, in order that it may fit tight. These wads may be attached with twine to the straps, or to the balls; or, they may be inserted, like other wads, after the ball.

MILITARY FIREWORKS.

Slow Match.

Preparation. Slow match is made of hemp, flax, or cotton rope, about 0.6 in. diameter, made with 3 strands, slightly twisted. Cotton rope well twisted forms a good match without any preparation.

To prepare hemp or flax rope: boil it 10 minutes in water holding in solution 1-20th of its weight of sugar of lead, or let it remain in the *cold* solution until it is thoroughly saturated—run it through the hands, to take the water from it—twist it hard by attaching one end to the hook of a twisting winch, and putting a stick in a loop at a convenient distance for twisting—smooth it by rubbing it smartly with coarse mats, hair cloth, or cuttings of buff leather, commencing at the winch and rubbing always in the same direction, until the diameter of the rope is reduced 0.1 in. and until the tension and hardness are even—stretch it on poles or on a fence to dry, and put it up in neat coils of 25 yards each.

100 yards of rope require 2.5 lbs. of sugar of lead.

Match thus prepared burns 4 inches in an hour. Cotton match burns 4½ inches in an hour.

If sugar of lead cannot be procured, the rope may be simply leached. For this purpose, it is put into a leach-tub, and steeped in pure water for 12 hours—this water is then drawn off and replaced by ley prepared in a boiler with a quantity of ashes equal to half the weight of the rope, to which 5 per cent. of quick lime is added—this ley, with the ashes, is put, after being warmed, into the hopper of the tub, and when it has run through and remained some time in the tub, it is drawn off, heated again, and poured back on the ashes. This operation is several times repeated in the course of 24 hours, which is the time required for the rope to be well leached. After being taken out and twisted with sticks, it is steeped for 5 minutes in hot water, being stirred at the same time, and the operation is finished as before. Match prepared in this manner burns 5 inches in an hour.

By treating bad match or old rope with sugar of lead, very good match may be made.

Slow match weighs from 3 to 5 oz. to the yard.

Packing. Slow match is packed in tight casks or boxes. A cask 40 in. high, 24 in. diameter (weighing 60 lbs.) contains 150 lbs. of match.

Dimensions of a box to hold 200 lbs. hemp or 220 lbs. cotton match; 44 in. long, 28 in. wide, 18 in. deep—weight 87 lbs.—It is made of boards 1 in. thick, ends 1¼ in.—It has corner pieces of hard wood 2.25 in. square. The casks and boxes should be marked with the kind and quantity of match, place and date of fabrication.

Quick Match.

Take cotton yarn, such as is used for candle wick, of such a size (generally 4 strands) that when doubled and twisted in the fingers, it may be 0.07 in. in diameter; wind it into a loose ball of convenient size, (say 1 lb., which will measure 1,000 yards,) and steep it in gummed brandy or whiskey, until the cotton is thoroughly soaked. In a wooden bowl or copper pan, put a layer about ¼ in. deep, of paste made of mealed powder and gummed spirits, of the consistency of flour paste; on this, spread a coil of the cotton by unrolling the ball and distributing it equally on the surface of the paste until there are 5 or 6 yarns over one another—put another layer of the paste, and proceed in this manner until the bowl is full, taking care not to entangle the strands; the last layer of paste should be a little deeper than the others. After the cotton has been 3 or 4 hours in the bowl, wind it on a reel, making it pass through a funnel filled with the paste, and taking care that the several turns of yarn do not touch each other. Before it is dry, dredge it with mealed powder; let it dry slowly, then cut it off from the reel and put it in bundles. The gum should be first dissolved in the smallest possible quantity of hot water or vinegar, and afterwards mixed with spirits.

Match thus prepared should be hard and stiff, and the composition should hold firmly on; 1 yard burns, in the open air, 13 seconds.

1,000 yards of quick match require 1 lb. of cotton yarn, 8 lbs. of mealed powder, 1¼ gallons of spirits, and 2½ oz. of gum arabic. Weight when dried, 9 lbs.

By using *vinegar*, a match is made which burns less rapidly in the proportion of 4 to 5; and with pure water, in the ratio of 4 to 6. *Alcohol* makes a quicker match, but it cannot be gummed, and the composition does not stick.

A slow kind of match is made by adding sulphur to the mealed powder; with one-sixth of sulphur, 1 yard of match burns 22 seconds; with one-fifth, 33 seconds; with one-third, 53 seconds; with one-half, 162 seconds.

Quick match enclosed in tubes burns more rapidly than in the open air, and more so in proportion as the tubes are smaller. To communicate fire very rapidly, it is enclosed in paper tubes called *leaders*.

Priming Tubes.

			In.
Dimensions of tubes.—Length			3.25
	Exterior diam.	at top	0.17
		at bottom	0.14
	Interior diam.	at top	0.12
		at bottom	0.09
	Exterior diam. of cup	at top	0.75
		at bottom	0.70
	Depth of cup	exterior	0.25
		interior	0.21

WEIGHT of 1000 tubes, empty—15 lbs.

Metal for tubes—50 lbs. Banca tin, 50 lbs. Lead, 1¼ lbs. Antimony — for 6,000 tubes.

Making tubes. The metal is melted in an iron pan, placed in the oven of a stove, and the moulds are kept heated, at the same time, so that their temperature may be high enough to scorch dry shavings. During the casting, the moulds should be smoked occasionally with rosin, or pine knots, to prevent the tubes from sticking. Six moulds should be used in casting, and they should not be cooled by wetting them. When not in use, the moulds must be kept well oiled and free from rust.

The tubes are drawn from the moulds by means of a lever fixed into the work bench; when the spindle withdraws, leaving the tube in the mould, a small screw is inserted into the tube, which, by being gently tapped with a hammer, loosens the tube and withdraws it.

Another method of making tubes, now generally practised, is to cut the metal into small discs, each of which is formed into a tube by being pressed through a die.

Tubes are *cupped* by running them through a groove, over which a plane is passed, turning in the edges of the cup.

CHARGING. Tubes are filled with mealed powder made liquid by spirits of wine, which is injected into them with a *tube injector* holding one quart. A better method is to make the mealed powder into a soft paste, which is pressed into the tube with the thumb.

A strand of quick match 2 in. long is placed across the cup, which is then filled with the same paste; a small brass wire, (No. 22,) is run through the tube and withdrawn after the composition is dry.

A paper cap is placed over the cup and twisted tightly around the tube, under the cup.

Composition to fill 1,000 *tubes:*

2½ lbs. mealed powder.
2 quarts of whiskey, or spirits of wine.

WEIGHT of 1000 tubes, filled—18 lbs.

QUILL TUBES. Priming tubes may be made also of quills; for this purpose the barrel of the quill is cut off at both ends, the largest end is slit into 7 pieces 0.5 in. long, which are bent outwards at right angles; fine woollen yarn is then woven into these slits, like basket work, or a perforated disc of paper is pasted on them. The tube is filled and finished as before.

The small end of the quill may be closed with sealing wax, and the tube charged with rifle powder.

These tubes are preferable for service on ship-board, or in casemates or block-houses, as there is no danger from the fragments blown out of the vent, which there may be with metallic tubes.

For mortar service, priming tubes may be made by inserting a strand of quick match in a cylinder of thin paper, of the same diameter and length as the metal tube. The match should project about 2 inches beyond the upper end of the tube.

Tubes are tied up in bundles of 10, wrapped in paper.

Portfires.

MAKING THE CASES. *Formers* for portfire cases are made of steel, turned smooth, 22 in. long, and 0.5 in. diameter, with a hole 0.2 in. diameter through one end, for the purpose of drawing it from the case. The length of the case is 18 inches; exterior diameter 0.65 in.; interior diameter 0.5 in. One sheet of paper, No. 4, makes two cases, and each case weighs 1 oz. The case is rolled hard with a hand rolling board, the sheet being pasted after one turn around the former.

DRIVING PORTFIRES. *Portfire moulds* are made of brass; they are 18 inches long, with a bore 0.65 in. diameter; the mould consists of two parts, 0.4 in. thick at top, and 0.6 in. at bottom, which are held together by a socket at bottom and by 4 strong bands.

Three *drifts* are used for driving portfires; they are made of steel, with brass tips, 0.5 in. long, upon the lower end. These drifts are 22 in., 15 in. and 10 in. long, and of a diameter 0.1 in. less than the interior diameter of the case. Four spiral grooves are cut upon the surface of the drifts, making one half of a revolution in 22 inches; the grooves are 0.15 in. wide, and 0.05 in. deep. The handles of the drifts are 6 inches long and 0.75 in. diameter, with the head enlarged to 1.25 in.

Mallets for driving portfires are turned of hard wood, and weigh one pound.

Put the case in the mould and drive on the rings—insert a small *funnel* in the top of the case—pass the long drift through the funnel to the bottom of the mould—fill the funnel with composition, and strike the drift about three blows every second, raising the drift about half an inch with the fingers of the left hand, between the blows. In this way the composition finds its way around the sides and through the grooves of the drift to the bottom, and is uniformly and compactly driven. The shorter drifts are used, as the case is filled. A man can drive 120 portfires in ten hours.

Portfires should not be primed with mealed powder. Before commencing the driving, a piece of paper should be pushed with the long drift to the bottom of the case, and after the portfire is driven, the top of the case should be turned in and beaten down; thus both ends of the composition are secured.

Composition for 100 portfires:

Nitre	13 lbs.
Sulphur	4.5 lbs.
Mealed powder	2.5 lbs.

The portfires made with this composition burn ten minutes.

The composition must be intimately mixed, by grinding with a muller on the mealing table, rubbing it through the hands, and passing it through a sieve, regrinding the coarse parts that remain, and adding them.

Portfires may be driven in a cylinder of sheet copper or tin, supported in a hole in a block of hard wood; but as they cannot be driven so hard in this way, the proportion of mealed powder in the composition should be reduced to $1\frac{1}{2}$ lb., in order that the portfire may not burn too fast.

INTERIOR DIMENSIONS OF BOXES FOR PORTFIRES.	100	200
	In.	In.
Length	18	18
Width	9.1	9.1
Depth	5.1	10.1
Weight, packed ....lbs.	38	70

The boxes are made of white pine boards 0.75 in. thick, the sides dovetailed together, and the top fastened with six $1\frac{1}{4}$ in. screws, the heads countersunk and covered with putty. They should be lined with water-proof paper, and painted with one coat of olive color—marked on one end with the number and kind of contents, and the year of fabrication.

Fuzes for Mortar Shells.—Plate 17.

DIMENSIONS AND WEIGHTS.	13-in.	10-in.	8-in.
	In.	In.	In.
Diameter of fuze { at upper end	1.85	1.7	1.25
Diameter of fuze { at lower end of first cone	1.65	1.55	1.15
Diameter of fuze { lower end of fuze	1.25	1.	0.9
Diameter of cup { at the top	1.25	1.	0.75
Diameter of cup { at the bottom	0.9	0.8	0.6
Diameter of the bore	0.4	0.3	0.3
Length of first cone	2.8	2.25	1.25
Depth of the cup	0.6	0.5	0.4
Thickness of wood at the bottom of the fuze	1.2	0.9	0.9
Length of composition	9.	8.	5.
Whole length of fuze	10.8	9.4	6.3
Length of 1st drift } exclusive of the handles	9.	8.	8.
Length of 2nd drift } exclusive of the handles	4.5	4.	4.
Diameter of drifts	0.36	0.27	0.27
	Lbs.	Lbs.	Lbs.
Weight of composition for 100 fuzes	8	4	$2\frac{1}{2}$
Weight of 100 fuzes, complete	54	33	16

Wooden fuzes for mortar service are made of beech, ash, or linden, seasoned and free from knots. They are bored in the lathe and the exterior is graduated into inches and tenths, (commencing at the bottom of the cup,) by means of a steel gauge applied to it in the lathe.

Compositions for Mortar Fuzes.

No.	Nitre.	Sulphur.	Mealed powder.	Time of burning 1 inch.	REMARKS.
1	2	1	3	3.8 sec.	For 10-inch and 8-inch mortars, light.
2	2	1	$2\frac{1}{4}$	5. sec.	For 13-inch and 10-inch mortars, heavy.
3	......	....	1	2.2 sec.	For 8-inch howitzers.

The composition must be well pulverized, thoroughly mixed with the hands and sifted. As the time of burning will vary a little according to the quality of the materials used, (especially of the mealed powder,) a few trials should be made to determine the exact composition in each case.

Driving. The articles necessary for driving fuzes are: *Blocks* with holes of the size of the fuze—*mallets*—*steel drifts*, shod with copper—*copper ladles*, to contain sufficient composition to make 1 diameter of the bore in height when driven—*copper pans*—*mealed powder*—*fuze composition*.

In driving fuzes, be careful to put in equal quantities of composition each time, by passing a drift over the ladle, to take off the composition along the edges; keep the strokes as regular as possible, giving always the same number and with the same force to each ladle full of composition. The pan with the composition must not be placed on the driving block, as the sulphur would collect together, and would separate from the rest of the composition.

13-in., 10-in., and 8-in. fuzes are driven with mallets that weigh 1 lb.; smaller fuzes, with mallets weighing $\frac{3}{4}$ lb. and $\frac{1}{2}$ lb.; 21 blows, in volleys of 3, are given to every ladleful of composition, in fuzes over 24-pdr., the drift being raised after each volley; 15 blows to each ladleful, in smaller fuzes.

One man, in 10 hours, can drive 50 13-in., 80 8-in., 120 to 150 smaller fuzes.

Fuzes must always be driven to the same height, for which purpose the last drift must be marked. They are primed with mealed powder, driven with the same force as is applied to a ladleful of composition. The space left in the bore of the fuze, for the mealed powder, is about 0.2 in. The cup is filled with mealed powder moistened with spirits of wine or strong whiskey; when dry, it is covered with a small piece of paper, over which is pasted a cap of strong, water-proof paper, marked with the number of seconds the fuze burns to the inch. For preservation and transportation, the fuze is capped with water-proof paper, linen, or serge, tied on, and lackered. Fuzes are packed with tow, in boxes lined with water-proof paper.

Fuzes may be driven with *blind fire composition*, which will not discover the flight of a shell in the night:

Compositions:	Mealed powder.	Sifted wood ashes.
1	6 parts	4 parts.
2	16 parts	9½ parts.

One ladleful of the common fuze composition, or of mealed powder, must be driven in the top of these fuzes.

Fuzes for Field Service.

The fuze for field shells and spherical case consists of a *paper case*, which is charged with fuze composition, and is inserted, at the time of loading the gun, into a *wooden plug* previously driven into the fuze hole, as described at *page* 254.

Making the paper cases. The case is made of a strip of smooth paper, rolled hard, on a mandril 0.35 inch diameter, and glued, after the first turn, with isinglass glue. The strip of paper is in the form of a rectangle joined to a trapezoid; it is rolled from the large end.

		Inches.
Whole length of the paper		18.
Length of the rectangular part		9.
Width of the rectangular part		1.5
Width at small end		0.4
Diameter of finished case, before being cut	At top	0.52
	At bottom	0.44

Log paper, (so called,) or thin drawing paper is suitable for making these cases. The dimensions of the strip of paper must be regulated by trial with the kind of paper used.

After the case is dry, it is smoothed by rubbing it with a fine file, and with sand paper.

FUZE COMPOSITIONS.	MEALED POWDER.	SULPHUR.	TIME OF BURNING 1 INCH.	COLOR OF FUZE.
1...............	1	0.	2 seconds.	Black.
2...............	8	3.	3 "	Red.
3...............	8	3.5	4 "	Green.
4...............	8	4.0	5 "	Yellow.

The materials must be thoroughly incorporated by being carefully ground together with a muller. The composition should always be tried before driving many fuzes, as the time of burning is subject to variation, according to the quality of the materials and their manipulation.

One pound of composition is required to charge 100 fuzes.

CHARGING THE FUZE. The case is set in a brass die, made in two parts which are held together by a strong ring or socket inserted in a block of wood. The composition is driven in the usual manner with a half pound mallet, with 15 blows to each ladleful of composition; one ladleful makes a length of 0.25 inch in the fuze.

CUTTING. The fuze is next put into an iron gauge, the bore of which has the same taper as the fuze, and it is cut off at both ends, with a saw, or sharp knife, to the proper length. It is then stained the proper color, according to the composition used.

Interior diameter of cutting gauge	at top..........	0.5	inch.
	at bottom.......	0.45	"
Length	....	1.	"

Fuzes for heavy Guns, Columbiads and Howitzers.

These fuzes are made in a similar manner to those for field service. Their dimensions are as follows:

Paper for the case.	Whole length......	19.	inches
	Length of rectangle.	6.	"
	Width of rectangle.	2.25	"
	Width of small end.	0.4	"
Fuze..	Diameter at top..............	0.53	"
	" at bottom...........	0.4	"
	Length......................	2.	"
	Diameter of composition.......	0.3	"

Fuze Compositions.

NO.	NITRE.	SULPHUR.	MEALED POWDER.	TIME OF BURNING 1 INCH.	REMARKS.
1	26	9	14	10 secs.	Materials procured from Dupont's powder mills.
2	26	9	12	14 "	
3	26	9	10	20 "	

The time of burning of these slow compositions is subject to considerable variations, according to the quality of the materials and the manipulation in mixing them. In making these fuzes, therefore, especial care should be taken to try the composition used, and to vary the proportions so as to produce the required result. The above table is given as an approximate guide.

PERCUSSION CAPS FOR SMALL ARMS.

MAKING THE CAPS. The cap for small arms is made of copper; it is very slightly conical, with a rim or flanch at the open end; it has four slits, extending about half the height of the cap.

The sheet copper for making the caps is No. 24, weighing about 13.5 oz. to the square foot. It is obtained in sheets 48 in. × 14 in., weighing 4 lbs.; the copper should be pure, well annealed, and rolled as evenly as possible.

The copper is cleaned by being immersed in a pickle made of 1 part (by measure) of sulphuric acid and 40 parts of water; it is then scoured by hand, with fine sand or saw dust, and washed clean in running water; after which it is slightly oiled by being rubbed with a rag dipped in clear neatsfoot oil.

The caps are formed by a machine which cuts a star or *blank* from the sheet and transfers it to a die in which the cap is shaped by means of a punch. For use in Boughton's machine, the copper is first cut into strips, from which the blanks are cut and the caps formed; Wright's machine cuts the blanks from the whole sheet and forms the cap. The first machine makes 2,196 caps, the second, 2,314 caps, from a sheet of the size above mentioned. Each machine can make about 5,000 caps an hour.

1,000,000 of caps, empty, weigh 1,162 lbs.

Before being charged, the caps are cleaned by being rolled in dry saw dust; but if only a small quantity of good oil is used, this operation is unnecessary.

PERCUSSION POWDER. The powder with which the caps are charged consists of *fulminate of mercury*, mixed with half its weight of saltpetre.

To prepare the fulminate of mercury. In a glass retort or bottle, holding about half a gallon, dissolve 10 oz. of pure mercury in 5.5 lbs. of nitric acid of the specific gravity of 1.40. The solution may be made at the ordinary temperature of the air in summer; in winter it is facilitated by placing the retort in a water bath heated to about 120°. The vapors which come over, being very deleterious, must not be inhaled.

When the solution is complete, pour the liquor into a glass vessel with a wide mouth, or a glazed stone jar, of the capacity of 8 or 10 gallons, into which 5.75 lbs. of alcohol, of the specific gravity of 0.85, have been previously poured—care must be taken to *pour the nitrate of mercury on the alcohol;* the reverse mode of mixing would be attended with danger. This operation must be performed at a safe distance from the fire, as the fumes of ether which escape are highly inflammable, and great heat is evolved during the effervescence which ensues from the mixture. When red fumes begin to appear, they must be reduced by adding a small quantity of alcohol. The proportion of alcohol used in the whole operation varies according to the quality of the acid and alcohol, and perhaps the state of the weather; the proper quantity is best determined by trial with the materials made use of.

When the effervescence has ceased, a precipitate of fulminate of mercury will be found at the bottom of the vessel; this must be repeatedly washed in soft water, until the water no longer reddens litmus paper. The fulminate is in the form of very small crystals, of a light grey color and brilliant surface. If the operation is well performed, no metallic mercury will be reproduced. The weight of the fulminate when dried is about 13 per cent. greater than that of the mercury used.

If the proper proportions are not used, (or if the materials are not of good quality,) the product will be, instead of fulminate, an impalpable, yellow powder, which is incombustible. When this is observed, the result may generally be corrected by varying the proportion of alcohol in the mixture.

The fulminate of mercury is kept under water, in jars or wide mouthed bottles, holding about 2 lbs. each, which should be preserved from frost.

To prepare the percussion powder: The water is drained from the fulminate, and the latter is partially dried, until it contains only 20 per cent. of moisture. In this state it is mixed with 60 per cent. of its weight of refined, pulverized saltpetre; the paste is worked with a spatula and a wooden muller, on a wooden table, until the ingredients are intimately mixed. While still in a moist state, the mixture is passed through a common hair sieve; it is then dried, with great care, in the sun, or in a room warmed by flues. When quite dry, it is again passed through a hair sieve, by rubbing it with the hand, or with a leather pad, so as to reduce it to a fine grained powder, but not to dust, when it is ready for use.

The dried powder is put into varnished wooden or paper boxes, holding about half a pound each, which should be kept in a small magazine, standing apart from other buildings.

Charging the caps. The charge of each cap is *half a grain* of percussion powder, which is put into the cap and compressed by machinery contrived for the purpose. In one of these machines, (made at Washington Arsenal,) the caps are placed by hand and the powder is supplied from a small hopper.

In Wright's machine, the charging is combined with the apparatus for making the caps. The caps are taken up as they are formed, and they are charged and pressed without handling; this machine, being supplied with the copper in sheets and the percussion powder, delivers the caps ready for being varnished, at the rate of 5,000 an hour.

Varnishing the caps. In order to fix the charge in the cap and to protect it from the effects of moisture, a drop of varnish is put into each cap.

To prepare the varnish. Dissolve 1 lb. of the best gum shellac in 1 quart of rectified alcohol, containing 95 per cent. of pure spirit. The solution is made at the ordinary temperature of the air in summer; it requires about 20 days, during which it must be frequently stirred. The operation is found to be much hastened and facilitated by putting the materials into a small rolling barrel made of tin, which is kept in motion by the power which moves the machines.

1 quart of alcohol and 1 lb. of shellac make 1.46 quart of varnish; a small quantity of alcohol is occasionally added for thinning the varnish when it is used.

To apply the varnish: The caps are put into holes in a board 15 in. by 12 in. and .25 in. thick; 500 in each board. This is quickly done by taking a parcel of caps on the board and shaking it sideways, the caps settling themselves in the holes. When the boards are filled, the defective caps and those which have lost their charge, are easily detected by the eye. The varnish is contained in a glass tube, furnished with a sliding valve of iron wire, which allows a drop of varnish to escape, when the tube is pressed in the bottom of the cap. In this manner a boy or a girl can varnish 5,000 or 6,000 an hour; or the varnish may be applied by means of a simple machine; about twenty boards are used; the caps remain in them 30 or 40 minutes, when the varnish is sufficiently set for them to be turned out into a tray, for drying. These trays may be 18 in. long, 12 in. wide, and 2 in. deep, to contain 5,000 caps each. The caps should be exposed for 24 hours in a room heated to about 100°; they are then put into bags and may be kept 2 or 3 days more in a temperature of about 120°, before they are packed in boxes.

Fifteen quarts of varnish are required for 1,000,000 of caps, and about 3 quarts of alcohol for thinning the varnish and cleaning the tubes.

Weight of 1,000,000 caps charged and varnished, 1,233 lbs.

Packing. The caps are put into bags of strong linen, 10,000 in a bag. These bags are made like cartridge bags for field service; 6 in. diameter and 13.5 in. deep. They are marked with the place and date of fabrication.

Weight of bag, with 10,000 caps, 12.5 lbs.

Ten of these bags are packed in one box.

The packing boxes are made of white pine, 1 in. thick; the sides and ends dovetailed together. The top is fastened with six 2-inch wood screws. They have brackets for rope handles, on the ends.

Interior dimensions of box: length 30 in.; width 12 in.; depth 9.5 in. Weight 30 lbs.

The bags are packed tight in tow. The boxes are lined with thick paper; they are painted olive color, and marked on the ends with the number and kind of contents and the date of fabrication. The place and date of fabrication are marked also on the inside of the cover.

Weight of box packed with 100,000 caps, 155 lbs.

Materials required for 1,000,000 *Caps.*

For the caps: 1,800 lbs. sheet copper, of which about one-third is returned in scraps.

For the powder: 43 lbs. mercury.
382 lbs. nitric acid.
400 lbs. alcohol.
24 lbs. saltpetre.

For the varnish: 10.25 lbs. gum shellac.
13 quarts alcohol.

For bags: 32 yards of brown linen, ¾ yard wide.

For boxes: 200 feet of white pine boards.

Friction Primers for Cannon.

A friction primer, for cannon, consists of a tube charged with gunpowder, to the top of which is fastened a cup containing friction powder, which is exploded by means of a slider pulled out with a lanyard.

The tube is made of sheet brass No. 22; it is formed by drawing a strip of brass .65 in. wide and 3 or 4 feet long, through a hole 0.195 in. diameter, and cutting it into lengths of 1.6 in. One end of the tube is slit into four parts 0.075 in. deep, for the purpose of fastening it to the cup.

The cup is made of sheet brass No. 30, cut with a punch into pieces 1.8 in. by 0.65 in., with a hole of the size of the tube.

The slit end of the tube is passed through the hole in the cup, and the ends are turned over and hammered down close, to secure it in place.

The slider is made of sheet brass No. 22, cut into strips 2.3 in. by 0.2 in. and doubled lengthwise over a mandril 0.2 in. diameter, which forms the eye for the hook of the lanyard.

The bottom of the cup and one side of the slider are made rough.

Charging. A charge of *four grains* of friction powder, in a moist state, is spread in the cup, and the slider is placed on it, with the rough side next the powder; the sides and ends of the cup are then doubled over the slider and pressed down firmly on it.

The tube is filled like common priming tubes, with a paste of mealed powder moistened with whiskey; a wire is passed in it, to leave an opening in the tube.

Varnishing. The primers are coated all over with a lacker of asphaltum dissolved in spirits of turpentine, or with shellac varnish. When dry, they are put up in bundles of 10, and wrapped in water-proof paper.

Friction powder. The powder is composed of equal parts of *chlorate of potash and sulphuret of antimony*, moistened with alcohol and mixed together in a wet state.

Lanyard. The lanyard, for pulling off the primers, is a piece of strong cod line (about .2 in. thick) 12 feet long; to one end is attached a small *iron hook*, with an eye for the line, and to the other end, a *wooden toggle* .75 in. diameter, and 4 inches long.

When the primers are kept dry, not more than one in a hundred will miss fire. If injured by moisture, they become serviceable again when dried.

Materials for making 1,000 Friction Primers.

Sheet brass No. 22	11.5	lbs.
Do. No. 30	4.5	"
Chlorate of potash	0.375	"
Sulphuret of antimony	0.375	"
Mealed powder	1.25	"
Whiskey	1	quart.

Weight of 1,000 primers finished, 13.25 lbs.

Percussion Primers for Cannon.

COMPOSITION: $\frac{1}{4}$ of fulminating mercury and $\frac{3}{4}$ of the following composition:

	oz.
Chlorate of potash	6
Sulphur	$1\frac{3}{4}$
Gunpowder	1
Antimony	$\frac{1}{2}$

To prepare this composition: Grind the chlorate of potash on a marble slab, with a little water; add the antimony and rub them well together, with water enough to make a stiff paste; then add the sulphur and the gunpowder successively, and mix the whole thoroughly. The composition must be kept in glass or tin; when dry it explodes by percussion.

To make the primers: Add the fulminating mercury to the above composition in a moist state, and mix them together, on glass or marble, with a wooden or ivory spatula; mould this paste into lozenges, 0.4 inch diameter and 0.04 inch thick; put the lozenges between two circular pieces of musket cartridge paper 0.8 inch diameter, which are united by isinglass glue and pressed firmly together; dry them and cut the paper with a circular cutter 0.6 inch in diameter.

Coat the primers with mastic varnish, or a solution of sealing wax in spirits of wine, or with other water proof varnish; keep them in glass bottles.

The cup of a quill tube may also be used to contain the fulminating composition, the barrel of the tube being charged with rifle powder.

Or the wafer may be made to form the bottom of a paper cap, which fits on the hammer of the lock.

FIREWORKS FOR SIGNALS, LIGHTS, AND INCENDIARY PURPOSES.

All dry compositions must be well mixed, first by the hands, and then by being passed several times through a fine hair sieve, in order that the ingredients may be thoroughly incorporated. In mixing compositions which require the use of fire, the greatest precautions are necessary, particularly for those in which gunpowder enters. The dry parts of the composition may, generally, be mixed together first, and put by degrees into the kettle when the other ingredients are fluid, being well stirred all the time. When the dry ingredients are very inflammable, the kettle must not only be taken off from the fire, but the bottom of it must be dipped in water, to prevent the possibility of accidents.

Signal Rockets.

IMPLEMENTS. *Formers*, for rolling the cases on—*rolling bench*—*callipers*, for measuring the diameter of the case—3 *hollow drifts*, bored to admit the spindle of the mould—1 *solid drift*—*former* for the cone—*former* for the pot—*mould and spindle*—*charging ladle*—*mallets*—*knives*—*scissors*—*gimlets*, for piercing the clay heads—*press* and *crank*, for rolling the cases—*choking machine*.

The dimensions of moulds, implements, and rockets are proportioned to the diameter of the orifice of the mould, or the exterior diameter of the rocket. The usual sizes are 1.5 in. and 2 in.

Height of the base of the mould		1	diameter of the orifice.
Height of the mould		$6\frac{1}{3}$	"
Exterior diameter of the mould		$1\frac{1}{3}$	"
Height of the spindle		$3\frac{1}{2}$	"
Nipple		$\frac{1}{2}$	"
Length of the screw of the spindle which passes through the foot of the mould		1	"
Thickness of the spindle	At the top	$\frac{1}{6}$	"
	At the bottom	$\frac{1}{3}$	"
Thickness of the nipple	At the top	$\frac{1}{3}$	"
	At the bottom	$\frac{2}{3}$	"

Thickness of the base equal to its height.

Moulds for rockets are cast in one piece and bored to the proper calibre.

Spindles, with their nipples, are made of cast steel; the base and screw, of iron.

Drifts and *formers* are made of brass, or of hard seasoned wood. The wooden drifts are tipped with copper $\frac{1}{8}$ of an inch thick, which is let into the wood without exceeding the size of the drift—the first drift is pierced so as to receive the whole length of the spindle; the second to receive $\frac{2}{3}$; the third, $\frac{1}{3}$; the fourth solid. Each drift has a handle 4 or 5 inches long, and somewhat larger than the body of the drift; the top strengthened by a band of copper. The diameter of the *former* for cases is $\frac{2}{3}$ that of the orifice of the mould—one end is pierced to receive the tap of a piece of the same diameter as the former, and $1\frac{2}{3}$ diam. long—the diameter of the tap or small part of this piece, which enters into the former, for choking the case, is $\frac{1}{8}$ of the interior diameter of the mould. The diameter of the *ladle* for charging a rocket is equal to the interior diameter of the rocket and the length $1\frac{1}{2}$ diam.—it holds as much composition as, when driven, will measure in height one-half of the interior diameter of the case.

Mallets for driving 1.5 in. and 2 in. rockets weigh about two and three pounds respectively.

Interior diameter of rocket case		$\frac{2}{3}$	exterior diameter.
Height of former		10	"
Length	1st drift without the handle	$5\frac{2}{3}$	"
	2nd drift do.	4	"
	3d drift do.	$2\frac{1}{3}$	"
	4th drift do.	$1\frac{2}{3}$	"
	former for pot	$2\frac{1}{3}$	"
	former for cone	$1\frac{2}{3}$	"
Diameter	former	$\frac{2}{3}$	"
	drift	$\frac{2}{3}$	"
	pot	1	"
	base of cone	$1\frac{2}{3}$	"

The former for cones has a handle 3 inches long in the centre of the base.

Making rocket cases. A sheet of paper No. 4 makes 2 strips for a 2-in. or an 1.5 in. rocket, by cutting it parallel to the short or the long side respectively. The former is first enveloped with a sheet of strong smooth paper which is pasted after the first turn, and rolled tight in the press; the other strips of paper are then rolled on the former in the same manner, until the case has attained the requisite size.

To choke the case. Wrap a piece of strong paper over it, at the joint in the former, to prevent the cord from chafing it; take a turn around it with the choking cord, and press on the treadle, turning the case at the same time, and drawing out the small part of the former as the paper contracts; wrap the choke firmly with strong twine. Let the case dry slowly, and when perfectly dry, trim it to the proper length, so that the distances from the middle of the choke to the bottom and top of the case shall be equal to the distance from the bottom of the spindle to the bottom and top of the mould respectively.

COMPOSITIONS.	Nitre.	Sulphur.	Charcoal.	Steel filings.
1	16	4	6	4
2	10	2	3	
3	8	2	3	

DRIVING ROCKETS. The composition must be well mixed by passing it through fine sieves and by rubbing it in the hands; the charcoal, being the lightest ingredient, must be added after the nitre and sulphur have been mixed; steel filings or antimony should be added after the charcoal. Whilst driving the rocket, the composition must be frequently stirred to prevent the settling of these heavy materials to the bottom. The clay which is driven in the top is pierced with a gimlet to the composition; through this hole the fire communicates to the bursting charge in the pot which contains the ornaments.

To put the case in the mould. Place it with the choked end down, over the spindle, and settle it with a mallet until it rests on the base of the spindle; then set the mould over it and key it to the base.

To drive the rocket. The hollow drifts are first used, taking the shorter drifts as the case fills, until the composition reaches the top of the spindle; then drive 1 diam. in height with the solid drift, cover this with a patch of stiff paper cut to fit the case, and over this patch drive a wad $\frac{1}{3}$ diam. high, of clay, or of plaster of Paris slightly moistened with water.

Rockets are sometimes driven solid throughout, and afterwards bored with a tap of the form of the spindle.

A rocket is primed with a piece of quick-match about 2 feet long, which is coiled in the bottom of the case, and covered with a cap of strong paper pasted down or tied in the choke.

The force to be employed in driving rockets depends on their size: A rocket 1.5 in. diam. receives 25 smart blows, and a 2 in., 30 blows of the mallet, on each ladleful of composition.

WEIGHT.	2-in.	1.5-in.
	Oz.	Oz.
Case ready for charging	9½	4
Case charged	16	8
Rocket finished	20	10

Pots for rockets, are made of rocket paper; two or three turns of paper are rolled upon a former of the same diameter as the rocket, being well pasted, except the interior or first turn upon the former. The pot is two diameters long, and is secured in its place on the rocket by paste and an exterior covering of fine paper. The interior depth of the pot, when attached to the rocket, is one diameter and a half.

Cones, are made of rocket paper, which is cut into circular pieces equal in diameter to twice the length of the cone intended to be made; each piece, being cut in half, makes two cones. They are rolled upon the former, pasted, and dried for use. In applying the cone to the rocket, its base is cut to the same diameter as the exterior of the rocket on which it rests; it is then filled with tow, to enable it the better to resist the action of the air, without much increasing its weight; it is confined in its position by another cone made of fine paper, about an inch longer than the interior cone; this outside cone must have its base cut in slips, which being well pasted, unite with the sides of the rocket or pot and firmly secure the interior cone; a narrow slip of fine paper is then pasted over the bottom of the exterior cone, as a finish to the head of the rocket.

Sticks for rockets, are made of dry pine or other light wood; the length is 49½ diameters, or 9 times the length of the case; the large end which is attached to the rocket is ⅓ the exterior diameter square, diminishing to one half of that thickness at the lower end; in the large end, a groove is made of a length ⅔ that of the rocket case, in which the rocket is tied; the end of the stick is beveled off, to present less resistance to the air; just below this bevel, and also opposite to the choke of the rocket, notches are cut out to receive the twine with which the rocket is fastened to the stick. The poise of rockets should be verified by balancing them on a knife edge. Those of an exterior diameter under 1¼ in. should be balanced at 3 diameters from the neck; those of a diameter between that and 2 in., at 2½ diameters; and those of greater dimensions, at 2 diameters. All these dimensions and precautions should be strictly observed, for if the stick be too light, the rocket will not rise vertically, and if the stick be too long and heavy, it will rise slowly and not arrive at its proper height.

Decorations for Rockets.

The pots of rockets are charged with various decorations, as *stars*, *serpents*, *gold rain*, *rain of fire*, *marrons*, *crackers*, &c., and with about half a charging ladleful of powder.

Stars are the most beautiful decorations of rockets. They are made by driving the composition, moistened with alcohol and a small quantity of gum arabic solution, in portfire moulds without any paper case, and with a moderate number of blows; they are cut into lengths of about ¾ of an inch and dredged with mealed powder. A more expeditious and better mode of making them is, to mould them in a brass cylinder of the diameter desired for the stars, and push them out with a rammer, cutting them into proper lengths as they are formed. Stars, after being dredged with mealed powder, must be dried in the shade. The gum arabic used in star composition is intended to give such consistency to the stars that the explosion of the head of the rocket may not break them in pieces and thereby destroy the effect.

COMPOSITIONS.	Nitre.	Sulphur.	Mealed powder.	Antimony.
1	16	8	3	
2	16	7	4	
3	16	8	4	1.5

SERPENTS are driven in small cases made of rocket paper or playing cards, rolled over a former 0.4 inch in diameter and covered with two thicknesses of strong fine paper, the last turn of which is pasted. When dry, these cases are choked at one end, without being entirely closed, and are then charged about $\frac{2}{3}$ of their length with composition, by means of a small mallet, a drift and a block of wood with a hole bored in it, to receive nearly the whole length of the case. The case is choked over the composition, and the remainder of it is nearly filled with mealed powder, upon which a small paper wad is placed; a clay head is then driven on it and the end of the case turned down, to secure it; the other end is opened with a punch and primed with priming paste, or a small strand of quick match. Serpents are placed perpendicularly in the pot, with the primed end downwards.

COMPOSITIONS.	Nitre.	Sulphur.	Mealed powder.	Charcoal.	Steel filings.
1	3	2	16	$\frac{1}{2}$	
2	15	4	–	$2\frac{1}{2}$	
3	16	2	4	6	
4	16	4	4	2	6

GOLD RAIN, is made in the same manner as stars, observing to cut or mould the composition into pieces of equal size. The effect of this decoration is beautiful and it is less troublesome than serpents.

COMPOSITIONS.	Nitre.	Sulphur.	Mealed powder.	Charcoal.	Pulverized soot.	German black.	Dissolved gum.
1	$\frac{1}{2}$	$1\frac{1}{2}$	8	–	$\frac{1}{2}$	$\frac{1}{2}$	$\frac{1}{2}$
2	16	10	6	4	–	2	
3	16	8	8	2	–	2	

RAIN OF FIRE, is made with small cases 0.3 in. diameter and 2 in. long; two thicknesses of paper are sufficient for them. The end of the case is closed and it is charged and primed like that for a serpent, omitting the powder for a cracker.

Composition. Mealed powder 16—Charcoal 6. Another kind which shows in sparks is made of camphor 16 parts, nitre 8, mealed powder 8, tow 8. The composition is formed into a very liquid paste with gummed brandy; tow chopped fine is put into the paste, and rolled into small balls about the size of buck-shot; when they have imbibed sufficient composition, they are rolled in mealed powder and dried.

MARRONS, are cubes filled with grained powder, and enveloped with two or three layers of strong twine or marline; to give them more consistency they are dipped in kit; they are primed by punching a small hole in one corner and inserting quick match. They are made of strong pasteboard, cut into the form of a parallelogram whose sides are in the proportion of 3 to 5, divided by 4 cuts from each side extending $\frac{1}{3}$ of the width and at equal distances apart, which prepare the paper for folding into the form of a cube of the size of one of the small squares thus marked out.

PACKING ROCKETS. The sticks are tied up in bundles; the rocket case is wrapped with tow so as to be larger than the pot, the tow being confined with a piece of twine long enough to tie on the stick. The rockets are placed in a box on a bed of tow laid under the choke, and they are pressed closely together; tow is then carefully stuffed in between the heads of the rockets; each tier is also covered with tow.

War Rockets.

The cases of war rockets are made of sheet iron, lined with paper, or wood veneer. The head is of cast iron, and may be either a solid shot, or a shell with a fuze communicating with the rocket composition. The case is usually charged solid, by means of a ram, or a press, and the core is then bored out.

The dimensions of war rockets are indicated by the exterior diameters of the cases.

These rockets have been made of two kinds, viz:

1. *The Congreve rocket,* which has a directing stick fastened to the tail piece, in the axis of the rocket.

2. *Hale's rocket,* which requires no stick, its direction being maintained by a peculiar arrangement of holes in the tail piece, through which the flame issues.

War rockets are usually fired from tubes or troughs, mounted on portable stands, or on light carriages.

For some memoranda of the ranges of Hale's rockets, *see* CHAPTER XIII.

Fire stone.

COMPOSITION.—Rosin.............................. 3 parts.
Sulphur............................ 4 "
Nitre...............................10 "
Regulus of antimony.............. 1 "

Pulverize these materials separately ; mix them with the hands, and sift them three times. In a furnace of the second kind, (p. 230,) or in an iron kettle in the open air, melt together 1 part of *mutton tallow* and 1 of *turpentine;* add the above composition, a small quantity at a time, stirring the mixture constantly with large wooden spatulas. Let one portion of the composition be melted before the next is added, and work with great precaution, to prevent it from taking fire.

The composition is cast into cakes, or into cylindrical moulds. These moulds are made of paper and are of two sizes: No. 1, for 13-in. and 10-in. shells; No. 2, for 8-inch, 42-pdr and 32-pdr. In the axis of the cylinder a small paper tube is placed, to contain the priming. The cases of the moulds are about .05 in. thick; they are made by rolling rocket paper on a former, and fastening it with glue. The priming tubes are made with 4 turns of musket cartridge paper.

The moulds are supported by a frame of wood, in the bottom part of which are fastened a number of spindles to support the priming tubes. To the upper part of this frame a tin pan is fixed, having cylindrical spouts attached to the under side, to support the upper ends of the moulds; the frame may contain 20 moulds in two rows.

When the composition has become solid, take the cylinders out of the frame, and trim them; charge the priming tubes with the composition No. 1 for mortar fuzes, driven with 21 blows of the mallet, and dip the ends of the cylinder in mealed powder.

DIMENSIONS OF CYLINDERS, ETC.	No. 1.	No. 2.
	In.	In.
Diameter of former for making the case	1.3	0.9
Length of ditto	12.	12.
Exterior diameter of the case	1.4	1.
Length of the case	3.	3.
Diameter of the former for priming tubes	0.25	0.25
Length of ditto	6.	6.
Diameter of the spindle of the mould	0.2	0.2
Length of ditto above the base	4.25	4.25
	Lbs.	Lbs.
Quantity of composition for 100 cylinders	18.	10.3

Valenciennes Composition.

Nitre..............................50 parts.
Sulphur............................28 "
Antimony...........................18 "
Rosin.............................. 6 "

The composition is cast in cylindrical copper moulds 6 inches long, of a diameter to suit the shell in which it is to be used. It is used as an incendiary composition, in charging shells, and is inserted along with the bursting charge, in pieces as large as the shell will admit without interfering with the fuze.

Carcasses.

CALIBRE - -	13-in.	10-in.	8-in.	42-pdr.	32-pdr.	24-pdr.	18-pdr.
	Lbs.	Lbs. oz.	Lbs. oz.	Lbs. oz.	Lb. oz.	Lb. oz.	Lb. oz.
Weight of composition - - -	19	7 8	4 4	2 8	1 14	1 10	1 1

COMPOSITION. A solution of equal parts of white turpentine and spirits of turpentine, incorporated with as much portfire composition as will give the whole a compressible consistency ; the portfire composition must be previously mixed with a small quantity of finely chopped tow. When properly incorporated, this composition is compactly pressed into the carcass with a drift, so as to fill it entirely. Sticks of wood of about ½ inch diameter are then inserted into each hole of the carcass, in such a manner as to meet in the centre of the composition, in order that, when they are withdrawn, as many holes shall remain in the composition, in the same direction ; in every hole thus formed, insert three strands of quick-match, of a length sufficient to allow of their being folded over the edge of the hole two or three inches ; some dry portfire composition must then be pressed into the interstices, to keep the quick-match fast in its place. Carcasses may be filled with the above composition, omitting the *tow*, or with *fire stone*, and the holes may be bored with a gunner's gimlet before the composition becomes hard. The quick match must be coiled into the holes and secured, until the carcass is wanted, by fastening a small cotton patch over the holes with kit.

Common shells may be loaded and used as carcasses in the following manner : The bursting charge is placed in the bottom of the shell in a flannel bag, over which carcass composition is driven until the shell is nearly filled ; then insert 4 or 5 strands of quick-match which must be secured by driving more composition upon it. These shells, after burning as a carcass, explode.

Fire Balls.

Fire balls are projectiles of an oval shape formed of sacks of canvas, filled with combustible composition. They are used to light up the enemy's works and are loaded with shells, to prevent them from being approached.

The sacks are made of strong and close canvas, (sail cloth,) which may be cut straight and gathered at the ends; or more neatly, cut in three gores or curved pieces, to form a ball. They are made of two or three thicknesses of stuff, according to its strength, and the pieces are sewed together with strong thread. One end is left open, or the bag may be attached to an iron hoop, forming a mouth for charging it; this mouth must be large enough to admit the shell with which the fire ball is loaded. After being sewed, the sack is turned, to bring the seams inside.

COMPOSITION.		13-in.	10-in.	8-in.
		Lbs.	Lbs.	Lbs.
Rosin		8.	5.5	2.75
Pitch		4.	2.75	1.25
Mutton tallow		1.5	1.	0.5
Spirits of turpentine		1.	0.66	0.33
Linseed oil		1.	0.66	0.33
Gunpowder		12.	8.	4.
Dry composition		10.	6.66	3.33
Chopped tow		1.	0.66	0.33
Dry composition, additional		2.	1.33	0.66
		In.	In.	In.
Height of composition.	Before inserting the tarred link and above the shell	1.	1.	0.5
	Whole height	12.	10.	8.
Tarred link.	Exterior diameter	6.5	6.	4.75
	Thickness	2.	1.75	1.5

The dry composition consists of:

Beeswax	0.66
Nitre	16.
Flowers of sulphur	6.
Inflammable saw dust	1.08
Regulus of antimony	2.66
Gunpowder	1.

Melt the beeswax over the fire and add the nitre to it; when the mixture is about to melt, take it off from the fire and stir in the sulphur; then add the saw dust, the antimony, and lastly, the powder, and mix them with the hands—Work with great caution against their taking fire.

To prepare the inflammable saw dust: Boil the saw dust in a solution of half its weight of nitre dissolved in an equal quantity of water—crude nitre or damaged gunpowder may be used for this purpose. Evaporate to dryness, stirring frequently; then spread out the saw dust, to become perfectly dry before being used.

To prepare the shell: A 32-pdr. shell is put into a 13-inch fire ball; a 24-pdr., into a 10-inch; a 12-pdr., into an 8-inch. The shell being charged with powder, put in a slow fuze. Dip the tarred link into the melted rosin, pitch, and tallow, and fasten it with twine to the shell, around the fuze hole.

To charge the sack: Put in the soft composition to the height indicated in the table, and level it with a spatula; put in the shell, with the tarred link, the fuze downwards; fasten the shell down with twine passed through the sides of the sack, or with a piece of canvas sewed to the sides. Fill the sack with composition to the proper height above the shell; put the additional quantity of dry composition in a heap in the centre of the sack, and finish filling it with the soft composition. Close the mouth by sewing, or tying the pieces together.

The iron bottom: The ball is furnished with an iron bottom, to prevent it from being broken by the force of the charge in the mortar. These bottoms are made of plate iron 3-16 in. thick.

DIMENSIONS.	13-in.	10-in.	8-in.
	In.	In.	In.
Inside diameter at top	10.5	8.25	6.5
Depth of concavity	2.75	2.25	2.2

The iron is cut in a circular form, heated and partly shaped with a set hammer, in a concave wooden former; it is again heated and finished in an iron former. It is then put into a lathe, where the outer edge is trimmed and chamfered to the thickness of $\frac{1}{8}$ in.

The iron bottom is attached to the ball with the following cement:

	Lbs.	Oz.
Beeswax	0	3
Pitch	2	
Rosin	1	
Turpentine	1	
Brick dust	0	9

The materials for the cement are melted successively over a slow fire, and the brick dust is stirred in last.

The iron bottom is filled about one-third full with the cement, and the loaded end of the fire ball is inserted in it and left to cool.

The ball is next covered and strengthened with a net work made of spun yarn or cord, from 0.25 to 0.5 inch thick, according to the size of the ball. This net work is commenced at the bottom of the sack, and terminates at the top in a strong loop, which forms a handle for carrying the ball. The ball, when finished, should pass through the large shell gauge. Fire balls are dipped in a composition of equal parts of pitch and rosin, made warm.

To prime the balls: Make 4 holes, about 3 in. below the top, by driving in greased wooden pins, 1 in. diam. and 2 in. deep. When the ball is to be primed take out these pins and fill the holes with fuzes, or with fuze composition, driven as in a fuze, and with two strands of quick match, held fast by the composition; leave room in the priming hole for coiling the quick match, and cover it with a piece of canvas fastened with 4 nails.

The balls are not primed until they are to be fired.

Light Balls.

Light balls are made in the same manner as fire balls, except that there is no shell in them, as they are used for lighting up our own works.

Tarred Links. (Tourteaux.)

Are used for lighting up a rampart, or for incendiary purposes. They consist of coils of soft rope placed on top of each other and loosely tied together; the exterior diameter is 6 inches, the interior 3 inches. They may be made of pieces of slow match about 15 feet long; immerse them for 10 minutes in a composition of 20 pitch and 1 tallow, and shape them under water; when dry, plunge them in a composition of equal parts of pitch and rosin, and roll them in tow or sawdust. In making them, the hands of the workmen should be covered with linseed oil.

A *link* takes from 1 lb. to $1\frac{1}{4}$ lb. of composition and $\frac{1}{2}$ lb. of tow. Two of them are put into a rampart grate, separated by shavings. They burn one hour in calm weather, half an hour in a high wind, and are not extinguished by rain. The grates are placed about 250 feet apart.

Pitched Fascines.

Fagots of vine twigs, or other very combustible wood, about 20 in. long and 4 in. in diameter, tied in three places with iron wire, may be treated in the same manner as *Links*, and used for the same purpose; their inflammability is increased by dipping the ends in melted fire stone.

Torches.

In a solution of equal parts of water and nitre, boil old rope or slow match well beaten and untwisted; let it dry perfectly, and cut it in pieces about 4 feet long; tie three or four of these pieces around a piece of pine wood about 2 in. diameter and 4 feet long; cover the whole with a mixture of equal parts of sulphur and mealed powder, moistened with brandy; fill the intervals between the cords with a paste of 3 parts of sulphur and 1 of quick lime. When it is dry, cover the whole torch with the following composition:

Pitch	3 parts.
Venice turpentine	3 "
Turpentine	½ "

Kit.

Composition: 9 rosin, 6 pitch, 6 beeswax, 1 tallow. To be melted together and poured into water; then worked with the hands until it becomes soft and pliable.

Incendiary Match.

Boil slow match in a saturated solution of nitre; let it dry; cut it into pieces, and plunge them into melted fire stone.

A yard of match requires about 1 lb. of fire stone.

Blue Lights.

Composition for 100 *Lights:*

	Lbs.	oz.
Saltpetre	9	10
Sulphur	2	6½
Red orpiment	0	11

The ingredients are pulverized, rubbed between the hands, and passed several times through a fine hair sieve; the brilliancy of the light depends on the purity and thorough incorporation of the materials.

The composition is pressed into a hemispherical cup about 2.5 in. diameter, made of well seasoned wood, (beech, linden, &c.,) with a stem or handle about the size of a 13 in. fuze. It is primed with a strand of quick match, and covered with paper which is pasted over the bottom of the cup.

STORAGE AND PRESERVATION OF AMMUNITION AND FIREWORKS.

Leaden balls are generally kept in cellars, on account of their weight; the boxes should be kept as dry as possible, and so piled as to admit the circulation of air about them.

Flints should be kept in cool, damp, and dark situations, generally in cellars; air, light, and heat seem to injure them; the occasional circulation of air is necessary for the preservation of the boxes or barrels containing them.

Cartridges for small arms are kept in magazines; the barrels or boxes being piled 3 or 4 tiers high at most. If barrels or boxes are not at hand, lay the bundles flat on a tarpaulin and pile them 10 high.

Fixed ammunition for cannon. If not in boxes, it should be placed in piles formed of two parallel rows of cartridges, with the sabots together; in 4 tiers for 12-pdr., and 5 for 6 pdr.; chock the lower tier with strips of wood fastened with small nails; put a layer of tow 2 in. thick between the shot; let the piles rest on planks, if there is no floor, and cover them with tarpaulins; have the place swept, and the cartridge bags brushed off. Leave a passage of 18 in. between the double rows, and keep them 2 feet from the walls.

Fixed ammunition should not be put into powder magazines, if it can be avoided; it should be kept in a dry place, above the ground floor if practicable; the store rooms should be always aired in fine weather; the piles should be taken down and made up again every six months at most, the bags examined and repaired, and the damaged cartridges broken up. A ticket on each pile should show the number and kind of cartridges, the additions to the pile, and the issues.

Canisters. Piled up like fixed ammunition, in 4 tiers for 24's and 18's; and 5, for 12's and 6's. Empty canisters in 10 or 12 tiers; the bottoms and covers separately.

Cartridge bags filled. Like fixed ammunition; or packed in boxes or barrels.

Paper cartridge bags. In bundles, packed in boxes or on shelves, in a dry place, with the precautions before indicated against worms and moths.

Loaded shells should never be put into magazines, except from absolute necessity; powder is not well preserved in them. They should be piled on the ground floor of a secure building—on planks, if the floor is not boarded; in 6 tiers at most; the fuzes of the lower tier in the vacant spaces between the shells; those of the other tiers turned downwards, like the fuze holes of empty shells; the pile should be covered with a tarpaulin.

Slow-match. In a dry place, such as a garret.

Quick-match. If not in boxes, it may be hung up in bundles, on ropes or pins, and covered with paper.

Priming tubes, Portfires, Fuzes, Signal Rockets. In safe and dry situations, packed in boxes.

Fire balls. In a cool place, separated from each other by shavings or straw, if they are piled up.

Tarred Links. Strung on a rope and hung up; for transportation they are packed in barrels, with straw between the tiers.

Fascines and Torches. Packed like the preceding.

Fire stone and Incendiary Compositions should not be kept in large quantities.

Percussion primers, in cool, dry places, apart from gunpowder and ammunition. Some cannon primers have exploded under circumstances which led to the opinion that their combustion was spontaneous. They should be carefully protected from rats, &c., by being enclosed in glass or tin.

BREAKING UP UNSERVICEABLE STORES.

Cartridges for small arms. 1 *Box*—1 *rectangular screen,* of brass wire, which fits in the box—1 *board,* with 4 *copper hooks,* placed across the middle of the screen—*boxes* for balls—*barrels* for powder—1 *paper press*—1 *sieve*—*stools.*

Put the bundles of cartridges on the screen, and open them there near the wire gauze; put the pieces of twine on the hooks, the papers on the board; the balls remain on the screen, and must be well washed. The serviceable papers are put under the press, the others thrown into water or burnt. The powder is dried and sifted, to separate the dust and the caked powder, which are laid by to be reworked, or to be melted for the saltpetre.

Fixed ammunition for cannon. 1 *Tarpaulin*—1 *box*—2 *barrels*—1 *knife*—2 *brushes*—1 *punch*—1 *hammer*—1 *scraper* (piece of *sword blade*)—*tow*—a *tub* half full of water, to clean the balls—*stools.*

One man holds the cartridge over the box, whilst another cuts the twine, takes off the strapped shot, brushes it, and stands it on the tarpaulin, on its sabot; the first man pours the good power into a barrel, the caked powder into another, turns the bag wrong side out, and cleans it. The strapped shot are taken to the door of the laboratory, where the shot which still require cleaning are separated from their sabots and immersed in the tub of water; after standing some time they are washed and cleaned. The others remain strapped. The serviceable, reparable, and unserviceable cartridge bags are separated from each other; the last are immersed in water. The breaking up of fixed ammunition requires many precautions and should never be done in the magazine.

CANISTERS. Turn up the slit ends of the canisters, take off the covers and empty the canisters, separating the shot and bottoms.

QUILTED GRAPE. Cut the quilting, open the bag and take out the shot; then separate the bag from the stool.

PORTFIRES. Split the paper, take out the composition and pulverize it by rolling for 2 hours. It may be made to burn more or less quickly by adding mealed powder or sulphur.

Unloading Shells.

This is necessary in order to save room in the store-houses, and to prevent accidents and the deterioration of the powder. It should be performed with great care, and at a distance from the magazines.

1 Artificer—1 helper.

IMPLEMENTS. 1 *Fuze extractor—a coil of rope*, or a *block*, to place the shell on—1 *brace*, with *bits* of the size of the bore of the fuzes—1 *copper chisel*—1 *wooden drift*—1 *mallet*—1 *copper hook*, and *rags*, to get out the powder and clean the interior of the shell—1 *knife*—a *tub* and a *basket* for the powder and fuzes—a *tarpaulin*—a *bucket of water*.

For large shells, in addition to the above: a *pair of shell hooks* and a *handspike*—2 *trestles* and a *frame*, to rest the shells on after extracting the fuze, for the purpose of emptying the shells over the tub.

Cut off the cap of the fuze; draw the fuze, and as soon as it is loose, hold the shell over the tub and empty it.

If the fuze breaks, or is bruised so that the extractor cannot hold it, pour water into the cup, and with the brace and bit bore out about 0.25 in. of composition; pour in more water, and proceed in the same manner until the composition is removed to the depth of 3 inches; then use the extractor again, or drive the fuze in with the wooden drift. If this cannot be done, bore out all the composition and wet the powder in the shell, by pouring water through the fuze; then drive in the fuze, and split it with the chisel, to get out the pieces.

Liniment for Burns.

Sweet oil, 8 parts; hartshorn, 1 part.

Or, equal parts of linseed oil and lime water.

CHAPTER ELEVENTH.

EQUIPMENT OF BATTERIES FOR FIELD, SIEGE, AND GARRISON SERVICE.

EQUIPMENT OF FIELD BATTERIES.

INTERIOR ARRANGEMENT OF AMMUNITION CHESTS FOR FIELD GUNS AND HOWITZERS.—Plate 18.

The principal divisions of a chest are designated as the *right half* and the *left half*, to a person facing the front of the chest.

The smaller divisions in each half, perpendicular to the sides, are designated as *first*, *second*, *third*, &c., from the principal partition, each way; the divisions parallel to the sides are designated as the *front*, *middle*, and *rear divisions*.

Ammunition Chest for the 6-*pounder Gun.*

Eight partitions, (POPLAR,) four in each half, perpendicular to the sides of the chest. The partitions are supported by *two strips* of wood at each end, forming a groove in which the partition slides; each strip is fastened to the side of the chest with *four copper nails.*

In the first division of the right half are *two bolsters*, for spherical case shot; one fastened to the principal partition by 3 *screws;* the other fastened to the first moveable partition by 3 *screws.*

One tray, for holding equipments, rests on the partitions in the left half of the chest. The tray has *two sides*, *two ends*, and *one bottom*, (POPLAR or WHITE PINE.) The sides and ends are dovetailed together and fastened by 12 *nails;* the bottom is fastened to the ends and sides by 14 *brass screws*. Three finger holes are bored in the inside of the ends, to lift the tray by; and a hole is bored through the middle of the bottom, to let the air escape when the tray is lifted out.

Ammunition Chest for the 12-pounder Gun.

Six partitions, three in each half, perpendicular to the sides of the chest, supported as in the 6-pounder chest.

Four bolsters, for spherical case shot; one of them fastened to the principal partition with 3 *screws;* two fastened to the first partition in the right half with 3 *screws*, and one to the left side of the second partition, right half, with 3 *screws*.

The second and third partitions in the right half are made higher than the others, to suit the height of the canisters fixed.

One tray, for equipments, in the left half; made like that for the 6-pdr. chest.

Ammunition Chest for the 12-pounder Howitzer.

Six partitions, three in each half, supported like those of the 6-pounder chest.

Twenty-one bolsters, for the lower tier of shells and spherical case shot. They are cupped out to receive the balls, and have holes bored through the bottom, for the fuzes to lie in. They are placed in the bottom of the chest, three in each division, except the first division in the right half; they are fastened to the bottom, each by 4 *sprigs*.

Twenty-eight props, for the upper tier of shells and spherical case. Four of the props are placed in each division, except the first one in the right half. Two of them are fastened to each end of the chest, two to the left side of the principal partition, and two to the right side of the first partition in the right half, each by 6 *copper nails*.

The rest of the props are fastened in pairs to the moveable partitions, each by 6 *copper nails*.

Six props for canisters, (OAK,) in the first division of the right half; three fastened to the principal partition, three to the moveable partition, each with 3 *screws*.

Ammunition Chest for the 24-pounder Howitzer.

Eight linings, two in each of the front and rear divisions, fastened to the ends of the chest and to the principal partition, each by 6 *copper nails*.

Four long partitions, two in each half, parallel to the sides of the chest; they are supported by the end linings and by *two upright strips*, fastened to the ends and principal partition, each by 4 *copper nails*.

Two short partitions for canisters, in the rear division of the right half; each of them is supported by 4 *strips*, fastened to the back of the chest and to the long partition, each by 3 *copper nails*.

Seven short partitions, for shells and spherical case shot: two in each of the front divisions; two in the rear division of the left half, and one in the middle division of the right half. These partitions slide into grooves made each by *two upright strips,* which are fastened to the sides and to the long partitions, each by 4 *copper nails;* each partition is formed of two pieces which slip into the grooves, one over the other.

Thirty-three bolsters for shells and spherical case. Seven of them are fastened, at the bottom of the chest, to the end linings of the two front divisions and the left rear division, and to the principal partition in the right middle division, each by 2 *screws.* Twenty-four of the bolsters are fastened in pairs on each side of the short partitions of the two front divisions and the left rear divisions; twelve to the lower half and twelve to the upper half of the partitions; each pair fastened by 3 *screws* which pass through the bolsters and the partition. Two bolsters are fastened to the left side of the middle partition in the right half, one to the lower and one to the upper part of the partition, each by 2 *screws.*

Ammunition Chest for the 32-pounder Howitzer.

Six long partitions, three in each half; one parallel to the ends, and two parallel to the sides of the chest; each partition is supported by 4 *strips* fastened to the sides and ends of the chest, or to the other partitions, each by 5 *copper nails.*

Four short partitions, one in the front and rear division of each half, made in two pieces and fastened in the same manner as those of the 24-pounder howitzer chest.

Twenty-one bolsters for shells and spherical case. Seven of them are fastened, at the bottom of the chest, to the ends and cross partitions, each by 2 *screws.* Twelve bolsters are fastened in pairs, as in the 24-pounder howitzer chest, to the short partitions in the left half, and in the rear division of the right half. Two bolsters are fastened, in like manner, on the right side of the short partition in the right front division.

Screws and Nails for interior of Ammunition Chests.

	DESIGNATION.	No.	Size.	Length.	Kind.
6-PDR. GUN.	*Screws* For 2 bolsters for spher. case..	6	No. 14	1.25	Iron.
	Screws " tray	14	No. 12	1.	Brass.
	Nails, for groove strips	128	3d	1.13	Copper.
12-PDR. GUN.	*Screws* For 2 single bolsters	6	No. 14	1.25	Iron.
	Screws " 2 double do	3	No. 14	2.	Do.
	Screws " tray	14	No. 12	1.	Brass.
	Nails, for groove strips	96	3d	1.13	Copper
12-PDR. HOW'R.	*Screws* For 3 bolsters for canisters	9	No. 14	1.25	Iron.
	Screws " 3 do	9	No. 14	1.5	Do.
	Nails.. " bottom bolsters	84	Sprigs.	1.5	Do.
	Nails.. " upper bolsters and strips	264	3d	1.13	Copper.
24-PDR. HOW'R.	*Screws* For 9 single bolsters	18	No. 14	1.5	Iron.
	Screws " 12 pairs double do	36	No. 14	2.	Do.
	Nails, for linings and strips	216	3d	1.13	Copper.
32-PDR. HOW'R.	*Screws* For 9 single bolsters	18	No. 14	1.5	Iron.
	Screws " 6 pairs double do	18	No. 14	2.	Do.
	Nails, for strips	200	3d	1.13	Copper.

Bill of Boards for interior of Ammunition Chests.

	DESIGNATION.	No. of pieces.	DIMENSIONS, (rough.) Length.	Width.	Thickness.	Quantity.	KIND.
			In.	In.	In.	Feet.	
6-PDR. GUN.	Partitions	1	168	11.	0.625	8.02	Poplar.
	Tray. bottom	1	22	20.	0.75	2.29	Poplar, or white pine.
	Tray. sides	1	22	10.	0.75	1.15	
	Tray. ends	1	20	11.	1.	1.53	
12-PDR. GUN.	Partitions	1	84	12.	0.75	5.25	Poplar.
		1	42	14.	0.75	3.06	Do.
	Tray. bottom	1	22	20.	0.75	2.29	Poplar, or white pine.
	Tray. sides	1	22	7.5	0.75	0.86	
	Tray. ends	1	20	9.	1.	1.25	
12-PDR. HOW'R.	Partitions	1	120	15.5	0.75	9.69	Poplar.
	Bolsters for lower tier	1	54	10.	2.	7.50	Do.
	Props for upper tier	1	90	12.	1.	7.5	Do.
	Bolsters for canisters	1	8	10.	1.5	1.87	Oak.
24-PDR. HOW'R.	Partitions	1	96	15.5	0.75	7.75	Poplar.
		1	13	10.5	1.	0.94	Do.
		1	96	8.25	1.	5.5	Do.
	Linings	1	54	15.5	1.	5.81	Do.
32-PDR. HOW'R.	Partitions	1	108	16.	1.	12.	Poplar.
		1	60	8.5	1.	3.54	Do.

Ammunition carried in each Chest.

KIND.	NO.	WEIGHT.	PLACE.
FOR 6-POUNDER GUN.		Lbs.	
Shot, fixed	35	266.	In the left half, and in 4th and 5th divisions of right half.
Spherical case, fixed	5	34.1	In 1st division, right half.
Canisters, fixed	10	84.	In 2nd and 3d divisions, right half.
Spare cartridges, $1\frac{1}{4}$ lb	2	2.6	On the spherical case.
Fuzes... 2 sec.—*Black*	2	0.1	In the fuze pouch, or in bundles in the tray.
Fuzes... 3 sec.—*Red*	5		
Fuzes... 4 sec.—*Green*	3		
Percussion primers	60	0.08	In the tube pouch, or in bundles in the tray.
Friction primers	40	0.52	
Priming tubes	20	0.30	
Slow match, yards	6	1.15	On the ammunition in right half.
Port fires	4	1.15	
		390.00	
FOR 12-POUNDER GUN.			
Shot, fixed	20	308.	In left half, and in 4th division of right half.
Spherical case, fixed	8	108.	In 1st and 2nd divisions, right half.
Canisters, fixed	4	67.64	In 3d division, right half.
Spare cartridges, $2\frac{1}{2}$ lbs	2	5.12	On the spherical case.
Fuzes... 2 sec.—*Black*	2	0.16	In fuze pouch, or in bundles in the tray.
Fuzes... 3 sec.—*Red*	8		
Fuzes... 4 sec.—*Green*	3		
Fuzes... 5 sec.—*Yellow*	3		
Percussion primers	40	0.05	In tube pouch, or in bundles in the tray.
Friction primers	25	0.33	
Priming tubes	20	0.30	
Slow match, yards	6	1.15	On the ammunition in right half.
Port fires	4	1.15	
		491.90	
FOR 12-PDR. HOWITZER.			
Shells, fixed	15	157.5	In 2nd, 3d, & 4th divisions, right half.
Spherical case, fixed	20	250.	In left half.
Canisters, fixed	4	47.4	In 1st division, right half.
Fuzes... 2 sec.—*Black*	17	0.7	In the fuze pouch, or in bundles, on the canisters, &c.
Fuzes... 3 sec.—*Red*	35		
Fuzes... 4 sec.—*Green*	18		
Percussion primers	50	0.06	In tube pouch, or in bundles, on the canisters, &c.
Friction primers	30	0.40	
Priming tubes	20	0.30	
Slow match, yards	6	1.15	On the canisters.
Port fires	4	1.15	
		458.66	

Ammunition carried in each Chest—Continued.

KIND.		NO.	WEIGHT.	PLACE.
FOR 24-PDR. HOWITZER.			Lbs.	
Shells, strapped		12	225.60	In left half.
Spherical case, strapped		8	184.00	In front and middle divisions of right half.
Canisters		3	63.75	In rear divisions of right half.
Cartridges	Small charge	23	53.82	12 in middle division, left half; 9 in middle division, right half; 2 on canisters.
	Large charge	2	5.40	On canisters.
Fuzes	2 sec.—*Black*	6	0.40	As for 12-pounder howitzer.
	3 sec.—*Red*	20		
	4 sec.—*Green*	7		
	5 sec.—*Yellow*	7		
Percussion primers		30	0.04	
Friction primers		20	0.26	
Priming tubes		10	0.15	
Slow match, yards		6	1.15	
Port fires		4	1.15	
			535.72	
FOR 32-PDR. HOWITZER.				
Shells, strapped		8	196.80	Front and rear divisions of left half.
Spherical case, strapped		6	186.00	Rear divisions, and right front division of right half.
Canister		1	28.50	Left front division, right half.
Cartridges	Small charge	15	46.50	1st division in each half.
	Large charge	1	3.88	
Fuzes	2 sec.—*Black*	4	0.28	In fuze pouch, or in the middle divisions.
	3 sec.—*Red*	14		
	4 sec.—*Green*	5		
	5 sec.—*Yellow*	5		
Percussion primers		20	0.03	In tube pouch, or in the middle divisions.
Friction primers		15	0.20	
Priming tubes		10	0.15	
Slow match, yards		6	1.15	In middle divisions.
Port fires		4	1.15	
			464.64	

Implements and Equipments for Field Carriages.

KIND.	NO.	WEIGHT.	PLACE.
FOR A GUN OR HOWITZER CARRIAGE.		Lbs.	
Sponges and rammers.....	2	....	12-pdr., 11.6 lbs.; 6 pdr., 9 lbs.
Sponge covers............	2	0.28	On the gun carriage.
Worm and staff..........	½	3.6	
Hand spikes.............	2	14.5	
Sponge bucket...........	1	10.	
Prolonge................	1	18.	
Linstock................	1	0.9	
Lock....................	1	2.75	On the gun.
Lock cover..............	1	0.9	
Tar bucket..............	1	7.	On the limber.
Water bucket, (leather)...	1	8.	
Gunner's havresacks......	2	3.72	In the implement trays, or in other vacant spaces in the ammunition chest.
Tube pouch..............	1	0.95	
Fuze pouch..............	1	0.95	
Vent punch..............	1	0.08	
Gunner's pincers.........	1	0.85	
Tow hook................	1	0.60	
Tangent scale............	1	0.21	
Thumb stalls.............	2	0.01	In the tube pouch.
Priming wire.............	1	0.08	
Lanyard for friction primers	1	0.10	
Gunner's gimlet..........	1	0.08	In the fuze pouch.
Fuze plug reamer.........	1	0.3	
Tarpaulin, large..........	1	54.	Strapped on the ammunition chest.
FOR A CAISSON.			
Felling axe..............	1	6.	In the places provided for them on the caisson body.
Shovel, long handle.......	1	4.75	
Pick axe................	1	6.5	
Spare handspike..........	1	7.25	
Spare pole..............	1	25.30	
Spare wheel.............	1	180.	
Tow hooks...............	2	1.2	One in the limber chest, and one in a caisson chest.
Tar bucket..............	1	7.	On the limber.
Watering bucket, (leather)	1	8.	
Tarpaulin, large..........	1	54.	Strapped on the limber chest.

Two pairs of straps for the tarpaulins are fastened with screws to the edges of the lid of the limber chest, at 10 inches from the ends. The straps are 1.25 inch wide; the front straps, 24 inches long; the rear, 10 inches long, with buckles; each fastened with two 1 inch screws.

Weights of Gun carriages and Caissons, equipped for Field Service.

DESIGNATION.	FOR GUNS.		FOR HOWITZERS.		
	6-pdr.	12-pdr.	12-pdr.	24-pdr.	32-pdr.
GUN CARRIAGE.	Lbs.	Lbs.	Lbs.	Lbs.	Lbs.
Gun	884	1,757	788	1,318	1,890
Gun carriage, without wheels	540	783	540	736	783
Two wheels	360	392	360	392	392
Limber body, without wheels	335	335	335	335	335
Two wheels	360	360	360	360	360
Ammunition chest, with interior divisions	185	182	206	198	192
Ammunition, packed	395	497	465	541	470
Large tarpaulin	54	54	54	54	54
Other implements and equipments	83	86	83	86	86
Total weight	3,196	4,446	3,191	4,020	4,562
Number of rounds of ammunition on each limber	50	32	39	23	15
CAISSON.	Lbs.	Lbs.	Lbs.	Lbs.	Lbs.
Body, without wheels	432	432	432	432	432
Two wheels	360	360	360	360	360
Two ammunition chests	370	364	412	396	384
Ammunition, packed in do.	790	994	930	1,082	940
Limber body, without wheels	335	335	335	335	335
Two wheels	360	360	360	360	360
Ammunition chest	185	182	206	198	192
Ammunition, packed in do.	395	497	465	541	470
Large tarpaulin	54	54	54	54	54
Other implements and spare parts	246	246	246	246	246
Total weight	3,527	3,824	3,800	4,004	3,773
Number of rounds of ammunition on each caisson and its limber	150	96	117	69	45

EQUIPMENT OF TRAVELLING FORGES AND BATTERY WAGONS.

One forge and one battery wagon accompany each field battery. They are furnished with the tools and materials required for shoeing horses and for ordinary repairs and preservation of carriages and harness.

Other forges and battery wagons, equipped for the general service of the army, accompany the field park which contains the general supplies of ordnance stores.

The forge for the field battery is designated by the letter A.
The forge for the field park " " " B.
The battery wagon for the field battery " " " C.
The battery wagon for the field park " " " D.

EQUIPMENT OF A FORGE FOR A FIELD BATTERY.

Interior arrangement of the Limber Chest.

The chest is marked: FORGE A.

There are *five boxes* for tools and stores; *one shoeing box*, and *one can* for oil.

The boxes are marked: A, Nos. 1, 2, 3, 4, 5.

They are made of white pine, .75 in. thick, with loose covers of the same thickness; the covers have three $\frac{3}{4}$ in. holes bored in each end, to lift them by.

Two handles of double leather are nailed on the inside of the ends of the boxes, so as not to interfere with the covers.

The sides and ends of all the boxes for the forges and battery wagons are dovetailed together, and fastened with 8*d. nails;* the covers are made with clamps on the ends.

Exterior dimensions of the Boxes for FORGE A.

DESIGNATION.	Length.	Width.	Depth.	Weight.	REMARKS.
	In.	In.	In.	Lbs.	
A, Nos. 1 & 3	17.8	13.25	7.5	8.25	
A, No. 2....	17.8	13.25	7.5	9.75	A parti'n at 4.5 in. from one end.
A, No. 4....	23.5	8.	6.5	8.	A partition for oil can, at 5.25 in. from one end.
A, No. 5....	39.8	9.8	6.5	14.5	
Shoeing box.	16.5	8.	6.5	4.7	

The *oil can* is made of tin, to hold one quart; it is five inches square and four inches high, with a neck for a cork, one inch diameter and .5 in. high, near one corner. Weight 0.9 lb. It is marked: A, SPERM OIL.

Boxes Nos, 1, 2, and 3, are placed in the bottom of the chest; No. 1 against the left hand; No. 2 in the middle.

No. 4 is placed on top of Nos. 1 and 2, against the left end and the back of the chest; the division for the oil can on the left hand.

No. 5 is placed on top of Nos. 1, 2, and 3, against the front of the chest.

The shoeing box is placed on No. 3, against the right end and the back of the chest.

The tools and stores in all the boxes, and in the forges and battery wagons, are securely packed with tow.

Contents of the Limber Chest of Forge A.

SMITH'S TOOLS AND STORES.	NO.	WEIGHT.	PLACE.
		Lbs.	
Horse shoes, Nos. 2 and 3..........lbs.	100	100.00	Box A, 1.
Horse shoes, Nos. 2 and 3..........lbs.	100	100.00	Box A, 3.
Horse shoe nails, Nos. 2 and 3......lbs.	50	50.00	Box A, 2; large div'n.
Washers and nuts, No. 2..............	30	5.25	In Box A, 2. 91.11 lbs.
Washers and nuts, No. 3..............	10	3.20	
Washers and nuts, No. 4..............	4	2.15	
Nails, No. 1, C....................lb.	1	1.00	
Nails, No. 2, C....................lb.	1	1.00	
Tire bolts............................	20	5.00	
Keys for ammunition chests...........	5	1.80	
Linch washers........................	8	7.30	
Linch pins...........................	12	8.37	
Chains, Nos. 1 and 2................ft.	2	1.54	
Cold shut *S* links, No. 3..............	50	2.50	
Cold shut *S* links, No. 5..............	12	2.00	
Hand cold chisels....................	2	2.00	In Box A, 4. 28.52 lbs.
Hardie...............................	1	0.75	
Files, assorted, with handles...........	12	10.00	
Buttress.............................	1	1.50	
Hand punches, round and square......	2	2.00	
Screw wrench.........................	1	2.42	
Hand screw driver....................	1	0.32	
Hand vice............................	1	1.00	
Pair smith's callipers................	1	0.40	
Taps...... } Nos. 1, 2, 3, and 4.......	4	1.50	
Pairs dies.. } Nos. 1, 2, 3, and 4.......	4	1.83	
Wood screws, 1 in., No. 14.......groce.	1	2.10	
Quart can of sperm oil................	1	2.70	
Carried forward..........	....	319.63	

Contents of the Limber Chest—Continued.

SMITH'S TOOLS AND STORES.	NO.	WEIGHT.	PLACE.
Brought forward	....	319.63	
Fire shovel	1	3.05	In Box A, 5. 80.05 lbs.
Poker	1	1.90	
Split broom	1	1.25	
Hand hammer	1	3.50	
Riveting hammer	1	1.05	
Nailing hammer	1	1.80	
Sledge hammer	1	10.50	
Chisels for hot iron	2	3.00	
Chisels for cold iron	2	3.00	
Smith's tongs	3	15.00	
Fore punch	1	1.00	
Creaser	1	1.00	
Fuller	1	2.40	
Nail claw	1	5.00	
Round punch	1	2.10	
Tap wrench	1	3.75	
Die stock	1	6.25	
Nave bands, developed	4	11.75	
Tire bands, developed	2	2.75	
Shoeing hammer	1	0.82	In shoeing box. 12.75 lbs.
Pair pincers	1	2.00	
Rasps, (12 inches)	2	2.15	
Shoeing knife	1	0.33	
Toe knife	1	0.30	
Pritchel	1	0.85	
Nail punch	1	0.80	
Clinching iron	1	1.00	
Oil stone	1	1.50	
Leather aprons	2	3.00	
Iron square	1	2.00	Fastened on inside of the chest cover with two copper clamps.
Padlock	1	0.50	On the chest.
Tar bucket	1	7.00	On its hook.
Boxes	6	53.45	
Tow for packing	....	5.00	
Total	....	480.38	

Contents of the Forge Body, A.

Box A, 6, of the same dimensions as A, 1, is carried in the iron room.

To put this box in, or take it out, loosen the thumb nuts and raise the rear of the bellows an inch.

TOOLS AND STORES.	NO.	WEIGHT.	PLACE.
		Lbs.	
Water bucket, wood	1	10.00	On its hook.
Anvil	1	100.00	On the fire place.
Vice	1	29.00	Fixed on the stock of the carriage.
Watering bucket, leather	1	8.00	On the vice.
Bituminous coal ... lbs.	250	250.00	In the coal box.
Coal shovel	1	4.75	
Padlock	1	0.50	On coal box.
Horse shoes, Nos. 2 and 3 ... lbs.	100	100.00	Box A, 6, in iron room.
Square iron, $\frac{1}{2}$ in. and $\frac{5}{8}$ in. ... lbs.	100	100.00	In the iron room. The bars not more than 3 feet long; the square iron in 2 bundles.
Flat iron, $1\frac{1}{4}$ in. $\times$ $\frac{5}{8}$ in., 1 in. $\times$ $\frac{1}{2}$ in. and $1\frac{1}{2}$ in. $\times$ $\frac{1}{4}$ in. ... lbs.	50	50.00	
Round iron, $\frac{3}{8}$ in. ... lbs.	50	50.00	
Cast steel, $\frac{5}{8}$ in. square ... lbs.	5	5.00	
English blister steel ... lbs.	5	5.00	
Box	1	8.25	
Tow	....	2.00	
Total, exclusive of vice	....	693 50	

NOTE.—100 lbs. of horse shoes, assorted, contain 90 shoes.
1 lb. horse shoe nails, No. 3, contains 140 nails.
1 lb. horse shoe nails, No. 2, contains 112 nails.

EQUIPMENT OF A BATTERY WAGON FOR A FIELD BATTERY.

Interior arrangement of Limber Chest.

The chest is marked: BATTERY WAGON, C.

The tools and stores are carried in *four boxes*, marked C, Nos. 1, 2, 3, and 4, respectively, and in *one oil can.*

The *boxes* are made of white pine .75 in. thick, with leather handles inside, and loose covers, like those of the limber chest of Forge A.

The covers of Nos. 1 and 2 are .75 in. thick; those of Nos. 3 and 4 are .5 in. thick.

Exterior dimensions of the Boxes.

DESIGNATION.	Length.	Width.	Depth.	Weight.
	In.	In.	In.	Lbs.
C, No. 1	17.8	13.25	7.5	8.25
C, No. 2	26.5	17.8	7.5	17.5
C, No. 3	39.8	9.8	6.25	12.5
C, No. 4	39.8	8.	6.25	11.

No. 3 has a partition, at 5.25 from one end, for the oil can.

No. 4 has two partitions perpendicular to the sides, making three divisions 15.8 in., 10 in., and 11 in. long, respectively.

The *oil can* is like that for the limber chest of Forge A, and is marked: C, SPERM OIL.

Boxes Nos. 1 and 2 occupy the bottom of the chest; No. 1 against the left end.

Nos. 3 and 4 are placed on top of Nos. 1 and 2; No. 3 against the rear of the chest.

Contents of Limber Chest for Battery Wagon, C.

TOOLS AND STORES.	NO.	WEIGHT.	PLACE.
CARRIAGE MAKER'S TOOLS.		Lbs.	
Hand saws	2	4.00	Fastened to the inside of chest cover.
Tenon saw, (14 in.)	1	1.50	
Jack plane	1	4.15	In Box C, 1. 17.20 lbs.
Smoothing plane	1	1.80	
Brace, with 24 bits	1	4.35	
Spoke shave	1	0.30	
Gauge	1	0.30	
Plane irons	2	1.05	
Saw set	1	0.25	
Rule, (2 feet)	1	0.14	
Gimlets	12	0.95	
Compasses, pair	1	0.18	
Chalk line	1	0.10	
Brad awls	2	0.17	
Scriber	1	0.15	
Saw files, (4½ in.)	12	0.87	
Wood files, (10 in.)	2	1.12	
Wood rasp, (10 in.)	1	0.40	
Trying square, (8 in.)	1	0.60	
Hand screw driver	1	0.32	
Carried forward	....	22.70	

Limber Chest for Battery Wagon, C—Continued.

TOOLS AND STORES.	NO.	WEIGHT.	PLACE.
		Lbs.	
Brought forward	....	22.70	
CARRIAGE MAKER'S TOOLS—Cont'd.			
Oil stone	1	1.50	In Box C, 2. 32.23 lbs.
Broad axe	1	6.00	
Hand axe	1	5.00	
Claw hatchet	1	2.00	
Claw hammer	1	1.50	
Pincers, (small) ... pair.	1	1.06	
Table vice	1	3.80	
Framing chisels, (1 in. and 2 in.)	2	3.00	
Firmer chisels, ($\frac{3}{4}$ in. and $1\frac{1}{2}$ in.)	2	1.00	
Framing gouges, (1 in. and $1\frac{1}{2}$ in)	2	2.60	
Augers and handles, ($\frac{1}{2}$ in. $\frac{5}{8}$ in. & $\frac{3}{4}$ in.)	3	2.35	
Screw wrench	1	2.42	
Felling axe } with handles	1	6.00	In Box C, 3. 23.25 lbs.
Adze } with handles	1	3.30	
Frame saw	1	4.50	
Quart can of sperm oil	1	2.70	
SADDLER'S TOOLS AND STORES.			
Mallet	1	1.75	
Clam	1	5.00	
Hammer	1	0.65	Box C, 4.
Shoe knife	1	0.09	
Half round knife	1	0.28	
Shears ... pair.	1	0.47	
Sand stone	1	1.54	
Rule, (2 feet)	1	0.14	
Needles	100	0.08	
Awls and handles	12	0.75	
Punches	2	0.22	
Pincers ... pair.	1	0.75	
Plyers ... pair.	1	0.22	
Claw tool	1	0.12	
Creaser	1	0.15	
Thimbles	4	0.06	
Strap awl	1	0.01	
Bees' wax ... lbs.	2	2.00	
Black wax ... lbs.	3	3.00	
Bristles ... oz.	8	0.50	
Shoe thread ... lbs.	5	5.00	
Patent thread ... lbs.	2	2.00	
Carried forward	....	96.21	

Limber Chest for Battery Wagon, C—Continued.

TOOLS AND STORES.	NO.	WEIGHT.	PLACE.
		Lbs.	
Brought forward..........	....	96.21	
SADDLER'S TOOLS AND STORES—Cont'd.			
Buckles, (assorted, .75 in. to 1.5 in).doz.	3	1.00	In Box C, 4. 20.66 lbs.
Tacks.............................M.	3	0.75	
Gunner's callipers	1	0.50	
Shoe knives..........................	2	0.18	
Scissors.......................pairs.	2	0.20	
Padlock..............................	1	0.50	
Tar bucket...........................	1	7.00	On its hook.
Boxes........................	4	49.25	
Tow for packing..............	....	7.00	
Total.................	....	162.59	

Interior arrangement of Wagon Body, C.

A TILL, 9 in. wide and 9.5 in. deep, is placed at the back or right side of the wagon body.

AN AXE RACK extends along the whole length of the body, on the left side, 11 inches from the bottom; it is 2 in. deep and 1.5 in. wide, and is fastened to the side by the middle rivets of the side studs, and by 5 wood screws. The rack has notches, to hold three axes, a hatchet, and three hand bills.

Four boxes, for stores, marked: C, Nos. 5, 6, 7, and 8.

One box, marked: C, CANDLES.

Exterior dimensions of Boxes for Wagon Body, C.

DESIGNATION.	Length.	Width.	Depth.	Weight.	REMARKS.	
	In.	In.	In.	Lbs.		
C, Nos. 5 & 6	23.	18.5	11.25	17.5	No covers..	Of hard wood, 0.75 in. thick.
C, No. 7....	23.5	20.25	14.	28.	Loose cover	
C, No. 8....	13.	13.	5.	6.	Div. into four parts	White pine, 0.625 in. thick, with covers, hinges, & locks.
Candle box..	11.	6.5	5.5	2.85		

Seven tin cans; two marked: C, NEATS' FOOT OIL; one marked: C, LINSEED OIL; one: C, TURPENTINE; two: C, OLIVE PAINT; one: C, BLACK PAINT.

Dimensions of Cans for Wagon Body, C.

KIND.	Capacity.	Diam.	Height.	Weight.	REMARKS.
		In.	In.	Lbs.	
For neats' foot oil..	2 gals.	8.	11.5	2.2	Rounded tops and necks for corks.
" linseed oil and turpentine....	1 gal.	6.	10.	1.37	
" olive paint.....	25 lbs.	9.75	10.25	3.	Flat tops; opening covered with a piece of tin, soldered on.
" black paint....	5 lbs.	7.	8.5	1.5	

Two kegs, for grease; exterior dimensions:

Diameter at the bilge...............	10.5 inches.
Diameter at the heads..............	9.75 "
Height..........................	12.5 "
Weight..........................	5 lbs.

Contents of the Wagon Body, C.

Box C, No. 5, is placed on the bottom of the wagon, next to the pile of harness which occupies the rear part of the body. Box No. 6 is on top of No. 5; No. 7 on the bottom of the wagon, in front of No. 5; No. 8 on top of No. 7. The candle box in No. 6.

TOOLS AND STORES.	NO.	WEIGHT.	PLACE.	
		Lbs.		
Linseed oil.........gal.	1	9.17	In 1 tin can	In Box C, 5. 80.44 lbs.
Spirits turpentine....gal.	1	8.77	" 1 do.	
Olive paint.........lbs.	50	56.	" 2 do.	
Black paint.........lbs.	5	6.5	" 1 do.	
Paint brushes..........	12	3.00	In candle box.	In Box C, 6. 28.73 lbs.
Sperm or wax candles, lbs	5	7.85		
Rammer heads.........	4	2.90		
Sponge heads..........	4	3.20		
Sponges...............	12	3.00		
Priming wires..........	3	0.24		
Gunner's gimlets.......	3	0.24		
Lanyards for friction tubes...............	4	0.40		
Cannon spikes.........	6	0.30		
Dark lanterns..........	3	3.		
Common lanterns......	4	4.60		
Carried forward....	....	109.17		

Contents of the Wagon Body, C—Continued.

TOOLS AND STORES.	NO.	WEIGHT.	PLACE.
		Lbs.	
Brought forward....	....	109.17	
Neats' foot oil .....gals.	4	32.80	In 2 tin cans. } In Box C, 7. 92.80 lbs.
Grease.............lbs.	50	60.	" 2 kegs.... } In Box C, 7. 92.80 lbs.
Nails, (4d, 6d, 8d, 10d) lbs.	20	20.	Box C, 8.
Felling axes...........	2	12.	In the axe rack.
Claw hatchet....... ...	1	2.	In the axe rack.
Hand bills.............	2	4.	In the axe rack.
Caisson stock..........	1	35.	Under the till, against the side and rear of the wagon.
Rammers and sponges..	3	13.5	On the caisson stock, against rear end.
Spokes................	40	72.	On the bottom; piled lengthwise against the front end.
Fellies................	24	160.	On the spokes, crosswise.
Grindstone, 14 in. × 4 in.	1	50.	On the fellies, against the left side of the wagon.
Arbor and crank for do..	1	6.5	On the fellies, against the left side of the wagon.
Screw jacks	3	75.	On the fellies, against the front and the till.
Wheel traces	10	47.5	In a pile occupying 30 inches at the rear end of the wagon, between the left side and the caisson stock, and up to the top of the till; the collars piled on each other, from the bottom.
Leading traces.........	10	57.5	(same)
Collars................	6	27.5	(same)
Girths................	16	11.	(same)
Whips.................	16	8.	(same)
Bridles................	6	18.	(same)
Halters	6	21.	(same)
Halter chains..........	12	15.5	(same)
Hame straps...........	25	4.5	(same)
Spare nose bags........	12	13.5	On the harness.
Sash cord ....pieces.	6	10.	On the harness.
Slow match........yds.	50	6.	On box No. 7, to the left of No. 8.
Elevating screw........	1	15.75	On the pile of harness.
Pole yoke.............	1	12.25	On the pile of harness.
Harness leather....side.	1	25.	Under the till, in front of the pile of harness, and against the caisson stock.
Bridle leather........do.	2	22.	Under the till, in front of the pile of harness, and against the caisson stock.
Prolonge..............	1	18.	On box No. 7, in front of No. 8.
Scythes...............	4	9.	In the till, against the front end.
Carried forward....	....	993.97	

Contents of the Wagon Body, C—Continued.

TOOLS AND STORES.	NO.	WEIGHT.	PLACE.
Brought forward	....	993.97	
Scythe stones	4	6.	In the curve of the scythes.
Spades	6	30.	In the till; the bits against the rear end.
Pick axes and handles	2	13.	Between the spade handles.
Corn sacks	24	20.	On the scythes.
Tarpaulins, 5 feet square.	2	18.	On the corn sacks, against front end.
Reaping hooks	4	3.85	Fastened to the ridge pole with a wooden clamp and a leather strap.
Scythe sneaths	4	12.	Fastened to the ridge pole with two leather straps and buckles.
Spare stock for battery wagon	1	90.	In the spare stock stirrup.
Padlock	1	0.5	
Watering bucket	1	8.	Tied to the forage rack.
Forage	....	....	In the forage rack.
Boxes	4	69.	
Tow	....	24.5	
Total	....	1288.82	Exclusive of forage.

EQUIPMENT OF A FORGE FOR THE FIELD PARK.

Interior arrangement of the Limber Chest.

The chest is marked: FORGE B.

Four boxes for tools and stores; *one shoeing box; one tin can* for oil.

The boxes are marked B, Nos. 1, 2, 3, and 4, respectively. They are made like those for the Forge A.

Exterior dimensions of boxes for Limber Chest of Forge B.

DESIGNATION.	Length.	Width.	Depth.	Weight.	REMARKS.
	In.	In.	In.	Lbs.	
B, No. 1	17.8	13.25	7.5	8.25	
B, No. 2	26.5	17.8	7.5	17.5	
B, No. 3	23.5	8.	6.5	8.	Partition for oil can, 5.25 in. from one end.
B, No. 4	39.8	9.8	6.5	14.5	
Shoeing box, B.	16.5	8.	6.5	4.7	

The oil can is like that for Forge A; it is marked: B, SPERM OIL.

Boxes Nos. 1 and 2 occupy the bottom of the limber chest; No. 1 against the left end.

No. 3 is placed on top of Nos. 1 and 2, against the left end and the back of the chest.

No. 4 on top of Nos. 1 and 2, against the front of the chest.

The shoeing box, on No. 2, against the right end and the back of the chest.

Contents of Limber Chest of Forge B.

TOOLS AND STORES.	NO.	WEIGHT.	PLACE.
		Lbs.	
Nuts and washers, No. 5..........	4	5.00	In Box B, 1. 83.40 lbs.
Nuts and washers, No. 4..........	6	3.22	
Nuts and washers, No. 3..........	10	3.20	
Nuts and washers, No. 2..........	45	7.88	
Nails, Nos. 1 and 2, C.........lbs.	2	2.00	
Tire bolts	20	5.00	
Rivets, for ammunition chests...lb.	1	1.00	
Washers for bolt heads, Nos. 3 & 4..	20	2.50	
Keys for ammunition chests........	5	1.80	
Pole prop socket and ferrule........	1	1.30	
Linch washers....................	8	7.00	
Shoulder washers.................	4	7.00	
Linch pins.......................	12	8.00	
Chain, No. 2................feet.	2	0.75	
Pintle hook......................	1	20.00	
Cap square	1	5.00	
Tire bands, (clips,) developed......	2	2.75	
Heading tools, for bolts............	2	12.00	In Box B, 2. 73.30 lbs.
Heading tool, for nails.............	1	4.00	
Tire punches, } with handles....	2	3.00	
Round punch, } with handles....	1	2.10	
Square punch, } with handles....	1	2.10	
Square hand punch...............	1	1.00	
Round hand punch................	1	1.00	
Centre punch.....................	1	0.50	
Key punch........................	1	1.00	
Set hammer, flat..................	1	2.85	
Set hammer, half round...........	1	3.00	
Chisels, for hot iron, } with handles.	3	4.50	
Chisels, for cold iron, } with handles.	2	3.00	
Hand cold chisels.................	2	2.00	
Smith's tongs	3	15.00	
Nail claw........................	1	5.00	
Tire circle.......................	1	1.35	
Bevel vice	1	1.75	
Hardie..........................	1	0.75	
Fuller..........................	1	2.40	
Hand axe........................	1	5.00	
Screws, 1 inch, No. 14......groce.	1	2.10	Box B, 3.
Small hand vice	1	1.00	
Hand screw driver................	1	0.32	
Taps } $\frac{1}{4}$, $\frac{3}{8}$, $\frac{1}{2}$, $\frac{5}{8}$, $\frac{3}{4}$, and 1 in.	6	2.85	
Dies } $\frac{1}{4}$, $\frac{3}{8}$, $\frac{1}{2}$, $\frac{5}{8}$, $\frac{3}{4}$, and 1 in. pairs.	6	2.75	
Gimlets, assorted................	12	0.95	
Small punches....................	3	0.75	
Carried forward......	....	167.42	

Contents of Limber Chest of Forge B.—Continued.

TOOLS AND STORES.	NO.	WEIGHT.	PLACE.
		Lbs.	
Brought forward	....	167.42	
Spring compasses.......pair.	1	0.15	In Box B, 3. 26.97 lbs.
Files, assorted, with handles	12	10.00	
Iron wire gauge	1	0.25	
Scribing awl	1	0.15	
Callipers.......pair.	1	0.40	
Bevel	1	0.35	
Trying square	1	0.60	
Scriber	1	0.15	
Buttress	1	1.50	
Quart can of sperm oil	1	2.70	
Nave bands, developed	4	11.75	In Box B, 4. 59.37 lbs.
Hand hammer	1	3.50	
Riveting hammer	1	1.05	
Nailing hammer	1	1.80	
Sledge	1	10.50	
Fore punch	1	1.00	
Creaser	1	1.00	
Screw wrench	1	2.42	
Smith's shovel	1	3.05	
Smith's poker	1	1.90	
Split broom	1	1.25	
Tap wrench, with 4 holes	1	3.75	
Die stock	1	6.25	
Tracing point	1	0.15	
Augers, ¾ in. and 1 in., (with handles)	2	2.50	
Framing chisel	1	1.50	
Felling axe	1	6.00	
Shoeing hammer	1	0.82	In shoeing box. 12.75 lbs.
Shoeing pincers	1	2.00	
Shoeing rasps	2	2.15	
Pritchel	1	0.85	
Nail punch	1	0.80	
Toe knife	1	0.30	
Clinching iron	1	1.00	
Shoeing knife	1	0.33	
Leather aprons	2	3.00	
Oil stone	1	1.50	
Iron square	1	2.00	Fastened inside chest cover.
Padlock	1	0.5	
Tar bucket	1	7.00	On its hook.
Boxes	5	52.95	
Tow	....	14.00	
Total	....	332.24	

Contents of Forge Body, B.

Boxes B, Nos. 5 and 6, of the same size as A, No. 1, are carried in the iron room. To put these boxes in place, loosen the thumb nuts and raise the rear of the bellows one inch.

TOOLS AND STORES.	NO.	WEIGHT.	PLACE.
		Lbs.	
Water bucket................	1	10.	On its hook.
Watering bucket, (leather).....	1	8.	On the vice.
Anvil........................	1	100.	On the fire place.
Vice..........................	1	....	On the stock of the forge.
Square iron, ($\frac{1}{2}$ to 1 in) ....lbs.	100	100.	In the iron room. Bars not more than 3 feet long. Square iron in two bundles.
Flat iron, ($1\frac{1}{4}\times\frac{5}{8}$, $1\times\frac{1}{2}$, $1\frac{1}{4}\times\frac{2}{10}$, $1\frac{1}{2}\times\frac{1}{4}$ in.)......lbs.	50	50.	
Round iron, ($\frac{3}{8}$ in.)........lbs.	50	50.	
Cast steel.................lbs.	10	10.	
English blistered steel......lbs.	5	5.	
Horseshoes, Nos. 2 & 3.....lbs.	200	200.	Boxes B, 5, and B, 6; half in each.
Horse shoe nails, Nos. 2 and 3.................lbs.	20	20.	
Bituminous coal....... ...lbs.	250	250.	In the coal box.
Coal shovel..................	1	4.75	
Padlock......................	1	0.50	On coal box.
Boxes................	2	16.5	
Tow..................	....	3.	
Total...........	....	827.75	Exclusive of vice.

EQUIPMENT OF A BATTERY WAGON FOR THE FIELD PARK.

Interior arrangement of Limber Chest.

The chest is marked: BATTERY WAGON, D.

Two cleats, of oak, are fastened to the ends of the chest, each with *four screws*, 1.5 in. No. 14. The cleats are .75 inch thick, and 1.75 inch wide; their upper edges are 7.5 inches from the bottom of the chest.

Two boxes, marked D, Nos. 1 and 2, occupy the upper part of the chest, resting on the cleats; No. 1 against the back of the chest. They are made of white pine, .75 in. thick, with leather handles and loose covers, .5 in. thick.

Each of the boxes is 39.8 in. long outside, and 6.25 in. deep.

No. 1 is 8 inches wide; it has two partitions 5.25 inches from one end, and 7.5 from the other, in the clear. Weight 11 lbs.

No. 2 is 9.8 inches wide, with two partitions, 14 inches from one end, and 11.8 inches from the other end. Weight 13 lbs.

One oil can, like that for the limber chest of Forge A, marked: D, SPERM OIL.

Five wooden clamps, for saws, are fastened to the interior of the chest cover, with *twelve screws*.

Two brass clamps, for webs or blades of frame saw, fastened to the interior of the cover, each with *six nails*.

Contents of Limber Chest, for Battery Wagon, D.

TOOLS AND STORES.	NO.	WEIGHT.	PLACE.
CARRIAGE MAKER'S TOOLS.		Lbs.	
Bench planes	4	16.00	Packed with tow in the bottom of the chest. 106.24 lbs.
Wood clamps	2	12.	
Oil stones	2	3.	
Broad axe	1	6.	
Hand axe	1	5.35	
Felling axe	1	6.	
Hand hammer	1	1.50	
Claw hatchet	1	2.	
Adze	1	3.30	
Table vice	1	3.80	
Holdfast	1	10.5	
Framing chisels	4	6.	
Firmer chisels	4	2.	
Gouges	4	5.	
Frame saw	1	4.50	
Screw wrenches	2	4.84	
Augers and handles	6	4.70	
Claw hammers	2	3.00	
Saddler's mallet	1	1.75	
Saddler's clam	1	5.	
Brace and 24 bits	1	4.35	Box D, 1.
Pincers, small.......pair	1	1.	
Callipers.......pair	1	0.40	
Spoke shaves	2	0.60	
Gauges	2	0.60	
Plane irons	6	3.15	
Saw set	1	0.25	
Trying square	1	0.60	
Bevel	1	0.35	
Rule, (2 feet)	1	0.14	
Gimlets	12	0.95	
Compasses.......pair	1	0.18	
Chalk line	1	0.10	
Brad awls	2	0.17	
Carried forward	....	119.08	

Contents of Limber Chest for Battery Wagon, D—Continued.

TOOLS AND STORES.	NO.	WEIGHT.	PLACE.
		Lbs.	
Brought forward	....	119.08	
Scriber	1	0.15	In Box D, 1. 27.52 lbs.
Taper files, (4½ inches)	12	0.87	
Wood files	6	3.36	
Wood rasps	2	0.80	
Compass saw	1	0.30	
Harness buckles....groce.	1	4.	
Tacks....M.	10	2.50	
Quart can sperm oil	1	2.70	
Hand saws	2	4.	Fastened to interior of chest cover, with wooden clamps.
Tenon saws	2	3.	
Webs or blades for frame saw	2	0.75	Do. with brass clamps.
SADDLER'S TOOLS AND STORES.			
Hammer	1	0.65	In Box D, 2. 30.24 lbs.
Shoe knives	6	0.54	
Half round knife	1	0.28	
Shears....pair.	1	0.47	
Sand stones	3	4.62	
Rule, (2 feet)	1	0.14	
Needles, assorted	600	0.50	
Collar needles	5	0.05	
Awls	36	2.25	
Awl handles	6	0.60	
Punches, (assorted)	6	0.66	
Pincers....pairs.	3	2.25	
Plyers....pairs.	6	1.32	
Claw tools	3	0.36	
Creasers	3	0.45	
Strap awls	3	0.03	
Gauge knife	1	0.80	
Compasses....pair.	1	0.18	
Thimbles	6	0.09	
Bristles....lb..	1	1.	
Beeswax....lbs.	3	3.	
Black wax....lbs.	5	5.	
Patent thread....lbs.	5	5.	
Padlock	1	0.50	
Tar bucket	1	7.	On its hook.
Boxes	2	24.	
Tow	....	5.25	
Total	....	208.50	

Interior arrangement of Wagon Body, D.

A till, on the right side of the wagon, } as in Battery Wagon C.
An axe rack, on the left side of the wagon body, } as in Battery Wagon C.

Eight boxes, for tools and stores, marked: D, Nos. 3, 4, 5, 6, 7, 8, 9, 10, respectively.

One shoeing box, marked D.

Exterior dimensions of Boxes for Battery Wagon, D.

DESIGNATION.	Length.	Width.	Depth.	Weight.	REMARKS.
	In.	In.	In.	Lbs.	
D, Nos. 3 & 5.	23.5	20.25	14.	28.	Hard wood .75 inch thick, with hinged covers, and hooks.
D, No. 4.....	27.5	23.5	14.	34.	
D, No. 6.....	19.5	19.5	10.5	21.	
D, No. 7.....	31.5	19.5	8.	26.	
D, No. 8.....	12.5	8.5	7.5	4.	White pine .625 inch thick; with hinges and hooks. No. 9 div. into 4 parts.
D, No. 9.....	13.	13.	5.	6.	
D, No. 10.....	14.5	6.	5.5	3.5	
Shoeing box...	16.5	8.	6.5	4.7	

Eight tin cans: Two of the capacity of *two gallons,* for NEATS' FOOT OIL and LINSEED OIL; three of *one gallon,* for the same oils, and for TURPENTINE; two, for *twenty-five pounds* each of OLIVE PAINT; and one, for *five pounds* of BLACK PAINT. They are made like those of the same capacity for Battery Wagon C.

Two kegs, for grease; like those in Battery Wagon C.

The *clamps* and other fixtures on the interior of the wagon cover, are mentioned in the list of contents.

Contents of Wagon Body, D.

TOOLS AND STORES.	NO.	WEIGHT.	PLACE.
		Lbs.	
Gun carriage stock, (ironed).	1	165.00	On the bottom of the wagon, against the right side, resting on two blocks to clear the rammer stop; the lunette to the rear.
Caisson stocks, (not ironed).	2	70.00	Against the left side and rear of the wagon; one on the other, the lunette ends in front.
Splinter bars	2	30.00	On the bottom, lying on each other against the caisson stocks and the rear of the wagon.
Tire bolts, nuts, and washers	28	11.75	On the bottom, against the front and right side.
Axletrees	2	234.00	On the bottom, against the gun carriage stock and the front end.
Half tires	4	140.00	Between the axletrees and the splinter bars.
Bar iron ....lbs.	200	200.00	In 5 bundles, not more than 3 feet long; on the half tires, against the front of the wagon.
Steel ....lbs.	50	50.00	
Pole yokes	3	37.00	On the bar iron towards the front.
Wheel traces	10	47.5	Piled on the bottom of the wagon, against the gun carriage stock and the till, and on the caisson stocks and splinter bars; occupying about 31 in. in length of the rear part of the wagon.
Leading traces	10	57.5	
Trace chains, staples, & rivets	20	26.00	
Collars	6	27.50	
Girths	16	11.00	
Whips	16	8.00	
Hames straps	25	4.50	
Bridles	6	18.00	
Halters	6	21.00	
Halter chains	12	15.50	
Harness leather ......sides.	3	75.00	Trimmed and rolled up tight; on the axletrees and tires, in front of the pile of harness.
Bridle leather.........sides.	2	22.00	
Rope, 2¾ in..........lbs.	30	30.00	Between the front ends of the caisson stocks and the bar iron.
Nose bags	12	13.50	On the pile of harness.
Slow match..........yds.	5	0.60	
Screw jacks	3	75.00	On the slow match.
Elevating screws	2	31.50	
Drag ropes	2	33.00	Coiled on the screw jacks.
Grindstone and arbor	1	56.50	On the drag ropes.
Felling axes	3	18.00	In the axe rack.
Hand bills	3	6.00	
Carried forward	....	1535.35	

Contents of Wagon Body, D.—Continued.

TOOLS AND STORES.	NO.	WEIGHT.	PLACE.
		Lbs.	
Brought forward.....	....	1535.35	
Neats' foot oil..........gals.	3	25.00	In 2 cans } In box D, 3; placed on the caisson stocks & the rolls of leather, against the front of the pile of harness.
Grease.................lbs.	50	60.00	" 2 kegs
Spirits turpentine ....gal.	1	8.77	" 1 can
LABORATORY TOOLS.			
Copper adze, with handle....	1	3.00	In box D, 4; placed on the caisson stocks and rolls of leather, next to No. 3.
Wooden bowls.............	4	6.00	
Bench brushes.............	2	0.90	
Callipers..............pair.	1	0.40	
Dredging box..............	1	1.00	
Rocket mould.. } For 1.5 in. rockets.	1	25.00	
Set of formers..	1	1.60	
Set of drifts....	1	1.75	
Formers for cylinders and caps, each calibre.....set.	1	7.50	
Copper funnels	4	4.00	
Shot and shell gauges....set.	1	15.00	
Gimlets..................	3	0.25	
Copper hammer	1	1.80	
Paste kettle................	1	9.00	
Lead ladle	1	2.00	
Stencils, for letters and figures ....set.	1	18.00	
Box for do...............	1	5.00	
Mallets..................	4	4.00	
Powder measures, 4 oz., 8 oz., 1 lb., and 2 lbs...........	4	2.00	
Brass mortar and pestle, small	1	6.00	
Moulds for musket and rifle balls, and buck shot...set.	1	23.00	
Wooden mullers...........	2	4.00	
Needles.........	50	0.04	
Paste brushes..............	3	1.25	
Copper pans, 10 or 12 in.....	3	5.00	
Rule, (2 feet,) not folded	1	0.15	
Sand stones	2	3.00	
Spring balance, 30 lbs.......	1	5.00	
Scissors..................	12	1.50	
Copper scoop, large.........	1	2.00	
Do. small	3	1.50	
Hair sieve................	1	0.80	
Hand screw drivers, large...	2	2.00	
Carried forward......	....	1792.56	

Contents of Wagon Body, D—Continued.

TOOLS AND STORES.	NO.	WEIGHT.	PLACE.
		Lbs.	
Brought forward...	....	1792.56	
Spatula..................	1	0.30	In Box D, 4. 176.88 lbs.
Thimbles.................	6	0.09	
Gunner's callipers..........	1	0.50	
Priming wires..............	6	0.50	
Gunner's gimlets...........	6	0.50	
Gunner's pincers...........	3	2.55	
Tinner's furnace............	1	9.00	
Linseed oil............gals.	3	26.5	In 2 cans; In box D, 5; placed on the pole yokes and rope, between No. 4 and the front of the wagon.
Olive paint.............lbs.	50	56.	In 2 cans
Black paint............lbs.	5	6.5	In 1 can
Tarpaulins, 5 feet square....	2	18.	On the gun carriage stock.
Do........do.........	2	18.	Between the till and boxes Nos. 3, 4, and 5.
Marline...............lbs.	10	10.	On box No. 3.
Sheep skins...............	6	12.	On boxes Nos. 4 and 5.
ARMORER'S TOOLS.			
Wire awls................	3	0.25	Box D, 6; placed on top of No. 5, against the front of the wagon.
Band set.................	1	0.50	
Drill brace................	1	2.60	
Hand brace...............	1	2.50	
Centre bits...............	6	0.40	
Hand brushes.............	2	0.60	
Bench brush..............	1	0.50	
Callipers.............pair.	1	0.30	
Centre punch.............	1	0.50	
Cold chisels...............	6	6.75	
Stocker's chisels..........	6	2.00	
Stocker's gouges..........	6	1.60	
Compasses...........pair.	1	0.18	
Spring clamps............	2	3.00	
Wood clamps.............	2	3.00	
Drill stock...............	1	0.45	
Drills, assorted............	6	0.25	
Die stock.................	1	0.75	
Dies.................set.	1	0.25	
Files, assorted............	72	21.50	
File handles..............	12	1.5	
Glue pot.................	1	2.15	
Carried forward...	....	2004.53	

Contents of Wagon Body, D—Continued.

TOOLS AND STORES.	NO.	WEIGHT.	PLACE.
		Lbs.	
Brought forward....	....	2004.53	
ARMORER'S TOOLS—(Cont'd.)			
Spring hooks..............	3	0.63	In Box D, 6. 100.92 lbs.
Bench hammers............	3	5.25	
Drawing knife.............	1	1.25	
Nippers..............pairs.	3	0.90	
Plyers...............pairs.	3	0.90	
Reamers, assorted..........	12	1.40	
Spring compasses......pair.	1	0.21	
Riffler....................	1	0.25	
Bench stake................	1	6.50	
Hack saw frame............	1	1.	
Hack saw blades...........	6	1.	
Armorer's punches.........	4	0.38	
Screw drivers, brace........	6	0.75	
Rule, 2 feet................	1	0.15	
Armorer's tongs............	2	2.50	
Screw taps.............set.	1	0.50	
Breeching vice.............	1	7.	
Hand vices.................	3	3.	
Bevel vice..................	1	1.75	
Breeching wrench..........	1	1.80	
Tap wrench................	1	1.20	
Straight edge..............	1	0.57	
Bayonet mandril...........	1	2.50	
Soldering irons............	2	3.50	
Screw wrench..............	1	2.42	
Oil cans, small............	2	0.22	
Tinner's shears........pair.	1	1.60	
Brass scale, 1 foot..........	1	0.20	
Flint screw wrench.........	1	0.06	
Haversacks................	12	22.32	In Box D, 7; placed on top of No. 4, and against No. 6. 37.46 lbs.
Tube pouches..............	8	7.60	
Thumb stalls..............	8	0.04	
Linen canvas.........yards.	15	7.50	
Sperm or wax candles...lbs.	10	10.	In box D, 8, on top of No. 3.
Nails, 4d. to 10d........lbs.	20	20.	Box D, 9, on No. 3 and on the till.
Shoeing tools...........set.	1	12.75	In shoeing box, on No. 3.
Spades.....................	6	30.	In the till, on each other; the bits against the back of the wagon.
Carried forward....	....	2164.13	

Contents of Wagon Body, D—Continued.

TOOLS AND STORES.	NO.	WEIGHT.	PLACE.
		Lbs.	
Brought forward...	....	2164.13	
Pick axes, without handles..	3	14.50	In the till, between the spade handles.
Handles for do............	3	5.	
Sash cord...........pieces.	24	40.	
Drill bow..................	1	0.45	In the till, lying on the bottom.
Barrel wiper and scraper....	1	2.5	
Quick match............lbs.	2	2.	Box D, 10; in the left side of the till, in front of the spade handles.
Shoe thread............lbs.	10	10.	In the till, in front of box No. 10.
Dark lanterns..............	3	3.	In the left side of the till, between the shoe thread & the front end.
Common lanterns	4	4.60	
Rammer heads.............	6	4.40	In the till, between the lanterns and the side of the wagon.
Sponges...................	12	3.	
Paint brushes..............	12	3.	On box No. 10, and by the side of it.
Rammer staves.............	6	13.5	In the wagon cover; three on each side of the ridge pole, secured with two wooden buttons, which are fastened to the ridge pole, each with one screw.
Reaping hooks.............	6	5.75	Fastened to the ridge pole with a wooden clamp and a leather strap passing through a staple in the ridge pole.
Cross cut saw..... without handles	1	9.	In the wagon cover, laid on each other, and fastened by 2 wooden clamps; the teeth of the cross cut saw against the right cover rail; the handle end of the pit saw against the rear board of the cover.
Pit saw........... without handles	1	15.	
Handles for do...........	4	3.	On the spade handles.
Spare stock for battery wagon	1	90.	On its hook.
Padlock..................	1	0.5	
Watering bucket...........	1	8.	
Boxes...........	8	155.20	
Tow	....	26.50	
Total........	....	2583.03	

Weights of Forges and Battery Wagons equipped for field service.

DESIGNATION.	For the Battery.	For the Park.
FORGE.	Lbs.	Lbs.
Body complete, without wheels	997	997
Two wheels	360	360
Anvil and water buckets	118	118
Stores in iron room	320	455
Stores in coal box	255	255
Limber body, without wheels	335	335
Two wheels	360	360
Limber chest, empty	158	158
Stores and tools on the limber	480	332
Total weight	3,383	3,370
BATTERY WAGON.	Lbs.	Lbs.
Body complete, without wheels	910	910
Two wheels	360	360
Stores in wagon body	1,289	2,583
Limber body, without wheels	335	335
Two wheels	360	360
Limber chest, empty	158	158
Stores and tools on the limber	162	209
Total weight, (exclusive of forage)	3,574	4,915

FIELD TRAIN.

Ordnance.

The proportion of artillery to other troops varies generally between the limits of 1 and 3 pieces to 1,000 men, according to the force of the army, the character of the troops of which it is composed, the force and character of the enemy, the nature of the country which is to be the theatre of war, and the character and objects of the war.

Similar considerations must regulate the selection of the kinds of ordnance and the proportions of the different kinds in the train.

The following principles may be observed in ordinary cases:

2 pieces to 1,000 men	$\frac{2}{3}$ guns, of which	$\frac{1}{4}$ are 12-pdrs.
		$\frac{3}{4}$ " 6-pdrs.
	$\frac{1}{3}$ howitzers, of which	$\frac{1}{4}$ " 24-pdrs. or 32-pdrs.
		$\frac{3}{4}$ " 12-pdrs.

Distributed as follows:

For the infantry: 1 piece to 1,000 men—6-pdr. guns and 12-pdr. howitzers, in batteries of foot artillery.

For the cavalry: 2 pieces to 1,000 men—6-pdr. guns and 12-pdr. howitzers, in batteries of horse artillery.

For the special and general parks of reserve:

1 piece to 1,000 men	$\frac{1}{2}$ in 12-pdr. batteries	of foot artillery.
	$\frac{1}{3}$ " 6-pdr. do.	
	$\frac{1}{6}$ " 6-pdr. batteries of horse artillery.	

Ammunition for Cannon.

200 rounds to each piece, both of the reserves and of the active batteries.

The ammunition which cannot be carried in the caissons attached to the pieces will be kept in boxes with the reserves.

Additional supplies of ordnance and ordnance stores are placed in convenient depôts, according to circumstances.

Ammunition for Small Arms.

100 rounds to each man; of which, for the musket, 40 rounds are in the cartridge box, 60 in the parks of reserve. In the same proportion for other small arms.

5 flints to 100 rounds, for arms with flint locks.

Percussion caps in the proportion of 12 caps to 10 cartridges.

Composition of a Battery on the War Establishment.

		KIND OF BATTERY	12-PDR.	6-PDR.
GUNS		12-pounders, mounted	4	
		6-pounders, do		4
HOWITZERS		24-pounder, do	2	
		12-pounder, do		2
Total number of pieces			6	6
CAISSONS		for guns	8	4
		for howitzers	4	2
			12	6
TRAVELLING FORGE			1	1
BATTERY WAGON			1	1
Whole number of carriages with a Battery			20	14
AMMUNITION	For 4 guns	Shot	560	560
		Spherical case	224	80
		Canisters	112	160
			896	800
	For 2 howitzers	Shells	168	120
		Spherical case	112	160
		Canisters	42	32
			322	312
Total number of rounds with a Battery			1,218	1,112
DRAUGHT HORSES		6 to each carriage	120	84
		Spare horses—one-twelfth	10	7
		Total	130	91

NOTE.—For two 32-pdr. howitzer carriages and 4 caissons, the number of rounds of ammunition is { Shells 112; Spherical case 84; Canisters 14 }

Shells	112
Spherical case	84
Canisters	14
Total	210

HARNESS, corresponding with the number of horses to the carriages.

Battery of Mountain Howitzers.

Howitzers	6	
Gun carriages	7	
Ammunition chests	36	(48 rounds for each howitzer.)
Forge and tools, in 2 chests	1	
Set of carriage makers' tools, in 2 chests	1	
Pack saddles and harness	33	
Horses or mules	33	

Such additional supplies of the above kinds as may be thought necessary will be carried with the park of reserve, together with the necessary ammunition for infantry, in packs.

A mountain howitzer ammunition chest will carry about 700 musket ball cartridges.

Rocket Battery.

No regular organization of a rocket battery has been arranged.

The nature and number of rockets, and of carriages or conductors, will be determined by the character of the service for which they may be required.

The Field Park.

The spare carriages, reserved supplies of ammunition, tools and materials for extensive repairs, and for making up ammunition, for the service of an army in the field, form the *Field Park*, to which should be attached also the batteries of reserve.

The quantities of these supplies must depend in a great measure on the particular circumstances of the campaign.

The ammunition required for artillery and small arms, (according to the proportions above stated,) in addition to what can be carried by the batteries and the troops, will be carried with the park, in caissons, or in store wagons.

The following carriages and stores, in due proportion, according to circumstances, will also form parts of the field park, viz:

Spare gun carriages, 1 to each field battery.
Travelling Forges, B } One or more of each.
Battery Wagons, D }
Spare spokes, 50 to each battery, } In store wagons.
Spare fellies, 20 to each battery, } In store wagons.
Spare harness } In boxes } In store wagons.
Horse shoes and nails, } In boxes } In store wagons.

Gunpowder.
Saltpetre.
Sulphur.
Charcoal.
Laboratory paper.
Percussion caps for small arms.
Cannon primers, percussion and friction.
Fuzes and fuze plugs for field service.
Stuff for cartridge bags.
Woollen yarn.
Cotton yarn.
Glue.

SIEGE TRAIN.

The number and kind of cannon for a siege train must be determined by the circumstances of each case, but the following general principles may be observed in assigning the proportion of different kinds and calibres, and the relative quantity of other supplies, for a Train of 100 pieces of ordnance.

Cannon.

GUNS..	24-pdr.	about one-half of the whole number	50
	18-pdr. or 12-pdr.	" one tenth "	10
HOWITZERS, 8-in. siege		" one-fourth "	25
MORTARS..	10-in. siege	" one-eighth "	12
	8-in. siege	"	3
STONE MORTARS		in addition to the 100 pieces	6
COEHORN MORTARS			6
WALL PIECES			40

Gun Carriages.

For 24-pdr. guns and 8-in. howitzers, one-fifth spare	90
For 18-pdr. and 12-pdr. guns........one-fifth spare	12
For 10-in. mortars and stone mortars, one-sixth spare	21
For 8-in. mortars	4

Other Carriages.

Mortar wagons. 1 for each 10-in. mortar and bed, for each stone mortar and bed, and for three 8-in. mortars and beds	38
Wagons, for transporting implements, intrenching and miner's tools, laboratory tools and utensils, and other stores—each loaded with about 2,700 lbs., say	140
Carts, (carrying balls, &c., on the march)	50
Park Battery wagons, fully equipped	28
Park Forges, do.	8
Sling carts, large	5
Do. hand	4

Draught Horses.

For each Gun and howitzer, with its carrriage	8
" Spare gun carriage	6
" Mortar wagon	8
" Battery wagon	6
" Forge	6

For each cart	2
" Sling cart, large	2
Spare horses	1-10th
Total, about	1,900 horses.

Projectiles and Ammunition.

FOR GUNS	Round shot. 800 to each 24-pdr	40,000
	Round shot. 1,000 to each 18 and 12-pdr	10,000
	Grape and canisters strapped, 20 rounds to each piece	1,200
	Spherical case strapped, 20 rounds to each piece	1,200
FOR HOWITZERS	Shells, 800 to each 8-inch howitzer	20,000
	Canisters strapped, 5 to each	125
	Spherical case strapped, 20 to each	500
FOR MORTARS	600 shells to each 10-inch	7,200
	800 " " 8-inch	2,400
	200 " " Coehorn	1,200

Gunpowder, in barrels ....lbs. 500,000

Computing for each 24-pounder round shot, one-third the weight of shot.

" " 18 & 12-pdr. " one-fourth " "

" " grape, canister, and spherical case, one-sixth the weight of shot.

" " round of howitzer ammunition	5 lbs.	including charge of shell.
" " " 10-inch mortar	7 "	including charge of shell.
" " " 8-inch "	3 "	including charge of shell.
" " " Coehorn	½ "	
" " " Stone mortar	1 "	

Cartridge bags, 1 for each round.

Cartridge paper, bundles 200

Wads—hay wads, made in the field.

Slow match ....lbs. 4,500

Port-fires 2,000

Priming tubes, for mortars 15,000

Fuzes, ¼ more than the number of shells 40,000

Wooden bottoms and baskets for stone mortars, 200 to each 1,200

Percussion primers, for pieces furnished with locks, ¼ to spare.

Friction tubes, for guns and howitzers, 1 to each round.

Cartridges for wall pieces, 500 rounds to each.

Cartridges, powder, percussion caps, flints and lead, for small arms, according to the force of the army.

Most of the ammunition is transported by hired wagons.

Implements and Equipments.

FOR EACH GUN.

2 Sponges—1 spare.
2 Rammers—1 do.
1 Worm to 4 pieces.
1 Ladle do.
8 Handspikes—2 spare.
1 Linstock.
1 Pass box to 4 pieces.
1 Tube pouch.
1 Havresack.
2 Thumbstalls.
2 Priming wires—1 spare.
1 Gunner's gimlet.
1 Tangent scale.
1 Vent cover, or lock cover.
1 Water bucket.
1 Broom.
1 Percussion lock and 2 lanyards.
2 Lanyards for friction tubes.

FOR EACH HOWITZER AND MORTAR.

IMPLEMENTS.	HOWITZER.	MORTAR.
Sponges and rammers	2—1 spare	2—1 spare
Handspikes, (2 shod, for mortar)	6—2 spare	6—2 spare
Linstocks	1	2—1 spare
Havresacks	1	1
Tube pouches	1	1
Priming wires	2—1 spare	2—1 spare
Gunner's gimlets	1	1
Quadrants	1	1
Fuze setters	2—1 spare	*2—1 spare
Fuze mallets	2—1 spare	*2—1 spare
Baskets	1	1
Chocks for wheels	2	
Loading tongs	1	
Tompions	1	1
Water bucket	1	1
Broom	1	1
Percussion locks and lanyards	1	
Lanyards for friction primers	2	
Plummets	....	1
Pointing wires	....	*2
Quoins	....	2
Shell hooks	....	*2—1 spare
Scrapers	....	1
Spatulas	....	*1
Gunner's sleeves (pair)	....	1
Wipers of tow linen	....	1

Scales and weights, or a spring balance, funnel, set of powder measures of 3 sizes, and fuze extractor, to each battery magazine.

Implements marked * are not required for the stone mortar.

The number of implements must be proportioned to the whole number of gun carriages, including the spare carriages.

One tar bucket to each travelling carriage.

Platforms.

For guns and howitzers........................ 1-10th spare.
For mortars................................ 1-8th do.

Embrasure Shutters.

For half the number of guns and howitzers.

Spare Parts of Carriages.

Proportion to the number of parts in the carriages:

Pintles for siege carriages	1-30th.
Nuts and washers, assorted	1-10th.
Linch pins	1-5th.
Axletrees	1-20th.
Wheels	1-15th.
Axle washers { Shoulder	1-20th.
Axle washers { Linch	1-10th.
Cap squares	1-15th.
Poles, one-half ironed	1-4th.
Elevating screws	1-8th.
Leading bars, one-half ironed	1-8th.

Spare parts of field carriages, as for field batteries.

Timber and other Materials for Repairs.

Proportion to the number of parts that enter into the construction of the carriages:

Axle bodies for siege carriages 1-50th—Breech bolsters 1-20th—Cheeks 1-30th—Fellies 1-50th—Spokes 1-30th—Fork saddles 1-30th—Poles 1-20th—Hounds 1-20th—Splinter bars 1-20th—Leading bars 1-10th—Square timber of various scantling—Plank—Wooden parts of mortar wagons; of each 1-20th.

Bar iron assorted, 80 lbs. to a piece, 8,000 lbs.—Steel, 5 lbs. to a piece, 500 lbs.—Sheet iron, 50 sheets—Iron wire, 400 lbs.—Tin, 225 sheets—Nails, assorted, 300 lbs.—Screws, assorted, 5 groce.

Machines and Ropes.

7 Gins, with tackle, complete—10 Lever Jacks—14 Screw Jacks—5 Lifting Jacks—20 Wheelbarrows, 1-5th for shells—7 Handbarrows—Balances, for weighing—10 Spare gin falls—75 Double prolonges—75 Single prolonges—

Drag ropes, 200—2¾ inch rope, 500 fathoms—Men's harness, 50—Small ropes, 200 lbs.—Twine, of various sizes, 50 lbs.

Tools.

Sets of carriage makers' and blacksmiths' tools—Pioneers' tools, for the artillery alone, 40 to a piece, say 4,000; of which 1,600 spades, 270 shovels, 2,000 mattocks, 130 picks—Spare tool handles, one-half.

Axes, 5 to a piece, 500—Bill hooks, 2 to a piece, 200—Saws, various kinds, 100—10-foot rods, 2-foot rules, mason's levels, 50 of each—Mauls, 200—Scythes, 8—Miners' tools—Baskets.

Laboratory Tools and Materials.

2 Sets of Laboratory tools; see CHAPTER X, *page* 231.

Nitre, pulverized........	1,500 lbs.	Twine..................	50 lbs.
Sulphur, pulverized......	100 "	Tarred rope yarn.......	200 "
Charcoal, pulverized.....	100 "	Copper wire...........	10 "
Sulphur, roll............	100 "	Brass wire.............	10 "
Pitch..................	150 "	Cotton yarn............	25 "
Rosin..................	150 "	Glue...................	10 "
Beeswax..............	50 "	Wrapping paper........	10 reams.
Camphor	20 "	Tar....................	2 barrels.
Spirits turpentine.......	10 gals.	Mealed powder.........	300 lbs.
Sperm oil..............	30 "	Quick match...........	150 "
Linseed oil.............	2 "	Torches................	100
Tow—Tarred links—Fire stone, &c.		Coal tar...............	1 barrel.

Implements for firing Hot Shot.

4 Sets—See CHAPTER XIII.

Instruments and Books.

2 Theodolites, or other instruments for measuring angles—2 Levels and staves —2 Compasses—4 Surveying chains—Diagonal scales—Cases of mathematical instruments—Spy glasses—Thermometer—Barometer.

Books. Ordnance Manual—Artillery for the land service—Tables of firing—Logarithmic tables—Drawing paper.

Miscellaneous Supplies.

Smiths' coal, 20 tons—Grease, 2,000 lbs., in 50 lb. kegs—Sand bags, 500 to each piece of ordnance—Chevaux de frise—Scaling ladders—Rampart grates, 50—Tarpaulins, various sizes, 100—2 Grindstones—Lanterns, 100—Sperm candles, 150 lbs.—Lamp lighter's torches—Canvas—Friction matches, in small tin cases.

ARMAMENT OF FORTIFICATIONS.

The kind and number of pieces of ordnance required for the armament of each of the fortifications are prescribed by the War Department, according to the character and extent of each work.

The carriages, ammunition, implements, equipments, and other supplies, for a fort placed on the war establishment, may be proportioned to the number of pieces on the following general principles, the application of which must, however, be regulated by the importance of the position, and by the peculiar circumstances of each case.

CARRIAGES.	For a front of attack.	For other land fronts and for sea-coast batteries.	
GUN CARRIAGES. Casemate	1-6th	1-20th	More than the number of pieces.
GUN CARRIAGES. Barbette	1-3d	1-10th	More than the number of pieces.
GUN CARRIAGES. Siege	1-3d	1-10th	More than the number of pieces.
GUN CARRIAGES. Field	1-3d		More than the number of pieces.
GUN CARRIAGES. Mortar beds	1-4th	1-10th	More than the number of pieces.
Trench carts, for advanced works	1 to 20 pieces		
Sling carts	1 to 25 pieces	1 to 25 pieces.	
Tumbrils or hand carts	1 to 20 pieces	1 to 20 pieces.	
Caissons	1 to each field piece.		
Forges, travelling, (besides permanent forges)	1 to 30 pieces of all kinds.		
AMMUNITION.			
For each 10-in. columbiad	400 rounds.		
For each gun and sea-coast howitzer and 8-in. columbiad	800 "	250 rounds.	1-20th Grape and canister
For each 24-pdr. howitzer	100 "	100 "	1-2nd Grape and canister
For each siege howitzer	600 "	200 "	1-20th Grape and canister
For each 10-in. mortar	400 "		
For each mortar		200 "	
For 8-in. mortar, stone mortar, and Coehorn	600 "		

Stone, 100 lbs. to each charge of a stone mortar.

Rampart grenades, 300 to a front of attack.

For each piece of artillery of a field battery for sorties, 200 rounds.

Gunpowder. The quantity of cannon powder may be calculated on the following principles:

For each charge of a gun—¼ of the weight of the shot.					
Do.	do.	10-in. columbiad,	21	lbs.	
Do.	do.	8 do.	12	"	
Do.	do.	24-pdr. howitzer,	2	"	
Do.	do.	8-in. siege howitzer,	4	"	
Do.	do.	10-in. sea-coast do.	12	"	
Do.	do.	8-in. do. do.	8	"	
Do.	do.	10-in. mortar, light,	7	"	including the charge of the shell.
Do.	do.	10-in. do. heavy,	15	"	
Do.	do.	8-in. do.	3	"	
Do.	do.	13 in. do.	30	"	
Do.	do.	Stone mortar	1	"	
Do.	do.	Coehorn	½	"	

To spare; for mining, fireworks, and waste, $\frac{1}{10}$ of the whole, including a proportion of mealed powder and its components, pulverized.

Fuzes, ¼ more than the number of shells.

Tubes, ½ the number of rounds.

Slow match, 40 lbs. to a piece.

Cannon cartridge paper, 1 sheet to a round.

Sabots.

Wooden bottoms for stone mortars.

Portfires, 1 to 50 rounds.

Percussion primers, ¼ more than the number of rounds, for pieces furnished with locks.

Friction primers, ½ the number of rounds.

Small Arms.

Muskets	⅓	more than the number of troops of the several kinds, supposed to be fully armed and equipped.
Musketoons	⅓	
Pistols	⅛	
Artillery and Infantry swords	$\frac{1}{25}$	
Cavalry sabots	⅕	

Wall pieces—50 to a front of attack, or a front exposed to escalade.

Ammunition: Musket cartridges, for each man....................400

Musketoon, pistol, and rifle cartridges................100

Cartridges for each wall piece 400

Spare powder for small arms, $\frac{1}{25}$ of the whole quantity required for the cartridges—Cartridge paper in proportion.

Flints, 1 to 10 rounds, for arms with flint locks.

Percussion caps, in addition to those packed with the cartridges, ¼ the number of rounds.

Implements and Equipments.

FOR EACH GUN.	FOR EACH HOWITZER.
2 Rammers—1 spare. 2 Sponges— 1 do. 1 Worm, } to 6 pieces. 1 Ladle, } 1 Linstock. 1 Pass box. 1 Budge barrel. 1 Tube pouch. 2 Thumbstalls—1 spare. 2 Priming wires—1 do. 1 Gunner's gimlet. 1 Hausse, or tangent scale. 1 Vent cover, or lock cover. 1 Percussion lock and 2 lanyards. 2 Lanyards for friction tubes. 1 Water bucket.	The same as for a gun, omitting *pass box*, and adding: 1 Haversack. 1 Fuze setter. 1 Fuze mallet. 1 Fuze extractor, to 6 pieces. 1 Quadrant. 1 Fuze saw. 1 Fuze gimlet.

FOR EACH MORTAR:

1 Sponge and rammer.
6 Handspikes—4 shod.
1 Linstock.
1 Haversack.
1 Tube pouch.
2 Priming wires.
1 Gunner's gimlet.
1 Quadrant.
1 Plummet.
2 Pointing wires.
2 Quoins.
1 Tompion.
1 Pair shell hooks.
1 Scraper.
1 Spatula.
1 Pair gunner's sleeves.
1 Wiper.
1 Fuze setter.
1 Mallet.
1 Fuze saw.
1 Fuze extractor, to 6 mortars.
1 Basket.
1 Broom.
1 Tarpaulin.

The implements for *shells* are not required for the stone mortar.

FOR EACH CASEMATE CARRIAGE: (including the spare carriages.)—2 Truck handspikes—2 Chocks—1 Broom.

FOR EACH BARBETTE CARRIAGE: 2 Manœuvring handspikes—1 Tarpaulin, or other cover—1 Platform and 1 maul; if the platform is not permanent.

FOR EACH SIEGE CARRIAGE: 4 Handspikes—1 Maul—1 Platform.

Spare Parts for repair of Carriages.

Proportion of the number of spare parts to that of similar parts which belong to the carriages:

Forks for traversing wheels of barbette carriages		1-20th.
Pintles for siege carriage limbers		1-30th.
Pintles for casemate carriages		1-20th.
Linch pins		1-5th..
Axletrees	for siege carriages	1-20th.
	for barbette carriages	1-40th.
	for casemate carriages	1-40th.
Rollers for casemate carriages		1-40th.
Bolster plates, for pintles not permanently fixed		1-40th.
Wheels	for siege carriages	1-15th.
	for barbette upper carriages, (including rollers,)	1-20th.
	for casemate do.	1-40th.
	for barbette chassis	1-40th.
	for casemate chassis	1-40th.
Axle washers,	shoulder	1-20th.
	linch	1-10th.
Poles, for siege carriage limbers, one-half ironed		1-4th..
Elevating screws		1-8th..
Tongues (iron) for casemate carriages		1-10th.
Nuts, assorted		1-10th.

Timber and other Materials for Repairs.

Cheeks, stocks, naves, spokes, fellies, for siege carriages; of each 1-20th—Cheeks of mortar beds, 1-12th. Handspikes, 4 to a piece—Tool handles, ½—Sets of timber for barbette carriages, 1-20th. Ditto, casemate, 1-40th—Iron assorted, 50 lbs. to each piece—Nails and screws assorted, 100 to each piece—Steel, 1 lb. to each piece—Sheet iron, 6 square feet to each piece—Tin, 5 sheets to each piece—Spare parts for small arms, see CHAP. VIII.

Machines, Ropes, &c.

Gins, casemate and rampart, as may be required, according to the extent of the fort—Screw Jacks—Capstans—Lever Jacks—Wheelbarrows, 1 to each piece—Handbarrow, for shells, 1 to each mortar—Sling handbarrow, or frame handbarrow with legs, 1 to 6 guns and howitzers—Platform balance, or scales and weights—Gin falls, 1-5th spare—Double prolonges, 2 to each gin—Drag ropes—$2\frac{1}{4}$ in. rope—Small rope, 5 lbs. to a piece—Handspikes, 7 feet long—Skids—Blocks—Rollers.

Tools.

Sets of carriage makers', smiths' and armorers' tools—Intrenching and miners' tools—Saws—Levels—Paviours' rammers—10-foot rods—2-foot rules—the number of each kind to be regulated by the particular circumstances of each case.

Tools and Materials for Fireworks.—See CHAPTER X.

Laboratory tools and materials, according to the extent and resources of the fort. See the proportion of those for a siege train.

For each night of a siege, or for each night on which the guns will probably be served, have 6 tarred links to each piece mounted on the ramparts of a front of attack, or of a sea-coast battery, and 5 fire balls for a front of attack—6 carcasses for each large mortar on a front of attack.

Signal rockets—Torches—Fire stone, &c.—according to circumstances.

Instruments, Books, and Stationery.

According to the character and extent of the fort—See *Siege Train.*

Miscellaneous Supplies.

Timber, plank, and boards—Wood for sabots, fascines, gabions, &c.—Pickets—Coal, 5 tons to a forge—Grease—Grindstones—Rampart grates, 2 to each piece on the ramparts—Sand bags, for the batteries of the front of attack—Lantern, 1 to each piece—Candles—Oil—Fire engine and buckets.

Field pieces, forming a part of the armament of a fortification, should be provided with their caissons, ammunition, &c., as for service in the field.

CHAPTER TWELFTH.

MECHANICAL MANŒUVRES.

A board of officers has been recently charged with revising and arranging the manœuvres of heavy ordnance; some general directions with regard to the mechanical manœuvres are retained here for present use.

FIELD ARTILLERY.

The manœuvres may be performed by the men attached to the piece, and require no other implements than those belonging to the piece.

Begin, in all cases, by unlimbering and taking off the implements attached to the carriage.

To change a Wheel.

Tighten the cap squares; raise the elevating screw to its whole height; raise the carriage by means of two handspikes, one in the bore of the piece, and the other crossed under the first; support the carriage whilst the wheel is changed. For the 12-pdr. carriage, dig a hole 6 in. deep under the wheel that is to remain, in order to prevent it from sliding.

To dismount a Piece.

Take off the cap-squares; run up the elevating screw to its whole height; raise the trail; stand the piece upon its muzzle on the ground, and withdraw the carriage.

To mount a Piece.

Put a handspike under the piece a little in rear of the rimbases, and another under the cascable; place 2 men at the first handspike, 4 at the second, and 2 at the handles, or, (if the piece has no handles,) 4 at each handspike, and raise the piece upon its muzzle; bring up the carriage, raise the trail, and put the piece in its place; put on the cap squares, and lower the trail, relieving the weight of the piece by raising the muzzle.

In this manœuvre and the preceding, it may be necessary, with the 12-pdr. and larger calibres, to make a hole in the ground for the muzzle.

When a piece is upset, separate it from its carriage and remount it as above.

To transport a Piece by means of the Limber.

Detach the prolonge ; place the limber over the piece so that the pintle hook shall be over the handles, (or over the rear of the trunnions,) with the breech toward the pole ; raise the pole, and elevate the muzzle of the piece ; lash the piece to the pintle hook, with the prolonge, by passing the ring of the prolonge twice through the handles, (or round the piece in rear of the trunnions,) and over the pintle hook ; with the loose end of the prolonge, lash the cascable to the fork of the limber.

Or, the gun may be placed on blocks at the proper height, and then lashed to the limber as before.

SIEGE ARTILLERY.

Implements.

6 *Handspikes;* 7 feet long.

1 *Lever;* 15 feet long, 5.5 in. square; the ends beveled.

1 *Lever jack;* or blocks for fulcrum.

3 *Short rollers,* for guns ; 12 inches long; 6 in. diameter for 12 and 18-pdrs.; 7 inches for 24-pdr. These rollers are hollowed out in the middle, to the depth of 0.25 in.

2 *Long rollers;* 42 inches long, 6 inches diameter.

1 *Small half roller;* 42 in. long, 3 in. diameter, 3 in. high.

1 *Large half roller;* 42 in. long, 6 in. diameter, 6 in. high.

2 *Skids;* 6 feet long, 8 inches square.

1 *Plank;* 67 in. long, 12 in. wide, 2.25 in. thick. The ends beveled on opposite sides.

4 *Blocks;* 20 in. long, 8 in. square.

4 *Half blocks;* 20 in. long, 8 in. wide, 4 in. thick.

2 *Quarter blocks;* pieces of plank, 20 in. long, 6 in. wide, 2 in. thick ; for manœuvre of mortar beds.

1 *Purchase block,* for a fulcrum ; 12.5 in. long, 7 in. wide, 5 in. thick, furnished with a handle 32 in. long, like a maul; a groove 1.75 in. wide and 1 in. deep is cut in one side and one end.

5 *Gun chocks;* wedges, 3.5 in. long, 2.75 in. wide, 2.5 in. high.

6 *Wheel chocks,* 7 in. long ; the cross section is triangular, base 6 in., height 3.25 in ; the upper angle rounded.

6 *Roller chocks;* made like the wheel chocks ; length 7 in., base 4 in., height 1.5 in.

2 *Long skids;* 15 feet long, 8 in. square; for rolling guns on.

1 *Hammer.*

1 *Wrench.*

Ropes.

1 *Double prolonge;* girth 3.25 in., length 78 feet; a loop 18 in. long at one end.

1 *Single prolonge;* girth 3 in., length 48 feet.

1 *Trace rope;* girth 2.25 in., length 30 feet.

1 *Lashing line;* girth 1.75 in., length 10 feet.

The prolonges used in the mechanical manœuvres with heavy pieces should be designated by their lengths, in order to distinguish them from those used for field service.

For the weight and strength of ropes, see CHAPTER XIV.

KNOTS; *Plate* 19.

A non-commissioned officer and 11 men are required for the manœuvres.

In order to avoid accidents, the functions of each man should be designated beforehand.

Preliminary Manœuvres.

IMPLEMENTS: 6 handspikes—1 lever jack—1 gun roller—1 small half roller—1 large half roller—4 blocks—2 half blocks—1 purchase block—2 gun chocks—4 roller chocks—6 wheel chocks.

1. *The gun being on the ground, to place blocks under the chase and reinforce.* Embar with four handspikes, two on each side, and raise first the chase and then the breech, to place the blocks.

To take them out, embar as before and remove the block from the breech first.

2. *The gun resting on two blocks, to place the half roller under the reinforce.* Place two blocks parallel to the piece, and by two purchases with the *lever,* under the knob of the cascable, raise the breech and lay the large half roller across these blocks The half roller is taken out by heaving as above, and the breech is supported by a block.

3. *The gun being mounted on its carriage and in the trunnion holes, either limbered or unlimbered, to place a roller under the reinforce, or to remove it:* Bear down on the muzzle; place or remove the roller.

4. *The gun being in the travelling position, and limbered up, to place a roller under the reinforce, or to remove it.* Heave under the base ring, with two handspikes supported on the purchase block, laid on the stock of the carriage; raise the breech, and place the roller, or remove it.

To place this roller nearer the centre of gravity of the piece; take a second purchase with the handspikes, supported on the small half roller laid on the purchase block. This roller is removed by raising the breech as above.

5. *The piece being in the trunnion holes, to unlimber.* Unhook the lashing chain; raise the trail by means of a handspike placed across under it, assisting the movement by bearing on a handspike inserted in the bore. When the pintle is disengaged, remove the limber and lower the trail to the ground.

6. *To limber up.* Raise the trail as before; back the limber, insert the pintle in the pintle hole, and hook the lashing chain.

7. *The piece being in the travelling position, to unlimber.* Bear down on the pole which will raise the stock sufficiently high to place 4 blocks and a half block under the middle of the stock; raise the pole to disengage the pintle and remove the limber.

To lower the trail on the ground. Take a purchase with the lever under the trail, shift the blocks under the manœuvring bolts, remove successively at each purchase a half block, or a block, as the lever will allow, and lay a chock in place of the lowest block, which can be removed with a lift of the lever, or with handspikes.

In the mortar wagon, first raise the pole, and lay a half roller on the end of the *fork* against the pintle; on lowering the pole, the stock is raised sufficiently to place the blocks as above.

8. *To limber up.* The trail is raised on four blocks and a half block by successive purchases with the lever, as in lowering it; placing a block or half block at each heave, as the lift will allow.

To change a piece from the Trunnion Holes to the Travelling Position.

Required: 11 men—6 handspikes—1 gun roller—1 small half roller—1 purchase block—2 gun chocks—4 roller chocks—6 wheel chocks—1 trace rope.

The carriage must be limbered up, or the trail raised upon 3 blocks and a half block.

Chock the wheels; depress the muzzle; remove the elevating screw, and place a roller under the reinforce.

Lift the muzzle, pushing the piece back, hauling at the same time on the trace rope attached to the knob of the cascable, until the trunnions come over their position. Remove the roller, and lower the breech on the bolster.

To change a piece from its Travelling Position to the Trunnion Holes.

The carriage being limbered up, or the trail resting on 4 blocks and 1 half block.

Place a roller under the reinforce as near as possible to the rimbases.

Raise the chase, and let the gun run forwards to its position, checking it with the trace rope attached to the knob of the cascable. As soon as the trunnions pass over the chin bolts, depress the muzzle, and the trunnions drop into their holes

Remove the roller, and put in the elevating screw.

To Change a Wheel.

11 Men—1 lever jack—2 wheel chocks.

Chock the wheel which is to remain; raise the carriage by means of the lever jack applied in front of the axletree, and support it until the wheel is changed.

To Mount a Piece on its Carriage.

11 Men—6 handspikes—1 lever and blocks (or a lever jack,)—1 gun roller—1 small half roller—1 large half roller—2 skids—4 blocks—4 half blocks—1 purchase block—2 gun chocks—4 roller chocks—6 wheel chocks—1 trace rope.

The gun resting on two blocks, bring up the carriage unlimbered, in line with it, the trail 2 yards from the muzzle: Place the large half roller in rear of the rimbases, resting it on the two skids; raise the chase by a handspike placed across under the neck, and run the carriage back until the swell of the muzzle rests on the bolster.—With the lever jack, raise the breech and place two blocks on the skids, one under each end of the large half roller. Lift the chase, and run back the carriage until the bolster touches the half roller; take a purchase under the breech, and continue to raise it until two half blocks are placed under each end of the half roller. Lift the muzzle, by inserting a handspike in it, and run back the carriage until the rear ends of the cheeks touch the half roller, and the trunnions are over their travelling position. Raise the trail with the lever, and remove the 4 blocks and a half block to the trail under the position of the manœuvring bolts. Lift the chase and insert a gun roller by the front as far as the half roller; depress the muzzle, to make the piece bear on the roller. Change the piece to the trunnion holes.

To Dismount a Piece.

The same implements required as for mounting it. Lift the trail by a handspike across under it, and support it on 3 blocks and a half block, under the manœuvring bolts.

Change the piece over the travelling trunnion bolts, and when the roller is removed, place the large half roller on the stock against the rear of the cheeks. Take a purchase under the trail, with the lever jack, and remove the blocks to the skids, placing 2 blocks and 2 half blocks on each skid under the ends of the half roller; as the trail comes to the ground, the ends bear on these blocks. Raise the muzzle, and run out the carriage until the muzzle, resting on the stock, is within 6 in. of the rear end of the cheeks. Raise the breech, and lower the half roller by a block on each side. Lift the muzzle and run out the carriage, until the swell of the muzzle rests on the bolster. Raise the breech and remove 1 block and 1 half block: lift the muzzle, remove the carriage, and let the muzzle rest on a block; take out the half roller and leave the piece on 2 blocks.

NOTE.—The manœuvre of mounting a gun may also be performed expeditiously, without the use of the lever jack, by raising the muzzle and the breech, in succession, and placing two sets of blocks under the piece, near the trunnions, until it is raised so as to rest on two skids, with four blocks and a large half roller in each set. In this position, by bearing down the muzzle and removing the rear set of blocks, the carriage, limbered up, may be run under the breech; a roller is then placed on the stock, and the gun is hauled back, with a rope attached to the knob of the cascable, until the trunnions are over the trunnion holes. Remove the front set of blocks and the roller, and lower the piece into its place.

This method requires 10 additional blocks, 20 inches long, 8 inches square.

The gun may be dismounted in like manner, by an inverse manœuvre.

To change a Carriage.

11 men—6 handspikes—3 gun rollers—1 small half roller—a plank with beveled ends—2 gun chocks—6 roller chocks—6 wheel chocks.

The carriage with the gun being unlimbered, bring up the new carriage limbered up, in line with the first; the head of its cheeks two yards from the trail of the other carriage. Place a gun roller under the reinforce of the gun, and lift up the muzzle, to raise the trunnions from the trunnion holes, into which insert the lower end of two handspikes, and let the trunnions rest on them. Run up the new carriage, over the stock of the first, until the wheels touch, taking care that they are in the same line. Slide the plank forwards between the cheeks, until it bears upon the heads of both stocks, and wedge one of the gun rollers on the stock of the first carriage, so that it will support the plank if the weight of the gun causes it to spring; place a roller on the plank near the rimbases, and make the trace rope fast to the knob of the cascable. Lift and push at the muzzle; haul on the rope, placing a second roller under and near the base ring, and let it clear the plank and rest on the stock, touching the plank, when the trunnions are over the chin bolts.

Take two or three turns with the rope around the manœuvring bolts, and hold taut on the rope. Raise the muzzle; take out the front roller by the head of the cheeks, and run the first carriage forward, lifting the muzzle and letting it rest on the stock as the carriage is moved off gradually. The trunnions will bear on the rear edges of the trunnion holes. When the first carriage is out of the way, remove the plank by the front, and insert a handspike in the muzzle; raise and work it, slacking off the rope at the same time sufficiently to let the trunnions drop into their places. Put in the elevating screw; remove the roller and rope, and put on the cap squares.

To place upon a Mortar Wagon a Mortar on its bed.

11 Men—6 handspikes—2 long rollers—1 block—2 half blocks—4 roller chocks—6 wheel chocks—2 quarter blocks—1 single prolonge.

The mortar being on its bed, the mortar wagon unlimbered is placed in the prolongation of the axis of the bed, the trail two yards from the rear of the bed. Place the quarter blocks under the heads of the cheeks; lift the rear of the bed by handspikes at the rear notches, and place a handspike under it, or support it by the half blocks under the cheeks. Use the block, with chocks on it, as a fulcrum; take a purchase under the rear part of the transom and lift it, placing a roller under the middle of the bed, its ends resting on the two half blocks. Run the wagon back, the stock under the middle of the bed; place the second roller on the stock above the nuts of the pintle plate bolts. Double the prolonge, and hook the middle of it on the hooks of the windlass; take a turn with each end round the windlass and carry the ends to the rear manœuvring bolts; take a turn round each and make the ends fast. Heave at the windlass; when the roller on the half blocks is free, replace it under the ends of the cheeks, as the mortar rises on the wagon, and draw it up until the rear ends of the cheeks touch the rear cross bar plate. The roller will be in front of the centre of gravity, and the ends of the cheeks will touch the bottom boards. Limber up. Take the rope from the roller; carry the bight to the front, draw the mortar forward to its proper position. By a purchase under the transom, with two handspikes, remove the roller and lower the bed on a handspike. Take a second purchase, with half blocks for supports, under the rear notches of the cheeks; remove the handspike, and let the mortar down on the wagon.

The Mortar on the Mortar Wagon, to lower it to the ground.

The same implements. Place the roller under the bed, by raising it in the same manner as for removing the roller. Fix the rope to the windlass and take as many turns round it as are required for drawing the mortar up. Attach the ends to the rear manœuvring bolts ; work the windlass and draw the mortar back, till the rear ends of the cheeks touch the rear cross bar. Unlimber. Lower away by unwinding the windlass, placing a second roller under the head of the cheeks, as the first passes the centre of gravity ; and when the latter is free, place it under the head of the cheeks, when they come near the two half blocks laid on each side of the trail. When the ropes no longer bear, take them off of the bolts. Place the quarter blocks under the head of the cheeks, and run the bed forward with handspikes, as into battery. Remove the wagon ; and by raising the rear of the bed, as at first, take out the roller and let the bed rest on the ground.

To mount a Siege Mortar on its Bed.

4 Handspikes ; 1 single prolonge ; 1 hammer ; 1 wrench.

Raise the mortar on its muzzle ; bring up the bed, the front transom within 6 in. of the mortar, the vent of which should be on the side opposite to the bed. Take a double turn with the middle of the rope round the mortar, close to the muzzle ring, the tie in front ; bring the ends up over the trunnions, and carry them to the rear. Place two handspikes under the trunnions, the lower ends resting on the platform, or on the ground. Heave and haul the mortar against the bolster ; place 1 handspike under each trunnion, the ends resting on the bolster, and two other handspikes between the heads of the cheeks and the mortar. Heave and haul, to raise the mortar on the bolster. As soon as it is sufficiently raised, shift one of the handspikes from under the piece to the bore ; heave again, and the mortar will fall into its place.

Remove the rope and put on the cap squares.

To put on or to remove the cap squares, it is necessary *to bring the mortar into a vertical position*. To do this, place 2 handspikes in the muzzle, and support them by a wheel chock or a piece of plank ; fasten the middle of the rope to the ends of the handspikes, and haul on the rope, assisted by two handspikes, with which the mortar is chocked, when it becomes upright.

To dismount a Mortar from its Bed.

Bring the mortar vertical as above described, and remove the cap squares ; take the handspikes out of the bore ; pass the middle of the rope around the mortar, just under the muzzle ring, and carry the ends to the rear; give a smart haul on the rope, assisted by two handspikes, and the mortar will fall over the transom and light on its muzzle.

A mortar standing on its face may be moved (cut) by means of two handspikes lashed to the trunnions.

The mortar wagon also serves for transporting a gun, which is drawn up on rollers, breech first, in a similar manner to the mortar and bed.

The piece can be shifted very quickly from this wagon to its carriage, both being limbered. The carriage and wagon are placed on the same line; the head of the cheeks next to the windlass, the wheels touching. Place 2 large rollers under the piece, and a gun roller on the head of the stock; make the middle of the trace rope fast to the knob of the cascable, and run the piece back until the trunnions are over the trunnion holes. Remove the wagon, and lower the trunnions into their holes. In a similar manner, the gun is changed from its carriage to the wagon.

The lifting jack, (a powerful geared screw jack,) is very useful with siege batteries. It may be used in place of the lever jack with fewer men, but requires more time. For any single operation, it is extremely convenient; as, with it, any part of a gun or carriage can be raised.

To Transport a Piece with a Sling Cart.

1st. *With the common sling cart.* 10 Men—1 piece of 5-in. rope—1 double prolonge, or 2 single ones—4 chocks for wheels—6 handspikes.

The piece being raised from the ground on blocks, bring up the sling cart over the piece, the breech towards the pole; raise the pole vertically, by hand and by means of a prolonge attached to the end of it, and keep it in that position by passing a handspike on each side of it between the spokes of the wheels. Sling the piece with the rope passed under it before and behind the trunnions, and over the bolster; take out the handspikes from between the spokes and lower the pole by means of the prolonge and by hand; lash the breech to it, and bring up the limber.

2nd. *With the screw sling cart.* 4 Men, with lashing ropes. The sling cart being in place, sling the gun with a rope or with chains passing under it and fastened to the hooks of the screw head, or with chains furnished with rings to embrace the trunnions. Raise the piece by turning the handles of the screw nut, and when it is sufficiently high, lash the load to the bolster and pole, so as to relieve the pressure on the screw. The manœuvre is easy but slow, and the machinery must be kept in good order. The piece may be slung more quickly by blocking it up as high as the axletree will permit.

To Move a Piece by Hand in the Trenches.

40 Men—8 handspikes—1 double prolonge—2 half prolonges, or men's harness.

The piece is on its carriage, without the limber, and may be moved with either the breech or the muzzle foremost. The first method is a little more expeditious, but, in turning sharp angles, it is attended with more danger to the men who support the trail. The second method is preferable. Double the double prolonge, or attach two single prolonges to the axletree; make loops in each part for 5 handspikes, the first under the chase, the others at 3 feet apart; put 4 men at each handspike; 4 behind the trail with handspikes; the rest on the sides, to push the wheels, and if necessary, to drag on them, as described in the next manœuvre: some of the men at the prolonge leave it to drag on the wheels; in short turnings, those who are at the first handspikes fall back to the others.

To extricate a Piece that is mired.

The number of men in proportion to the difficulty—2 prolonges—handspikes.

Attach a prolonge by one end to one of the lower spokes of each wheel, and bring the other end round to the front, over the tire. The men drag on the prolonges directly, or on the handspikes passed through loops in them.

GARRISON ARTILLERY.

To lower, from its Chassis, a Barbette Carriage with its Piece mounted.

This carriage can transport its piece with the assistance of the limber of a field piece, from which the ammunition box is removed—18 men are required to remove a 24-pdr.—4 handspikes—1 large block—2 skids—2 short pieces of skidding.

The piece being in battery, lower the elevating screw a little; chock the rollers behind; pass a handspike through the manœuvring loop at the end of the tongue; place two men at each end of this handspike, and two at each end of another passed under the tongue. Raise the chassis, take out the forks and traverse wheels, and lay them on the ground; lower the rear of the chassis on the traversing platform. Put a skid or plank on each side of the chassis, raised on blocks at one end, so that it nearly touches the wheel. Roll the carriage back till the wheels rest upon this skid and the muzzle clears the parapet about three or four feet; put a handspike in the bore, another across the top of the chase, a third through the manœuvring staples, and a fourth under the lunette plate; place two men at the first handspike, and four at each of the three others; raise the trail of the carriage, and place a block under the rear transom. Back up the limber and insert the pintle hook into the lunette. Lighten up the trail, to remove the block; key the pintle hook, and lower the elevating screw. All the men working at the wheels of the carriage and limber, and at the pole, lower the piece gently from the platform. Horses may then be attached to the limber, if necessary.

To raise on its Chassis a Barbette Carriage with its Piece mounted.

The same number of men and the same implements as in the preceding manœuvre. The chassis having been lowered, as in the first part of the preceding manœuvre, bring the carriage up to the rear of the platform and place opposite to each wheel a plank resting on two blocks, making a gentle slope to roll the carriage up on the traversing platform—place skids as before on each side of the chassis—move the carriage forward until the rollers nearly rest upon the rails—run up the elevating screw—lighten up the trail, to disengage the pintle hook—remove the limber, and lower the lunette plate on a block placed upon the tongue—raise the trail again, to remove the block—lower the trail transom upon the tongue—run the carriage up to battery—replace the traverse wheels in the same manner as directed for taking them out, in the preceding manœuvre.

In situations where it may be required, the carriage can be used without its chassis; in this manner it may be applied to the embrasures of field works, by placing it in battery on a common platform for a siege piece, and resting the trail on a skid attached to the front hurter by a pintle. The rear of this skid may rest on a block so as to give it the same inclination as the tongue of the chassis.

To place a Casemate Carriage in Battery and mount its Gun.

14 to 16 Men required. The gun is brought to the casemate with the sling cart, and carried through the galleries on a truck.

The carriage for the embrasure farthest from the door of entrance is to be placed first, and its gun mounted before the next carriage is placed. The tongue of the chassis is inserted into the tongue hole, and the pintle in its hole, through the end of the tongue.

The top carriage is lifted by hand and placed on the chassis, which is traversed on one side, and the gun is laid near the middle of the casemate on blocks, the muzzle towards the embrasure. The casemate gin (legs 14 feet long) is placed over the carriage and gun; the legs and the roller over the gun, the pry-pole over the chassis. The gin is equipped and the gun slung in the usual manner. When the gun is raised sufficiently high, the chassis is traversed under it, and the upper carriage so placed that the trunnion holes come exactly under the trunnions of the gun, which is then lowered carefully to its place. Unsling the gun and remove the gin.

MANŒUVRES OF THE FIELD AND SIEGE GIN.

10 Men, including a non-commissioned officer as director—5 handspikes—1 gin fall—2 lines—a number of pulley blocks, single or double, according to the manner in which the gin is to be equipped.

The gin fall is 4-in. rope, 90 feet long.

To put the Gin together.

Lay the legs on the ground, the outer sides up, the bevels towards each other; place the windlass; connect the heads of the cheeks by the assembling bolt; and insert successively the 1st, 2nd, and 3d cross bars, and key them.

To carry the Gin.

Put six men at the legs, viz., 2 abreast of the windlass, 2 abreast of the second cross bar, and 2 near the head; 2 men, with a handspike, carry the fall coiled up, with the blocks hooked to it; one man carries the prypole, another the remaining handspikes and the lines.

To set up the Gin.

6 Men, placed in the same manner as for carrying the gin, set it up; 2 men place their feet against the bottom of the legs, or their handspikes against the lower cross bar; one sets up the prypole, two paces in front of the head of the gin, facing it. The director assists by putting the end of a handspike into the slit for the tongue of the prypole. When the prypole is in place, the foot of it should be equally distant from the two legs, 12 feet from the lower cross bar; the pullies should be over the middle of the weight to be raised.

To equip the Gin.

The gin equipped with one pulley, can raise a 12-pounder garrison gun; with 2, an 18-pounder; with 3, a 24-pounder; with 5 or 6, a 32 or 42-pounder. It is generally proper to use more pulleys than are absolutely necessary, in order to avoid straining the fall.

1st. *To equip the gin with 1 pulley.* Pass one end of the fall over the windlass, and take three turns from left to right, the loose end being outside. Put a handspike in one of the mortises of the windlass, or let down the pall, if there is one; overhaul the fall, letting it wrap round the windlass; pass the end through the right hand pulley of the head, and secure it to the sling round the gun by a capstan knot.

2nd. *With 2 pulleys.* Hang a single block on the second cross bar, the point of the hook outwards; proceed as in the first case; pass the end of the fall through the block on the cross bar, and tie it round the head of the gin, the loose end of the rope hanging on the left side and pinched against the leg. Hook the block to the sling round the gun, the point of the hook towards the left side of the gin.

3d. *With* 3 *pulleys*. Proceed as for two; pass the end of the fall through the left hand pulley at the head of the gin, from the outside; tie it to the sling on the side towards the prypole, and hook the block to it on the other side, the point inwards.

4th. *With* 4 *pulleys*. Hang a second block (or a double block) on the second cross bar. Proceed as in the last case; pass the end of the fall into the second block, and fasten it to the head of the gin as in the second case; hook both blocks to the sling, the points of the hooks inwards.

If a double block is used, place the pin perpendicular to the cross bar, the head towards the prypole; pass the fall the first time through the sheave next the prypole, the second time through that next the legs; hook the block to the sling, the point towards the left side of the gin.

5th. *With* 5 *pulleys*. Hang two single blocks, or a double block, on the second cross bar; fasten a third block to the head of the gin, on the left side, by a collar or coil of rope; the point of the hook being outwards, and the head of the pin towards the gin. Proceed as in the last case; pass the end of the fall into the third block, and fasten the end to the sling round the piece, to which the blocks are also to be hooked.

6th. *With* 6 *pulleys*. Fix a single block to the head of the gin, another on the second cross bar near the right leg, and a double block on the same cross bar near the left leg. Proceed as in the last case; pass the fall through the single block on the cross bar, and secure it to the head of the gin, the loose end of the rope hanging on the left side, and the third block hooked into the knot. Hook the double block and the other single block to the sling.

The man who directs the manœuvres, or the most intelligent man, should be charged with passing the fall through the pullies at the head of the gin, and with tying the knots, fixing slings, &c. If he is too much exposed by mounting on the third cross bar, the gin must be laid down, the head resting on the gun, and equipped in that position.

To lay the gin down, the men are placed in the same positions as for setting it up. If the gin has a clevis at the top, the fall may be reeved in the blocks, and the upper block then hooked to the clevis.

To Sling a Piece.

A piece without handles may be slung by means of a rope, the two ends of which are tied together and which is passed under the piece, one-half before and the other behind the trunnions.

If this is not convenient, as when the gun lies on the ground, or is to be placed on its carriage, a sling may be made by splicing together the ends of a 5-inch hawser a little more than twice the length of the piece (about 26 feet) or by passing a strong rope several times, according to the weight, over the piece lengthwise, under the cascable and under the handspike or a block of wood inserted in the muzzle. The two sides of this sling may be brought together by another just behind the trunnions.

To Work the Gin.

4 Men put their handspikes alternately, 2 by 2, in the mortises of the windlass; 2 others assist in heaving; 3 overhaul the slack of the rope; the non-commissioned officer or director steadies the piece or the load, by means of a guy or of a handspike in the bore.

To make fast. If the gin has no ratchet wheel and pall, put a handspike across the legs, and let the heaving handspikes in the mortises rest against it; cross the slack round the turns on the windlass, drawing it tight round the last turn, and pass it under the lower cross bar from the inside, tying it in a loop in which the point of a handspike is inserted; during this operation, one man bears with both hands on the turns round the windlass, to prevent the rope from slipping. The men and 4 handspikes are then no longer required.

To shift the rope on the windlass. When the turns on the windlass, commencing at the left, reach the other end, make fast with the handspikes resting as before. Tie a lashing line to the fall with an artificer's knot, 1 foot above the second cross bar; wrap both ends of the line several times round the fall and pass it round the leg, under the cross bar, lashing the fall and the cross bar together. Let the windlass turn so as to bring the weight to bear on the lashing line; then slip the rope to the left end of the windlass.

The gin may be worked, if necessary, by less than 10 men. The men at the slack may be saved by equipping the gin without taking the 3 turns on the windlass; pass the fall over the windlass, and bring it round underneath, placing the slack across the windlass, so that the fall may coil over it. By steadying the piece with a rope attached to the prypole and to one leg, and by equipping the gin with a greater number of blocks, 3 men may work it, 2 holding the handspikes, and the 3d assisting them alternately.

To use the Gin as a Derrick.

12 Men, 2 being for the guys. Additional implements: 1 double prolonge, or 2 single ones—4 strong pickets, 4 or 5 feet long—2 mauls—and sometimes a second fall and a drag rope.

If the derrick is to be established on a parapet, or on earth which is not firm, lay a strong plank across two others, with holes in the first for the points of the feet; ram the earth about them and secure them with pickets.

Lay the gin down, the outer side underneath, and the feet of the legs resting on a skid.

The director steps 5 paces from the head of the gin, in a direction perpendicular to the cross bars, and then 4 paces to the right and left, where he marks the places for the two first pickets; the two others are placed 30 feet beyond the first, in the direction which the guys will take.

Drive the pickets inclining off from the gin; if necessary, strengthen them by putting a plank or a fascine behind each, and ramming the earth firmly about it.

Equip the gin as it lies; fasten the guys to the head of it with an artificer's knot, if they are formed of one rope; with German knots, if of two. The gin being raised almost vertically, 2 men take a turn of the guys around the first pickets, and the director makes them fast to the second pickets with an artificer's knot. Let down the fall and tackles, and prepare to work the windlass. On a parapet, the feet of the derrick should be 2 feet from the exterior crest; as the guys, by stretching, are apt to give the derrick too great an inclination, place it at first 4 feet from the crest, and after taking a few turns, let the load down again, and move the derrick to its proper place.

If the fall should not be long enough, join another to it by a flat knot, tied at 4 or 5 yards from the end of the second rope, passing a piece of round wood, of the size of a tool handle, through the knot, to prevent its tightening too much. The first fall passes only through the right hand pulley of the head of the derrick and over the windlass; when the knot comes up near the pulley, cease heaving and make fast; coil a drag rope round the head of the gin and tie it to the second fall by 5 or 6 loops, below the knot. Let go the windlass and bring the weight to bear on the drag rope. Undo the knot, and pass the end of the second fall through the pulley; take 3 turns with it round the windlass, and join the first fall to it, to lengthen the slack.

GARRISON AND CASEMATE GINS.

The fall for these gins is 5-inch rope, 120 feet long. They are equipped with a pair of blocks adapted to receive such a number of ropes as may be necessary, according to the weight to be raised; the upper block being hung on the clevis at the head of the gin. They are worked like the field and siege gin.

CHAPTER THIRTEENTH.

ARTILLERY PRACTICE.

The plan of this work does not include the details relative to the service of artillery, either in the field or in garrison; but in the absence of more full and accurate tables of firing, it is thought useful to give here the mean results of such trials of the ranges of our ordnance as have been made, from time to time, by the Ordnance Department, together with some other practical information derived from authentic sources.

Ranges of Field Guns and Howitzers.

The range of a shot or shell in this table is the first graze of the ball on horizontal ground, the piece being mounted on its appropriate field carriage.

The range of a spherical case shot is the distance at which the shot bursts near the ground, in the time given; thus showing the elevation and the length of fuze required for certain distances.

For the range of the Mountain Howitzer—see CHAP. VI.

KIND OF ORDNANCE.	Powder.	Ball.	Elevation.	Range.	REMARKS.
	Lbs.		° ′	Yards.	
6-PDR. FIELD GUN.	1.25	Shot	0	318	
		"	1	674	
		"	2	867	
		"	3	1138	
		"	4	1256	
		"	5	1523	
	1.	Sph. case shot.	2	650	Time of flight 2 secs.
			2 30	840	" 3 "
		"	3	1050	" 4 "

Ranges of Field Guns and Howitzers.

KIND OF ORDNANCE.	Powder.	Ball.	Elevation.	Range.	REMARKS.
	Lbs.		° ′	Yards.	
12-PDR. FIELD GUN.	2.5	Shot	0	347	
		"	1	662	
		"	1 30	785	
		"	2	909	
		"	3	1269	
		"	4	1455	
		"	5	1663	
	1.5	Sph.case.	1	670	Time 2 seconds.
		"	1 45	950	" 3 "
		"	2 30	1250	" 4 "
12-PDR. FIELD HOWITZER	1.	Shell	0	195	
		"	1	539	
		"	2	640	
		"	3	847	
		"	4	975	
		"	5	1072	
	0.75	Sph. case	2 15	485	Time 2 seconds.
		"	3 15	715	" 3 "
		"	3 45	1050	" 4 "
24-PDR. FIELD HOWITZER	2.	Shell	0	295	
		"	1	516	
		"	2	793	
		"	3	976	
		"	4	1272	
		"	5	1322	
	1.75	Sph. case	2	600	Time 2 seconds.
		"	3	800	" 3 "
		"	5 30	1050	" 4 "
	2.	"	3 30	880	" 3 "
32-PDR. FIELD HOWITZER	2.5	Shell	0	290	
		"	1	531	
		"	2	779	
		"	3	1029	
		"	4	1203	
		"	5	1504	
	2.5	Sph. case	3	800	Time 2.75 seconds.

Ranges of Heavy Ordnance.

The *range* of a gun or howitzer in this table is the first graze of the ball on the horizontal plane on which the carriage stands.

KIND OF ORDNANCE.	Powder.	Ball.	Elevation	Range.	REMARKS.
	Lbs.		° ′	Yards.	
18-PDR. SIEGE AND GARRISON GUN. On barbette carriage.	4.5	Shot	1	641	
		"	2	950	
		"	3	1256	
		"	4	1450	
		"	5	1592	
24-PDR. SIEGE AND GARRISON GUN. On siege carriage.	6.	Shot	0	412	
		"	1	842	
		"	1 30	953	
		"	2	1147	
		"	3	1417	
		"	4	1666	
		"	5	1901	
	8.	"	1	883	
		"	2	1170	
		"	3	1454	
		"	4	1639	
		"	5	1834	
32-PDR. SEA-COAST GUN. On barbette carriage.	6.	Shot	1 45	900	
	8.	"	1	713	
		"	1 30	800	
		"	1 35	900	
		"	2	1100	
		"	3	1433	
		"	4	1684	
		"	5	1922	
	10.67	"	1	780	
		"	2	1155	
		"	3	1517	
42-PDR. SEA-COAST GUN. On barbette carriage.	10.5	Shot	1	775	
		"	2	1010	
		"	3	1300	
		"	4	1600	
		"	5	1955	
	14.	"	1	770	
		"	2	1128	
		"	3	1380	
		"	4	1687	
		"	5	1915	

Ranges of Heavy Ordnance.

KIND OF ORDNANCE.	Powder.	Ball.	Elevation.	Range	REMARKS.
	Lbs.	Shell	° ′	Yards.	
8-INCH SIEGE HOWITZER. On siege carriage.	4.	45 lbs.	0	251	
		"	1	435	
		"	2	618	
		"	3	720	
		"	4	992	
		"	5	1241	
		"	12 30	2280	
		Shell			
8-INCH SEA-COAST HOWITZER. On barbette carriage.	4.	45 lbs.	1	405	
		"	2	652	
		"	3	875	
		"	4	1110	
		"	5	1300	
	6.	"	1	572	
		"	2	828	
		"	3	947	
		"	4	1168	
		"	5	1463	
	8.	"	1	646	
		"	2	909	
		"	3	1190	
		"	4	1532	
		"	5	1800	
		Shell			
10-INCH SEA-COAST HOWITZER. On barbette carriage.	12.	90 lbs.	1	580	
		"	2	891	Time, flight 3. sec.
		"	3	1185	" " 4. "
		"	3 30	1300	
		"	4	1426	" " 5.25 "
		"	5	1650	" " 6. "
		Shot			
8-INCH COLUMBIAD. On barbette carriage.	10.	65 lbs.	1	932	Axis of gun 16 feet above the water.
		"	2	1116	
		"	3	1402	
		"	4	1608	
		"	5	1847	
		"	6	2010	
		"	8	2397	Shot ceased to ricochet on the water.
		"	10	2834	
		"	15	3583	
		"	20	4322	
		"	25	4875	
		"	27	4481	
	15.	"	27 30	4812	

Ranges of Heavy Ordnance.

KIND OF ORDNANCE.	Powder.	Ball.	Elevation.	Range.	REMARKS.
8-INCH COLUMBIAD—Continued.	Lbs.	Shell	° ′	Yards.	
	10.	50 lbs.	1	919	
		"	2	1209	
		"	3	1409	
		"	4	1697	
		"	5	1813	
		"	6	1985	
		"	8	2203	
		"	10	2657	
		"	15	3556	
		"	20	3716	
		"	25	4387	
		"	27	4171	
	15.	"	27 30	4468	
10-INCH COLUMBIAD. On barbette carriage.	18.	Shot	0	394	Axis of gun 16 feet above the water.
		128 lbs.	1	752	
		"	2	1002	
		"	3	1230	
		"	4	1570	
		"	5	1814	
		"	6	2037	Shot ceased to ricochet on water.
		"	8	2519	
		"	10	2777	
		"	15	3525	
		"	20	4020	
		"	25	4304	
		"	30	4761	
		"	35	5433	
	20.	"	39 15	5654	
	12.	Shell	1	800	
		100 lbs.	2	1012	
		"	3	1184	
		"	4	1443	
		"	5	1604	
	18.	"	0	448	
		"	1	747	
		"	2	1100	
		"	3	1239	
		"	4	1611	
		"	5	1865	
		"	6	2209	
		"	8	2489	
		"	10	2848	
		"	15	3200	
		"	20	3885	
		"	25	4150	
		"	30	4651	
		"	35	4828	Time of flight 35 sec.

Ranges of Heavy Ordnance.

KIND OF ORDNANCE.	Powder.	Ball.	Elevation.	Range.	REMARKS.
	Lbs.	Shell,	° ′	Yards.	
12-INCH COLUMBIAD....	20.	172 lbs.	10	2770	Time of flight 11 sec.
		"	15	3731	" 16 "
		"	22	4280	" 20 "
		"	25	4718	" 26 "
		"	30	5004	
		"	35	5339	" 32 "
		"	37	5266	" 31 "
		"	39	5064	
	25.	"	10	2881	" 11.5 "
		"	15	3542	" 15 "
		"	30	5102	
		"	35	5409	" 32 "
		"	37	5373	" 32 "
		"	39	5506	" 36 "
		Shell,	35	5644	
		180 lbs.	39	5615	
	28.	"	35	5671	
		"	39	5761	$3\frac{1}{3}$ miles. Time 36 sec.
13-IN. SEA-COAST MORTAR	20.	Shell, 200 lbs.	45	4325	
12-IN. SEA-COAST MORTAR	20.	Shell, 200 lbs.	45	4625	Experimental.
10-IN. SEA-COAST MORTAR	10.	Shell, 98 lbs.	45	4250	Time of flight 36 sec.
10-INCH SIEGE MORTAR..	1.	Shell,	45	300	Time of flight 6.5 sec.
	1.5	90 lbs.	45	700	" 12 "
	2.	"	45	1000	" 14 "
	2.5	"	45	1300	" 16 "
	3.	"	45	1600	" 18 "
	3.5	"	45	1800	" 19 "
	4.	"	45	2100	" 21 "
	Lbs. oz.	Shell,			
8-INCH SIEGE MORTAR. (From Griffith's Artillerist's Manual.)	0 $10\frac{3}{4}$	46 lbs.	45	500	Time of flight 10 sec.
	$13\frac{3}{4}$	"	"	600	" 11 "
	1	"	"	750	" $12\frac{1}{4}$ "
	1 2	"	"	900	" 13 "
	1 $3\frac{1}{2}$	"	"	1000	" $13\frac{1}{2}$ "
	1 $4\frac{3}{4}$	"	"	1100	" 14 "
	1 6	"	"	1200	" $14\frac{1}{2}$ "

Ranges of Heavy Ordnance.

KIND OF ORDNANCE.	Powder.	Ball.	Elevation.	Range.	REMARKS.
	Oz.	Shell,	°	Yards.	
24-POUNDER COEHORN MORTAR.	0.5	17 lbs.	45	25	
	1.	"	"	68	
	1.5	"	"	104	
	1.75	"	"	143	
	2.	"	"	165	
	2.75	"	"	260	
	4.	"	"	422	
	6.	"	"	900	
	8.	"	"	1200	

Ranges of Hale's War Rockets.

ELEVATION.	RANGE, (FIRST GRAZE.)		REMARKS.
	$2\frac{1}{4}$-inch.	$3\frac{1}{4}$-inch.	
	Yards.	Yards.	
4° to 5°	500 to 600	500 to 600	The rockets were fired from a trough 10 feet long.
8°	700	800 to 1000	
10°	800 to 900	1000 to 1200	
15°	1200	1200 to 1400	Weight of $2\frac{1}{4}$-inch rocket, 6 lbs.
47°	1760	2200	" $3\frac{1}{4}$-inch " 16 lbs.

INITIAL VELOCITIES OF CANNON BALLS.

From experiments made with the ballistic pendulum, at Washington Arsenal.

Kind of Ordnance.	PROJECTILE.		Charge of powder.	Initial velocity.
	Kind.	Weight.		
		Lbs.	Lbs.	Feet.
6-pdr. field gun.	Shot.......	6.15	1.25	1439
			1.5	1563
			2.	1741
	Sph. case...	5.5	1.	1357
	Canister....	6.8	1.	1230
12-pdr. field gun.	Shot.......	12.3	2.5	1486
			3.	1597
			4.	1826
	Sph. case...	11.	2.	1392
	Canister....	13.5	2.	1262

Initial Velocities—Continued.

Kind of Ordnance.	PROJECTILE.		Charge of powder.	Initial velocity.
	Kind.	Weight.		
		Lbs.	Lbs.	Feet.
12-pdr. field howzer.	Shell.......	8.9	1.	1054
			1.25	1178
	Sph. case...	11.	1.	953
	Canister....	9.64	1.	1015
12-pdr. siege and garrison gun.	Shot.......	12.3	2.	1378
			3.	1674
			4.	1906
	Shell.......	8.9	2.	1611
			3.	1929
12-pdr. gun 25 cal. long.	Shot.......	12.3	2.	1411
			3.	1734
			4.	1933
			5.	2098
			6.	2239
			7.	2300
			8.	2324
24-pdr. siege and garrison gun.	Shot.......	24.25	3.	1240
			4.	1440
			6.	1680
			8.	1870
	Shell.......	17.	3.	1470
			4.	1670
	Canister....	29.	3.	1135
			4.	1303
	Grape......	30.6	3.	1108
			4.	1272
32-pdr. sea-coast gun.	Shot.......	32.3	4.	1250
			5.33	1430
			8.	1640
			10.67	1780
	Shell.......	23.4	4.	1450
			5.33	1657
	Canister....	37.	4.	1172
			5.33	1342
	Grape......	39.75	4.	1133
			5.33	1297

Initial velocities of Balls fired from Small Arms.

KIND OF ARM.	Charge.	No. of balls to the lb.	Initial velocity.
	Grains.		Feet.
Musket........	110	17	1500
Rifle..........	70	32	1750
Hall's Carbine..	70	"	1240
Pistol.........	35	"	947

Loss of velocity by the Windage of the Ball.

KIND OF GUN.	Charge of powder.	Initial velocity of ball		Loss of velocity by a windage of $\frac{1}{40}$ diameter.	
		Without windage.	With windage of $\frac{1}{40}$ diameter.		
	Lbs.	Feet.	Feet.	Feet.	Per ct.
32-PDR. SEA-COAST...........	4.	1444	1271	173	12
24-PDR. SIEGE............	4.	1600	1433	167	10
	6.	1890	1723	167	9
12-PDR., 25 calibres........	2.	1617	1444	173	11
	3.	1915	1742	173	9
	4.	2124	1951	173	8
12-PDR. FIELD, 16 calibres...	2.	1528	1370	158	10
	3.	1793	1635	158	9
	4.	1992	1834	158	8
6-PDR. FIELD................	1.5	1734	1560	174	10

The loss of velocity by a given windage is directly as the windage and inversely as the diameter of the bore, very nearly.

For a formula for computing the initial velocity of a ball, see CHAP. XV ; Article *Ballistics*.

PENETRATION OF SHOT AND SHELLS.

The following tables and notes, (when not otherwise specified,) are extracted from a report of experiments made at Metz in 1834.

The charges, when expressed in fractions, denote the proportion of powder to the nominal weight of the shot; the calibres are those of the French guns, the exact relation of which to those of the United States ordnance will be found by reference to the table of foreign ordnance in CHAPTER I.

The French 36-pdr. corresponds nearly with our 42-pdr; the 16-pdr. with our 18-pdr.; the 8-pdr. with our 9-pdr.; and the 6-inch with our 32-pdr. The diameter of the French 8-inch howitzer is 8.782 inches in our measure. The musket is of the same calibre as ours.

Penetration of Shot in Masonry.

Rubble work of good quality; scarp wall built by Vauban.

Calibre.	Charge.	DISTANCE IN YARDS.								
		27	55	109	219	328	438	656	875	1094
		In.	In.	In.	In.	In.	In.	In.	In.	In.
36	1-3d	26.78	26.39	25.60	23.83	22.25	20.87	17.92	14.96	12.21
24	1-2nd	25.60	25.20	24.22	22.45	20.87	19.30	16.25	13.39	10.83
	1-3d	24.22	23.83	22.84	21.07	19.50	18.12	15.16	12.21	9.85
	1-4th	22.65	22.25	21.46	19.89	18.22	16 74	13.78	11.23	9.06
	1-6th	20.08	19.69	18.90	17.33	15.75	14.38	11.81	9.65	7.88
	1-8th	17.33	16.93	16.15	14.57	13 20	11.81	9.65	7.88	6.50
16	1-2nd	22.45	21.86	20.87	19.10	17.53	15.95	12.80	10.05	7.68
	1-3d	21.07	20.68	19.69	17.92	16.35	14.77	11.81	9.26	7.29
	1-4th	19.50	19.10	18.22	16.74	15.16	13.78	10.83	8.47	6.69
	1-6th	17.13	16.74	16.15	14.57	13.00	11.62	9.06	7.29	5.91
	1-8th	14.96	14.57	13.78	12.21	10.83	9.45	7.48	6.11	5.12
12	1-3d	18.90	18.51	17.53	15.95	14.57	13.00	10.05	7.68	6.11
	1-4th	17.72	17.33	16.54	14.96	13 39	11.81	8.86	6.89	5.51
	1-6th	15.56	15.16	14.38	13.00	11.42	10.05	7.48	6.11	4.93
	1-8th	13.78	13.39	12.60	11.03	9.65	8.27	6.50	7.68	4.33
8	1-3d	15.95	15.56	14.77	13.19	11.62	10.24	7.48	5.51	4.14

By multiplying the numbers expressing the penetrations in this table by 1.25, we have the penetration in masonry of medium quality; by 1.75, in brick masonry; by 0.46, in hard calcareous stone (solid.)

According to the experiments, the holes made in masonry such as that referred to in the table, by shot striking it perpendicularly at a short distance, are formed of an exterior, funnel-shaped opening, the mean diameter of which is about 5 times that of the shot, and of an interior part nearly cylindrical. The exterior cone appears to be produced by the reaction of the masonry, some fragments of which are projected backwards, to the distance of 45 or 50 yards. The train of fragments in front of the hole extends about 20 feet. Around the exterior opening, the masonry is loosened to a distance about one-half greater than the diameter of the opening; say 45 in. by the 24-pounder shot; 35.5 inches by the 16-pdr.; 31.5 in. by the 12-pounder. This loosening indicates the proper distance between the first shots from a breaching battery. Nearly all the shot are broken, even at the charge of one-fourth, and the fracture is generally in meridional planes, the pole of which is the point which strikes first. On the shot which are not broken, and on the fragments of those which are broken, small cracks or furrows, sometimes 0.02 in. deep, are observed, radiating from the same point.

The effect of shells fired horizontally against masonry is very small; they are broken at the moment of striking, or if fired with very low charges, so as not to break, they produce a very slight impression.

Penetration in Oak Wood.

CALIBRE.	CHARGE.	DISTANCE IN YARDS.								
		27	55	109	219	328	438	656	875	1094
Guns.		In.	In.	In.	In.	In.	In.	In	In.	In.
36	1 3d	65.4	64.2	62.2	58.3	54.3	50.8	44.1	37.4	31.5
	1-2nd	63.0	61.4	59.1	54.7	50.8	47.3	40.2	33.5	27.6
	1 3d	59.1	57.9	55.9	51.6	47.6	44.1	37.4	30.7	24.8
24	1-4th	55.5	54.3	52.3	48.4	44.9	41.3	35.0	28.4	22.8
	1-6th	49.2	48.4	46.5	42.9	39.4	36.2	29.5	24.0	19.3
	1 8th	42.5	41.6	40.2	36.6	32.7	30.3	24.4	19.7	15.8
	1 2nd	54.7	53 2	50.8	46.5	42.5	39.0	31.9	25.6	19.7
	1-3d	51.2	50.0	48.0	43.7	40.2	36.6	29.9	23.6	18.5
16	1-4th	47.7	46.5	44.5	40.9	37.4	33.9	27.6	21.7	16.9
	1 6th	42.1	41.4	39.8	36 2	32.7	29.5	23.2	17.7	14.2
	1-8th	37.0	36.2	34.3	30.7	27.6	24.4	19.3	15.0	11.8
	1-3d	46.1	44.9	42.9	38 6	35.0	31.9	25.6	19.7	14.6
12	1-4th	43.3	42.1	40.2	36.6	33.1	29.9	23.6	18.1	13.4
	1-6th	37.8	37.0	35.4	31.9	28.4	25.2	19.3	15.0	11.4
	1-8th	33.9	33.1	31.1	27.6	24.4	21.7	16.5	13.0	9.8
8	1-3d	39.4	38.2	36.2	32.3	28 7	25.6	19.3	13.8	10.6
Howitzers.	Lbs.									
	4.4	28.4	27.6	26.0	22.4	19.3	16.5	13.0	10.6	9.1
8-in. Siege.	3.3	23.2	22.4	20 9	18.1	15.8	13.8	11.0	9.5	8.3
	2.2	16.1	15.4	14.2	12 6	11.4	10.2	8.7	7.9	7.5
	1.1	39.1	8.7	8.3	8.3	7.5	7.1	6.7	6.3	5.9
	3.3	33.1	31.9	30 3	26.8	23.6	20.5	15.0	11.8	9.8
6-in.	2.2	27.6	26.8	25.2	21.7	18.5	15.8	11.4	9.1	7.9
	1.65	22.8	22.1	20.5	17.3	14.6	12.6	9.8	8.3	7.1
24 pdr.	2.2	27.6	26.8	25.2	21.7	18.1	15.0	10.2	7.9	6.3
	1.1	18.9	18.1	16.5	13.4	11.0	9.5	7.5	6.3	5.1
12-pdr. Mountain.	0.6	15.0	14.2	12.6	10.2	8.3	7.1	5.9	4.7	3.9
	Grains.									
Musket Balls - - -	154	3.35	3.15	2.56	1.77	1.06	0.71	0.32		

The penetrations in other kinds of wood are deduced from those in the preceding table by multiplying by 1, for beech and ash; by 1.3, for elm; by 1.8, for white pine and birch; by, 2 for poplar.

In oak, the fibres are displaced laterally by the passage of the shot and afterwards close up again, so as to leave an opening scarcely sufficient for measuring the depth of penetration. This effect explains the cause of vessels not being always sunk by shot striking below the water line; but the timber is split longitudinally even by the smallest shot, in a length of 6.5 feet; the splinters are driven to the distance of 42 to 50 feet, and the largest timbers are soon destroyed.

In white pine nearly all the fibres struck by the shot are broken, but the effect does not extend much beyond the opening made; this material is therefore preferable to oak for structures which are not intended to be proof against cannon shot.

Penetration in Compact Earth, (half sand, half clay.)

CALIBRE.		CHARGE.	DISTANCE IN YARDS.								
			27	55	109	219	328	438	656	875	1094
			In.	In.	In.	In.	In.	In.	In.	In.	In.
Guns.	36	1 3d	109.1	106.3	102.4	97.3	93.4	89.4	82.3	75.6	69.7
	24	1-2nd	108.2	107.2	99.3	91.0	84.3	79.6	72.5	66.2	60.6
		1 3d	100.4	97.7	92.6	85.9	81.1	77.2	70.1	63.8	58.3
		1-4th	92.6	90.2	86.6	81.5	77.6	74.0	67.3	61.8	57.1
		1-6th	83.5	82.3	79.9	75.6	72 2	68.9	62.6	57.1	52.4
		1-8th	76.4	74.8	72.4	68.9	65.8	63.0	57.5	52.0	47.3
	16	1-2nd	94.5	91.0	85 9	77.6	72.2	67.7	61.4	55.9	50.4
		1-3d	86.6	83 5	79.6	73.6	69.3	65.8	59.9	54.4	49.2
		1-4th	80.7	78.3	75.2	69.7	66.5	63.4	57.9	52.4	47.3
		1-6th	72.9	70.9	68.1	65.0	61.8	59.1	53.6	48.8	44.5
		1-8th	63.0	65.4	63.8	60.6	57.9	55.1	50.4	45.7	41.3
	12	1 3d	65.0	63 4	59.9	54.7	50.8	48.2	42.9	38.6	35.0
		1 4th	60.6	59.1	55.9	52.0	48.8	46.1	41.3	37.4	33.9
		1-6th	54.7	53.6	50.8	48.2	45.3	42.9	38.6	35.0	32.3
		1-8th	50 0	48.8	47.3	44.5	41.7	39.8	36.2	33.1	30.7
	8	1-3d	56.3	54.7	52.0	46.9	43.3	40.2	35.4	31.9	28.7
Howitzers.		Lbs.									
8-in. Siege.		4.4	48.4*	47.3*	45.3*	41.7	38.6	35.4	30 3	26.0	23.2
		3.3	42 9*	41.7	40.2	37.0	33.9	31.1	27.2	24.0	21.7
		2.2	34.7	33.9	32.3	29.5	27.6	25.6	22.8	20.9	19.3
		1.1	22.8	22.4	21.7	20.9	20.1	19.3	17.7	16.5	15.8
6-in.		3.3	52.8*	51.2*	48.8	45.0	41.0	37.4	30.7	25.2	22.1
		2.2	45.3	44.1	42.5	38.6	35.0	31.9	26.4	22.4	19.7
		1.65	39.8	38.6	37.0	33.5	30.7	28.0	23.6	20 5	18.1
24-pdr.		2.2	44.5*	42.9*	41.0*	36.6	32.7	29.1	23.2	18.9	16.1
		1.1	33.5	32.3	30.7	27.6	24.8	22.4	18.1	15.4	13.4
Mountain 12-pdr.		0.6	27.2	26.4	24.8	21.7	19.3	17.3	14.6	12.2	10.2
		Grains.									
Musket Balls - - -		154	9.85	9.45	8.66	5.91	4.33	3.15	1.58		

*With these charges, and at these distances, the shells were often broken.

The penetrations in other kinds of earth are found by multiplying the above by 0.63, for sand mixed with gravel.

" 0.87, for earth mixed with sand and gravel, and weighing twice as much as water.

" 1.09, for compact mould and fresh earth mixed with sand, or half clay.

" 1.44, for wet potter's clay.

" 1.50, for light earth, settled.

" 1.90, for do. fresh.

In general, sand, sandy earth mixed with gravel or small stones, chalk and tufa, resist shot better than the productive earths, or clay, or earth that retains water.

Penetration of Shells.

Elevation.	Distance.	In compact earth.			In oak wood.			In masonry.		
		8-in.	10-in.	12-in.	8 in.	10-in.	12-in.	8-in.	10-in.	12-in.
	Yds.	In.	In.	In.	In.	In.	In.	In.	In.	In.
30°	656	7.88	17.72	19.69	3.94	7.88	8.66	1.97	3.54	3.94
	1312	9.85	25.60	27.57	4.73	11.81	13.78	2.36	4.73	5.12
45°	656	11.81	19.69	21.66	5.91	9.85	10.63	3.15	3.94	4.33
	1312	15.75	27.57	29.54	7.88	13.78	15.75	3.94	5.51	5.91
60°	656	19.69	29.54	31.50	8.66	13.00	14.57	4.33	5.91	6.30
	1312	21.66	31.50	33.47	9.85	13.78	15.75	4.73	6 30	6.69
Falling with maximum velocity		23.63	33.47	35 44	9.85	13.78	15.75	4 73	6.69	7.09

The penetrations in other kinds of earth, wood, and stone, may be obtained by using the co-efficients given for the other tables.

Penetration in Fascines, Wool, &c.

At the distance of 24 yards, a musket ball penetrates 20 in. into a gabion stuffed with sap fagots; the ball from a wall piece, 23.63 in. The resistance of fascines decreases very rapidly by the twigs being broken or separated by the balls.

A *rolling gabion*, stuffed with fascines, is proof against the ball of a wall piece at 15 yards; at the distance of 200 yards, and even more, it is pierced through by cannon balls of the smallest calibre.

The penetration of balls in wool is more than double of that in compact earth, even when the wool is contained in close, well quilted matrasses, pressed between hurdles. At 40 yards, a musket ball penetrates more than 40 inches into woollen matrasses thus placed together.

Effects of Shot on Cast Iron.

Shot projected with even a small velocity will break pieces of cast iron of very large dimensions. A 24-pdr. ball fired with a charge of 1-12th and moving with a velocity of 883 feet in a second, split, in two shots, to the depth of 40 inches, a block of cast iron 12 inches wide by 40 inches thick. The fragments of the block and of the broken shot are projected with sufficient velocity to produce the most destructive effects.

According to these results, cast iron cannot be advantageously used either for gun carriages, or for revetments of fortifications.

Penetration in Masonry.

Experiments at Fort Monroe Arsenal, in 1839.

CALIBRE.	Charge.	Distance.	MEAN PENETRATION.		
			Dressed granite.	Potomac free stone,	Hard brick.
	Lbs.	Yards.	In.	In.	In.
Shot. 32-pounder gun...........	8	880	3.5	12.	15.25
Shell. 8-inch sea-coast howitzer...	6	880	1.	4.5	8.5

The solid shot broke against the granite, but not against the free stone or brick.

The shells broke into small fragments against each of the three materials.

The circumstances attending the penetration of the shot and shells corresponded with those above stated in the experiments at Metz. The wall used as a target was built of dressed stone and of the best bricks, laid in hydraulic cement; but being an isolated wall, (10 feet square of each material, and 5 feet thick, with 3 counterforts,) and being battered before the masonry was perfectly set, the effect of the projectiles in *shattering* the masonry around the point struck was greater than indicated by the experiments referred to.

Penetration in a Target of White Oak Timber, 5 feet thick.

Experiment in New York Harbor, in 1814.

GUN.	Charge.	Distance.	Diameter.	REMARKS.
	Lbs.	Yards.	Inches.	
32-pdr.	11	100	60	Shot wrapped with leather, so as
	11	150	54	to destroy the windage.

Penetration of Lead Balls in Seasoned White Oak.

Experiments at Washington Arsenal, in 1839.

ARM.	Charge.	Distance.	Penetration.	REMARKS.
	Grains.	Yards.	Inches.	
Musket............	144	5	3.00	Arms loaded with new musket powder.
Common rifle........	100	"	2.05	
Hall's rifle..........	100	"	2.00	
Hall's carbine, musket calibre...........	70	"	0.60	
	80	"	0.80	
	90	"	1.10	Charges too great for service.
	100	"	1.20	
Pistol..............	51	"	0.725	

Experiments made at West Point, in 1837.

ARM.	Charge.	DISTANCE IN YARDS.							REMARKS.
		3½	9	50	100	150	200	300	
	Grains.	In.	In.	In.	In.	In.	In.	In.	
Musket	134	2 00	1.60	1.43	1.	0.66	0.55	0.00*	*1 Ball in 10 imbedded.
	125	1.60							
	90	1.60							
Common rifle	92	2.10	1.80	1.43	0.94	0.65	0.29	0.00†	†Indentation 0.2 in.
Hall's rifle	70	1.12	1.70	0.63	0.53	0.40	0.00‡	–	‡2 Balls in 10 imbedded.

The musket fired at 9 yards distance, with a charge of 134 grains, 1 ball and 3 buckshot, gave for the ball, a penetration of 1.15 in.; buckshot, 0.41 in.

Penetration in a bundle of Musket Ball Cartridge Paper, No. 1.

Musket, with 134 grains, at 13⅓ yards............653 sheets.

Common rifle, 92 grains, at 13⅓ yards............500 sheets.

FIRING HOT SHOT.

Furnaces for heating shot are erected at the forts on the sea-coast. These furnaces hold 60 or more shot. The shot being placed, and the furnace cold, it requires 1 hour and 15 minutes to heat them to a red heat. After the furnace is once heated, a 24-pdr. shot is brought to a red heat in 25 minutes; the 32 and 42 require a few minutes longer. Two or three men are required to attend a furnace.

Grates. In siege batteries, or in other situations where there are no furnaces, a *grate* is used for heating shot. This grate consists of 4 bars, 1.75 in. square, 3 feet long, placed diagonally, 4 in. apart, resting on 3 iron stands with legs 1 foot high.

To use the grate: Make an excavation 1 foot deep and 1 foot wide, with no slope at the sides or in rear, open in front. Place the grate in it, on stones or bricks, rising about 4.5 in. above the bottom; make a roof over it with hoops of flat iron, covered with sods and with 18 in. of earth, leaving in the back part a chimney 6 in. square. Put the shot on the grate, leaving about one-fourth of the length free, in front; on this part, and under the front of the grate, put the wood, cut into pieces about 14 in. long and 2 in. or 2.5 in. thick. Make use of a thick sod, as a register, to regulate the draught of the chimney, so that no flame shall issue from the front of the furnace. This little furnace, which will contain about fifteen 24-pdr. balls, heats them to a red heat in 1 hour, and will supply 3 guns; it requires the attendance of one man.

Implements. 2 *Pokers*, for stirring the fire, made of $\frac{3}{4}$ in. round iron, $5\frac{1}{2}$ feet long, the end bent at a right angle—2 *Iron forks*, for taking out the shot. These forks are immersed alternately in water to cool them—1 *Rasp*, to rub the scales from the balls when they have been overheated—1 *Pair tongs* with circular jaws, for taking up shot—1 *Iron rake*, to remove the cinders, &c., from the ash pit—1 *Trough or tub*—1 *Bucket*—1 *Barrel*—1 *Rammer*, with the head covered by a circular plate of sheet iron, of rather larger diameter than the ball; to remove the clay which may stick to the sides of the bore when clay wads are used—1 *Ladle*, (to each piece,) for carrying the balls, formed of an iron ring the interior of which is beveled to fit the ball, with 2 arms inserted into wooden handles; for small calibres it is made with 1 handle.

Wads, may be made of good clay, free from sand or gravel, moistened just enough to work well; the wads are cylindrical, 1 calibre long. But it is preferable to use *hay wads* that have been steeped in water for 15 minutes and allowed to drip.

Cartridges for hot shot, are made of cannon cartridge paper or parchment well pasted, to prevent the powder from sifting out; they should be carefully examined before use, to see that there are no holes in them. It is best to use two cartridge bags, one within the other.

Manner of loading. Elevate the muzzle sufficiently to allow the ball to roll in; ram the cartridge home carefully, and a *dry* hay wad over it; then a wet hay or clay wad; prick and prime; insert the ball, and put a wet hay or clay wad over it; this second clay wad may be only ½ calibre long. It is a good precaution also to pass a wet sponge into the gun just before putting in the shot. When wet hay wads are used, steam is seen to issue from the vent as soon as the ball gets home; this is the effect of the heat of the ball upon the water contained in the wad; no danger can result from it, as the ball may be allowed to cool in the gun without the charge taking fire; but it is better to fire without much delay, as this steam would injure the powder.

The penetrations of cold and hot shot into wood are equal under the same circumstances. A red hot shot retains sufficient heat to set fire to wood after having struck the water several times. The fire is communicated more rapidly and certainly to the wood when the ball does not penetrate more than 10 or 12 inches, because at a greater depth the communication with the external air is not sufficiently free. It is proper therefore to fire with small charges, ¼ to ⅙ wt. of the shot, according to the distance, in order that the shot may remain in the wood and not penetrate too deep.

Expansion of Shot heated to a white heat.

CALIBRE.	8-IN.	42	32	24	18	12
Expansion ....In.	0.149	0.11	0.10	0.08	0.06	0.04

Heated shot do not return to their original dimensions on cooling, but retain a permanent enlargement, as will appear from the following table, giving the mean of 16 trials by Lieutenant Rodman, of the Ordnance Department:

8-inch Shot.	FIRST HEATING.			SECOND HEATING.		
	Diam.	Expansion.		Diam.	Expansion.	
	In.	In.	Per cent.	In.	In.	Per cent.
Original..........	7.840	....	0.000			
White heat........	7.989	0.149	.019	8.017	0.177	0.022
Cherry red.........	7.963	.123	.016			
After cooling.......	7.895	.054	.007	7.939	.099	.012

CHAPTER FOURTEENTH.

MATERIALS.

TIMBER.

The kinds of wood principally used in ordnance constructions are the following:

WHITE OAK, (*Quercus alba.*) The bark is white, the leaf long, narrow and deeply indented; the wood is of a straw color, with a somewhat reddish tinge, tough and pliable. It is the principal timber used for ordnance purposes, being employed for all kinds of artillery carriages.

WHITE BEECH—RED BEECH, (*Fagus sylvestris—Fugus ferruginea,*) are the most suitable for fuzes and mallets; also for plane stocks and various other tools.

WHITE ASH, (*Fraxinus Americana,*) is straight grained, tough, and elastic, and is therefore suitable for light carriage shafts; in artillery, it is used chiefly for sponge and rammer staves; sometimes for handspikes, and for sabots and tool handles.

ELM, (*Ulmus Americana,*) is well suited for fellies and for small naves.

HICKORY, (*Juglans tomentosa,*) is very tough and flexible; the most suitable wood for handspikes and tool handles, and for wooden axletrees.

BLACK WALNUT, (*Juglans nigre,*) is hard and fine grained; it is sometimes used for naves, and the plank for ammunition boxes; it is used exclusively for the stocks of small arms.

WHITE POPLAR, OR TULIP TREE, (*Liriodendron tulipifera,*) is a soft, light, fine grained wood, which grows to a great size; it is used for sabots, cartridge blocks, &c., and for the lining of ammunition boxes.

WHITE PINE, (*Pinus strobus,*) is used for arm chests and packing boxes generally, and for building purposes.

CYPRESS, (*Cupressus disticha,*) is a soft, light, straight grained wood, which grows to a very large size. On account of the difficulty of procuring oak of suitable kind in the Southern States, cypress has been sometimes used for sea-coast and garrison carriages. It resists better than oak the alternate action of heat and moisture to which sea-coast carriages are particularly exposed in casemates; but being of inferior strength, a larger scantling of cypress than of oak is required for the same purpose, and on account of its softness it does not resist sufficiently the friction and shocks to which such carriages are liable.

Bass wood or American lime, (*Tilia Americana*,) is very light, not easily split, and is excellent for sabots and cartridge blocks.

Dog wood, (*Cornus florida*,) is hard and fine grained, suitable for mallets, drifts, &c.

Selection of standing Trees.

The principal circumstances which affect the quality of growing trees are *soil*, *climate*, and *aspect*.

In a moist soil, the wood is less firm and decays sooner than in a dry, sandy soil, but in the latter the timber is seldom fine; the best is that which grows in a dark soil, mixed with stones and gravel; this remark does not apply to the poplar, willow, cypress, and other light woods, which grow best in wet situations.

In the United States, the climate of the Northern and Middle States is most favorable to the growth of the timber used for ordnance purposes, except the cypress.

Trees growing in the centre of a forest, or on a plain, are generally straighter and more free from limbs than those growing on the edge of the forest, in open ground, or on the sides of hills, but the former are at the same time less hard. The aspect most sheltered from the prevalent winds is generally most favorable to the growth of timber. The vicinity of salt water is favorable to the strength and hardness of white oak.

The selection of timber trees should be made before the fall of the leaf. A healthy tree is indicated by the top branches being vigorous and well covered with leaves; the bark is clear, smooth, and of a uniform color. If the top has a regular, rounded form; if the bark is dull, scabby, and covered with white and red spots, caused by running water or sap, the tree is unsound. The decay of the uppermost branches, and the separation of the bark from the wood, are infallible signs of the decline of the tree.

Felling Timber.

The most suitable season for felling timber is that in which vegetation is at rest, which is the case in midwinter and in midsummer. Recent experiments incline to give preference to the latter season, say the month of July; but the usual practice is to fell trees for timber between the first of December and the middle of March.

The tree should be allowed to obtain its full maturity before being felled; this period in oak timber is generally at the age of from 75 to 100 years or upwards, according to circumstances. The age of hard wood is determined by the number of rings which may be counted in a section of the tree.

The tree should be cut as near the ground as possible, the lower part being the best timber; the quality of the wood is in some degree indicated by the color, which should be nearly uniform in the heart wood, a little deeper towards the centre, and without sudden transitions.

Felled timber should be immediately stripped of its bark, and raised from the ground.

Defects of Timber Trees, (especially of Oak.)

Sap, the white wood next to the bark, which very soon rots, and should never be used, except that of hickory. There are sometimes found rings of light colored wood surrounded by good hard wood; this may be called the *second sap;* it should cause the rejection of the tree in which it occurs.

Brash wood, is a defect generally consequent on the decline of the tree from age; the pores of the wood are open, the wood is reddish colored, it breaks short, without splinters, and the chips crumble to pieces. This wood is entirely unfit for artillery carriages.

Wood which has died before being felled should in general be rejected; so should *knotty trees,* and those which are covered with tubercles or excrescences.

Twisted wood, the grain of which ascends in a spiral form, is unfit for use in large scantling; but if the defect is not very decided, the wood may be used for naves and for some light pieces.

Spilts, checks, and cracks, extending towards the centre, if deep and strongly marked, make the wood unfit for use, unless it is intended to be split.

Wind shakes, are cracks separating the concentric layers of wood from each other; if the shake extends through the entire circle, it is a ruinous defect.

All the abovementioned defects are to be guarded against in procuring timber for use in artillery constructions. The *centre heart* is also to be rejected, except in timber of very large size which cannot generally be procured free from it.

Seasoning and Preserving Timber.

As soon as practicable after the tree is felled, the sap wood should be taken off and the timber reduced, either by sawing or splitting, nearly to the dimensions required for use. Pieces of large scantling, or of peculiar form, such as those for the bodies of gun carriages and for chassis, are got out with the saw; those of smaller dimensions, such as spokes, are split with wedges. Naves should be cut to the proper length and bored, through the axis, with a 1½ in. auger, to facilitate their seasoning and to prevent cracking as much as possible. They should be cut from the butt of the tree.

Timber of large dimensions is improved by *immersion in water* for some weeks, according to its size, after which it is less subject to warp and crack in seasoning.

For the purpose of seasoning, timber should be piled under shelter, where it may be kept dry, but not exposed to a strong current of air; at the same time, there should be a free circulation of air about the timber, with which view slats or blocks of wood should be placed between the pieces that lie over each other, near enough together to prevent the timber from bending. In the sheds, the pieces of timber should be piled in this way, or in square piles, and classed according to age and kind. Each pile should be distinctly marked with the number and kind of pieces, and their age, or the date of receiving them. The piles should be taken down and made over again at intervals, varying with the length of time which the timber has been cut. The seasoning of timber requires from 2 to 8 years, according to its size.

Gradual drying and seasoning in this manner is considered the most favorable to the durability and strength of timber, but various methods have been proposed for hastening the process. For this purpose, *steaming* timber has been applied with success; and the result of experiments with Mr. Kyan's process of saturating timber with a solution of corrosive sublimate, have been highly satisfactory; this is said to harden and season the wood, at the same time that it secures it from the dry rot and from the attacks of worms. The process of Mr. Earle, which consists in saturating the wood with a hot solution of copperas and blue vitriol mixed together, has been tried by the Ordnance Department, but the results have not been favorable, as regards its effect on the strength or preservation of the timber. *Kiln drying* is serviceable only for boards and pieces of small dimensions, and is apt to cause cracks and to impair the strength of wood, unless performed very slowly. *Charring* or *painting* is highly injurious to any but seasoned timber, as it effectually prevents the drying of the inner part of the wood, in which consequently fermentation and decay soon take place.

Oak timber loses about *one-fifth of its weight* in seasoning, and about *one-third of its weight* in becoming perfectly dry.

Measuring Timber.

Sawed or hewn timber is measured by the cubic foot, or more commonly by *board measure*, the unit of which is a superficial foot of a board 1 in. thick. Small pieces, especially those which are got out by splitting, (such as spokes,) and *shapes*, or pieces roughed out to a particular pattern, (such as stocks for small arms,) are often purchased by the piece.

Usual rule for measuring round timber:

Multiply the length by the square of one-fourth the mean girth, for the solid contents; or, $\frac{LC^2}{16}$; *L* being the length of the log, and *C* half the sum of the circumferences of the two ends. But when round timber is procured for use in the Ordnance Department, it should be measured according to the square of good timber which can be obtained from the log.

Table, *showing the Superficial Feet in one lineal foot of Boards of various widths.*

WIDTH.	AREA.	WIDTH.	AREA.	WIDTH.	AREA.
In.	Sup. ft.	In.	Sup. ft.	In.	Sup. ft.
0.25	0.0208	4.25	0.3542	8.25	0.6875
0.5	0.0417	4.5	0.375	8.5	0.7083
0.75	0.0625	4.75	0.3958	8.75	0.7292
1.	0.0833	5.	0.4167	9.	0.75
1.25	0.1042	5.25	0.4375	9.25	0.7708
1.5	0.125	5.5	0.4583	9.5	0.7917
1.75	0.1458	5.75	0.4792	9.75	0.8125
2.	0.1667	6.	0.5	10.	0.8333
2.25	0.1875	6.25	0.5208	10.25	0.8542
2.5	0.2083	6.5	0.5417	10.5	0.875
2.75	0.2292	6.75	0.5625	10.75	0.8958
3.	0.25	7.	0.5833	11.	0.9167
3.25	0.2708	7.25	0.6042	11.25	0.9375
3.5	0.2917	7.5	0.625	11.5	0.9583
3.75	0.3125	7.75	0.6458	11.75	0.9792
4.	0.3333	8.	0.6667	12.	1.0000

To find the number of feet, *board measure*, in any piece of timber of a given width, multiply the tabular *area*, for that width, by the length in feet and the thickness in inches.

IRON.

Iron is obtained from ores in which it generally exists in the state of an oxide, combined with earthy or stony matters, and sometimes with *sulphur*, *arsenic*, *magnesia*, *manganese*, &c. Iron ores are classed and named according to their different combinations, as, *magnetic*, *specular*, *micaceous*, *red hematite*, *brown hematite;* the last named is the ore from which the Salisbury and the Juniata irons are extracted.

Making Pig Iron.

Roasting. To obtain pig iron, the ore is first roasted, to separate such of the foreign substances as can be consumed or volatilized by a moderate heat. For this purpose the ore is distributed in layers alternately with refuse coal or charcoal, and burnt in the open air, or in a kiln similar to that used for burning lime; when sufficiently calcined, the ore is easily broken into pieces of the proper size for smelting.

Smelting, separates the iron from the refractory substances with which it is combined in the ore. It is effected in the blast furnace, by exposing the ore to a great heat, in conjunction with a suitable flux of limestone or clay, which combining with the earthy matter runs off over the dam, in a cinder, leaving the iron to settle at the bottom of the furnace, where it is protected from the blast by the cinder, and kept hot and fluid, until it is drawn off into open channels or moulds, in the form of *pigs*, which is usually done every twelve hours.

The kinds of fuel used for smelting are charcoal, bituminous coal, coke, and recently, anthracite coal. For many purposes, such as sheets for tinning, bars for converting into steel, *charcoal iron* is exclusively used, and for bar iron, it is superior to that made with bituminous coal; but for castings, the latter may be often used with advantage.

Pig iron, according to the proportion of carbon which it contains, is divided into *foundry iron* and *forge iron*, the latter being adapted only to converting into malleable iron; while the former, containing the largest proportion of carbon, can be used either for casting or for making bar iron.

Malleable Iron.

Malleable iron may be made directly from the pigs, by means of the bloomery, or puddling furnace; but when it is desired to obtain iron homogeneous and of the best quality, the pig iron should invariably be *refined*, otherwise the bar iron will be full of black specks and cinder holes.

REFINING. This important operation deprives the iron of a considerable portion of its carbon; it is effected in a *blast furnace* where the iron is melted by means of charcoal or coke, and exposed for some time to the action of a great heat; the metal is then run into a cast iron mould, by which it is formed into a large, broad plate, about 2.5 in. thick. As soon as the surface of the plate is chilled, cold water is poured on plentifully, to render it brittle.

The next process is to convert the metal into malleable iron, by depriving it of its remaining carbon and oxigen, which in the United States is usually effected in the *bloomery fire;* in England, by means of a *puddling furnace.*

BLOOMERY. The bloomery resembles a large forge fire, where charcoal and a strong blast are used, and the refined metal or the pig iron, after being broken into pieces of the proper size, is placed before the blast, directly in contact with the charcoal; as the metal fuzes, it falls into a cavity left for that purpose below the blast, where the bloomer works it into the shape of a *ball,* which he places again before the blast, surrounded with fresh charcoal; this operation is generally again repeated, when the ball is ready for the *shingler.*

PUDDLING, is effected in a reverberatory furnace, where the flame of bituminous coal is made to act directly on the metal, which has been previously broken into small pieces. When melted, it is thoroughly worked by the puddler, who separates his charge, on the cast iron bottom or hearth of the furnace, into five or six *puddlers' balls,* weighing from 80 to 100 pounds each. These balls are next passed to the shingler.

SHINGLING, is best performed under the *tilt hammer* weighing from two to four tons, although it is sometimes done under a *squeezer;* it has a double object, to form the ball into a shape to be received by the puddle rolls, and to express the liquid cinder which may remain in the ball; this is effected by from fifteen to twenty blows with the hammer; the ball, now called a *bloom,* is ready for being rolled or hammered.

PUDDLE ROLLS. By passing through different grooves in these rolls, the bloom is reduced to a *rough bar* from three to four feet in length, its name conveying an idea of its condition, which is rough and imperfect.

The bloom may be *broken down* under the hammer, instead of rollers; for this purpose, the shingler works the bloom as long as the heat will permit, when it is re-heated and hammered, until it is reduced to one or more *anconies,* according to the size of bar which it is intended to make; these are again heated and reduced to the required size and shape.

PILING. To prepare rough bars for this operation, they are cut, either hot or cold, by means of a strong pair of *shears,* into such lengths as are best adapted to the size of the finished bar required ; the sheared bars are piled, one over the other, to the number of from two to six or more pieces, according to the size required, when the pile is ready for balling.

BALLING. This operation is performed in the balling furnace, which is similar to the puddling furnace, except that its bottom or hearth is made up, from time to time, with sand instead of cast iron ; it is used to give a welding heat to the piles to prepare them for rolling.

FINISHING ROLLS. The *balls* are passed successively between rollers of various forms and sizes according to the shape of the finished bar required.

These bars are straightened on a cast iron bed, with heavy wooden beetles.

PROPERTIES OF BAR IRON. All iron contains more or less carbon, the hardest containing the least, and the proportion varies from ½ to 2 per cent. It expands 1-812th part from 32° to 212° Fahr., and 1-140th part, from 32° to a red heat—Specific gravity, 7,788.

To test the quality of bar iron. The most convenient test is by the fracture ; but this is not always sufficient, as the same iron will present different appearances, according to the manner in which it has been forged, and the degree of heat to which it has been subjected. In testing by the fracture, the sample should be 1 inch square, or if a flat bar, ½ inch thick ; cut a notch on one side with a cold chisel, and bend the bar down over the edge of an anvil, or give it a heavy blow, when lying flat on the ground, with a sledge hammer; if the fracture exhibits long silky fibres, of a leaden gray color, cohering together and twisting or pulling apart before breaking, it denotes a tough, soft iron, which is easy to work and hard to break, suitable for sheet iron, wire, &c., but it may weld badly. A medium, even grain, mixed with fibres as above, but without bright specks or dark spots, is also a favorable indication. In general, a short, blackish fibre indicates iron badly refined and mixed with carbon, plumbago, or oxide; if worked very hot, it may be improved, but there will be a great waste. *A very fine, close grain* denotes a hard, steely iron, which is apt to be *cold-short,* hard to work with the hammer or file. *A coarse grain,* with a brilliant, crystallized fracture, or yellow or brown spots, denotes a brittle iron, inclined to be *cold-short,* but working easily when heated, and making a good weld. Numerous cracks on the edges of the bar generally indicate a *hot-short* iron, which cracks or breaks when punched or worked at a red heat, and will not weld ; it is strong when cold, and may be useful in that state, but if worked, care should be taken not to subject it to strains at a red heat. *Blisters, flaws,* and *cinder holes,* are caused by imperfect welding at too low a heat, or by the iron not being properly worked, and do not always indicate an inferior quality. The above mentioned characters are not often found separate in iron, and its quality must be determined by their combination, and by the predominance of one or the other of them. In general good iron is readily heated, is soft under the hammer, and throws out but few sparks when taken from the fire.

The best test for bar iron is to have a piece forged into the shape in which it is intended to use it. *Another test for iron when cold* is to cut a screw thread on a square bar, and bend it by striking the end with a hammer; also by punching or drilling pieces which are to have holes in them; in the case of the square bar, it should be bent in different directions at sharp angles, and if the bar is heavy, place the end on the corner of the anvil, and strike it with a heavy sledge until the piece is forced off. Examine the welding of pieces which are *jumped on*, or *upset*.

To test iron when hot. Draw out the iron, bend and twist it—split it, and turn back the two parts, to see if the split extends up—punch a long hole in the direction of the fibre and another at right angles to it—punch holes of different forms—weld the iron to iron and steel—make chains from small rods—observe if cracks or flaws weld easily—finally, forge some of the most difficult pieces for which the iron is intended.

NOTE ON FORGING. Good iron is often injured by being unskilfully worked. Care should be taken that the iron while heating, is not exposed to the air, which would assist in forming scales of oxide on its surface; it is to prevent this that the workman from time to time throws sand or clay on his iron to protect it. When iron is at a white heat, immediate contact with coal tends to carbonize it and make it *steely*. Iron heated for any purpose, and especially for welding, should be heated as rapidly as possible, in order to expose it the least possible time to the action of the air and coal; for this purpose, the strongest fuel, with an abundant, steady blast, is necessary. Defects in iron, caused by unskilful working may be remedied in part; if, for example, iron has been *burned*, give it a smart heat, protected as much as possible from the air; if the iron has been injured by *cold hammering*, a moderate annealing heat will restore it; if the iron has become hard and steely, give it one or more smart heats, to extract the carbon.

Cast Iron.

Iron castings for ordnance purposes are made of the pig metal obtained from the smelting furnace. There are many varieties of cast iron, differing from each other by almost insensible shades; the two principal divisions are *grey* and *white*, so called from the color of the fracture when recent.

Grey iron, is softer and less brittle than white iron; it is in a slight degree malleable and flexible, and is not sonorous; it can be easily drilled and turned in the lathe, and does not resist the file. It has a brilliant fracture, of a grey, or sometimes a bluish grey color; the color is lighter as the grain becomes closer, and its hardness increases at the same time. A medium sized grain, bright grey color, lively aspect, fracture sharp to the touch, and a close compact texture, indicate a good quality of iron. A grain either very large or very small, a dull, earthy aspect, loose texture, dissimilar crystals mixed together, indicate an inferior quality.

Grey iron melts at a lower heat than white iron, becomes more fluid, and preserves its fluidity longer; it runs smoothly; the color of the fluid metal is red, and deeper in proportion as the heat is lower; it does not stick to the ladle; it fills the moulds well, contracts less and contains fewer cavities than white iron; the edges of a casting are sharp and the surface smooth, convex, and covered with carburet of iron. Grey iron is the only kind suitable for making castings which require great strength, such as cannon. Its tenacity and specific gravity are *diminished* by annealing. Its mean specific gravity is 7,200.

White iron is very brittle and sonorous; it resists the file and the chisel, and is susceptible of high polish; the surface of a casting is concave; the fracture presents a silvery appearance, generally fine grained and compact, sometimes radiating, or lamellar.

When melted it is white, and throws off a great number of sparks, and its qualities are the reverse of those of grey iron; it is therefore unsuitable for ordnance purposes. Its tenacity is *increased* and its specific gravity *diminished* by annealing. Its mean specific gravity, 7,500.

Mottled iron is a mixture of white and grey; it has a spotted appearance; it flows well and with few sparks; the casting has a plane surface, with edges slightly rounded. It is suitable for making shot and shells.

Besides these general divisions the manufacturers distinguish more particularly the different varieties of pig metal by numbers, according to their relative hardness.

No. 1 is the softest iron, possessing in the highest degree the qualities described as belonging to grey iron; it has not much strength, but on account of its fluidity when melted and of its mixing advantageously with old or scrap iron, and with the harder kinds of cast iron, it is of great use to the founder, and commands the highest price.

No. 2 is harder, closer grained, and stronger than No. 1; it has a grey color and considerable lustre. It is the kind of iron most suitable, in general, for making shot and shells.

No. 3 is still harder than No. 2. Its color is grey, but inclining to white; it has considerable strength, but it is principally used by the founder for mixing with other kinds of iron.

No. 4 is *bright* iron. No. 5, *mottled*. No. 6, *white*, which is unfit for general use by itself.

The qualities of these various kinds of iron seem to depend on the proportion of carbon, and on the state in which it is found in the metal. In the darker kinds of iron, where the proportion is sometimes 7 per cent. of carbon, it exists partly in the state of graphite or plumbago, which makes the iron soft. In white iron, the carbon is thoroughly combined with the metal, as in steel.

Cast iron frequently retains a portion of foreign ingredients from the ore, such as earths, or oxides of other metals, and sometimes sulphur and phosphorus, which are all injurious to its quality. Sulphur hardens the iron, and unless in a very small proportion, destroys its tenacity.

These foreign substances, and also a portion of the carbon, are separated by melting the iron in contact with air, and soft iron is thus rendered harder and stronger. The effect of remelting varies with the nature of the iron and the kind of ore from which it has been extracted; that from the hard ores, such as the magnetic oxides, undergoes less alteration than that from the hematites; the latter being sometimes changed from *No.* 1 to *white* by a single remelting in the air furnace. The kind of iron most suitable for any special purpose, such as the casting of cannon, should be ascertained by trial for that purpose in the furnace in which it is to be used.

All cast iron expands forcibly at the moment of becoming solid, and again contracts in cooling; grey iron, as before remarked, expands more and contracts less than other iron.

The color and texture of cast iron depend greatly on the size of the casting and the rapidity of cooling; a small casting, which cools quickly, is almost always *white*, and the surface of large castings partakes more of the qualities of white metal than the interior.

STEEL.

Steel is a compound of iron and carbon, in which the proportion of the latter is from 5 to 1 per cent., and even less, in some kinds. Steel may be distinguished from iron by its fine grain; its susceptibility of hardening by immersion, when hot, into cold water; and with certainty, by the action of diluted nitric acid, which leaves a black spot on steel, and on iron a spot which is lighter colored in proportion as the iron contains less carbon.

There are many varieties of steel, the principal of which are:

Natural steel, which is obtained by reducing the rich and pure kinds of iron ore with charcoal, and refining the cast iron, so as to deprive it of a sufficient portion of carbon to bring it to a malleable state. It is made principally in Germany and is used for making files and other tools.

The India steel called *Wootz* is said to be a natural steel, containing a small portion of other metals.

Blistered steel, or steel of cementation, is prepared by the direct combination of iron and carbon. For this purpose, the iron in bars is put in layers alternating with powdered charcoal, in a close furnace, and exposed for 7 or 8 days to a heat of about 70° Wedgewood, and then suffered to cool for as many days more. The bars on being taken out are covered with blisters, have acquired a brittle quality, and exhibit in the fracture a uniform crystalline appearance. The degree of carbonization is varied according to the purposes for which the steel is intended, and the best qualities of iron (Russian and Swedish) are used for the finest kinds of steel.

Tilted steel, is made from blistered steel moderately heated and subjected to the action of a tilt hammer, by which means its tenacity and density are increased, and it is thus adapted to use.

Shear steel, is made from blistered or natural steel refined by piling thin bars into faggots, which are brought to a welding heat in a reverberatory furnace, and hammered or rolled again into bars; this operation is repeated several times to produce the finest kinds of shear steel, which are distinguished by the names of *half-shear*, *single-shear*, and *double-shear*, or steel of 1 *mark*, of 2 *marks*, of 3 *marks*, &c., according to the number of times it has been piled.

Cast steel, is made by breaking blistered steel into small pieces and melting it in close crucibles from which it is poured into iron moulds; the *ingot* is then reduced to a bar by hammering or rolling, as described under the head of malleable iron, these operations being performed with great care. Cast steel is the finest kind of steel and best adapted for most purposes; it is known by a very fine, even, and close grain, and a silvery homogeneous fracture; it is very brittle and acquires extreme hardness, but is difficult to weld without the use of a flux. The other kinds of steel have a similar appearance to cast steel, but the grain is coarser and less homogeneous; they are softer and less brittle, and weld more readily. A fibrous or lamellar appearance in the fracture indicates an imperfect steel. A material of great toughness and elasticity, as well as hardness, is made by forging together steel and iron, forming the celebrated *damask steel*, which is used for sword blades, springs, &c.; the damasked appearance is produced by the action of a diluted acid, which gives a black tint to the steel parts, whilst the iron remains white.

Various *fancy steels*, or alloys of steel with *silver*, *platinum*, *rhodium*, *aluminium*, have been made with a view to imitating the Damascus steel, wootz, &c., and improving the fabrication of some of the finer kinds of surgical and other instruments.

PROPERTIES OF STEEL. The best steel possesses the following characters: heated to redness and plunged into cold water, it becomes hard enough to scratch glass, and to resist the best files; the hardness is uniform throughout the piece; after being tempered it is not easily broken; it welds readily; it does not crack or split; it bears a very high heat and preserves the capability of hardening after repeated working; the grain is fine, even, and homogeneous, and it receives a brilliant polish. Its specific gravity is 7,816, being greater than that of iron.

Test. Break a few bars, taken at random; make tools of them and try them in the severest manner.

HARDENING AND TEMPERING STEEL. On these operations the quality of manufactured steel in a great measure depends.

Hardening, is effected by heating the steel to a cherry red, or until the scales of oxide are loosened on the surface, and plunging it into a liquid, or placing it in contact with some cooling substance; the degree of hardness depends on the heat and the rapidity of cooling. Steel is thus rendered so hard as to resist the hardest files, and it becomes at the same time extremely brittle. The degree of heat and the temperature and nature of the cooling medium must be chosen with reference to the quality of the steel and the purpose for which it is intended. Cold water, mercury, and acids give the greatest hardness; oils and fatty substances, sand, wet iron scales or cinders, &c., give an inferior degree of hardness, but prevent the cracks which are caused by too rapid cooling. The lower the heat at which the steel becomes hard, the better.

Tempering. Steel in its hardest state being too brittle for most purposes, the requisite strength and elasticity are obtained by tempering, or *letting down the temper*, as the workmen term it, which is performed by heating the hardened steel to a certain degree and letting it cool gradually. The requisite heat is usually ascertained by the color which the surface of the steel assumes from the film of oxide thus formed. The degrees of heat to which these several colors correspond, are as follows:

At 430° Fahr.,	a very faint yellow.	Suitable for hard instruments; as hammer faces, drills for hard substances, &c.
At 450° "	a pale straw color.	
At 470° "	a full yellow......	For instruments requiring hard edges without elasticity; as shears, scissors, tools for turning iron and steel.
At 490° "	a brown color.....	

At 510° Fahr.,	brown, with purple spots..........	For tools for cutting wood and soft metals; such as plane irons, chisels, knives, &c.
At 530° "	purple..........	
At 550° "	dark blue.........	For tools requiring strong edges without extreme hardness; as cold chisels, axes, table cutlery, &c., which will break before bending.
At 560° "	full blue..........	
At 600° "	greyish blue, verging on black....	For spring temper, which will bend before breaking; saws, sword blades, &c.

If the steel is heated higher than this, the effect of the hardening process is destroyed.

Case hardening, is the conversion of the surface of wrought iron into steel, for the purpose of adapting it to receive a polish, or to bear friction, &c.; this is effected by heating the iron to a cherry red, in a close vessel, in contact with carbonaceous materials, and then plunging it into cold water. Bones, leather, hoofs and horns of animals, are generally used for this purpose, after having been burnt or roasted, so that they can be pulverized. Soot is also frequently used.

Welding Composition, for Iron or Steel.

Borax..	10 parts.
Sal ammoniac....................................	1 "

Pound them together, and melt them in a crucible into a clear liquid; pour it out on an iron plate, and when cold pulverize it for use.

SHEET IRON.

Sheet iron is made by rolling. It should be soft and tough, its surface very smooth, without holes or thick scales; it is generally of a bluish color, sometimes clouded; the sheet should be of regular thickness, elastic, and crackling when bent in the hands. When bent at a right angle, there should be no appearance of fracture on the exterior.

Russia sheet iron has a planished, glossy and smooth surface of grey oxide of iron; it should be free from rust or flaws, and be very soft and tough.

The severest test of sheet iron consists in hammering a part of the sheet into a concave form.

Sheet steel, should have the same qualities as sheet iron, with greater elasticity and hardness in a thinner sheet.

For the weight of sheet iron, see Tables on pages 406 and 407.

SHEET TIN.

Sheet tin is made by coating sheet iron with tin. The iron is first *scoured*, or thoroughly cleaned, by means of an acid, and then immersed in melted tin. There are two kinds, called *single tin* and *double tin*, differing in thickness and in the quantity of tin with which the iron is coated. The surface of the sheets should be bright and smooth, free from specks, beads and blisters.

KIND.	SIZE.	MEAN THICKNESS.		WEIGHT.	REMARKS.
	In.	Wire gauge.	In.	Lbs.	
Single Tin.	10×14	31	0.0125	0.5	There are usually 225 sheets in a box.
Double X..	10×14	27	0.018	0.75	
Roofing....	20×14	27	0.018	1.5	112 sheets in a box.

A *square* of roof (100 square feet) requires about 71 sheets of roofing tin.

Pickle for cleaning Iron.—To a mixture of equal parts of nitric and muriatic acids, add twelve times their joint volume of water.

Liquor for Tinning, or Soldering.—Dissolve 3 ounces of zinc in a pint of muriatic acid, letting it stand in a warm place about 8 hours; strain the solution through a cotton or linen cloth; add a teaspoonful of pulverized sal ammoniac to a pint of the solution, and let it boil for 10 minutes; when cool it is fit for use.

To TIN IRON. Immerse the iron in the cleaning pickle; if the surface is rough, let it remain in the pickle about 4 hours, or until all the scales can be rubbed off. Then dip the iron into the solution of zinc, and immediately afterwards into the melted tin, which must be kept a little above the melting point. Let it remain in the melted tin until the latter has ceased to be agitated, when the iron will have become warm enough for the tin to adhere; on taking it out, wipe or shake off the surplus tin.

To TIN COPPER. It is only necessary to dip the copper into the solution of zinc and then into the bath of tin; or to clean the copper with diluted sulphuric acid, before immersing it in the tin.

SOLDERING, WITH SOFT SOLDER. Dip a sponge or mop into the solution of zinc and pass it over the part to be soldered, before applying the soldering iron; this will cause the solder to flow freely, without using rosin, or cleaning the surface with a file.

FILES AND RASPS.

List of Files and Rasps required for use at an Arsenal of Construction.

No.	KIND.	Length.	Width.	Thickness.	Weight.		REMARKS.
		In.	In.	In.	Lbs.	oz.	
1	Flat rough (ruffs)..	14.	1.35	0.35	1	4	Flat, tapering.
2	Do. do...........	12.	1.17	0.3	0	15	
3	Do. bastards.......	12.	1.17	0.3	0	14	
4	Do. do..........	8.	0.7	0.2	0	5	
5	Half round bastards	12.	1.14	0.32	0	11	
6	Do. do....	9.	0.85	0.25	0	5½	
7	Do. do....	6.	0.56	0.2	0	1½	
8	Round do....	12.	....	0.5	0	8½	
9	Do. do....	9.	....	0.23	0	2	
10	Do. do....	6.	....	0.23	0	¾	
11	Do. do....	4.5	....	0.16	0	¼	
12	Square do....	12.	0.5	0.5	0	9	
13	Do. do....	8.	0.32	0.32	0	3	
14	Do. do....	6.	0.24	0.24	0	2	
15	Do. do....	4.	0.2	0.2	0	¾	
16	Flat, single cut, (floats)..........	12.	1.12	0.22	0	10½	1 edge rounded.
17	Flat, hand, smooth.	12.	1.16	0.31	1	2	Safe edge.
18	Do. do.	9.	0.96	0.27	0	10	Do.
19	Do. do.	8.	0.83	0.2	0	6	Do.
20	Do. do.	4.	0.44	0.1	0	¾	Do.
21	Half round, hand, do.	12.	1.15	0.33	0	12	
22	Do. do.	9.	0.84	0.27	0	5½	
23	Do. do.	6.	0.6	0.18	0	1½	
24	Taper, hand saw...	4.5	Δ	0.4	0	1¼	
25	Flat, shoeing rasp..	14.	1.5	0.35	1	8	
26	Half round do...	12.	1.14	0.32	0	11	Without tang.

English files are generally used at the Arsenals and Armories.

Files should be made of the best cast steel. The teeth are generally cut at an angle of 60° with the centre line; at a smaller angle, the teeth are apt to choke, and at a greater angle, they do not cut.

In choosing files, they should be examined to see that they are straight, that they are free from cracks and flaws, and that they are cut regularly. The teeth should not be turned or broken by filing on iron or tempered steel. One out of each dozen may be tried on a piece of tempered steel, such as the tang of a file screwed in a vice; the file should "take" in its whole length, both on the flat and edge, and should not cut in drawing back; it should not make furrows, or show a tendency to deviate from the direction given to it by the hand. The quality of the steel may be determined by breaking some of the files, and working the steel in the forge.

ALLOYS.

Bronze—Gun metal: 90 copper and 10 tin.

Bell metal: 78 copper and 22 tin.

Fine brass: 2 copper and 1 zinc.

Brass for parts of small arms and of gun carriages: 80 copper, 17 zinc, and 3 tin.

Sheet brass: 3 copper and 1 zinc.

Hard solder: 1 zinc and 2 brass.

Plumber's solder: 1 tin and 1 lead.

Tinner's solder: 1 tin and 2 lead.

Pewterer's solder: 2 tin and 1 lead.

Pewter: 4 tin and 1 lead.

An alloy that expands in cooling: 9 lead, 2 antimony and 1 bismuth; useful for filling small cavities in cast iron.

Babbit's metal, for journal boxes: 9 tin and 1 copper.

STORAGE AND PRESERVATION OF METALS.

Metals are stored on the ground floors of dry and well aired buildings, which should be kept open in fine weather only.

Bar iron and *steel,* and pieces rough forged, (*shapes,*) divided according to kind and size, on racks, or standing upright in frames—*unserviceable iron* and *scraps,* in piles marked with the weight. *Sheet iron* and *tin,* oiled, and placed on edge, in frames. *Wire,* oiled, in coils, hung on hooks; arranged according to kind and size.

Heavy chains, coiled up in piles—*Small chains,* in bundles of 10 or 20, in boxes or on shelves.

Finished work, according to kind, in piles or in boxes.

Pig metal, in square piles; the flat sides lying together.

The iron and steel parts of implements, &c., covered with a black varnish, made of white varnish and lampblack, for intrenching, and other heavy tools; of white varnish and ivory black, for polished tools. See Chapter VII.

Artificer's tools and *files,* according to kind, in a dry place, with suitable divisions; they should be sprinkled with powdered charcoal, or fine quick lime, to protect them from rust.

Nails, according to kind and size, in bins or kegs. *Anvils* and other heavy pieces, on skids on the floor. Every division, bin, pile and box, should be marked with a label showing the character of the article contained in it, its kind, its distinctive number or size, the quantity, weight, &c.

ROPES.

The size of a rope is designated by the circumference or girth measured with a thread ; thus, a 3-inch rope measures 3 inches round. *The length* is usually expressed in fathoms.

STRENGTH. The utmost strength of good hemp rope is 6,400 lbs. to the square inch ; the weight which it will bear before breaking is expressed in *tons* by *one-fifth of the square of the girth in inches;* in practice, a rope should not be subjected to more than half this strain. It stretches from 1-7th to 1-5th, and its diameter is diminished from 1-7th to 1-4th, before breaking. A difference in the quality of the hemp may produce a difference of 1-4th in the strength of ropes of the same size.

White rope is stronger than tarred rope, and the difference is increased by age and service; therefore such ropes only as are to be immersed in water should be tarred.

The strength of Manilla rope is less than that of hemp rope.

QUALITY. The quality of hemp is in some measure indicated by its color; the best is of a pearl grey ; the next, greenish ; then, the yellow; a brown color indicates the beginning of decay ; the odour should be strong, but free from a musty, tainted smell. It should be well combed, pliant, and clear of stalks. The yarns should be fine spun and slightly twisted ; they are from $\frac{1}{4}$ to $\frac{1}{5}$ of an inch in girth. A rope is defective when the yarns are of unequal sizes, or unequally twisted ; when it is fuzzy before being used ; and when it contains pieces of stalk, indicating that the hemp was not well combed.

TWISTING OR LAYING. The number of *yarns* in a *strand* of cordage varies from 16 to 25, and several strands are combined or *laid*, to form a large rope. A rope is said to be twisted $\frac{1}{3}$ or $\frac{1}{4}$, when it is $\frac{1}{3}$ or $\frac{1}{4}$ shorter than the strand. For artillery service, ropes should be twisted $\frac{1}{4}$.

The degree of twisting may be determined by constructing a right-angled triangle, the base of which is the circumference of the rope, and the height, the length of one revolution of the strand, measured parallel to the axis; the difference between this height and the hypotheneuse is the quantity by which the rope is twisted.

SPLICING, is the joining of two ends of rope without a knot; the instrument used for the purpose is a *marline spike*. There are two kinds of splice; see *Plate* 19.

Short splice. Untwist from 4 to 8 inches of each of the two ends of rope, and interlock the strands up to the close parts of the rope, those of the two ends alternating; hold in the left hand one end of rope with the loose strands in front, and cross each strand of that end over the strand of the other end which is to the left hand of it; then by means of the marline spike, pass it under the same strand of the second end, and draw firmly on the strand which is passed through. Pursue the same course with the strands of the second rope. To increase the strength of the splice, pass each strand round the one on its left a second time, and cut off the loose ends.

Long splice. For a rope which is to pass through a pulley, the short splice would be too thick. Untwist about 18 inches of the two ends, and interlock them as before; untwist a strand of one end from the close part of the rope and replace it by the strand of the other rope which comes to hand; cross the end of the latter strand over the one which is replaced, and pass it under the adjacent strands. Substitute, in this manner, every other strand of one rope by a strand of the other rope, and cut off the loose ends.

PRESERVATION IN STORE. Ropes should be placed in the upper stories of a building, coiled up and labeled; large ropes on skids, so as to allow the circulation of air; small ropes hung up to the joists, on pins or hooks. Ropes should not be coiled until they are perfectly dry; they should be uncoiled every year, and stretched out for several days at the beginning of the dry season.

COAL.

Charcoal.

Charcoal of good quality burns slowly in the air, without flame; it is clean, hard, compact, brittle, sonorous, and of a fine black colour; its fracture is shining, irridescent, and of a conchoidal form.

When not perfectly charred, it is tough, of a greyish colour, and burns with a white flame and smoke. When too much burnt, it is of a dull black, soft and unelastic. By exposure to the air, charcoal absorbs from 10 to 20 per cent. of moisture, and its qualities are thereby impaired; it should therefore be kept under cover.

Charcoal is made from either hard or soft wood; that from the former, such as oak, maple, beech, chesnut, is the most serviceable, giving the greatest quantity of heat for an equal weight of coal.

Making charcoal. For ordinary purposes, wood is charred in heaps or stacks, in the following manner: Select sound wood; it may be burnt immediately after being felled; wood which has been exposed for a year after felling gives inferior charcoal. Cut it into pieces about 4 or 5 feet long, and split those which are more than 4 inches in thickness.

Level the ground on which the stack is to be made, choosing a dry and sheltered spot. Plant a stake in the middle of the space, and cover the bottom of the pile with wood placed in a direction converging towards the centre, the intervals being filled up with small sticks; place the rest of the wood around the stake, the pieces nearly upright and close together, in several tiers, covering the whole with a layer of wood placed as close together as possible; leave one or more horizontal openings near the ground, from the exterior to the centre. Cover the stack, commencing at the top, with leaves and a coat of wet sod about 4 inches thick, leaving open a space 6 inches high, all round the bottom, for the escape of the air and steam.

Draw out the stake, and set fire to the pile, either by means of the hole left by the stake, or through the horizontal gallery, which may have been previously filled with combustible materials. Push the fire actively until the flame comes out at the top of the stack, in order to ignite the whole of the bottom part, and to expel the steam which would otherwise occasion explosions. Then close the hole at the top, and cover the lower part of the pile, leaving small openings at intervals; the smoke should now escape equally from all parts of the stack, except towards the top, which is kept closed in order to prevent a draught. When the stack has *sweated* sufficiently, increase the thickness of the coating of earth; moderate the fire, and direct it, by means of openings on the sides, in such a manner that the combustion may be equal in every part, and that the fire may be always drawn towards the bottom. Leave the holes open as long as the smoke is black and thick, and close them when it becomes light and of a bluish color. The charring is completed when the flame escapes through the openings at the bottom; then stop the holes and cover the pile well with earth, which should be renewed after 24 hours; extinguish the fire entirely, and let the pile stand 12 or 24 hours more. Open it on one side only; select the coal, and separate what is imperfectly burnt. Wood furnishes in this way, on an average, about 16 or 17 per cent. of charcoal.

The stack should be formed of one kind of wood; if soft and hard woods are used in the same pile, put the former on the outside. Large stacks are the most advantageous; as much as 50 or 60 cords of wood may be put into one.

Pit Coal.

BITUMINOUS COAL. There are two principal varieties:

Open burning coal kindles quickly and burns well, but produces much flame and smoke, and is soon consumed; it lies open in the fire and does not cake. Of this kind is the English cannel coal.

Close burning coal melts and swells in the fire and runs together, forming what blacksmiths call a *hollow fire*, or a dome over the nozzle of the bellows, under which the iron is heated equally, and covered from the air. This kind of coal forms a very hot fire and leaves little residuum; it is, therefore, the most suitable for smiths' use. The Newcastle coal, and the Virginia, Maryland, and Pennsylvania bituminous coals are of this kind.

ANTHRACITE COAL, is now extensively used for the forge in fire places specially contrived for the purpose. It ignites with difficulty, and does not cake or melt in the smallest degree, but produces a very hot, open fire.

Coal is not injured, but on the contrary rather improved, by exposure to air and moisture.

Mean Weight of Coals.

KIND.	Specific gravity.	Weight of 1 cubic foot.	Cubic feet to 1 ton.
		Lbs.	
Bituminous........	1,355	51.4	43.58
Anthracite..........	1,500	53.	42.21

Coke.

Coke is produced by charring bituminous coal, in order to expel the bitumen and sulphur; this is usually done in close furnaces or ovens. Good coke has a dull fracture, is very porous, and cellular; it gives very little ashes when burnt; it is injured, like wood charcoal, by absorbing water.

Coal furnishes 60 to 70 per cent. of coke by weight; the volume being increased 5 to 20 per cent.

COAL TAR is a bituminous product obtained by the distillation of coal, in making gas, &c.

TAR, PITCH, TURPENTINE.

The following are the principal varieties of products from resinous trees, such as the pine.

TURPENTINE. This is extracted from the tree in warm weather, by cutting a deep notch, or *box*, near the base, and scoring the tree by scraping off the bark above the box; the first year's running produces the *virgin* or *white turpentine*, and the second year's is nearly as good; after that, the turpentine becomes each year darker and stiffer, the tree yielding less of what is called *dippings*, and more *scrapings;* the latter kind of turpentine is hard and yellow. A tree will bear tapping 14 to 16 years, on two sides alternately, the scoring being extended upwards from 12 to 15 inches each year.

SPIRITS OF TURPENTINE, is the *essential oil* obtained by distillation from the native turpentine.

ROSIN, OR COLOPHONY, is the residuum of the distillation of turpentine. Its quality depends on that of the turpentine and on the care used in distillation; the finest quality is of a light straw color.

TAR is obtained from the heart of the pine tree, by *smouldering*, or a smothered combustion, effected in stacks, nearly in the manner described for making charcoal. The tar runs off into trenches dug for the purpose. Tar is semi-fluid, transparent in thin portions, and of a reddish color; it has a strong, peculiar odor. It is rendered more fluid by heat; and it burns with a bright flame, leaving a light and dry coal. It is refined by heating it in an iron vessel, and pouring it off, after it has been kept for some time in a liquid state; by this means, water and pyroligneous acid are driven off, and the earthy particles are separated by settling.

It is used for coating cordage, and for wood which is not to be immersed in water.

PITCH, is made by boiling tar down to the requisite consistency, either by itself or combined with a portion of rosin; it becomes solid on cooling, but is soon softened by the heat of the hand, in which state it is very adhesive; when of good quality it is clear and hard.

It is used for coating wood which is to be immersed in water, and is applied hot, with a *mop*.

VENICE TURPENTINE is obtained from the *larch*; but what is commonly called by that name is a compound of melted rosin and spirits of turpentine.

STRENGTH AND WEIGHT OF MATERIALS.

Relative Ductility of Metals.

Gold—Silver—Platinum—Iron—Copper—Zinc—Tin—Lead.

Relative Malleability.

Gold—Silver—Copper—Tin—Platinum—Lead—Zinc—Iron.

Tenacity of various Materials.

S represents the weight required to break a rod whose cross section, a, is one square inch, when pulled in the direction of its length; for rods of other dimensions, the breaking weight $W = S\,a$; the weight of the rod being neglected.

METALS.		Value of S	
Cast steel		134,000 lbs.	
Bar iron.	Swedish	72,000	Experiments of Franklin Institute, on bars whose cross section was about one-fifth of a square inch.
	Salisbury, Conn.	66,000	
	Bellefonte, Pa.	58,500	
	English	56,000	
	Pittsfield, Mass.	57,000	Experiments by Major W. Wade, for the Ordnance Department, on pieces whose cross section was nearly 1 square inch.
Cast iron	Pig metal	15,000	
	Good, common castings	20,000	
	Specimens from gun heads	24,000 / 39,500	
Cast steel		128,000	
Bronze—gun metal		30,000 / 42,000	
Copper, cast; (Lake Superior)		24,138	
Brass		18,000	
Copper..	Wrought	34,000	
	Cast	19,000	
Tin, cast		4,800	
Zinc		3,500	
Platinum		56,000	
Silver		40,000	
Gold		30,000	
Lead		1,800	
WOODS.			
Ash		15,800	
Mahogany		11,500	
Oak		11,600	
White pine		11,800	
Walnut		7,700	

In general, the tenacity of metals is increased by hammering and wiredrawing.

The strength of Pittsfield bar iron, given in the above table, is the mean of four trials, with cylinders 1 in. long and 0.9 in. diameter. They were extended in length, before fracture, to 1.4 in., and they were reduced in diameter to 0.6 in. in the middle.

A bar of wrought iron is extended about one-hundredth part of its length for every ton of strain on a square inch.

Transverse Strength.

S = the weight in pounds required to break a beam 1 in. square and 1 in. long, fixed at one end and loaded at the other; b the breadth, d the depth, and l the length, in inches, of any other beam of the same material, and W the weight which will cause it to break, neglecting the weight of the beam itself.

1. *If the beam is supported at one end and loaded at the other:*

$$W = S\,\frac{b\,d^2}{l}$$

2. *If the beam is supported at one end and the load distributed over its whole length:*

$$W = 2\,S\,\frac{b\,d^2}{l}$$

3. *If the beam is supported at both ends and loaded in the middle:*

$$W = 4\,S\,\frac{b\,d^2}{l}$$

4. *If the beam is supported at both ends and loaded uniformly over its whole length:*

$$W = 8\,S\,\frac{b\,d^2}{l}$$

5. *If the beam is supported at both ends and loaded at the distance m from one end:*

$$W = S\,\frac{l\,b\,d^2}{m\,(l-m)}$$

Values of the co-efficient S, deduced from Mr. Barlow's experiments.

Good English bar iron	6,150	Ash	2,025
Cast iron	7,644	Pitch pine	1,632
English oak	1,200	Riga fir	1,128

In practice, about one-half or one-third of these values should be used, in computing the strain to which a beam should be subjected.

Resistance to longitudinal Compression.

S = the weight required to crush a bar 1 inch square, in the direction of its length. The area of the cross section of any other bar being denoted by a, the weight required to crush it is $W = S\,a$; the length of the bar being not more than three times, nor less than once and a half, its breadth.

Practical Formulæ for computing the weight which a column will sustain.

[From WEALE's Engineer's Pocket Book.]

b, the side of a square column, in inches;

d, the diameter of a cylindrical column, in inches;

l, the length of the column, in feet;

W, the weight it will sustain, in pounds.

MATERIAL.	SOLID SQUARE COLUMN.	SOLID CYLINDRICAL COLUMN.
Cast iron..........	$W=\frac{15300\, lb^3}{4b^2+.18\,l^2}$	$W=\frac{9562\, d^4}{4d^2+.18\,l^2}$
Wrought iron......	$W=\frac{17800\, lb^3}{4b^2+.16\,l^2}$	$W=\frac{11125\, d^4}{4d^2+.16\,l^2}$
Oak...............	$W=\frac{3960\, lb^3}{4b^2+.5\,l^2}$	$W=\frac{2470\, d^4}{4d^2+.5\,l^2}$

Resistance to Torsion.

S = the weight in pounds required to break, by twisting, a solid cylinder, 1 inch diameter; the weight acting at the distance of 1 inch from the axis of the cylinder; d, the diameter in inches of any other cylinder of the same material; r, the distance from its axis to the point where the breaking weight W is applied, then:

$$W = S\frac{d^3}{r}$$

Torsional strength of Hollow Cylinders.

Practical formula deduced by Lieut. Rodman, Ordnance Department, from Major Wade's experiments.

D, the exterior, and d, the interior diameter of the cylinder in inches; S, W and r, as before.

$$W = S\frac{D^4-d^4}{D\,r}$$

Relative torsional strength of cast iron shafts, of different forms, having equal areas of cross sections.

From Major Wade's experiments on shafts whose cross sections were 1, 2, and 3 square inches.

SOLID CYLINDER.	SOLID SQUARE.	Hollow cylinders, whose interior and exterior diameters are in the proportion of				
		4 to 10	5 to 10	6 to 10	7 to 10	8 to 10
1.0000	0.8750	1.2656	1.4433	1.7000	2.0864	2.7377

Values of the co-efficients S for the strength of certain metals.

From experiments made by Major Wm. Wade, for the Ordnance Department.

KIND OF METAL.	Values of S. Tenacity.	Transverse strength.	Compression.	Torsion.	Specific gravity.
	Lbs.	Lbs.	Lbs.	Lbs.	
CAST IRON. Mean results. Common pig iron	15,000	6,000	-	-	7.000
CAST IRON. Mean results. Good, common castings	20,000	7,500	-	7,000	7.180
CAST IRON. Mean results. Gun iron, from gun heads, (Boston and West Point, 1848 & '49)	32,000	-	105,000	-	7.280
CAST IRON. Mean results. Gun iron, cast in small bars	34,000	9,500	130,000	9,000	7.320
CAST IRON. Extremes. Least	9,000	5,000	-	-	6.900
CAST IRON. Extremes. Greatest	39,500	11,500	-	10,000	7.724
CAST STEEL	128,000	23,000	-	-	7.846
WROUGHT IRON. Begins to yield, taking a permanent set	31,000	6,500	40,000	3,600	7.855
WROUGHT IRON. Ultimate strength	57,000	-	-	-	
WROUGHT IRON. Bends and endures without breaking	-	-	116,000	7,700	
BRONZE. Begins to yield, taking a permanent set	19,000	-	-	2,300	8.710
BRONZE. Ultimate strength	42,000	-	-	-	
BRONZE. Bends and endures without breaking	-	-	-	5,500	
CAST COPPER, (Lake Superior,) ultimate strength	24,138	-	-	-	8.712

The torsional strains, which the wrought iron and bronze endured without breaking, twisted the cylinders about 100°.

Weight and Strength of Iron Chains.

Diam. of iron for the links.	Weight of 1 foot of chain.	Breaking weight.	Proof weight.	REMARKS.
In.	Lbs.	Lbs.	Lbs.	
0.1875	0.325	2,240	948	Extracted from a table furnished by Col. Denison, for the Aide Mémoire of Military Sciences.
0.25	0.65	4,256	1,680	
0.3125	0.967	6,720	2,464	
0.375	1.383	9,634	3,584	
0.4375	1.767	13,216	5,152	The proof weights are computed at the rate of 420 lbs. to one-eighth of an inch diameter of the iron for the links.
0.5	2.633	17,248	6,720	
0.5625	3.333	21,728	8,512	
0.625	4.217	26,880	10,304	
0.6875	4.833	32,704	12,544	
0.75	5.75	38,752	15,232	
0.8125	6.667	45,696	17,696	
0.875	7.5	51,744	20,384	
0.9375	9.333	58,464	23,520	
1.	10.817	65,632	26,880	

Weight and Strength of Hemp and Iron Wire Ropes.

HEMP ROPE.					IRON WIRE ROPE.		
Circumference.	Hawser-laid 3 strands.		Cable-laid.		Circumference.	Weight of 1 foot.	Breaking weight.
	Weight of 1 foot.	Breaking weight.	Weight of 1 foot.	Breaking weight.			
In.	Lbs.	Lbs.	Lbs.	Lbs.	In.	Lbs.	Lbs.
0.75	0.028	291	....	....	0.75	0.070	2,240
1.	0.038	560	....	....	1.	0.125	3,360
1.5	0.087	1,120	....	....	1.5	0.280	6,160
2.	0.153	2,016	....	....	2.375	0.680	15,680
2.5	0.238	3,136	....	....	2.625	0.860	16,800
3.	0.343	4,256	0.301	3,674	3.125	1.230	24,520
3.5	0.467	5,824	0.422	4,480	3.75	1.770	30,244
4.	0.612	7,616	0.552	6,440	4.125	2.140	44,800
4.5	0.773	9,428	0.697	8,154			
5.	0.955	11,872	0.862	10,060			
5.5	1.155	14,336	1.042	12,183			
6.	1.375	17,044	1.240	14,515			
6.5	1.613	19,936	1.455	17,024			
7.	1.872	23,072	1.687	19,712			
7.5	2.148	26,432	1.928	22,400			
8.	2.445	30,016	2.138	25,805			
8.5	2.760	34,048	2.613	29,120			
9.	3.095	38,080	2.850	32,660			
9.5	3.533	42,336	3.088	36,378			
10.	3.822	44,800	3.327	40,320			

The above table is taken chiefly from the "Aide Mēmoire to the Military Sciences." The breaking weights of the hawser-laid rope are a good deal below the results obtained with ropes of the same sizes at Woolwich Dockyard; but the lowest results have been taken in preference. The wire rope was made by Kuper & Co.

Weight of one foot in length of Flat and Square Bar Iron.

Width.	Thickness.	Weight.	Width.	Thickness.	Weight.	Width.	Thickness.	Weight.
In.	In.	Lbs.	In.	In.	Lbs.	In.	In.	Lbs.
0.25	0.25	0.21	1.375	1.	4.62	2.	1.125	7.56
0.3	0.3	0.03	.	1.125	5.19	.	1.25	8.40
0.375	0.375	0.47	.	1.25	5.77	.	1.375	9.24
0.5	0.125	0.21	.	1.375	6.35	.	1.5	10.08
.	0.1875	0.31	1.5	0.125	0.63	.	1.75	11.76
.	0.25	0.42	.	0.1875	0.94	.	2.	13.44
.	0.375	0.63	.	0.25	1.26	2.25	0.125	0.94
.	0.5	0.84	.	0.375	1.89	.	0.1875	1.41
0.625	0.625	1.34	.	0.5	2.52	.	0.25	1.89
0.75	0.125	0.31	.	0.625	3.15	.	0.375	2.83
.	0.1875	0.47	.	0.75	3.78	.	0.5	3.78
.	0.25	0.63	.	0.875	4.41	.	0.625	4.72
.	0.375	0.94	.	1.	5.04	.	0.75	5.66
.	0.5	1.26	.	1.125	5.67	.	0.875	6.61
.	0.625	1.57	.	1.25	6.30	.	1.	7.56
.	0.75	1.89	.	1.5	7.56	.	1.125	8.50
0.875	0.875	2.57	1.625	0.125	0.68	.	1.25	9.45
1.	0.125	0.42	.	0.25	1.36	.	1.375	10.39
.	0.1875	0.63	.	0.5	2.73	.	1.5	11.34
.	0.25	0.84	.	0.75	4.20	.	1.75	13.22
.	0.375	1.26	.	1.	5.46	.	2.	15.12
.	0.5	1.68	.	1.625	8.87	.	2.25	17.01
.	0.625	2.10	1.75	0.125	0.73	2.5	0.125	1.05
.	0.75	2.52	.	0.1875	1.10	.	0.1875	1.57
.	0.875	2.94	.	0.25	1.47	.	0.25	2.10
.	1.	3.36	.	0.375	2.20	.	0.375	3.15
1.125	1.125	4.25	.	0.5	2.94	.	0.5	4.20
1.25	0.125	0.52	.	0.625	3.67	.	0.625	5.25
.	0.1875	0.78	.	0.75	4.41	.	0.75	6.30
.	0.25	1.05	.	0.875	5.14	.	0.875	7.35
.	0.375	1.57	.	1.	5.87	.	1.	8.40
.	0.5	2.10	.	1.125	6.60	.	1.125	9.55
.	0.625	2.62	.	1.25	7.35	.	1.25	10.50
.	0.75	3.15	.	1.375	8.07	.	1.5	12.60
.	0.875	3.67	.	1.5	8.80	.	1.75	14.70
.	1.	4.20	.	1.75	10.29	.	2.	16.80
.	1.125	4.72	1.875	1.875	11.81	.	2.5	21.
.	1.25	5.25	2.	0.125	0.84	2.75	0.125	1.15
1.375	0.125	0.57	.	0.1875	1.26	.	0.1875	1.73
.	0.1875	0.86	.	0.25	1.68	.	0.25	2.31
.	0.25	1.15	.	0.375	2.52	.	0.375	3.46
.	0.375	1.73	.	0.5	3.36	.	0.5	4.62
.	0.5	2.31	.	0.625	4.20	.	0.625	5.77
.	0.625	2.88	.	0.75	5.04	.	0.75	6.93
.	0.75	3.46	.	0.875	5.88	.	0.875	8.08
.	0.875	4.04	.	1.	6.72	.	1.	9.24

Flat and Square Bar Iron.—Continued.

Width.	Thick-ness.	Weight.	Width.	Thick-ness.	Weight.	Width.	Thick-ness.	Weight.
In.	In.	Lbs.	In.	In.	Lbs.	In.	In.	Lbs.
2.75	1.125	10.39	3.5	0.375	4.41	4.	3.	40.32
.	1.25	11.55	.	0.5	5.88	.	3.5	47.04
.	1.5	13.86	.	0.625	7.35	.	4.	53.76
.	2.	18.48	.	0.75	8.82	4.25	0.125	1.78
.	2.5	23.10	.	0.875	10.29	.	0.25	3.57
.	2.75	25.41	.	1.	11.76	.	0.375	5.35
3.	0.125	1.26	.	1.25	14.70	.	0.5	7.14
.	0.1875	1.89	.	1.5	17.64	.	1.	14.28
.	0.25	2.52	.	2.	23.52	.	4.25	60.69
.	0.375	3.78	.	2.5	29.40	4.5	0.125	1.89
.	0.5	5.04	.	3.	35.28	.	0.25	3.78
.	0.625	6.30	.	3.5	41.16	.	0.375	5.66
.	0.75	7.56	3.75	0.125	1.57	.	0.5	7.56
.	0.875	8.82	.	0.1875	2.36	.	1.	15.12
.	1.	10.08	.	0.25	3.15	.	4.5	68.04
.	1.125	11.34	.	0.375	4.72	4.75	0.125	2.
.	1.25	12.60	.	0.5	6.30	.	0.25	4.
.	1.5	15.12	.	0.625	7.87	.	0.375	6.
.	2.	20.16	.	0.75	9.45	.	0.5	7.98
.	2.5	25.20	.	0.875	11.02	.	1.	15.96
.	3.	30.24	.	1.	12.60	.	4.75	75.81
3.25	0.125	1.36	.	1.25	15.75	5.	0.125	2.10
.	0.1875	2.04	.	1.5	18.90	.	0.25	4.20
.	0.25	2.73	.	2.	25.20	.	0.375	6.30
.	0.375	4.09	.	2.5	31.50	.	0.5	8.40
.	0.5	5.46	.	3.	37.80	.	1.	16.80
.	0.625	6.82	.	3.75	47.25	.	5.	84.
.	0.75	8.19	4.	0.125	1.68	5.25	0.25	4.41
.	0.875	9.55	.	0.1875	2.52	.	1.	17.64
.	1.	10.92	.	0.25	3.36	5.5	0.25	4.62
.	1.125	12.28	.	0.375	5.04	.	1.	18.48
.	1.25	13.65	.	0.5	6.72	5.75	0.25	4.83
.	1.5	16.38	.	0.625	8.40	.	1.	19.32
.	2.	21.84	.	0.75	10.08	6.	0.25	5.04
.	2.5	27.39	.	0.875	11.76	.	1.	20.16
.	3.	32.76	.	1.	13.44	.	6.	120.96
.	3.25	35.5	.	1.25	16.80	6.5	0.25	5.46
3.5	0.125	1.47	.	1.5	20.18	.	1.	21.84
.	0.1875	2.20	.	2.	26.88	.	6.5	142.
.	0.25	2.94	.	2.5	33.65	7.	7.	164.64

Weight of one foot in length of Round Bar Iron.

Diam.	Weight.	Diam.	Weight.	Diam.	Weight.	Diam.	Weight.
In.	Lbs.	In.	Lbs.	In.	Lbs.	In.	Lbs.
0.15	0.059	1.625	6.91	3.25	27.65	4.75	59.06
0.2	0.105	1.75	8.01	3.375	29.82	4.875	62.21
0.25	0.163	1.875	9.2	3.5	32.07	5.	65.45
0.375	0.368	2.	10.47	3.625	34.4	5.125	68.76
0.5	0.654	2.125	11.82	3.75	36.81	5.25	72.16
0.625	1.02	2.25	13.25	3.875	39.31	5.375	75.63
0.75	1.47	2.375	14.76	4.	41.89	5.5	79.19
0.875	2.	2.5	16.36	4.125	44.54	5.625	82.83
1.	2.61	2.625	18.03	4.25	47.28	5.75	86.56
1.125	3.31	2.75	19.79	4.375	50.11	5.875	90.36
1.25	4.09	2.875	21.63	4.5	53.01	6.	94.25
1.375	4.94	3.	23.56	4.625	56.	6.185	100.
1.5	5.89	3.125	25.56				

Weight of one square foot of rolled Iron Plate.

Thick-ness.	Weight.	Thick-ness.	Weight.	Thick-ness.	Weight.	Thick-ness.	Weight.
In.	Lbs.	In.	Lbs.	In.	Lbs.	In.	Lbs.
0.01	0.406	0.06	2.434	0.1	4.057	0.6	24.344
0.02	0.811	0.07	2.840	0.2	8.114	0.7	28.401
0.03	1.217	0.08	3.246	0.3	12.172	0.8	32.458
0.04	1.623	0.09	3.651	0.4	16.232	0.9	36.516
0.05	2.029	0.10	4.057	0.5	20.286	1.	40.573

Multipliers for finding the Weights of other Metals, from the three preceding Tables.

Metals.	Multipliers.	Metals.	Multipliers.
Platinum, laminated.......	2.846	Copper, cast...........	1.128
Platinum, purified........	2.503	Brass, wire............	1.096
Pure gold, hammered.....	2.486	Brass, cast............	1.080
Pure gold, cast...........	2.47	Steel..................	1.003
Lead:..................	1.457	Iron, wrought..........	1.
Pure silver, hammered....	1.350	Iron, cast.............	0.925
Pure silver, cast..........	1.344	Pewter................	0.960
Copper, wire	1.136	Tin, cast..............	0.937
Copper, hammered........	1.132		

Weight of one square foot of various Metals.

THICKNESS.	WEIGHT.				
	Wrought Iron	Cast Iron.	Copper.	Brass.	Lead.
In.	Lbs.	Lbs.	Lbs.	Lbs.	Lbs.
0.0625	2.535	2.345	2.860	2.738	3.693
0.125	5.070	4.690	5.720	5.476	7.386
0.1875	7.605	7.035	8.580	8.214	11.079
0.25	10.140	9.380	11.440	10.952	14.772
0.3125	12.675	11.725	14.300	13.690	18.465
0.375	15.216	14.670	17.160	16.428	22.158
0.4375	17.851	16.415	20.020	19.166	25.851
0.5	20.280	18.760	22.880	21.904	29.544
0.5625	22.815	21.105	25.740	24.642	33.237
0.625	25.350	23.450	28.600	27.380	36.930
0.6875	27.885	25.795	31.640	30.118	40.623
0.75	30.410	28.140	34.320	32.856	44.316
0.8125	32.945	30.485	37.180	35.594	48.009
0.875	35.480	32.880	40.040	38.332	51.702
0.9375	38.015	35.225	42.900	41.170	55.405
1.	40.550	37.570	45.760	43.908	59.098

Table of equivalent Vulgar and Decimal Fractions.

Vulgar.	Decimal.	Vulgar.	Decimal.
$\frac{1}{16}$	0.0625	$\frac{9}{16}$	0.5625
$\frac{1}{8}$	0.125	$\frac{5}{8}$	0.625
$\frac{3}{16}$	0.1875	$\frac{11}{16}$	0.6875
$\frac{1}{4}$	0.25	$\frac{3}{4}$	0.75
$\frac{5}{16}$	0.3125	$\frac{13}{16}$	0.8125
$\frac{3}{8}$	0.375	$\frac{7}{8}$	0.875
$\frac{7}{16}$	0.4375	$\frac{15}{16}$	0.9375
$\frac{1}{2}$	0.5		

Weight of 1 foot in length of Cast Iron Pipes of different thickness.

DIAM. OF BORE.	¼ Inch.	⅜ Inch.	½ Inch.	⅝ Inch.	¾ Inch.	⅞ Inch.	1 Inch.
In.	Lbs.	Lbs.	Lbs.	Lbs.	Lbs.	Lbs.	Lbs.
1	3.06	5.06	7.36	9.97	12.89	16.11	19.63
1¼	3.68	5.98	8.59	11.51	14.73	18.25	22.09
1½	4.29	6.9	9.82	13.04	16.56	20.4	24.54
1¾	4.91	7.83	11.05	14.57	18.41	22.55	27.
2	5.53	8.75	12.27	16.11	20.25	24.7	29.45
2¼	6.14	9.66	13.5	17.64	22.09	26.84	31.85
2½	6.74	10.58	14.72	19.17	23.92	28.93	34.36
2¾	7.36	11.5	15.95	20.7	25.71	31.14	36.81
3	7.98	12.43	17.18	22.19	27.62	33.29	39.28
3¼	8.59	13.34	18.35	23.78	29.45	35.44	41.72
3½	9.2	14.21	19.64	25.31	31.3	37.58	44.18
3¾	9.76	15.19	20.86	26.85	33.13	39.73	46.63
4	10.44	16.11	22.1	28.38	34.98	41.88	49.1
4¼	11.1	17.08	23.37	29.97	36.87	44.08	51.6
4½	11.66	17.94	24.54	31.44	38.65	46.17	54.
4¾	12.27	18.87	25.77	32.98	40.5	48.32	56.45
5	12.80	19.78	26.99	34.51	42.33	50.46	59.
5¼	13.5	20.71	28.23	36.05	44.18	52.62	61.36
5½	14.11	21.63	29.45	37.58	46.02	54.76	63.81
5¾	14.73	22.55	30.68	39.12	47.86	56.91	66.27
6	15.34	23.47	31.91	40.65	49.7	59.06	68.73
6¼	15.95	24.39	33.13	42.18	51.54	61.21	72.
6½	16.57	25.31	34.36	43.72	53.39	63.36	73.41
6¾	17.18	26.23	35.59	45.26	55.23	65.28	76.1
7	17.79	27.15	36.82	46.79	56.84	67.65	78.53
7¼	18.41	28.08	38.05	48.1	58.91	69.79	81.
7½	19.03	29.	39.05	49.86	60.74	71.95	83.45
7¾	19.64	29.69	40.5	51.38	62.59	74.09	86.
8	20.02	30.83	41.71	52.92	64.42	76.23	88.35
8¼	20.86	31.74	42.95	54.45	66.26	78.38	90.81
8½	21.69	32.9	44.4	56.21	68.33	80.76	93.49
8¾	22.09	33.59	45.4	57.52	69.95	82.68	95.72
9	22.71	34.52	46.64	59.07	71.8	84.84	98.18
9¼	23.31	35.43	47.86	60.59	73.63	86.97	100.63
9½	23.93	36.36	49.09	62.13	75.47	89.13	103.1
9¾	24.55	37.28	50.32	63.66	77.32	91.28	105.54
10	25.16	38.2	51.54	65.2	79.16	93.42	108.
10¼	25.77	39.11	52.77	66.73	80.99	95.57	110.44
10½	26.38	40.04	54.	68.26	82.84	97.71	113.
10¾	27.	40.96	55.22	69.8	84.67	99.86	115.35
11	27.62	41.88	56.46	71.33	86.52	102.01	117.81
11¼	28.22	42.8	57.67	72.86	88.35	104.15	120.26
11½	28.84	43.71	58.9	74.39	90.19	106.3	122.71
11¾	29.45	44.64	60.13	75.93	92.04	108.45	125.18
12	30.06	45.55	61.35	77.46	93.6	110.6	127.6

Specific Gravities.

SOLIDS.	Specific gravity.	Weight of 1 cubic inch.
		Lbs.
Antimony, cast	6,712	0.2428
Brass, cast	8,396	0.3037
Bronze, gun metal	8,700	0.3147
Copper, cast	8,788	0.3179
Do. wire	8,878	0.3211
Gold, cast	19,258	0.6966
Do. hammered	19,361	0.7003
Iron, bar	7,788	0.2817
Do. cast	7,207	0.2607
Lead, cast	11,352	0.4106
Mercury, at 32°	13,598	0.4918
Do. at 60°	13,580	0.4912
Platinum, rolled	22,069	0.7982
Do. hammered	20,337	0.7356
Silver, cast	10,474	0.3788
Do. hammered	10,511	0.3806
Steel, soft	7,833	0.2833
Do. hardened and tempered	7,818	0.2828
Tin, cast	7,291	0.2637
Zinc, cast	6,861	0.2482
Amber	1,078	0.0390
Beeswax	965	0.0349
Bricks	1,900	0.0690
Borax	1,714	0.0620
Camphor	989	0.0358
Chalk	2,784	0.1007
Charcoal	441	0.0160
Do. triturated	1,380	0.0499
Clay	1,930	0.0700
Coal, bituminous, Eng.	1,270	0.0460
Diamond	3,521	0.1274
Earth, common	1,500	0.0543
Gunpowder, loose	900	0.0326
Do. shaken	1,000	0.0362
Do. solid	1,550 1,800	0.0561 0.0652
Gypsum	2,168	0.0784
Ice	930	0.0336
Ivory	1,822	0.0659
Limestone	3,180	0.1150
Lime, quick	804	0.0291
Marble, Parian	2,838	0.1027
Marble, common	2,686	0.0972

SOLIDS.	Specific gravity.	Weight of 1 cubic inch.
		Lbs.
Salt, common	2,130	0.0774
Saltpetre	2,090	0.0756
Sand	1,800	0.0652
Slate	2,672	0.0959
Stone, common	2,520	0.0911
Sulphur, native	2,033	0.0735
Tallow	945	0.0342
Wood, (dry,) Apple	793	0.0287
Ash	845	0.0306
Beech	852	0.0308
Box	912	0.0330
Cedar	596	0.0216
Cherry	715	0.0259
Cork	240	0.0087
Cypress	644	0.0233
Elm	671	0.0243
Fir	700	0.0253
Lignum vitæ	1,333	0.0482
Mahogany	854	0.0309
Maple	750	0.0271
Oak, English	932	0.0337
Do. do. heart, 60 years old	1,170	0.0423
Pine, yellow	660	0.0239
Do. white	554	0.0200
Poplar	383	0.0139
Walnut	671	0.0243
Seasoned American Wood. Ash	722	0.0261
Beech	624	0.0226
Cherry	606	0.0219
Cypress	441	0.0160
Hickory, red	838	0.0303
Mahogany, (St. Domingo)	720	0.0260
Oak, white, (Upland)	687	0.0248
Oak, white, (James river)	759	0.0275
Pine, yellow	541	0.0196
Do. white	473	0.0171
Poplar, (Tulip tree)	587	0.0212
WATER	1,000	0.0362

Specific Gravities—Continued.

LIQUIDS.	Specific gravity.	ELASTIC FLUIDS.	Specific gravity.
Acid, nitric	1,217	Air, atmospheric	1,000
Do. sulphuric	1,841	Ammoniacal gas	597
Alcohol, absolute	792	Azote	976
Ether, sulphuric	715	Carbonic acid	1,524
Oil, linseed	940	Carburetted hydrogen	555
Do. olive	915	Chlorine	2,470
Do. essential, of turpentine	870	Chloro carbonic	3,389
Do. whale	923	Hydrogen	70
Turpentine, liquid	991	Oxygen	1,104
Water, distilled	1,000	Phosphuretted hydrogen	870
Do. sea	1,026	Sulphuretted hydrogen	1,777
Wine	992	Sulphurous acid	2,120
		Vapor of alcohol	1,613
		Do. spirits of turpentine	5,013
		Do. sulphuric ether	2,586
		Do. water	623

The weight of dry atmospheric air at the temperature of 32°, the barometer being at 30 in., is $\frac{1}{770}$ of that of distilled water.

The weight of a cubic foot of distilled water *at the maximum density* being nearly 1,000 ounces avoirdupois, the specific gravity of a solid or liquid body expresses the weight of a cubic foot, in ounces; therefore the weight of such a body in ounces will be found by multiplying its contents in cubic feet by its specific gravity.

According to Mr. Hassler's comparisons, the weight of a cubic foot of water at its maximum density, the barometer being at 30 in., is 998.068 oz.

According to the British imperial standards, the weight of a cubic foot of water, at 62°, the barometer being at 30 in., is 997.136 oz; this would give for the cubic foot of water, at the maximum density, 998.224 oz.

By the investigations of Prof. R. S. McCulloch, the maximum density of water is at the temperature of 39°.6 Fahr; this agrees very nearly with Mr. Hassler's determination of the maximum density, 39°.83.

For a table of the density of water at different temperatures, see CHAP. XV.

CHAPTER FIFTEENTH.

MISCELLANEOUS INFORMATION.

WEIGHTS AND MEASURES.

Measures of Length.

Inches.	Feet.	Yards.	Rods or Poles.	Furlongs.	Mile.
12	1				
36	3	1			
198	16½	5½	1		
7920	660	220	40	1	
63360	5280	1760	320	8	1

The inch was formerly divided into three parts, called *barley corns*, and also into 12 parts called *lines*, neither of which denominations is now in common use. Scales and measuring rules are generally divided into *inches*, *quarters*, *eighths* and *sixteenths;* or into *inches* and *decimal parts;* the latter of these divisions is used in the Ordnance Department.

For surveying land: 7.92 Inches = 1 link } Gunter's chain.
100 Links = 4 poles, or 22 yards, or 66 feet.

For map making: Chains are often made of 50 links, each 1 foot in length.

For measuring ropes and soundings: 1 Fathom = 6 feet.
1 Cable's length = 120 fathoms.

For measuring cloth: 1 Nail = 2¼ inches = 1-16th of a yard.
1 Quarter = 4 nails.
1 Yard = 4 quarters.
1 Ell English = 5 quarters.

For measuring horses: 1 Hand = 4 inches.

Geographical measure: 1 Degree of a great circle of the earth = 69.77 miles.
1 Geographical or nautical mile = 1-60th of a degree of the earth = 2025 yards.
1 Nautical league = 3 miles.

A standard measure has been adopted for the United States, copies of which are distributed to various parts of the country, for the purpose of establishing a uniform system. This standard is measured on a brass bar and copied from the British standard *yard.* For the proportion which it bears to the French *metre*, see below.

Foreign Measures of Length.

GREAT BRITAIN. The Imperial standard yard of Great Britain, adopted in 1825, is referred to a natural standard, which is the distance between the axis of suspension and the centre of oscillation of a pendulum which shall vibrate seconds in vacuo, in London, at the level of the sea; that distance measured on a brass rod, at the temperature of 62° Fahr., is declared to be 39.1393 *imperial inches.*

FRANCE.—*Old system:*

1 Point		= 0.0074	Eng. inches.	
1 Line	= 12 points	= 0.08884	"	
1 Inch	= 12 lines	= 1.06577	"	
1 Foot	= 12 inches	= 12.7892	"	
1 Ell	= 43 in. 10 lines	= 46.716	"	= 1.298 yd.
1 Toise	= 6 feet	= 76.735	"	= 2.132 "

1 Perch (Paris) = 18 feet.

1 Perch (royal) = 22 "

1 League, (common,) 25 to a degree = 2280 toises = 4861 yds., = 2.76 miles.

1 League, (post,) = 2000 toises = 4264 yds. = 2.42 miles.

1 Fathom (*Brasse*) = 5 feet French = 63.946 inches, or $5\frac{1}{3}$ feet Eng. nearly.

1 Cable length = 100 toises = 120 fathoms Fr., = $106\frac{2}{3}$ fathoms English.

1 Pace (pas) = $\frac{2}{3}$ metre = 26.5 in. nearly.

TABLE *for reducing old French Measures to English.*

French feet.	English inches.	Fr. feet or inch.	English feet or inches.	French lines.	English inches.	French points.	English inches.
1	12.7892	1	1.0658	1	0.0888	1	0.0074
2	25.5784	2	2.1315	2	0.1776	2	0.0148
3	38.3676	3	3.1973	3	0.2664	3	0.0222
4	51.1568	4	4.2631	4	0.3553	4	0.0296
5	63.9460	5	5.3288	5	0.4441	5	0.0370
6	76.7352	6	6.3946	6	0.5329	6	0.0444
7	89.5244	7	7.4604	7	0.6217	7	0.0518
8	102.3136	8	8.5261	8	0.7105	8	0.0592
9	115.1028	9	9.5919	9	0.7993	9	0.0666
10	127.8920	10	10.6577	10	0.8881	10	0.0740
11	140.6812	11	11.7234	11	0.9770	11	0.0814

New French System. The basis of the new French system of measures is the measure of a meridian of the earth, a quadrant of which is 10,000,000 *metres*, measured at the temperature of 32° Fahr. The multiples and divisions of it are decimal, viz: 1 metre = 10 decimetres = 100 centimetres = 1000 millimetres = 39.3707971 English inches, or 3.2809 feet.

Road measure. Myriametre = 10,000 metres. Kilometre = 1,000 metres. Decametre = 10 metres. Metre = 0.51317 toise.

TABLE FOR REDUCING METRES TO INCHES.

According to Capt. Kater's comparison, 1 metre = 39.37079 English inches.

Metres.	Inches.	Metres.	Inches.	Metres.	Inches.	Metres.	Inches.
0.001	0.039371	0.026	1.023641	0.051	2.007910	0.076	2.992180
2	0.078742	27	1.063011	52	2.047281	77	3.031551
3	0.118112	28	1.102382	53	2.086652	78	3.070922
4	0.157483	29	1.141753	54	2.126023	79	3.110292
5	0.196854	0.030	1.181124	55	2.165393	0.080	3.149663
6	0.236225	31	1.220494	56	2.204764	81	3.189034
7	0.275596	32	1.259865	57	2.244135	82	3.228405
8	0.314966	33	1.299236	58	2.283506	83	3.267776
9	0.354337	34	1.338607	59	2.322877	84	3.307146
0.010	0.393708	35	1.377978	0.060	2.362247	85	3.346517
11	0.433078	36	1.417348	61	2.401618	86	3.385888
12	0.472449	37	1.456719	62	2.440989	87	3.425259
13	0.511820	38	1.496090	63	2.480358	88	3.464630
14	0.551191	39	1.535461	64	2.519731	89	3.504000
15	0.590562	0.040	1.574832	65	2.559101	0.090	3.543371
16	0.629933	41	1.614202	66	2.598472	91	3.582742
17	0.669303	42	1.653573	67	2.637843	92	3.622113
18	0.708674	43	1.692944	68	2.677214	93	3.661483
19	0.748045	44	1.732315	69	2.716585	94	3.700854
0.020	0.787416	45	1.771686	0.070	2.755955	95	3.740225
21	0.826787	46	1.811056	71	2.795326	96	3.779596
22	0.866157	47	1.850427	72	2.834697	97	3.818967
23	0.905528	48	1.889798	73	2.874068	98	3.858337
24	0.944899	49	1.929169	74	2.913438	99	3.897708
25	0.984270	0.050	1.968540	75	2.952809	0.100	3.937079

		English.
Austria.—	1 Foot = 12.445 English inches	= 1.0371 feet.
	1 Mile = 4,000 toises	= 5 miles nearly.
Prussia.—	1 Rhineland foot = 12.3557 English inches	= 1.0296 feet.
	1 Mile = 8,552 yards, English	= 5 miles nearly.
Russia.—	1 Foot = 21.1874 English inches	= 1.7656 feet.
	For the artillery, the English foot and inch are used.	
	1 Verst = 2,000 Russian feet	= 1,177 yards.

SPAIN.— 1 Foot = 11.1284 English inches.
1 Vara = 3 feet = 0.9274 English yard.
1 League Royal = 25,000 Spanish feet = $4\frac{1}{3}$ miles, nearly.
1 Common league = 19,800 do. = $3\frac{1}{2}$ "
1 Judicial league = 15,000 do. = $2\frac{5}{8}$ "
MEXICO.—1 Common league = 15,000 do. = $2\frac{5}{8}$ "
SWEDEN.—1 Foot = 11.6865 English inches.

Measures of Surface.

Square measure. 144 Square inches = 1 square foot.
9 Square feet = 1 square yard.
Land measure. $30\frac{1}{4}$ Square yards = 1 square perch or pole.
40 Perches = 1 rood.
160 Perches = 4 roods = 1 acre = 10 square chains. (Gunter's) = 4,840 square yards = 70 yards square nearly.
640 Acres = 1 square mile.

French Superficial Measures.

Old system. 1 Square inch = 1.13587 English square inch.
1 Arpent (Paris) = 100 square perches (Paris) or 900 square toises = 4,088 square yards, or 5-6ths of an acre, nearly.
1 Arpent (woodland) = 100 square perches (royal) = 6,108 square yards, or 1 acre, 1 rood, 1 perch.
New, or *Decimal system.* 1 Are = 100 square metres = 119.603 square yds.
1 Decare = 10 ares. 1 Hecatare = 100 ares.

Measures of Solidity.

Cubic or *Solid measure.* 1 Cubic foot = 1,728 cubic inches.
1 Cubic yard = 46,656 " " = 27 cubic feet.

Measuring stone. In different parts of the United States the *perch* of stone denotes a different quantity, but it is usually $24\frac{3}{4}$ cubic feet.

Measuring wood. 1 Cord is a prism 4 ft. square and 8 ft. long = 128 cubic ft.

French Solid Measures.

1 Cubic inch = 1.2106 cubic inch, English.
1 Cubic foot = 2091.85 cubic inches, English.
1 Cubic decimetre = 61.0271 " "
1 Stere = 1 cubic metre = 61027.1 cubic in. = 35.3166 cubic feet = 1.308 cubic yard.

Measures of Capacity.

Liquid Measure.

Gills.	Pints.	Quarts.	Gallons.
4	1		
8	2	1	
32	8	4	1

The standard gallon of the United States is the old wine gallon, which measures 231 cubic inches, and contains, (as determined by Mr. Hassler,) 58373 Troy grains, or 8.3388822 avoirdupois pounds, of distilled water at the maximum density (39°.83 Fahr.); the barometer being at 30 inches.

A cubic foot contains 7.48 gallons.

A box 6 × 6 × 6.42 inches contains 1 gallon.

A box 4 × 4 × 3.61 inches contains 1 quart.

Dry Measure.

Pints.	Quarts.	Gallons.	Pecks.	Bushels.
2	1			
8	4	1		
16	8	2	1	
64	32	8	4	1

The standard bushel of the United States is the Winchester bushel, which measures 2150.4 cubic inches, and contains 543391.89 Troy grains, or 77.627413 lbs. avoirdupois, of distilled water, under the circumstances above stated.

A cubic yard contains 21.69 bushels.

A cylinder 14 in. diam. × 14 in. deep } contains 1 bushel.
Or a box 16 × 16.8 × 8 inches }

A box 12 × 11.2 × 8 inches contains ½ bushel.

A box 8 × 8.4 × 8 inches contains 1 peck.

N. B.—It will be observed that the pint, quart, and gallon of dry measure are not the same as for liquid measure.

Foreign Measures of Capacity.

Great Britain.—The British imperial gallon measures 277.274 cubic inches, containing ten pounds avoirdupois of distilled water, weighed in air, at the temperature of 62°, the barometer being at 30 in. The same measure is used for liquids as for dry goods which are not measured by heaped measure; for the latter, the bushel is to be heaped in the form of a cone not less than 6 inches high, the base being 19½ inches. The old distinctions of wine measure, ale and beer measure, and dry measure are discontinued.

For grain. 8 bushels = 1 quarter = 10.269 cubic feet.
5 quarters = 1 load = 51.347 cubic feet.

For coal or *heaped measure.* 1 sack = 3 bushels = 4.89 cubic feet nearly.
1 chaldron = 12 sacks = 36 bushels = 58.68 cubic feet.

For timber. 1 load = 40 cubic feet.

Former wine gallon = 231 cubic inches.

Former ale gallon = 282 cubic inches.

Imperial gallon = 277.274 cubic inches, (as above.)

France. 1 Litre = 1 cubic decimetre = 61.0271 cubic inches = 1.057 U.S. quart = 1.761 imperial pint of Great Britain.
1 Boisseau = 13 litres = 793.364 cub. in. = 3.4344 U. S. gals.
1 Pinte = 0.931 litre = 56.816 cub. in. = 0.98383 U. S. quart.

Spain. 1 Wine arroba = 4.2455 U. S. gallons.
1 Fanega, (corn measure) = 1.593 U. S. bushel.

Measures of Weight.

Avoirdupois Weight.

Drams.	Ounces.	Pounds.	Quarters.	Cwt.	Ton.
16	1				
256	16	1			
7168	448	28	1		
28672	1792	112	4	1	
573440	35840	2240	80	20	1

The standard avoirdupois pound of the United States, as determined by Mr. Hassler, is the weight of 27.7015 cubic inches of distilled water weighed in air, at the temperature of the maximum density, (39°.83;) the barometer being at 30 inches.

Troy Weight.

Grains.	Dwt.	Ounce.	Pound.
24	1		
480	20	1	
5760	240	12	1

The pound, ounce, and grain are the same in Apothecaries' and Troy weight; in the former, the ounce is divided into 8 drachms, the drachm into 3 scruples, and the scruple into 20 grains.

7000 Troy grains = 1 lb. Avoirdupois.
175 Troy pounds = 144 lbs. Avoirdupois.
175 Troy ounces = 192 oz. Avoirdupois.
437½ Troy grains = 1 oz. Avoirdupois.

Foreign Weights.

GREAT BRITAIN. The imperial avoirdupois pound is the weight of 27.7274 cubic inches of distilled water weighed in air, with brass weights, at the temperature of 62° Fahr.; barometer, 30 inches. Therefore,

1 cubic inch of distilled water at 62° weighs 252.458 grains.

0.003961 cubic inch weighs 1 grain.

22.815689 cubic inches weigh 1 troy pound.

Horseman's weight: 1 stone = 14 pounds.

FRANCE. *Old system.* 1 Livre = 16 onces = 1.0780 lb. avoirdupois.
1 Once = 8 gros = 1.0780 oz. do.
1 Gros = 72 grains = 58.9548 grains troy.
1 Grain............ = 0.8188 do.

New system. The basis of the system of weights is the weight, in vacuo, of a litre, or a cubic decimetre, of distilled water, at the temperature of 39°.2 Fahr; $\frac{1}{1000}$ th part of this weight is a *gramme*, the multiples of which are: 1 Decagramme = 10 grammes: 1 Hectogramme = 100 grammes: 1 Kilogramme = 1000 gram's. The divisions are: 1 Decigramme = $\frac{1}{10}$th gramme: 1 Centigramme = $\frac{1}{100}$th gramme: 1 Milligramme = $\frac{1}{1000}$th gramme.

1 Quintal = 100 kilogrammes.
1 Millier = 1000 kilogrammes = 1 ton sea weight, (French.)
1 Kilogramme = 2.204737 pounds avoirdupois.
1 Gramme = 15.433159 grains troy = 0.03528 oz. avoirdupois.
1 Pound avoirdupois = 0.4535685 kilogramme.
1 Pound troy = 0.3732223 kilogramme.

SPAIN. 1 Pound = 1.0152 pound avoirdupois.
SWEDEN. 1 Pound = 0.9376 " "
AUSTRIA. 1 Pound = 1.2351 " "
PRUSSIA. 1 Pound = 1.0333 " "

27

Measures of Value.

All calculations of value in the military service of the United States are expressed in *Dollars* and *Cents*, although the denominations of *shillings* and *pence* are still in common use as a nominal currency in many of the States.

The standard of gold and silver is 900 parts of pure metal and 100 of alloy, in 1000 parts of coin. The alloy of gold coin is 25 silver and 75 copper; the alloy of silver is copper.

Weight of Dollar	412.5	grains troy.	Other coins in proportion.
" Eagle	258	"	
" Cent	168	"	

Relative Mint Value of United States and Foreign Coins.

GREAT BRITAIN	1 Guinea = 21 shillings	= 5.059	dollars.
	1 Sovereign, or 1 pound = 20 shillings	= 4.845	"
	1 Crown = 5 shillings	= 1.08	"
	1 Shilling = 12 pence	= 0.217	"
	1 Penny	= 0.018	"
FRANCE	5 Francs	= 0.932	"
	1 Franc = 20 sous	= 0.185	"
	1 Sous	= 0.0093	"
SPAIN	1 Doubloon, or 1 ounce	= 15.57	"
AUSTRIA	1 Ducat	= 2.275	"
	1 Crown, or rix dollar	= 0.97	"
	20 Kreutzers	= 0.16	"
PRUSSIA	1 Double Frederick	= 8.00	"
	1 Thaler	= 0.693	"
RUSSIA	1 Half-Imperial = 5 roubles	= 3.967	"
	1 Rouble	= 0.75	"
SWEDEN	1 Ducat	= 2.267	"
	1 Specie daler	= 1.042	"
TURKEY	20 Piastres	= 0.82	"

DIMENSIONS OF DRAWING PAPER.

Demy	1 ft.	7½ in.	×	1 ft.	3½	inches.
Medium	1 "	10 "	×	1 "	6	"
Royal	2 "	0 "	×	1 "	7	"
Super royal	2 "	3 "	×	1 "	7	"
Imperial	2 "	5 "	×	1 "	9¼	"
Elephant	2 "	3¾ "	×	1 "	10¼	"
Columbier	2 "	9¾ "	×	1 "	11	"
Atlas	2 "	9 "	×	2 "	2	"
Double elephant	3 "	4 "	×	2 "	2	"
Antiquarian	4 "	4 "	×	2 "	7	"

PHYSICAL DATA.

Working Power of Men and Horses.

MEN. *A foot soldier* travels in 1 minute, in common time, 90 steps = 70 yds.
In quick time 110 " = 86 "
In double quick 140 " = 109 "

He occupies in the ranks a front of 20 in., and a depth of 13 in., without the knapsack; the interval between the ranks is 13 in. 5 Men can stand in a space of 1 square yard. Average weight of men, 150 lbs. each.

A *man* travels, without a load, on level ground, during 8½ hours a day, at the rate of 3.7 miles an hour, or 31¼ miles a day. He can carry 111 lbs., 11 miles in a day. A porter going short distances and returning unloaded, carries 135 lbs., 7 miles a day. He can carry in a wheelbarrow 150 lbs., 10 miles a day.

The maximum power of a strong man, exerted for 2½ minutes, may be stated at 18,000 lbs. raised 1 foot in a minute.—*Mr. Field's experiments*, 1838.

A man of ordinary strength exerts a force of 30 lbs. for 10 hours a day, with a velocity of 2½ feet in a second = 4500 lbs. raised 1 foot in a minute = *one-fifth* the work of a horse.

Daily allowance of water for a man, 1 gallon, for all purposes.

HORSES. *A horse* travels the distance of 400 yards, at a walk, in 4½ minutes; at a trot, in 2 minutes; at a gallop, in 1 minute.

He occupies in the ranks a front of 40 in., a depth of 10 feet; in a stall, from 3½ to 4½ feet front; at picket, 3 feet by 9. Average weight of horses, 1000 lbs. each.

A horse carrying a soldier and his equipments, (say 225 lbs.,) travels 25 miles in a day (8 hours.)

A *pack horse* can carry 250 to 300 lbs., 20 miles a day.

A *draught horse* can draw 1600 lbs. 23 miles a day; weight of carriage included.

Artillery horses should not be made to draw more than 700 lbs. each, the weight of the carriage included.

The ordinary work of a horse for 8 hours a day may be stated at 22,500 lbs. raised 1 foot in a minute.

In a horse mill, the horse moves at the rate of 3 feet in a second. The diameter of the path should not be less than 25 or 30 feet.

Daily allowance of water for a horse, 4 gallons.

Forage. Hay, pressed in bundles; 11 lbs. to the cubic foot.
Oats: 40 lbs. to the bushel, or 32.14 lbs. to the cubic foot.
Wheat: 60 lbs. to the bushel, or 48.21 lbs. to the cubic foot.

A horse power in steam engines, is estimated at 33,000 lbs. raised 1 foot in a minute; but as a horse can exert that force but 6 hours a day, one steam horse power is equivalent to that of 4 horses.

The number of horse-powers, in a single stroke engine, is expressed by $.0000238\ d^2\ n\ p\ l$; d being the diameter of the piston in inches, n the number of strokes in a minute, l the length of stroke in feet, and p the pressure of steam on a square inch, (diminished usually by $\frac{1}{5}$ for friction and inertia.) In a double stroke engine the power is double the above.

Electricity.

Relative conducting Power of Metals.

Copper	10,000	Iron	1,580
Gold	9,360	Tin	1,550
Silver	7,360	Lead	830
Zinc	2,850	Mercury	345
Platinum	1,880	Potassium	133

The conducting power of rods of the same metal, of equal diameter, is inversely as their lengths; of rods of equal lengths, it is proportional to the mass and not to the surface.

The conducting power is increased by lowering the temperature, and diminished and finally destroyed, by raising the temperature.

The metals are infinitely better conductors than any other substances. Charcoal which has been exposed to a strong heat is one of the best conductors, but greatly inferior in this respect to iron and platinum.

Heat.

Thermometers.

FIXED POINTS.	Fahrenheit.	Reaumer.	Centigrade.
Freezing point of water	32°	0°	0°
Boiling do. do	212°	80°	100°

The zero of Wedgewood's pyrometer corresponds with 1077° Fahr., and 1° Wedgewood is equal to 130° Fahr. Hence for converting from one scale to another, $F^\circ = \frac{C^\circ \times 9}{5} + 32^\circ = \frac{R^\circ \times 9}{4} + 32^\circ = W^\circ \times 130^\circ + 1077.$

Note.—The indications of Wedgewood's pyrometer are no longer relied on for high temperatures.

Relative Conducting Power.

Gold	10,000	Tin	3,039
Platinum	9,810	Lead	1,796
Silver	9,730	Marble	236
Copper	8,932	Porcelain	122
Iron	3,743	Brick clay	114
Zinc	3,638		

Relative Radiating Power.

Water	100	Tin, blackened	100
Lampblack	100	Do. bright	12
Glass	90	Ice	85
Silver	12	Iron, polished	15
Lead, bright	19	Copper	12

Relative Specific Heat, of equal weights.

Water	10,000	Silver	557
Sulphur	1,880	Tin	515
Glass	1,770	Mercury	330
Iron	1,000	Platinum	314
Copper	949	Gold	298
Zinc	927	Lead	293

Relative Capacity for Heat, of equal weights.

Water	100	Zinc	102
Glass	187	Silver	82
Iron	126	Tin	60
Brass	116	Gold	50
Copper	114	Lead	43

The capacity for caloric increases with the temperature, and diminishes as the density of the body increases. Air reduced rapidly to *one-fifth* of its volume evolves heat enough to set fire to tinder.

Latent Heat.

Fluids.		*Vapors.*	
Ice	140°	Steam	990°
Sulphur	144	Vinegar	875
Lead	162	Ammonia	860
Bees' wax	175	Alcohol	442
Zinc	493	Ether	302

Expansion by Heat.

Linear Expansion of Solids, from 32° to 212°.

Zinc	0.00296
Lead	0.00285
Tin, refined	0.00247
Silver, fine	0.00215
Brass	0.00190
Copper	0.00172
Gold	0.00150
Steel, tempered	0.00119
Iron, soft, hammered	0.00124
Do. cast	0.00111
Steel, not tempered	0.00108
Platinum	0.00086
Roman cement	0.00144
Marble, Sicilian	0.00141
Do. Carrara	0.00119
Sandstone	0.00117
Slate	0.00104
Granite	0.00080
Glass, flint	0.00082
Brick, stock	0.00055
Do. fire	0.00049
Marble, black Galway	0.00045
Oak, dry	0.00006

The expansion in surface is expressed by numbers *double* of the above, and the expansion in volume by *triple* numbers.

Expansion of Fluids in bulk, from 32° to 212°.

Mercury	0.01808
Water, distilled	0.04330
Water, saturated with salt	0.05000
Alcohol	0.11000
Sulphuric acid	0.05882
Oil (olive and linseed)	0.08333
Spirits turpentine	0.07143
Gases, and air	0.37500

The rate of expansion of solids and liquids increases with the temperature; that of the gases is uniform for all temperatures.

Linear Expansion of Solids, (according to Daniell.)

	LINEAR EXPANSION FROM 62°.			Temperature of melting point.
	To 212°.	To 662°.	To melting point.	
Black lead ware	1.000244	1.000703		Fahrenh't.
Wedgewood ware	1.000735	1.002995		
Platinum	1.000735	1.002995	1.009926	3280°
Wrought iron	1.000984	1.004483	1.018378	3280
Cast iron	1.000893	1.003943	1.016389	2786
Gold	1.001025	1.004238	....	2016
Copper	1.001430	1.006347	1.024376	1996
Silver	1.001626	1.006886	1.020640	1873
Brass (zinc ¼)	1.001787	1.007207	1.021841	1800
Bronze (tin ¼)	1.001541	1.007053	1.016336	1500
Zinc	1.002480	1.008527	1.012621	746
Lead	1.002323	....	1.009072	612*
Tin	1.001472	....	1.003798	442*
Pewter (tin ⅕)	1.001696	....	1.003776	403

*Experiments of Franklin Institute.

3280° was the highest heat attained with an air furnace. Platinum does not *melt* at this temperature, but undergoes a change, which renders it unfit for further use in Daniell's pyrometer.

Density of Water at different Temperatures.

From a report made to Prof. A. D. Bache, by Prof. R. S. M'Culloch, December, 1849.

Temperature.	Density.	Temperature.	Density.
Fahr.		Fahr.	
20°	99901	65°	99863
25	99944	70	99807
30	99984	75	99741
35	99999	80	99666
40	1,00000	85	99581
45	99993	90	99487
50	99975	95	99383
55	99947	100	99270
60	99910		

Melting Points of Solids.

Platinum, palladium, rhodium, lime, silex, fine porcelain, can be melted in small quantities, by means of strong lenses, or of the hydro-oxygen blow pipe.

Iron red hot, in day light, 1077° Fahr.; in the dark, 752°.

	Wrought iron melts	3,280° Fahr.	
	Cast iron	2,786	
	Gold	2,016	
	Silver	1,873	
	Copper	1,996	
	Brass	1,900	
	Flint glass	2,377	
	Antimony	809	
	Zinc	746	
	Saltpetre	660	
	Lead	612	Experiments of committee of the Franklin Institute.
	Bismuth	506	″
	Tin	442	″
Alloys.	Lead 2, tin 1 (common solder)	475	″
Alloys.	Lead 1, tin 1	393	″
Alloys.	Lead 1, tin 2 (soft solder)	360	″
Alloys.	Lead 1, tin 1, bismuth 1	272	″
Alloys.	Lead 2, tin 3, bismuth 5	212	
	Sulphur	220	
	Beeswax, bleached	155	
	Do. common	149	
	Tallow	127	
	Gunpowder explodes	600	

Freezing Points of Liquids.

Olive oil	36° Fahr.	Strong wines	20° Fahr.
Water	32	Sulphuric acid	1
Milk	30	Brandy	— 7
Vinegar	28	Mercury	—39
Spirits of turpentine	16	Nitric acid	—55

Boiling Points of Liquids. (Bar. 30 in.)

Sulphuric ether	98°	Phosphorus	554°
Ammonia	140	Spirits of turpentine	560
Alcohol	174	Sulphur	570
Water, and essential oils	212	Sulphuric acid	590
Water, saturated with salt	224	Linseed oil	600
Nitric acid	248	Mercury	660

Liquids boil at a much lower temperature in vacuo, or under diminished pressure of the atmosphere. At the altitude of about 17,500 feet above the sea, where the barometer stands at 15.35 in., water boils at 180°.

Frigorific Mixtures.

Nitrate of ammonia 1, water 1; thermometer falls from	50° to 4°
Sulph. soda 8, muriatic acid 5	50° to 0°
Phosphate of soda 9, nitrate of ammonia 6, diluted nitric acid, 4	50° to —21°
Common salt 1, snow or ice 2	32° to — 4°
Cryst. chloride of lime 3, snow 2	32° to —50°

Heating Power of Different Combustibles.

The *calorific unit* is the quantity of heat required to raise 1° the temperature of a weight of water equal to that of the combustible used.

The following table gives the quantity of water which would be heated from 32° to 212° by an equal weight of several kinds of fuel, supposing no heat to be lost.

Hydrogen	234
Olive oil	100
Tallow	75
Pit coal, coke, or good charcoal	70
Wood, perfectly dry, (mean)	35
Wood, common, 1 year after felling; turf	26

The heating power of different kinds of wood (taking equal weights) does not vary more than in the proportion of 13 to 14, for the extremes.

Nearly six times as much heat is required to evaporate a given quantity of water as is required to raise its temperature to the boiling point; dividing the above numbers by 6, we have therefore the quantity of water which each kind of fuel will evaporate.

In even the best apparatus, not more than *half* the heat produced by the combustion of fuel is economized.

Elastic Force of Steam at Different Temperatures.

[From experiments of Committee of Franklin Institute.]

The unit is the atmospheric pressure, or 1 atmosphere = 30 inches of mercury.

Temp.	Press.	Temp.	Press.	Temp.	Press.	Temp.	Press.	Temp.	Press.
212	1	275	3	304½	5	326	7	345	9
235	1½	284	3½	310	5½	331	7½	349	9½
250	2	291½	4	315½	6	336	8	352½	10
264	2½	298½	4½	321	6½	340½	8½		

Strength of Ice.

Ice 2 inches thick will bear infantry.
4 " cavalry or light guns.
6 " heavy field guns.
8 " 24-pdr. gun, on sledges; weight not more than 1,000 lbs. to a square foot.

Velocity of Sound.

At the temperature of 33° the mean velocity of sound is 1100 feet in a second. It is increased or diminished *half a foot* for each degree of temperature above or below 33°.

Velocity and Force of the Wind.

VELOCITY.		Pressure on 1 square foot.	Common designations of the force of the winds.
In 1 hour.	In 1 second.		
Miles.	Feet.	Lbs.	
1	1.47	0.005	Hardly perceptible.
2	2.93	.020	Just perceptible.
3	4.40	.044	
4	5.87	.079	Gentle, pleasant wind.
5	7.33	.123	
10	14.67	.492	Pleasant, brisk breeze.
15	22.00	1.107	
20	29.34	1.968	Very brisk.
25	36.67	3.075	
30	44.01	4.429	High wind.
35	51.34	6.027	
40	58.68	7.873	Very high.
45	66.01	9.963	
50	73.35	12.300	A storm or tempest
60	88.02	17.715	A great storm.
80	117.36	31.490	A hurricane.
100	146.70	49.200	A hurricane that tears up trees, carries buildings before it, &c.

Measurement of Heights by means of the Barometer.

1. $X = 60345.51\ [1 + .00111111\ (T + T' - 64)]$

$$\times \text{Log.}\ \frac{H}{H'} \times \frac{1}{1 + .0001\ (t - t')} \times (1 + .002695 \cos. 2\ L.)$$

X is the required difference of height, in feet;

T, the temperature of the air, in degrees of Fahrenheit,
t, the temperature of mercury,
H, the height of mercury,
} at the lower station.

T', the temperature of the air,
t', the temperature of mercury,
H' the height of mercury,
} at the upper station.

L, the latitude of the place.

2. Neglecting the corrections for the latitude of the place and for the difference between the temperature of the air and that of the mercury in the barometers at the two stations, the difference of height, in feet, may be expressed approximately by $X = 67.0505\ (T + T' + 836) \times \text{Log.}\ \frac{H}{H'}$.

3. *Approximate rule:* For a mean temperature of 55° the difference of height in feet is, $X = 55{,}000 \times \frac{H - H'}{H + H'}$. Add 1-440th of this result for each degree which the mean temperature of the air at the two stations exceeds 55°, and deduct as much for each degree below 55°.

The average quantity of water which falls in rain and snow at Philadelphia is 36 inches in a year.

Limits of vegetation, in the Temperate Zone. The vine ceases to grow at the height of about 2,300 feet above the level of the sea; Indian corn, 2,800; oak, 3,350; walnut, 3,600; ash, 4,800; yellow pine, 6,200; fir, 6,700.

Perpetual Snow. Under the equator, at 15,800 feet above the level of the sea; in latitude 45°, at 8,400; in latitude 65°, at 5,000.

Declination of the Magnetic Needle. At London.....in 1580..11° 5' E.
1657.. 0 0
1832..24° 17' W.
1844..23° 15' W.
At West Point, N. Y., 1837.. 6° 44' 30" W.
1849.. 7° 20' 39" W.

Dip of the Needle. London................1844.............69°
West Point............1849.............73° 21'

Force of Gravity.

MOTION OF FALLING BODIES: Let t be the time of descent in seconds, of a body falling freely, in vacuo; h, the space described in the time t; v, the velocity acquired at the end of that time, and g the velocity acquired at the end of one second of time; then:

$$h = \tfrac{1}{2} g t^2; \qquad v = g t = \sqrt{2 g h}$$

The velocity g, which is the measure of the force of gravity, varies with the latitude of the place, and with its altitude above the level of the sea.

The force of gravity at the latitude of $45^\circ = 32.1803$ feet; at any other latitude L; $g = 32.1803$ feet $- 0.0821$ cos. $2 L$. If g' represents the force of gravity at the height h above the sea, and r the radius of the earth, the force of gravity at the level of the sea will be $g = g' (1 + \frac{5 h}{4 r})$.

In the latitude of London, at the level of the sea, $g = 32.191$ feet.

Do. Washington, do. do., $g = 32.155$ feet.

Pendulums.

The times of vibration of pendulums are proportional to the square roots of their lengths.

$$T = \pi \sqrt{\frac{l}{g}}$$

Therefore, if l be the length of a pendulum vibrating seconds, and l' the length of any other simple pendulum, or the distance from the point of suspension to the centre of oscillation of a compound pendulum, vibrating in the time t at the same place, then: $l' = l t^2$.

The length of a pendulum vibrating seconds is in a constant ratio to the force of gravity:

$$\frac{g}{l} = 9.8696044$$

Length of a pendulum vibrating seconds at the level of the sea, in various latitudes.

At the Equator		39.0152 inches.
Washington,	Lat. 38° 53′ 23″	39.0958 "
New York,	Lat. 40° 42′ 40″	39.1017 "
London,	Lat. 51° 31′	39.1393 "
	Lat. 45°	39.1270 "
	Lat. L	39.1270 in.—0.09982 cos. 2 L

BALLISTICS.

Motion of a body projected vertically upwards, in vacuo.

Let t, represent any time of ascent, in seconds.

h, the height } at the end of the time t.
v, the velocity }

g, the velocity acquired by a falling body in 1 second.

V, the initial velocity of projection.

H, the whole height of ascent.

T, the whole time of ascent.

Then:

$$h = Vt - \tfrac{1}{2} g t^2. \qquad v = V - g t.$$

$$H = \frac{V^2}{2g}. \qquad T = \frac{V}{g}.$$

Motion of a Projectile in vacuo.

The trajectory of a body projected obliquely, in vacuo, is a parabola, the axis of which is vertical.

The formulæ for the parabolic trajectory apply also, approximately, to the path of a body projected in the air, with a small velocity; such as a shell fired with a light charge from a mortar, or the ball of a mortar eprouvette.

Let V represent the initial velocity $= \sqrt{2gH}$

φ, the angle of projection, above the horizontal plane.

x, y, the horizontal and vertical co-ordinates of any point m in the trajectory, from the point of departure as the origin.

v, the velocity of the projectile, at the point m.

t, the time of flight, to the same point.

θ, the inclination of the tangent at that point.

X, the whole horizontal range.

Y, the greatest height of ascent.

T, the whole time of flight, for the range X.

1. *Equation of the trajectory.*

$$y = x \text{ tang. } \varphi - \frac{x}{4 H \cos.^2 \varphi}.$$

$$y = Vt \sin. \varphi - \tfrac{1}{2} g t^2. \qquad x = Vt \cos. \varphi.$$

2. $$X = 2H \sin. 2\varphi = \frac{V^2 \sin. 2\varphi}{g}.$$

$$Y = H \sin.^2 \varphi = \frac{V^2 \sin.^2 \varphi}{2g}.$$

$$T = \frac{2V \sin. \varphi}{g}.$$

3. The angle of greatest range is $\varphi = 45°$.

In that case, $X = 2\,H = 4\,Y$; $Y = \frac{1}{2}\,H$; $V = \sqrt{g\,X}$; $T = \sqrt{\frac{2\,X}{g}}$.

The ranges are equal at angles equidistant from 45°.

4. Under a given angle of projection the initial velocities are as the square roots of the ranges.

When the initial velocities are equal, the ranges are proportional to the sines of double the angles of elevation.

5. $v = \sqrt{2g\,(H - y)}$.

The velocities are equal in the two branches of the trajectory, at the same height.

The least velocity is at the summit, and is $= V \cos.\ \varphi$.

6. $\text{Tang.}\ \theta = \text{tang.}\ \varphi - \frac{x}{2\,H \cos.^2 \varphi}$.

On horizontal ground, the angle of descent is equal to the angle of projection, and the final velocity is equal to the initial velocity.

7. $t = \frac{x}{V \cos.\ \varphi}$.

When $\varphi = 45°$, $t = 1.4142\,\frac{x}{V}$.

8. *To find the initial velocity, or the angle of projection, necessary for striking a given point.*

Let a and b be the horizontal and vertical co-ordinates of the point, and ε its angle of elevation, making $\text{tang.}\ \varepsilon = \frac{b}{a}$; then:

$$H = \frac{a}{4 \sin.\ (\varphi - \varepsilon)} \cdot \frac{\cos.\ \varepsilon}{\cos.\ \varphi}. \qquad V = \sqrt{\frac{a\,g}{2 \sin.\ (\varphi - \varepsilon)} \cdot \frac{\cos.\ \varepsilon}{\cos.\ \varphi}}.$$

$$\text{Tang.}\ \varphi = \frac{2}{a}\left(H \pm \sqrt{(H\,(H - b) - \tfrac{1}{4}\,a^2)}\right)$$

Motion of a Projectile in the air.

The normal trajectory in the air is a continuous plane curve, which can be cut by a right line in not more than two points; it has two asymptotes, one vertical, the other inclined.

The actual trajectory of a ball is generally a curve of double curvature. It differs from the normal trajectory in consequence of the deviations, both lateral and vertical, produced by the eccentricity of the ball, its position in the gun, the motion of the air, and other circumstances, which cause the ball to revolve about an uncertain and variable axis, and to depart from the vertical plane of projection.

The equation of the trajectory is transcendental, and difficult of computation, but there are some cases which admit of simplification, giving useful approximate results.

Poisson's Equation of the Trajectory in the air.

$$y = x \text{ tang. } \varphi - \frac{1}{8\, c^2\, H \cos.^2 \varphi} \left(e^{2\, cx} - 2\, c\, x - 1\right)$$

y is the ordinate and x the abscissa of the curve; φ the angle of projection; H, the height corresponding to the initial velocity $V = \sqrt{2 g H}$; $e = 2.7182818$, the number whose hyperbolic logarithm is 1; $c = \frac{3\, n\, a}{16\, R\, D}$, in which a is the density of the air, and D that of the ball, the density of water being 1,000; R, the radius of the ball; n, a co-efficient for the resistance of the air, the value of which, for different velocities, is given by Hutton, as follows:

VELOCITY IN FEET.	600	800	1000	1100	1200	1300	1400	1500	1600	1700	1800	1900	2000
Value of n..	1.50	1.62	1.77	1.84	1.91	1.98	2.03	2.06	2.08	2.07	2.06	2.03	2.00

The above form of the equation supposes that the resistance of the air is proportional to the square of the velocity, and that the ball does not depart very far from a horizontal line drawn through the muzzle of the piece.

By developing the exponential function,

$$e^{2cx} = 1 + 2\, cx + \frac{4\, c^2\, x^2}{1.2} + \frac{8\, c^3\, x^3}{1.2.3} + \&c.,$$

the equation becomes

$$y = x \text{ tang. } \varphi - \frac{1}{8\, c^2\, H \cos.^2 \varphi} \left(\frac{4\, c^2\, x^2}{1.2} + \frac{8\, c^3\, x^3}{1.2.3} + \&c.\right)$$

If the angle of projection is small and the range x not greater than 2000 feet, the terms of this series above the third power may be neglected, and we may consider $\cos. \varphi = 1$; the equation will then take the form,

$$y = x \text{ tang. } \varphi - \frac{1}{2\, H} \left(\frac{x^2}{2} + \frac{c\, x^3}{3}\right).$$

Substituting for $2\, H$ its value $\frac{V^2}{g}$, and putting $m = \frac{1}{c}$, we have,

$$y = x \text{ tang. } \varphi - \frac{g\, x^2}{6\, m\, V^2} (3\, m + 2\, x)$$

In this form the equation may be used for cases of firing at low angles, with ranges not exceeding 650 yards.

Recent experiments in France, on the resistance of the air to the motion of projectiles, have furnished a more accurate (but more complicated) expression for the relation between the resistance and the velocity, than that given by Hutton, which has been generally used heretofore. This expression is of the form:

$$\rho = A \pi R^2 v^2 \left(1 + \frac{v}{r}\right)$$

in which R is the radius of the ball; A and $\frac{1}{r}$, co-efficients depending on the density and diameter of the ball, and the density of the air.

Considering the mean density of the air as 1-828th part of that of water, and expressing the dimensions and velocity in feet, the mean value of A, for artillery projectiles, may be taken $= 0.0085$.

For the resistance to solid shot, $r = 1427$ feet; for shells, $r = 2735$ feet.

The loss of velocity, by the resistance of the air, in any *small* distance x, will be expressed by

$$V - v = x \frac{3 A g}{4 R D} \left(1 + \frac{v}{r}\right) v$$

This formula may be used in experiments with the ballistic pendulum, for computing the velocity lost by the ball in passing from the gun to the pendulum block.

Final velocity of descent in the air.

The velocity of a projectile diminishes from the commencement of its flight to a point a little beyond the summit of the trajectory; it then increases to a certain limit, dependent on the diameter and density of the ball. The final velocity is given by the equation

$$v^2 \left(1 + \frac{v}{r}\right) = \frac{4 R D}{3 A}$$

	Shot.					Shells.				Musket ball.
Calibre...	42	24	18	12	6	13-in.	10-in.	8-in.	24-pdr.	
Final velocity of descent in feet per second...	485	455	425	410	360	585	505	445	375	213

General Formula for computing the Initial Velocity of a Ball.

$$V = \gamma \sqrt{\frac{\mu}{m + \frac{1}{3}\mu} \log. \frac{M}{\mu} - \Delta \frac{C^2 - R^2}{C^2}}.$$

In which V, is the initial velocity of the ball.

C, the radius of the bore.

R, the radius of the ball.

m, the weight of the ball, with the wad, or sabot, &c., used in loading.

μ, the weight of the charge of powder.

M, the weight of powder (loose) which would fill the bore of the gun.

Log. the common logarithms.

γ and Δ, co-efficients, depending on the nature of ordnance and the quality of the powder used; to be determined experimentally by means of some known velocity, and given difference of windage.

Δ may probably, without sensible error, be regarded as constant for the same quality of powder, though used in different kinds of ordnance; but the value of γ should be computed from the known velocity in a case approaching nearest to that to which the formula is to be applied.

In ordinary cases of windage, (W) we may consider $\frac{C^2 - R^2}{C^2} = \frac{2(C-R)}{C} = \frac{W}{C}$.

According to the experiments made with the ballistic pendulum at Washington Arsenal, the mean values of the co-efficients γ and Δ, for Dupont's powder, in guns of various calibres, (from 6-pounder to 32-pounder,) are: $\gamma = 3500$ feet; $\Delta = 3200$ feet.

The above formulæ, for the resistance of the air and for the initial velocity, are obtained from the "Traité de Balistique, par Didion, 1848;" a work which may be consulted for a full discussion of the theory of the motion of projectiles, and the deviations produced by their eccentricity and other causes.

MECHANICAL POWERS.

Conditions of Equilibrium of simple Machines.

LEVER. The *effective arm* of a lever is the perpendicular distance from the fulcrum to the line of direction of the power or weight.

The power is to the weight inversely as the effective arms of the lever:

$$P\,D = w\,d.$$

The pressure on the fulcrum is the resultant of the power and weight.

FIXED PULLEY. The power is equal to the weight. The pressure Q on the axis is to the power or weight as the chord c of the arc enveloped by the rope is to the radius r of the pulley. $P = w = \frac{Q\,r}{c}$.

MOVEABLE PULLEY. The power is to the weight, as the radius of the pulley is to the chord of the arc enveloped by the rope.

The pressure on the fixed end of the rope is equal to the power: $P = Q = \frac{w\,r}{c}$.

In a system of n moveable pulleys, the power is to the weight, as the product of the radii of the pulleys is to the product of the chords of the arcs enveloped by the rope: $P = w \frac{r\,r'\,r'' \,..\, n}{c\,c'\,c'' \,..\, n}$.

If the ropes are parallel, $c = 2\,r$, and $P = \frac{w}{2^n}$.

BLOCK AND TACKLE. The power is equal to the weight divided by the number of ropes attached to the lower block, or by twice the number of rising pulleys.

WHEEL AND AXLE. The power is to the weight, as the radius r, of the axle, is to the radius R, of the wheel.

$$P = \frac{w\,r}{R}.$$

SYSTEM OF WHEELS AND PINIONS. The power is to the weight, as the product of the radii, (or number of teeth,) r, r', r'', &c., of the pinions is to the product of the radii, (or number of teeth,) R, R', R'', &c., of the wheels:

$$P = w\,\frac{r\,r'\,r''\,....}{R\,R'\,R''\,....}$$

INCLINED PLANE. If the direction of the power is horizontal, the power is to the weight, as the height of the plane h is to its base b. $P = \frac{w\,h}{b}$.

The pressure on the plane, $Q = \frac{P\,l}{h} = \frac{w\,l}{b}$; l being the length of the plane.

If the direction of the power is parallel to the plane, the power is to the weight as the height of the plane to its length. $P = \frac{w\,h}{l}$. The pressure on the plane, $Q = \frac{P\,b}{h} = \frac{w\,b}{l}$.

SCREW. The power, applied perpendicular to the axis, is to the weight, as the *pitch* of the screw s, or the distance between two threads, is to the circumference described by the point to which the power is applied. Thus, if the power is applied by means of a lever l,

$$P = \frac{w\,s}{2\,\pi\,l}.$$

WEDGE. The power is to the resistance acting perpendicularly *on each side* of the wedge, as the thickness of the back of the wedge is to the length of the side.

BALANCE. The common balance is a simple lever, the arms of which are equal. If the balance is not accurate, the true weight of a body may be found, by taking the square root of the product of the weights which counterpoise it successively in each scale. A better and more convenient method of eliminating the error of a balance, is to place the body in one scale and counterpoise it by any weights in the opposite scale ; then remove the body and replace it by known weights, until the equilibrium is again restored. The sum of the latter weights will be that of the body required.

Friction.

In the foregoing conditions of equilibrium of machines, no account is taken of the resistance caused by friction, and by the stiffness of ropes, chains, &c.

Numerous experiments on friction have been made in France by M. Morin, from which the following general results are obtained :

1. The friction of any two bodies in motion is proportional to the pressure, whether the surfaces are dry or covered with an unguent. The ratio between the pressure and the friction is called the *co-efficient of friction*.

2. The amount of friction is independent of the surface of contact and of the velocity of the motion. It depends only on the pressure, the nature of the surfaces in contact, and the kind of unguent interposed.

3. In general, friction is less between bodies of different kinds, than between those of the same kind.

4. When two surfaces have been long in contact at rest, an adhesion takes place between them, the force of which is proportional to the extent of the surface of contact, and independent of the pressure.

5. When a continuous stratum of an unguent is constantly interposed between the surfaces of contact, the amount of friction depends on the nature of the unguent, and not on that of the surfaces.

6. With the unguents, hog's lard and olive oil, the co-efficient of friction is nearly the same for surfaces of wood moving on metals, wood on wood, metal on wood, and metal on metal, being in all cases between 0.07 and 0.08.

The co-efficient for the unguent tallow is the same, except in the case of metal on metal, for which it appears to be less suited than the others, giving a co-efficient of about 0.10.

7. The friction of axles is generally a little less than that of plane surfaces, under similar circumstances. The amount of friction is here also proportional to the pressure, and independent of the velocity of the motion.

MATHEMATICAL FORMULÆ AND DATA.

Mensuration.

Lines.

CIRCLE. *Ratio of circumference to diameter*, $\pi = 3.1415926536 = \frac{355}{113}$ nearly.

Length of an arc $= \frac{a \pi r}{180}$; r being the radius of the circle, and a the number of degrees in the arc; or, nearly $= \frac{8c' - c}{3}$; c being the chord of the arc, and c' the chord of half the arc, which is $= \sqrt{\frac{1}{4} c^2 + \text{versine}^2}$.

Length of 1 *degree* $= 0.0174533$; radius being 1.
Length of 1 *minute* $= 0.0002909$.
Length of 1 *second* $= 0.0000048$.

ELLIPSE. *Circumference* $= \frac{180}{200} \pi \sqrt{\frac{1}{2} (a^2 + b^2)}$, nearly; a and b being the axes.

PARABOLA: *Length of an arc*, commencing at the vertex, $= \sqrt{\left(\frac{4 a^2}{3} + \sqrt{b}\right)}$ nearly; a being the abscissa, and b the ordinate.

Surfaces.

Triangle. Half the base $\times$ the height; or half the product of two sides $\times$ the sine of the included angle, $(\frac{1}{2} a b \frac{\sin. C}{R})$; or, $\sqrt{s (s - a) (s - b) (s - c)}$; a, b, c being the sides, and $s = \frac{a + b + c.}{2}$

Parallelogram. The base $\times$ the height.

Trapezoid. Half the sum of the parallel sides $\times$ the height.

Any Quadrilateral. Half the product of the diagonals $\times$ the sine of their angle.

Any irregular plane figure bounded by curves. Divide the figure into any *even* number of parts by parallel equidistant ordinates; let a be the sum of the first and last ordinates, b the sum of the *even* ordinates, c that of the *odd* ones, except the first and last; d the common distance between them; then will the area $= \frac{1}{3} d (a + 4 b + 2 c)$. *Five* ordinates will generally be found sufficient.

Circle. πr^2; or diam.$^2 \times .7854$; or, circum.$^2 \times .07958$.

Circular sector. $\frac{r a}{2}$; a being the length of the arc in linear measure.

Circular segment. The difference between the sector, and the triangle formed by the cord and the radii; or $\frac{r\,a - r^2 \sin. A}{2}$; or nearly $= .4\,v\,(c + \frac{4}{3}\sqrt{\frac{1}{4}c^2 + v^2})$; c being the cord and v the versed sine.

Ellipse. $.7854\,a\,b$; a and b being the axes.

Parabola. $\frac{2}{3}\,a\,b$; a being the abscissa, and b the double ordinate.

Right prism or cylinder. Curved surface = height × perimeter of base.

Right pyramid or cone. Half the slant height × perimeter of base.

Frustum of a right prism or cylinder. The perimeter of the base multiplied by the distance from the centre of gravity of the upper section to the base. If the prism or cylinder is oblique, multiply this product by the sine of the angle of inclination.

Frustum of a right pyramid or cone. The slant height × half the sum of the perimeters of the two ends.

Sphere. $4\,\pi\,r^2$; or, diam. × circum.; or, diam.^{2} × 3.1416

Spherical zone or segment. $2\,\pi\,r\,h$; or, the height of the zone or segment multiplied by the circumference of the sphere.

Circular spindle. $2\,\pi\,(r\,c - a\sqrt{r^2 - \frac{1}{4}c^2})$; a being the length of the arc, and c its chord, or the length of the spindle.

Spherical triangle. $\pi\,r^2\,\frac{s - 180^\circ}{180^\circ}$; s being the sum of the three angles.

Any surface of revolution. $2\,\pi\,r\,l$; or, the length of the generating element multiplied by the circumference described by its centre of gravity.

Table of Regular Polygons.

No. of sides.	Name.	Area.	Radius of circumscribing circle.	Side of inscribed polygon.
3	Triangle.	0.4330127	0.5773503	1.732051
4	Square.	1.0000000	0.7071068	1.414214
5	Pentagon.	1.7204774	0.8506508	1.175570
6	Hexagon.	2.5980762	1.0000000	1.000000
7	Heptagon.	3.6339124	1.1523824	0.867767
8	Octagon.	4.8284271	1.3065628	0.765367
9	Nonagon.	6.1818242	1.4619022	0.684040
10	Decagon.	7.6942088	1.6180340	0.618034
11	Undecagon.	9.3656399	1.7747324	0.563465
12	Dodecagon.	11.1961524	1.9318517	0.517638

The column of *areas*, in the foregoing table, gives the number by which the *square of the side* is to be multiplied, to find the area of the polygon.

The next column gives the multiplier for the *side of a polygon*, to find the radius of the circumscribing circle.

The last column gives the multiplier for the *radius of a circle*, to find the side of the inscribed polygon.

Solids.

Prism or *cylinder*. Area of base multiplied by the height.

Pyramid or *cone*. Area of base multiplied by one-third of the height.

Frustum of a pyramid or cone. $\frac{1}{3} h \ (B + b + \sqrt{B b})$; h being the height; B and b the areas of the two ends. Or, for a conic frustum :

$\frac{1}{3} h \times .7854 \times \left(\frac{D^3 - d^3}{D - d}\right)$; D and d being the diameters of the two ends.

Frustum of a right triangular prism. The base $\times \frac{1}{3} \ (H + H' + H'')$.

Frustum of any right prism. The base multiplied by its distance from the centre of gravity of the section.

Cylindrical segment, contained between the base and an oblique plane passing through a diameter of the base: two-thirds of the height multiplied by the great triangular section ; or $\frac{2}{3} r h^2$; r being the radius of the base, and h the area of the height.

Sphere. $\frac{4 \pi r^3}{3}$; or, $.5236 \ d^3$; r being the radius and d the diameter.

Spherical segment. $\frac{1}{3} \pi h^2 (3 r - h) = \frac{\pi h}{6} \ (3 b^2 + h^2)$; b being the radius of the base, h, the height of the segment, and r the radius of the sphere. $\frac{\pi}{6} = 0.5236$.

Spherical zone. $\frac{\pi h}{6} \ (3 B^2 + 3 b^2 + h^2)$; B, b being the radii of the bases.

Spherical sector. $\frac{1}{3} r \times$ the surface of the segment or zone, or, $\frac{2}{3} \pi r^2 h$.

Ellipsoid. $\frac{\pi a^2 b}{6}$; a being the revolving diameter and b the axis of revolution.

Paraboloid. Half the area of the base multiplied by the height.

Circular spindle. $\pi \ (\frac{1}{6} c^3 - 2 s \sqrt{r^2 - \frac{1}{4} c^2})$; s being the area of the revolving segment and c its chord.

Any solid of revolution. $2 \pi r s$; or, the area of the generating surface multiplied by the circumference described by its centre of gravity.

Any irregular solid, bounded by a curved surface. Use the rule for finding the area of an irregular plane figure, substituting *sections* for *ordinates*.

Cask gauging. 1. — By the preceding rule:

The content of a cask $= \frac{\pi}{24}\, l\,(d^2 + D^2 + 4\,M^2)$; l being the length, d, D, the head and bung diameters, and M, a diameter midway between them, all measured in the clear, inside; $\frac{\pi}{24} = 0.1309$

The same formula may be thus stated: $\frac{1}{6}\, l\,(A + B + C)$; l being the length; A and B, the areas of the head and bung sections; and C, that of the section midway between them.

2. Contents of a cask, nearly, $= \frac{\pi}{12}\, l\,(2\,D^2 + d^2)$; or, $l \times$ the area of a circle whose diameter is $\frac{2\,D + d}{3}$

Centres of Gravity.

Lines.

Circular arc. At a distance from the centre $= \frac{r\,c}{l}$; r being the radius, c the chord, and l the length of the arc.

Areas.

Triangle. On a line drawn from any angle to the middle of the opposite side, at two-thirds of the distance from the angle to the side.

Trapezoid. On a line a joining the middle points of the two parallel sides, B, b; distance from $B = \frac{a}{3}\left(\frac{B + 2\,b}{B + b}\right)$

Semicircle. Distance from the centre $= \frac{4\,r}{3\,\pi}$

Circular segment. Distance from the centre $= \frac{c^3}{12\,A}$; c being the chord of the segment, and A its area.

Circular sector. Distance from the centre $= \frac{2\,r\,c}{3\,l}$; c being the chord, and l the length of the arc.

Parabolic segment. Distance from the vertex = three-fifths of the abscissa.

Surface of a right cylinder, cone, or *frustum of a cone.* The centre of gravity is at the same distance from the base as that of the parallelogram, triangle or trapezoid, which is a right section of the same.

Surface of a spherical zone or *segment.* At the middle of the height.

Solids.

Prism or *cylinder*. At the middle of the line joining the centres of gravity of the two ends.

Pyramid or *cone*. The distance from the base is one-fourth of the line joining the vertex with the centre of gravity of the base.

Frustum of a cone. Distance from the centre of the smaller end =
$\frac{1}{4} h \times \frac{(R+r)^2 + 2R^2}{(R+r)^2 - Rr}$; or, $\frac{1}{4} h \times \frac{3R^2 + 2Rr + r^2}{R^2 + Rr + r^2}$; h being the height, R and r the radii of the greater and less ends.

Distance from the large end $= \frac{1}{4} h \frac{3r^2 + 2Rr + R^2}{R^2 + Rr + r^2}$

Spherical segment. Distance from the centre $= \frac{3(r - \frac{1}{2}h)^2}{3r - h} = \frac{\pi h^2 (r - \frac{1}{2}h)^2}{S}$; r being the radius of the sphere, h the height of the segment, and S its solid contents. Distance from the vertex $= h \frac{8r - 3h}{12r - 4h}$

Spherical sector. Distance from the centre $= \frac{3}{4}(r - \frac{1}{2}h)$.

Distance from the vertex $= \frac{2r + 3h}{8}$

Hemisphere. Distance from the centre $= \frac{3}{8} r$.

Paraboloid. Distance from the vertex $= \frac{2}{3} h$.

Any system of bodies. Distance of the common centre of gravity from a given plane $= \frac{BD + B'D' + B''D'' + \&c.}{B + B' + B'' + \&c.}$; B, B', B'' being the masses or solid contents of the bodies, and D, D', D'', the distances of their respective centres of gravity from the given plane.

Arithmetical Progression.

a, the first term; d, the common difference; n, the number of terms; l, the nth term; s, the sum of n terms.

$$l = a + d(n - 1); \; s = \frac{n}{2}(a + l)$$

Geometrical Progression.

r, the common ratio; the rest as above.

$$l = a r^{n-1}; \; s = \frac{lr - a}{r - 1} = a \frac{(r^n - 1)}{r - 1}$$

Logarithms.

x, the common logarithm of the number a; e, the base of the hyperbolic logarithms $= 2.7182818$; x', the hyperbolic logarithm of a.

$a = 10^x = e^{x'}$; $x = x'$ Log. e; Log. $e = 0.4342945$.

Plane Trigonometry.

A, B, C, the three angles; a, b, c, the three sides respectively opposite to them; R, the tabular radius; S, the area of the triangle; $p = \frac{1}{2}(a + b + c)$.

Right angled Triangles: A being the right angle.

$$a = \sqrt{b^2 + c^2}\,;\quad b = c\,\frac{\text{tang. } B}{R} = a\,\frac{\text{sin. } B}{R}$$

Oblique angled Triangles:

$$\frac{a}{\text{sin. } A} = \frac{b}{\text{sin. } B} = \frac{c}{\text{sin. } C}$$

$$\text{Tang. } \tfrac{1}{2}(A - B) = \text{tang. } \tfrac{1}{2}(A + B) \times \frac{a - b}{a + b}$$

$$c = \sqrt{\left((a - b)^2 + \frac{4\,a\,b\,\text{sin.}^2\,\frac{1}{2}C}{R^2}\right)} = \sqrt{\left(a^2 + b^2 - \frac{2\,a\,b\,\text{cos. } C}{R}\right)}$$

$$\text{Cos. } \tfrac{1}{2}A = R\sqrt{\frac{p\,(p - a)}{b\,c}}\,;\quad \text{Sin. } \tfrac{1}{2}A = R\sqrt{\frac{(p - b)\,(p - c)}{b\,c}}$$

$$S = \tfrac{1}{2}\,a\,b\,\frac{\text{sin. } C}{R} = \sqrt{p\,(p - a)\,(p - b)\,(p - c)}$$

General Formulæ:

$$R.\ \text{sin. } (a \pm b) = \text{sin. } a \text{ cos. } b \pm \text{sin. } b \text{ cos. } a.$$

$$R.\ \text{cos. } (a \pm b) = \text{cos. } a \text{ cos. } b \pm \text{sin. } a \text{ sin. } b.$$

$$R.\ (\text{sin. } a \pm \text{sin. } b) = 2 \text{ sin. } \tfrac{1}{2}(a \pm b) \text{ cos. } \tfrac{1}{2}(a \pm b).$$

$$R.\ (\text{cos. } a + \text{cos. } b) = 2 \text{ cos. } \tfrac{1}{2}(a + b) \text{ cos. } \tfrac{1}{2}(a - b).$$

$$R.\ (\text{cos. } a - \text{cos. } b) = 2 \text{ sin. } \tfrac{1}{2}(a + b) \text{ sin. } \tfrac{1}{2}(a - b).$$

$$\frac{\text{sin. } a + \text{sin. } b}{\text{sin. } a - \text{sin. } b} = \frac{\text{tang. } \frac{1}{2}(a + b) \text{ cot. } \frac{1}{2}(a - b).}{R^2}$$

$$\text{sin. } \tfrac{1}{2}a = \sqrt{\left(\frac{R^2 - R \text{ cos. } a}{2}\right)}\,;\quad \text{tang. } \tfrac{1}{2}a = R\sqrt{\left(\frac{R - \text{cos. } a}{R + \text{cos. } a}\right)}$$

Chord of $A = 2$ sin. $\frac{1}{2}A$

Table of Natural Sines and Tangents.

Deg.	Min.	Sine.	Tangent.	Deg.	Min.	Sine.	Tangent.
0	10	0029089	0029089	12	30	2164396	2216947
	15	0043633	0043634		45	2206974	2262769
	30	0087265	0087269	13	00	2249511	2308682
	45	0130896	0130907		15	2292004	2354687
1	00	0174524	0174551		30	2334454	2400788
	15	0218149	0218201		45	2376859	2446984
	30	0261769	0261859	14	00	2419219	2493280
	45	0305385	0305528		15	2461533	2539676
2	00	0348995	0349208		30	2503800	2586176
	15	0392598	0392901		45	2546019	2632780
	30	0436194	0436609	15	00	2588190	2679492
	45	0479781	0480334		15	2630312	2726313
3	00	0523360	0524078		30	2672384	2773245
	15	0566928	0567841		45	2714404	2820292
	30	0610485	0611626	16	00	2756374	2867454
	45	0654031	0655435		15	2798290	2914734
4	00	0697565	0699268		30	2840153	2962135
	15	0741085	0743128		45	2881963	3009658
	30	0784591	0787017	17	00	2923717	3057307
	45	0828082	0830936		15	2965416	3105083
5	00	0871557	0874887		30	3007058	3152988
	15	0915016	0918871		45	3048643	3201025
	30	0958458	0962890	18	00	3090170	3249197
	45	1001881	1006947		15	3131638	3297505
6	00	1045285	1051042		30	3173047	3345953
	15	1088669	1095178		45	3214395	3394543
	30	1132032	1139356	19	00	3255682	3443276
	45	1175374	1183578		15	3296906	3492156
7	00	1218693	1227846		30	3338069	3541186
	15	1261990	1272161		45	3379167	3590367
	30	1305262	1316525	20	00	3420201	3639702
	45	1348509	1360940		15	3461171	3689195
8	00	1391731	1405408		30	3502074	3738847
	15	1434926	1449931		45	3542910	3788661
	30	1478094	1494510	21	00	3583679	3838640
	45	1521234	1539147		15	3624380	3888787
9	00	1564345	1583844		30	3665012	3939105
	15	1607426	1628603		45	3705574	3989595
	30	1650476	1673426	22	00	3746066	4040262
	45	1693495	1718314		15	3786486	4091108
10	00	1736482	1763270		30	3826834	4142136
	15	1779435	1808295		45	3867110	4193348
	30	1822355	1853390	23	00	3907311	4244748
	45	1865240	1898559		15	3947439	4296339
11	00	1908090	1943803		30	3987491	4348124
	15	1950903	1989124		45	4027467	4400105
	30	1993679	2034523	24	00	4067366	4452287
	45	2036418	2080003		15	4107189	4504672
12	00	2079117	2125566		30	4146932	4557263
	15	2121777	2171213		45	4186597	4610063

Table of Natural Sines and Tangents—Continued.

Deg.	Min.	Sine.	Tangent.	Deg.	Min.	Sine.	Tangent.
25	00	4226183	4663077	50	00	7660444	11917536
	30	4305111	4769755		30	7716246	12130970
26	00	4383711	4877326	51	00	7771460	12348972
	30	4461978	4985816		30	7826082	12571723
27	00	4539905	5095254	52	00	7880108	12799416
	30	4617486	5205671		30	7933533	13032254
28	00	4694716	5317094	53	00	7986355	13270448
	30	4771588	5429557		30	8038569	13514224
29	00	4848096	5543091	54	00	8090170	13763819
	30	4924236	5657728		30	8141155	14019483
30	00	5000000	5773503	55	00	8191520	14281480
	30	5075384	5890450		30	8241262	14550090
31	00	5150381	6008606	56	00	8290376	14825610
	30	5224986	6128008		30	8338858	15108352
32	00	5299193	6248694	57	00	8386706	15398650
	30	5372996	6370703		30	8433914	15696856
33	00	5446390	6494076	58	00	8480481	16003345
	30	5519370	6618856		30	8526402	16318517
34	00	5591929	6745085	59	00	8571673	16642795
	30	5664062	6872810		30	8616292	16976631
35	00	5735764	7002075	60	00	8660254	17320508
	30	5807030	7132931	61	00	8746197	18040478
36	00	5877853	7265425	62	00	8829476	18807265
	30	5948228	7399611	63	00	8910065	19626105
37	00	6018150	7535541	64	00	8987940	20503038
	30	6087614	7673270	65	00	9063078	21445069
38	00	6156615	7812856	66	00	9135455	22460368
	30	6225146	7954359	67	00	9205049	23558524
39	00	6293204	8097840	68	00	9271839	24750869
	30	6360782	8243364	69	00	9335804	26050891
40	00	6427876	8390996	70	00	9396926	27474774
	30	6494480	8540807	71	00	9455186	29042109
41	00	6560590	8692867	72	00	9510565	30776835
	30	6626200	8847253	73	00	9563048	32708526
42	00	6691306	9004040	74	00	9612617	34874144
	30	6755902	9163312	75	00	9659258	37320508
43	00	6819984	9325151	76	00	9702957	40107809
	30	6883546	9489646	77	00	9743701	43314759
44	00	6946584	9656888	78	00	9781476	47046301
	30	7009093	9826973	79	00	9816272	51445540
45	00	7071068	10000000	80	00	9848078	56712818
	30	7132504	10176074	81	00	9876883	63137515
46	00	7193398	10355303	82	00	9902681	71153697
	30	7253744	10537801	83	00	9925462	81443464
47	00	7313537	10723687	84	00	9945219	95143645
	30	7372773	10913085	85	00	9961947	114300520
48	00	7431448	11106125	86	00	9975641	143006660
	30	7489557	11302944	87	00	9986295	190811370
49	00	7547096	11503684	88	00	9993908	286362530
	30	7604060	11708496	89	00	9998477	572899620
				90	00	10000000	Infinite.

Diameter.	Area.	Circum.	Diameter.	Area.	Circum.
0.	0.	0.	6.	28.274	18.849
.125	.012	.393	.125	29.464	19.242
.25	.049	.785	.25	30.680	19.635
.375	.110	1.178	.375	31.919	20.027
.5	.196	1.571	.5	33.183	20.420
.625	.307	1.963	.625	34.471	20.813
.75	.442	2.356	.75	35.785	21.205
.875	.601	2.749	.875	37.122	21.598
1.	.785	3.142	7.	38.484	21.991
.125	.994	3.534	.125	39.871	22.383
.25	1.227	3.927	.25	41.282	22.776
.375	1.485	4.320	.375	42.718	23.169
.5	1.767	4.712	.5	44.179	23.562
.625	2.074	5.105	.625	45.663	23.954
.75	2.405	5.498	.75	47.173	24.347
.875	2.761	5.891	.875	48.707	24.740
2.	3.142	6.283	8.	50.265	25.132
.125	3.547	6.676	.125	51.848	25.515
.25	3.976	7.069	.25	53.456	25.918
.375	4.430	7.461	.375	55.088	26.310
.5	4.909	7.854	.5	56.745	26.703
.625	5.412	8.247	.625	58.426	27.096
.75	5.940	8.639	.75	60.132	27.489
.875	6.492	9.032	.875	61.862	27.881
3.	7.069	9.425	9.	63.617	28.274
.125	7.670	9.818	.125	65.396	28.662
.25	8.296	10.210	.25	67.200	29.060
.375	8.946	10.602	.375	69.029	29.452
.5	9.621	10.995	.5	70.882	29.845
.625	10.320	11.388	.625	72.759	30.237
.75	11.045	11.781	.75	74.662	30.630
.875	11.793	12.173	.875	76.588	31.023
4.	12.566	12.566	10.	78.540	31.416
.125	13.364	12.959	.125	80.515	31.808
.25	14.186	13.351	.25	82.516	32.201
.375	15.033	13.744	.375	84.540	32.594
.5	15.904	14.137	.5	86.590	32.987
.625	16.800	14.529	.625	88.664	33.379
.75	17.720	14.922	.75	90.762	33.772
.875	18.665	15.315	.875	92.885	34.164
5.	19.635	15.708	11.	95.033	34.558
.125	20.629	16.100	.125	97.205	34.950
.25	21.647	16.493	.25	99.402	35.343
.375	22.690	16.886	.375	101.623	35.735
.5	23.758	17.278	.5	103.869	36.128
.625	24.850	17.671	.625	106.139	36.521
.75	25.967	18.064	.75	108.434	36.913
.875	27.108	18.457	.875	110.753	37.306

Diameter.	Area.	Circum.	Diameter.	Area.	Circum.
12.	113.097	37.699	18.	254.47	56.55
.125	115.466	38.091	.125	258.02	56.94
.25	117.859	38.484	.25	261.59	57.33
.375	120.276	38.877	.375	265.18	57.73
.5	122.718	39.270	.5	268.80	58.12
.625	125.184	39.662	.625	272.45	58.51
.75	127.676	40.055	.75	276.12	58.90
.875	130.192	40.448	.875	279.81	59.30
13.	132.73	40.84	19.	283.53	59.69
125	135.30	41.23	.125	287.27	60.08
.25	137.89	41.63	.25	291.04	60.48
.375	140.50	42.02	.375	294.83	60.87
.5	143.14	42.41	.5	298.65	61.26
.625	145.80	42.80	.625	302.49	61.65
.75	148.49	43.20	.75	306.35	62.05
.875	151.20	43.59	.875	310.25	62.44
14.	153.94	43.98	20.	314.16	62.83
.125	156.70	44.38	.125	318.10	63.22
.25	159.48	44.77	.25	322.06	63.62
.375	162.29	45.16	.375	326.05	64.01
.5	165.13	45.55	.5	330.06	64.40
.625	167.99	45.95	.625	334.10	64.79
.75	170.87	46.34	.75	338.16	65.19
.875	173.78	46.73	.875	342.25	65.58
15.	176.71	47.12	21.	346.36	65.97
.125	179.67	47.52	.125	350.50	66.37
.25	182.65	47.91	.25	354.66	66.76
.375	185.66	48.30	.375	358.84	67.15
.5	188.69	48.69	.5	363.05	67.54
.625	191.75	49.09	.625	367.28	67.94
.75	194.83	49.48	.75	371.54	68.33
.875	197.93	49.87	.875	375.83	68.72
16.	201.06	50.27	22.	380.13	69.12
.125	204.22	50.66	.125	384.46	69.51
.25	207.39	51.05	.25	388.82	69.90
.375	210.60	51.44	.375	393.20	70.29
.5	213.82	51.84	.5	397.61	70.69
.625	217.08	52.23	.625	402.04	71.08
.75	220.35	52.62	.75	406.49	71.47
.875	223.65	53.01	.875	410.97	71.86
17.	226.98	53.41	23.	415.48	72.26
.125	230.33	53.80	.125	420.00	72.65
.25	233.70	54.19	.25	424.56	73.04
.375	237.10	54.59	.375	429.13	73.43
.5	240.53	54.98	.5	433.74	73.83
.625	243.98	55.37	.625	438.36	74.22
.75	247.45	55.76	.75	443.01	74.61
.875	250.95	56.16	.875	447.70	75.00

Diameter.	Area.	Circum.	Diameter.	Area.	Circum.
24.	452.39	75.40	30.	706.86	94.25
.125	457.11	75.79	.125	712.76	94.64
.25	461.86	76.18	.25	718.69	95.03
.375	466.64	76.58	.375	724.64	95.43
.5	471.44	76.97	.5	730.62	95.82
.625	476.26	77.36	.625	736.62	96.21
.75	481.11	77.75	.75	742.64	96.60
.875	485.98	78.15	.875	748.69	97.00
25.	490.87	78.54	31.	754.77	97.39
.125	495.80	78.93	.125	760.87	97.78
.25	500.74	79.33	.25	766.99	98.17
.375	505.71	79.72	.375	773.14	98.57
.5	510.71	80.11	.5	779.31	98.97
.625	515.72	80.50	.625	785.51	99.35
.75	520.77	80.90	.75	791.73	99.75
.875	525.84	81.29	.875	797.98	100.14
26.	530.93	81.68	32.	804.25	100.53
.125	536.05	82.07	.125	810.54	100.92
.25	541.19	82.47	.25	816.86	101.32
.375	546.36	82.86	.375	823.21	101.71
.5	551.55	83.25	.5	829.58	102.10
.625	556.76	83.64	.625	835.97	102.49
.75	562.00	84.04	.75	842.39	102.89
.875	567.27	84.43	.875	848.83	103.28
27.	572.56	84.82	33.	855.30	103.67
.125	577.87	85.21	.125	861.79	104.06
.25	583.21	85.61	.25	868.30	104.46
.375	588.57	86.00	.375	874.84	104.85
.5	593.96	86.39	.5	881.41	105.24
.625	599.37	86.79	.625	888.00	105.64
.75	604.81	87.18	.75	894.62	106.03
.875	610.27	87.57	.875	901.25	106.42
28.	615.75	87.96	34.	907.92	106.81
.125	621.26	88.36	.125	914.61	107.21
.25	626.80	88.75	.25	921.32	107.60
.375	632.36	89.14	.375	928.06	107.99
.5	637.94	89.54	.5	934.82	108.39
.625	643.55	89.93	.625	941.60	108.78
.75	649.18	90.32	.75	948.42	109.17
.875	654.84	90.71	.875	955.25	109.56
29.	660.52	91.11	35.	962.11	109.96
.125	666.23	91.50	.125	968.99	110.35
.25	671.96	91.89	.25	975.91	110.74
.375	677.71	92.28	.375	982.84	111.13
.5	683.49	92.68	.5	989.80	111.53
.625	689.30	93.07	.625	996.78	111.92
.75	695.13	93.46	.75	1003.79	112.31
.875	700.98	93.85	.875	1010.80	112.70

Diameter.	Area.	Circum.	Diameter.	Area.	Circum.
36.	1017.88	113.10	42.	1385.4	131.9
.125	1024.95	113.49	.125	1393.7	132.3
.25	1032.06	113.88	.25	1402.0	132.7
.375	1039.19	114.28	.375	1410.3	133.1
.5	1046.35	114.67	.5	1418.6	133.5
.625	1053.52	115.06	.625	1427.0	133.9
.75	1060.73	115.45	.75	1435.4	134.3
.875	1067.95	115.85	.875	1443.8	134.7
37.	1075.2	116.2	43.	1452.2	135.1
.125	1082.5	116.6	.125	1460.6	135.5
.25	1089.8	117.0	.25	1469.1	135.9
.375	1097.1	117.4	.375	1477.6	136.3
.5	1104.5	117.8	.5	1486.2	136.7
.625	1111.8	118.2	.625	1494.7	137.1
.75	1119.2	118.6	.75	1503.3	137.4
.875	1126.7	119.0	.875	1511.9	137.8
38.	1134.1	119.4	44.	1520.5	138.2
.125	1141.6	119.8	.125	1529.2	138.6
.25	1149.1	120.2	.25	1537.9	139.0
.375	1156.6	120.6	.375	1546.5	139.4
.5	1164.2	121.0	.5	1555.3	139.8
.625	1171.7	121.3	.625	1564.0	140.2
.75	1179.3	121.7	.75	1572.8	140.6
.875	1186.9	122.1	.875	1581.6	141.0
39.	1194.6	122.5	45.	1590.4	141.4
.125	1202.3	122.9	.125	1599.3	141.8
.25	1210.0	123.3	.25	1608.2	142.2
.375	1217.7	123.7	.375	1617.0	142.6
.5	1225.4	124.1	.5	1626.0	142.9
.625	1233.2	124.5	.625	1634.9	143.3
.75	1241.0	124.9	.75	1643.9	143.7
.875	1248.8	125.3	.875	1652.9	144.1
40.	1256.6	125.6	46.	1661.9	144.5
.125	1264.5	126.0	.125	1671.0	144.9
.25	1272.4	126.4	.25	1680.0	145.3
.375	1280.3	126.8	.375	1689.1	145.7
.5	1288.2	127.2	.5	1698.2	146.1
.625	1296.2	127.6	.625	1707.4	146.5
.75	1304.2	128.0	.75	1716.5	146.9
.875	1312.2	128.4	.875	1725.7	147.3
41.	1320.3	128.8	47.	1734.9	147.7
.125	1328.3	129.2	.125	1744.2	148.0
.25	1336.4	129.6	.25	1753.5	148.4
.375	1344.5	130.0	.375	1762.7	148.8
.5	1352.7	130.4	.5	1772.1	149.2
.625	1360.8	130.8	.625	1781.4	149.6
.75	1369.0	131.2	.75	1790.8	150.0
.875	1377.2	131.6	.875	1800.1	150.4

Diameter.	Area.	Circum.	Diameter.	Area.	Circum.
48.	1809.6	150.8	54.	2290.2	169.6
.125	1819.0	151.2	.125	2300.8	170.0
.25	1828.5	151.6	.25	2311.5	170.4
.375	1837.9	152.0	.375	2322.1	170.8
.5	1847.5	152.4	.5	2332.8	171.2
.625	1857.0	152.8	.625	2343.5	171.6
.75	1866.5	153.2	.75	2354.3	172.0
.875	1876.1	153.5	.875	2365.0	172.3
49.	1885.7	153.9	55.	2375.8	172.8
.125	1895.4	154.3	.125	2386.6	173.1
.25	1905.0	154.7	.25	2397.5	173.6
.375	1914.7	155.1	.375	2408.3	173.9
.5	1924.4	155.5	.5	2419.2	174.4
.625	1934.1	155.9	.625	2430.1	174.7
.75	1943.9	156.3	.75	2441.0	175.1
.875	1953.7	156.7	.875	2452.0	175.5
50.	1963.5	157.1	56.	2463.0	175.9
.125	1973.3	157.4	.125	2474.0	176.3
.25	1983.2	158.0	.25	2485.0	176.7
.375	1993.0	158.2	.375	2496.1	177.1
.5	2003.0	158.7	.5	2507.2	177.5
.625	2012.8	159.0	.625	2518.2	177.8
.75	2022.8	159.4	.75	2529.4	178.3
.875	2032.8	159.8	.875	2540.5	178.6
51.	2042.8	160.2	57.	2551.8	179.1
.125	2052.8	160.6	.125	2562.9	179.4
.25	2062.9	161.0	.25	2574.2	179.9
.375	2072.9	161.3	.375	2585.4	180.2
.5	2083.1	161.8	.5	2596.7	180.6
.625	2093.2	162.1	.625	2608.0	181.0
.75	2103.3	162.6	.75	2619.4	181.4
.875	2113.5	162.9	.875	2630.7	181.8
52.	2123.7	163.4	58.	2642.1	182.2
.125	2133.9	163.7	.125	2653.4	182.6
.25	2144.2	164.1	.25	2664.9	183.0
.375	2154.4	164.5	.375	2676.3	183.3
.5	2164.8	164.9	.5	2687.8	183.8
.625	2175.0	165.3	.625	2699.3	184.1
.75	2185.4	165.7	.75	2710.9	184.6
.875	2195.7	166.1	.875	2722.4	184.9
53.	2206.2	166.5	59.	2734.0	185.4
.125	2216.6	166.8	.125	2745.5	185.7
.25	2227.0	167.3	.25	2757.2	186.1
.375	2237.5	167.6	.375	2768.8	186.5
.5	2248.0	168.1	.5	2780.5	186.9
.625	2258.5	168.4	.625	2792.2	187.3
.75	2269.0	168.9	.75	2803.9	187.7
.875	2279.6	169.2	.875	2815.6	188.1

Diameter.	Area.	Circum.	Diameter.	Area.	Circum.
60.	2827.4	188.5	66.	3421.2	207.3
.125	2839.2	188.8	.125	3434.1	207.7
.25	2851.0	189.3	.25	3447.2	208.1
.375	2862.8	189.6	.375	3460.1	208.5
.5	2874.8	190.1	.5	3473.2	208.9
.625	2886.6	190.4	.625	3486.3	209.3
.75	2898.5	190.9	.75	3499.4	209.7
.875	2910.6	191.2	.875	3512.5	210.0
61.	2922.5	191.6	67.	3525.6	210.5
.125	2934.4	192.0	.125	3538.8	210.8
.25	2946.5	192.4	.25	3552.0	211.3
.375	2958.5	192.8	.375	3565.2	211.6
.5	2970.6	193.2	.5	3578.5	212.1
.625	2982.6	193.6	.625	3591.7	212.4
.75	2994.8	194.0	.75	3605.0	212.8
.875	3006.9	194.3	.875	3618.3	213.2
62.	3019.1	194.8	68.	3631.7	213.6
.125	3031.2	195.1	.125	3645.0	214.0
.25	3043.5	195.6	.25	3658.4	214.4
.375	3055.7	195.9	.375	3671.8	214.8
.5	3068.0	196.3	.5	3685.3	215.2
.625	3080.2	196.7	.625	3698.7	215.5
.75	3092.6	197.1	.75	3712.2	215.9
.875	3104.8	197.5	.875	3725.7	216.3
63.	3117.2	197.9	69.	3739.3	216.7
.125	3129.6	198.3	.125	3752.8	217.1
.25	3142.0	198.7	.25	3766.4	217.5
.375	3154.4	199.0	.375	3780.0	217.9
.5	3166.9	199.5	.5	3793.7	218.3
.625	3179.4	199.8	.625	3807.3	218.7
.75	3191.9	200.3	.75	3821.0	219.1
.875	3204.4	200.6	.875	3834.7	219.5
64.	3217.0	201.1	70.	3848.5	219.9
.125	3229.5	201.4	.125	3862.2	220.3
.25	3242.2	201.8	.25	3876.0	220.7
.375	3254.8	202.2	.375	3889.8	221.0
.5	3267.5	202.6	.5	3903.6	221.5
.625	3280.1	203.0	.625	3917.4	221.8
.75	3292.8	203.4	.75	3931.4	222.2
.875	3305.5	203.8	.875	3945.2	222.6
65.	3318.3	204.2	71.	3959.2	223.0
.125	3331.0	204.5	.125	3973.1	223.4
.25	3343.9	205.0	.25	3987.1	223.8
.375	3356.7	205.3	.375	4001.1	224.2
.5	3369.6	205.8	.5	4015.2	224.6
.625	3382.4	206.1	.625	4029.2	225.0
.75	3395.3	206.6	.75	4043.3	225.4
.875	3408.2	206.9	.875	4057.4	225.8

Diameter.	Area.	Circum.	Diameter.	Area.	Circum.
72.	4071.5	226.2	78.	4778.4	245.0
.125	4085.6	226.5	.125	4793.7	245.4
.25	4099.8	227.0	.25	4809.0	245.8
.375	4114.0	227.3	.375	4824.4	246.2
.5	4128.2	227.7	.5	4839.8	246.6
.625	4142.5	228.1	.625	4855.2	247.0
.75	4156.8	228.5	.75	4870.8	247.4
.875	4171.0	228.9	.875	4886.1	247.7
73.	4185.4	229.3	79.	4901.7	248.2
.125	4199.7	229.7	.125	4917.2	248.5
.25	4214.1	230.1	.25	4932.7	249.0
.375	4228.5	230.5	.375	4948.3	249.3
.5	4242.9	230.9	.5	4963.9	249.8
.625	4257.3	231.3	.625	4979.5	250.1
.75	4271.8	231.7	.75	4995.2	250.5
.875	4286.3	232.0	.875	5010.8	250.9
74.	4300.8	232.5	80.	5026.5	251.3
.125	4315.3	232.8	.125	5042.2	251.7
.25	4329.9	233.3	.25	5058.0	252.1
.375	4344.5	233.6	.375	5073.7	252.5
.5	4359.2	234.0	.5	5089.6	252.9
.625	4373.8	234.4	.625	5105.4	253.3
.75	4388.5	234.8	.75	5121.2	253.7
.875	4403.1	235.2	.875	5137.1	254.1
75.	4417.9	235.6	81.	5153.0	254.5
.125	4432.6	236.0	.125	5168.9	254.9
.25	4447.4	236.4	.25	5184.9	255.3
.375	4462.1	236.7	.375	5200.8	255.6
.5	4477.0	237.2	.5	5216.8	256.0
.625	4491.8	237.5	.625	5232.8	256.4
.75	4506.7	238.0	.75	5248.9	256.8
.875	4521.5	238.3	.875	5264.9	257.2
76.	4536.5	238.8	82.	5281.0	257.6
.125	4551.4	239.1	.125	5297.1	258.0
.25	4566.4	239.5	.25	5313.3	258.4
.375	4581.3	239.9	.375	5329.4	258.8
.5	4596.3	240.3	.5	5345.6	259.2
.625	4611.3	240.7	.625	5361.8	259.6
.75	4626.4	241.1	.75	5378.1	260.0
.875	4641.5	241.5	.875	5394.3	260.4
77.	4656.6	241.9	83.	5410.6	260.8
.125	4671.7	242.2	.125	5426.9	261.1
.25	4686.9	242.7	.25	5443.3	261.5
.375	4702.1	243.0	.375	5459.6	261.9
.5	4717.3	243.5	.5	5476.0	262.3
.625	4732.5	243.8	.625	5492.4	262.7
.75	4747.8	244.3	.75	5508.8	263.1
.875	4763.0	244.6	.875	5525.3	263.5

29

Diameter.	Area.	Circum.	Diameter.	Area.	Circum.
84.	5541.8	263.9	90.	6361.7	282.7
.125	5558.3	264.3	.125	6379.4	283.1
.25	5574.8	264.7	.25	6397.1	283.5
.375	5591.3	265.0	.375	6414.8	283.9
.5	5607.9	265.5	.5	6432.6	284.3
.625	5624.5	265.8	.625	6450.4	284.7
.75	5641.2	266.2	.75	6468.2	285.1
.875	5657.8	266.6	.875	6486.0	285.5
85.	5674.5	267.0	91.	6503.9	285.9
.125	5691.2	267.4	.125	6521.7	286.3
.25	5707.9	267.8	.25	6539.7	286.7
.375	5724.6	268.2	.375	6557.6	287.1
.5	5741.5	268.6	.5	6575.5	287.5
.625	5758.2	268.9	.625	6593.5	287.8
.75	5775.1	269.4	.75	6611.5	288.2
.875	5791.9	269.7	.875	6629.5	288.6
86.	5808.8	270.2	92.	6647.6	289.0
.125	5825.7	270.5	.125	6665.7	289.4
.25	5842.6	271.0	.25	6683.8	289.8
.375	5859.5	271.3	.375	6701.9	290.2
.5	5876.5	271.7	.5	6720.1	290.6
.625	5893.5	272.1	.625	6738.2	291.0
.75	5910.6	272.5	.75	6756.4	291.4
.875	5927.6	272.9	.875	6774.7	291.8
87.	5944.7	273.3	93.	6792.9	292.2
.125	5961.7	273.7	.125	6811.1	292.6
.25	5978.9	274.1	.25	6829.5	293.0
.375	5996.0	274.4	.375	6847.8	293.4
.5	6013.2	274.9	.5	6866.1	293.7
.625	6030.4	275.2	.625	6884.5	294.1
.75	6047.6	275.7	.75	6902.9	294.5
.875	6064.8	276.0	.875	6921.3	294.9
88.	6082.1	276.5	94.	6939.8	295.3
.125	6099.4	276.8	.125	6958.2	295.7
.25	6116.7	277.2	.25	6976.7	296.1
.375	6134.0	277.6	.375	6995.2	296.5
.5	6151.4	278.0	.5	7013.8	296.9
.625	6168.8	278.4	.625	7032.3	297.3
.75	6186.2	278.8	.75	7051.0	297.7
.875	6203.6	279.2	.875	7069.5	298.1
89.	6221.1	279.6	95.	7088.2	298.5
.125	6238.6	280.0	.125	7106.9	298.8
.25	6256.1	280.4	.25	7125.6	299.2
.375	6273.6	280.8	.375	7144.3	299.6
.5	6291.2	281.2	.5	7163.0	300.0
.625	6308.8	281.6	.625	7181.8	300.4
.75	6326.4	282.0	.75	7200.6	300.8
.875	6344.0	282.3	.875	7219.4	301.2

Diameter.	Area.	Circum.	Diameter.	Area.	Circum.
96.	7238.2	301.6	98.	7543.0	307.9
.125	7257.1	302.0	.125	7562.2	308.3
.25	7276.0	302.4	.25	7581.5	308.7
.375	7294.9	302.8	.375	7600.8	309.0
.5	7313.8	303.2	.5	7620.1	309.4
.625	7332.8	303.5	.625	7639.4	309.8
.75	7351.8	303.9	.75	7658.9	310.2
.875	7370.7	304.3	.875	7678.2	310.6
97.	7389.8	304.7	99.	7697.7	311.0
.125	7408.8	305.1	.125	7717.1	311.4
.25	7428.0	305.5	.25	7736.6	311.8
.375	7447.0	305.9	.375	7756.1	312.2
.5	7466.2	306.3	.5	7775.6	312.6
.625	7485.3	306.7	.625	7795.2	313.0
.75	7504.5	307.1	.75	7814.8	313.4
.875	7523.7	307.5	.875	7834.3	313.8
			100.	7854.0	314.2

TO FIND THE AREA OF A CIRCULAR SEGMENT.

Divide the height of the segment by the diameter of the circle, and look for the quotient in the column H, in the following table, opposite to which will be found a number in column Area, which multiplied by the square of the diameter will give the area of the segment. Should the height of the segment be greater than half the diameter, find the area of the remaining segment, and substract this from the area of the whole circle.

H.	Area.	H.	Area.	H.	Area.	H.	Area.
.01	.001329	.14	.066833	.27	.171089	.40	.293369
.02	.003748	.15	.073874	.28	.180019	.41	.303187
.03	.006865	.16	.081112	.29	.189047	.42	.313041
.04	.010537	.17	.088535	.30	.198168	.43	.322928
.05	.014681	.18	.096134	.31	.207376	.44	.332843
.06	.019239	.19	.103900	.32	.216666	.45	.342782
.07	.024168	.20	.111823	.33	.226033	.46	.352742
.08	.029435	.21	.119897	.34	.235473	.47	.362717
.09	.035011	.22	.128113	.35	.244980	.48	.372704
.10	.040875	.23	.136465	.36	.254550	.49	.382699
.11	.047005	.24	.144944	.37	.264178	.50	.392699
.12	.053385	.25	.153546	.38	.273861	.001	.000042
.13	.059999	.26	.162263	.39	.283592	.002	.000119

POWERS—ROOTS—CIRCLES.

No.	Square.	Cube.	Sq. Root.	Cu.Root.	Area.	Circum.
1	1	1	1.000	1.000	0.7854	3.1416
2	4	8	1.414	1.260	3.1416	6.2832
3	9	27	1.732	1.442	7.0686	9.4248
4	16	64	2.000	1.587	12.5664	12.5664
5	25	125	2.236	1.710	19.6350	15.7080
6	36	216	2.449	1.817	28.2743	18.8496
7	49	343	2.646	1.913	38.4846	21.9911
8	64	512	2.828	2.000	50.2655	25.1327
9	81	729	3.000	2.080	63.6173	28.2743
10	100	1000	3.162	2.154	78.5398	31.4159
11	121	1331	3.317	2.224	95.0332	34.5575
12	144	1728	3.464	2.289	113.0973	37.6991
13	169	2197	3.606	2.351	132 7323	40.8407
14	196	2744	3.742	2.410	153.9380	43.9823
15	225	3375	3.873	2.466	176.7146	47.1239
16	256	4096	4.000	2.520	201.0619	50.2655
17	289	4913	4.123	2.571	226.9801	53.4071
18	324	5832	4.243	2.621	254.4690	56.5487
19	361	6859	4.359	2.668	283.5287	59.6903
20	400	8000	4.472	2.714	314.1593	62.8319
21	441	9261	4.583	2.759	346.3606	65.9734
22	484	10648	4.690	2.802	380.1327	69.1150
23	529	12167	4.796	2.844	415.4756	72.2566
24	576	13824	4.899	2.884	452.3893	75.3982
25	625	15625	5.000	2.924	490.8739	78.5398
26	676	17576	5.099	2.962	530.9292	81.6814
27	729	19683	5.196	3.000	572.5552	84.8230
28	784	21952	5.292	3.037	615.7522	87.9646
29	841	24389	5.385	3.072	660.5199	91.1062
30	900	27000	5.477	3.107	706.8583	94.2478
31	961	29791	5.568	3.141	754.7676	97.3894
32	1024	32768	5.657	3.175	804.2477	100.5310
33	1089	35937	5.745	3.208	855.2986	103.6726
34	1156	39304	5.831	3.240	907.9203	106.8142
35	1225	42875	5.916	3.271	962.1128	109.9557
36	1296	46656	6.000	3.302	1017.8760	113.0973
37	1369	50653	6.083	3.332	1075.2101	116.2389
38	1444	54872	6.164	3.362	1134.1149	119.3805
39	1521	59319	6.245	3.391	1194.5906	122.5221
40	1600	64000	6.325	3.420	1256.6370	125.6637
41	1681	68921	6.403	3.448	1320.2543	128.8053
42	1764	74088	6.481	3.476	1385.4424	131.9469
43	1849	79507	6.557	3.503	1452.2012	135.0885
44	1936	85184	6.633	3.530	1520.5308	138.2301
45	2025	91125	6.708	3.557	1590.4313	141.3717
46	2116	97336	6.782	3.583	1661.9025	144.5133
47	2209	103823	6.856	3.609	1734.9445	147.6549
48	2304	110592	6.928	3.634	1809.5574	150.7964
49	2401	117649	7.000	3.659	1885.7410	153.9380
50	2500	125000	7.071	3.684	1963.4954	157.0796

No.	Square.	Cube.	Sq. Root.	Cu.Root.	Area.	Circum.
51	2601	132651	7.141	3.708	2042.8206	160.2212
52	2704	140608	7.211	3.733	2123.7166	163.3628
53	2809	148877	7.280	3.756	2206.1834	166.5044
54	2916	157464	7.348	3.780	2290.2210	169.6460
55	3025	166375	7.416	3.803	2375.8294	172.7876
56	3136	175616	7.483	3.826	2463.0086	175.9292
57	3249	185193	7.550	3.849	2551.7586	179.0708
58	3364	195112	7.616	3.871	2642.0794	182.2124
59	3481	205379	7.681	3.893	2733.9710	185.3540
60	3600	216000	7.746	3.915	2827.4334	188.4956
61	3721	226981	7.810	3.936	2922.4666	191.6372
62	3844	238328	7.874	3.958	3019.0705	194.7787
63	3969	250047	7.937	3.979	3117.2453	197.9203
64	4096	262144	8.000	4.000	3216.9909	201.0619
65	4225	274625	8.062	4.021	3318.3072	204.2035
66	4356	287496	8.124	4.041	3421.1944	207.3451
67	4489	300763	8.185	4.062	3525.6524	210.4867
68	4624	314432	8.246	4.082	3631.6811	213.6283
69	4761	328509	8.307	4.102	3739.2807	216.7699
70	4900	343000	8.367	4.121	3848.4510	219.9115
71	5041	357911	8.426	4.141	3959.1921	223.0531
72	5184	373248	8.485	4.160	4071.5041	226.1947
73	5329	389017	8.544	4.179	4185.3868	229.3363
74	5476	405224	8.602	4.198	4300.8403	232.4779
75	5625	421875	8.660	4.217	4417.8647	235.6194
76	5776	438976	8.718	4.236	4536.4598	238.7610
77	5929	456533	8.775	4.254	4656.6257	241.9026
78	6084	474552	8.832	4.273	4778.3624	245.0442
79	6241	493039	8.888	4.291	4901.6699	248.1858
80	6400	512000	8.944	4.309	5026.5482	251.3274
81	6561	531441	9.000	4.327	5152.9974	254.4690
82	6724	551368	9.055	4.344	5281.0173	257.6106
83	6889	571787	9.110	4.362	5410.6079	260.7522
84	7056	592704	9.165	4.380	5541.7694	263.8938
85	7225	614125	9.220	4.397	5674.5017	267.0354
86	7396	636056	9.274	4.414	5808.8048	270.1770
87	7569	658503	9.327	4.431	5944.6787	273.3186
88	7744	681472	9.381	4.448	6082.1234	276.4602
89	7921	704969	9.434	4.465	6221.1389	279.6017
90	8100	729000	9.487	4.481	6361.7251	282.7433
91	8281	753571	9.539	4.498	6503.8822	285.8849
92	8464	778688	9.592	4.514	6647.6101	289.0265
93	8649	804357	9.644	4.531	6792.9087	292.1681
94	8836	830584	9.695	4.547	6939.7782	295.3097
95	9025	857375	9.747	4.563	7088.2184	298.4513
96	9216	884736	9.798	4.579	7238.2295	301.5929
97	9409	912673	9.849	4.595	7389.8113	304.7345
98	9604	941192	9.899	4.610	7542.9640	307.8761
99	9801	970299	9.950	4.626	7697.6874	311.0177
100	10000	1000000	10.000	4.642	7853.9816	314.1593

No.	Square.	Cube.	Sq. Root.	Cu.Root.	Area.	Circum.
101	10201	1030301	10.050	4.657	8011.847	317.301
102	10404	1061201	10.100	4.672	8171.282	320.442
103	10609	1092727	10.149	4.688	8332.289	323.584
104	10816	1124864	10.198	4.703	8494.867	326.726
105	11025	1157625	10.247	4.718	8659.015	329.867
106	11236	1191016	10.296	4.733	8824.734	333.009
107	11449	1225043	10.344	4.747	8992.024	336.150
108	11664	1259712	10.392	4.762	9160.884	339.292
109	11881	1295029	10.440	4.777	9331.316	342.434
110	12100	1331000	10.488	4.791	9503.318	345.575
111	12321	1367631	10.536	4.806	9676.891	348.717
112	12544	1404928	10.583	4.820	9852.035	351.858
113	12769	1442897	10.630	4.835	10028.749	355.000
114	12996	1481544	10.677	4.849	10207.035	358.142
115	13225	1520875	10.724	4 863	10386.891	361.283
116	13456	1560896	10.771	4.877	10568.318	364.425
117	13689	1601613	10.817	4.891	10751.315	367.566
118	13924	1643032	10.863	4.905	10935.884	370.708
119	14161	1685159	10.909	4.919	11122.023	373.849
120	14400	1728000	10.954	4.932	11309.734	376.991
121	14641	1771561	11.000	4.946	11499.015	380.133
122	14884	1815848	11.045	4.960	11689.866	383.274
123	15129	1860867	11.091	4.973	11882.289	386.416
124	15376	1906624	11.136	4.987	12076.282	389.557
125	15625	1953125	11.180	5.000	12271.846	392.699
126	15876	2000376	11.225	5.013	12468.981	395.841
127	16129	2048383	11.269	5.027	12667.687	398.982
128	16384	2097152	11.314	5.040	12867.963	402.123
129	16641	2146689	11.358	5.053	13069.811	405.265
130	16900	2197000	11.402	5.066	13273.229	408.407
131	17161	2248091	11.446	5.079	13478.218	411.549
132	17424	2299968	11.489	5.092	13684.778	414.690
133	17689	2352637	11.533	5.104	13892.908	417.832
134	17956	2406104	11.576	5.117	14102.609	420.973
135	18225	2460375	11.619	5.130	14313.882	424.115
136	18496	2515456	11.662	5.143	14526.724	427.257
137	18769	2571353	11.705	5.155	14741.138	430.398
138	19044	2628072	11.747	5.168	14956.123	433.540
139	19321	2685619	11.790	5.180	15174.678	436.681
140	19600	2744000	11.832	5.192	15393.804	439.823
141	19881	2803221	11.874	5.205	15614.501	442.965
142	20164	2863288	11.916	5.217	15836.769	446.106
143	20449	2924207	11.958	5.229	16060.607	449.248
144	20736	2985984	12.000	5.241	16286.016	452.389
145	21025	3048625	12.042	5.254	16512.996	455.531
146	21316	3112136	12.083	5.266	16741.547	458.673
147	21609	3176523	12.124	5.278	16971.669	461.814
148	21904	3241792	12.166	5.290	17203.361	464.956
149	22201	3307949	12.207	5.301	17436.625	468.097
150	22500	3375000	12.247	5.313	17671.459	471.239

No.	Square.	Cube.	Sq. Root.	Cu.Root.	Area.	Circum.
151	22801	3442951	12.288	5.325	17907.864	474.380
152	23104	3511808	12.329	5.337	18145.839	477.522
153	23409	3581577	12.369	5.348	18385.386	480.664
154	23716	3652264	12.410	5.360	18626.503	483.805
155	24025	3723875	12.450	5.372	18869.191	486.947
156	24336	3796416	12.490	5.383	19113.450	490.088
157	24649	3869893	12.530	5.395	19359.279	493.230
158	24964	3944312	12.570	5.406	19606.680	496.372
159	25281	4019679	12.610	5.418	19855.651	499.513
160	25600	4096000	12.650	5.429	20106.193	502.655
161	25921	4173281	12.689	5.440	20358.306	505.796
162	26244	4251528	12.728	5.451	20611.989	508.938
163	26569	4330747	12.767	5.463	20867.244	512.080
164	26896	4410944	12.806	5.474	21124.069	515.221
165	27225	4492125	12.845	5.485	21382.465	518.363
166	27556	4574296	12.884	5.496	21642.432	521.504
167	27889	4657463	12.923	5.507	21903.969	524.646
168	28224	4741632	12.961	5.518	22167.078	527.788
169	28561	4826809	13.000	5.529	22431.757	530.929
170	28900	4913000	13.038	5.540	22698.007	534.071
171	29241	5000211	13.077	5.550	22965.824	537.212
172	29584	5088448	13.115	5.561	23235.219	540.354
173	29929	5177717	13.153	5.572	23506.182	543.496
174	30276	5268024	13.191	5.583	23778.715	546.637
175	30625	5359375	13.229	5.593	24052.819	549.779
176	30976	5451776	13.266	5.604	24328.493	552.920
177	31329	5545233	13.304	5.615	24605.739	556.062
178	31684	5639752	13.342	5.625	24884.555	559.203
179	32041	5735339	13.379	5.636	25164.943	562.345
180	32400	5832000	13.416	5.646	25446.900	565.487
181	32761	5929741	13.454	5.657	25730.429	568.628
182	33124	6028568	13.491	5.667	26015.529	571.770
183	33489	6128487	13.528	5.677	26302.199	574.911
184	33856	6229504	13.565	5.688	26590.440	578.053
185	34225	6331625	13.601	5.698	26880.252	581.195
186	34596	6434856	13.638	5.708	27171.635	584.336
187	34969	6539203	13.675	5.718	27464.588	587.478
188	35344	6644672	13.711	5.729	27759.113	590.619
189	35721	6751269	13.748	5.739	28055.208	593.761
190	36100	6859000	13.784	5.749	28352.874	596.903
191	36481	6967871	13.820	5.759	28652.110	600.044
192	36864	7077888	13.856	5.769	28952.918	603.186
193	37249	7189057	13.892	5.779	29255.296	606.327
194	37636	7301384	13.928	5.789	29559.245	609.469
195	38025	7414875	13.964	5.799	29864.765	612.611
196	38416	7529536	14.000	5.809	30171.856	615.752
197	38809	7645373	14.036	5.819	30480.517	618.894
198	39204	7762392	14.071	5.828	30790.749	622.035
199	39601	7880599	14.107	5.838	31102.553	625.177
200	40000	8000000	14.142	5.848	31415.927	628.319

No.	Square.	Cube.	Sq. Root.	Cu.Root.	Area.	Circum.
201	40401	8120601	14.177	5.858	31730.871	631.460
202	40804	8242408	14.213	5.867	32047.386	634.602
203	41209	8365427	14.248	5.877	32365.473	637.743
204	41616	8489664	14.283	5.887	32685.129	640.885
205	42025	8615125	14.318	5.896	33006.358	644.026
206	42436	8741816	14.353	5.906	33329.156	647.168
207	42849	8869743	14.387	5.915	33653.526	650.310
208	43264	8998912	14.422	5.925	33979.468	653.452
209	43681	9123329	14.457	5.934	34306.977	656.593
210	44100	9261000	14.491	5.944	34636.059	659.734
211	44521	9393931	14.526	5.953	34966.712	662.876
212	44944	9528128	14.560	5.963	35298.936	666.018
213	45369	9663597	14.595	5.972	35632.729	669.159
214	45796	9800344	14.629	5.981	35968.096	672.300
215	46225	9938375	14.663	5.991	36305.030	675.442
216	46656	10077696	14.697	6.000	36643.536	678.584
217	47089	10218313	14.731	6.009	36983.614	681.726
218	47524	10360232	14.765	6.018	37325.264	684.868
219	47961	10503459	14.799	6.028	37668.480	688.008
220	48400	10648000	14.832	6.037	38013.271	691.150
221	48841	10793861	14.866	6.046	38359.632	694.292
222	49284	10941048	14.900	6.055	38707.564	697.434
223	49729	11089567	14.933	6.064	39057.069	700.575
224	50176	11239424	14.967	6.073	39408.140	703.716
225	50625	11390625	15.000	6.082	39760.782	706.858
226	51076	11543176	15.033	6.091	40114.996	710.000
227	51529	11697083	15.067	6.100	40470.782	713.141
228	51984	11852352	15.100	6.109	40828.140	716.284
229	52441	12008989	15.133	6.118	41187.065	719.424
230	52900	12167000	15.166	6.127	41547.563	722.566
231	53361	12326391	15.199	6.136	41909.631	725.707
232	53824	12487168	15.232	6.145	42273.272	728.850
233	54289	12649337	15.264	6.153	42638.481	731.991
234	54756	12812904	15.297	6.162	43005.260	735.132
235	55225	12977875	15.330	6.171	43373.614	738.274
236	55696	13144256	15.362	6.180	43743.536	741.416
237	56169	13312053	15.395	6.188	44115.029	744.557
238	56644	13481272	15.427	6.197	44488.092	747.698
239	57121	13651919	15.460	6.206	44862.728	750.841
240	57600	13824000	15.492	6.214	45238.934	753.982
241	58081	13997521	15.524	6.223	45616.710	757.124
242	58564	14172488	15.556	6.232	45996.060	760.266
243	59049	14348907	15.588	6.240	46376.976	763.407
244	59536	14526784	15.620	6.249	46759.465	766.548
245	60025	14706125	15.652	6.257	47143.525	769.690
246	60516	14886936	15.684	6.266	47529.155	772.832
247	61009	15069223	15.716	6.274	47916.356	775.973
248	61504	15252992	15.748	6.283	48305.129	779.115
249	62001	15438249	15.780	6.291	48695.471	782.257
250	62500	15625000	15.811	6.300	49087.385	785.398

No.	Square.	Cube.	Sq. Root.	Cu.Root.	Area.	Circum.
251	63001	15813251	15.843	6.308	49480.870	788.540
252	63504	16003008	15.875	6.316	49875.925	791.681
253	64009	16194277	15.906	6.325	50272.550	794.823
254	64516	16387064	15.937	6.333	50670.748	797.964
255	65025	16581375	15.969	6.341	51070.516	801.106
256	65536	16777216	16.000	6.350	51471.854	804.248
257	66049	16974593	16.031	6.358	51874.763	807.389
258	66564	17173512	16.062	6.366	52279.243	810.531
259	67081	17373979	16.093	6.374	52685.294	813.672
260	67600	17576000	16.125	6.383	53092.916	816.814
261	68121	17779581	16.155	6.391	53502.109	819.956
262	68644	17984728	16.186	6.399	53912.872	823.097
263	69169	18191447	16.217	6.407	54325.205	826.239
264	69696	18399744	16.248	6.415	54739.110	829.380
265	70225	18609625	16.279	6.423	55154.586	832.522
266	70756	18821096	16.310	6.431	55571.632	835.664
267	71289	19034163	16.340	6.439	55990.250	838.805
268	71824	19248832	16.371	6.447	56410.438	841.947
269	72361	19465109	16.401	6.455	56832.196	845.088
270	72900	19683000	16.432	6.463	57255.526	848.230
271	73441	19902511	16.462	6.471	57680.426	851.372
272	73984	20123648	16.492	6.479	58106.898	854.513
273	74529	20346417	16.523	6.487	58534.940	857.655
274	75076	20570824	16.553	6.495	58964.552	860.796
275	75625	20796875	16.583	6.503	59395.736	863.938
276	76176	21024576	16.613	6.511	59824.490	867.080
277	76729	21253933	16.643	6.519	60260.815	870.221
278	77284	21484952	16.673	6.527	60698.711	873.363
279	77841	21717639	16.703	6.534	61136.178	876.484
280	78400	21952000	16.733	6.542	61575.216	879.646
281	78961	22188041	16.763	6.550	62015.824	882.788
282	79524	22425768	16.793	6.558	62458.003	885.929
283	80089	22665187	16.823	6.565	62901.753	889.071
284	80656	22906304	16.852	6.573	63347.074	892.212
285	81225	23149125	16.882	6.581	63793.966	895.354
286	81796	23393656	16.912	6.589	64242.428	898.495
287	82369	23639903	16.941	6.596	64692.461	901.637
288	82944	23887872	16.971	6.604	65144.065	904.779
289	83521	24137569	17.000	6.611	65597.240	907.920
290	84100	24389000	17.029	6.619	66051.986	911.062
291	84681	24642171	17.059	6.627	66508.302	914.203
292	85264	24897088	17.088	6.634	66966.189	917.345
293	85849	25153757	17.117	6.642	67425.647	920.466
294	86436	25412184	17.146	6.649	67886.675	923.628
295	87025	25672375	17.176	6.657	68349.275	926.770
296	87616	25934336	17.205	6.664	68813.445	929.911
297	88209	26198073	17.234	6.672	69279.186	933.053
298	88804	26463592	17.263	6.679	69746.498	936.195
299	89401	26730899	17.292	6.687	70215.381	939.336
300	90000	27000000	17.321	6.694	70685.835	942.478

No.	Square.	Cube.	Sq. Root.	Cu. Root.	Area.	Circum.
301	90601	27270901	17.349	6.702	71157.859	945.619
302	91204	27543608	17.378	6.709	71631.454	948.761
303	91809	27818127	17.407	6.717	72106.620	951.903
304	92416	28094464	17.436	6.724	72583.356	955.044
305	93025	28372625	17.464	6.731	73061.664	958.186
306	93636	28652616	17.493	6.739	73541.542	961.327
307	94249	28934443	17.521	6.746	74022.991	964.469
308	94864	29218112	17.550	6.753	74506.008	967.610
309	95481	29503629	17.578	6.761	74990.602	970.752
310	96100	29791000	17.607	6.768	75476.764	973.894
311	96721	30080231	17.635	6.775	75964.496	977.035
312	97344	30371328	17.664	6.782	76453.798	980.177
313	97969	30664297	17.692	6.790	76944.673	983.318
314	98596	30959144	17.720	6.797	77437.117	986.460
315	99225	31255875	17.748	6.804	77931.133	989.602
316	99856	31554496	17.776	6.811	78426.719	992.743
317	100489	31855013	17.804	6.818	78923.876	995.885
318	101124	32157432	17.833	6.826	79422.604	999.026
319	101761	32461759	17.861	6.833	79922.902	1002.168
320	102400	32768000	17.889	6.840	80424.772	1005.310
321	103041	33076161	17.916	6.847	80928.212	1008.451
322	103684	33386248	17.944	6.854	81433.223	1011.593
323	104329	33698267	17.972	6.861	81939.805	1014.734
324	104976	34012224	18.000	6.868	82447.958	1017.876
325	105625	34328125	18.028	6.875	82957.681	1021.018
326	106276	34645976	18.055	6.882	83468.975	1024.159
327	106929	34965783	18.083	6.889	83981.840	1027.303
328	107584	35287552	18.111	6.896	84496.276	1030.442
329	108241	35611289	18.138	6.903	85012.282	1033.584
330	108900	35937000	18.166	6.910	85529.860	1036.726
331	109561	36264691	18.193	6.917	86049.008	1039.867
332	110224	36594368	18.221	6.924	86569.727	1043.009
333	110889	36926037	18.248	6.931	87092.016	1046.150
334	111556	37259704	18.276	6.938	87615.877	1049.292
335	112225	37595375	18.303	6.945	88141.309	1052.434
336	112896	37933056	18.330	6.952	88668.311	1055.575
337	113569	38272753	18.358	6.959	89196.884	1058.717
338	114244	38614472	18.385	6.966	89727.028	1061.858
339	114921	38958219	18.412	6.973	90258.742	1065.000
340	115600	39304000	18.439	6.980	90792.028	1068.142
341	116281	39651821	18.466	6.986	91326.884	1071.283
342	116964	40001688	18.493	6.993	91863.311	1074.425
343	117649	40353607	18.520	7.000	92401.308	1077.566
344	118336	40707584	18.547	7.007	92940.877	1080.708
345	119025	41063625	18.574	7.014	93482.016	1083.849
346	119716	41421736	18.601	7.020	94024.726	1086.991
347	120409	41781923	18.628	7.027	94569.007	1090.132
348	121104	42144192	18.655	7.034	95114.859	1093.274
349	121801	42508549	18.682	7.041	95662.282	1096.418
350	122500	42875000	18.708	7.047	96211.275	1099.557

No.	Square.	Cube.	Sq. Root.	Cu.Root.	Area.	Circum.
351	123201	43243551	18.735	7.054	96761.84	1102.699
352	123904	43614208	18.762	7.061	97313.97	1105.840
353	124609	43986977	18.788	7.067	97867.16	1108.982
354	125316	44361864	18.815	7.074	98422.96	1112.124
355	126025	44738875	18.841	7.081	98979.80	1115.265
356	126736	45118016	18.868	7.087	99538.22	1118.407
357	127449	45499293	18.894	7.094	100098.21	1121.548
358	128164	45882712	18.921	7.101	100659.37	1124.690
359	128881	46268279	18.947	7.107	101222.90	1127.832
360	129600	46656000	18.974	7.114	101787.60	1130.973
361	130321	47045881	19.000	7.120	102353.87	1134.115
362	131044	47437928	19.026	7.127	102921.72	1137.256
363	131769	47832147	19.053	7.133	103491.13	1140.398
364	132496	48228544	19.079	7.140	104062.11	1143.540
365	133225	48627125	19.105	7.147	104634.67	1146.681
366	133956	49027896	19.131	7.153	105208.79	1149.823
367	134689	49430863	19.157	7.160	105784.49	1152.964
368	135424	49836032	19.183	7.166	106361.76	1156.106
369	136161	50243409	19.209	7.173	106940.60	1159.248
370	136900	50653000	19.235	7.179	107521.01	1162.389
371	137641	51064811	19.261	7.186	108102.99	1165.531
372	138384	51478848	19.287	7.192	108686.54	1168.672
373	139129	51895117	19.313	7.198	109271.66	1171.814
374	139876	52313624	19.339	7.205	109858.35	1174.956
375	140625	52734375	19.365	7.211	110446.62	1178.097
376	141376	53157376	19.391	7.218	111036.45	1181.238
377	142129	53582633	19.416	7.224	111627.86	1184.380
378	142884	54010152	19.442	7.230	112220.83	1187.522
379	143641	54439939	19.468	7.237	112815.38	1190.663
380	144400	54872000	19.494	7.243	113411.49	1193.805
381	145161	55306341	19.519	7.250	114009.28	1196.947
382	145924	55742968	19.545	7.256	114608.44	1200.088
383	146689	56181887	19.570	7.262	115209.27	1203.230
384	147456	56623104	19.596	7.268	115811.67	1206.372
385	148225	57066625	19.621	7.275	116415.64	1209.513
386	148996	57512456	19.647	7.281	117021.18	1212.654
387	149769	57960603	19.672	7.287	117628.30	1215.796
388	150544	58411072	19.698	7.294	118236.98	1218.938
389	151321	58863869	19.723	7.300	118847.24	1222.079
390	152100	59319000	19.748	7.306	119459.06	1225.221
391	152881	59776471	19.774	7.312	120072.46	1228.363
392	153664	60236288	10.799	7.319	120687.42	1231.504
393	154449	60698457	19.824	7.325	121303.96	1234.646
394	155236	61162984	19.849	7.331	121922.07	1237.788
395	156025	61629875	19.875	7.337	122541.75	1240.929
396	156816	62099136	19.900	7.343	123163.00	1244.071
397	157609	62570773	19.925	7.350	123785.82	1247.212
398	158404	63044792	19.950	7.356	124410.21	1250.354
399	159201	63521199	19.975	7.362	125036.17	1253.495
400	160000	64000000	20.000	7.368	125663.70	1256.637

No.	Square.	Cube.	Sq. Root.	Cu. Root.	Area.	Circum.
401	160801	64481201	20.025	7.374	126292.81	1259.778
402	161604	64964808	20.050	7.380	126923.48	1262.920
403	162409	65450827	20.075	7.386	127555.73	1266.062
404	163216	65939264	20.100	7.393	128189.54	1269.204
405	164025	66430125	20.125	7.399	128824.93	1272.345
406	164836	66923416	20.149	7.405	129461.89	1275.486
407	165649	67419143	20.174	7.411	130100.42	1278.628
408	166464	67911312	20.199	7.417	130740.52	1281.770
409	167281	68417929	20.224	7.423	131382.19	1284.911
410	168100	68921000	20.248	7.429	132025.43	1288.053
411	168921	69426531	20.273	7.435	132670.24	1291.194
412	169744	69934528	20.298	7.441	133316.62	1294.336
413	170569	70444997	20.322	7.447	133964.58	1297.478
414	171396	70951944	20.347	7.453	134614.10	1300.620
415	172225	71473375	20.372	7.459	135265.20	1303.761
416	173056	71991296	20.396	7.465	135917.87	1306.902
417	173889	72511713	20.421	7.471	136572.10	1310.043
418	174724	73034632	20.445	7.477	137227.91	1313.186
419	175561	73560059	20.469	7.483	137885.29	1316.327
420	176400	74088000	20.494	7.489	138544.24	1319.469
421	177241	74618461	20.518	7.495	139204.76	1322.610
422	178084	75151448	20.543	7.501	139866.85	1325.752
423	178929	75686967	20.567	7.507	140530.51	1328.895
424	179776	76225024	20.591	7.513	141195.74	1332.036
425	180625	76765625	20.616	7.518	141862.54	1335.177
426	181476	77308776	20.640	7.524	142530.91	1338.318
427	182329	77854483	20.664	7.530	143200.86	1341.459
428	183184	78402752	20.688	7.536	143872.38	1344.600
429	184041	78953589	20.712	7.542	144545.46	1347.744
430	184900	79507000	20.736	7.548	145220.12	1350.885
431	185761	80062991	20.761	7.554	145896.35	1354.027
432	186624	80621568	20.785	7.560	146574.14	1357.168
433	187489	81182737	20.809	7.565	147253.51	1360.310
434	188356	81746504	20.833	7.571	147934.46	1363.452
435	189225	82312875	20.857	7.577	148616.97	1366.593
436	190096	82881856	20.881	7.583	149301.06	1369.736
437	190969	83453453	20.905	7.589	149986.71	1372.877
438	191844	84027672	20.928	7.594	150673.92	1376.019
439	192721	84604519	20.952	7.600	151362.72	1379.160
440	193600	85184000	20.976	7.606	152053.08	1382.301
441	194481	85766121	21.000	7.612	152745.02	1385.442
442	195364	86350888	21.024	7.617	153438.53	1388.584
443	196249	86938307	21.048	7.623	154135.18	1391.726
444	197136	87528384	21.071	7.629	154830.26	1394.868
445	198025	88121125	21.095	7.635	155528.47	1398.009
446	198916	88716536	21.119	7.640	156228.28	1401.150
447	199809	89314623	21.142	7.646	156929.63	1404.291
448	200704	89915392	21.166	7.652	157632.56	1407.432
449	201601	90518849	21.190	7.657	158337.06	1410.574
450	202500	91125000	21.213	7.663	159043.13	1413.717

No.	Square.	Cube.	Sq. Root.	Cu. Root.	Area.	Circum.
451	203401	91733851	21.237	7.669	159750.78	1416.858
452	204304	92345408	21.260	7.674	160459.98	1420.000
453	205209	92959677	21.284	7.680	161170.78	1423.140
454	206116	93576664	21.307	7.686	161883.13	1426.282
455	207025	94196375	21.331	7.691	162597.05	1429.425
456	207936	94818816	21.354	7.697	163312.56	1432.568
457	208849	95443993	21.378	7.703	164029.63	1435.710
458	209764	96071912	21.401	7.708	164748.26	1438.848
459	210681	96702579	21.424	7.714	165468.47	1441.992
460	211600	97336000	21.448	7.719	166190.25	1445.133
461	212521	97972181	21.471	7.725	166913.61	1448.274
462	213444	98611128	21.494	7.731	167638.52	1451.416
463	214369	99252847	21.517	7.736	168365.02	1454.558
464	215296	99897344	21.541	7.742	169093.09	1457.700
465	216225	100544625	21.564	7.747	169822.72	1460.841
466	217156	101194696	21.587	7.753	170553.92	1463.982
467	218089	101847563	21.610	7.758	171286.70	1467.123
468	219024	102503232	21.633	7.764	172021.04	1470.264
469	219961	103161709	21.656	7.769	172756.96	1473.406
470	220900	103823000	21.679	7.775	173494.45	1476.549
471	221841	104487111	21.703	7.780	174233.51	1479.690
472	222784	105154048	21.726	7.786	174974.14	1482.832
473	223729	105823817	21.749	7.791	175716.34	1485.973
474	224676	106496424	21.772	7.797	176460.11	1489.114
475	225625	107171875	21.794	7.802	177205.46	1492.257
476	226576	107850176	21.817	7.808	177952.37	1495.398
477	227529	108531333	21.840	7.813	178700.86	1498.539
478	228484	109215352	21.863	7.819	179450.91	1501.682
479	229441	109902239	21.886	7.824	180202.54	1504.823
480	230400	110592000	21.909	7.830	180955.74	1507.964
481	231361	111284641	21.932	7.835	181710.51	1511.106
482	232324	111980168	21.954	7.841	182466.84	1514.248
483	233289	112678587	21.977	7.846	183224.75	1517.388
484	234256	113379904	22.000	7.851	183984.24	1520.532
485	235225	114084125	22.023	7.857	184745.28	1523.672
486	236196	114791256	22.045	7.862	185507.90	1526.814
487	237169	115501303	22.068	7.868	186272.09	1529.955
488	238144	116214272	22.091	7.873	187037.86	1533.096
489	239121	116930169	22.113	7.878	187805.20	1536.240
490	240100	117649000	22.136	7.884	188574.10	1539.380
491	241081	118370771	22.159	7.889	189344.58	1542.522
492	242064	119095488	22.181	7.894	190116.62	1545.664
493	243049	119823157	22.204	7.900	190890.24	1548.802
494	244036	120553784	22.226	7.905	191665.42	1551.946
495	245025	121287375	22.249	7.910	192442.18	1555.088
496	246016	122023936	22.271	7.916	193220.51	1558.230
497	247009	122763473	22.293	7.921	193998.62	1561.372
498	248004	123505992	22.316	7.926	194781.88	1564.514
499	249001	124251499	22.338	7.932	195564.92	1567.655
500	250000	125000000	22.361	7.937	196349.54	1570.796

No.	Square.	Cube.	Sq. Root.	Cu.Root.	Area.	Circum.
501	251001	125751501	22.383	7.942	197135.72	1573.938
502	252004	126506008	22.405	7.948	197923.48	1577.080
503	253009	127263527	22.428	7.953	198712.81	1580.221
504	254016	128024064	22.450	7.958	199503.70	1583.362
505	255025	128787625	22.472	7.963	200296.17	1586.504
506	256036	129554216	22.494	7.969	201090.20	1589.646
507	257049	130323843	22.517	7.974	201885.81	1592.787
508	258064	131096512	22.539	7.979	202682.99	1595.928
509	259081	131872229	22.561	7.984	203480.96	1599.070
510	260100	132651000	22.583	7.990	204282.06	1602.212
511	261121	133432831	22.605	7.995	205083.95	1605.354
512	262144	134217728	22.627	8.000	205887.42	1608.496
513	263169	135005697	22.650	8.005	206692.46	1611.637
514	264196	135796744	22.672	8.010	207499.05	1614.778
515	265225	136590875	22.694	8.016	208307.23	1617.920
516	266256	137388096	22.716	8.021	209116.97	1621.062
517	267289	138188413	22.738	8.026	209928.29	1624.203
518	268324	138991832	22.760	8.031	210741.18	1627.344
519	269361	139798359	22.782	8.036	211555.64	1630.488
520	270400	140608000	22.804	8.041	212371.66	1633.628
521	271441	141420761	22.825	8.047	213189.26	1636.770
522	272484	142236648	22.847	8.052	214008.44	1639.912
523	273529	143055667	22.869	8.057	214829.18	1643.053
524	274576	143877824	22.891	8.062	215651.49	1646.194
525	275625	144703125	22.913	8.067	216475.37	1649.336
526	276676	145315576	22.935	8.072	217300.82	1652.478
527	277729	146383183	22.956	8.077	218127.85	1655.619
528	278784	147197952	22.978	8.082	218956.44	1658.760
529	279841	148035889	23.000	8.088	219786.61	1661.902
530	280900	148877000	23.022	8.093	220618.34	1665.044
531	281961	149721291	23.043	8.098	221451.65	1668.186
532	283024	150568768	23.065	8.103	222286.53	1671.328
533	284089	151419437	23.087	8.108	223122.98	1674.469
534	285156	152273304	23.108	8.113	223961.00	1677.610
535	286225	153130375	23.130	8.118	224800.59	1680.752
536	287296	153990656	23.152	8.123	225641.75	1683.894
537	288369	154854153	23.173	8.128	226484.48	1687.035
538	289444	155720872	23.195	8.133	227328.78	1690.176
539	290521	156590819	23.216	8.138	228174.66	1693.318
540	291600	157464000	23.238	8.143	229022.10	1696.460
541	292681	158340421	23.259	8.148	229870.33	1699.602
542	293764	159220088	23.281	8.153	230721.70	1702.744
543	294849	160103007	23.302	8.158	231573.86	1705.884
544	295936	160989184	23.324	8.163	232427.59	1709.026
545	297025	161878625	23.345	8.168	233282.89	1712.168
546	298116	162771336	23.367	8.173	234139.76	1715.310
547	299209	163667323	23.388	8.178	234998.20	1718.451
548	300304	164566592	23.409	8.183	235858.21	1721.592
549	301401	165469149	23.431	8.188	236719.79	1724.733
550	302500	166375000	23.452	8.193	237582.94	1727.876

No.	Square.	Cube.	Sq. Root.	Cu. Root.	Area.	Circum.
551	303601	167284151	23.473	8.198	238447.67	1731.018
552	304704	168196608	23.495	8.203	239297.96	1734.160
553	305809	169112377	23.516	8.208	240165.83	1737.301
554	306916	170031464	23.537	8.213	241043.26	1740.442
555	308025	170953875	23.558	8.218	241922.27	1743.584
556	309136	171879616	23.580	8.223	242794.84	1746.726
557	310249	172808693	23.601	8.228	243668.99	1749.867
558	311364	173741112	23.622	8.233	244544.71	1752.968
559	312481	174676879	23.643	8.238	245442.00	1756.110
560	313600	175616000	23.664	8.243	246300.86	1759.292
561	314721	176558481	23.685	8.248	247181.29	1762.434
562	315844	177504328	23.707	8.253	248063.30	1765.576
563	316969	178453547	23.728	8.258	248946.87	1768.717
564	318096	179406144	23.749	8.262	249832.01	1771.858
565	319225	180362125	23.770	8.267	250718.73	1775.000
566	320356	181321496	23.791	8.272	251607.01	1778.142
567	321489	182284263	23.812	8.277	252496.87	1781.283
568	322624	183250432	23.833	8.282	253388.30	1784.424
569	323761	184220009	23.854	8.286	254281.30	1787.566
570	324900	185193000	23.875	8.291	255175.86	1790.708
571	326041	186169411	23.896	8.296	256072.00	1793.849
572	327184	187149248	23.917	8.301	256969.71	1796.990
573	328329	188132517	23.937	8.306	257868.99	1800.132
574	329476	189119224	23.958	8.311	258769.84	1803.274
575	330625	190109375	23.979	8.316	259672.27	1806.416
576	331776	191102976	24.000	8.320	260576.26	1809.558
577	332929	192100033	24.021	8.325	261481.83	1812.699
578	334084	193100552	24.042	8.330	262388.96	1815.840
579	335241	194104539	24.062	8.335	263297.66	1818.981
580	336400	195112000	24.083	8.340	264207.94	1822.124
581	337561	196122941	24.104	8.344	265119.79	1825.265
582	338724	197137368	24.125	8.349	266033.21	1828.406
583	339889	198155287	24.145	8.354	266948.20	1831.548
584	341056	199176704	24.166	8.359	267864.76	1834.690
585	342225	200201625	24.187	8.363	268782.89	1837.832
586	343396	201230056	24.207	8.368	269702.59	1840.933
587	344569	202262003	24.228	8.373	270623.87	1844.074
588	345744	203297472	24.249	8.378	271546.70	1847.256
589	346921	204336469	24.269	8.382	272470.33	1850.398
590	348100	205379000	24.290	8.387	273397.10	1853.540
591	349281	206425071	24.310	8.392	274324.65	1856.682
592	350464	207474688	24.331	8.397	275253.78	1859.823
593	351649	208527857	24.352	8.401	276184.48	1862.964
594	352836	209584584	24.372	8.406	277116.74	1866.106
595	354025	210644875	24.393	8.411	278050.58	1869.248
596	355216	211708736	24.413	8.416	278985.99	1872.390
597	356409	212776173	24.434	8.420	279922.98	1875.531
598	357604	213847192	24.454	8.425	280861.52	1878.672
599	358801	214921799	24.474	8.430	281801.64	1881.814
600	360000	216000000	24.495	8.434	282743.34	1884.956

No.	Square.	Cube.	Sq. Root.	Cu.Root.	Area.	Circum.
601	361201	217081801	24.515	8.439	283686.61	1888.097
602	362404	218167208	24.536	8.444	284631.44	1891.238
603	363609	219256227	24.556	8.448	285577.84	1894.380
604	364816	220348864	24.576	8.453	286525.82	1897.522
605	366025	221445125	24.597	8.458	287475.36	1900.664
606	367236	222545016	24.617	8.462	288426.48	1903.806
607	368449	223648543	24.637	8.467	289379.17	1906.947
608	369664	224755712	24.658	8.472	290333.42	1910.088
609	370881	225866529	24.678	8.476	291289.26	1913.229
610	372100	226981000	24.698	8.481	292246.66	1916.372
611	373321	228099131	24.718	8.486	293205.63	1919.513
612	374544	229220928	24.739	8.490	294166.17	1922.654
613	375769	230346397	24.759	8.495	295129.86	1925.796
614	376996	231475544	24.779	8.499	296091.96	1928.938
615	378225	232608375	24.799	8.504	297057.22	1932.079
616	379456	233744896	24.819	8.509	298024.05	1935.221
617	380689	234885113	24.839	8.513	298992.45	1938.362
618	381924	236029032	24.860	8.518	299962.40	1941.504
619	383161	237176659	24.880	8.522	300933.94	1944.645
620	384400	238328000	24.900	8.527	301907.05	1947.787
621	385641	239483061	24.920	8.532	302881.73	1950.928
622	386884	240641848	24.940	8.536	303857.98	1954.070
623	388129	241804367	24.960	8.541	304837.16	1957.211
624	389376	242970624	24.980	8.545	305815.19	1960.353
625	390625	244140625	25.000	8.550	306796.16	1963.495
626	391876	245314376	25.020	8.554	307778.69	1966.636
627	393129	246491883	25.040	8.559	308762.79	1969.778
628	394384	247673152	25.060	8.564	309748.47	1972.919
629	395641	248858189	25.080	8.568	310735.72	1976.061
630	396900	250047000	25.100	8.573	311724.53	1979.203
631	398161	251239591	25.120	8.577	312714.92	1982.344
632	399424	252435968	25.140	8.582	313706.87	1985.486
633	400689	253636137	25.160	8.586	314700.41	1988.628
634	401956	254840104	25.180	8.591	315695.50	1991.769
635	403225	256047875	25.200	8.595	316692.17	1994.911
636	404496	257259456	25.220	8.600	317690.42	1998.052
637	405769	258474853	25.239	8.604	318690.24	2001.194
638	407044	259694072	25.259	8.609	319691.61	2004.335
639	408321	260917119	25.278	8.613	320694.56	2007.477
640	409600	262144000	25.298	8.618	321699.09	2010.619
641	410881	263374721	25.318	8.622	322705.19	2013.760
642	412164	264609288	25.338	8.627	323712.85	2016.902
643	413449	265847707	25.357	8.631	324720.52	2020.043
644	414736	267089984	25.377	8.636	325732.89	2023.185
645	416025	268336125	25.397	8.640	326745.27	2026.327
646	417316	269586136	25.417	8.645	327759.22	2029.468
647	418609	270840023	25.436	8.649	328774.74	2032.610
648	419904	272097792	25.456	8.653	329791.82	2035.751
649	421201	273359449	25.475	8.658	330810.48	2038.893
650	422500	274625000	25.495	8.662	331830.72	2042.035

No.	Square.	Cube.	Sq. Root.	Cu.Root.	Area.	Circum.
651	423801	275894451	25.515	8.667	332852.53	2045.177
652	425104	277167808	25.534	8.671	333875.90	2048.318
653	426409	278445077	25.554	8.676	334900.85	2051.460
654	427716	279726264	25.573	8.680	335927.38	2054.602
655	429025	281011375	25.593	8.685	336955.45	2057.743
656	430336	282300416	25.612	8.689	337985.10	2060.885
657	431649	283593393	25.632	8.693	339016.32	2064.026
658	432964	284890312	25.652	8.698	340049.13	2067.167
659	434281	286191179	25.671	8.702	341083.50	2070.309
660	435600	287496000	25.690	8.707	342119.44	2073.451
661	436921	288804781	25.710	8.711	343156.95	2076.592
662	438244	290117528	25.720	8.715	344196.03	2079.734
663	439569	291434247	25.749	8.720	345236.69	2082.876
664	440896	292754944	25.768	8.724	346278.91	2086.017
665	442225	294079625	25.788	8.729	347322.70	2089.159
666	443556	295408296	25.807	8.733	348368.08	2092.300
667	444889	296740963	25.826	8.737	349415.02	2095.442
668	446224	298077632	25.846	8.742	350463.51	2098.583
669	447561	299418309	25.865	8.746	351513.62	2101.725
670	448900	300763000	25.884	8.750	352565.24	2104.867
671	450241	302111711	25.904	8.755	353618.46	2108.008
672	451584	303464448	25.923	8.759	354673.26	2111.150
673	452929	304821217	25.942	8.763	355729.62	2114.291
674	454276	306182024	25.962	8.768	356787.54	2117.433
675	455625	307546875	25.981	8.772	357847.04	2120.575
676	456976	308915776	26.000	8.776	358908.11	2123.716
677	458329	310288733	26.019	8.781	359970.76	2126.858
678	459684	311665752	26.038	8.785	361034.96	2130.000
679	461041	313046839	26.058	8.789	362100.75	2133.141
680	462400	314432000	26.077	8.794	363168.11	2136.283
681	463761	315821241	26.096	8.798	364237.04	2139.425
682	465124	317214568	26.115	8.802	365307.54	2142.566
683	466489	318611987	26.134	8.807	366384.56	2145.708
684	467856	320013504	26.153	8.811	367453.18	2148.849
685	469225	321419125	26.173	8.815	368528.45	2151.991
686	470596	322828856	26.192	8.819	369605.23	2155.133
687	471969	324242703	26.211	8.824	370683.59	2158.274
688	473344	325660672	26.230	8.828	371763.50	2161.416
689	474721	327082769	26.249	8.832	372845.00	2164.557
690	476100	328509000	26.268	8.837	373928.07	2167.699
691	477481	329939371	26.287	8.841	375012.71	2170.840
692	478864	331373888	26.306	8.845	376098.91	2173.982
693	480249	332812557	26.325	8.849	377186.68	2177.124
694	481636	334255384	26.344	8.854	378276.03	2180.265
695	483025	335702375	26.363	8.858	379366.95	2183.407
696	484416	337153536	26.382	8.862	380459.44	2186.548
697	485809	338608873	26.401	8.866	381553.50	2189.690
698	487204	340068392	26.420	8.871	382649.13	2192.832
699	488601	341532099	26.439	8.875	383746.33	2195.973
700	490000	343000000	26.458	8.879	384845.10	2199.115

No.	Square.	Cube.	Sq. Root.	Cu.Root.	Area.	Circum.
701	491401	344472101	26.476	8.883	385945.45	2202.256
702	492804	345948008	26.495	8.887	387047.34	2205.398
703	494209	347428927	26.514	8.892	388150.83	2208.539
704	495616	348913664	26.532	8.896	389255.89	2211.681
705	497025	350402625	26.552	8.900	390362.52	2214.823
706	498436	351895816	26.571	8.904	391470.72	2217.964
707	499849	353393243	26.589	8.909	392580.49	2221.106
708	501264	354894912	26.608	8.913	393691.82	2224.248
709	502681	356400829	26.627	8.917	394804.73	2227.389
710	504100	357911000	26.646	8.921	395919.21	2230.531
711	505521	359425431	26.665	8.925	397035.26	2233.672
712	506944	360944128	26.683	8.929	398152.88	2236.814
713	508369	362467097	26.702	8.934	399272.07	2239.956
714	509796	363994344	26.721	8.938	400392.83	2243.097
715	511225	365525875	26.739	8.942	401515.18	2246.239
716	512656	367061696	26.758	8.946	402639.09	2249.380
717	514089	368601813	26.777	8.950	403764.55	2252.522
718	515524	370146232	26.796	8.955	404891.60	2255.664
719	516961	371694959	26.814	8.959	406020.22	2258.805
720	518400	373248000	26.833	8.963	407150.41	2261.947
721	519841	374805361	26.851	8.967	408282.17	2265.088
722	521284	376367048	26.870	8.971	409415.50	2268.230
723	522729	377933067	26.889	8.975	410550.39	2271.371
724	524176	379503424	26.907	8.979	411686.86	2274.513
725	525625	381078125	26.926	8.984	412824.91	2277.655
726	527076	382657176	26.944	8.988	413964.54	2280.796
727	528529	384240583	26.963	8.992	415105.72	2283.938
728	529984	385828352	26.981	8.996	416248.46	2287.079
729	531441	387420489	27.000	9.000	417392.78	2290.221
730	532900	389017000	27.019	9.004	418538.68	2293.363
731	534361	390617891	27.037	9.008	419684.58	2296.504
732	535824	392223168	27.055	9.012	420835.18	2299.646
733	537289	393832837	27.074	9.016	421985.79	2302.787
734	538756	395446904	27.092	9.021	423137.97	2305.829
735	540225	397065375	27.111	9.025	424291.72	2309.071
736	541696	398688256	27.129	9.029	425447.04	2312.212
737	543169	400315553	27.148	9.033	426603.93	2315.353
738	544644	401947272	27.166	9.037	427762.40	2318.495
739	546121	403583419	27.185	9.041	428922.43	2321.637
740	547600	405224000	27.203	9.045	430084.03	2324.779
741	549081	406869021	27.221	9.049	431247.20	2327.920
742	550564	408518488	27.240	9.053	432411.95	2331.062
743	552049	410172407	27.258	9.057	433576.70	2334.203
744	553536	411830784	27.276	9.061	434746.16	2337.345
745	555025	413493625	27.295	9.065	435915.62	2340.487
746	556516	415160936	27.313	9.069	437086.65	2343.628
747	558009	416832723	27.331	9.073	438259.24	2346.769
748	559504	418508992	27.350	9.078	439433.41	2349.910
749	561001	420189749	27.368	9.082	440609.05	2353.052
750	562500	421875000	27.386	9.086	441786.47	2356.194

No.	Square.	Cube.	Sq. Root.	Cu.Root.	Area.	Circum.
751	564001	423564751	27.404	9.090	442965.37	2359.335
752	565504	425259008	27.423	9.094	444145.81	2362.477
753	567009	426957777	27.441	9.098	445327.83	2365.619
754	568516	428661064	27.459	9.102	446511.42	2368.760
755	570025	430368875	27.477	9.106	447696.59	2371.902
756	571536	432081216	27.495	9.110	448883.33	2375.044
757	573049	433798093	27.514	9.114	450071.63	2378.185
758	574564	435519512	27.532	9.118	451261.51	2381.327
759	576081	437245479	27.550	9.122	452453.05	2384.469
760	577600	438976000	27.568	9.126	453645.98	2387.610
761	579121	440711081	27.586	9.130	454840.57	2390.752
762	580644	442450728	27.604	9.134	456036.73	2393.893
763	582169	444194947	27.622	9.138	457234.46	2397.035
764	583696	445943744	27.641	9.142	458433.76	2400.176
765	585225	447697125	27.659	9.146	459634.64	2403.318
766	586756	449455096	27.677	9.150	460837.08	2406.459
767	588289	451217663	27.695	9.154	462041.09	2409.601
768	589824	452984832	27.713	9.158	463246.69	2412.742
769	591361	454756609	27.731	9.162	464453.84	2415.884
770	592900	456533000	27.749	9.166	465662.57	2419.026
771	594441	458314011	27.767	9.170	466872.87	2422.167
772	595984	460099648	27.785	9.174	468084.74	2425.309
773	597529	461889917	27.803	9.178	469296.61	2428.451
774	599076	463684824	27.821	9.182	470513.19	2431.593
775	600625	465484375	27.839	9.185	471729.77	2434.734
776	602176	467288576	27.857	9.189	472947.92	2437.876
777	603729	469097433	27.875	9.193	474167.65	2441.017
778	605284	470910952	27.893	9.197	475388.94	2444.159
779	606841	472729139	27.911	9.201	476611.80	2447.300
780	608400	474552000	27.928	9.205	477836.24	2450.442
781	609961	476379541	27.946	9.209	479062.25	2453.583
782	611524	478211768	27.964	9.213	480289.83	2456.725
783	613089	480048687	27.982	9.217	481518.98	2459.867
784	614656	481890304	28.000	9.221	482749.70	2463.009
785	616225	483736025	28.018	9.225	483981.98	2466.150
786	617796	485587656	28.036	9.229	485215.85	2469.292
787	619369	487443403	28.054	9.233	486451.27	2472.433
788	620944	489303872	28.071	9.238	487688.27	2475.575
789	622521	491169069	28.089	9.240	488926.85	2478.716
790	624100	493039000	28.107	9.244	490166.99	2481.858
791	625681	494913671	28.125	9.248	491408.71	2485.000
792	627264	496793088	28.142	9.252	492651.98	2488.131
793	628849	498677257	28.160	9.256	493896.85	2491.272
794	630436	500566184	28.178	9.260	495143.28	2494.414
795	632025	502459875	28.196	9.264	496391.27	2497.566
796	633616	504358336	28.213	9.268	497640.85	2500.708
797	635209	506261573	28.231	9.272	498891.98	2503.849
798	636804	508169592	28.249	9.275	500144.69	2506.991
799	638401	510082399	28.267	9.279	501398.97	2509.132
800	640000	512000000	28.284	9.283	502654.82	2513.274

No.	Square.	Cube.	Sq. Root.	Cu.Root.	Area.	Circum.
801	641601	513922401	28.302	9.287	503912.25	2516.416
802	643204	515849608	28.320	9.291	505171.24	2519.557
803	644809	517781627	28.337	9.295	506431.80	2522.698
804	646416	519718464	28.355	9.299	507693.94	2525.840
805	648025	521660125	28.373	9.302	508957.64	2528.982
806	649636	523606616	28.390	9.306	510222.92	2532.123
807	651249	525557943	28.408	9.310	511489.76	2535.265
808	652864	527514112	28.425	9.314	512758.18	2538.406
809	654481	529475129	28.443	9.318	514028.18	2541.548
810	656100	531441000	28.460	9.322	515299.74	2544.690
811	657721	533411731	28.478	9.326	516572.87	2547.831
812	659344	535387328	28.496	9.329	517847.57	2550.973
813	660969	537366797	28.513	9.333	519123.83	2554.115
814	662596	539353144	28.531	9.337	520401.69	2557.256
815	664225	541343375	28.548	9.341	521681.10	2560.398
816	665856	543338496	28.566	9.345	522962.08	2563.540
817	667489	545338513	28.583	9.348	524244.64	2566.681
818	669124	547343432	28.601	9.352	525528.77	2569.823
819	670761	549353259	28.618	9.356	526814.46	2572.964
820	672400	551368000	28.636	9.360	528101.73	2576.106
821	674041	553387661	28.653	9.364	529390.57	2579.247
822	675684	555412248	28.671	9.368	530680.97	2582.388
823	677329	557441767	28.688	9.371	531972.95	2585.530
824	678976	559476224	28.705	9.375	533266.50	2588.672
825	680625	561515625	28.723	9.379	534561.62	2591.814
826	682276	563559976	28.740	9.383	535858.32	2594.955
827	683929	565609283	28.758	9.386	537156.58	2598.097
828	685584	567663552	28.775	9.390	538456.42	2601.239
829	687241	569722789	28.792	9.394	539757.81	2604.380
830	688900	571787000	28.810	9.398	541060.79	2607.522
831	690561	573856191	28.827	9.402	542347.34	2610.663
832	692224	575930368	28.844	9.405	543671.49	2613.805
833	693889	578009537	28.862	9.409	544979.15	2616.946
834	695556	580093704	28.879	9.413	546288.40	2620.088
835	697225	582182875	28.896	9.417	547599.23	2623.230
836	698896	584277056	28.914	9.420	548911.63	2626.371
837	700569	586376253	28.931	9.424	550225.60	2629.513
838	702244	588480472	28.948	9.428	551541.14	2632.654
839	703921	590589719	28.965	9.432	552858.26	2635.796
840	705600	592704000	28.983	9.435	554176.94	2638.938
841	707281	594823321	29.000	9.439	555497.19	2642.079
842	708964	596947688	29.017	9.443	556819.02	2645.221
843	710649	599077107	29.034	9.447	558142.42	2648.363
844	712336	601211584	29.052	9.450	559467.39	2651.504
845	714025	603351125	29.069	9.454	560793.92	2654.646
846	715716	605495736	29.086	9.458	562122.03	2657.787
847	717409	607645423	29.103	9.462	563451.71	2660.929
848	719104	609800192	29.120	9.465	564782.98	2664.071
849	720801	611960049	29.138	9.469	566115.78	2667.212
850	722500	614125000	29.155	9.473	567450.17	2670.354

No.	Square.	Cube.	Sq. Root.	Cu.Root	Area.	Circum.
851	724201	616295051	29.172	9.476	568786.13	2673.495
852	725904	618470208	29.189	9.480	570123.66	2676.637
853	727609	620650477	29.206	9.484	571462.77	2679.778
854	729316	622835864	29.223	9.488	572803.45	2682.920
855	731025	625026375	29.240	9.491	574145.69	2686.062
856	732736	627222016	29.257	9.495	575489.54	2689.203
857	734449	629422793	29.275	9.499	576834.89	2692.345
858	736164	631628712	29.292	9.502	578181.85	2695.486
859	737881	633839779	29.309	9.506	579530.38	2698.628
860	739600	636056000	29.326	9.510	580880.48	2701.770
861	741321	638277381	29.343	9.513	582232.15	2704.911
862	743044	640503928	29.360	9.517	583585.39	2708.053
863	744769	642735647	29.377	9.521	584940.20	2711.194
864	746496	644972544	29.394	9.524	586296.58	2714.336
865	748225	647214625	29.411	9.528	587654.54	2717.478
866	749956	649461896	29.428	9.532	589014.06	2720.619
867	751689	651714363	29.445	9.535	590375.16	2723.760
868	753424	653972032	29.462	9.539	591737.82	2726.902
869	755161	656234909	29.479	9.543	593102.06	2730.044
870	756900	658503000	29.496	9.546	594467.87	2733.186
871	758641	660776311	29.513	9.550	595835.25	2736.327
872	760384	663054848	29.530	9.554	597204.22	2739.469
873	762129	665338617	29.547	9.557	598574.72	2742.610
874	763876	667627624	29.563	9.561	599946.81	2745.752
875	765625	669921875	29.580	9.565	601320.47	2748.894
876	767376	672221376	29.597	9.568	602695.70	2752.035
877	769129	674526133	29.614	9.572	604072.51	2755.177
878	770884	676836152	29.631	9.576	605450.88	2758.318
879	772641	679151439	29.648	9.579	606830.82	2761.460
880	774400	681472000	29.665	9.583	608212.34	2764.602
881	776161	683797841	29.682	9.586	609595.43	2767.743
882	777924	686128968	29.698	9.590	610980.08	2770.885
883	779689	688465387	29.715	9.594	612366.31	2774.026
884	781456	690807104	29.732	9.597	613754.12	2777.168
885	783225	693154125	29.749	9.601	615143.48	2780.309
886	784996	695506456	29.766	9.605	616534.42	2783.451
887	786769	697864103	29.783	9.608	617926.93	2786.592
888	788544	700227072	29.799	9.612	619321.02	2789.734
889	790321	702595369	29.816	9.615	620716.66	2792.876
890	792100	704969000	29.833	9.619	622113.89	2796.017
891	793881	707347971	29.850	9.623	623512.67	2799.159
892	795664	709732288	29.866	9.626	624913.10	2802.300
893	797449	712121957	29.883	9.630	626314.98	2805.442
894	799236	714516984	29.900	9.633	627718.48	2808.584
895	801025	716917375	29.917	9.637	629123.56	2811.725
896	802816	719323136	29.933	9.641	630530.24	2814.867
897	804609	721734273	29.950	9.644	631938.43	2818.009
898	806404	724150792	29.967	9.648	633348.22	2821.150
899	808201	726572699	29.983	9.651	634759.58	2824.292
900	810000	729000000	30.000	9.655	636172.51	2827.433

No.	Square.	Cube.	Sq. Root.	Cu. Root.	Area.	Circum.
901	811801	731432701	30.017	9.658	637587.01	2830.575
902	813604	733870808	30.033	9.662	639003.08	2833.716
903	815409	736314327	30.050	9.666	640420.73	2836.858
904	817216	738763264	30.067	9.669	641839.94	2840.000
905	819025	741217625	30.083	9.673	643260.73	2843.141
906	820836	743677416	30.100	9.676	644683.09	2846.283
907	822649	746142643	30.116	9.680	646107.01	2849.424
908	824464	748613312	30.133	9.683	647532.51	2852.566
909	826281	751089429	30.150	9.687	648959.58	2855.707
910	828100	753571000	30.166	9.691	650388.22	2858.849
911	829921	756058031	30.183	9.694	651818.43	2861.990
912	831744	758550528	30.199	9.698	653250.20	2865.132
913	833569	761048497	30.216	9.701	654683.56	2868.273
914	835396	763551944	30.232	9.705	656118.48	2871.415
915	837225	766060875	30.249	9.708	657554.98	2874.557
916	839056	768575296	30.265	9.712	658993.04	2877.698
917	840889	771095213	30.282	9.715	660432.68	2880.840
918	842724	773620632	30.299	9.719	661873.88	2883.982
919	844561	776151559	30.315	9.722	663316.66	2887.123
920	846400	778688000	30.332	9.726	664761.01	2890.265
921	848241	781229961	30.348	9.729	666206.92	2893.407
922	850084	783777448	30.364	9.733	667654.42	2896.548
923	851929	786330467	30.381	9.736	669103.47	2899.690
924	853776	788889024	30.397	9.740	670554.07	2902.832
925	855625	791453125	30.414	9.743	672006.30	2905.973
926	857476	794022776	30.430	9.747	673460.07	2909.115
927	859329	796597983	30.447	9.750	674915.42	2912.256
928	861184	799178752	30.463	9.754	676372.35	2915.398
929	863041	801765089	30.480	9.758	677830.82	2918.539
930	864900	804357000	30.496	9.761	679290.87	2921.681
931	866761	806954491	30.512	9.764	680752.49	2924.822
932	868624	809557568	30.529	9.768	682215.70	2927.964
933	870489	812166237	30.545	9.771	683680.46	2931.106
934	872356	814780504	30.561	9.775	685146.80	2934.247
935	874225	817400375	30.578	9.778	686614.71	2937.389
936	876096	820025856	30.594	9.783	688084.18	2940.531
937	877969	822656953	30.610	9.785	689555.24	2943.672
938	879844	825293672	30.627	9.789	691027.86	2946.814
939	881721	827936019	30.643	9.792	692502.06	2949.955
940	883600	830584000	30.659	9.796	693977.82	2953.097
941	885481	833237621	30.676	9.799	695455.15	2956.238
942	887364	835896888	30.692	9.803	696934.05	2959.380
943	889249	838561807	30.708	9.806	698414.59	2962.521
944	891136	841232384	30.725	9.810	699896.58	2965.663
945	893025	843908625	30.741	9.813	701380.19	2968.805
946	894916	846590536	30.757	9.817	702865.38	2971.946
947	896809	849278123	30.773	9.820	704351.35	2975.088
948	898704	851971392	30.790	9.824	705840.47	2978.230
949	900601	854670349	30.806	9.827	707330.37	2981.371
950	902500	857375000	30.822	9.830	708821.84	2984.513

No.	Square.	Cube.	Sq. Root.	Cu. Root.	Area.	Circum.
951	904401	860085351	30.838	9.834	710314.88	2987.655
952	906304	862801408	30.854	9.837	711809.47	2990.796
953	908209	865523177	30.871	9.841	713305.68	2993.938
954	910116	868250664	30.887	9.844	714803.44	2997.079
955	912025	870983875	30.903	9.848	716302.76	3000.221
956	913936	873722816	30.919	9.851	717803.65	3003.362
957	915849	876467493	30.935	9.855	719306.12	3006.504
958	917764	879217912	30.952	9.858	720810.16	3009.645
959	919681	881974079	30.968	9.861	722315.77	3012.787
960	921600	884736000	30.984	9.865	723822.95	3015.929
961	923521	887503681	31.000	9.868	725331.70	3019.070
962	925444	890277128	31.016	9.872	726842.02	3022.212
963	927369	893056347	31.032	9.875	728353.91	3025.353
964	929296	895841344	31.048	9.879	729867.36	3028.495
965	931225	898632125	31.064	9.882	731382.40	3031.637
966	933156	901428696	31.081	9.885	732899.01	3034.778
967	935089	904231063	31.097	9.889	734417.18	3037.920
968	937024	907039232	31.113	9.892	735936.96	3041.061
969	938961	909853209	31.129	9.896	737458.25	3044.203
970	940900	912673000	31.145	9.899	738981.13	3047.345
971	942841	915498611	31.161	9.902	740505.59	3050.486
972	944784	918330048	31.177	9.906	742031.62	3053.628
973	946729	921167317	31.193	9.909	743559.22	3056.769
974	948676	924010424	31.209	9.913	745088.39	3059.911
975	950625	926859375	31.225	9.916	746619.13	3063.053
976	952576	929714176	31.241	9.919	748151.44	3066.194
977	954529	932574833	31.257	9.923	749685.32	3069.336
978	956484	935441352	31.273	9.926	751220.78	3072.478
979	958441	938313739	31.289	9.930	752757.80	3075.619
980	960400	941192000	31.305	9.933	754296.40	3078.761
981	962361	944076141	31.321	9.936	755836.56	3081.902
982	964324	946966168	31.337	9.940	757378.30	3085.044
983	966289	949862087	31.353	9.943	758921.60	3088.185
984	968256	952763904	31.369	9.946	760466.48	3091.327
985	970225	955671625	31.385	9.950	762012.93	3094.469
986	972196	958585256	31.401	9.953	763560.95	3097.610
987	974169	961504803	31.417	9.956	765109.54	3100.752
988	976144	964430272	31.432	9.960	766661.70	3103.893
989	978121	967361669	31.448	9.963	768214.44	3107.035
990	980100	970299000	31.464	9.967	769768.74	3110.177
991	982081	973242271	31.480	9.970	771324.61	3113.318
992	984064	976191488	31.496	9.973	772882.06	3116.460
993	986049	979146657	31.512	9.977	774441.07	3119.601
994	988036	982107784	31.528	9.980	776001.66	3122.743
995	990025	985074875	31.544	9.983	777563.82	3125.885
996	992016	988047936	31.560	9.987	779127.55	3129.026
997	994009	991026973	31.575	9.990	780692.85	3132.168
998	996004	994011992	31.591	9.993	782259.72	3135.310
999	998001	997002999	31.607	9.997	783828.14	3138.451
1000	1000000	1000000000	31.623	10.000	785398.16	3141.593

List of useful Books of reference.

Bélidor, Bombardier Français.. 1731
Saint Rémy, Mémoires d'artillerie.. 1745
Dupuget, Essai sur l'usage de l'artillerie dans la guerre de campagne et celle de siége.. 1771
Saint Auban, Mémoires sur les nouveaux systèmes d'artillerie.......... 1774
Müller, Treatise on Artillery.. 1780
Jones, Artificial Fire Works.. 1786
Lombard, Tables de tir des Canons et Obusiers........................ 1787
Antoni, On Gunpowder.. 1789
Texier de Norbec, Recherches sur l'artillerie en général................ 1792
Monge, Description de l'art de fabriquer les canons.................. 1793
Vandemonde, Procédé sur la fabrication des armes blanches............ 1793
Durtubie, Manuel de l'artilleur.. 1796
Lombard, Traité du mouvement des projectiles........................ 1798
Scheel, Treatise on Artillery (Translated from the German)............ 1800
Morel, Traité pratique des feux d'artifice........................ 1800
Cornibert, Manuel du canonnier marin........................ 1800
James, Military Dictionary.. 1802
Robins, New principles of gunnery.. 1805
Cotty, Mémoires sur la fabrication des armes portatives................ 1806
Cossigny, Recherches sur la poudre.. 1807
—*Idem*—Supplément.. 1808
Renaud, Fabrication de la poudre.. 1808
Toussard, American Artillerist's Companion........................ 1809
Cornibert, Tables des portées des canons et carronades de la marine..... 1809
Bigot, Traité d'artifices de guerre.. 1809
Dartein, Traité élémentaire de la fabrication des bouches à feu.......... 1810
Bottée et Riffault, Traité de l'art de fabriquer la poudre à canon......... 1811
Bottée et Riffault, L'art du Salpêtrier.. 1812
Hoyer, Dictionary of Artillery (German).. 1812
Hutton, New experiments in gunnery, (Hutton's Tracts).............. 1812
Herbin de Halles, Des bois propres au service des Arsenaux............ 1813
Hulot, Instruction sur le service de l'artillerie........................ 1813
Duane, Military Dictionary.. 1813
Bigot, Manœuvres de force.. 1814
D'Obenheim, Balistique.. 1814
Scharnhorst, Treatise on Artillery, German [translated into French, 1840] 1814

Poumet, Essai sur l'art de pointer 1816
Douglass, Essay on Military Bridges 1816
Lamartillière, Réflexions sur la fabrication des bouches ā feu 1817
D'Obenheim, Mémoire sur la planchette du canonnier 1818
Gassendi, Aide-Mémoire 1819
Observations on the use of Artillery, at the sieges of Badajos, St. Sebastian, &c 1819
Dupin, Force Militaire de la Grande Bretagne 1820
Lallemand, Treatise on Artillery 1820
Ruggieri, Elémens de Pyrotechnie 1821
Paixhans, Nouvelle force maritime 1822
Cotty, Dictionnaire d'artillerie 1822
Vergnaud, Poudres fulminantes 1824
Culman, Manuel de la métallurgie du fer 1824
Pyrotechnie Militaire, traduit de l'Allemand par R. de Peretsdorff 1824
Journal des Sciences Militaires; commencé en 1825
Cutbush, Pyrotechny 1825
Decker, Traité élémentaire d'artillerie 1825
Montgéry, Fusées de guerre 1826
Hervé, Documens sur la matiére ā canons 1827
Allix, Observations sur le nouveau système d'artillerie 1827
Allix, Système d'artillerie de campagne 1827
Adye, Pocket Gunner 1827
Congreve, On the Rocket system 1827
Serres, Essai sur l'art des fontes 1827
Proust, Receuil de Mémoires sur la poudre ā canon .... 1827–'8
Michel, Mémorial de l'artilleur marin 1828
Poumet, Observations sur le nouveau système d'artillerie 1828
Mémorial de l'artillerie, 5 parties .... 1827, '28, '30, '37, '42
Spearman, British Gunner 1828
Montgéry, Régles de pointage ā bord des vaisseaux 1828
Douglass, Naval Gunnery 1829
Karsten, Métallurgie du fer, traduit de L'Allemand par Culman 1830
Grewenitz, Traité de l'organisation et de la tactique de l'artillerie, traduit de l'Allemand par Peretsdorff 1831
Cotty, Supplément au dictionnaire d'artillerie 1832
Braddock, Memoir on Gunpowder 1832
Paulin-Desormeaux, Manuel de l'armurier 1832

Journal des Armes Spéciales..............................begun in 1834

Meyer, Expériences sur la fabrication et la durée des bouches à feu en fer et en bronze; traduit de l'Allemand par Peretsdorff.......... 1834

Thiéry, Applications du fer aux constructions de l'artillerie............ 1834

Lebas, Aide-Mémoire d'art militaire.................................. 1834

Mémorial à l'usage de l'armée Belge................................ 1835

Instructions and Regulations for the service and management of heavy ordnance in the British service.................................. 1835

Expériences sur les principes du tir, faites à Metz en 1834............. 1836

Piobert, Traité d'artillerie théorique et pratique; Partie élémentaire...... 1836

Bonaparte, (*Napoleon Louis*,) Manuel d'artillerie à l'usage des officiers de la République Helvétique................ 1836

Le Bourg, Essai sur l'organisation de l'artillerie, 2 parties........... 1836–'7

Expériences comparatives entre des bouches à feu en fonte de fer, d'origine Française, Anglaise, et Suédoise; faites à Gâvres en 1836............ 1837

Expériences faites à Brest en 1831 sur les canons Paixhans............ 1837

Expériences sur des projectiles creux, faites en 1829, '30, '31.......... 1837

Decker, Instruction pratique sur l'emploi des projectiles, traduit de l'Allemand par Peretsdorff.................................. 1837

Simmons, Effects of heavy ordnance as applied to ships of war......... 1837

Maguin, Expériences sur les poudres de guerre, faites à Esquerdes en 1832, '33, '34, '35.................................. 1837

Thiroux, Instruction théorique et pratique d'artillerie, à l'usage des élèves de St. Cyr.................................. 1837

Cours sur le service des officiers d'artillerie dans les forges............ 1837

Meyer, Manuel Historique de la technologie des armes à feu; traduit de l'Allemand par M. Rieffel, 2 parties.................. 1837–'38

Poisson, Formules relatives aux effets du tir sur l'affût................ 1838

Morin, Aide-Mémoire de mécanique pratique........................ 1838

Vergnaud, Manuel de l'artificier.................................. 1838

Jacobi, Etat actuel de l'artillerie de campagne de toutes les puissances de l'Europe; traduit par Mazé:

Artillerie Anglaisé ....
" Française ....
" Bavaroise..........
" Néerlandaise.......
" Wurtembergeoise ..
" Suédoise...........
}...................... 1838 to 1849

(Other parts have been published in German.)

Cours sur le service des officiers d'artillerie dans les fonderies.......... 1839
Huguenin, Description de la fabrication des bouches à feu à la fonderie royale de Liège.. 1839
Timmerhans, Poudre à Canon.. 1839
Zeni et Des Hays, Renseignements sur le matériel de l'artillerie navale de la Grande Bretagne.............................. 1840
Migout et Bergery, Théorie des affûts et des voitures de l'artillerie........ 1840
Handbuch für die K. K. Oesterreichische artillerie-offiziere, [*Manual for the Austrian artillery officers*].......................... 1840
Saamlung von steindruckzeichnungen der Preussischen artillerie, mit erläuterungen—[*Collection of plates of the Prussian artillery, with explanatory text*].. 1837 to 1840
Collection de plans des fonderies de Ruelle et St. Gervais..............
Corréard, Histoire des fusées de guerre—Tome 1er, (a reprint of Montgéry's work).. 1841
Timmerhans, Construction des bouches à feu.......................... 1841
Laisné, Aide-Mémoire des officiers du Génie.......................... 1840
Aide-Mémoire d'Artillerie.. 1844
Aide-Mémoire to the Military Sciences (English)............begun in 1845
Experiments on gunpowder at Washington Arsenal; First Report...... 1845
Griffith, Artillerist's Manual.. 1847
Piobert, Traité d'artillerie—Partie théorique et expérimentale (Poudres de guerre).. 1847
Decker, Expériences sur les shrapnels.................................. 1847
Marion, Receuil des bouches à feu les plus remarquables.............. 1847
Didion, Traité de Balistique.. 1848
Cavalli, Mémoire sur les canons se chargeans par la culasse............ 1849
Cours sur les armes à feu portatives, par l'instructeur à l'école de St. Omer 1849
Experiments on gunpowder at Washington Arsenal; Second Report... 1849
Gregory's Mathematics for Practical Men.
Weale's Engineer's pocket book.

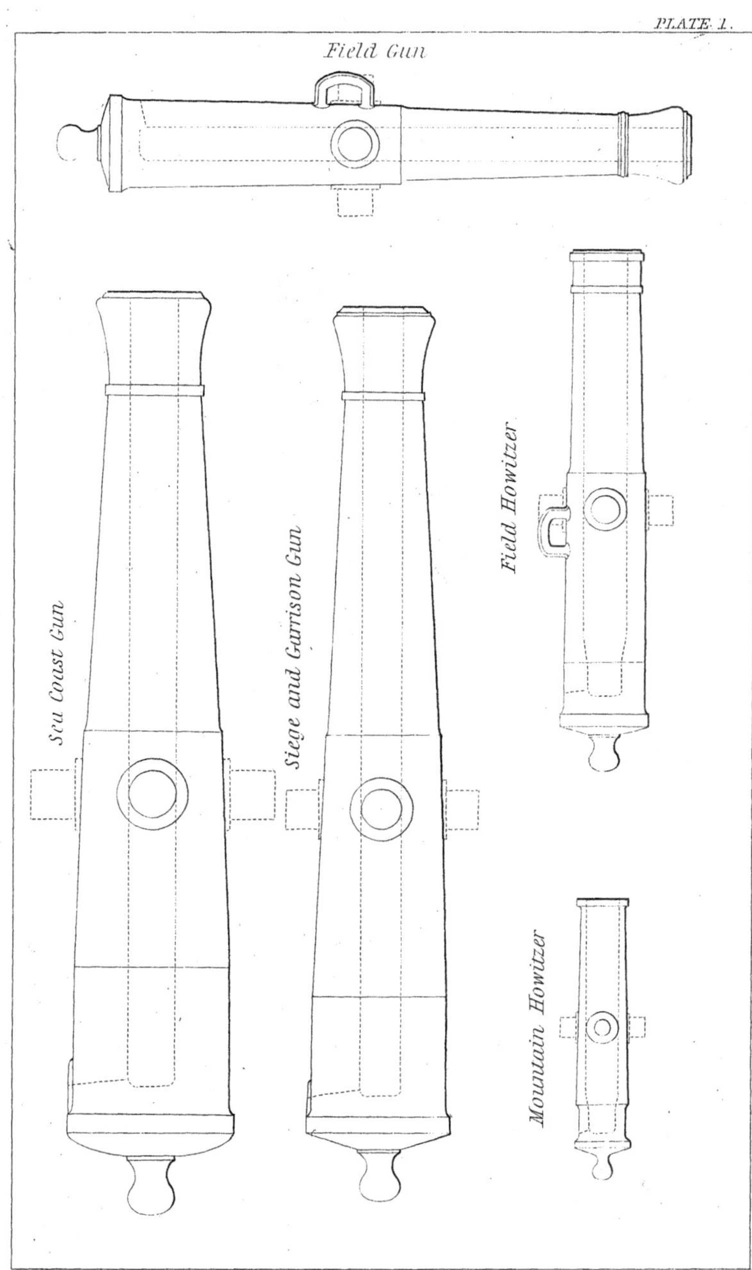

J.W.Butler Delt.

D.McClelland Sc.Wash^{n} D.C.

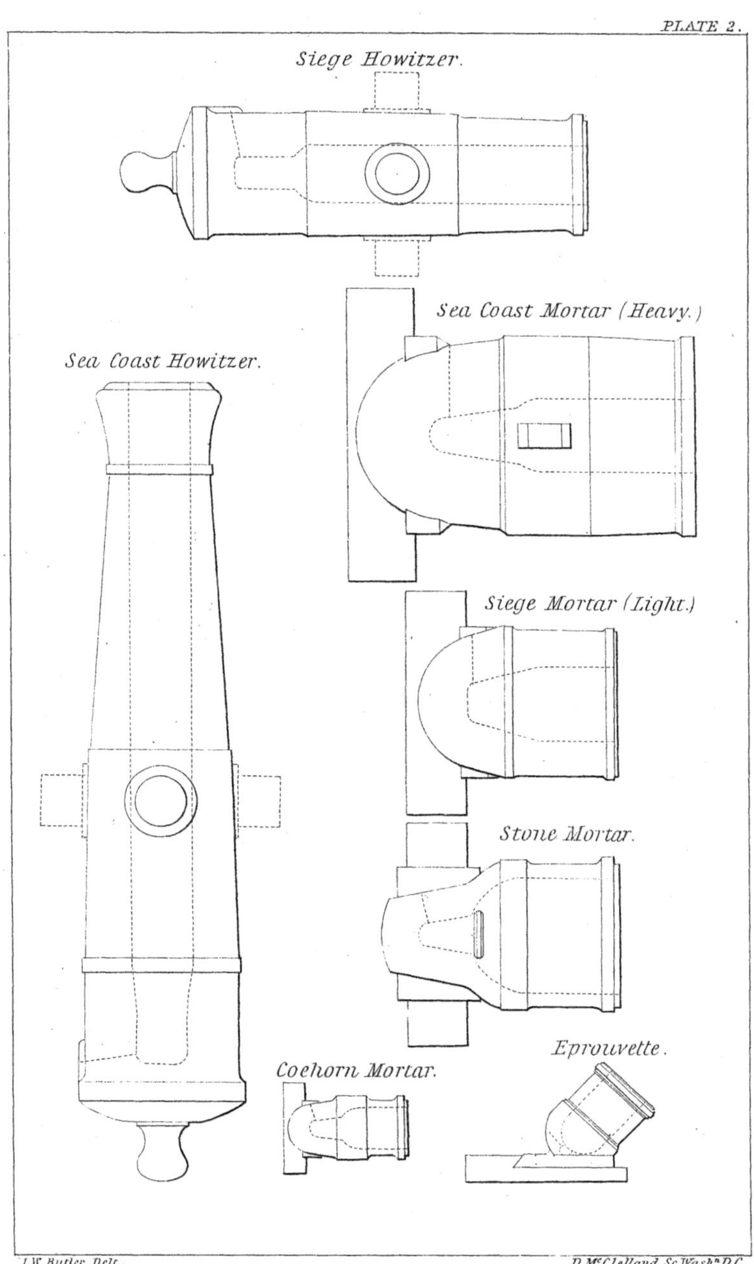

J.W. Butler Delt. D.McClelland Sc.Washn D.C.

Field Gun Carriage.

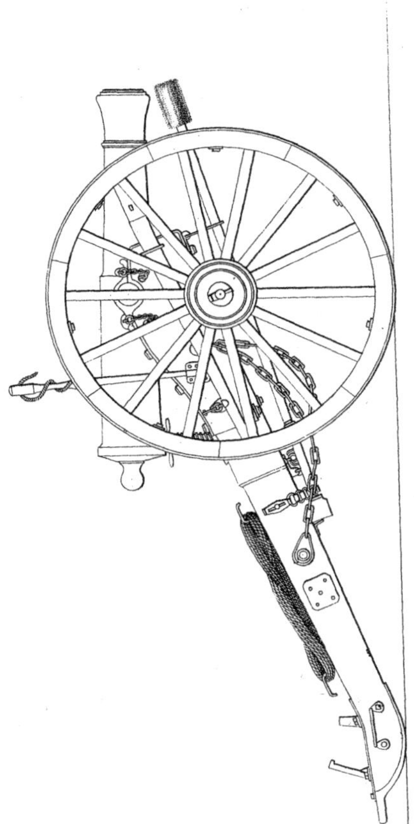

J. W. Butler Delt.

D. McClelland Sc. Washn. D.C.

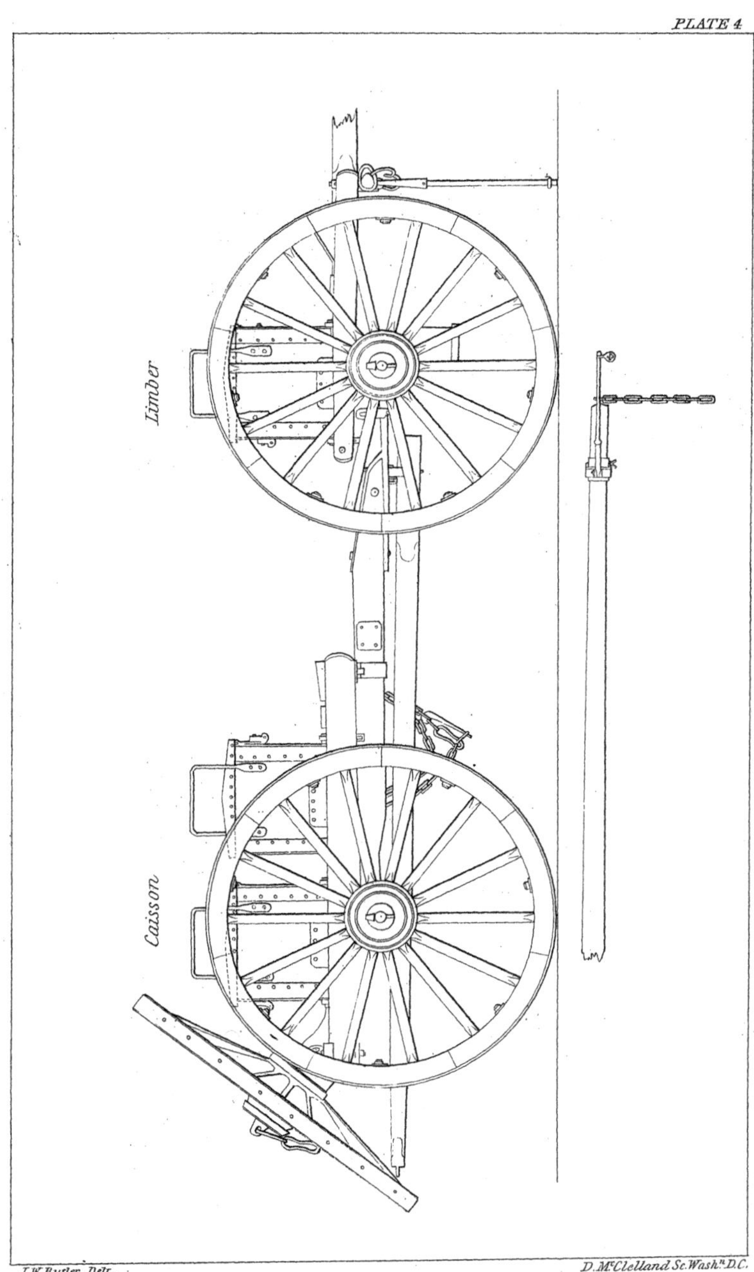

J. W. Butler Delt.

D. McClelland Sc. Washn. D.C.

PLATE 5.

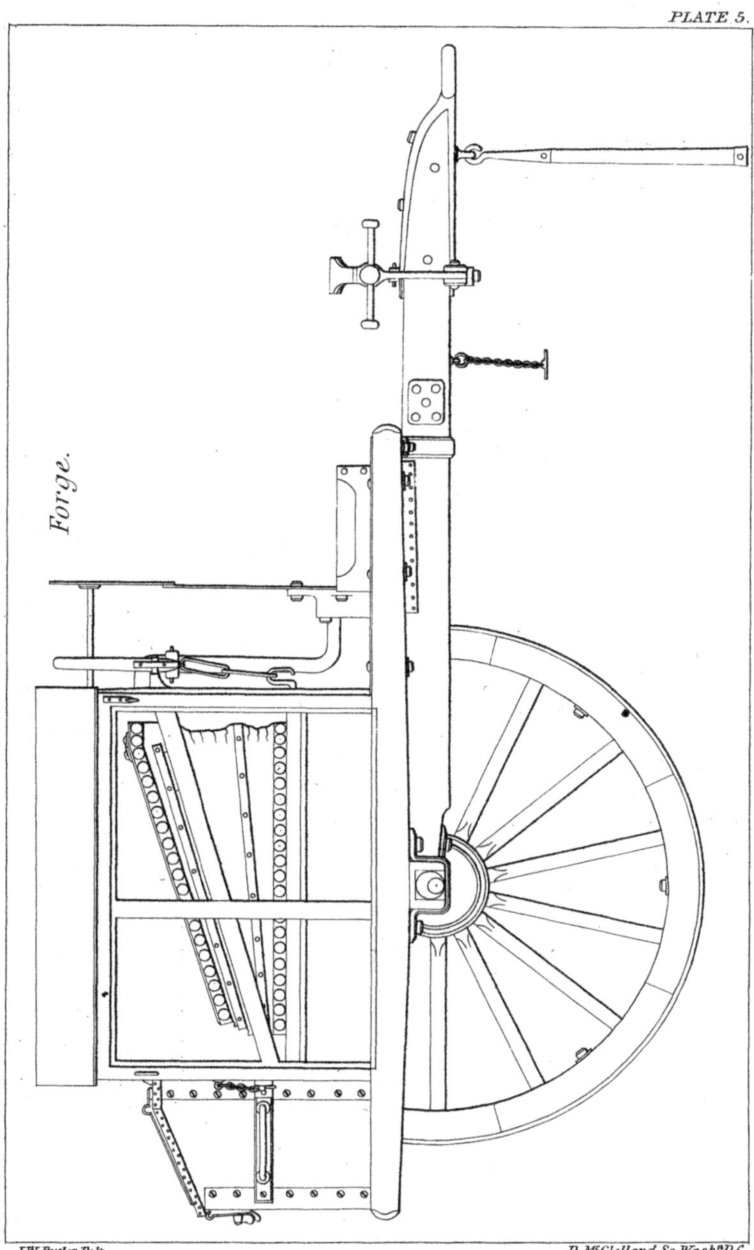

J. W. Butler Delt. D. McClelland Sc. Washn. D.C.

PLATE 6.

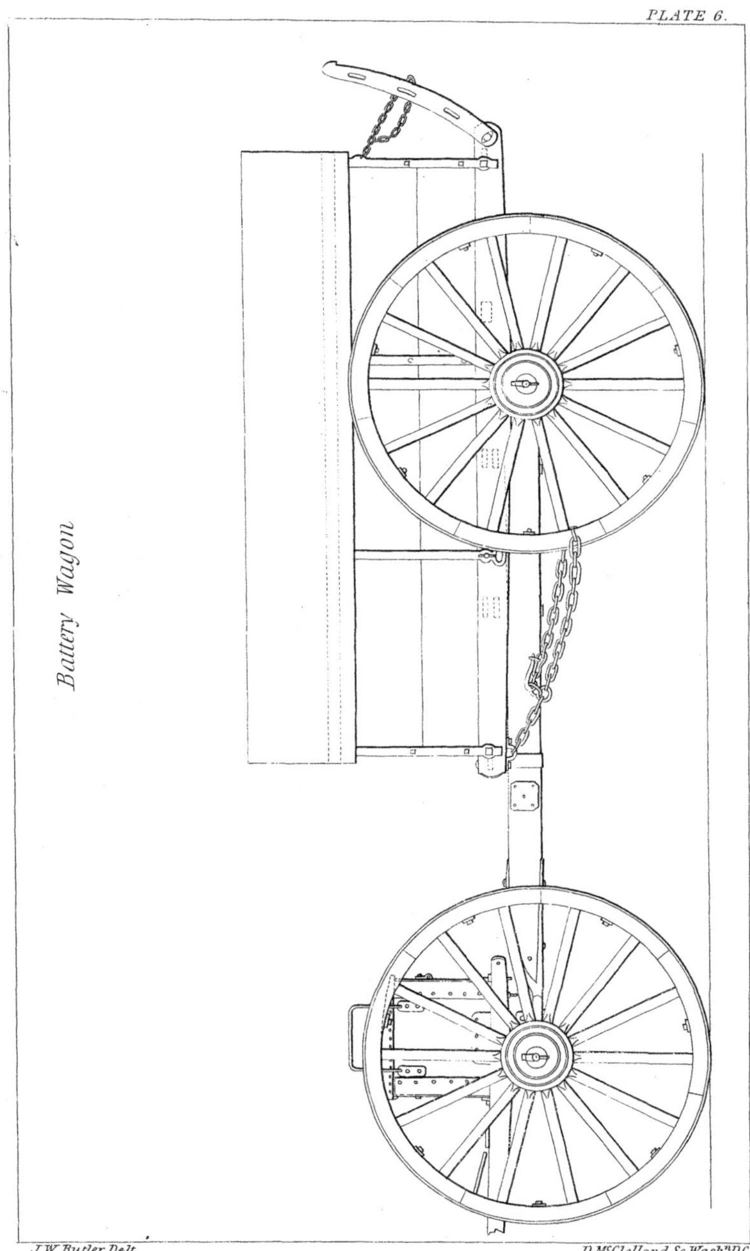

Battery Wagon

J. W. Butler Delt.

D. McClelland Sc. Washn. D.C.

PLATE 7

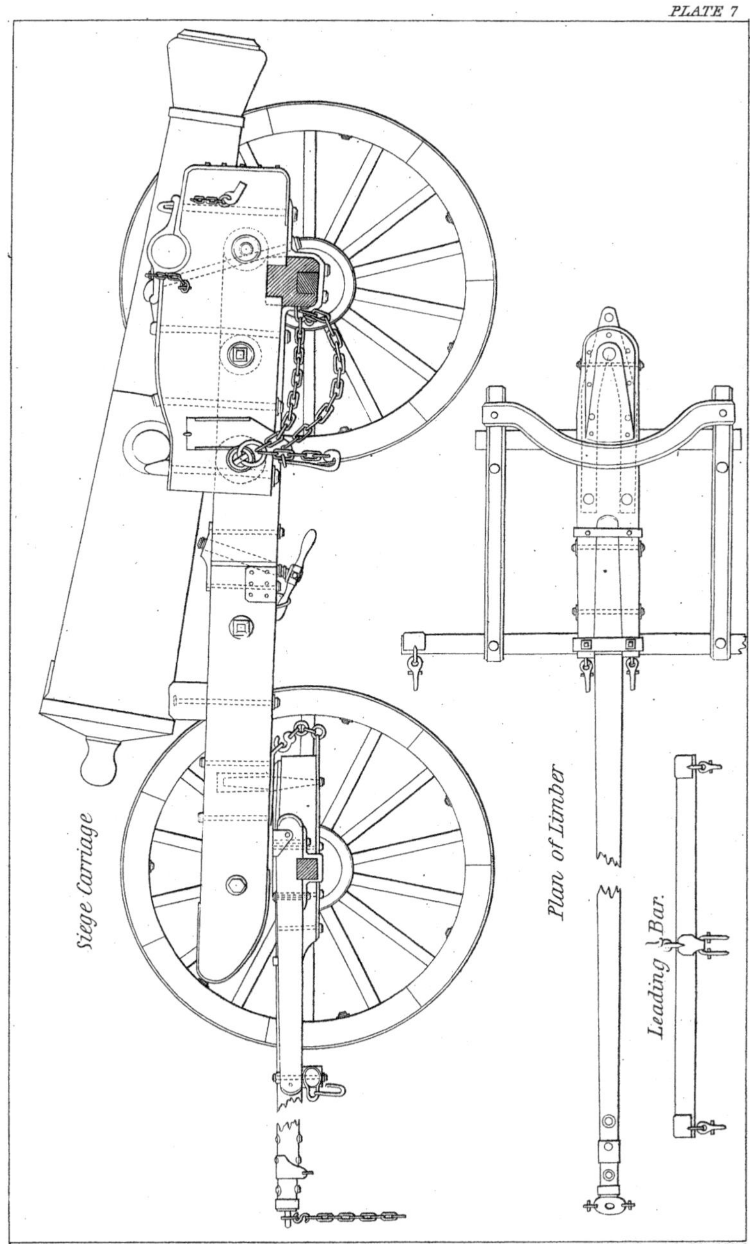

J.W.Butler Delt. D.McClelland Sc.Washn.D.C.

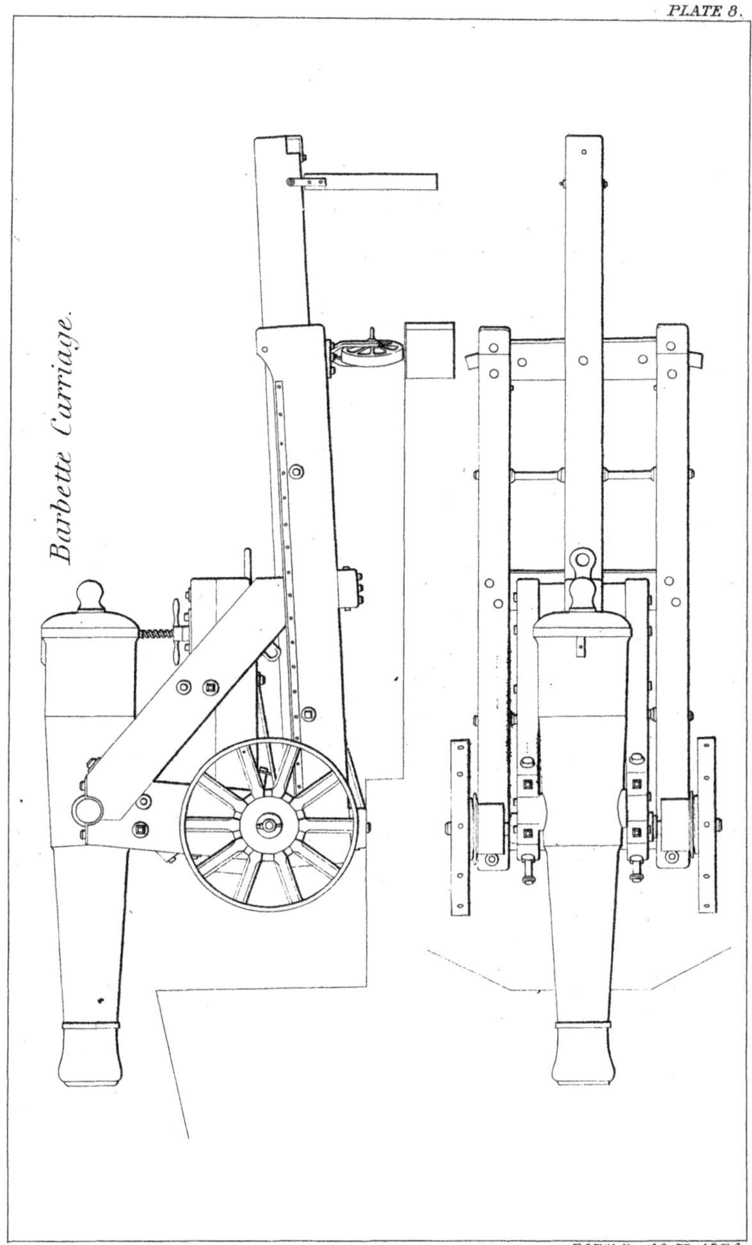

J. G. Benton Lieut. Ordn. Delt. D. McClelland Sc. Washn. D.C.

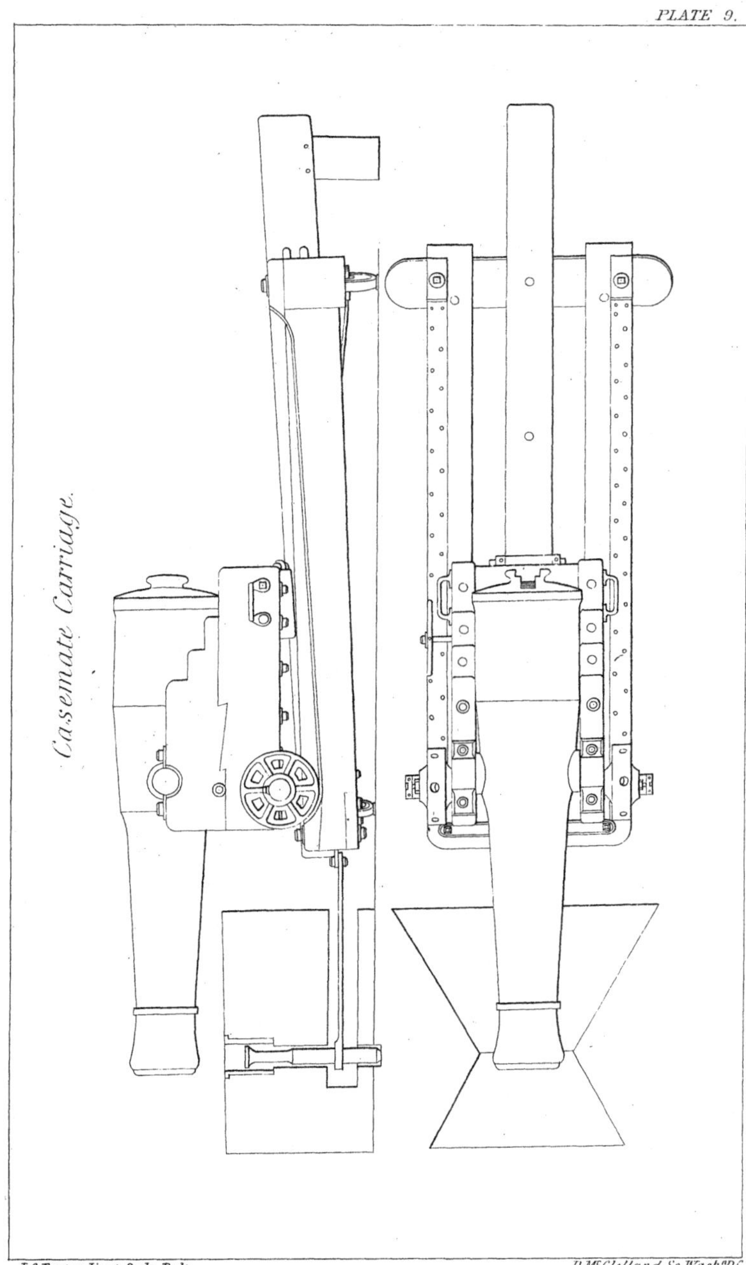

Casemate Carriage.

J. G. Benton Lieut. Ordn. Delt.

D. McClelland Sc. Wash. D.C.

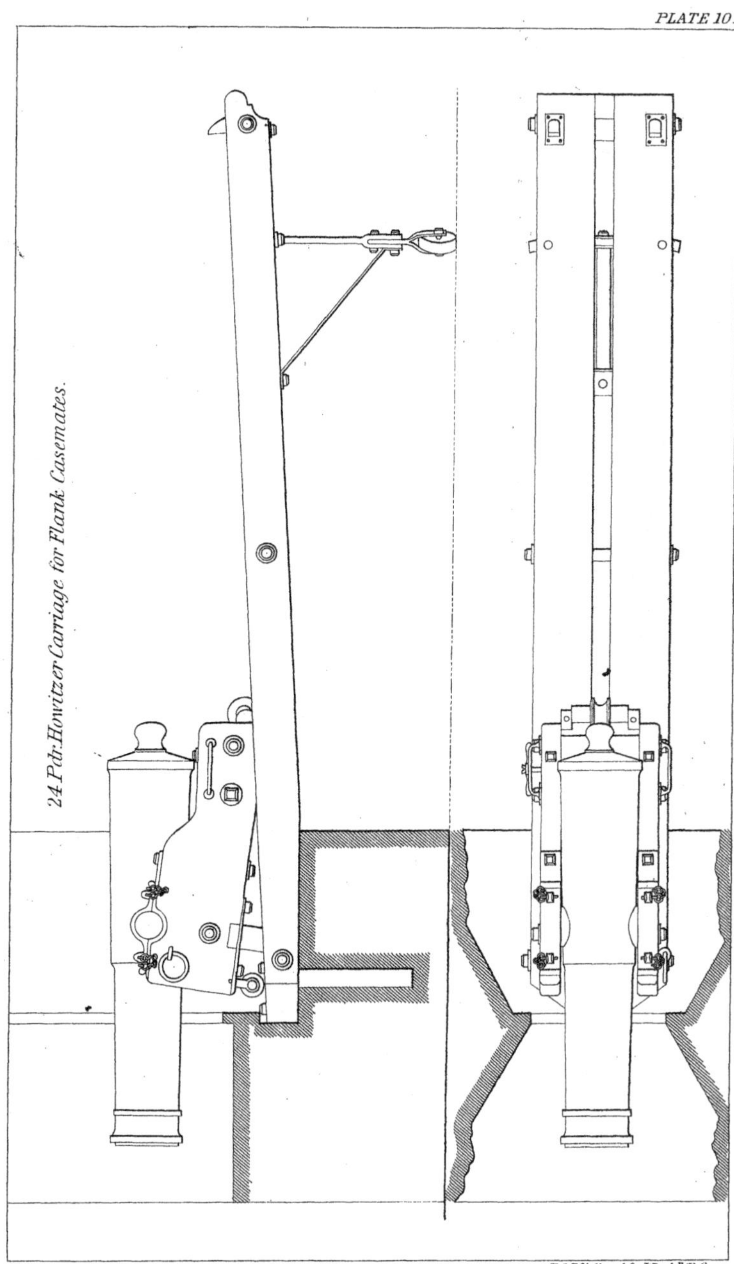

24 Pdr. Howitzer Carriage for Flank Casemates.

J. W. Butler Delt.

D. McClelland Sc. Washn. D.C.

Garrison Gin.

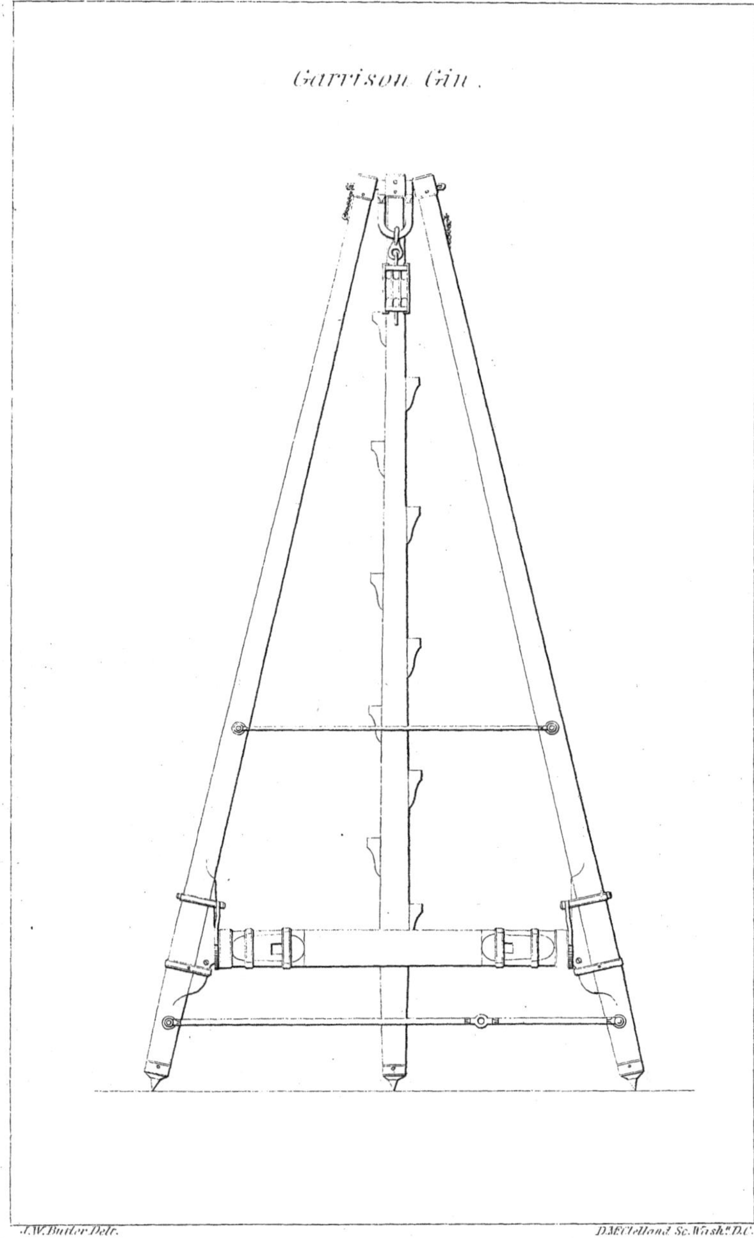

J.W. Butler Delr. D.McClelland Sc. Wash.n D.C.

Sling Cart.

Trunnion Chain.

J.W. Butler Del.

D. McClelland Sc. Wash. D.C.

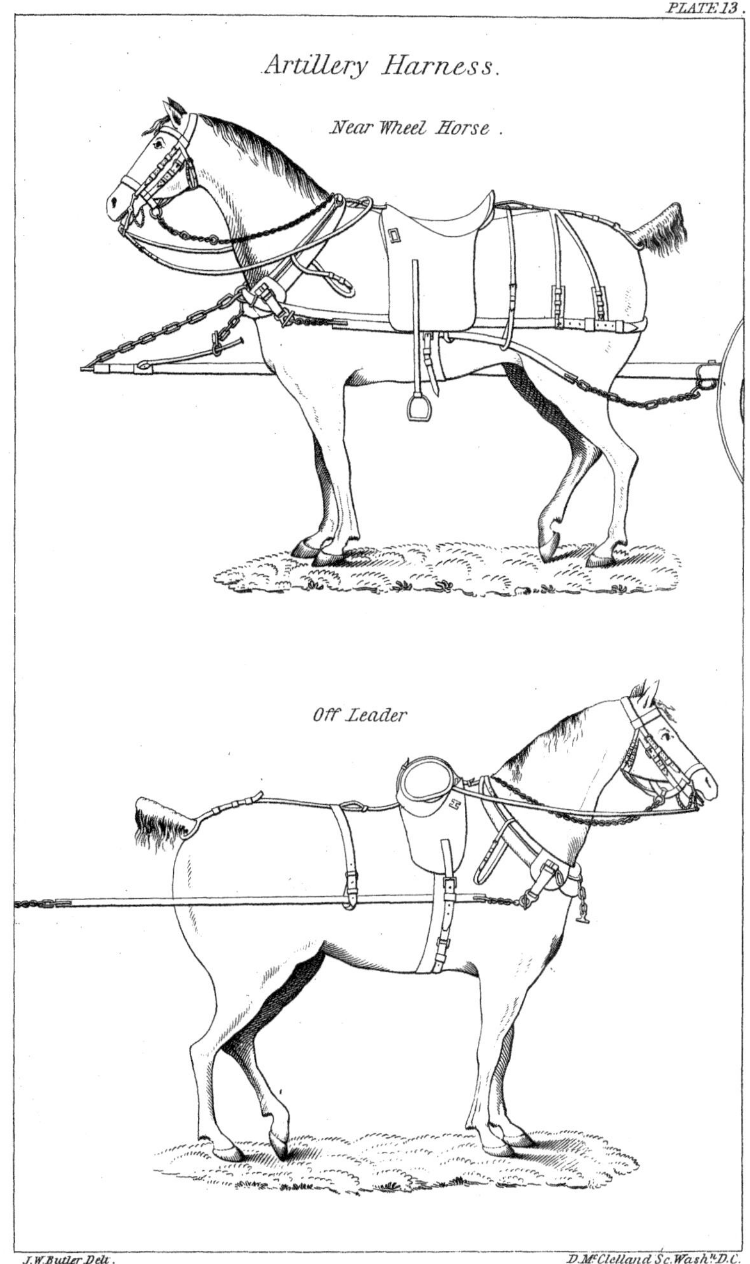
PLATE 13.
Artillery Harness.
Near Wheel Horse.
Off Leader
J.W.Butler Delt.
D.McClelland Sc.Wash.n D.C.

PLATE 14.

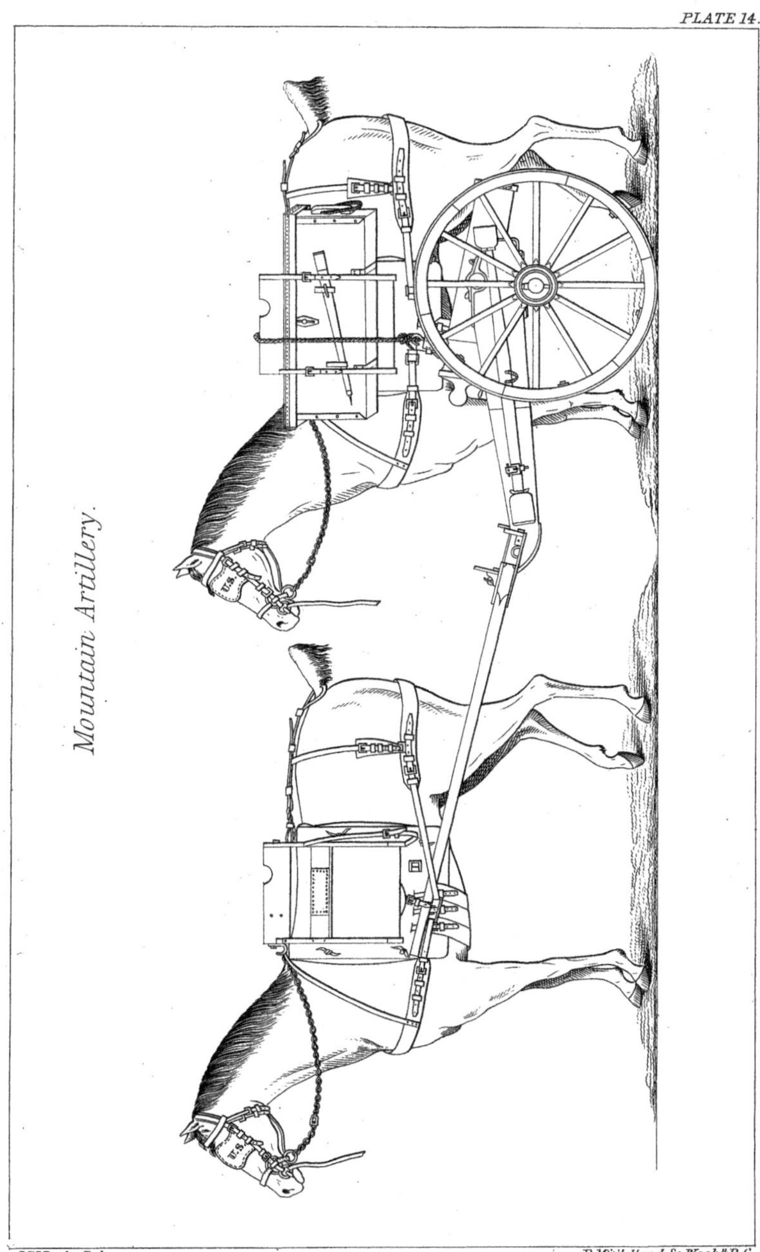

Mountain Artillery.

J.W.Butler Delt. D.McClelland Sc.Wash.n D.C.

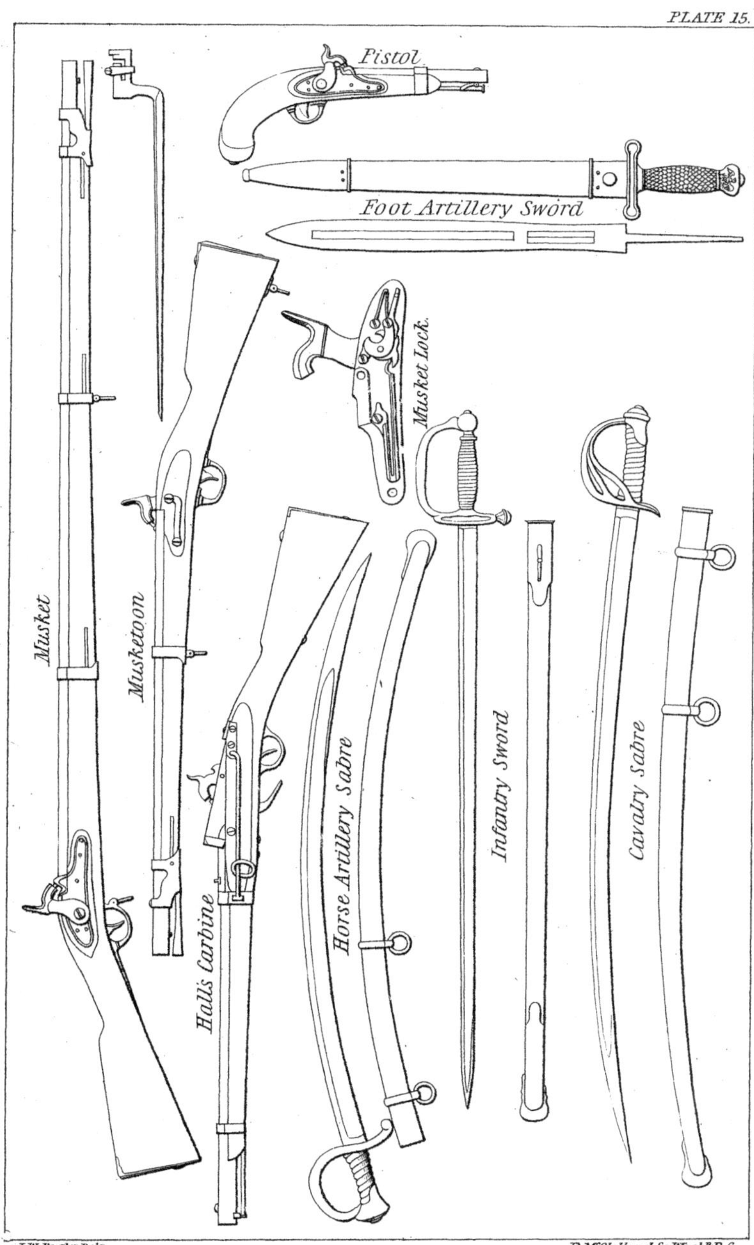

J. W. Butler Delt.

D. McClelland Sc. Washn. D.C.

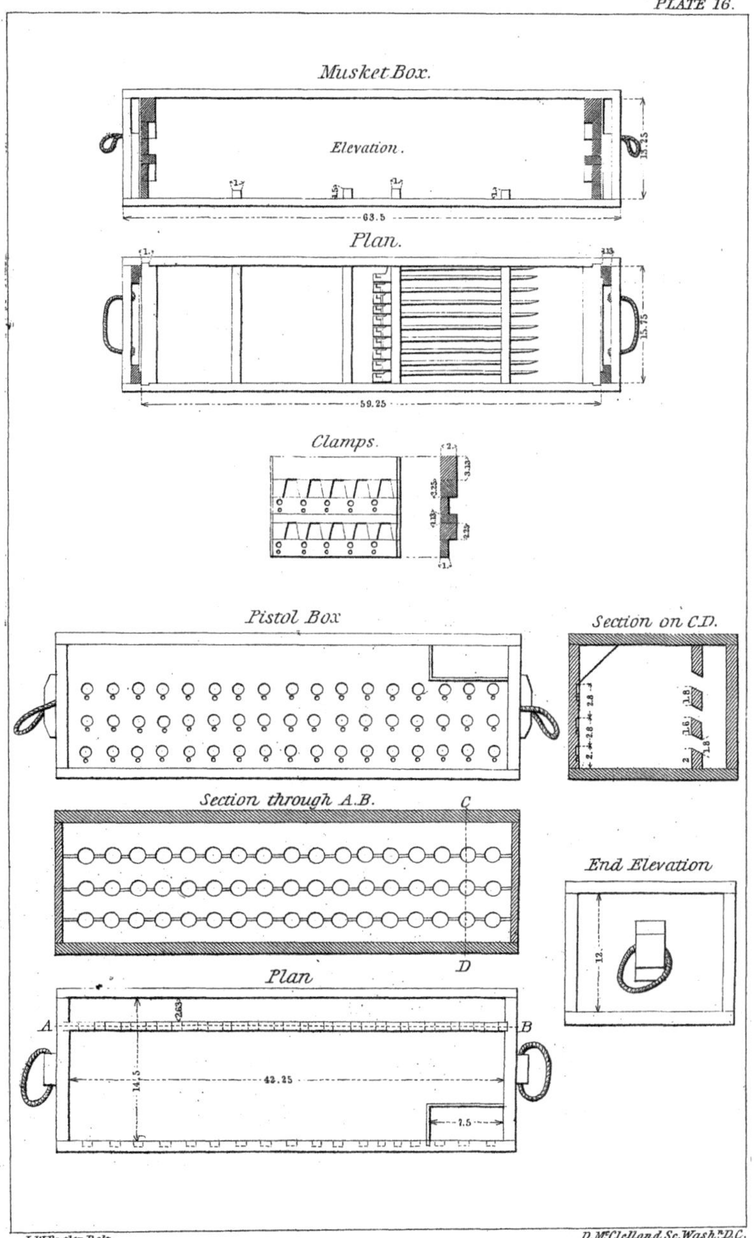

J. W. Butler Delt.

D. McClelland Sc. Wash^n. D.C.

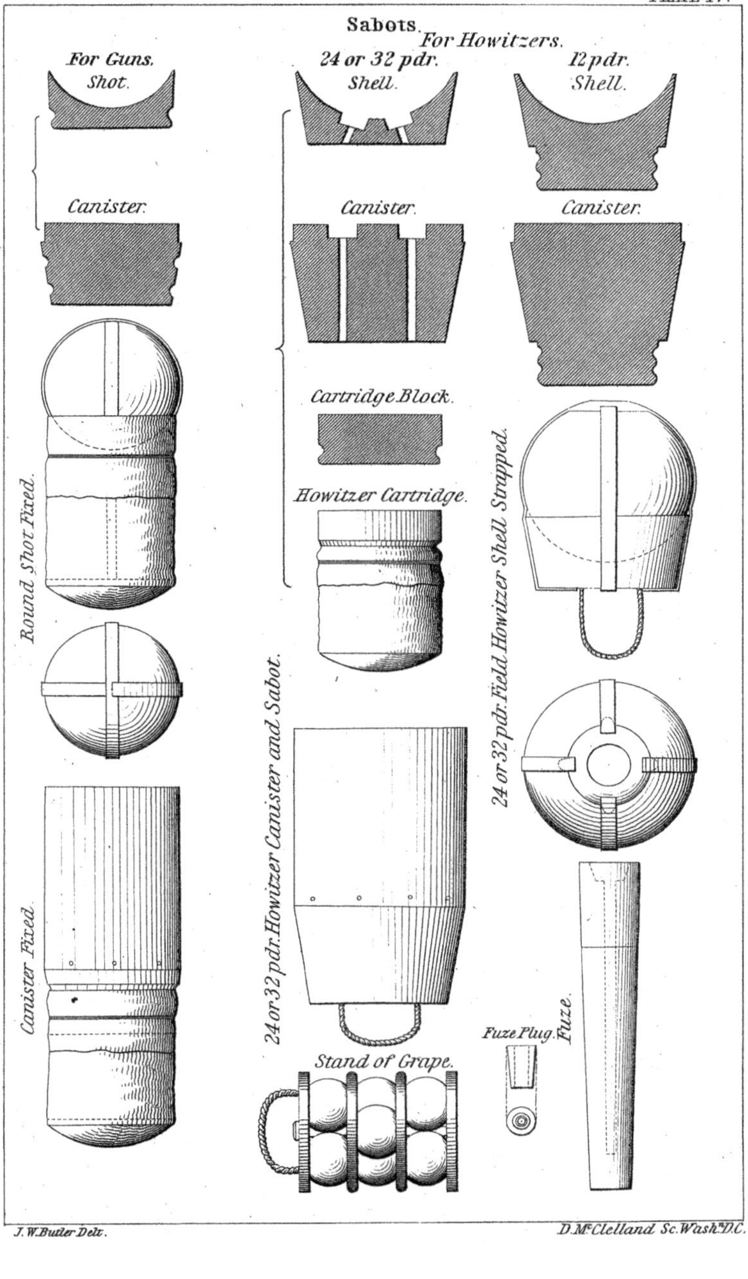

Sabots.

For Guns.
Shot.

For Howitzers.
24 or 32 pdr.
Shell.

12 pdr.
Shell.

Canister.

Canister.

Canister.

Cartridge Block.

Howitzer Cartridge.

Round Shot Fixed.

24 or 32 pdr. Howitzer Canister and Sabot.

24 or 32 pdr. Field Howitzer Shell Strapped.

Canister Fixed.

Stand of Grape.

Fuze Plug.

Fuze.

J. W. Butler Delt.

D. McClelland Sc. Washn. D.C.

Ammunition Chests.

6 Pdr. Gun.

Plan.  *Elevation.*

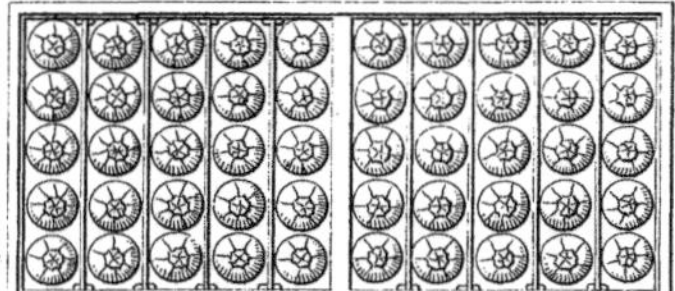

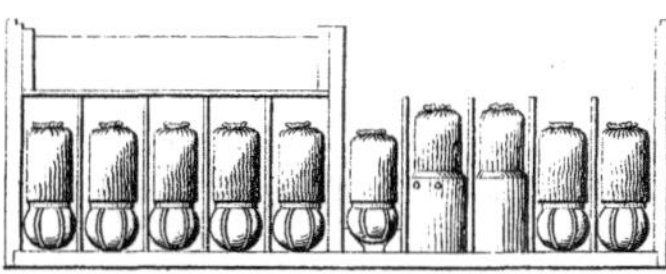

12 Pdr. Gun.

Plan. *Elevation.*

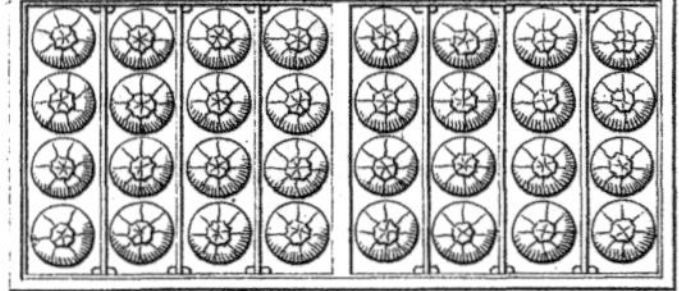

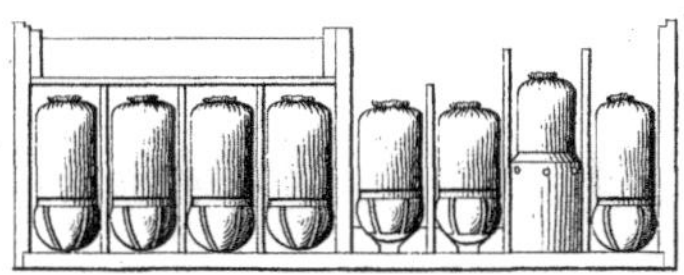

12 Pdr. Howitzer.

Plan. *Elevation.*

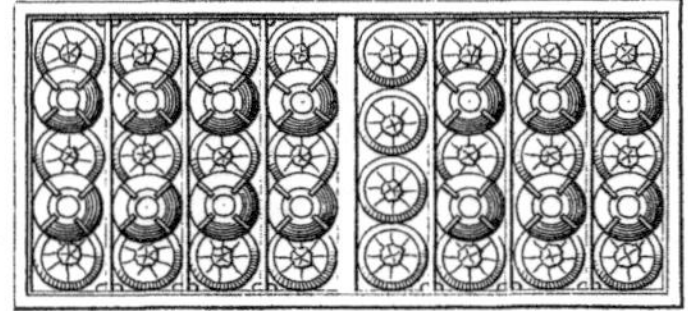

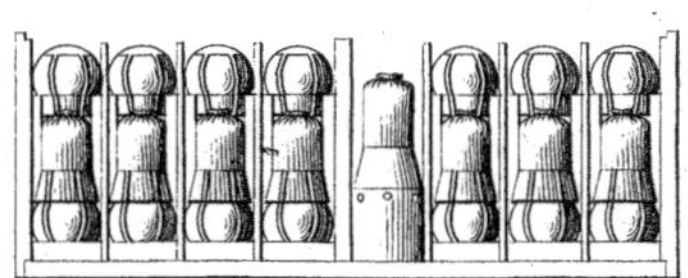

24 Pdr. Howitzer.

Plan. *Elevation.*

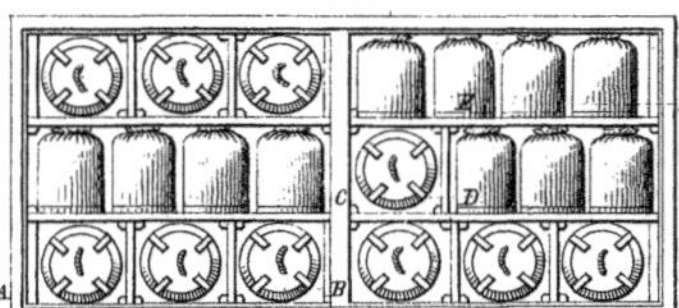

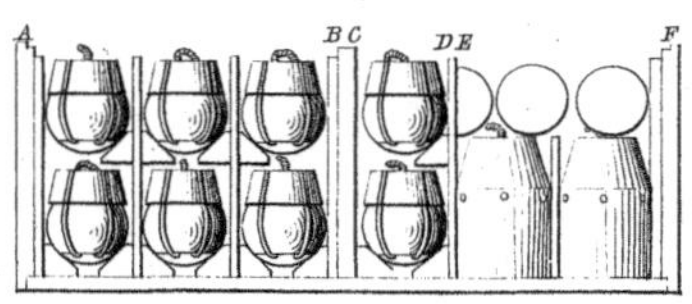

32 Pdr Howitzer.

Plan. *Elevation.*

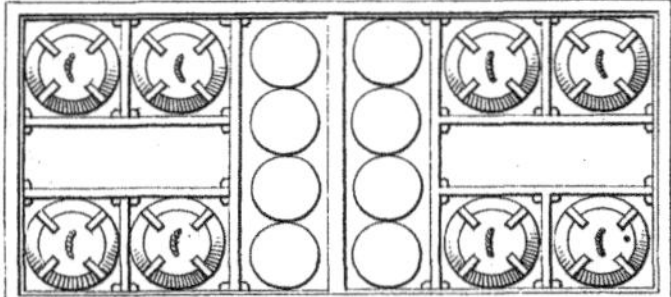

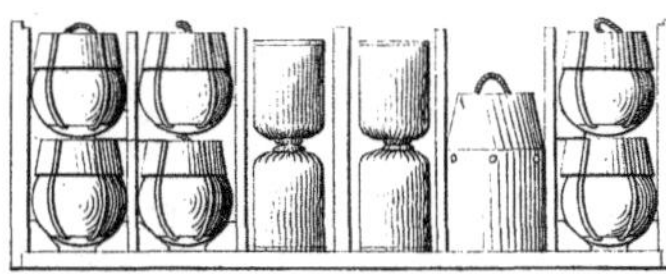

J. W. Butler Delt. *D. McClelland Sc. Washn. D. C.*

PLATE 19.

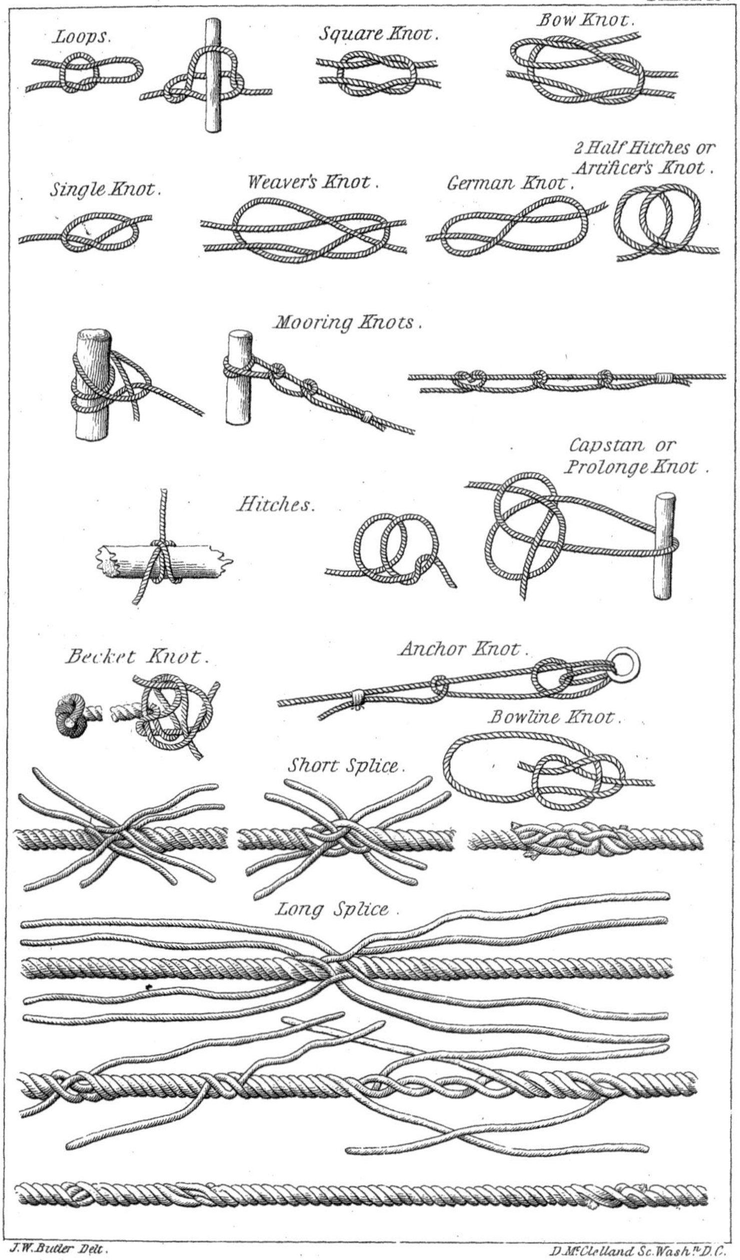

Loops.

Square Knot.

Bow Knot.

Single Knot.

Weaver's Knot.

German Knot.

2 Half Hitches or Artificer's Knot.

Mooring Knots.

Hitches.

Capstan or Prolonge Knot.

Becket Knot.

Anchor Knot.

Bowline Knot.

Short Splice.

Long Splice.

J.W. Butler Delt.

D. McClelland Sc. Washn. D.C.

www.ingramcontent.com/pod-product-compliance
Lightning Source LLC
LaVergne TN
LVHW021303110826
845150LV00003B/464

* 9 7 8 1 4 2 5 5 5 9 7 1 7 *